D0848512

AND NOW YOU HAVE DEALT US ANOTHER BLOW BY APPOINTING AS YOUR FOREIGN SECRETARY THE UNFAMILIAR, ALMOST UN-CARICATURABLE MR. SELWYN LLOYD!

I EARNESTLY BEG OF YOU TO ASK MR. LLOYD TO GROW A MOUSTACHE AND WEAR AN 'EDEN' HAT.

THIS WOULD NOT ONLY HELP US BUT WOULD ALSO SYMBOLISE THE CONTINUITY OF YOUR FOREIGN POLICY.

THANKING YOU IN ANTICIPATION, I REMAIN YOURS SINCERELY

VICKY

SELWYN LLOYD

by the same author

THE UNCROWNED PRIME MINISTERS
A Study of Sir Austen Chamberlain,
Lord Curzon and Lord Butler

SELWYN LLOYD

D. R. Thorpe

JONATHAN CAPE
THIRTY-TWO BEDFORD SQUARE LONDON

First published 1989
Copyright © 1989 by D. R. Thorpe
Jonathan Cape Ltd, 32 Bedford Square, London WC1B 3SG

A CIP catalogue record for this book
is available from the British Library

ISBN 0 224 02828 6

Photoset by Rowland Phototypesetting Ltd
Bury St Edmunds, Suffolk
Printed in Great Britain by
Mackays of Chatham PLC, Chatham, Kent

For Michael Fraser

Calm's not life's crown, though calm is well.
'Tis all perhaps which man acquires,
But 'tis not what our youth desires.

MATTHEW ARNOLD, *Youth and Calm*

Contents

Illustrations

CARTOONS

Preface

Political biographies come in many shapes and sizes but until recently have tended to fall into one of two categories. There are the biographies written shortly after the death of the subject, such as Keith Feiling's *Life of Neville Chamberlain* or Nigel Fisher's *Iain Macleod*, that have the benefit of personal knowledge of the contemporary personalities, but without access to the public records. On the other hand there are the biographies, such as Roy Jenkins's *Asquith* or David Marquand's *Ramsay Macdonald*, written a generation or more after the events they describe, with the gain of a longer historical perspective and full access to the public as well as the private papers. Both approaches have their obvious advantages and disadvantages.

The relaxation under the Thirty Year Rule since 1967 has, however, increasingly led to a further type of political biography, Ben Pimlott's *Hugh Dalton* for instance, in which the advantages of both the 'historical' and the 'contemporary' approach can be judiciously combined. Now a biographer can see at the Public Record Office the correspondence and minutes of a political figure he may be interviewing later in the same week, an experience which can sometimes be as disconcerting for the politician as it can be rewarding for the interviewer. Whether this more open policy will lead, as many politicians now 'on view' at the Public Record Office think, to a greater caution in expressing frank opinions on paper and an increasing blandness in future Cabinet minutes and conclusions, it does at present provide a vivid opportunity for chronicling the lives of those who took up high government office in the decade after the Second World War. The biographies of figures such as Attlee, Bevin, Butler, Eden and Gaitskell are radically different from those initially written about the comparable figures of the 1920s and 1930s.

It has been my aim in writing the life of Selwyn Lloyd to combine the immediacy of personal recollections with a study of both the government records and the relevant private archives. The sudden and comparatively early death of Selwyn Lloyd in 1978 enabled me to interview nearly 400 of his political contemporaries (those who had pre-deceased him I had in the main interviewed in connection with an earlier book in the 1970s), while under the Thirty Year Rule I have been able to see material in the public domain up to the end of 1957, including, with the permission of the Lord Chancellor, a few selected papers dated between 1957 and 1960 which deal with some later aspects of the Suez Canal crisis and which were made available ahead of the usual thirty-year period.[1]

Selwyn Lloyd's career in post-war politics was unique both for its variety and for the bitter controversies it generated. His name will always be linked with the Suez crisis and with his attempt, as Chancellor of the Exchequer, at an incomes policy. For a man of great sensitivity who did his best in personal relationships to avoid 'the life of telegrams and anger' it was a source of great pain that in 1962 some constituents would shun him in the streets of West Kirby as 'the man who was unfair to nurses'.[2]

There is more to Selwyn Lloyd's career than Suez and the 'pay pause', large though both loom, and there is more than one paradox. The range of offices he held between 1951 and 1976 is without political parallel in recent times. Like Bottom the Weaver (a role he once played at school) he 'undertook' many parts. Although Selwyn Lloyd was never Home Secretary (he was, however, offered the post), he held the other two great offices of state – Foreign Secretary and Chancellor of the Exchequer – and remains the only twentieth-century example of a Leader of the House of Commons becoming Speaker and, despite other former ministers such as W. S. Morrison (later Lord Dunrossil) and George Thomas (later Lord Tonypandy), the only Speaker to have held such high, and controversial, office beforehand. One has to go back to the days of Grenville and Addington at the turn of the eighteenth century to find Speakers (both of whom became Prime Minister) for whom the Speakership was but one staging post in a long line of important offices. The fact that Selwyn Lloyd could be embroiled in the bitterness of Suez and the passions aroused by the pay pause, yet subsequently become Speaker of the House of Commons, is one of the central paradoxes and one of the most significant facts in an understanding of the view his contemporaries held of him. Other paradoxes are that at certain times he appeared to be a cipher, the staff officer for the leading general, yet at other times (particularly during his membership of the Beveridge Committee on Broadcasting) he was innovative and independent; under harsh parliamentary questioning he often seemed like a stuck machine gun – the words would not come out – yet in committee and on paper he was efficiently fluid, though never prolix.

Selwyn Lloyd was always conscious of the part that luck played in politics. Unlike many of his Labour Party friends, Sidney Silverman for instance, he had the good fortune that thirteen years of Conservative rule coincided with the time he was at the appropriate level of seniority within his party and consequently he spent twelve of those thirteen years on the front bench. After the General Election of October 1951 he was appointed Minister of State, the last politician to hold that Foreign Office post by himself. In October 1954 he was promoted to the Ministry of Supply ('Supply of what?' asked one colleague when congratulating him) and when Anthony Eden became Prime Minister in April 1955 he made Selwyn Lloyd Minister of Defence, the crucial promotion into the first division of Cabinet posts. By now he was firmly on the ladder and eight months later was Foreign Secretary. But as Selwyn Lloyd was later to write, 'All was well until I became Foreign Secretary.'[3] In retrospect the Foreign Office was the wrong square of the chessboard on which to have alighted at that particular moment and how differently things might have turned out if he had been Chancellor of the Exchequer first, like Sir Austen Chamberlain before him and Sir Geoffrey Howe afterwards. Despite Suez (or rather because of it) Harold Macmillan retained Selwyn Lloyd as Foreign Secretary on becoming Prime Minister in January 1957, commenting that one head on a charger was enough. Unfortunately for Selwyn Lloyd this was not a principle that operated on Friday 13 July 1962 when his two-year tenure of the Treasury ended in the most dramatic political blood-letting of the post-war era. Yet just over a year later the central victim of the Night of the Long Knives was back as Leader of the House of Commons and in 1971 came the most surprising apotheosis of all as he crowned his career with the Speakership.

Selwyn Lloyd was always determined that his biography should be written one day, suggesting to Bertie Hesmondalgh at the Foreign Office that he might like to take it on. In the 1960s Emrys Hughes, a prolific biographer of contemporary figures, began desultory preparations but they did not come to fruition. After his death Selwyn Lloyd's papers were deposited at Churchill College, Cambridge ('I have done my best to sort out my papers and leave them in as convenient form as possible for anyone who wishes to take the trouble to look at them', wrote Selwyn)[4] and in 1984 I was invited to be his biographer. When Harold Nicolson began his biography of King George V he wrote in his diary that it was rather like setting out in a taxi to Vladivostock. Now I can sympathise with this feeling and would like to record my gratitude to all those who have made my journey possible.

My first and most manifold debt is to the literary executors of the Lord Selwyn-Lloyd estate – Mr Michael Marshall, Mr Anthony Shone and Mr Christopher Spence – for entrusting me with the responsibility of writing Selwyn Lloyd's biography, for granting me access to the vast collection of his papers at Churchill College, for introducing me to his relations and for welcoming me among their own families at so many stages during the realisation of this project. If the completed biography gives an accurate account of Selwyn Lloyd's life it is in large part owing to the unstinted help and encouragement I have received from his literary executors, who have put every facility at my disposal but who have never sought to alter my view of him or the way in which I have used those facilities.

I would next like to thank the Hon. Joanna Lloyd for talking to me about her father and for the many insights she was uniquely able to afford me. I am much indebted also to Mrs Martin Lubbock for her understanding and sympathetic help in speaking to me about her former husband and for her help over the biography.

At the outset of the project I was able to speak to Mrs A. Howard Shone, Selwyn Lloyd's eldest sister, about her brother's life from the time of his birth to the Memorial Service in Westminster Abbey and it is my greatest regret that Mrs Shone was not to live to read the biography of a brother who was devoted to her. To Mrs Ronald Clayton, Selwyn Lloyd's youngest sister, I extend my grateful thanks for speaking to me on several occasions about her brother, for introducing me to members of her family, all of whom had their own individual memories to offer and for reading the book in typescript. Other members of the family have been very generous with their hospitality and time and I would particularly like to thank Mrs Anthony Shone for all her kindness and cheerful encouragement. I would also like to record my gratitude to Mrs John Keighley, Mr and Mrs David Shone, Mr John Shone, Mr and Mrs Patrick Shone and Brigadier David and Mrs Stileman; to Mrs Michael Marshall; to Miss Anne Clayton, Mr Christopher Clayton and Mr David Clayton; and to Miss Emma Shone, Miss Lucy Shone and Mr Peter Shone.

In the early stages I received vital help from Dr Eric Anderson, Lord Fraser of Kilmorack, Mr Anthony Howard, Lord Jenkins of Hillhead and Mr Kenneth Rose and to them I would like to record my special thanks.

The bulk of the book is based upon the 495 boxes of private and political papers deposited in the Archives Centre at Churchill

College, Cambridge (Catalogue SELO); on other private family papers, not at Churchill College; on the Government records in the Public Record Office at Kew and on many other private archives, details of which can be found in the bibliography.

Although the movements of modern political life are not recorded in correspondence to anything like the same extent as was customary among politicians in the first thirty years of the century (Sir Austen Chamberlain's family letters were in themselves the basis of a large autobiographical volume), but have usually vanished on whatever desert air surrounded the telephone or taxi of the moment, Selwyn Lloyd has left through his correspondence with his family in the Wirral, a comprehensive and weekly record of his political activity over fifty years. This, like the Chamberlain family letters, essentially derived from the combination of having a metropolitan political base and a provincial constituency where the roots were strong and enduring. On 29 January 1922 Selwyn Lloyd wrote home to his parents from Fettes College, 'I am reading Morley's *Life of Gladstone* at present. I notice one of the things Morley says is "Youth will commonly do anything rather than write letters" – a true enough remark in the majority of cases, but certainly not in mine.'[5] Such correspondence has been invaluable in the preparation of this biography.

Among the effects of Max Beerbohm's wife were boxes labelled *Pieces of string too small to use.* Selwyn Lloyd, in part because of his legal training, had a similar passion for hoarding and aimed to keep, within the rules for servants of the Crown, every document of family or public significance. The archive at Churchill College therefore contains the paperwork of a lifetime. There is scarcely a single file within the 495 boxes that does not yield up some insight into Selwyn Lloyd's life and times. Dr Edwin Brooks, MP from 1966–70 for the neighbouring constituency of Bebington, vividly recalls Selwyn Lloyd remonstrating with him over what Selwyn thought his some-what cavalier attitude to the retention of his parliamentary papers, which had just been sent to the Bebington Council's furnaces for disposal. Selwyn Lloyd was of the firm belief that it was the res-ponsibility of all politicians to keep their papers for the use of future historians, one of many ways in which he differed from Iain Macleod.

If it is important to understand the machinery of government, it is equally important to understand the men who operate that machine. I have, therefore, sought help from figures who were closely involved in the events described and have spoken with many who have recalled their memories of Selwyn Lloyd, given me generous hospitality, found photographs, memorabilia, documents and given leads to further useful contacts. Without such help I would not have been able to complete this study. As many of these interviews were on a non-attributable basis the reader will find few direct references in the notes as to the source of such verbal information. However, no fact is included unless it came from an unimpeachable source or was independently corroborated. Among those who spoke to me about Selwyn Lloyd, and to whom I am deeply indebted, were: Sir Antony Acland, the Hon. Lady Aitken, Mr Jonathan Aitken, the Rev. William and Mrs Aitken, Lord Aldington, Mr John Foster Allan, Mr Julian Amery, Major the Hon. Sir John Astor, the Countess of Avon, Lord Barber, Sir Harold Beeley, Mr John Behrend, Mr and Mrs Glanvill Benn, Mr Ray Bernie, Col. T. S. Bigland, His Honour Judge Bingham, Lord and Lady Blake, Lord Boyd-Carpenter, Sir Ashley Bramall, Lord Briggs, Dr Edwin Brooks, Lord and Lady Broxbourne, Lady Butler of Saffron Walden, Sir Robin Butler, Lord Caccia, Sir Alec Cairncross, Dame Olwen Carey Evans, Lord Carr, Lord and Lady Carrington, Miss Susan Carter, Sir Bryan Cartledge, Mr E. G. Cass, Mr T. H. Caulcott, Mrs Charles-Edwards, His Honour Gordon Clover and Mrs Clover, the late Sir John Colville, Mr John Corner, Sir John Coulson, M. Maurice Couve de Murville, Mr and Mrs Donald Crichton-Miller, the late Lord Crowther-Hunt, Mr T. O. Crundwell, Sir John Davis, Sir Patrick Dean, Lord Deedes, Lord and Lady Devlin, Professor David Dilks, Mr P. V. Dixon, Sir Douglas Dodds-Parker, the late Lord Drumalbyn, Sir Antony Duff, Sir James Dunnett, Mr Neil Durden-Smith, Dr James and Mrs Dyce, Mr George Eustance, the Rt Rev. Douglas Feaver, Mr Clive Fenn-Smith, Sir Nigel and Lady Fisher, Sir John Ford, Lord Franks, Lord and Lady Fraser of Kilmorack, Sir Edward Gardner, Lord and Lady Gladwyn, Lord Glendevon, Sgt W.S. and Mrs Golding, Sir Samuel Goldman, the late Sir William Gorell Barnes, Lady Gorell Barnes, Sir John Graham, Mr John Graham, the late Sir Hugh Greene, Lord Grimond, Sir Michael Hadow, Lord Hailsham, Mr W. N. Hanna, Brigadier Sir Geoffrey Hardy-Roberts, the late Lady Hardy-Roberts, Mr Leslie Hargreaves, Sir Thomas Harley, the late Mr Ian Harvey, Lord Harvington, Sir William and Lady Hayter, the Rev. Andrew Henderson, Mr Peter Hennessy, Mr Bertram Hesmondalgh, Mrs Kathleen Hill, Lord Home of the Hirsel, Sir Peter Hope, Mr Alistair Horne, Lord Houghton, the late Mr Bill Housden, Mr Michael Howard, Mrs Joy Howard Davies, the late Mr T. E. B. Howarth, Sir Geoffrey Howe, Mr David Hubback, Mr David Hunt, Mrs Irene Hunter, Mr Anthony Hunter-Tilney, Lord Inchyra, Lord Jenkins of Hillhead, Sir Alexander Johnston, Mr Aubrey Jones, Mrs

John Kemp-Welch, His Honour Alan King-Hamilton, Dr Lionel and Mrs King-Lewis, Mr Peter King-Lewis, Mr Keith Kyle, Lord Lambton, Mr R. J. Langridge, the late Sir Denis Laskey, Lady Laskey, Sir John Leahy, Lord Leverhulme, Sir Donald Logan, Mr Martin Lubbock, Mr and Mrs P. B. Lucas, Mr C. D. Lush, Mr Michael McAfee, Mr Alasdair Macdonald, Mr David Machin, Mr and Mrs Michael McRitchie, the late Lord Mancroft, Lord Mayhew, Lord Mellish, Mr Norman Miscampbell, the Hon. Sir Charles Morrison, Mr Ferdinand Mount, His Honour Judge Nance, Sir John Nicholson, Sir Anthony Nutting, Mr Roger Opie, Lord Orr-Ewing, Col. Michael Osborn, Sir Thomas and Lady Padmore, Mr Colin Peterson, Lord Peyton, Sir David Pitblado, Mr Enoch Powell, Sir Richard Powell, Sir John and Lady Prideaux, Major Robert Priestley, Mr and Mrs John Profumo, Lord and Lady Pym, the late Lord Ramsey of Canterbury, Lady Ramsey, Mr James Reeve, Sir Patrick Reilly, Mr Robert Rhodes James, Sir Brooks Richards, Sir Derek Riches, Sir Denis and Lady Rickett, the late Lord Roberthall, Mr Peter Robinson, Mr Kenneth Rose, Sir Archibald and Lady Ross, Mr and Mrs Ian Samuel, Mr and Mrs Hugh Scurfield, Lord Shawcross, Lord Sherfield, Sir Robert Shone, Sir Evelyn and Lady Shuckburgh, the late Mr Henry Silcock, Mr Nicholas Smith, the late Lord Soames, Sir Robert and Lady Speed, Mr C. J. Spence, Mr Anthony Steen, Mr Gilbert Stephenson, the late Lord Stockton, Vice Admiral Sir FitzRoy Talbot, Mr Cecil Taylor, Sir John Temple, Lord Thomas of Swynnerton, Mr Bruce Thompson, Sir Peter Thorne, Lord Thorneycroft, Sir John and Dame Guinevere Tilney, Lord Tonypandy, Councillor F. W. Venables, Brigadier Richard Vernon, Mr Peter Vinter, Mr Peter Walker, Sir Douglas Wass, Lord and Lady Watkinson, Mr and Mrs J. S. Watson, Mr Bernard Weatherill, Lord Whitelaw, Sir Michael Wilford, Lord Wilson of Rievaulx, Mr Bill Wood, Miss Emily Wright, Mr Harold Wright and Sir Philip de Zulueta.

I was also able to talk earlier about the political scene in the 1950s and 1960s with public figures now dead: Lord Boothby, Lord Butler of Saffron Walden, Sir Knox Cunningham, Mr Peter Goldman, Mr Reginald Maudling and Sir Austin Strutt, all of whom gave me insights into issues raised in this book.

The following corresponded with me about Selwyn Lloyd and I am grateful to them for their contributions: Nayef Al-Kadi, Mr Charles Appleton, Mr L. J. Campbell, Lord Eccles, Señor Josep Ensesa, Mr Peter Henderson, Lord Hill of Luton, Mr George Hodson, Sir Bryan Hopkin, Mr C. I. R. Hunter, M. Marwan S. Kasim, Dr Joseph Luns, Sir Donald MacDougall, Mr Nigel Nicolson, Mr Michael Noakes, M. Christian Pineau, Mr Timothy Raison, Mr John Rigg, Mrs John

Barry Ryan, the late Lord Shinwell, Miss Helen Snow and Her Grace Viola, the late Dowager Duchess of Westminster.

It was said by the Duke of Windsor that nobody could understand his father, King George V, who had not seen York Cottage, Sandringham. I believe that the 'spirit of place' is the third vital area of research for a biographer and I am grateful to those who have shown me or afforded me access to places of importance in Selwyn Lloyd's life. Firstly I am grateful to Mr Anthony Shone and Mr Christopher Spence for taking me to the houses in which Selwyn lived, from his birth place, Red Bank in West Kirby, to Lower Farm House, Preston Crowmarsh, where he died. I am particularly grateful to Mr George Eustance for arranging a tour of 32 Queen's Road, Hoylake, now an Abbeyfield Home. Thanks to the Rev. Ronald Pearce and Mr A. Hall I was able to visit the Westbourne Road Methodist Church, West Kirby and see the Baptismal Register there. In Liverpool I was able to see the various properties in Rodney Street associated with the Lloyd family and to visit the Shaftesbury Hotel. The late Mr Henry Silcock, Headmaster of the Leas School, Hoylake, took me on a tour of Selwyn Lloyd's preparatory school (in what proved to be the last months before its closure), did research for me in the records there and made available otherwise unobtainable material. To the former headmaster of Fettes College, Edinburgh, Mr Cameron Cochrane, I owe grateful thanks for giving me residential facilities at Fettes to study Selwyn Lloyd's books in the Selwyn Lloyd Memorial Library (including his marked copies of *Hansard*) and for finding much correspondence in the records at Fettes in connection with Selwyn Lloyd, in particular his charitable activities for the school. I would also like to thank Mr R. A. Cole-Hamilton, Mr Kenneth Collier and Mr Michael Leslie, who helped over the Fettes section. At Cambridge I am grateful to Mr N. J. Hancock for making available to me the records of the Union Society, now deposited at the University Library, and for arranging my visit to the Union itself. The staff of the University Library, particularly in the Official Publications Department, were of great help, as was Dr Timothy Hobbs and the staff of Trinity College Library for their help over Lord Butler of Saffron Walden's papers. I was also able to visit the Pepys Library at Magdalene College and other places of Cambridge association. Rear Admiral C. M. Bevan, Treasurer of Gray's Inn, afforded me every facility for visiting Selwyn Lloyd's Inn of Court and I am grateful to Mrs Thom, the Librarian, for showing me round and providing copies of material at Gray's Inn relating to Selwyn Lloyd's legal career. In the Wirral, Mrs C. A. Prato, Information Officer at the Town Hall,

Hoylake, showed me round the former Council Chamber of the Hoylake Urban District Council. In 1984, the 40th anniversary of D-Day, public access was possible to HMS *Dryad*, Southwick House and places associated with the final logistical planning of the Overlord operation. The Prime Minister gave permission for me to see the complex of government offices based in 10 Downing Street and I am grateful to Sir Robin Butler for showing me the Cabinet Room, the State Dining Room (where Selwyn Lloyd in company with Anthony Eden heard news of the nationalisation of the Suez Canal on 26 July 1956) and other rooms in 11 and 12 Downing Street connected with the Chancellor of the Exchequer and the Whips Office. The Prime Minister and the Trustees of the Chequers Estate generously allowed me to visit Chequers where Selwyn Lloyd lived intermittently between 1957 and 1962. I am grateful to Mr Kenneth Stacey, Secretary to the Chequers Estate, for arranging this visit and to the late Wing Commander Vera Thomas, Curator of Chequers, and to Chief Petty Officer Wren Dorothy Haynes for showing me round this historic property and for providing information about Selwyn Lloyd's tenure. The Chequers Visitors' Book, as it related to Selwyn Lloyd's career, was of inestimable help in establishing his movements at certain key moments. The Foreign Secretary, Sir Geoffrey Howe, kindly arranged for me to visit the Foreign Office and in addition to showing me the Secretary of State's room there and the accommodation at 1 Carlton Gardens, the Foreign Secretary's official London residence, provided a full tour of the Foreign Office. I am particularly grateful for this privilege and to Mr Albert Marshall, who conducted me on my visit to the Minister of State's offices. I am grateful to Mr P. V. Dixon, Secretary to the Council of the National Economic Development Office, who arranged my visit to the NEDC and provided me with the records of Selwyn Lloyd's time as Chairman. The Speaker of the House of Commons, Mr Bernard Weatherill, kindly showed me the private apartments of Speaker's House, and arranged a tour for me of the public rooms. I am grateful to Mr R. J. Canter and Mr P. L. Warwick for their help over this visit.

None of this would have been possible without the understanding help of the Governing Body of Charterhouse and the Headmaster, Mr Peter Attenborough, who afforded me sabbatical leave to research the book. I am grateful to the Master of Churchill College, Cambridge, Sir Hermann Bondi, the Fellows and the Archives Committee of the College for then electing me to an Archives Fellow Commonership. The Churchill Archives Centre, which holds the papers of nearly three hundred persons, is the only British equivalent of one of the great American Presidential libraries and I am most grateful to Mr Correlli Barnett, Keeper of the Archives, for guiding me through the many collections in his custody, to Miss Marion Stewart, the former Archivist, and Miss Leslie James, Assistant Archivist, and to Mr Victor Brown, the Conservationist, for their daily help while I was in residence at Churchill. Miss Mary Beveridge, Registrar, and Mr Hywel George, Bursar, helped greatly in the general arrangements for my visiting Fellowship. In the stimulating atmosphere of the College I much appreciated the help and encouragement given to me by Dr Edward Craig, Dr Mark Goldie, Director of Studies in History, Professor Frank Hahn and Dr Michael Hoskin.

I would finally like to thank Dr Sarah Street, Keeper of the Conservative Party Archives at the Bodleian Library, Oxford, for making available the records of Selwyn Lloyd's Party activities, especially the Selwyn Lloyd Report into the Conservative Party Organisation in 1962–3; Mrs Clare Brown of the BBC Written Archives Centre, Caversham; the staff of the Foreign and Commonwealth Office Library, especially Miss Patricia M. Barnes; Dr J. A. Edwards, Keeper of Archives and Manuscripts at the University of Reading; Miss Patricia Methven, Archivist, and Mr A. J. B. Mussell, Assistant Archivist, at the Liddell Hart Centre for Military Archives, Kings College; Dr J. B. Post and his staff in the Search Department and Stacks at the Public Record Office, Kew; the staff at Godalming Public Library; Miss Rosemary Aimetti, personal secretary to the late Earl of Stockton; Mr James Bayliss; Dr Ian Blake; Mr Clive Carter; Major Michael Chignell; Mr Richard Crawford; Mr Colin Davies; Dr Robert Frost; Mr Cary Gilbart-Smith; Lord Goodman; Mr Leonard Halcrow; Dr David Holloway; Mrs M. J. Hopkins of Wirral Newspapers Ltd for access to fifty years of back numbers of *Wirral News* and associated publications; Mr Robert Ingram; Dr Paul Johnson; Mr Graham Jones; sixth formers at Kingswood School, Bath; Mr Gregor Macmillan; Dr Giles Mercer; Mrs F. M. Myles; Mr David Natzler; Mr John Peters; Mr and Mrs Neville Randall; Mr Brian Souter; Mr R. L. Stewart; Col. Owen Taylor; the Twenty-Five Club of Liverpool and its secretary, Mr J. B. Bibby, for the pre-war minutes of the club; Mrs Christopher Wheeler; Mr Frank Wiseman, and Mr Nicholas Wright of Schott & Co.

I am grateful to Mr Jonathan Aitken, Lord Fraser of Kilmorack, Sir Donald Logan and Mr Kenneth Rose for sparing the time to read the book at the typescript stage and to Mr John Corner of the Department of Communication Studies, Liverpool University, for reading the chapter on commercial television. Their comments have been of great value, although I would add the customary *caveat* that any inaccuracies or misinterpretations which may remain are entirely my own.

At Jonathan Cape I owe more than I can say to Mr Graham C. Greene for his guidance over this project and for his own insights into the career of Selwyn Lloyd, whose two books were published by Cape. I am also greatly indebted to Tony Colwell and Jill Sutcliffe at Jonathan Cape for their work in preparing the book for publication.

While acknowledging with gratitude all the help I have been given, I would add that the views expressed in this book are not, of course, to be taken as representing the views of those mentioned above. The project has been greatly aided by way of a generous grant from the Trustees of the Leverhulme Trust.

Godalming, 1988   D. R. THORPE

Acknowledgments

I am grateful to the following for permission to quote copyright material: Jonathan Aitken MP (diary extracts and correspondence); Julian Amery MP (letter); The Hon. Sir John Astor (two letters); The Earl Attlee (letter written by his father, the first Earl, and extract from the Attlee papers at Churchill College, Cambridge); The Countess of Avon (letters by the first Earl of Avon); Correlli Barnett (extract from *The Audit of War*, Macmillan); The BBC Written Archives Centre (material at the Centre, Caversham Park, Reading); Sir Alec Cairncross (diary extracts); The Master, Fellows and Scholars of Churchill College in the University of Cambridge for extracts from the papers of Sir Dingle Foot, Lord Gordon-Walker and Lord Strang; Mr Rupert Colville and the executors of the late Sir John Colville (letter); The Chairman of the Conservative Party (extracts from Conservative Research Department material in the Conservative Party Archives, the Department of Western Manuscripts, the Bodleian Library, Oxford); Crown copyright material in the Public Record Office is reproduced by permission of the Controller of Her Majesty's Stationery Office, as is *The Selwyn Lloyd Minority Report* Command Paper 8116 (1950); Lord Devlin (letter); Professor David Dilks (extract from *Neville Chamberlain*, Volume 1 1869–1929, Cambridge University Press); Sir Nigel Fisher (extracts from two letters and extract from *The Tory Leaders*, Weidenfeld & Nicolson); Sir Edward Gardner QC (extract from the Selwyn Lloyd obituary, published in *Graya*, the magazine for Gray's Inn); Lord Gladwyn (extracts from his papers and correspondence); Edward Heath MP (letter); Mrs Kathleen Hill (letters); George Hodson (letter); The Ismay family and the Trustees of the Liddell Hart Centre for Military Archives (extract from the Ismay papers); The trustees of the Liddell Hart Centre for Military Archives (extract from the Pyman papers); Sir Donald Logan (letter); Viscount Montgomery of

Alamein CBE (letter written by his father, Field Marshal Viscount Montgomery of Alamein); The National Economic Development Office (extracts from the minutes of National Economic Development Council meetings); Nigel Nicolson (letter); Michael Noakes (letters); Sir Anthony Nutting, Bt., (extracts from *No End of a Lesson*, Constable, and letter); Colonel Michael Osborn (letter); Enoch Powell (letter); the late Lord Ramsey of Canterbury (extract from his Selwyn Lloyd obituary published in the *Magdalene College Magazine and Record* and correspondence); Sir Patrick Reilly (extracts from his papers and correspondence); Lady Roberthall (letter written by her husband the late Lord Roberthall); Lord Shawcross (letter); Lord Sherfield (extracts from his personal correspondence); Patrick Shone (diary extract); The Earl of Stockton (letters written by his grandfather, the first Earl); Cecil Taylor (letter); Lord Thomas of Swynnerton (letter); The Master and Fellows of Trinity College, Cambridge for extracts from Lord Butler of Saffron Walden's papers; Her Grace Viola, the late Dowager Duchess of Westminster (letter); J. S. Watson (letter); Sir Nicholas Williamson (extracts from the papers of Lord Hailes at Churchill College, Cambridge).

I am grateful to the following for lending me photographic material from their private collections: Mr Jonathan Aitken, Mr Glanvill Benn, Mrs Ronald Clayton, His Honour Judge Gordon Clover, Mr Donald Crichton-Miller, Mr George Eustance, Mr Michael McAfee, Mr Anthony Shone and Mrs David Stileman.

Abbreviations

ARP	Air-Raid Precautions
BBC	British Broadcasting Corporation
BMRA	Brigade Major Royal Artillery
CBI	Confederation of British Industry
CENTO	Central Treaty Organisation
CH	Companion of Honour
CIA	Central Intelligence Agency
CRA	Commander Royal Artillery
DBE	Dame Commander of the Order of the British Empire
DEA	Department of Economic Affairs
EDC	European Defence Community
EEC	European Economic Community
EFTA	European Free Trade Association
ENSA	Entertainments National Services Association
FBI	Federation of British Industries
GATT	General Agreement on Tariffs and Trade
HMG	Her Majesty's Government
HMSO	Her Majesty's Stationery Office
HQ	Headquarters
IMF	International Monetary Fund
ITA	Independent Television Authority
ITV	Independent Television
KC	King's Counsel
LCC	London County Council
LLB	Bachelor of Laws
MC	Military Cross
NAAFI	Navy, Army and Air Force Institutes
NATO	North Atlantic Treaty Organisation
NCB	National Coal Board
NEDC	National Economic Development Council

NEDO	National Economic Development Office
NHS	National Health Service
NIC	National Incomes Commission
OTC	Officers' Training Corps
PPS	Parliamentary Private Secretary
RAF	Royal Air Force
RAMC	Royal Army Medical Corps
RHA	Royal Horse Artillery
SC	Staff Course
SCUA	Suez Canal Users' Association
SEATO	South-East Asia Treaty Organisation
TA	Territorial Army
TUC	Trades Union Congress
UDC	Urban Distict Council
UDI	Unilateral Declaration of Independence
UHF	Ultra High Frequency
UN	United Nations
VHF	Very High Frequency
WASP	Wirral Action Schools Project
YVFF	Young Volunteer Force Foundation
ZANU	Zimbabwe African National Union
ZAPU	Zimbabwe African People's Union

I

A Middle Class Lawyer
from Liverpool

The memoirs of retired politicians are often more interesting for what they hide than for what they reveal. Even the titles can be deceptive. Behind the barrier of *A Prime Minister Remembers* retreated an unforthcoming and forgetful Attlee; Duff Cooper's *Old Men Forget* on the other hand was open to the world, a fulfilled and generous testimony. Towards the end of a long political life Selwyn Lloyd too began to plan his autobiography. He had already written, with some misgivings, a narrative of his Speakership and, with fewer misgivings, had embarked in the latter part of 1976 on the research for his personal account of the Suez crisis, a book he did not intend to publish until after the death of Anthony Eden. The suddenness of his own final illness meant that plans for the third and most extensive of his books remained largely unrealised, though chapters exist in draft form among his papers. But of one thing he was certain from the start. 'I shall call it *A Middle Class Lawyer from Liverpool*', he told his friends and when they politely demurred, suggesting it to be a rather ponderous title, he delighted in explaining, 'But it is what Harold Macmillan calls me behind my back.'[1]

The title had about it the terrible fluidity of self-revelation. In the first place, as Selwyn Lloyd wrote in those memoirs, 'the description was wholly accurate.'[2] More than that, though, his delight in the mischievous recycling of an uncomplimentary remark about himself had an openness and self-effacing quality that was entirely in character, revealing the edge that was always present behind the exterior of the most dramatic of all his political relationships, as well as the honesty and simple candour of his personality. Humility may be a difficult virtue to achieve, but it was one that Selwyn Lloyd compassed.[3] Nevertheless he did not underestimate the ebb and flow of his life's experience. 'It would be false modesty for me to pretend that I have not had a remarkable and intensely interesting life.'[4] Born into the suburban world of Edwardian professional life, he never ceased to be grateful for the opportunities which enabled him to walk with the captains and the kings.

Although the Lloyds had been established in Liverpool for three generations when Selwyn was born in 1904, their roots as a family lay deep in Welsh soil and Selwyn was proud of his Celtic ancestry. In a speech on St David's Day in 1961 he told his audience that he had been 'born and bred in sight of the Welsh hills across the estuary of the River Dee.'[5] These Welsh origins contributed to his early radicalism (nurtured in the company of the Lloyd Georges at Criccieth), to his feelings for the under-dog and to an intense ambition which never left him. The Nonconformist upbringing of his childhood combined with the business drive of his mother's forbears and gave him the determination to set his foot on the ladder of three different and distinctive careers. The modest, often casual appearance that Selwyn gave to the world belied this inner resolve. 'That Welsh lawyer', was the American Secretary of State Dean Acheson's phrase for him, any accompanying adjective (and there were many) indicating the independence or intransigence that Selwyn had shown in negotiation. Acheson once stooped to calling him 'a crooked Welsh lawyer',[6] but it did not make it any easier to conquer. 'Why hasn't he a K?', asked Selwyn of his staff in mock puzzlement as the guardsmanlike figure of the immaculately attired *Mister* Acheson was announced.

Selwyn Lloyd never forgot the Welsh stock from which he sprang. With the application of a Soames Forsyte, if not the tenacity of a Curzon, Selwyn delighted in tracing his family roots back over two centuries to the earliest recorded Lloyds, keeping elaborate genealogical trees which he updated at the subsequent births of great nephews and nieces. On his father's side the origins were small hill farmers from Merioneth and a tanner and weaver from the small textile town of Llanidloes; on his mother's Warhurst side there was a great-grandfather who was a customs officer and a grandfather who, with considerable entrepreneurial skill, had built up a chain of chemist shops in Bootle and North West Liverpool. The patriarch of the Lloyd family was the weaver David Lloyd Bach, who was born in Llanidloes in 1742. His son William (1767–1841) was also a weaver and the father of eleven children by Jane, the daughter of John Morgan, a tanner from Machynlleth, 'a thoroughly Welsh town', as George Borrow described it.[7] The town was to be of considerable importance in the early history of the Lloyd family for among the eleven children of William Lloyd was John Lloyd (Selwyn's great-grandfather) who, as the Rev. John Lloyd, was to be the Methodist minister in charge of the twelve preaching stations of the Machynlleth circuit.

John Lloyd was born in 1802 (the date of his birth is uncertain, but he was baptised on 2 September) and brought up in a devout and strict home. There were few educational opportunities owing to the size of the family and the general atmosphere of economic depression. Llanidloes had been a principal textile centre, providing wares for the American slave trade and for the Army in the Peninsular campaign, but with the introduction of machinery in the North of England demand for the wares of the Severn Valley weavers fell and before the Repeal of the Corn Laws in 1846, over a quarter of the population of two thousand was regularly in receipt of parish relief. It was against this background that John Lloyd spent his impressionable adolescent years, his unpampered upbringing doing much to foster the drive and energy of his adult years. Though poor on the material side, Llanidloes was richly endowed on the spiritual and as it was on the old coaching route from Shrewsbury to Aberystwyth it became a gateway for travelling preachers. John Wesley, after whom both Selwyn's grandfather and father were to be named, had preached there and in April 1819 the town was the focus of the 'Great Revival' which converted many to Methodism, including the sixteen-year-old John Lloyd, who subsequently joined the local Band Meeting and acted as a local preacher. In 1826 he became a full-time circuit Minister and travelled the circuits of Wales from Caernarvon to Merthyr before living in London for a spell in 1836. By that time, the Rev. John Lloyd had married Elizabeth Thomas, the daughter of Alderman Thomas of Cowbridge. Their first son (Selwyn's grandfather) was born in April 1836 and christened John Wesley Lloyd. 'A Welshman born in London', was how this son described himself in adult life, but he settled permanently neither in Wales nor London, nor did he follow his father's profession. John Wesley Lloyd qualified instead as a dentist and eventually established himself in practice in Liverpool. When the Rev. John Lloyd retired in 1865 (his last mission was near Cardiff) he too moved to Liverpool, sometimes called the capital of Wales, to be near his son and, by then, the growing company of grandchildren. So the Lloyds left their native Welsh background and set down new roots on Merseyside. The Rev. John Lloyd had an active retirement, teaching the children at the Shaw Street Chapel Sunday School. It was in June 1869 after taking one of these classes that he fell ill. He died on 2 September, the anniversary of his baptism, and was buried in the Lloyd family vault which had been purchased in the Anfield Cemetery, Liverpool.

Much of the pragmatic thoroughness of the family (and their transition to professional status) stemmed from the Rev. John Lloyd and, as his biographer recorded, 'he played the game nobly, heroically, without bragging and without grumbling'[8] – qualities which he sought to instil in his own offspring. To this end he educated his eldest son at Kingswood School, then in Bristol. John Wesley had started this school, the oldest of Methodist foundations, in 1748 and when Selwyn's grandfather entered the school in July 1847 all pupils by statute were the sons of Methodist Ministers. Self-help, hard work and a religious vocation were the touchstones. John Wesley Lloyd was of quick intelligence and made the most of his opportunities. When he left in 1850, just before the school moved to its present site at Bath, his final memorandum, as reports were called at Kingswood, summed up simply 'a good boy'.[9] He was deeply religious and in his chosen profession of dentistry something of a pioneer. He practised briefly at Machynlleth and like his father before him chose a Machynlleth bride, Anne Jones.

After their marriage the Lloyds moved to Liverpool in search of broader horizons and established themselves at 30 Mount Pleasant. On the family tree John Wesley Lloyd is described as Dentist of Machynlleth and Liverpool,[10] but it was in Liverpool that the practice flourished, first at 30 Mount Pleasant, later in Rodney Street, the Harley Street of the North, where the physicians and surgeons colonised – a prestigious address for the dentists who followed. John Wesley Lloyd bought as his main residence 43 Rodney Street, opposite the birthplace of W. E. Gladstone, with a second property, 1a, as the surgery. John Wesley Lloyd was forward-looking in his professional life and was one of the first provincial dentists to make use of nitrous oxide gas as an anaesthetic for his patients. He experimented on himself and was sometimes found on the floor of his surgery under the influence of the gas. This pioneering spirit was held up to his young grandson Selwyn as an example of the diligence needed to succeed in life, not that this much impressed the young boy who caused raised eyebrows at tea-parties by asking his own father's dental patients if they had gas when they went to the surgery. 'But of course', replied one satisfied customer. 'I wouldn't if I were you', warned Selwyn impishly, 'that's when they go through your pockets.'

The Lloyds were forward-looking in their politics too. As Nonconformist chapel-going people they were staunch Liberals, largely because of the commitment to Free Trade, at a time when the Liberal Party was the voice of the Nonconformist conscience, and Liverpool an important repository of that conscience. In 1876 John Wesley Lloyd met Gladstone himself at the time of the Bulgarian atrocities. 'What has Liverpool to say?', was the question Gladstone put to John Wesley Lloyd of the massacre of some 12,000 Bulgarians by Turkish irregular troops. Conservatism in nineteenth-century Liverpool was

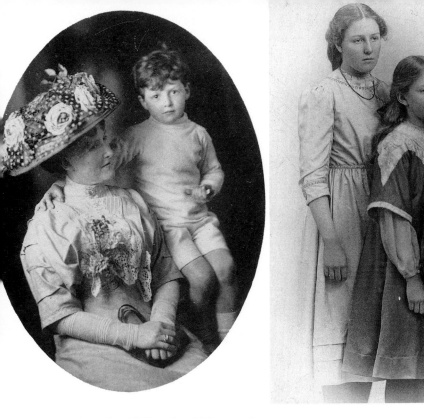

1 Selwyn in early childhood, with his mother.
2 Dorice and Eileen with their younger brother Selwyn.
3 Selwyn and his youngest sister Rachel.

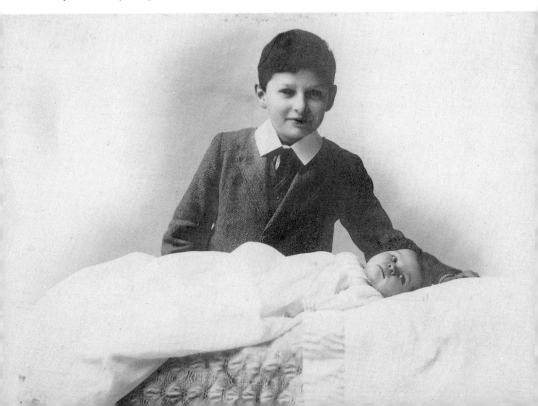

4 Edwardian motoring: Dr and Mrs Lloyd in 1906.

5 Selwyn at Number 2 in a Fettes tug-of-war, 1923.

seen as the preserve of the landed gentry, while the emerging radicalism of Socialist organisations had an essentially working class base, not that any of the Lloyds ever had a trace of snobbery. The Lloyds remained mainstream Liberals even though confused and shocked by the diversionary controversies of Irish Home Rule and the Parnell divorce case.

The family grew, as did the practice. John Wesley Lloyd's sons were born in 1865 and 1870. The eldest (Selwyn's father) was inevitably christened John Wesley, though to avoid confusion he was known as Jack. The second son was called Henry William, known to the family as Harry. There were also two daughters in their family, Anne, who died in infancy, and Elizabeth. All were brought up in the Methodist faith. John Wesley Lloyd's commitment to the Church, as in all things, was essentially practical and down-to-earth. His was not a Christianity of the pew. He welcomed many young Circuit preachers to the Shaw Street Chapel and to his own Rodney Street home. He was conscious of the temptations that a city like Liverpool offered the young. Determined to protect them from the flesh-pots of Lime Street, he bought up two houses in Mount Pleasant and two in Newington to form one block in 1878 and turned them into a Temperance Hotel for visiting preachers. In 1927 the old family residence, No. 30, was also incorporated. Eventually 'Mount Pleasant', as it was always known to the Lloyds, was renamed the Shaftesbury Hotel after (and by permission of) the great social reformer Lord Shaftesbury. Some of Selwyn Lloyd's earliest memories were of 'Mount Pleasant' where, as he later recalled, Grandfather Lloyd 'kept open house for Wesleyan Ministers and friends and relations rather in that order of precedence.'[11] Grandfather Lloyd's business acumen, so marked in his professional life, did not extend to the Shaftesbury, which belonged rather to his heart. The hotel was retained as a Liverpool pied-à-terre after the family had moved 'over the water' to West Kirby and, under the management of a distant cousin, Matilda Jones, was maintained on a more even financial keel and was a steady source of income for the family through to the 1950s, long after it had ceased to be an exclusively Circuit lodging house. Thanks to his generosity to visiting preachers, whom he rarely charged, Grandfather Lloyd had died in debt in 1915, but because of the skilful management of the Shaftesbury by Matilda Jones from the early 1920s, Dr Lloyd (Selwyn's father) was able to retire in 1930 at the age of 65 in an era when retirement at that age was less usual than it is now. Dr Lloyd would often go to Mount Pleasant for a few days (he died there in 1954) and in Selwyn's early days in Parliament he himself would stop over at the Shaftesbury when the timings of

London trains were at inconvenient domestic hours. Nephews and nieces would be taken to the hotel for lunch before a Christmas pantomime where the novelty of the tinned grapefruit (how *did* they manage the transformation?) was always remembered as a special treat. After the death of Selwyn Lloyd's mother in 1959 the premises were sold and flourished as a licensed commercial hotel. In this new guise the Shaftesbury featured as a location in the 1985 film *Letter to Brezhnev*, though it was used there by its young Liverpudlian clients for purposes very different from those intended by its original founder.

That founder was a formidable Victorian grandfather figure to the young Selwyn. Even at the age of 75 he was still at his desk by six every morning. His correspondence, kept in Selwyn's papers, is in an immaculate copperplate. It was said of him that 'a glance at the stamps on his morning correspondence testified at once to the wideness of his interests and the greatness of his heart.'[12] As a child Selwyn was allowed into the surgery to collect the brightly coloured foreign stamps from the morning mail, always wanting to know the whereabouts of the far-off Imperial outposts. John Wesley Lloyd held prayers twice a day in his household, for family and visitors alike, at 9 a.m. in the dining room (by which time a substantial part of the day's work was accomplished) and at 5 p.m. in the drawing-room. The afternoon service was more elaborate but less severe, John Wesley Lloyd accompanying the hymns on the harmonium. Anne Lloyd was a gentler figure than her redoubtable husband, never angry or flurried, and a particular favourite of the young Selwyn. John Wesley Lloyd died in February 1915, but his widow lived on to her 88th year. When she died in May 1923 it was a distinct break with the old world of Machynlleth, but by then the family were firmly established on Merseyside.

'A Liverpool dentist of comparatively modest means',[13] was Selwyn's description of his father. Dr Lloyd, however modest the initial means, had inherited from his father the same sense of purpose and willpower that had led to the burgeoning of the Rodney Street –Mount Pleasant axis and was brought up to believe that there was nothing in this world that was not gained by hard work (values he stressed to his four children) and that one's behaviour should be conducted according to the principles of some higher power. His early schooling was at the Liverpool Institute High School, but in January 1880 he was sent to board at the Leys School, Cambridge, which had been founded five years earlier by a group of leading Methodists. The school to which he was sent was a largely untried quantity, but until 1922 laymen were not eligible to send their sons to Kingswood School, and so began an important family link with Cambridge. The aim of the Leys School was to build on Christian but non-sectarian principles and the school was 'perfectly open to boys belonging to other churches',[14] but when Selwyn's father was there the majority of the boys had Kingswoodian grandfathers who were Methodist Ministers.

John Wesley Lloyd was an energetic boy at the Leys and his diaries show him to have been a devout, serious-minded pupil. His house-master in Schoolhouse was the founding headmaster of the Leys, Dr W. F. Moulton, and after hearing one sermon of Dr Moulton's in November 1882, John Wesley Lloyd wrote 'I intend to give myself up entirely to Christ & his work, seeing him not in my own strength but in his.'[15] It was a time of muscular Christianity and John Wesley Lloyd became Gymnasium Champion, President of the Boat Club and eventually a prefect.

On leaving the Leys John Wesley Lloyd studied medicine at University College, Liverpool, on the continent and at Edinburgh University for a time in 1896. At that stage it was planned that his younger brother Harry would take over the father's dental practice, but when that did not materialise John Wesley Lloyd added – a more common practice in those days – dental qualifications to the benefit of his patients. Early diagnosis of wider medical problems often followed routine dental work. 'He was in fact always known as Dr Lloyd', recalled Selwyn, 'and served as a Doctor in the Army.'[16] He became engaged to Miss Rachel Warhurst and was married in June 1896.

Dr Lloyd's household was to mirror that of his parents. There was a devout Methodism and a strict teetotal atmosphere. Like his father, Dr Lloyd practised in Rodney Street, but was persuaded by a prominent local doctor, William McAfee, of the advantages of setting up a one-day-a-week additional practice in the summer at West Kirby. Dr Lloyd became the consultant to the West Kirby Conva-lescent Hospital for children with Dr McAfee (who was to bring both Eileen and Selwyn into the world) and, in his 'additional' career, a delegate to the international Dental Congress in London in 1914. Mrs Lloyd did not care for the bustle of Liverpool and through their friendship with Dr McAfee, like many professional families of the time, the Lloyds established a holiday residence in the Wirral. 'My parents spent the winter at 1a Rodney Street where my father had his main surgery', wrote Selwyn, 'and the summer at the West Kirby House, where my father saw practice on Thursdays.'[17] Their first child, Dorice Amelia, was born in May 1897 at Rodney

Street, but a second daughter, Eileen Moyra, was born in March 1900 at Inglehurst, West Kirby. 'My parents moved house quite a bit', wrote Selwyn and all four Lloyd children were to be born at different addresses.[18] Each move, because of the expanding family, was up what would now be called the housing ladder, to a more secluded spot, or in the case of Red Bank, Banks Road (Selwyn's birthplace), a more prominent corner site. Unlike later custom the houses were rented, not bought, and Selwyn was never to buy a house outright in his life. Red Bank, as with the Rodney Street house, was in the centre of a colony of doctors, a friendly relaxed colony with doctors as family friends. Sometimes when they called to see a sick child they spent so long chatting downstairs that they forgot the reason for the visit. Although his main consultations were in Liverpool, Dr Lloyd soon set up in practice in West Kirby to fill the long summer months. Initially he spent only the summer in West Kirby, but gradually the pattern changed and he worked one day in the Banks Road surgery and four in Liverpool. The station master at West Kirby (the line had been extended there in 1878) said that he could set his watch by the time that Dr Lloyd appeared on the platform each morning. On Saturdays, ostensibly his day off, Dr Lloyd would work *gratis* at the Convalescent Home for Children. Eventually the centre of gravity switched to West Kirby and it was into this industrious and well-ordered life that Selwyn was born on 28 July 1904.

This third child of the Lloyds was late in arriving (one of the few occasions in Selwyn's life when he was unpunctual) and on 24 July an anxious Mrs Lloyd wrote to her mother-in-law: 'It is the same old story and I am "the late Mrs Lloyd" as the Doctor says.'[19] But four days later all was well and to the tune of a hurdy-gurdy in Banks Road playing *There's a girl wanted there* their first and only son made his appearance at Red Bank. Dr Lloyd wrote the next day to his parents:

> July 29 04 Te deum laudamus   My dear mother & father I am glad to say we have a son and heir, he arrived on Thursday afternoon at 3.30 weighs 8¾ lbs and is healthy and of good appearance. He has a very superior look on his face as if he did not think much of his surroundings.[20]

His father wished to christen the new arrival John Wesley, the third Lloyd son to commemorate the founder of Methodism, but his mother felt that two John Wesleys in the family were quite enough. 'My mother was an Anglican and she dug in her toes at having another John Wesley', recalled Selwyn.[21] So as a compromise they chose one name each, the father opting for John, Wesley's name, while his mother, to bring Anglican balance, settled on Selwyn, after Bishop Selwyn of New Zealand and Lichfield and later the dedicatee of Selwyn College, Cambridge. As a fresh name with no religious connections they jointly settled on Brooke, but from the start the child was known simply as Selwyn. If there had been dispute over the name, there was to be none over the christening, which was in the new Methodist Church in Westbourne Road, 400 yards away. Selwyn was the first boy to be christened there, though not, as his parents intended, the first child. A holiday-maker's daughter had been christened there, denying the Lloyds priority. Entry No. 40 in the West Kirby Register records that the boy was christened John Selwyn Brooke Lloyd by the Rev. Henry Burton on 9 October 1904.[22]

From the start Selwyn was doted upon by aunts and distant relatives alike and until the arrival of his youngest sister Rachel (who was born in 1915) was not displaced – if then – as the family's Benjamin. The unusual Christian name was later to be of great benefit politically in that he joined a small group of public figures – Austen Chamberlain, Winston Churchill and Nye Bevan among them – who were instantly identified by a single name. Selwyn's status as the Benjamin of the family was reinforced by his delicate health. He was vulnerable to infection and suffered from pneumonia on more than one occasion. (When he was called to the Bar in January 1930 he was congratulated by a West Kirby neighbour who reminded him that when 18 months old 'both you and my little fellow about the same age were at death's door with pneumonia'.)[23] Even when quite recovered from childhood illnesses he was never allowed to undertake such jobs as bringing down the luggage. All such jobs devolved upon Dorice and Eileen.

The style of middle class life before the First World War has now largely vanished, but for Selwyn it was the fabric of his upbringing. Red Bank, his birthplace, was a three-storeyed semi-detached house with three large rooms on each floor, a huge kitchen with a coal range, a back kitchen and large larder, no central heating and no refrigerator but a large, cool 'keeping cellar'. The Lloyds had two servants, a cook general at £30 a year and a housemaid at £22 a year, eventually rising to £26. There was never any alcohol in the house. Selwyn's mother was a skilful housekeeper and everything was made to go a long way. There was a joint a week, delicious sausages on toast for Sunday breakfast, and sometimes black pudding too; chicken was always regarded as a great luxury. If there were visitors on Saturday or Sunday evening, Mrs Lloyd served cold salmon and profuse salads. Clothes were important. There were large hats for the ladies, and many of the men wore knickerbocker suits. Miss Foster, the local dressmaker, used to come about once a month for a wage that eventually rose to 7s. 6d. a day, though it was tacitly understood that she expected a good square meal for her labours. Inevitably she left pins all over the carpet. All Dorice and Eileen's dresses were made up by Miss Foster. Dr Lloyd would take the children for a walk in the afternoons at the weekend. As Selwyn grew up they went to watch the rugby at Birkenhead Park. From the Rodney Street home Dorice could remember Dr Lloyd setting off on horseback over Sefton Park and at the docks being shown the remains of the irons that had been used for the slave trade. But Selwyn's main childhood memories were of West Kirby, which underwent many changes in the first quarter of the century from being a small, village-like community, largely of retired people, to one of independent businessmen, commuters and a large self-governing urban district council. It was a world in which people played no tennis or golf on Sundays (a time for improving books, for novels were frowned on) and a visit to the Philharmonic Orchestra in Liverpool meant white tie and tails. 'It was the age of hansom cabs, waggonettes and "growlers"', recalled Selwyn.[24]

Church loomed large. There were two services on Sunday, Dr Lloyd attending in his frock-coat and top-hat. Pew rent was paid. Owing to Selwyn's restlessness and constant fidgeting during the sermons, the family moved to the back pew of the Westbourne Road Church where he could fidget to his heart's content. But even then the pew had to have a door put on it as during the longer sermons Selwyn would slip out and run up and down the aisle. The only way they could get him to keep quiet was to allow him to play with his father's gold sovereign purse. 'I did not then know much about getting quarts into pint pots, but trying to get a sovereign into the half sovereign side was a challenge to be met every week.'[25] Mrs Lloyd sometimes attended the Anglican Churches of St Bridget, where there were fierce gargoyles depicting Gladstone and Disraeli (which represented the devil was not specified) or St Andrew, where Selwyn was to be married in 1951.

Selwyn remembered little of Red Bank for they moved when he was five to No. 10, The Oatlands, a more secluded house set at the end of its own cul-de-sac, and near to Avalon School where Dorice and Eileen were pupils. One memory of his birthplace, however, was retained with particular vividness. 'When we had some friends to stay, the Buntings from Accrington, a lot of powerful pills were left in the piano', recalled Selwyn. As these pills had gone missing the assumption was that Selwyn had swallowed them.

> Fervent denials availed me nought. I was shaken upside down, sideways and longways. Every kind of emetic was vigorously used

against me. I parted with all that my little inside contained. Shortly afterwards the bottle of pills was found in Mrs Bunting's bedroom. The result was a lesson for life. I received no sympathy or offer of compensation. My sufferings were overlooked and soon forgotten. What a lesson! I wondered whether this was a foretaste of what fortune, at certain times, had in store for me.[26]

More formal lessons were learned in a succession of West Kirby schools. He went first to a local kindergarten, Miss Poore's Academy, where he was the only boy in a class with twelve girls. Fortunately, this experience was short-lived, thanks to the timely intervention of three shadowy figures who hovered in the background of Selwyn's childhood, the three 'Misses' – Nellie, Susie and Fairy Jones – who were patients of Dr Lloyd in West Kirby. Miss Susie Jones walked the sea-front and was a mysterious spinster to the young. Selwyn said he would marry her when he grew up and she took to referring to him as her dear future husband. The house of the three Misses overlooked Miss Poore's Academy and it was they who told Dr Lloyd that they had seen poor Selwyn surrounded by the girls of the school who were kissing him in a ring-a-roses game. After that Selwyn was promptly moved to the Mount, a pre-preparatory school in a red brick house in its own grounds on the Caldy Road, and within walking distance of Oatlands. Here the five-year-olds were taught the different disciplines of Latin and Greek by the headmaster, Mr E. Temple Churton.

The Mount was rather grand, its prospectus giving many references from titled people. Of more appeal to the Lloyds was the emphasis on the healthy importance of physical pursuits, though even this could not be simply stated in the curriculum. 'The boys are exercised daily in physical drill and breathing exercises and the holidays generally coincide with those of Eton.'[27] The predominant memory that Selwyn had of the Mount was his inability through ill health to join in games, yet he prospered in his work and one of the teachers at the Mount told Dr Lloyd, 'if this boy is given his health he will go far'.[28] When the others were at games Selwyn read voraciously. He was an alert, inquisitive child and was fascinated by history. He would take his history books upstairs and on returning to the drawing room would fire off questions to his parents such as, 'Who married Catherine of Aragon?', as well as more considered inquiries.[29] The war played havoc with the children's education and with his elder sisters away at St Felix School, Southwold he was very much left to his own devices at the Oatlands and his upbringing at times was more like that of an only child. His imagination was stimulated by his reading. As he recalled,

'I loved G. A. Henty, because not only was there a story, but there were great chunks of history, a subject in which I was very interested. I was also very fond of books like *Treasure Island*, Herbert Strang's *Adventure Story*, Ian Hay's *Pip*, *The Right Stuff*, *Man's Man* and *Safety Match*. Another book I liked very much was *The Little Duke* by Charlotte Mary Yonge.'[30] But his favourite book, which he read over and over again, was *Little Lord Fauntleroy* and he took delight some sixty years later in referring to his Speaker's robes as his Little Lord Fauntleroy suit when he was sitting for his official portrait.[31] His fort and toy soldiers occupied him for hours (only by placing these soldiers near the artist who painted his first portrait, a life-size pastel, could his parents get Selwyn to sit still long enough for a likeness to be drawn) and he arranged great battles against foreign foes, battles which he then chronicled in his notebooks. These little adventures, profusely illustrated by Selwyn and with titles like *My Adventures* and *A Tale of A King*, were romantic legends of derring-do, usually featuring a thinly disguised Selwyn as the millionaire commander of an equivalent number of troops storming the battlements of some distant imperial outpost. His particular childhood heroes were Henry V, Drake, Marlborough, Wolfe, Nelson, Wellington and Joan of Arc and there are distinct echoes of Agincourt in Selwyn's *A Tale of A King*, written when he was eight years old:

> The French King had brought an army to England meaning to get to London but he was met by King Edward's army at Windsor. Courage was fighting the Scots in the North so the King asked Edward if he would fight the French. So Edward went and beat the French at the battle of Windsor. There were only about ten French left out of ten million, and out of ten thousand English there were nine thousand left.[32]

Selwyn was ten when the First World War broke out. His tenth birthday on 28 July 1914 was the date on which Austria and Hungary chose to declare war on Serbia and on his father's 49th birthday Britain went to war with Germany. Once a week until then a German band used to play in Oatlands Park. When the war came Selwyn was convinced they were German spies.

Dr Lloyd had been in the Territorial Army in Liverpool before the war (he always believed in getting involved in the local community) and he joined up as a Surgeon-Major in the Royal Army Medical Corps. He had always longed to make more of his life, to cut a figure, to shine, to make speeches, and he had a feeling, despite his un-doubted professional success in combining two careers, that he had not done with his life what he wanted. The war was a liberating opportunity, as it was for his son in 1939. The last years of peace were something of a golden age for the family. Finances were comfortable, with Dr Lloyd earning £1,500 a year. He still retained 1a Rodney Street, had two houses in West Kirby (one for Thursday surgeries), two domestic servants, two housekeepers. His three children were all being educated privately. Yet life was not lavish; Selwyn remembered the two great treats of the week as an ounce of boiled sweets and a good long donkey ride on the sands, each costing 1d. Dr Lloyd was always determined to do the best for his family and was philosophical and unhurried in his ways. He was practical, a creature of habit, and liked photography, fishing, the mechanics of cars and early bed. Mrs Lloyd on the other hand tended to worry and become dejected. If a visit was called off at the last minute it could temporarily seem like the end of the world, whereas Dr Lloyd would mutter consolingly, 'Well, we'll go another time.' Mrs Lloyd was an intensely beautiful lady and dressed with style and elegance. Yet she brought up her children to feel for the unfortunate and impoverished. 'At home, my mother always had about a dozen people to whom it was our duty to take week by week flowers or fruit or little household delicacies or small gifts of money. This was quite apart from the wider charitable commitments with which my parents busied themselves.'[33]

The Lloyds were devoted to each other, but were so different in temperament that they seldom agreed and hardly a day passed without disagreement. Every few weeks there would be a storm and father would not speak for a couple of days, or worse still, would go and live at Mount Pleasant for a while; a cloud would hang over the household and the children would be miserable. Dr Lloyd could be brusque with his tongue, a characteristic he handed on to his son. When a prospective son-in-law asked for the hand of one of his daughters in marriage he advised, 'I wouldn't if I were you, women are queer cattle at the best of times.' In older age when someone asked him, 'How are you keeping?', more likely than not he would receive the reply, 'Why? Do I smell?'. Selwyn recalled breakfast as a particularly dangerous time, quite a lot of the strain revolving (unnecessarily) round money, though the medical practice inevitably declined when Dr Lloyd was serving in the war. Selwyn began to take a vicarious interest in stocks and shares and when travelling locally could be seen making notes of his mock investments.[34] It was made clear to him that if he was to go on to a public school he would have to win a scholarship.

With Dr Lloyd away at the war Selwyn went to board at the Mount for the first time, but numbers were falling (the Wirral coastline was thought a possible place for German invasion) and Mrs Lloyd was left to find another school for Selwyn. He was entered as a day boy at the

Leas School, Hoylake, from January 1916 and, with Mrs Lloyd's fourth child expected, and so that it would be easier for him to walk there, the family moved in 1915 from The Oatlands to Netherton in Banks Road.

'I examined your boy today', wrote Percy Dealtry, the headmaster of the Leas, to Mrs Lloyd on 20 January 1916, 'and he seemed to me most intelligent with capacities distinctly above the average.'[35] With such encouraging reports Selwyn entered a school very different from Miss Poore's Academy or the Mount. If his home life was of quiet, ordered regularity the eccentricities of his future mentors more than contrasted. The Leas had been founded in 1898 by two Liverpool schoolmasters, Percy Dealtry ('Doll-tree' to the boys) and Jackie Barr, who were joint proprietors. The school occupied cold, grey buildings, its windows open to all seasons and weathers. The distinctive school ornament, remembered by generations of Leasians, was an armadillo, yellowed with age. Dealtry and Barr aimed for a blend of the best values of Merseyside business and Cheshire gentility. They wanted to show the Liverpool merchants over the water that there was more to life than brass and toil and the Wirral residents that sweetness and light were not enough. They judged their market well and the school was one of the most successful in the North West. Dealtry's practical, down-to-earth approach suited Selwyn well and he responded at once to the challenging atmosphere. A regimental sergeant-major from the Afghan wars was in charge of boxing; classics were taught by Ken Sutton and 'Old' Mr Hadley (and very well too judging by the honours board), though Jackie Barr tended to be rather forgetful. Selwyn remembered how he would fall asleep in form and then give the boys the excuse he had been staying up to watch the stars.[36] Parental contacts were left to Percy Dealtry and, as he was later to greet a visitor during his last illness with, 'You're too late with the fruit and too early for the flowers', these tended to be brusque and to the point.[37]

Selwyn's years at the Leas, though academically successful, were sombre ones. Most of the fathers were serving abroad and the school magazines were filled with the lists of the Fallen. A leather-bound book was kept by Miss Stockqueller in a place of honour. By November 1918 20 per cent of serving old boys were dead. School life continued as best it could under the shadow of war and endless news of casualties, and not surprisingly one of Selwyn's contemporaries remembers him as 'a solemn, square boy.'[38] Nevertheless, the worst of childhood illness was behind him and he played football for the second eleven – generally he was a second eleven type of schoolboy. 'Lloyd at times has played brilliantly in goal', recorded *The Leas*

School Magazine in December 1917 and (a pre-echo of his political role) 'has saved the situation on several occasions.'[39] But golf became his main interest. The Royal Liverpool links bordered the school grounds and he twice won the sons of members' competition over a course where he had been taken to see J. H. Taylor win the Open in 1913. He progressed in his school work too, justifying the confidence Percy Dealtry had placed in him. 'Will do great things',[40] wrote Dealtry in November 1916. By this time Dr Lloyd had been invalided out of the RAMC (though he remained on the reserve list) and took an active part with Dealtry in planning the next phase of his son's education. Initially he favoured the Leys School, Cambridge, though when this did not work out he rationalised the decision to go elsewhere. There would be the broadening experience of a Non-Methodist school and also if Selwyn went up to Cambridge, which Dr Lloyd planned, then a public school elsewhere would give additional variety. But a scholarship was the first requisite. 'I was brought up to believe that I had to get a scholarship to go to a public school.'[41] Malvern was a possibility, but eventually Uppingham was chosen. Selwyn recorded the outcome laconically: 'In June 1918 I was to sit a scholarship for Uppingham. 3 days before I got mumps. I did two papers, under some difficulty. I failed. Of the schools with scholarship examinations in July, Fettes was adjudged the best. This time I succeeded.'[42]

Percy Dealtry was delighted. 'Fettes I regard as likely to suit him well, and from a financial point of view actually seems certainly the best', he wrote to Dr Lloyd.[43] Dr Lloyd felt that the bracing climate of Edinburgh would be preferable to the dank air of Uppingham and he had heard great reports of Selwyn's prospective housemaster, K. P. Wilson, so was well pleased with the turn of events. On 17 July 1918 Dr Heard, the headmaster of Fettes, wrote to the Lloyds offering their son a scholarship of £40 a year and Mr Hadley's latest success was duly inscribed on a retrospective and much later dining-hall honours board.

Selwyn always held the Leas in great affection and Percy Dealtry was the first of his many mentors in life, *My Masters* as he called them in a book of that title sketched out in retirement. When he became Member of Parliament for the Wirral in July 1945 he hastened the return of the school premises from the RAF. He presented prizes at speech days, even when more public events clamoured, and nephews and great-nephews followed him there as pupils. For its part, the school held almost proprietorial links, the joint Headmasters A. F. Fetherstanhaugh and Henry Silcock sending telegrams of congratulations on behalf of the school as Selwyn ascended successive rungs of the ministerial ladder. It was a bold young master who inquired what they were going to send after one of Selwyn's rare reverses.[44]

In September 1918, as the First World War entered its final phase, Selwyn travelled to Edinburgh with his father to take up his place at Fettes. As an open scholar he was not sent to School House, this was reserved for foundationers, but was placed in Glencorse, the house of K. P. Wilson. Fettes had been founded in 1870 and was named after Sir William Fettes, a prosperous man of commerce, who had endowed the College in his will. The governors of the Fettes trust engaged as architect David Bryce, who created by the Comely Bank Estates of Sir William Fettes a building which combined the Scottish baronial style with the French châteaux of the period of François Ier, a building encrusted with gargoyles and decorated with gilded bees. But it was not for these delights that Selwyn had eyes: 'I walked down with my father from the Hotel to the school in a frame of mind which was a mixture of curiosity and exaltation', wrote Selwyn. 'The terrible icy fear that grips the heart of every new boy sooner or later had not yet set in.'

The first sight of Glencorse was not reassuring. 'Its Northern aspect would daunt the boldest heart. While waiting on the doorstep, I thought again of the picture I had drawn for my mind's eye of K. P. Wilson . . . We were admitted by an aged domestic, afterwards to prove a firm friend . . . K.P. was standing in his hall . . . clad in a homely suit of plus-fours, above the average height, bald except for a fringe of white at the back, a large whitish moustache, his cheeks tanned by long exposure to the Edinburgh winds.'[45]

In this manner did Selwyn first meet K.P. (as he was universally known), the second mentor of his life and a friend until his death in 1949. For Selwyn he was 'the schoolmaster par excellence – the epitome of the Edwardian schoolmaster.' He was an eccentric bachelor, a housemaster of thirty years standing, first of School House and from 1900 of Glencorse. He had intense likes and dislikes, loathing the house matron Miss Webster, but devoted to his crochety housekeeper Mrs Raggett (the 'aged domestic'). His *bête noire*, however, was D. W. Tanqueray, the Second Master and housemaster of neighbouring Moredun, and the dislike was heartily reciprocated. (It was part of Fettes folklore that when K.P. had almost died in a cricketing accident in 1887 – he had been a prolific games player – a blood transfusion from Tanqueray had saved his life.) K.P. dressed abominably. 'In the afternoon he would walk about with a threadbare shirt with no collar and an old handkerchief round his neck – accompanied by an aged and bad tempered dog. He spent a lot of time digging in his kitchen garden. He was numbed by the deaths of World War I – of 1,000 Old Fettesians who served 250 were killed.'[46]

K.P. was intimidating to parents and boys alike. 'I've brought up five boys', proclaimed one mother. 'Madam, I've brought up hundreds', he retorted. On one report he wrote: 'dull, plodding, platitudinous – would make a good parent.'[47] Fortunately for Selwyn he was on the side of the angels from the start. K.P.'s appearance – Selwyn wrote home to say that he looked like 'a fifteenth rate plough-boy'[48] – belied the care he took over 'his' boys, though like many schoolmasters of that time he delegated too much to autonomous and often sadistic seniors. At Fettes it was a case of Glencorse versus the rest and in that battle Selwyn was to play a commander's role. 'K.P. seems to be quite decent', he wrote home after a fortnight, 'only he is reported to be a terror in form.'[49]

But there were other terrors. As a new man, the Fettes term for newcomers, Selwyn did not have an easy time. The worst things he confided only in letters to his eldest sister Dorice (Eileen was studying medicine from that autumn at Liverpool University). 'I do not believe that I have ever explained to you the different ranks at Fettes', he wrote on 19 November 1918. 'First and foremost there are the school prefects (commonly known as the Schoolies) who have the power of life and death over you, in other words can cane you without asking permission from Dr Heard (commonly known as the Gussy or the Bulge).' And so on down to the most menial level of house prefects ('the prefs') who not only indulged in ritual beatings of new men but also had the power of 'rabbiting'. 'To be rabbited', Selwyn explained for his sister's edification, 'is to be chased round the study area by the prefs, with hockey sticks etc. You can be rabbited for leaving your clothes about and those sort of things.'[50] Bullying was rife and the general toughening process was intensified by the unofficial system whereby second year men bullied new men and so on up the scale to the Olympian heights of the head of house who had total autonomy. Selwyn had few friends. The only old Leasian was three years older and in another house. By the schoolboy code of the day he could have inhabited a different planet. Morals too were at a low ebb. Selwyn was a good-looking boy and, together with others in his year, soon attracted the attentions of a group of senior boys, three of whom were subsequently expelled. His initials J.S.B. earned him the nickname of Jezebel and in Fettes slang he was dubbed a 'Greaser' for ingratiating himself with the masters, notably K.P. The truth was that Selwyn had been brought up largely in the company of adults and was more at home with them.

He was placed in the lower fifth form of H. R. Pyatt. In the same

form was a Foundation Scholar from School House, Michael Tippett,
later to achieve fame as a composer. Fettes had always had a Spartan
reputation (potato bread and oatcakes with margarine was the staple
diet on many days in the rationing of war) and there were those, such
as Michael Tippett's parents, who sent their sons to the school
because of its 'manliness'.[51] This Spartan atmosphere left many by
the wayside. 'This school will either make you or break you', said one
boy, 'and it's broken me.' But it was all part of the accepted
toughening process.[52] When Tippett's parents heard of the conditions they removed their son forthwith and were instrumental in
alerting the authorities. Dr Heard, who had stayed on to see the
school through the war, moved into accelerated retirement in the
summer of 1919 and was succeeded by A. H. Ashcroft in the autumn.
'We have got a new headmaster this term', wrote Selwyn to his
grandmother in October 1919, 'he is far younger and more energetic
than the old one.'[53] He had been Headmaster of Birkenhead School
and this Wirral connection was to prove beneficial to Selwyn. In fact
the upturn in Selwyn's Fettes fortunes can be dated from the arrival of
Ashcroft, for after the sackings he forged ahead determined to make
a place for himself one day at the top of the house. His industry, his
brusqueness (inherited partly from his father) and the underlying
sense of insecurity can all be traced back to this period at Fettes. Yet
the resilience he showed in adversity and his ability to cope with set-
backs also stemmed from this time. When asked what he had done in
the French Revolution, the Abbé Siéyès said that he had survived.
The same could be said of Selwyn. He was already one of the survivors
of life. If he could survive as a new man in the Fettes of 1918 then
Aneurin Bevan in full cry in the Suez debates of 1956 was manageable.

His sister Dorice was not the only recipient of his voluminous
letters. Percy Dealtry soon got wind of his initial unhappiness. 'I
believe in time you will thank your stars that you went to Fettes', he
wrote reassuringly during Selwyn's first term, 'and will someday be a
big swell there.'[54] And so it proved. 'I learned to love Fettes', Selwyn
recalled, 'but that was not my feeling at all for the first two years. I
loathed it. The saving grace was my housemaster K. P. Wilson, one of
the outstanding schoolmasters of his generation. When it was discovered in my third year that I could play Rugby football, my life
became much easier.'[55]

Ashcroft appointed younger masters and gradually the atmosphere
improved. He attracted a first-rate staff in the post-war years. W. C.
Sellar, of later *1066 and all that* fame, was one who inspired Selwyn
with his wit and scholarship. ('Stormy petrol' was mis-spelt by one
boy in a history essay for Sellar. 'Hail to thee blithe Spirit, Bird thou

never wert', came the correction.) Ashcroft was popular with the boys, though it was more his prowess as a rugby international than his having a double first that commended him. As at the Mount and the Leas, Selwyn's main interest was history. 'His report came to hand this morning', wrote Dr Lloyd to K. P. Wilson at the end of Selwyn's first year. 'I find history mentioned in it for the first time. He was extraordinarily keen as a small boy in that subject & exhausted the stock of books in that subject in our district & he was a terror to his master at his last school when he (the master) made a slip.'[56] In the summer of 1919 Selwyn was taken by his father to see the battlefields of North West Europe where he would one day serve. One of the places they visited was Ypres. 'Mile after mile of barren waste, broken here and there with the stump of a dead tree, littered with debris of every description', noted Selwyn in his diary. 'We stayed 1 hour at Ypres where we got a British soldier to take us around the dug outs.'[57] The visit made a profound impression on the 15-year-old boy.

   Belgium was a pilgrimage rather than a holiday. From 1917 the Lloyds – with Dorice, Eileen, Selwyn and 'baby' Rachel – had holidayed in Criccieth in North Wales and these holidays awakened Selwyn's political interest. For Criccieth was the home of Lloyd George, then at the height of his fame as Prime Minister. From 1925 the Lloyd family stayed at a respectable temperance hotel, Henfaes, on the Portmadoc road, run by Miss Evans (whom Selwyn remembered as frightfully proper) and her niece Dilys Williams, both from a local leading family through whom the Lloyds first met the Lloyd Georges. Selwyn was fascinated by Lloyd George once they were on visiting terms with the Lloyd Georges, Selwyn thus consolidating his first Cambridge contacts with the Welsh Wizard. Selwyn soon got to know Olwen Carey Evans and her younger sister Megan Lloyd George on visits to Brynawelon, the Lloyd George family home. 'It was a fascinating place', remembered Selwyn. 'There were famous people to see. Brynawelon was an enchanting house to visit. Dame Margaret was a delightful personality, full of humour and commonsense. We all loved her. Lloyd George himself was more formidable, charming, scintillating, but dominating.'[58] Selwyn used to listen to Lloyd George at the local village functions and listen spell-bound to that gaunt Celtic romanticism which stirred his own Welsh blood and determined him that, come what may, one day he too would sit in the House of Commons. He was a great hero-worshipper and would hear no evil of his idol. ('I'm Lloyd George's daughter', said Megan in one of the Criccieth shops. 'Aren't we all, dearie?' came the reply. Selwyn was not amused.) He became a devoted Lloyd George Liberal from the age of 17 and followed the Prime Minister's career in the

newspapers, renewing the flame at Criccieth each summer. The first
big political event he remembered was the Genoa conference in
March 1922, but shortly after that Lloyd George fell from power
never to hold office again. This only intensified the young Selwyn's
commitment to the cause. 'I remember reading with resentment J. L.
Garvin's attack on him at the time of the Genoa conference.'[59] Back
at Fettes he envied two masters who took the train to Glasgow to hear
Lloyd George and F. E. Smith speak at a big political meeting during
the 1922 General Election.

As his hero's star waned on the national stage, so Selwyn's rose at
Fettes. 'Shows vigour and character in his life here, generally speaking', reported K. P. Wilson, 'he ought someday to be of importance.'
But K. P. noted (February 1922) that 'expression with him does not
come very easily', and that (June 1922), 'he is much in earnest and
even anxious',[60] characteristics of his later parliamentary career.
Nevertheless he received accelerated promotion in the OTC and
reached the 2nd XV. He acted in Shakespeare plays and by the
autumn of 1922 was a house prefect (though he disdained the
privilege of 'rabbiting') writing to his parents, 'It will be a pleasant
surprise for you, though it was not to me, as K.P. told me last holiday
at the Lakes.'[61] Already he had been marked out as a Cambridge
scholarship candidate by K.P. and was included in the reading parties
at his housemaster's Lake District cottage. He became Editor of *The
Fettesian* ('Rigid economy is still necessary if we are to avoid being
restricted to a single number a term', he warned in his first editorial)
and in November 1922 a member of the 1st XV ('A forward rush by
Lloyd recovered all the lost ground').[62] The Fettes motto *Industria*
(its emblem a bee) could have been Selwyn's own.

A new generation was coming to the top of the school. In Glencorse there were the Scott brothers, W.B. and J.M., and in College
G.P.S. Macpherson and his brother Niall (later Lord Drumalbyn and a
government colleague of Selwyn). With Selwyn they were the 'bloods',
but no longer the despots of war-time Fettes, and they did much to
civilise the school. Selwyn remembered his own unhappy start and
was sensitive to the sufferings of others. When he had joined the school,
custom had forbidden contact with a Leasian three years his senior.
Now the roles were reversed. On 21 September 1922, at the start of
his final year at Fettes, he received a letter from Percy Dealtry. 'Just
a line to beg you to seek for a boy called Hodson, G. B. He lost his
father, who lived at Heswall, in the War, and his mother at the beginning of July. Please condescend to speak to him & ask him to refer to
you as an O.L. if he is in doubt or difficulty.'[63] Selwyn did just that and
sixty-three years later George Hodson could still recall the outcome.

As a new man in September 1922 I came down the steps after Chapel on the first morning to be accosted by a very senior person who asked if my name was Hodson. This was Selwyn Lloyd, who was in his last year and a School Prefect. He said that if I was in any difficulty or wanted any help I was to get in touch with him . . . What struck me at the time and has done ever since is how on earth he picked me out . . . That he should have taken the trouble even to speak to me, let alone find out which of so many I was seems typical of one who cares, and I think Selwyn always did that.[64]

As Selwyn had been fortunate in the advice of Percy Dealtry over his Fettes scholarship, so now he received expert guidance from K.P. and Dr Ashcroft about Cambridge. Ashcroft and K.P. were both Cambridge men (at Caius and Pembroke respectively) and knew how to place Fettesians around the colleges. It was K.P.'s idea that Selwyn should apply for Magdalene. K.P.'s sister was married to A. S. Ramsey (a mathematics master at Fettes in the 1890s), now the President (or Vice-Master) of Magdalene. To be the Magdalene 'nominee' was a special mark of favour for Selwyn and, as in later life, he grasped the opportunity that this presented. Dr Ashcroft, who coached Selwyn, said that he wrote the best Greek prose of his generation.[65] The examination was in December and K.P. was confident of success. After his first interview Selwyn wrote home:

Imagine one large dark oak-panelled room at 6 p.m., imagine seven learned dons, imagine seven shaded candles, imagine one wretched affrighted mortal sitting in a chair in front of them, imagine all this and you will have in your mind's eye a picture of your only son undergoing an interview with the dons of Magdalene College, Cambridge. I have just come back from it and am feeling more dead than alive.[66]

Among the dons who interviewed Selwyn were A. C. Benson, A. S. Ramsey, Frank Salter and Owen Morshead (later Librarian of Windsor Castle). One of Selwyn's fellow candidates was Michael Ramsey, the future Archbishop of Canterbury, son of A. S. Ramsey and thus K.P.'s nephew. Michael Ramsey had stayed many times in Glencorse with his uncle and as a result the young Reptonian struck up an immediate affinity with Selwyn. Their friendship was to last a lifetime. Many years later Selwyn said to Michael Ramsey that nobody would have thought in December 1922 that their respective careers would end in Palaces at opposite ends of Westminster Bridge. When the examinations were over they shared a train journey to Derby, where Ramsey went back to Repton and Selwyn changed for Chester *en route* for West Kirby. Selwyn had permission to miss the last week of the Fettes term to the amused admiration of Ramsey who had no such leave. On the train they had set the world to rights. Ramsey was as fiercely pro-Asquith in his politics as Selwyn was pro-Lloyd George, so the arguments occupied many a mile. On 22 December 1922 Michael Ramsey wrote to Selwyn:

> Dear Lloyd,
>
> You made me contradict myself so many times and abandon so many attitudes on the way to Derby that I felt sure you had done well and that I would be out of it altogether.

On the train they had argued also over Greece, Sparta, the British Empire and the public school system. In the light of their experiences Michael Ramsey concluded that Repton stood for reason and Fettes for force.

> But if I go on much longer I shall soon be involved in a denunciation of that timeserver George, and a panegyric upon the honesty, shrewdness, and statesmanship of Mr. Asquith.
> Wishing you a very happy Christmas (I hope really it won't be happy. Your Nonconformist conscience should trouble you for not being a Passive resister.)
> Yours sincerely, A. M. Ramsey.[67]

The news was good for both of them and the *Vive-La* (the annual Fettes song recording the year's achievements) noted with sincere sentiments, albeit execrable rhyme:

> In our scholarship work who can say we've been dawdlin',
> When Lloyd as a Scholar's accepted at Magdalene.[68]

Although Selwyn had gained a Classics Scholarship, as his subsequent academic career at Cambridge was to show, it was not really a very strong one, and he did not win a leaving exhibition from the Fettes governors to supplement the Magdalene scholarship ('a deep disappointment to Selwyn', wrote K.P., 'though he is taking it perfectly.')[69]

Another disappointment had been the failure to become head of school in September 1922. There were three candidates for this post, including W. B. Scott and Selwyn. It was a great surprise that K.P. nominated Scott and not Selwyn. The rumour then spread – unlike many schoolboy rumours it was an accurate one – that Ashcroft had wanted Selwyn as Head of School (and thus automatically Head of Glencorse) but that K.P. had vetoed this – even headmasters bowed before K.P. – because he did not think Selwyn could afford the time if he was to get his scholarship. In this, as in so many things, Selwyn owed much to K.P.'s foresight.

With his Magdalene scholarship safely secured, Selwyn entered upon one of the happiest years of his life, perhaps only matched later by his year as Leader of the House of Commons from October 1963. He was the 'observed of all observers', though always more popular with the masters than the boys, in the first teams for rugby and cricket, Company Sergeant-Major of the OTC, impeccably smart and conscientious. The OTC was where he made his mark with his peers. When he gave an order it was obeyed. It was a heady mixture, but all very different from the previous five years.

Selwyn's farewell to Fettes came as Bottom the Weaver in the Founder's Day performance of *A Midsummer Night's Dream* in July 1923. Peter Quince was played by his friend Alasdair Macdonald who rehearsed with Selwyn the Pyramus and Thisbe scenes where Bottom wished to play all the parts. 'Well, I will undertake it', said Bottom of the part he was given, as Selwyn later did of the many other parts in life he was given to play. His political career was to be one in which, like Bottom, he did play all the parts. He left his inhibitions behind him that day. 'I will undertake it', declared Selwyn in a riotously successful performance. 'I can hear him saying it now', recalled Alasdair Macdonald over sixty years later.[70]

'I always felt Fettes would do you more good than any other school', wrote Percy Dealtry to Selwyn that July. 'But above all else you met K.P. and he appreciated you. I've never met K.P. more's the pity, but for years I've felt he was one of those rare people, who combine by their influence the strength of Sparta with the grace of Athens . . . I rather envy you your next four years.'[71] Such was the tribute of Selwyn's first 'Master' to his second.

K.P. bade farewell to Selwyn with real regret. In his final report in July 1923 he wrote: 'To a certain gentleness of character he has added or developed this year a very considerable capacity for lead and command.'[72] He offered to make each year a payment of £40 (the equivalent of a Fettes leaving exhibition), an offer Dr Lloyd declined. Instead K.P. paid for Selwyn to become a full member of the Royal Liverpool Golf Club. He was convinced that Selwyn was destined for a special career, an impression which was communicated to other Glencorse boys the next year when Selwyn visited the house from Cambridge. K.P. lent Selwyn his car, which Selwyn drove to Mussel-burgh for the needle Loretto rugby match. As the car trundled up the tracks to New Field, laden with Glencorse prefects, Selwyn passed various Fettes masters humbly proceeding on foot from the station. Neither Selwyn nor his passengers paid any attention to them. In due

course Selwyn was established on the front row of the pavilion with
Dr Ashcroft and his Loretto counterpart. For those who witnessed it,
it was a lordly display which they never forgot.[73]

T. S. Eliot said that no man can wholly escape from the kind of
culture which he acquired from his early environment.[74] This was true
in a marked degree with Selwyn Lloyd. The work ethic had been
instilled in him from the start and was reinforced at the Leas and
Fettes. The episode of Mrs Bunting's pills was an early lesson in how
to keep his emotions in check and not to complain. He developed a
chameleon-like ability to blend in with people. At Fettes he cultivated quite a 'hearty' image on the parade ground and rugger field
(though to K.P., bloods were 'great big lumps of football swagger'),
yet underneath there was often the vein of insecurity and anxiety. At
an impressionable age Lloyd George and his family had left a
vicarious whiff of adventure and power. There was a world beyond
the Wirral and he was determined to be part of it. His upbringing
could have been called parochial (and was by many who were to sneer
in later years), but there was a firm sense of what was right and wrong
(grandfather Lloyd and his own parents had seen to that), and a
sympathy always with the underdog. He was emotionally reserved
and cultivated the defensive mechanism of the teasing comment, one
contemporary recalling that Selwyn never knew the difference between pulling one's leg and breaking one's leg. But the brusqueness
was the cover for his ambitious industry. His childhood could have
been an early chapter from Samuel Smiles's *Self Help*. 'Men who are
resolved to find a way for themselves will always find opportunities
enough', wrote Smiles, 'and if they do not lie ready to their hand, they
will make them.'[75] Selwyn made his opportunities. Although his was
not to be a career built on a flamboyant personality there were truer
values beneath. The foundations were firm and the faults venial.
By birth and upbringing he was an archetypal example of the professional middle class (not at that time the term of abuse it
subsequently became). 'I belong to the middle class', said Joseph
Chamberlain of his origins, 'and I am proud of the ability, the
shrewdness, the industry, the providence and the thrift by which they
are distinguished.'[76] He could have been speaking of the Lloyds of
Rodney Street and West Kirby. With two children now established at
university, Dr Lloyd looked to the next phase. Eileen's path in
medicine was clear. After some alarms and excursions, Selwyn
settled on the law at Cambridge. But it proved a staging post.
Although he was to become Harold Macmillan's 'Middle Class
Lawyer from Liverpool', he had already succumbed to the lure of
Westminster. This, above all, was to be the passion of his life.

2

Cambridge and Liberalism

In his book *Recollections of the Cambridge Union*, Percy Cradock notes that in the biographies of Cambridge politicians there is invariably a section which runs along the following lines:

> In addition to his other activities, so successfully prosecuted, he became an assiduous speaker at the Union, that nursery of statesmen. Here his natural humour and eloquence soon brought him to the front, and, despite one or two setbacks, he passed rapidly through the usual stages of Secretary and Treasurer, finally attaining the office of President.[1]

Things were not to run so smoothly for Selwyn Lloyd. Indeed it was only by staying up for an unprecedented fifth year that he eventually became President. But it was a goal he was determined to achieve and achieve it he did.

He went up to Magdalene in October 1923 and as a scholar was given lodgings at the top of the Pepys building with a view over the Cam. 'I am really very lucky, compared with some people whose rooms I have seen', he wrote home.[2] Across the small landing were the rooms of Michael Ramsey, whose friendship Selwyn consolidated during his first year. (In 1978 Lord Ramsey was to write Selwyn's obituary for the *Magdalene College Magazine and Record*). Both of them were, in their different ways, untypical Magdalene men. Of the yearly intake of seventy undergraduates, the majority were Etonians and Magdalene was, in those days, a small, select College. There was an air of wealth and privilege that contrasted sharply with the Nonconformist Wirral background. Selwyn was unduly pessimistic about his finances in this company ('The tariff issued by the College kitchens seems to be rather expensive, and I shall probably cook my own breakfasts and lunches')[3] as he had his scholarship and an additional £30 exhibition specially arranged by Dr Ashcroft from Fettes. Eileen had taken her degree at Liverpool in July and Dr Lloyd made Selwyn a yearly allowance of £200. He soon discovered the attractions of the Union (Liebfraumilch 1921, 4s.) and unusually for a Freshman was invited to join the Hawks Club. But he lived very inexpensively during vacations and never went up to London or abroad. Though keen on Rugby football (he played in the Freshmen's Rugby trials and was disappointed not to get a Blue in his time at Cambridge) he rarely went to the Varsity match at Twickenham because of the expense. There were ample attractions in Cambridge, which was a revelation for him.

'Cambridge was a new adventure', he recalled. 'My parents had a friend called Meirion Thomas who had fought in the war, and was up as a research student at Cambridge 1919–1923. He used to come and see us quite a lot, and it was from him that I got some atmosphere. He first planted in my mind the idea that the University was the place to make friends, to talk about everything under the sun to everyone at all times of the day and night, to try to understand human relationships and above all not stick just to the books.'[4]

The 1920s were something of a golden age in Magdalene's history. A. C. Benson was the Master, delighting at 'the feeling of being the unquestioned boss of the very modest show.'[5] For the rather raw and inexperienced Selwyn it was very far from being a modest show. Vernon Jones became Selwyn's supervisor in Classics and a harsh taskmaster whenever Selwyn fell (as in Tripos) from the high standards required of a scholar. F. S. Salter was also a great influence, particularly from 1927. But Selwyn was not to make his mark in the academic field. He had too many irons in the fire and was always prepared for the 'glorious third' of his Law Degree rather than the 'undistinguished first', though he gained Seconds in Classics and History. Nevertheless his scholarship was reduced in June 1925, Vernon Jones explaining, 'Your second was neither a very good one nor a bad one, but just a mean between the two.'[6] He joined the Liberal Club (of which he was to become President) and became quite clubbable, always ready of an evening to play bridge or join in the discussions, particularly when they were political. He continued his arguments with Ramsey, 'a gaunt, ascetic, dedicated and rather grim Liberal, devoted to Asquith, hostile to Lloyd George and his supporters.'[7] Liberalism in any guise was at odds with the prevailing High Toryism of many of the Magdalene undergraduates ('I found myself propelled at once into a stratum of society of which I knew little'),[8] though the greater contrast was to be political at all in a largely apolitical college.

In the University at large the academic feel was for Liberalism, Cambridge Socialism never gaining the equivalent Oxford foothold. One of the first motions Selwyn proposed at the Union was: 'That in the opinion of this House, the hope for the future of this country lies in the revival of Liberalism rather than in the growth of Socialism.' Michael Ramsey thought it 'a superbly good debate, well opened by Selwyn',[9] who carried the day by 161 votes to 109. But achieving Union office was to prove a long haul. To begin with Selwyn dabbled at too many things ('I am pretty busy all the time, Captain of rugger, President of Liberal Club, and President of College Classical Society, a pretty heterogeneous combination')[10] and laboured under the disadvantage that Magdalene was a comparatively small college at a time when Union votes came mainly from College connections. He worked hard with the Liberal Club to learn his politics and cultivated a rather languid Magdalene air (an example, as with his 'heartiness' at Fettes, of his ability to blend), giving the impression of never being in a hurry about anything. He soon became a Cambridge man rather than a Magdalene one and most of his important contacts and friendships were eventually to be formed outside Magdalene. He got to know people across a wide political and social spectrum at the Union, figures such as R. A. Butler, Patrick Devlin, Hugh Foot, Gilbert Harding, Alan King-Hamilton and Geoffrey Lloyd. 'It was the time', he recalled, 'for the dreaming of dreams, forming of new faiths, founding of new parties in the conviction that one knew how to reform the world. After the strict discipline of a public school, it was the time to think, to talk, to listen, to drink.'[11] At the Liberal Club he met Asquith, Herbert Samuel and John Simon; at the Union he debated with Prime Ministers and Foreign Secretaries. 'I remember Stanley Baldwin describing oratory (or on this occasion was it the owning of newspapers?) as the harlot of the arts; F. E. Smith, Lord Birkenhead, listening for two hours without taking a note and then, the supreme courtesy, dealing faithfully and not always politely with every single undergraduate argument put forward in the debate; G. K. Chesterton was not a success, I think Hilaire Belloc was, largely because he lost his temper, or was it the other way round?'[12]

Of the speakers of his own generation he noted three as being outstanding. The first was Michael Ramsey ('tough and critical in debate and already an orator'), the second, Patrick Devlin ('a brilliant debater who never gave a point away, a keen politician, ambitious and one would have guessed then a natural selection for an outstanding parliamentary career') and the third, Gilbert Harding ('he had a rumbustious manner all his own').[13] The Union was seen, not least by its own members, as a House of Commons in embryo and from the vague schoolboy feeling that he would like to go into politics came a real determination on Selwyn's part to secure nomination as a Liberal candidate. The Baldwin government had been returned with a strong majority at the October 1924 Election and, after Baldwin's disastrous early dissolution in December 1923, it was clearly going to be a full five years before the country went to the polls again. A General Election in 1929 suited Selwyn's plans well. He would have graduated from Cambridge, established himself on the first rungs of a profession and would have had time to do the rounds of Liberal constituency organisations in the North. Not many local Liberals would have had the contacts Selwyn now assiduously built at the highest levels of the party. In March 1925 he entertained Asquith in Magdalene after a Liberal meeting in the Cambridge Guildhall. 'He came back to the Magdalene guest-room for a drink, and incidentally had half a tumbler full of whisky neat. "Margot" was with him. He showed a great mastery of diction and expression in his speech, and considerable charm of manner when talking to me; but he seemed very old and finished.'[14] Asquith and Lloyd George by this time were in a state of uneasy reconciliation with a combined total of only forty MPs. At Criccieth that summer Selwyn compared the two and was in no doubt that the future lay with Lloyd George (who became Liberal leader in 1926). 'He was quite the reverse of Asquith, very full of vitality, and seemed absolutely at the height of his intellectual vigour.' At Brynawelon ('he spoke to me for quite a long time in a very friendly manner')[15] their talks centred on Selwyn's possible parliamentary candidature.

Selwyn was determined that the Liberals should not be outsmarted by the Conservatives in Cambridge Union matters and this led to a curious incident in March 1925, the month of his meeting with Asquith. Not content with socialising with a former Liberal Prime Minister and Chancellor of The Exchequer, he met the former Conservative Foreign Secretary, Lord Curzon, when he came to Cambridge on 5 March to dine with the Conservative Club.

I was there representing the Liberal Club. He broke down just before the dinner, as is well known. I overheard Sir Geoffrey Butler tell P. A. Devlin, the Conservative Treasurer, to send round some flowers in the morning, and it struck me that it would be rather a good plan to send some from the Liberal Club first. I sent 10s. worth of carnations and received the following letter in reply addressed to Selwyn Lloyd, Esq., Magdalene College, with the Lord President of the Council's seal on the back of the envelope.

Christ's College,
Cambridge
March 6th 1925

My dear Sir,

Allow me to thank you most cordially for your exceedingly kind thought of me as well as for the lovely flowers and the message of sympathy from the Liberal Club. I begin to think that my illness was opportune since, had I spoken, I might have said something disrespectful of the party with which you are identified and which has treated me with so much courtesy.

I am
Yours very truly
Curzon.[16]

It was a little letter from a former Foreign Secretary to a future one, but one of the last that Curzon penned, for he died a fortnight later on 20 March.

Throughout the summer months of the early 1920s the Lloyd family returned regularly to Criccieth, coincidentally meeting up with the West Kirby family of Roland Marshall, a well-known Liverpool solicitor and solicitor to the Hoylake Urban District Council. Eileen had completed her medical studies at Liverpool University in the summer of 1923 and was engaged to be married to Bill McKerrow. The McKerrows were also a West Kirby family and as Bill was shortly to take up a post with the Royal Insurance Company in Bombay for two years, much talk centred on the venue and timing of Eileen's forthcoming wedding. Selwyn's eldest sister Dorice was engaged to Howard Shone, a prominent local miller, whom she married in May 1924, so despite Dr Lloyd's reluctance to assume father-in-law status they were smaller family gatherings at Henfaes. The holidays were a mixture of beach for 'Baby' Rachel, though she was by now past that stage, golf for Selwyn and his father, reading and relaxation for his mother, but – even after his fall from power in October 1922 – there was always the predominating influence of Lloyd George. With Olwen Lloyd George now married to the distinguished surgeon, Tom Carey Evans, and his sisters with their 'young men', Selwyn was thrown very much into the company of Megan Lloyd George, who was to remain a life-long friend, a possible bride in the eyes of the Press and (until his break with the Liberals) a political associate also. They were happy halcyon days – the time of the flapper and the Charleston – of charades and midnight bathing. On one occasion Olwen Carey Evans was wheeled in on the Brynawelon kitchen table

under a sheet for a mock operation at the hands of Selwyn and Tom
Carey Evans, who spirited in a leg of Welsh lamb, which was raised
aloft at the appropriate moment by Selwyn to the horrified amuse-
ment of the assembled guests. For the first time in his life Selwyn let
himself go. He was 'mad', great fun in the company of those he knew.
'I can see him now playing cricket charades in a corridor at
Brynawelon with two pillows attached to his legs', recalled Dame
Olwen Carey Evans over sixty years later. 'My father had been
Chancellor of the Exchequer. Who would have thought that one day
Peter would follow in his footsteps?'[17]

Peter was a name that Selwyn had been given at Cambridge. Just as
Oswald Mosley was always known as Tom to his closest friends, so
Selwyn was rechristened Peter in the 1920s and (despite his wish to
shed it in the 1950s) it was a name that stuck to the end, especially
among his Cambridge contemporaries. Selwyn tended to compart-
mentalise his friends – the Wirral ones were kept separate from the
Cambridge ones, the Cambridge ones from the Criccieth and later
Macclesfield ones. But the common factor in the 1920s for the
Cambridge people was the name Peter. It came about because, in the
nineteenth century, Selwyn College had not been a full collegiate
member of Cambridge University and was seen by the Magdalene set
as a socially dim place full of earnest clergymen and quiet grammar
school boys. 'You can't be called Selwyn if you're in Magdalene',
his friends said. 'We shall call you Peter.' Thus was Bishop Selwyn
indirectly responsible both for Selwyn's christening and re-
christening.

In Criccieth Selwyn broke away from the rather stiff, unbending
world of the Lloyd family. He was a great tease and deflator of
romanticism, jesting at scars that had never felt a wound. One night
the young ones went for a midnight bathe. 'Isn't this romantic,
swimming in the ocean by moonlight?', called out Olwen Carey
Evans. 'You're five feet off Criccieth sea front and it's a street lamp',
replied Selwyn.[18]

But the carefree atmosphere of those days when the world was
young was not to last and the family tragedy that ensued in 1925 was
one of the major turning points of Selwyn's life.

It was decided towards the end of 1924 that Eileen should be
married in India. Bill McKerrow was not due to return to England for
two years and Eileen felt she could profitably practise as a doctor in
India rather than wait for her fiancé to return. Her university career,
her determination to practise, the desire to travel and set up her home
in a far-off land in the very year that the fictional Adela Quested made
her passage to India, all marked Eileen out as the exception among

her generation. For the 1920s this was pioneering work and Dr Lloyd was justifiably proud of his second daughter. Mrs Lloyd was not so keen and had a premonition that all would not be well. Many years before Eileen had set out for India she had had her palm read at a fair. 'I see elephants and death in a far land', was the message she was given.[19] The family saw Eileen off from Birkenhead at the end of October 1924. The waters were dark and the smell of the oil oppressive as the family went on board. Indians went below deck to work the engines as they took their leave. Apart from Dr Lloyd they were never to see Eileen again.

Mrs Lloyd had been planning to travel as far as Naples with her daughter but when she was unable to go, Dr Lloyd travelled in her place and Mrs Lloyd always regretted that she had not been the last of the immediate family to bid farewell to Eileen. The fact that Dr Lloyd was able to afford the time (and the money) to travel to Naples tells a great deal of the improvement in the family's finances in the preceding ten years. It was a quietly prosperous father and his daughter who set sail for the Mediterranean.

The boat, *The City of Cairo*, made its leisurely way to Naples and then India. It was a time of hope and excitement. Letters came back to West Kirby full of the romance of adventure. On 15 November Eileen passed through the Suez Canal. 'The sea is as blue as blue & land quite near. I was sorry we passed through the Canal when it was dark but everyone said it was much nicer, with the moon shining it looks much more romantic – in the daylight it is just a stretch of land on either side & then water – the Bitter Lakes – beyond.'[20] The McKerrows were married at the United Free Church of Scotland in Bombay on 27 November. Inside the ring was engraved the single word *Inseparable*. The local papers in West Kirby contained pictures of the wedding, but with an ominous footnote to say that the bride was reportedly very ill. The news became worse, telegrams arriving regularly from the subcontinent. Mrs Lloyd planned to sail to India and letters continued to arrive even after the crisis. A virus had turned into amoebic dysentery and on 16 January 1925, some six weeks after her marriage and two months short of her 25th birthday, Eileen died. In her delirium she had called for her mother. Bill McKerrow telegrammed to West Kirby:

Mummy all my sympathy to you and her daddy in our great loss
My dearest one passed away peacefully last evening will tell all soon
Hope sail 24th
Broken hearted   Bill.[21]

From this grievous blow some feel that Mrs Lloyd in particular never recovered. Selwyn was back at Magdalene when the telegram came. 'In Cambridge alone at this time we are thinking & talking a great deal about you', wrote his mother. 'Write to Daddy he is frightfully cut up.'[22] Selwyn wrote separately to both his parents. To his father he wrote, 'I only wish that I could be at home with you all at this terrible time of trouble. It seems strange that God has seen fit to give her so short a period of happiness with her husband, after all her plucky achievements before. But HE knows best, and we who are left behind to keep her precious memory ever fresh, must remember our love for her, and our grief at her loss, and be by these more closely bound together in our love for one another.' To his mother he wrote, 'Be brave now, as she would have been.'[23] But Mrs Lloyd could not rest until Eileen's body had been brought home. In December 1925 the body was reinterred in the Grange Cemetery at West Kirby. 'Since Jan. 16th this year we have felt that she should rest in our own country', wrote Dr Lloyd in his diary.[24]

By those springs of action which spur a compensatory ambition, Selwyn now felt it incumbent upon himself to achieve in his sphere what had been denied to Eileen in hers. The career that Eileen never had meant that the hopes of the family were transferred to Selwyn. Anything he could achieve would be a posthumous tribute to the sister who had lived so short a time. In the spring of 1925 Selwyn flung himself into work – the History Tripos, the Union, the Liberal Club – with a kind of frenzied urgency as grief took hold. At this time Morley's *Life of Gladstone* made a great impact. 'What a wonderful book that is!', noted Selwyn in his diary. 'I find a continual stimulus in it; reading of his reflections, his readings, his writings, his incredible industry, and above all his high moral purpose.' Gladstone who, like so many of the Lloyds, had begun his life in Rodney Street, became the new inspiration. 'After reading this book, one cannot help being moved to the hope that one may be able to regulate one's own life in faint imitation of him.'[25] There was an emotional loneliness in Selwyn's life at this time that sought a vicarious fulfilment in hero-worship. In the autumn when he moved out of College over the road to 17 Magdalene Street the first thing he did was to put a picture of Rupert Brooke over his desk. 'I must be careful of the light upon him, because with a certain light & shade he looks almost sullen', he noted in his diary. 'Above my desk he cannot fail to be a constant inspiration: it is consoling to remember that he too got a 2nd in Classics.'[26] He succumbed to the whole emotional spell of Grantchester, unforgettable and unforgotten, its summer haze, its orchard, its friendships. Academically, history became his main preoccupation.

Even at the Liberal Club the focus was more on the academic than the political side at the time of the visit of Philip Guedalla in November. 'I went back with him to Trinity where he was staying, after the meeting: he spent 1½ hours explaining his book on Palmerston which is to come out in about a year's time.'[27] The Union was not his main hunting ground in 1925 and he who goes hunting elsewhere loses his place. So it proved with the elections to Union office at the end of that Michaelmas Term. 'I thought I had done well at the Union, until the results of the terminal elections were announced: Devlin got the Secretaryship. I must confess I was very disappointed at this term's result. King-Hamilton's success practically rules out my chances of the Secretaryship', noted Selwyn, though adding with a determination of which K.P. would have approved, 'it must be hoped that this set-back will make me redouble my efforts next term.'[28]

But the Lent Term of 1926 was largely taken up with considerations of his future career, which assumed some urgency if he was to take up Law. K. P. Wilson had told Dr Lloyd that Selwyn would not be suited to a medical career, but there was an open offer of a schoolmastering position at Fettes from Dr Ashcroft after graduation. Dr Lloyd was very much against this and steered Selwyn towards Law. Selwyn was not keen on the idea of being financially dependent upon his father, as became clear in a letter he wrote on 5 February 1926:

It will cost about £120 before I can start to keep my Bar terms, £50 of which is refunded at the end. I have to keep 12 Bar terms, which will take three years: the way I keep them is to eat dinners in London, 3 each term, which can be done on consecutive nights. There are 6 Bar Exams which I can take at my leisure during the three years. Personally I think it would be a good scheme for me to enrol myself as quickly as possible and start eating my dinners and keeping my terms, so that the date of my being called to the Bar will be as soon as possible. Secondly, I think it would be a good scheme for me to read law up here, for a fourth year and get an L.L.B., possibly taking the odd Bar Exam at the same time. Then in between the time I come down from Cambridge (June 1927) and the time I am called to the Bar (say March 1929) I will have nearly two years at my disposal to go into Chambers or somewhere and try and learn the job, or else get some politico-secretarial job which will give me time to read law at the same time for my uncompleted Bar Exams. What do you think of this? Please despatch considered opinion and objections, remembering always that the suggestion about Law emanated from yourself.[29]

The most significant detail in this letter is the reference to the
'politico-secretarial job', and there were many revealing points in Dr
Lloyd's reply from 1a Rodney Street on 8 Feburary:

> With reference to the step which you are about to take, I think that
> it is a wise one because you will have more scope in the legal
> profession than you would have in the scholastic. Anyhow I do not
> see how a barrister could not enter into any other profession very
> easily afterwards if he got tired of the law and I know of some who
> have taken up business and who have been selected for their
> position on account of their acquaintance with the law.
>   It is a great advantage also from the social side. You are in touch
> with men of high intellectual ability and your tastes will be similar
> and it is eminently a gentlemanly occupation. You really mix with
> the best.

Dr Lloyd did not consider this to be the case with schoolmastering
and added a further *caveat*:

> You are entering a cul-de-sac and very few find their way out and
> make a good living for themselves.

He knew that Selwyn was worried about the monetary aspect but
sought to allay his fears:

> As to the monetary part, I am quite willing to put up the money
> because it would be exceedingly interesting to me to follow your
> career and then if you come and practise in the Northern Circuit
> you will be near to us and be a comfort to us in our declining years.
> You know that a father's feeling is that of living again in his son and
> he likes to see him doing what he would like to have done himself if
> he had had the opportunity.
>   I am told that careful attention and seriousness about getting on
> makes it quite possible for a young barrister to support himself in a
> reasonable time in the Northern Circuit and for those who are
> fortunate enough to get the chance there are opportunities in
> Liverpool which have been taken by men who have prepared
> themselves and which have landed them in the highest posts in the
> country. The time spent in diligent labour will bring in a golden
> harvest.[30]

So the die was cast and in the midst of the celebrations of the birth
of the Duchess of York's first daughter (later Queen Elizabeth II)
Selwyn wrote to his father:

April 25th 1926 I have taken the plunge in the law question, and on the advice of the Law man here, have taken the first steps to join Gray's Inn.[31]

He went as a pupil to Mr J. H. Layton, a solicitor who for many years practised at the Bar, to obtain preliminary experience of the early stages of litigation. On May Day 1926 Selwyn took his first dinner at Gray's Inn, travelling with Patrick Devlin on the train to Liverpool Street, then the Underground to Chancery Lane (2*d.* in those days), dined at 7 and then back in time for locking-in at College. It was a journey repeated many times and in the same company over the next three years. But 1 May 1926 was to be significant for other reasons. The General Strike had arrived, that litmus paper test of political attitudes in the mid-1920s.

Like Suez in 1956, the issues divided a whole generation and the split was not entirely on class lines, even among undergraduates. From the start Selwyn was firmly on the side of the government, though his allegiance was not uncritical. 'I hope that you will still be alive when this reaches you and that the mobs of Birkenhead will not have razed the ancestral home to the ground', he wrote home on 5 May. 'Things are perfectly quiet here: it is rather a backwater from the point of view of excitement, but the "jeunesse dorée" of the 20th century is responding gallantly to the call that England expects every man to do his duty. All day long there is a long line of volunteers going into the Guildhall to register for voluntary service. 50 undergraduates have gone off to do dockers' work at Dover today.'[32] Selwyn's experience was very different from that of Hugh Gaitskell, for instance, at New College, Oxford who simultaneously was enrolling as a driver, but at the Oxford Strike Committee headquarters.[33] Cambridge opinion was much more for the government.[34] In an interesting pre-echo of the philosophical issue at the heart of the February 1974 General Election, Selwyn told his parents, 'The opinion here is that things are pretty serious, and that either the government or the Trade Union movement will be smashed. I think the govt. have been most provocative over the whole business, but as they do, however inadequately, represent law and order as organised in this country, we must, I am afraid, support them.'[35] The coal miners were locked out on 1 May, the day of Selwyn's first dinner at Gray's Inn, and after the strike had officially begun on 3 May, Selwyn in company with many of his Magdalene contemporaries became a special Police Constable in Lemon Street, London. 'We march each day to the Tower but that is all of about ½ a mile. We are supposed to occupy a very good strategic position, and have six buses in the street all night to rush us off where we are wanted.'[36] They were quartered in a warehouse in Whitechapel, settling down to barrack life with straw mattresses and army blankets. A convoy of 180 cars took them to their quarters and back to Cambridge when the strike was called off on 12 May. They were paid £2 5s. 0d. for their work. 'All things considered it was a great success', summed up Selwyn at the end of the strike.[37] Like many of his generation, Selwyn experienced only the middle class excitement of the nine days' wonder with none of the lingering working-class bitterness. Selwyn's reflective instincts were on the liberal side and subsequently he was deeply concerned at the way in which he felt Stanley Baldwin was being pulled away from his centrist position by the Conservative die-hards. 'There seem to be fewer and fewer reasons each day why one should not join the Labour party!! Perhaps the result will be yet another great political sensation in about September when Mr J. S. B. Lloyd leaves the Liberal party.'[38] Though written with an element of tongue-in-cheek, this letter to his parents showed Selwyn's growing tendency to take himself very seriously, a habit that his contemporaries seized on with cheerful mockery, though not often to much effect.

The General Strike had two effects on Selwyn's Cambridge career. As the Strike had coincided with Tripos examinations those who had volunteered for work were encouraged by their colleges to take an extra year, an encouragement which in more spacious days fitted in very well with Selwyn's plans. His fourth year, to which he had alluded in a letter to his father about his future career plans, was thus to become a fifth year. Secondly, the subsequent debate at the Union in Michaelmas Term 1926 was to mark the resurgence of Selwyn on the Union stage (thus paving the way for his Presidency in June 1927) and to bring him notice in the national Press. It may be convenient to consider the events surrounding the debate at this stage before turning to his extensive political activity in the summer of 1926.

Selwyn had always been instrumental in persuading speakers of the highest calibre and importance to appear in debates – Baldwin, Lloyd George, Herbert Samuel and F. E. Smith were all enticed to Cambridge during Selwyn's time. (In his retiring Presidential Debate on 29 November 1927 three future Foreign Secretaries spoke, Sam Hoare, Rab Butler and Selwyn himself.) Therefore he believed that any debate on the General Strike would be incomplete without the presence of A. J. Cook, the miners' leader. At this suggestion both the University authorities and the City Fathers took fright. There was a considerable toing and froing as to whether Cook should be allowed to come. The most vociferous opponent of the suggestion was the Town Clerk who had a stormy meeting in Patrick Devlin's rooms in

6 Graduation day at Cambridge: Selwyn with his parents outside the Senate House.

7 When the world was young: Selwyn and his sister Rachel beside the family's Essex car at Netherton, Banks Road, 1926.

8 David Lloyd George at Criccieth. 'He was very affable', wrote Selwyn in his diary.

Christ's (pacing the floor and agitatedly referring to him as Mr *Delvin*) with Selwyn, Alan King-Hamilton and Devlin himself. Selwyn stuck to his guns and refused to be deflected. Cook was billed to appear with Selwyn against the motion: 'That the power of Trade Unionism in England has increased, is increasing and ought to be diminished'. At the last moment Cook could not appear so Selwyn persuaded Walter Citrine, General Secretary of the Trades Union Congress, to speak with him. It was one of the Union Society's most memorable debates of the 1920s. 'So large was the attendance that all the seats in the body of the hall and the gallery were occupied', reported the *Cambridge Daily News* the next day, 'and members were glad to sit on the window sills and the floor of the House.'[39] Geoffrey Crowther spoke for the motion. Selwyn opened his reply:

> We regret that Mr Cook is not here, although there was a corres-ponding relief on the part of the Mayor of Cambridge and the Senior Proctor of the University. These gentlemen were so mis-guided as to think that there was a prospect of disorder in these hallowed walls. If the university authorities come nearer home and look into the records of the Senate House they will find it has been the happier hunting ground of riot and turbulence.[40]

The Daily Herald (Motto: Strike and Strike Hard) seized on this in its report of the debate. ('It is something of which to be proud to have been *quoted verbatim* by the *Daily Herald*!', wrote Selwyn to his parents.)[41] Selwyn declared that it was only because of very hard-fought strikes in the past that the standard of living of the workers was as high as it was today. The Trade Unions, he claimed, wanted to strengthen trade unionism until a time came when industry was organised, not on the basis of speculation, but of real livelihood in the fullest sense of the word. Against prevailing Cambridge trends Selwyn carried the day by 378 votes to 237.[42] He carried the day in Union Elections too. In January 1927 he was elected Secretary (the crucial stage), in March Vice-President and was installed as President of the Union on 7 June for the following Michaelmas Term. After the Leas and Fettes, the Union was the third institution to which Selwyn became devoted. He had a great love of the reassurance of corporate life and there was a side of him that found the worn leather armchair deeply satisfying.

In the summer of 1926 Selwyn became more directly involved with the propagation of Liberal policies. His successor as President of the Liberal Club at Cambridge, and fellow member of the Union Com-mittee, was Hugh Foot (later Lord Caradon). Together they set off

on a tour of the West Country in the latter part of August, to extol the
virtues of the Liberal Land Policy in a campaign that took them round
the rural areas most affected by the drift of population from the
traditional farming centres to the industrial and urban employment
centres. Lloyd George had set up a Land Inquiry to look at this
problem, part of the whole policy review of Liberal philosophy he
undertook in the years leading up to the 1929 Election. Selwyn, as
usual, had spent the first fortnight in August at Criccieth and had
discussed his forthcoming tour with Lloyd George at Brynawelon.
'He was very affable', wrote Selwyn in his diary, 'especially when he
heard that I was going on a Land & Nation League van, propagating
Liberal Land Reform.'[43] Megan also was enthusiastic. Policy documents were flooding from the Liberal presses in those years – *Coal
and Power*, *Land and the Nation* (the 'Green' book because of its
cover), *Towns and the Land*, *Britain's Industrial Future* (the famous
'Yellow' book) culminating in the assertive and central 'Orange'
Book, *We Can Conquer Unemployment*. From this came the questioning slogan, 'Can Lloyd George Do It?' (which in some quarters
led to rather scabrous replies). The effect of these documents –
intellectually perhaps the most cogent manifestos placed before the
electorate before the similar period of policy reassessment undertaken by Rab Butler in the Conservative Party after 1945 (and with
which Selwyn was also to be involved) – proved a mixed blessing. If
an opposition party spells out the minutiae of policy it runs the risk of
burdening itself with unfulfillable commitments (a danger of which
Churchill was well aware), and also sows the seeds of internal party
division on those policies, which was what happened when *The Land
and the Nation* was published. Walter Runciman, the Asquithian
Liberal MP for Swansea West, regarded Lloyd George's proposals
for a system of 'cultivating ownership' (with the state possessing
agricultural lands and granting fixed secure tenure to those who
worked their land conscientiously) as land nationalisation. A three-
day Land Convention in London had only added fuel to the fire as
elder statesmen, such as Sir Alfred Mond, Liberal MP for
Carmarthen, who defected to the Conservatives on this issue, turned
up to add their criticisms.

Against this background, Selwyn set off to the West Country with
Hugh Foot to show (as Selwyn put it in his diary for 27 August) 'that
the Liberal Party was still alive and kicking.'[44] The Foot dynasty in
radical politics has sometimes been seen as a kind of West Country
Hatfield. Sir Isaac Foot, with whom Selwyn stayed at the outset of the
campaign, was the father of Hugh and the Liberal Member for
South-East Cornwall (when he won the seat at the 1922 Election, Sir

John Simon telegrammed, 'Dear Foot, Congratulations on your magnificent feat'),[45] and, as Selwyn noted, 'a name to conjure with in Devon.'[46] Selwyn and Hugh Foot left Plymouth on the morning of 23 August in a travelling van, like latter-day revivalist preachers. Their reception – ranging from indifference to hostility – was a salutary blooding in the political realities of the hustings. The first stop was at Ilfracombe where they spoke on Urban and Rural land policy to people consisting in the main of holiday crowds, 'rather the opposite of what we had bargained for.'[47] But worse was to follow. 'The police would not allow us to come down on the front, but told us that the Market Square was the place for us. The Market Square turned out to be fifteen yards by twenty, and a constant stream of cars passed right through the middle of it.' The meetings, Selwyn noted, were 'uphill work'.[48] Nor did things improve overmuch at Lynmouth on 26 August. 'Lynmouth is a place upon which the sun never sets, for the simple reason that after about noon it gets no sun at all, owing to the fact that it is tucked away on the Eastern side of a large hill . . . We were to hold the evening meeting on the promenade and spent the afternoon watching the tide come in until by the time the meeting commenced it was beating against the prom. and occasionally splashing over. We had a terrible fight to make our voices heard above the waves.'[49] But they persevered and visited Brendon and Seaton ('The people staying here are of a terrifying respectability'),[50] spreading the Liberal gospel wherever they went. By the end of the tour they had addressed 600 people, who definitely stopped to listen for some time, distributed literature to about 1,000, but showed six times that number that there was a definite land campaign in progress. When Michael Foot took formal leave of Selwyn as Speaker on Selwyn's retirement in 1976 he made specific reference to those days which had been long remembered in the Foot family.

The Liberal Land Campaign, though of little long-term political consequence, was a valuable educative experience for Selwyn. It was one thing to address an informed undergraduate audience at the Union, quite another to contend with the petrol fumes and indifference of a Devon market square. It was his first direct experience of the hustings, a process which Selwyn always regarded as an unenviable chore rather than a challenge to relish. More important, it brought him into contact with another great Liberal family, that of Isaac Foot, and reinforced his fascination with the political game. But he was more at home in the cerebral atmosphere of the Liberal summer schools, now a regular feature of his long vacations. By the next year he was a leading light in the organisation of the Cambridge school, writing to his father on 31 July 1927:

The summer school is going splendidly. There are about 150 more than there were last year, and everyone is bright and hopeful. Sir Herbert Samuel gave a brilliant opening lecture on the relations between Liberals and Labour. It is primarily an Industrial school, and Henderson, the Editor of the *Nation*, Layton, the Editor of *The Economist*, J. M. Keynes and several others are reading papers on the various aspects of the industrial problem. It is all very interesting. I am attending all the lectures and discussions with diligence, taking notes etc, leaving my frivolous coevals to lie abed of the mornings and go to the Cinema in the evenings. Such is the stern necessity of Candidature, with its expected Omniscience.[51]

Selwyn had been adopted (at the age of 22) as the Liberal Party's parliamentary candidate for the Macclesfield Division after a selection meeting over lunch at the Manchester Reform Club in April 1927.[52] It was not his first offer of a candidacy. He had been approached with a view to becoming Liberal Candidate for Cambridge County the previous October, but did not think it geographically suitable. 'It would be difficult to reconcile law in Liverpool with Liberalism in Cambridge County', he noted. 'That seems to be the determining factor.'[53] With commendable maturity he did not rush at the first offer. The approach from Cambridge County coincided with a visit to the Liberal Club for a lunch and a speech by Sir John Simon, the former Home Secretary in Asquith's coalition government until his resignation over conscription in January 1916. 'He refused to go without his weekend exercise, and so I had to play golf with him on the Gogs in the morning', wrote Selwyn in his diary. 'His handicap is 18, and he is a bit better than that, but proved no match for youth and fervour. In spite of advice to the contrary, I was so indiscreet as to beat him, five and four. He was very pleasant and we had three points of contact – Fettes, Liberalism and the Bar. He talked a lot about all three.'[54]

Simon's advice was to go for a North West constituency, which he could combine with practice on the Northern Circuit, first as a candidate and hopefully later as Member. So Macclesfield was just the kind of constituency that fitted the bill. He was the unanimous choice of the selection committee. Dr Lloyd tells the story in his diary:

2 May 1927   The newspapers have the notice of Selwyn's selection by the Macclesfield Liberal Consultative Committee as their candidate to contest the parliamentary seat at the next election. A month ago he was asked to go & speak to the delegates there, about 150,

afterwards he was unanimously asked to consent. He interviewed Sir Herbert Samuel in London who had previously asked him to call upon him.[55]

The Lloyds were delighted, but Macclesfield too were pleased with their catch. Selwyn was just the kind of candidate – President of the Union, member of Gray's Inn, politically enthusiastic and hard-working – the Liberals were going to have to field (and in large numbers) at the forthcoming General Election if they were to have any chance of breaking the stranglehold of the Labour Party on the anti-Conservative vote. History shows that it was the Labour Party that moved decisively in the 1920s into the position of being the main party of opposition to the Conservatives, but this was certainly not seen by Liberals at the time as being inevitable. As Maurice Cowling has pointed out, 'it is important to avoid assuming, as a permanent factor in these years, that the Liberal party was doomed.'[56] In the next two years Selwyn flung himself into the task of winning Macclesfield from the sitting Conservative member, John Remer, a task combined with work for his Cambridge finals and his Bar Exams in London. 'I have to flit up to town again on March 26th for three days to lead my Macclesfield delegation at the Liberal Industrial Convention to consider the new Liberal Industrial policy', he wrote home on 19 February 1928. 'I see from the Macclesfield paper that there are now 1,000 Young Liberals in the Division, which on the whole is very good indeed. I begin to think that I shall get it!'[57]

The Macclesfield candidacy confirmed Selwyn's place in the various strands of the Liberal Party in the late 1920s. The Criccieth holiday in 1927 had been one long fortnight of political talk (he lunched and dined with Megan Lloyd George on 22 August, when she enlisted to speak for him at Macclesfield meetings). He had accompanied Lloyd George and the various grandchildren at weekend visits to the cinema and was very much at home at Brynawelon. In February 1928 a reception for Liberal candidates was held in London. 'I had a word with Lloyd George himself later in a room downstairs.' He asked Selwyn about Macclesfield and they reminisced over Criccieth. 'Herbert Samuel also recognised me, and asked how the organisation was progressing, in his own sibilant fashion', recorded Selwyn. 'I had quite a long chat with Sir Archie Sinclair.'[58] In one evening he was thus speaking to the three politicians who led or were to lead the Liberal Party from 1926–45. At Cambridge he dined the Speaker of the House of Commons, John Whitley, former Liberal MP and member for Halifax.[59] Not an iron was left unheated. Macclesfield Liberals welcomed him, therefore, as a great recruit for the cause. 'He comes from a stout Liberal family, highly esteemed in the neighbourhood where he lives', said Lord Leverhulme by way of introduction at the 1928 Annual General Meeting of the Macclesfield Division Liberals. 'He is a Liberal of conviction and a sincere Liberal, the type of Liberal that we want at the present time. I congratulate you on securing him as your candidate.'[60] He was even introduced at one meeting as Megan Lloyd George's fiancé ('she was very amused', he wrote home).[61]

The meetings in the spring of 1928 were held under the shadow of the death of Asquith, on 15 February. This served only to intensify the commitment of party workers, particularly in Macclesfield, to the forthcoming electoral fight. On 28 March Selwyn travelled to Macclesfield with Megan for a speaking weekend around the various wards, fresh from organising a visit to the Cambridge Liberals by Lloyd George. 'The great event here this past week has been Lloyd George's visit', Selwyn wrote home. 'About 220 people came. I went down to the station with (Hugh) Foot to meet him in the afternoon. The excellent result of the Ilford by-election had just come out, and he was as pleased as Punch about it. We had tea with him in a private sitting room at the Varsity Arms. He spoke superbly in the evening: "the ark of the covenant of reform was hewn out of the wood of Liberalism".'[62] The national Press covered the visit and there was a feature with photographs in the *Observer*, Selwyn's regular Sunday paper at this time.

Selwyn's days at Cambridge were coming to an end, not in a blaze of academic triumph, but certainly in the limelight of more than parochial political attention. Meirion Thomas's advice about not just sticking to the books had certainly been heeded. Cambridge proved the Clapham Junction of Selwyn's career. Before, he was travelling hopefully; after passing through he was on the verge of arriving. Increasingly his thoughts turned to the possibility of a General Election early in 1929 and the certainty of one before the year was out. But Stanley Baldwin, who had had one disastrous early flirtation with the electorate in the 'Protection' Election of December 1923, showed no signs of seeking another premature dissolution. In the end this suited Selwyn rather well in that it allowed him – in the inevitable lull between the excitement of adoption and the call to battle – to concentrate on his Bar Exams, which he completed at the end of 1929. As a result the next institution to win a place in his heart, Gray's Inn, began to assume ever greater importance at this time. 'I went up for my third Bar dinner', he wrote home in the hiatus before the election. 'Birkenhead was dining at the High Table, and Furneaux, his son, among the members. Birkenhead looked very fat and bloated in the distance. I dined with Pat Devlin: he looked rather ill, he is in a solicitor's office and working very hard.'[63]

Uncertainty over the election date continued. 'The time is getting very short before the election', Selwyn wrote home after one of his visits to Gray's Inn, 'and everyone in London said that it had been fixed for the second week in June, which will suit me very well.'[64] Selwyn's prediction was not far out. Parliament was dissolved on 10 May and Stanley Baldwin announced that Polling Day would be on 30 May. At the age of 24 Selwyn prepared to fight his first parliamentary election.

3

Mr Hoylake UDC

For the Liberal Party and for Lloyd George the 1929 General
Election was to prove a climacteric. On 1 March Lloyd George had
given his pledge that unemployment (the dominating issue of the
election) would be reduced to 'normal' levels within a year under a
Liberal administration. This was a very different Return to Normality
from that promised in the aftermath of the First World War. Yet only
the Liberal Party offered in its manifestos a challenge to the economic
orthodoxies of the day, guarded by the gaunt and brooding presence
of the Governor of the Bank of England, Montagu Norman, and
(after the Election) reinforced by the neophyte-like Chancellor of the
Exchequer, Philip Snowden. The battle in 1929 was not between
capitalism and socialism (though the two main parties liked to see it in
those terms); it was between economic orthodoxy and economic
unorthodoxy, and was a battle fought not entirely on party lines. If
one camp was dominated by Montagu Norman and the economic
establishment, the followers of J. M. Keynes were a diverse band,
incorporating at various times, and in varying degrees of commitment, figures such as Ernest Bevin, General Secretary of the Transport and General Workers' Union since 1922; leftish Tories such as
Robert Boothby and Harold Macmillan; the mercurial figure of
Oswald Mosley, soon to be Chancellor of the Duchy of Lancaster in
the new Labour Government, and just as soon after the rejection of
his 'Memorandum' in May 1930, in the political wilderness; and,
of course, the wizard of Criccieth himself. But who was listening?
The Liberal Party suffered the fate of all third parties under the
British electoral system since the Reform Bills. It was squeezed. The
extinction of Selwyn's high hopes for a centre party was a bitter
disappointment.

The Conservatives, under the uninspiring slogan of 'Safety First'
(much play was made of 'Captain' Baldwin steering the ship of state

to harbour), had high expectations of being returned. Although unemployment was rising (in January 1929 it had stood at 1,466,000, was to rise by December 1930 to 2,500,000, and reach a peak of 2,955,000 in January 1932) Baldwin appealed to the instincts, as he felt, of the British people for an unchanged system. If Change there had to be, let it not also be accompanied by Decay. The Labour Party entered the campaign wary of the Liberal Party's appeal to the non-Conservative voter. Its main election pamphlet (G. D. H. Cole's *How to Conquer Unemployment: Labour's Reply to Lloyd George*) fell between two stools and, as Lloyd George neatly pointed out in a speech before the dissolution, 'The Labour Party could not make up its mind whether to treat the Liberal plan as a freak or to claim its paternity.'[1] That Liberal Plan, based on the famous 'Orange Book' of March 1929, was for an interventionist degree of government planning, unprecedented at the time, and deeply influenced by the economic thinking of J. M. Keynes. With 513 candidates in the field the Liberals made a sustained push for power, proclaiming the policies thrashed out in countless Liberal Summer Schools since 1925. Selwyn, and Megan Lloyd George who had been adopted as Liberal candidate for Anglesey, embraced those policies enthusiastically. It was all to no avail. The Conservatives may have offered Safety First, but the electorate showed that it wanted Labour First. When the results were declared, the Labour Party had won 288 seats, the Conservatives 260 and the Liberals (with 23.4 per cent of the vote) a mere 59.* Although the Liberals held the balance of power in the new Parliament, the limit of their realistic ambitions at subsequent elections, it was a poor reward for their efforts.

Selwyn fared no better at Macclesfield, where he faced an uphill task if he was to unseat the sitting Conservative member, John Remer. But if it was an uphill task, it was also an opportunity. Macclesfield was the kind of industrial constituency which, because of its disproportionate reliance on one manufacturing base (the silk trade), had experienced particular hardship in the economic recession. At the 1924 Election the Liberals had trailed a poor third behind Labour, yet Selwyn genuinely believed he could win the seat, or at worst push the Labour candidate, J. Williams, into third place. He was to be roundly disabused.

With its backcloth of the Pennines, its fiercely Nonconformist tradition (the King Edward Street Unitarian Chapel had been one of the earliest Free Churches), its unemployment and its proud local sense of community, Macclesfield had something of the air of an old

* In February 1974, 23.6 per cent of the popular vote produced only 14 seats for the Liberals.

hill-town on the defensive. Selwyn began his onslaught with characteristic thoroughness. On 11 May, the day after the dissolution of the
previous Parliament, Selwyn travelled with his father to Macclesfield
for his adoption meeting. He was due to take his Bar Finals in London
during the first week of the election (though he never used that
election as an excuse for his third) and wanted to put in an early
appearance. The Macclesfield Liberals welcomed him warmly. 'Most
enthusiastic', noted Dr Lloyd in his diary that night. '250 people stood
& sang For he's a jolly good fellow & cheered him. Many encouraging
observations & prophecies as to his future.'[2] Selwyn had carefully
cultivated the constituency over the previous two years (he had held
over 50 meetings) in association with Frank W. Duncalf, the Secretary of the Macclesfield Division Liberal Association.[3] Duncalf had
advised him to adopt a more aggressive stance than the previous
Liberal candidate, W. Tudor Davies, a Welsh barrister from the
Middle Temple. Selwyn's antecedents may have been similar but his
campaign was that of a later era. 'End Liberalism and you begin the
class war,' he declared to the silk operatives in a slogan-dominated
speech, 'end Socialism and you remove a bar to progress; end
Toryism and Save the Nation.'[4] At one meeting on the subject of
women's franchise (under the Representation of the People Act of
1928 the Baldwin Government had extended the franchise to women
over the age of 21) one lady told Selwyn that in her opinion nobody
should have the vote before the age of 25. Selwyn asked what the lady
thought, therefore, of his being her MP as he was only 24. For some
time the local press had been reporting 'Conservative perturbation' at
Selwyn's youthful candidature and *The People* pointed out that at
Macclesfield, 'where the girls are numerous and pretty, the only thing
that is really worrying the sage Conservatives is that the Liberals have
as their candidate an entrancing Ivor Novello young gentleman of 24
for whom all the lovely silk weavers are falling.'[5] During the last week
of the campaign Megan Lloyd George came over from Anglesey
(unlike Selwyn she was to win her seat) to speak for him and this led to
further press speculation that Selwyn would soon be announcing his
engagement to Megan. Great things were predicted for a Lloyd who
would soon also be a Lloyd George by marriage. Selwyn and Megan
canvassed in the vicinity of the mills, often to the strains of the
Macclesfield Liberals campaign song *Young Lloyd* (to the tune of
John Peel):

> D'ye ken young Lloyd with his smile so gay?
> D'ye ken young Lloyd at the break of day?
> D'ye ken young Lloyd on the broad highway?
> With his Van and his horn in the morning.

Chorus: For the sound of his horn brought me to the street,
          The cheer of the crowds was quite a treat,
          Young Lloyd has proved we are not effete,
          We shall win at the poll next Thursday.

          Yes – I ken young Lloyd and Lloyd George too,
          The Liberal pledge and the programme true,
          From reaction to progress for me and for you,
          From the dole to good work in the morning.[6]

Not all campaigning was so good humoured. Selwyn took an uncharacteristic personal dislike to his Conservative opponent, John Remer, a feeling strongly reciprocated. Increasingly bitter letters passed between them with allegations and counter-allegations of what would later be known as 'dirty tricks'. Remer's continual harrying of Selwyn suggests that he regarded the Liberals rather than Labour as his main challengers. An extract from Selwyn's letter of 21 May gives some indication of the acrimony that developed:

Dear Mr Remer,

    Since our conversation at the Town Hall on Nomination Day it has come to my knowledge that you have been publicly accusing Liberal canvassers and workers of underhand tactics . . . I resent most strongly your public attempts to saddle the Liberal Party in this Division, its official canvassers and workers, with this charge. It appears to me to be nothing more nor less than an electioneering device.[7]

Selwyn held his eve of poll meeting at Congleton Town Hall. He had taken copies of the Yellow and Orange books to all his meetings and his campaign notes have copious pages on such topics as Sankey and the Coal Commission.* Most people were more interested in heckling. 'I was only 22 when I was adopted as a Parliamentary candidate', he said at a meeting at Ashton Hall. A voice from the back, 'Well done, laddie.'[8] In his final address he said, 'It has been a strenuous campaign. I have enjoyed every minute of it, and I hope that I have made many new friends. My sole regret is that I have not been able to meet and to talk to every elector. I have done my best, but the size of the great division has made it impossible to become personally acquainted with all.'[9] Further insults were traded with John Remer and then Selwyn awaited the verdict of the electors. Dr Lloyd attended the count and recorded the outcome in his diary:

* A government inquiry into the Coal Industry in 1919, headed by Sir John Sankey, a judge of the King's Bench. It was largely a device by Lloyd George to buy time.

On 30th May the polling took place & the following day Friday the results declared. Remer 1st with 19,329 votes Williams 2nd with 13,919* Lloyd 3rd with 12,891. S doubled the Liberal votes of the last election but was sorry not to at least beat Williams the Labour man.

I assisted at the Town Hall at the counting & it was very tiring. S stood the strain very well & he looked well after it all. He is now at Hawarden Castle with the Gladstones.[10]

Selwyn was not too despondent about the result. He had taken on a difficult seat (only in the next six years did it become clear how virtually all seats were to be difficult for the Liberals, and whereas there were 513 official Liberal candidates in 1929, by 1935 this had dwindled to 161) and had gained valuable political experience. But on the national level the defeat of the Lloyd George programme in *We Can Conquer Unemployment* was still remembered by Selwyn over forty years later as one of the great disappointments of his life in politics.[11] The Macclesfield campaign, the only Parliamentary election that Selwyn lost, was a formative experience. He soon learned that politics was not roses and cheering silk operatives all the way, but was all too frequently leavened by personal bitterness and enmity, often on the slenderest foundation. In fact his greatest doubt about seeking a political career had been whether it would be fair to subject his family, even vicariously, to inevitable abuse.[12] Yet there were compensations. He had enjoyed the involvement in Macclesfield, particularly the insights it had brought a rather protected, earnest young Cambridge graduate into industrial problems, insights that were to stand him in good stead in his forthcoming legal career, and he was delighted with Megan's success in Anglesey. Despite press speculation, Selwyn never became emotionally involved with Megan. For most of his life he was on his guard against emotional closeness and Megan, who never married, was, like Selwyn, essentially wedded to work. Their involvement was as though they were close cousins in the large and sometimes frenetic family firm of Lloyd George Ltd. Their break, when it came in 1945, was political and Megan never really forgave Selwyn (or her brother Gwilym) for joining the Conservatives, though she was to join the Labour Party in 1955.[13] Macclesfield was a false start in Selwyn's political career. The 1930s were to be the decade not of national, but of local politics, and far from strengthening the links with the Liberals (*pace* Criccieth and Hawarden) Macclesfield was the beginning of the break with Liberalism, a break symbolised by his refusal to stand there again in 1931.

* The vote was actually 13,911. The Liberal vote in 1924 had been 6,434.

The first minority Labour government in 1924 had lasted nine months. Although the Labour Party was now the single largest party, it still depended on the 59 Liberals for survival, support which was by no means guaranteed on all issues, not least because the Parliamentary Liberal Party was itself divided on many of them, notably the Coal Bill of December 1929. As another election could follow at any time, many Liberal Associations moved to secure the best candidates for their constituencies. In December the local Wirral Liberals asked Selwyn if he would transfer his candidacy from Macclesfield and enter the lists next time in his home constituency against the sitting Conservative member, Sir Christopher Clayton. Selwyn was as unenthusiastic about standing for the Wirral as he had been earlier about the prospect of Cambridge County. 'Re politics, of course I would not dream of Wirral for three good reasons', he wrote to his parents on 6 December. '(a) one might get in (b) it would be terrible to live in the constituency one was nursing (c) it is too near one's bread and butter.'[14]

That bread and butter was now firmly centred on the law. As Dr Lloyd noted in his diary, which was increasingly full of Selwyn's activities: '1930 Jan 14 *The Times* of today has Selwyn's name amongst those who have successfully passed the final Bar exam (3rd class). He has now done with exams for ever I hope. He goes to the chambers of Mr Sellers barrister 10 Cook St to arrange his plans for the future.'[15] From 1926 he had been a pupil of J. H. Layton, a solicitor who for many years practised at the Bar, but now he began his professional life in earnest. He was in chambers first with Frederick Sellers (and later Frederick Pritchard) and was brought up in the immediate tradition of the great names of the Liverpool Bar – Rigby Swift, Greer, Kiffyn-Taylor and the most brilliant of them all, F. E. Smith. When he went to 10 Cook Street he could still see under the varnish of the door the name, F. E. Smith.[16]

The Chambers at 10 Cook Street, to be demolished by a bomb in the Second World War, contained Master Sellers' practice. Selwyn found this 'very high grade – his Admiralty and commercial cases far above my head.' Before long he left that 'rarefied and respectful atmosphere for the coarser and earthier surroundings of Master Pritchard's.'[17] Here, at 3 Cook Street, he worked with Pritchard, Rice Jones and Probyn Jones. Pupillage was different in the 1920s in that barristers could practise from time to time when pupils, and Selwyn had already gained experience with J. H. Layton. He soon became known as a very solid junior barrister. Although he had a wide clientele he preferred to appear for the defence, and with the devoted help of Edward Kentish Burns, his intensely loyal clerk, he

established a valuable personal injuries practice through links with
insurance companies. Burns kept him informed of possible leads,
devilling well for his master (the first time Selwyn had been in that
role), going out into the Liverpool pubs touting for business, generally keeping his ears open as a good legal clerk should. (During the war
Edward Burns wrote weekly letters to Selwyn telling him of the state
of the practice – by then in Castle Street – and general Liverpool and
Northern circuit gossip).

It was during this first year on the Northern circuit that Selwyn
began to realise how much he had owed and how much he loved
Gray's Inn, its history, the grace of its buildings, the statue of Sir
Francis Bacon on the South Court lawn, the timeless rituals of Hall,
the links with the great F. E. Smith. In his more fanciful moods
Selwyn liked to think of himself as a latter-day F.E. – Gray's Inn, the
Northern circuit, politics, even the prospect of the Lord Chancellorship, his great unfulfilled ambition. At the end of his life Selwyn's
last London address was 7 Gray's Inn, the flat in which he drafted
Suez 1956. Gray's Inn was a constant thread in his life. He was
admitted to the Inn in 1926, called in 1930, became a KC in 1947 and a
Bencher in 1951. (One of his enduring disappointments was that
largely because of the timing of these things a vacancy did not occur in
the Office of Treasurer [the titular head of the Inn, a yearly unpaid
post] at a time when he was also free of constraining ministerial
commitments, though he was greatly pleased that his first legal
mentor, Sir Frederick Sellers, should be Treasurer in 1952 at the time
Selwyn was first making his mark in government circles and dining
again at Gray's Inn. And after the Speakership he was pleased that,
like Mr Perker, that intelligent attorney in *Pickwick Papers*, he kept
an office in Gray's Inn Square.)

Selwyn was an energetic recruit to the Liverpool legal scene in
1930. His first brief on 10 February was a Settling Report from Layton
& Co, for which he was paid five guineas.[18] Briefs came in regularly
and Patrick Devlin wrote to Selwyn at this time telling him how wise
he had been to start on the Northern Circuit as work was proving very
difficult to obtain in London. Selwyn travelled the length and breadth
of his Circuit over the next nine years, appearing at Appleby and
Carlisle, Lancaster, Manchester and Liverpool. '4 or 5 weeks after I
was called to the Bar I conducted my very first criminal case in front of
Mr Justice Swift, and I can recall now the feelings of trepidation and
awe with which I confronted that formidable presence.'[19] Mr Justice
Rigby Swift was a hard taskmaster, but a master of the disguised
compliment as Selwyn found when he appeared before him in a case
concerning an Indian who was accused of cutting a man's Achilles

tendon. The injured man, who spoke only Urdu, was brought in on a stretcher. There was an interpreter, whom Selwyn addressed directly to cut out what he called 'meaningless' talk to the injured party. But an interpreter in court cannot be addressed directly as a substitute witness and Judge Rigby Swift at once seized on Selwyn's error. 'Mr. Lloyd, I do not expect that from you', he said, knowing that Selwyn would not wittingly have made such a slip and that his skill in advocacy was well equal to the task.[20]

By the end of 1930 Selwyn had earned fees of £240, 'a record for 1st year for a young L'pool barrister', as Dr Lloyd noted in his diary on 22 December. 'Starting in the chambers of Mr Sellers he came home one day with a smile on his face with his first brief from Layton & Co. Since then his success has been striking & his briefs perhaps 30 or 40 have come in with regularity. Two cases from the Public Prosecutor have brought him into some prominence & a poor person's Vitriol throwing at a sweetheart 6 yr sentence reduced to 1½ on appeal was prominent through the Country in the Press.'[21] Dr Lloyd had always stressed to Selwyn that a legal career would entail mixing with the best professional minds of his generation. And so it proved. In the 1930s Selwyn worked alongside figures such as David Maxwell Fyfe (later as Lord Kilmuir destined to be a joint victim with Selwyn of the Night of the Long Knives in July 1962), Hartley Shawcross (a friend for life and one whose wig he wore throughout his tenure of the Speakership) and an ebullient solicitor, Sidney Silverman, whose company he much enjoyed. 'It was always an excitement to be briefed by him, the little figure bouncing up and down, pulling one's gown, passing notes in his almost completely illegible handwriting. We won some notable victories together.'[22] In the 1940s, on opposite sides of the House of Commons, they campaigned vigorously together for the abolition of capital punishment and Silverman became one of Selwyn's most important cross-floor political friendships.

Selwyn's legal methods were very precise. In his notebooks of forthcoming cases he always established first the chronology of events (in the case of William Neill v. Pease in 1948 when he was leading silk, for example, there was an almost continuous daily calendar of events from 8 September 1945 to 17 February 1947)[23] before drawing up a suggested order of witnesses. Nobody who engaged Selwyn as their barrister had cause to complain of lack of preparation. His clients, even when on the losing side, frequently wrote to thank him for the trouble he had taken. A letter he received on 6 October 1936 runs:

I am more sorry than I can say that the time & care which you expended on the perusal of all the documents in the case & the 'getting up' of the structure & strains of cargo vessels should in the event have been wasted in the result. If it is any small consolation to you I can say in all truthfulness that for myself any labours I may have expended in the matter have been more than compensated for by the pleasure of having such an enthusiastic & energetic colleague to work up & present my case for me.[24]

For Selwyn legal work was never merely a means of making money. He was deeply moved by injustice of any kind and was happier when briefed for the defence rather than the prosecution. He had no time for the dead wood of the legal profession. 'I can think of one or two magistrates,' he wrote in his legal notebook, 'who used to use the Magistrates' room as a sort of Club room – go there every day & sit every day – although long past efficient work', lamenting that, 'busy men of affairs [were] only too ready to leave it to them.'[25] Like his father before him he waived fees. 'I have three poor person's divorces to do (for which I shall not be paid)', he wrote home from the County Hotel, Carlisle on 18 October 1930, 'so I am looking forward to a cheery time.'[26] He could be sharp, and even disrespectful to the Bench. Selwyn was sitting in court one Holy Week and as the case was almost finished the judge asked if everybody could come back to sit on the Friday morning. Selwyn said that the last judge to have sat on Good Friday was Pontius Pilate, so that was the end of that suggestion.[27]

Although he was an assiduous worker on the Circuit, his colleagues never felt he was interested in its life as such. He treated it all rather lightheartedly – though never unconscientiously – giving the impression, even in the early 1930s, that this was not to be the central occupation of his life. After the war, when he became an MP, he rather dropped out, despite holding positions such as the Recordership of Wigan. It was as though he had confidence in the future. Although his bread and butter was in the law he did not really apply himself in the way that he would have done if his ambition had been to become a High Court Judge. He was a tease and (within limits) he liked to be teased. On one occasion he was about to go on a holiday cruise when some of his fellow barristers made up a bulky set of papers for him purporting to be a brief from a valued client with instructions to settle a form of pleading, for an opinion and an early conference, marked *Urgent*. His face fell in dismay when he saw the papers. On his 34th birthday in 1938 a reverse joke was played. He had been pompous and busy and said that he had no time to take on a minor case. A spoof call came from London about a House of Lords brief. He dropped everything and spoke for half an hour about how important it was that he should undertake it. One perennial joke into which he entered was the end-of-circuit dinner at Appleby. The hotel where the barristers dined had on its first-floor landing a stuffed otter which had been the hunting memento of some local sportsman. This otter stood upright, paws aloft and beakish nose in the air. At the end of the dinner the custom was for this otter to be brought down, installed in the place of honour at the top table, dressed in wig and bands and from then on be referred to as 'Mr. Selwyn Lloyd, addressing the jury.'[28]

Yet despite such diversions and doubts as to his long-term commitment, Selwyn worked hard in these years. ('Selwyn starts the year very busily engaged in professional work', wrote Dr Lloyd at the beginning of his 1933 Diary. 'Tomorrow Jan 9th he has seven cases in different courts.')[29] Some indication of Selwyn's material success at the Bar in the 1930s (at a time when 75 per cent of families in Britain had incomes of less than four pounds a week) can be seen by looking at his legal fee book for Coronation week in May 1937:

May 10	Banks Kendall	£5 – 5 – 0	Brief
May 10	Taylor & Gorst	£1 – 1 – 0	Conference
May 11	Wood Lord & Co	£5 – 5 – 0	Brief
May 11	Wood Lord & Co	£1 – 1 – 0	Conference
	Wednesday May 12th	Coronation Day	
May 13	Wood Lord & Co	£3 – 3 – 0	Defence
May 13	Laces & Co	£3 – 3 – 0	Defence
May 13	R & W Ashcroft	£3 – 3 – 0	Defence
May 14	Wood Lord & Co	£5 – 5 – 0	Brief
May 14	Wood Lord & Co	£1 – 1 – 0	Conference.[30]

Not only was this at least seven times the average industrial wage (and in a week shortened by the Coronation festivities), but as a bachelor living quietly at home with his parents and youngest sister Rachel, Selwyn had few outgoings. Dr Lloyd, as we have seen, retired in 1930, Mount Pleasant was doing well, and he had time and means for a comfortable leisure. In 1936 the family had moved from Netherton in Banks Road to the Rushes at 27, Stanley Road, a substantial house, overlooking the short 13th hole ('the short, wicked 13th', as it has been described, 'jiggety, tricky, witty, deplorable')[31] of the Royal Liverpool links, a hole after which the house was named. As an investment Selwyn had contributed financially to the move. ('The family very pleased as the Rushes is very suitable for all of us', wrote Dr Lloyd. 'Each one will derive some separate pleasure in addition to the general improvement for all of us.')[32] This was one form of investment for Selwyn but he also managed his stocks and

shares shrewdly, no more mock calculations on the top deck of
Liverpool Corporation buses. His tastes, however, remained simple:
a quiet evening at home, and bridge until 9.30 with his parents and
Rachel (though there were often difficulties when changing from
Contract to Auction Bridge), then up to his room to work on the next
day's briefs until 1 or even 2 in the morning. When Rachel's fiancé,
Ronald Clayton, a solicitor, came on the scene he would take the
hand at bridge, enabling Selwyn to work even harder at the briefs,
though finding time at the weekends for new interests such as amateur
dramatics, taking the lead with great success in a play called *The
Truth Game*, in which Ivor Novello was then starring in London.

By this time he was No. 2 to Fred Pritchard in the Chambers at 25
Castle Street. Others in the substantial practice included Hugh
Macneil, A. T. Miller, J. S. Watson (always known as 'Watty'),
Gordon Clover, T. M. Banks, Glyn Burrell and, as Selwyn's pupil
from 17 March 1937, Frank Nance. The boot was now on the other
foot with Selwyn as the demanding pupil master, calling Nance 'the
Chief Noman' because of the number of times Nance used the word
'No' in Chambers' Conferences. Selwyn made Nance work, 'Get an
answer to this', he would say as more papers came in, and to a
younger colleague there was an element of unapproachability about
him. Selwyn drove in a little open 2-seater with Nance to the Assizes
at Appleby, Carlisle and Lancaster, and the two came to work well
together. Of his other colleagues, 'Watty' and Gordon Clover (for
whom Selwyn acted as best man after the war) were particular
friends. His contemporaries regarded him professionally as being
possessed of a first-class legal brain, though never in the top rank
of advocates. But this was in comparison with such impressive
adornments of the Northern Circuit as Maxwell Fyfe and Hartley
Shawcross, whose voices rang with effortless superiority. Selwyn was
never in that league of advocate.

Nevertheless, he had his successes. In addition to the vitriol-
throwing case Dr Lloyd had noted, Selwyn also came to national
prominence in a case heard at Manchester Assizes on 7 December
1937 when he defended a man against a charge of having wounded Sir
Oswald Mosley with intent to cause grievous bodily harm. This was
one of his last cases with Sidney Silverman and one that gave both a
great deal of satisfaction. 'Our defence, putting it crudely, was that
the brick which our client admittedly threw, was not the one which hit
Mosley. It was not a very easy argument to make convincing but we
procured a disagreement in the jury at Manchester Assizes, and the
prosecution did not pursue the case.'[33] He could show passion when
cross-examining, especially when convinced a witness was lying. In

March 1939 Selwyn defended a chaplain from a local Mersey mission who had been accused of sexual offences against a 15-year-old boy. 'Counsel in Duel with Solicitor', ran the headline in the *Liverpool Daily Post* of the several heated scenes between Mr John Behn, prosecuting for the police, and Selwyn who said that it would be monstrous if the man were sent for trial on uncorroborated evidence. 'The boy is about as abandoned a piece of work as you could find in this city and is a bareface liar', said Selwyn. 'No court, no jury, would consider this case for a moment.' The case was not proceeded with.[34]

There were failures too. In 1939 Selwyn appeared for the defence in a capital case at Carlisle Assizes, 'in which a youth convicted of murder was hanged although in my view he should have been reprieved on each of three grounds, his youth, the circumstances of the crime and the medical history of the family.'[35] This experience confirmed Selwyn's views on capital punishment. By instinct and conviction he was an abolitionist ahead of his time. Even then he was under no illusions that his views were very much against the populist stance and the day of the 'law and order' debate at Conservative Party conferences in the 1950s was one he came particularly to loathe. This attitude was to have profound effects upon his political career and was one of the reasons why he never became Home Secretary, though he was offered the post by one Prime Minister who had temporarily and inadvertently forgotten Selwyn's views on the death penalty. Selwyn made it clear that had he been Home Secretary he would have administered the law as it stood, but it was never a post he coveted. When anyone 'joked' about capital punishment in his presence he was deeply offended. From the gruesome and unsolved Wallace case in Liverpool in January 1931, which he observed as a young barrister, to the case at Carlisle Assizes just before the outbreak of war, all his legal experience confirmed him in his view that the judicial taking of human life was morally indefensible.

The law was only one part of Selwyn's life in the 1930s. His overriding interest remained the political process. By 1931 Selwyn had broken with the Macclesfield Liberals and effectively with the National Liberals (whether in Lloyd George or Simonite colours) and with Herbert Samuel, who led the main group of Liberal MPs from 4 November that year. As the door of Liberal politics closed that of local politics opened, but before considering this part of Selwyn's career it is necessary to look at the reasons for the schism with the Liberals as in the long-term this was one of the more significant developments of his life.

Against the background of rising unemployment and increasing financial crisis Ramsay Macdonald had formed a National Government (consisting of Baldwin's Conservatives, Samuel's Liberals and 4 National Labour MPs) on 24 August 1931. Like Peel and Gladstone before him, Macdonald split his party for a generation. In October Macdonald sought his 'Doctor's Mandate' for further measures of financial stringency. At the centre of the package which he presented to the electorate was Tariff Reform. The Conservatives were traditionally for Protection (especially Neville Chamberlain at this time), but the Liberals (under Samuel) were for Free Trade. It was a difficult tightrope for Macdonald, but one that in the end saw him leading a National Government of Conservatives and Liberals against his former colleagues in the Labour Party. The ramifications of this for the Labour Party have been well documented.[36] For Liberals too it was a time of soul searching and it was on the rock of Free Trade that Selwyn's association with the Liberal Party foundered. The 1931 Election severed many of the old political links. Should Liberals who believed in Free Trade stand against National Conservative candidates who advocated Tariffs? If the National Government candidate was the former Conservative member then a possible splitting of the 'patriotic' vote might reduce the mandate that Macdonald now sought. (Even Maurice Hankey, the impeccably neutral Cabinet Secretary, was urged by King George V to vote for the National Government, so strong was the King's desire for a resounding endorsement of the Government's position.)[37] This polarisation between the 'patriotic' and the supposedly 'unpatriotic' had disastrous consequences for the Labour Party, who were reduced to a mere 46 seats, the level of a quarter of a century earlier. 'The importance of the election', as C. L. Mowat wrote, 'was that it gave the Conservatives, under false colours, an overwhelming strength in parliament which they could hardly have won unaided.'[38] The Conservatives won 473 seats and three groupings of Liberals won 72 seats. Although he did not stand in this 1931 Election, the events surrounding the campaign proved a crucial staging-post on Selwyn's journey to the Conservative ranks.

Macclesfield was one of those constituencies where the sitting member (John Remer, Selwyn's adversary from 1929) was a National Conservative. When the election was announced Frank Duncalf, Secretary, and T. A. Edwards, Chairman, from the local Liberal association asked Selwyn if he would stand again. Selwyn had cultivated the constituency in a desultory way, attending church services and quasi-social and political events, so the Macclesfield Liberals assumed as a matter of course that he would stand.[39] Selwyn, however, thought differently. 'I disagreed with the Liberals over

Tariffs. They still were standing out for complete Free Trade. I thought when we had massive unemployment of over 2½ millions to let all foreign goods come into this country unrestricted was quite wrong . . . so I really left them on that.'[40] Five years earlier he had jokingly referred to the possibility of joining the Labour Party. Now, if he remained in active politics, there was only one party. On 29 September 1931 Selwyn outlined his position to Frank Duncalf:

> In the event of the Government continuing in office, I should like to see the component parts pledge themselves to carry on, say, for two years without an Election. In either case, I should favour the Government being given a free hand to employ the weapon of an emergency tariff to restrict imports if the present devaluation of the pound does not rectify our trade balance (as presumably it would not, if most other countries went off the gold standard).

The Government had taken Britain off the Gold Standard on 21 September 1931 and the era of managed currencies had begun. Selwyn continued in his letter:

> If the government carries on, the question of the next election is postponed. If it comes to the country as a National Government with the Liberal leaders in it, then no doubt Mr Remer would be approved as the National candidate for this constituency and our task – a disagreeable one but nevertheless a clear one, would be not to oppose him. The extent of our support might be considered later![41]

From the national point of view Selwyn considered that, undesirable though a general tariff would be, a Conservative government, 'would mean financial stability and confidence abroad and among industrialists at home'. In the light of this situation Selwyn had no doubt as to his course of action. He would not oppose Remer, the National candidate.

> I hope that these rather frank observations will help the Committee. The situation, whatever else it is, is not simple. The national situation is far more serious than most people imagine and party tactics must definitely be the last thing to be considered.
> As regards my personal position, I appreciate that there is no reason why the Committee should pay any particular regard to my views. If it feels that I no longer represent it, I will place my resignation in its hands without any ill feeling whatsoever. I shall always remember with gratitude and affection the pleasant times I have had in the Macclesfield Division.[42]

The Committee asked him to reconsider and meet the party executive, but Selwyn refused to depart from the terms of his letter of 29 September. Duncalf was deeply disappointed and in his reply of 5 October said that Liberals in Macclesfield would be effectively disenfranchised as they could not be expected to support an extreme Protectionist (the Remer position), or the Labour candidate who would be subject to Trades Union Congress control and who was a member of the party 'which had shirked responsibility in the recent crisis.'[43] But Selwyn would not stand and on 12 October wrote an open letter to the Macclesfield Liberals:

> To those Liberals to whom this decision may be unpalatable, I would say that I have given the matter the most earnest and conscientious consideration, and that bitter though the temporary disappointment may be, I am convinced that neither an individual nor a party eventually regrets having put National Duty before personal consideration.[44]

Duncalf accepted the inevitable and the Liberals put up no candidate against Remer. Selwyn was asked not to make any public statement in support of Remer. To this he agreed, but he did speak on behalf of Sir Christopher Clayton, Conservative candidate in the Wirral.[45] *The Hoylake and West Kirby Advertiser* headed its report, 'A Liberal's Patriotism: Mr. J. S. B. Lloyd's sacrifice at Macclesfield', and Dr Lloyd wrote in his diary the day after the election:

> Oct 28 This has led to considerable disappointment on the side of his old constituency but S thinks he has done right & it looks as if it was so . . . At both local meetings he received quite an ovation and many said they wished he had been standing for Wirral (he was asked & refused two years ago, also for Wrexham). The whole country has been intensely excited & is now definitely delighted at the crushing blow the Socialists have recd about only 50 returned.[46]

Remer, like so many National candidates, was returned with an increased majority. But this was not quite the end of the Macclesfield story for Selwyn. On 9 April 1934 the new Secretary and Agent, K. L. Spencer, approached Selwyn with the unanimous wish of his Committee that he should stand again for them at the next General Election. Selwyn, who was by then deeply involved in Urban District Council affairs, declined and with the choice of John L. Poole as Selwyn's successor at Macclesfield for the 1935 General Election, Selwyn's Liberal days were effectively at an end. It was a move he took with regret and letters from Liberal luminaries such as Sir John Simon, saying that he was 'one of the rising hopes of the Liberal

Party',[47] were kept as a reminder of what might have been if the course of politics in the 1930s had taken a different turning.

When it was known that Selwyn was not standing at Macclesfield in 1931 the Conservative Association in Clitheroe approached him about being put on the candidates list at Conservative Central Office. This initiative came from the Assheton family at Downham Hall, Clitheroe, who felt that he was the kind of young political figure who should now be encouraged to join the Conservatives.[48] After the war Ralph Assheton (later Lord Clitheroe), Chairman of the Party from 1944–6 and member of Churchill's Shadow Cabinet, was to be one of Selwyn's important North West contacts when he entered Parliament, but in 1931 he declined the invitation. Not only was he establishing himself in his legal career, but he had temporarily turned aside from national to concentrate on local politics. The Hoylake Urban District Council was where he learned the basics of his trade and was the next phase in his political apprenticeship.

Selwyn attended his first meeting of the Hoylake UDC on 19 April 1932, Mr Walker and Mr Doleman proposing: 'That Mr. Lloyd be a member of the Committee.'[49] This period of local government work, which lasted until the outbreak of war, unglamorous and unexciting as it may have seemed to a later metropolitan audience, was a vital part of his political training. Politics is one of the few professions where no qualification, other than that of satisfying the electors (or in most cases the selecting committee of the local constituency association), is required. The British political tradition has been one of learning by experience. For Selwyn that experience was on his own doorstep.

In the 1930s local government really was *local* government. The Hoylake UDC to which Selwyn was elected in 1932 owned its own electricity, gas and water works, and maintained two swimming pools and a municipal golf-links. Although the work was essentially apolitical Selwyn no longer wished to be associated with free trade Liberalism and always stood as an independent.[50] Selwyn was representative for the Grange Ward and served on every committee. For three years he was Chairman of the Estates Finance Committee, handling an annual budget in excess of a quarter of a million pounds. 'My three years as Chancellor of the Exchequer of that Authority were happy and entertaining,' Selwyn recalled in a speech in 1949, 'particularly as two large and covetous County Councils were continually casting greedy eyes upon us.'[51] The difficult balance which the UDC had to maintain in the 1930s was how to keep West Kirby a pleasant, quiet residential district, while at the same time attracting holidaymakers. The four sources of revenue were boating at West Kirby, bathing, the speed-boat pool at Hoylake, and the municipal golf-links, though many visitors were attracted to Hoylake by the Royal Liverpool links, which hosted two Open Championships in the 1930s. (In 1930 the American golfer Bobby Jones won the second leg of his impregnable quadrilateral of the Open and Amateur championships of Great Britain and the United States at Hoylake, for Selwyn the greatest of all sporting achievements. By 1936 when the championship returned not all welcomed the influx of visitors. 'Glad it is over', wrote Dr Lloyd in his diary, 'A rowdy crowd at the Club.')[52] A penny rate brought in £1,000. In Selwyn's first year as Finance Committee Chairman 495 new houses were built, rateable value increased from £223,407 to £236,674, 3½ miles of new sewers were laid and many new streets of which over 2 miles were adopted as public highways. The mastering of such local government detail was the best possible training for later departmental work. Although opinions differed as to Selwyn's effectiveness as a Minister, particularly on the communicative side, none denied his ability to master a brief. This stemmed not only from his legal work, but from the hundreds of meetings he attended in the 1930s as Councillor, Finance Committee Chairman, and eventually Chairman of the Hoylake UDC. (In the year ending 14 April 1934 he attended 72 meetings and in subsequent years 49, 32 and 70 meetings.)[53] Selwyn presented his last 'Budget' on 16 March 1937 (the day before Frank Nance became his pupil in chambers) and was thanked by the Council for his efforts. 'So far as the Budget itself is concerned the whole council and its officers share with Councillor Lloyd the distinction of bringing a listing ship back to an even keel, and to have accomplished this with a promise of the policy's continuance, without increasing the rates is a notable feat.'[54] In dealing with the estimates for the coming year, Selwyn referred to the fact that this would be Coronation year and the Council desired to play their part in marking the event. But Selwyn was determined that a lot of money should not be spent on ephemeral pageantry which would soon be forgotten. His policy was to ensure that certain improvements should be completed during the year as permanent amenities. The Coronation gardens, which were opened on 9 April by his friend Sir John Nicholson, still serve as a recreational area to this day. Selwyn was determined that Coronation Day itself, 12 May, should largely be a day for the local children. Selwyn was an unabashed Monarchist and, like his father, had been appalled by the Abdication. ('Feeling is very strong that he had done a serious disservice to the Monarchy', wrote Dr Lloyd in his diary. 'I have just heard the parting message from Edward VIII . . . there was something disappointing and unconvincing in the speech.')[55] He kept among his papers many of the illustrated royal supplements of the time – the Kent and Gloucester weddings in 1935, George V's funeral, and the Coronation programme of 1937. By Coronation Day he was Chairman of the UDC – he had been unanimously elected to that post on 20 April at the age of 32, the youngest chairman the Council had ever had[56] – and in charge of all the local festivities. Dr Lloyd wrote:

> Wed 12 May Sel very busy, service at St Hildeburg's, march past the Town Hall of scouts, guides, fire brigade, sports events, Cinema for children. Turning on new lights in main road.[57]

The rest of the year was not so happy. No sooner were the Coronation celebrations over than the Council turned its attention to air-raid precautions and Civil Defence measures. Selwyn chaired a meeting of the League of Nations union at the local cinema in October and later attended a conference on air-raids as the shadows of approaching war lengthened.[58]

As Chairman, Selwyn had the UDC in the palm of his hand, he knew how to handle it and blend the disparate voices into one united front. He knew how to identify the opposition, mollify it if possible, and if not overcome it, and it was in this world of local affairs that he cut his political teeth.[59] Yet this episode in Selwyn's life, where he learned at first hand about administration and committee work in a self-financing, autonomous local authority has been commonly held up as an example of his narrow parochialism and provincial bearing. Mr Hoylake UDC was one of the most persistent barbs aimed in Selwyn's direction, particularly when he was Chancellor of the Exchequer.[60] The truth is that there were worse ways of serving a pragmatic political apprenticeship.

In the 1930s Selwyn lived the life of a small-town professional man, the kind of world that Ibsen drew in his social prose dramas; the world of the doctor, the newspaper editor, the solicitor, the retired military officer. It was a quiet, comfortable and largely untroubled existence, but it was not one that entirely satisfied Selwyn or gave him fulfilment. He was intensely ambitious, even edgy. There was an element of wanting 'to show them' in the wider world. Many thought this would be in the London legal world, taking silk and moving on as a High Court Judge in due course. In the Wirral he was a creature of habit, living a structured and ordered life in which the church, golf, the Bar and the work of the Council all took their compartmentalised and allotted place in the week. West Kirby contained an interconnecting group of communities and families. In 1936 when the Lloyds moved to the Rushes, they became the third point of a triangle at the edge of the links. Howard and Dorice Shone were now established at Stanmore by the fifth green with their growing family (they were to have four sons and two daughters) and one of the visiting customs of childhood was walking down the out of bounds alongside the fairway of the old third hole to be met half way by the family from the Rushes, with strict instructions to wait in the hut for an adult lest by their toings and froings they should encroach on the golf.[61] Selwyn's work on the UDC had also brought him increasingly into contact with Roland Marshall, whose family were established at Sandhills at the far end of the course where the 9th hole turns for the homeward leg. Eventually these bonds were to be strengthened when Selwyn married the Marshalls' daughter Elizabeth in 1951.

In many ways Selwyn did not have much 'fun' before the war, that came more in the last decade of his life. He took his responsibilities extremely seriously at a time when many of his contemporaries were living it up after the privations of war. The world of the Charleston was not the world of West Kirby. Michael Ramsey, who had a parish in Liverpool after Cambridge, came to stay from time to time. When he came down to breakfast without a tie Dr Lloyd was horrified. It was a conservative milieu. (Like his father, Selwyn voted for Baldwin's government in 1935 and increasingly became something of a Baldwin figure in his own right.) One of his few extravagances (for such was how Dr Lloyd viewed it) was to go on holiday cruises on the SS *Orontes*, visiting places such as Constantinople, Athens and (the place that fascinated him most) Gallipoli. He was always immaculately dressed, long white stockings on deck by day, black tie by night, and still talking politics. On one of these cruises he met Lord Mancroft, a former Financial Secretary to the Treasury, and his son, telling them that as he had had experience of local politics, one day he hoped to go into national politics and was, therefore, learning to speak. Lord Mancroft told him that the important thing in politics was to learn how to listen. Many years later he told the 2nd Lord Mancroft that this was a lesson he had never forgotten.[62]

Another friendship from the *Orontes* days was with Pamela Bowring-Toms. In a desultory, and yet at other times militaristic way he sought her hand in marriage. His campaign was not helped by the intervention of his intended's younger Etonian brother, who addressed Selwyn in letters as my F.A. (Faithful Ally) and followed the wooing with voyeuristic, but unsuccessful, enthusiasm. The final correspondence between all three was acrimonious and tearful. For a long time the family believed that he would marry a local girl, Erica Carter. This also was an engagement that blew hot and cold. Selwyn proposed and was refused. Later Erica Carter went back on her refusal, but Selwyn in his turn refused. These were skirmishes, not emotional involvements. Selwyn was increasingly seen as 'a confirmed bachelor' and 'not the marrying kind' as he settled to the comforts of home life. In a more innocent age these phrases were not intended as euphemisms. Yet Selwyn was never entirely at ease in female company outside the family circle. In later life he was to owe much to the wives of his friends, particularly those with strong-willed personalities and a capacity for organisation, but his real friendships were in the context of clubbable, institutional worlds. In 1936, for instance, he joined the Northern Bar Lodge and much enjoyed his social life in the 25 Club of Wirral. In the last phase of his life too he enjoyed the company of the personable young and although reticent personally he could be fulsome in his letters. It was part of his niceness and his naïvety that he did not see how this could be open to misinterpretation.

The 25 Club, which still flourishes, was a debating group that met on a monthly rota basis at members' houses (hence the upper limit of twenty-five) for semi-serious topical argument. To be elected was a signal honour and a sign of rising prominence among the Liverpool professional classes. Selwyn was elected to the Club in November 1932 and remained a member for 15 years. On 12 December 1934 Selwyn spoke against the motion that 'Romance is stronger than ambition'. He quoted Jacob and Esau ('Jacob won'), the Roundheads had beaten the Cavaliers. 'People who had given way to their romantic and sentimental instincts had failed.' As the 1930s drew to a close the motions took on an increasingly darker tinge and by 1938 had largely given way to discussions on the international situation. On 27 October 1938, less than a month after the Munich Agreement, Selwyn led a discussion on Civil Defence and began a programme of co-ordination of UDC and Territorial Army activities.[63] He believed there should be much firmer central control by some government department and had no confidence in the role played by Sir Thomas Inskip as Minister of Co-ordination for Defence.

Macclesfield had not entirely given up its hold on him. In October 1935 his successor as Liberal candidate, John L. Poole, wanted Selwyn to speak in the election campaign for old time's sake. But Selwyn was increasingly moving in Conservative circles, the Asshetons at Clitheroe and, from 1933, with Bill Aitken, a nephew of Lord Beaverbrook, who was to become one of his closest friends and a political colleague in the post-war House of Commons. His last dinner with Lloyd George was at Criccieth on 13 September 1934.[64]

As Liberalism gave way to Conservatism, so peace gave way to war. The Munich agreement was to Selwyn the postponing of the inevitable, at best a temporary respite. In 1918 he had regretted that he had been too young for military service. Twenty-one years later, the shadow of war once more lay over the land. In the last weeks of peace – on 8 July 1939 – his youngest sister Rachel married Ronnie Clayton. By this time Selwyn was already involved in the initial stages of his military service. Instead of the London legal world being the process by which he was drawn on to the wider stage, it was Hitler's war, and the next six years were to lead, not to a Circuit bench but to Westminster. The days as Mr Hoylake UDC were over.

4

Willingly to War

For many of the generation that was too young to serve in 1914, the Second World War, for all its atrocities and sufferings, was an opportunity (perhaps the only one) to rid the world of Nazi oppression and tyranny and to atone for the sins of omission, for what Churchill called the years of the locust. It was a war that was actually 'about' something, unlike its messy, almost accidental predecessor. Selwyn certainly did not go into the war 'ardent for some desperate glory',[1] but he was fascinated by its experience, by the camaraderie, and, as he assumed high rank in Second Army, by the international co-operation that was focused on a common sense of purpose. He came out of the war, like many of his colleagues who were to make their name in Labour politics, with a feeling that there had to be a better and more secure future. The six years of that war were arguably the most intense of his life.

'Soldiering was an urge or a fixation which had always possessed me', wrote Selwyn. 'Why I know not. The splendid fort I was given on my 8th birthday; the platoons of toy soldiers, guardsmen, camel corps, Zulus etc; G. A. Henty and his fascinating accounts of military campaigns throughout the ages, Hannibal over the Alps, Titus and the fall of Jerusalem, the Crusades, Agincourt, India, the Napoleonic wars, I suppose all this contributed.'[2] The Anschluss, the union of Austria and Germany in March 1938, was the event through which an urge became a reality. 'In the thirties I was too busy, trying to earn a living at the Bar, to worry too much about international affairs or the T.A. The occupation of the Rhineland by Hitler made no significant impact. The Anschluss did. I began to be worried. I joined the Officers' Emergency Reserve. I wrote a polite letter to the War Office saying that although I was a lawyer, I had no intention of being a lawyer in War, and could I please be an Infantry Officer.'[3] The letter he got by return was polite, but blunt. The only situation in which he would be any use to the Army would be in the Judge Advocate's department. As so often, once Selwyn had set his mind on something, he was not so easily deflected.

In the Wirral he was at the hub of local defence preparations. Not only Chairman of the Council and of its Finance Committee, he also headed the ARP Committee. On 17 May 1938, two months after the Anschluss, Selwyn noted of his recruiting drive that, 'the district had the highest number of volunteers of any Borough or Urban or Rural District in the County'.[4] At the time of the Munich Agreement in September 1938 he had a row with the County Council over ARP equipment and issued an appeal locally for funds to purchase essential training stores. He raised £1,000 in voluntary donations in a week. The County Council at first were furious. The Clerk and his officials came to a rally of Air Raid Wardens that Selwyn held at the cinema in West Kirby. Selwyn explained their purpose in diplomatic terms. He told the Council that they had raised their own money and would buy their training equipment independently, but this was no reflection on the County Council, it simply showed how keen they were. The meeting ended amicably and the fund served an unexpectedly useful purpose in that it proved impossible to spend the whole £1,000, because then the equipment began to come through at a faster rate.

On 2 January 1939 Maurice Hankey, recently retired Cabinet Secretary, wrote to the War Secretary, Leslie Hore-Belisha, urging an expansion of the Territorial Army, conditional only on financial viability.[5] With the collapse of Czechoslovakia in March (what Selwyn called 'the encircling gloom of Nazi pretensions'),[6] Hore-Belisha announced a doubling of the Territorial Army from 13 to 26 divisions on 29 March. As Chairman of the Council Selwyn was told early in April that a second line unit of 106 RHA, a Liverpool unit, was going to be raised in the Wirral, either in Hoylake or Wallasey. Selwyn was determined it would be Hoylake and arranged a recruiting week in the district, taking the chair at the final meeting of the campaign in the Winter Gardens Cinema at Hoylake. By coincidence the film showing that week was *The Warning* and Selwyn arranged for the foyer to be used for propaganda and recruiting purposes. Brigadier Cherry, the CRA of the 55th West Lancashire Division, was the principal speaker but Selwyn established himself as the overseer of the whole operation. 'No sooner had I done this than the thought presented itself – how could I, 34 years old, appeal to my contemporaries and others to join this new unit, unless I set the proper example myself? Accordingly when the fateful night came I announced my own intention to apply for a Commission, having *ex abundante controle* ascertained from Brigadier Cherry that my application would be accepted.'[7]

On the evening of the meeting a carnival atmosphere prevailed. It was Coronation week again with a military flavour. A mechanised unit of the 10th Regiment RHA gave a demonstration of manoeuvres on the sands, the Band of the 87th 1st Lancs Field Regiment played as crowds entered the Winter Gardens Cinema to hear Brigadier Cherry appeal for at least 500 volunteers for what would be the first Royal Horse Artillery Unit in the Wirral. Recruiting started on 26 April and the 149 RHA – known affectionately from the start as the Hoylake Horse – was raised in 6 days with some 470 officers and other ranks. Godfrey Castle, a Liverpool solicitor (and an MC from the First World War), was put in command. The uniforms, field boots, mess dress were ordered at once, Selwyn working very closely at this time with Captain Alan Graham, his predecessor as Wirral's Conservative MP. The Royal Horse Artillery had, as Selwyn recalled, neither artillery nor horses, but a loyalty to the Crown and some buildings near the gas-works which provided temporary accommodation. They began to study gunnery and deployment and went on weekend exercises. 'In for a penny, in for a pound', was Selwyn's reaction when he was commissioned as a second lieutenant in June.[8] He told Brigadier Cherry that he intended to take six weeks holiday from his legal practice and as Cherry was spending those six weeks visiting T.A. units at their summer camps he took Selwyn along as his acting Brigade Major. So at the end of July with three pips on his shoulder – his substantive rank was still Captain – and the Coronation Medal of May 1937, Selwyn was accepted as a Territorial of long-standing. He went to camps in Derbyshire and at Trawsfynydd in North Wales, lecturing on deployment.

As the international situation deteriorated Hore-Belisha wrote to the Prime Minister Neville Chamberlain on 24 August asking for permission to call out the whole of the Regular Army and to embody the Territorials.[9] On 1 September Selwyn returned to Hoylake from the TA Camp at Buxton and as he pulled into the drive of the Rushes was surprised to see his father 'coming out of the house looking rather pale to say it has begun.'[10] The Germans had invaded Poland. The Hoylake Horse was embodied at once. When Selwyn reported to Colonel Castle he was told that the Adjutant, W. F. A. Preston, had been appointed second-in-command and that he would be the new Adjutant. His military career, which was to end as Brigadier Deputy Chief of Staff Second Army, had begun in earnest. The Army was to be as liberating an experience for Selwyn as Magdalene had been. The TA camps, for instance, had been boozy affairs and in the next six months Selwyn had many of the peace-time spots knocked off him. For the next fortnight, however, the Hoylake Horse had little to do except dig trenches and clear the cascades of paper descending from higher authority. On the morning of 3 September Selwyn heard Chamberlain's declaration of war at his office desk, 'very moving', he wrote in his diary.[11] The Hoylake Horse contained many legal men and Selwyn's friend Gordon Clover was billeted at the Rushes. It was a time of PT on the shore, swims in the open-air pools, and mess life in the Municipal Golf-Course Club House. The work had a distinct 'Dad's Army' feel to it. One of Selwyn's tasks was to work with a 'Director', a three-legged surveying instrument which he set up on training nights on the lawn at the Rushes. As the machine was a relic of the Boer War many hours were spent puzzling how to work it. But Selwyn's days with the Hoylake Horse were numbered.

Brigadier Cherry – the next in the growing line of 'My Masters' – had no illusions about war, he knew the quality of men who would be needed and he had marked out Selwyn as suitable for the Staff Officers' Course at Camberley. On 13 September there was a letter for Selwyn at the Rushes with an instruction for Acting Captain J. S. B. Lloyd to report that day to the Staff College at Camberley for the first war-time short course for potential staff officers. Selwyn at once rang Brigadier Cherry to find out what it was all about. Cherry told him that a vacancy had arisen at the last moment and he had nominated Selwyn for it. The nomination had been accepted and he must go. Selwyn loaded up his car at once (the instructions said he had to report by 1800 that evening), said goodbye to Godfrey Castle and others who were around, including a tearful Mrs Lloyd who was under the impression that he was going to the front. 'Goodbye to the 149 never to see them again', recorded Selwyn laconically.[12]

So Selwyn's lot was thrown in with the staff officers, not the infantry posting he had desired. At key moments in his life – and the Staff Officers' Course at Camberley was the most significant to date in his ambition to spread his wings beyond the Wirral peninsula – Selwyn had the good fortune to come up against men of real ability in their fields.'The instructors there', he later recalled, 'really were men of very great ability indeed.'[13] The Commandant was General Paget and the instructors included Brian Horrocks and Charles Keightley (whose career was to overlap with Selwyn's again in 1956 when the Suez invasion was launched). For Selwyn to be accepted into this company in September 1939 was a stroke of great fortune. Places on the Staff College course were like gold-dust and he must have been spotted as a potential high-flier to have been taken in with the first batch as a Territorial.

9 Megan Lloyd George at the time of the 1929 General Election.

10 Selwyn at a Liberal Summer School, Thorneycroft Hall, near Macclesfield, 1927.

11 Chairman of the Hoylake Council: Selwyn on A.R.P. stretcher drill, 1938.

12 The first meeting on French soil of General Sir Bernard Montgomery
    with his invasion commanders, Lt-General Omar Bradley and
    Lt-General Miles Dempsey, Port en Bessin, 10 June 1944, four days
    after D Day.

13 HM King George VI knighting Dempsey in the field, 15 October 1944.

He reached Camberley on the afternoon of 13 September and was billeted in the town. When the course got underway the instructors were very disappointed with their pupils, who were a strange and ill-assorted hotch-potch; staff officers from the First World War, reserve staff, long-serving Territorials and, finally, raw recruits like Selwyn. It soon became clear that it was among the ranks of these raw recruits that the staff officers of the future would be selected. Shortly after the course had started Paget went off to command a division and was succeeded by Brian Horrocks. He was a gruelling task-master and Selwyn found him abrasive. In addition there was argument about Selwyn's future posting. But Horrocks's demands were born of the atmosphere of the time, which he recalled in his memoirs:

> Most of the officers selected to attend No. 1 war staff were successful young barristers, business men, schoolmasters, dons . . . including Selwyn Lloyd (Capt. J. S. B. Lloyd) and 2nd Lt. D. C. Walker-Smith.* They were a brilliant collection of young men and instead of the usual shop to which we had become hardened the ante-room now resounded to fierce arguments ranging over every possible topic in the world. We thoroughly enjoyed trying to teach them the art of war, and it was encouraging to learn that they in their turn were quite impressed with our standard and method of instruction.[14]

Selwyn found it a fascinating three months and was surprised and gratified by the tolerance shown to him when he requested permission to go up to London to appear in what was to be his last case for six years, in the House of Lords, Selwyn in uniform led by Fred Sellers, with Hartley Shawcross on the other side. The disappointment of defeat was softened by the fee (100 guineas), it later transpiring that this fee (far more than any instructor was receiving at Camberley) was the reason Selwyn had been allowed to go by an impressed Commandant.[15] Otherwise there was a melancholy running down of his legal interests. On 8 October his father wrote to him, 'I called at 27 Lord Street & saw Burrell & Watson & gave up the keys of your chambers.'[16] Mrs Lloyd went to the old stomping ground of Henfaes Hotel at Criccieth. It may have been the time of the Phoney War, but for Selwyn it was the beginning of his real military training as the days of TA camps and Directors on the back lawn gave way to an intense, although necessarily abbreviated course from some of the finest theorists in the British Army.

Despite the disparity of age and experience (the recent doubling of

---

* Later Lord Broxbourne and a government colleague of Selwyn.

the Territorials meant that there were some very raw recruits at Camberley) it was, as one of Selwyn's colleagues of the time recalled, 'a very friendly show', in which people were bound together by a common sense of purpose. Officers were placed in individual syndicates under their respective Directing Staff. Under this system Selwyn showed great aptitude in mastering the brief (as later in his political life) and was widely seen as 'the man most likely to succeed', first in whatever Staff Appointment the Military Secretary's Department at the War Office might arrange, and second in the post-war world. He had a 'very early grasp of things', and was appreciative of General Paget's skilful talks to the assembled syndicates. Although as a potential Staff Officer at this time Selwyn proved himself *'facile princeps'* this did not give him undue cause for celebration.

The Staff College course was highly competitive and there were regular siftings-out. Selwyn had a strong sense of pessimism in his character (which later was to surface at election times) and he held out little personal hope for a successful completion to the course. 'There was another purge from this place on Saturday with people being sent back to their units as unsuitable', he wrote to his parents on 6 November. 'I have just managed to survive, but will probably fall before long.'[17] His account of the atmosphere at Camberley gives some indication of the sense of war-time urgency:

> We get lectured to for almost 6 hours a day and have about another 3–4 hours reading to do just to keep abreast of the lectures. There are 115 student officers, and 15 Colonels or brevet colonels to teach and the Commandant who is a Major-General + a full Colonel and a Lieut-Col who act as the directors of studies, which works out at about 1 senior officer to 6 student officers, therefore I think they must regard us as rather important . . . We are supposed to be doing a 12 months course in 14 weeks. When it is over, if we are lucky, we get the job of sticking on the stamps and counting the petty cash at some Divisional HQ somewhere.[18]

Political discussion filled many of the hours. 'Churchill made another very good speech last night. They all tip him as the next Prime Minister – he certainly seems to be the only one with any personality', Selwyn wrote home on 9 November. 'Our M.Ps. from here went up to heckle Hore-Belisha – they all hate him like poison – and he never tells the truth publicly about the Army or the state of its equipment.'[19]

On 12 November Brigadier Cherry, Selwyn's original sponsor for the staff course, asked for Selwyn to be posted as his Brigade Major. ('I hope that it would suit your book – or shall I say "Ambition"!! –

to rejoin me', wrote Cherry.)[20] By December Selwyn's pessimism was proved unfounded. 'I understand 22 officers out of the 110 here have been passed as fit for immediate posting to staff appointments', wrote Selwyn to his parents. 'Strange as it may seem, I am among the 22.'[21] Throughout his life Selwyn always had great respect for the professional, the expert in his chosen field. This was the case at Camberley. 'I left with mixed feelings, some idea of what an operation order was, respect for the Regular soldiers and the certain knowledge that I was quite unfit to be B.M.R.A., not knowing anything about guns etc.'[22] Selwyn took seven days leave at the end of his course and reported to Loughborough on 31 December. He was now Brigade Major RA 55th West Lancashire Division under Brigadier Cherry.

Selwyn was billeted in an old-fashioned Victorian house, Mountfield, in Loughborough. It was a cold, depressing time, enlivened for Selwyn only by the news of the removal of Hore-Belisha from the War Office.* 'What do you think about Hore-Belisha being kicked out?', he enquired of his parents in a letter of 7 January 1940, two days after the Cabinet changes were announced. 'Everyone here is very pleased – the view being that he is completely untrustworthy.'[23] The military work was not demanding (especially after Camberley), the rations meagre and the temperature arctic. Eventually Selwyn, whose health had always been unreliable as a child, fell seriously ill and was removed to Leicester Royal Infirmary in February. 'The regimental doctor came to see me and said there was nothing much wrong', recalled Selwyn. 'I felt worse and worse.' Pneumonia was diagnosed and Selwyn's morale was not improved when he was placed next to the bed where the dying were put. 'I spent my nights listening to the death rattle.'[24] The Chairman of the hospital, Mr Pickard, had been at the Leys School, Cambridge with Dr Lloyd and sent an alarmist message which brought Selwyn's father to Leicester at once through the deprivations of a wartime February, fearing the worst. The new M & B 'miracle' pills saved the day, but Selwyn's position with the 55th West Lancs Division was affected, as Cherry explained when he came to see his protégé in hospital. If he stayed away from duty for 21 days – a time-limit that was rapidly approaching – his post automatically became vacant despite anything that Cherry might do. So highly did Cherry regard Selwyn's capabilities as his Number 2 that he concocted a plan whereby Selwyn would return to Loughborough on the twentieth day and then go on

* Hore-Belisha was succeeded as War Secretary by Oliver Stanley, with whom Selwyn's own career was to overlap before the decade was over.

leave for ten days. This plan was actually carried out (to the annoyance of the commanding Major-General) and Selwyn went to Criccieth to recuperate. Here he met Megan Lloyd George, with whom he discussed the latest political developments, whether Churchill was going to become Prime Minister and Megan's assessment of Hitler. 'Megan gave account of meeting with Hitler, who she said was normal except when the greatness of German nation was mentioned.'[25] When Selwyn returned to Loughborough he found that Cherry had been sacked, officially on grounds of health, in effect because of the personality clashes that had arisen, Cherry not being a man who suffered fools gladly and whose fierce temper frequently got the better of him. As Selwyn was known to be Cherry's nominee he was in a very exposed position on his return. Cherry's successor was Brigadier C. B. Robertson, a completely different leader, 'One of the most charming and likeable people I have ever met', Selwyn recalled.[26] Robertson had been at the French Staff College and, in Selwyn's opinion, consequently had an exaggerated regard for the efficiency of the French Army, never believing that Paris would fall as it did in June 1940. Selwyn adapted well to the change of leadership in the Division, though privately he became the recipient of increasingly anguished letters from a superannuated Cherry, to whom he owed much. It was his first experience of the disadvantage of being too closely hitched to someone else's star.

Shortly after Robertson's arrival the division moved to Suffolk to defend sixty miles of coastline. 'We are now comfortably encased in our new HQ', wrote Selwyn to his parents on 21 April from Parham Hall, Framlingham. 'It is a yellow brick country house – 70–80 years old I should say – much larger than the Loughborough house and much more comfortable.'[27] He even found time to visit (for the first time) his sisters' old school at Southwold. But within two weeks Neville Chamberlain had been replaced by Winston Churchill as Prime Minister and one of the first places Churchill visited in his inspection of coastal defences was the 55th Division. Selwyn sent an account of the visit home to his parents: 'He went round the area with the Divisional Commander: he was in a very bad temper, which was only to some extent relieved when he saw some German aeroplanes come over and shoot up the barrage balloons over Harwich. He observed with obvious satisfaction that this would annoy Lord Beaverbrook.'[28]

Three incidents from his time at Framlingham in 1940 stuck with Selwyn. One day a number of bi-planes flew slowly over the house and Selwyn thought that if the British had been reduced to them then we must be in a bad way. In fact they were going to drop supplies on

Calais. Shortly afterwards a German aeroplane was shot down near Woodbridge. Selwyn was in the party that went to investigate. 'I saw my first dead German of the war – the pilot', he wrote home on 19 May, 'very young.'[29] On Sunday 5 May Selwyn was detailed to be host to a lawyer politician. 'We have had a very social day – Lord Ullswater and a granddaughter came over to call. His name was Lowther and he was Speaker of the House of Commons.' Over tea one past and one future Speaker discussed the political scene. Selwyn asked Ullswater who had been the most impressive parliamentarian who had appeared before him in his sixteen years in the chair. 'He said without doubt Asquith – he could put a case in 20 minutes with superb clarity.'[30]

By this time Selwyn's batman was a gunner called Colfer, who stayed with him until the end of the war. 'I owed a great deal to him', wrote Selwyn, who remembered Colfer in a will made on the eve of D-Day in 1944. He did his best to reciprocate, noting in June, 'All leave is stopped except on compassionate grounds – my batman wants to go on leave to get married – I suggested that that was compassionate grounds but even so it was refused.'[31] Dunkirk found Selwyn very dispirited. 'It is very sad, and disturbing for this country, but we have had worse perils in the past. I expect people were much more anxious when the Spanish Armada was in the offing and when old Napoleon was at Boulogne – I think he (Hitler) will find us a much tougher proposition than he expects.'[32] Although Selwyn was now very much the professional staff officer the seamier side of war repulsed him. There was the incident of the dead German pilot that affected him deeply and when in September the Blitz led to reprisal raids he noted (11 September), 'It seems a poor sort of reply to go and kill a lot of women and children in Berlin.'[33] He was fascinated by the political implications of war. 'Churchill made another very good speech', he noted on 7 September. 'He seems amazingly skilful at catching the mood of the moment and striking the right note. They say that General Ironside was sacked because he had collapsed mentally – not insane but just gave under the strain and became incapable of giving a decision about anything.' He followed events in America closely too, recording in November, 'I think it was a big plus for us that Roosevelt got elected. America will be in the war in 12 months time.'[34] The Division was now in the Cotswolds, where Selwyn worked in an icy-cold office in a tin hut and became involved in the aftermath of the Coventry bombing raids. In February 1941 Selwyn prepared to move with the Division to Heathfield in Sussex, but promotion intervened. Brigadier Robertson had written the following report on Selwyn for Major-General

Charles Allfrey, commander of 43rd Wessex Division, part of 12 Corps:

> Has done a short course at Camberley & obtained an S.C. certificate. He has a first class brain, extremely clear, quick & logical with great capacity for work. He is very adaptable & possesses great initiative and ingenuity . . . He possesses marked tact & a strong sense of duty. I consider him outstanding.[35]

This was one of the more significant promotions of Selwyn's army career, for not only did it bring him into contact with Charles Allfrey, another of 'My Masters', but from April 1941 General Bernard Montgomery, the new commander of 12 Corps. Selwyn was delighted with the move. 'The Divisional Commander is called Allfrey, a gunner – very nice – very silent and I have not had much chance of converse with him yet', he wrote home to his parents. 'The worst of the Army seems to be that no sooner do you know one set of people thoroughly than you are plucked out by the roots and sent on somewhere else.'[36] With the arrival of Monty the pace of life quickened considerably with many 6 a.m. exercises in the Canterbury – Maidstone – Deal areas. 'A new Corps Commander has just been appointed called General Montgomery', he wrote home on 25 April. 'He is mad on runs every afternoon and physical exercises before breakfast every morning . . . his great expression is 100% binge, not meaning alcoholic entertainment but physical fitness.'[37] As G2 Selwyn met Monty from time to time and what impressed him most was Monty's gift for communication. Various units had been assembled in South East Command after Dunkirk, expecting the possibility of German invasion in the spring of 1941. After six weeks of Monty everybody in 12 Corps knew what the plan was – 'Three fortresses Dover, Ashford, Canterbury to be held at all costs, and then the Boche will come up the middle and I'll hit him for six with my mobile reserve.'[38] Gradually Selwyn was creeping up the ladder of command and observing the decision-making processes of war at ever closer levels. Charles Allfrey became a particular friend and mentor. Selwyn never forgot their days together, writing to Allfrey on 11 December 1961 when Chancellor of the Exchequer, 'Being your G2 during Binge, Much Binge and Great Binge was a lot more fun than my present assignment.'[39] Monty continued to impress also, whether laying plans for knocking the Boche for six or addressing commandos in a Haywards Heath cinema, after which Selwyn noted that he was 'v. polite, v. incisive, full of self confidence.'[40] Another commander from whom Selwyn learned was General Alan Brooke, GOC Home Forces. 'His tongue goes at about 2000 words a minute', he wrote after one course at Camberley (a nostalgic return) in October 1941, 'but even so cannot keep up with his brain, which works perceptibly ahead of his tongue.'[41] Visits to Camberley gave Selwyn a chance to see K. P. Wilson, now in retirement at Crowthorne, still with Mrs Raggett and the latest in the dynasty of bad-tempered dogs. Selwyn never forgot the old friends and K.P.'s delight is evident in his letter to Mrs Lloyd, which gives a good indication of the kind of milieu in which Selwyn was operating in 1941:

> I have been wanting to write to you for a long time and now I have a good excuse, a visit from Selwyn, who turned up here in style with 2 motor cars and 2 soldier attendants. He looked very well and tells me he is now a Major. I expect his civil ambitions at the bar are quite eclipsed by his military occupations; he never even mentioned them.[42]

Like many non-regulars on home postings Selwyn wondered if he would ever see overseas service. But after his somewhat peripatetic existence in uniform so far, Selwyn was on the verge of his longest continuous spell in one posting before joining Second Army in May 1943. He may not have been abroad as yet, but he had caught Monty's eye. The commander kept a little black book with the names of promising men to bring on.[43] Selwyn's inclusion in it led to his move to South East Command at Reigate on 18 December 1941. Again there was the significant move up the ladder and intense hours of work ('My hours of work are colossal,' he wrote home on 20 December, 'never finished before midnight').[44] He was soon promoted GSO 1 and had high hopes of going to Africa with Monty, who had been appointed to the command of 8th Army on 8 August.[45] 'I am extremely busy here – the Army Commander is away for reasons of which you may shortly hear', he wrote home on 9 August 1942. 'I had quarter of an hour with him just before he left. He was very affable and said that he hoped we should meet again. He said that he was delighted to go, as he had spent two years in this country and it was high time that he went off to fight the Germans again. He was delighted at having to take on a Field Marshal, i.e. Rommel. I hope he cleans up Egypt and then comes back here.'[46] At their meeting Selwyn said that he had joined the Army to fight. Monty told him that he must realise that temporary soldiers were not really in the Army to command men, but that they were very good – better in fact than the regulars – at staff duties. This was to be his métier and he would have his chance before the war was over.[47]

For the moment it was more conferences and paper work. 'We have just got our new Army Commander appointed – a man called Swayne', he wrote home on 6 September. 'He has quite a good reputation, but is not the fellow Monty was . . . I was up in London on Tuesday with the Acting Army Commander & saw the Commander in Chief . . . Old Paget looked in very good form. I also saw Brooke . . . he looked pale, I thought – too much of Churchill for too long, I should think.'[48] One of Selwyn's tasks was to pin-point faults in administration and methods. He wrote frank critiques. In the autumn of 1942 he felt there were excessive staffs, too many specialists, mediocre brigade and divisional commanders, insufficient ability to use personal weapons with rifle and grenade, too many complete passengers, i.e. soldiers not taught to fight. He thought there was insufficient study of the art of war, a lack of offensive spirit and imagination and a complete failure to train battle *teams*, lack of austerity in the Army (the influence of Monty), a lack of co-operation between arms and a lack of discipline in higher spheres. He felt that when the onslaught on Europe came these faults would need re-medying if the invasion was to be successful and in his small way (his phrase) tried in his immediate circle to remedy what faults he could, especially with his staff-college background. He found a kindred spirit at Reigate in Maurice Chilton, with whom his career in Second Army was to be intimately connected.

By Christmas 1942 Selwyn was contemplating what his next posting might be. 'I shall have to be thinking of my own next move soon – probably back to regimental soldiering for a spell as 2nd in command of something like an anti-tank regiment – irritating to come down a pip in rank, but preferable to spending the whole war in an office.'[49] In many ways he felt it had been an unsatisfactory progress. He had joined the Officers' Emergency Reserve in 1937, became a T.A. Captain in August 1939 (not a private as stated in *The Times* obituary),[50] beginning the war as an adjutant in 149 RHA. He had met and worked with commanders as diverse as Paget, Horrocks, Cherry, Robertson, Allfrey, Montgomery and now Chilton – but he had never heard a shot fired in anger. ('I wish I was over in Belgium having a crack at the Boche', he had written in Framlingham days.)[51] Montgomery had told him that he was never destined to be a combatant. Reluctantly Selwyn came to terms with the fact that the staff officer too had a vital role to play, that of:

> The still and mental parts,
> That do contrive how many hands shall strike
> When fitness calls them on and know by measure
> Of their observant toil the enemy's weight.[52]

In the spring of 1943 came the crucial move in his military career when he was posted to Oxford to join the newly formed Second Army on 10 May. He wrote home from Reigate for the last time:

My last letter to you from this address. My new one will be
GSO1   ◎
HQ Second Army
Home Forces

I go there on Monday, and will plunge into a whirl of activity trying to get the new place organised and trained as quickly as possible.[53]

Second Army was formed to head the invasion of Europe, the long-awaited second front. Its foundation was an indication that the tide of war was truly on the turn. From the time of the retreat of the British Expeditionary Force from Dunkirk in 1940 it had always been the intention that an invading force would at some undefined future stage of the war liberate occupied Europe. As the threat of German invasion of Britain receded so more forces in Southern England were assembled for training for the 'Overlord' operation.

Selwyn's experience in the previous 3½ years of war made him a natural candidate for a role on the staff side of this operation. His application and industry to the exclusion of all social life marked him out as a man totally dedicated to the military task in hand. (The wife of one of Selwyn's closest friends remembers being invited to a Mess night at Reigate and being left to her own devices while Selwyn memorised the next batch of ops orders.)[54] From June 1943 to January 1944 Second Army was under the command of General Kenneth Anderson, 'a good plain cook general', as Montgomery was later to refer to him disparagingly. But from 2 January 1944, the date of the arrival of Montgomery in England to take up his appointment as Commander of 21st Army Group (of which Second Army was a part), Anderson's days were numbered. To his intense disappointment he was transferred to Eastern Command and his place taken by General Miles Dempsey, with effect from 26 January.[55]

In his time in the 55th Wessex Division Selwyn had seen the sudden departure of Cherry and his replacement by Robertson. Now the pattern repeated itself (on a higher level) with the arrival of Dempsey. An uneasy political atmosphere prevailed for some time and not all adapted as well to the change as Selwyn, who had not been close to Anderson and, therefore, found that his ability to cope with the unexpected was not as severely tested as it had been in Loughborough. Dempsey's modest and self-effacing personality (which concealed professional determination and integrity) was much to

Selwyn's liking and it was not long before Dempsey became the most important 'Master' of Selwyn's life so far. From Ashley Gardens, London (where the headquarters were established on 26 January) to Belsen in 1945 was a long and dramatic journey, which Selwyn made largely in Dempsey's company. He became the indispensable staff officer. 'I will never forget Miles and his friendship', wrote Selwyn to Dempsey's widow in July 1969. 'He was always a great influence – was one at all measuring up to his standards was a pretty constant thought.'[56]

Dempsey had been appointed Commander of XIII Corps of 8th Army six weeks after El Alamein and played a crucial part with Montgomery in planning the invasion of Sicily. His winter campaign in Italy in 1943 confirmed him in Montgomery's eyes as the man to command Second Army as it prepared for the invasion of Europe. It was not a time for good, plain cooks. Dempsey headed a joint military, naval and air force planning group at Ashley Gardens. Eastern Naval Task Force (part of Second Army) was headed by Rear-Admiral Sir Philip Vian, whose qualities of offensive spirit Selwyn much admired; 83 Group Royal Air Force was under the command of Air-Vice-Marshal Harry Broadhurst, a similarly uncompromising figure. Montgomery's great skill in January 1944 lay in his blending of the Desert 'veterans' with the home-based trainees and Selwyn, unlike some at Ashley Gardens, listened to the experienced battle-scarred campaigners and learned from them. His immediate superior was Maurice Chilton, a formidable, dark and cadaverous Chief of Staff. At Ashley Gardens, Selwyn is remembered as something of a legend by those who worked there in the hectic months before D-Day and as the real guts behind the logistical planning.[57] His main contribution lay in the preparation of the loading tables. The allocation of craft to assault formations was one problem, but the real complexity lay in loading everything in precisely the right order so that on disembarking the sharp end of the assault formations would be first ashore, followed by the relevant support groupings and supplies. Of the thousands of craft that sailed in the invasion flotilla scarcely a formation did not benefit from Selwyn's blueprints. His second responsibility was the plan for rapid build-up from D + 1 onwards. The comparison between Estimated and Actual Rates of Build-Up shows that only minor adjustments had to be made on D + 4 and D + 10.[58] The one unforeseeable difficulty in the field was the outbreak of malaria on D + 20 in 1st Corps at Troarn in France, where pits, flooded to prevent German paratroopers from landing, had led to mosquitoes swarming around the camps. Selwyn solved the problem of vaccines through contacts he had in Burma. All other aspects such as ammunition and petrol were already in hand from the planning at Ashley Gardens from January to April 1944.[59]

The foundations of this logistical success were laid in 1943 before Ashley Gardens had been established and while Anderson was still in command of Second Army. But it was not a success based only on paper work and theory. Selwyn was deeply conscious that he had not been abroad and experienced battle conditions at first-hand. With sixteen colleagues from Second Army HQ at Oxford he planned a Mediterranean visit to the theatres of war to learn as much as possible about amphibious warfare. So in June 1943 he went to North Africa, Malta and Sicily on observation exercises in connection with the D-Day landings. He sailed on 17 June from Liverpool docks, Dr Lloyd noting in his diary, 'Went over to L'pool to meet Sel who is going to N Africa as an observer at HQ . . . He is very pleased to go and expects to return end of August as he is a key man in the 2nd Army & cannot be spared for long.'[60] This was the beginning of the most interesting part of the war for Selwyn. From D-Day to the liberation of Belsen, his service was entirely abroad. The reconnaiss-ance of 1943 was a hint of things to come. His impressions are recorded in his diaries and letters:

> 31 July Algiers was absolutely crowded with troops of all national-ities, it is the usual type of French colonial city with the usual smells and dirt . . .
>
> Tunis was not much damaged except in the area of the docks and airport. The aerodrome buildings were smashed to pieces and there was a huge pile of smashed German aeroplanes – a very pleasant sight . . .[61]

He met up again with General Allfrey, attended Intelligence Conferences, had talks with Monty's Chief of Staff, Major General de Guingand, and saw General Alexander. But the highlight of his North African visit was his meeting with Monty on 9 July. He jotted down his recollections of Monty's frank views of the time:

> Saw Monty in Ops room had 20 mins talk with him – he asked after all the old Seco boys – saw how good his main HQ was – that he would not allow us into Sicily until he gave the word – said Anderson had been given 2nd Army a great pity – 1 Army HQ had always been most unhappy – he said a staff not trained in battle did not matter so long as the cmmd had had battle experience – introduced me to his Chief of Staff as his former G1 O and said that I had followed him about a good deal.[62]

From North Africa Selwyn flew with seventeen others in a rickety aircraft to Malta, taking a circuitous route to keep out of the way of

German planes. 'Malta was very much damaged – quite up to what we expected – worse really taking the whole area of Valetta than any place I have seen in England. The people however looked very cheerful. The island was full of troops and aeroplanes and there was a mass of shipping.'[63] He attended a conference at which Eisenhower and Admiral Cunningham spoke and also met up for the first time with Dick Vernon, his future G1 Ops after D-Day, and Toby Low (later Lord Aldington) a post-war parliamentary colleague. From Malta Selwyn had a brief visit to Cap Passero on the south-eastern tip of Sicily and had a look at the beaches there, testing out landing-craft and investigating the obstacles (natural and man-made) that might be found on the invasion beaches. Selwyn later recalled that the biggest body blow of all was discovering three days before D-Day that one line of rocks was 3½ feet higher than anticipated. This meant that the time of the invasion had to be altered to cope with the tides and this was solved by a complex staggering of times, 'the sort of thing that came right at the last minute when we thought everything had been planned and reconnoitred.'[64] The Mediterranean trip was field work for these problems.

By the beginning of August Selwyn was back at Oxford. 'We are very busy here and have a large party going next week with a mass of generals and people coming to spend a week in studying war', he wrote home on 3 August. The visit of the top brass went well, as Selwyn reported in his next letter on 13 August. 'We have got rid of all our visitors and I now have a moment to breathe – 4 Lt Generals, 9 Major Generals and about 40 Brigadiers. I had to make 4 speeches to them in the course of the week, ending up with an hour on my recent trip.' Many of the lessons learned in the Mediterranean were incorporated into the next big training exercise. 'Just a line from the field', wrote Selwyn on 23 August. 'We have a big exercise just coming off and we are up to the eyes – the real thing as I witnessed it in N Africa is very much less trouble.'[65]

The time for the Second Front was approaching and for once Selwyn did not show his accustomed pessimism, noting in a letter on 31 October, 'Everyone here is still very optimistic about a speedy conclusion to this European part of the War . . . I doubt whether they (the Germans) will make very serious preparations for a prolonged war in N Western Europe.'[66] With the end of the war in sight Selwyn had many discussions with his Army contemporaries about the way in which the peace would be won. 'It will be interesting to see what the Brave New World will be like', he wrote on 28 November. 'Everyone is talking a good deal about it and there is great controversy on how much the State should do.'[67] Selwyn believed that it was inevitable that the State would take a greater role than in pre-war days and that in certain areas of social provision this was desirable, but he was opposed to absolute interventionism. The immediate priority, however, was to win the war.

With the return of Montgomery from North Africa in January 1944 the crucial dispositions for the opening of the Second Front were about to be made. Selwyn wondered what his place in the team would be. 'I had a few words with General Montgomery last Thursday', he wrote home on 12 January 1944. 'He looked very well, and was in tremendous form, and I saw him again on Saturday for a moment or two. At present I still hold my appointment, but I expect at any moment to be relegated to some haven of rest like the Hebrides as garrison adjutant in favour of some battle scarred warrior from the Mediterranean.' But the major changes were to be at a higher level and when Selwyn's role was more clearly defined in Monty's shake up he wrote to his parents on 20 February:

> I have got a new G1 Ops a boy called Dick Vernon aged 26, who has come back from Italy and the 8th Army, after being through all their battles . . . An Army Commander has a Chief of Staff called a Brigadier General Staff, and that is Brigadier Chilton, and there is now a Deputy Chief of Staff called a Colonel General Staff and that is Lloyd . . . I suppose you saw about Anderson in the paper: he was very disappointed at having to leave us – he was not a bad chap, quite modest and high principled, but a dour Scot who became querulous under the slightest pressure – not being sure of himself, he became fretful and nagging – and would have been very difficult in battle. It is bad luck on him in a way, but a good thing for the war effort. Psychologically he was quite unfit to handle men. However he was very nice to me and did his best for me.[68]

Under Montgomery and Dempsey the pace quickened appreciably, first at Ashley Gardens and, from April 1944, at Portsmouth. Selwyn was able to observe men in high command at close quarters and was himself working harder than at any time in his life. (Later at the height of the Suez crisis in October 1956 he said that the pressures were more intense at Ashley Gardens in the spring of 1944.) He met Eisenhower again on 26 March ('very jovial and pleasant – quite young looking') and received the OBE Military Division at Buckingham Palace ('The investiture went off v. well. H.M. was very affable and asked me what I had been doing during the war'). On Sunday 21 May, as D-Day approached, Selwyn wrote home. 'I had an extremely interesting trip to London during the week to attend a very select meeting addressed by the King, Churchill, Smuts, Eisenhower and a few other celebrities.' This was the meeting at St Paul's School on 15 May at which the final OVERLORD plans were revealed to the Allied High Command. 'I went with the Army Commander; the King spoke very well, his stammer hardly interfering at all. Churchill was in tremendous form, looking very much better than when I last heard him . . . Yesterday we had a tremendous address from Monty – he spoke extremely well, and gave a firm date for the end of the war, which curiously enough coincided with the date*which I have always given you.'[69] Selwyn was acutely conscious of being caught up in great events, though in later years he could only rarely be prevailed upon to talk of his experiences. On 28 May, with D-Day little more than a week away, Selwyn was the senior officer detailed to take the Secretary of State for War, P. J. Grigg, round the Headquarters at Fort Southwick behind Portsmouth. The time of waiting was almost over, but because of the bad weather over the Channel, on 4 June Eisenhower postponed the invasion. On the same day representatives of Second Army, Dempsey, Chilton and Selwyn among them, attended a service at Christ Church, Portsdown (as they were to do on all post-war Sundays nearest 6 June up to the time of Dempsey's death in 1969), a voluntary act of dedication before the great armada set off. 'We had a good church parade this morning. The Army Commander did *not* read the lesson. Very different from Monty who loved doing it.'[70] In the next twenty-four hours as the storms continued to rage Eisenhower took one of the great decisions of history; at a 4 a.m. meeting on 5 June, despite the reservations of Air-Chief-Marshal Tedder, Deputy Supreme Commander, and Air-Marshal Leigh-Mallory, commander Allied Expeditionary Air Force, the irrevocable order was given. OVERLORD was on. Selwyn spent the night of 5 June 1944 at Fort Southwick as the winds whipped up from the Channel. When the news came that Eisenhower had finally decided to go ahead Selwyn was convinced that he had made the wrong decision. It was one of the low-spots of his life and the eve of its greatest adventure. He penned letters home to his parents to be opened in the event of his death, franked *Second Army HQ* and dated 6 June 44. The letters were sent in a packet to his brother-in-law, Howard Shone, 'in case anything happens'. Selwyn added, 'I know you will keep to yourself the fact that they were sent to you.' After adding various codicils to his will, which with a lawyer's apprehension he *hoped* would be valid (the most interesting of which was, 'The Governors of Fettes gave me £30 a year for four years while I was at the University which made a lot of difference and which I appreciated

---

* The date was 31 October 1944.

very much. I should like that £120 returned for them to do likewise for someone else'), he addressed his parents, in a letter they never saw. In it Selwyn surveyed his life to this moment:

If and when you read this, I shall be dead or missing. You will already have had the shock of receiving the telegram and will be much upset. The purpose of this letter is to tell you how I feel about it myself, in the hope that it will alter your view and be a measure of comfort to you.

I do not want you to grieve for me: in fact my last request to you is that you should not do so. I feel that there is really nothing tragic about what has happened. I am not trying to be melodramatic when I say that it is a proud moment for me.

I have had an extremely happy life, thanks largely to both of you. It has been interesting and, I think, not unsuccessful – The Leas, Fettes, Magdalene, The Union, Macclesfield, the Council, the Northern Circuit and now the Army. I have had many friends and received much kindness, and throughout have felt myself protected by your love and care.

After all that, I can think of nothing more fitting than to die in the service of one's country and for the generations to come. When you think of the various kinds of death that can come to one, – accident, disease etc – possibly reaching one disillusioned with life and discontented with oneself, having lost faith in one's fellows, and possibly even in God, you must admit how much better and finer it is to die in some sort of higher service, when still in the prime of life and still believing in it all.

If you say how sad it is when you think of what I might have done or become, my answer is that I have finished on a high note. If I had survived, who can tell what dark places full of unhappiness and doubt might have had to be traversed.

If you say how sad it is for you to be separated from me, in fact that separation is likely to be much shorter than otherwise it might have been. I have no doubt at all that this life is a preparation for another life and in that belief I know that we shall meet again soon. I do believe in a just God and in the immortality of the human soul and so I ask you to be of good cheer and not to grieve about what has happened to me. It is only an incident in something far bigger.[71]

Selwyn was within two months of his fortieth birthday. This letter was the exequy to the first half of his life.

As Deputy Chief of Staff, Second Army, Selwyn boarded the destroyer *Impulsive* at first light with Miles Dempsey on 6 June. Under a

grey cloudy sky the destroyer turned into the wind-tossed Channel in
the wake of the invasion flotilla. Selwyn went up on to the bridge with
Dempsey. To their surprise there was no enemy action, yet many
craft were turning back owing to the rough weather. Selwyn again
wondered whether Eisenhower had taken the right decision as he
scanned the seas. 'It was the most remarkable sight – all the aeroplanes, flotillas of aeroplanes going backwards and forwards, or
flights of aeroplanes and flotillas of ships, big ships, little ships,
warships, a lot streaming back from taking the first flight and others
going along with the follow up and one thought of the amount of
money that had been spent and the amount of human effort that had
been put into it and if only that could go into peaceful purposes what a
different place the world might have been. However it was necessary
at that time in order to win the war.'[72] Selwyn went ashore with
Dempsey on D + 1 at the small port of Courseulles. Tac[tical]
Headquarters was established and by 1810 hours radio contact was
established with Main Headquarters at Portsmouth. Maurice Chilton
and Selwyn had written the orders to get Second Army established on
French soil and now they had seen the first phase of the plans
accomplished.[73] Chilton and Selwyn had under them 180 officers and
970 men and were now in charge of setting up, and then moving, the
various Tac, Main and Rear Headquarters and ensuring proper
channels of supply. The first Main HQ was established at Creully on
12 June 1944; just over a year later on 13 June 1945 the last main HQ
was established at Bunde in Germany, eighteen HQs later. Selwyn's
permanent base was normally Main HQ (with Dempsey), but he
visited daily both Tac and Rear HQ, journeys which were made
perilous not merely by war conditions, but by the fact that pockets of
German resistance often crossed the arterial roads that separated
HQs sometimes miles apart. At times of rapid advance Main HQ
could be 80 miles from Rear HQ, yet Selwyn was responsible for
maintaining contact between 'G' (the General Staff side) and 'Q' (the
Supply side). Chilton was incisive, yet with a gentle side like
Dempsey, and the partnership with Selwyn was a fruitful one. The
other friendships that Selwyn made at this time – with Geoffrey
Hardy-Roberts, 'Spud' Murphy, Mike Osborn ('Selwyn played a
great part in my life and I feel very privileged to have been able to
claim him as a friend'),[74] John Prideaux, Robert Priestley (a veteran
of Alam Halfa and El Alamein) and Dick Vernon – were to remain
with him. In the war-time conditions of the next year there were all
the ingredients for some first-class rows – the regulars versus the
non-regulars, the clash of differing personalities, those with 'sand in
their hair' versus those who had never heard a shot fired in anger, the

European experience versus the desert experience – yet the recipes for resentment never came to anything. The winning of the war and the subjugation of self were the joint priorities. One example of Selwyn's part in this came with the Phantom system. In the Western Desert there was an informal system known as Phantom, where the bright young officers used to go out and gather information and squadron commanders were allocated to each Corps for unofficial intelligence gathering. As the Regular Army is chain-of-command conscious, such a system could have led to friction. Yet Selwyn heard from the desert soldiers of Phantom and introduced it into Second Army, but managed to bring together the official and the unofficial, thus getting the best of both worlds. He liaised with the 'Ultra' officers and when Dempsey moved up to Forward Tac HQ (as in the aftermath of the battle for Caen to draw the German fire) was the essential conduit through which information passed to Rear HQ, where Geoffrey Hardy-Roberts was based. Alan Moorehead, the doyen of war correspondents, gained much of his information from Selwyn and also accepted his guidance on what could not at any particular stage be released. (The two of them were to enter Belsen together.) It was, in the words of one veteran, 'a 23½ hour day', and when operations like MARKET GARDEN were being planned they lived on Benzedrine to keep awake. Selwyn brought a lawyer's mind to the logistical problems of Second Army, as later he was to do over fiscal control as Chancellor of the Exchequer. Many non-regulars felt in the face of the 8th Army veterans that 'they knew it all'. Selwyn was one of the few who did, but he was also one of the few who did not show that he did. It was at this time that he gave voice to his belief that there is no limit to what man might achieve as long as people do not mind who gets the credit. The sensibilities had to be subordinated. With Dempsey in command this was an example that came from the top. (Dempsey would never have a photograph taken of himself if at all possible. The photograph of George VI knighting him in the field is thus rare on two accounts.) It truly was a 'band of brothers'.[75]

Two days after landing in France, Selwyn wrote to his parents:

9 June 44 Just a line from the field. I had a very pleasant trip over in a destroyer on the first day with the Commander, getting here in the afternoon – the sight of the beaches and all the way over was quite astounding. There was a complete procession of ships, large and small all the way from England to France, almost equal proportions, going and coming. There was a mass of ships off the beaches themselves and every conceivable type of launch, motor boat and other ferry craft. We stayed aboard the first night in one of

the ships and disembarked on Wednesday – it seems about a month ago although they tell me it is only the day before yesterday. We went ashore in a launch, thumbed a lift closer in on an amphibian full of stores, picked up a jeep on the beach and made our way to a rendezvous where one of our own vehicles was waiting. I walked for about ½ mile along the beaches where part of the assault had taken place, it was getting very well organised and it was just like one of those pictures of Dunkirk except that people were going the other way, and a lot of vehicles were being discharged.[76]

Dempsey held his first big conference to review the situation before the battle for Caen on 19 June. (The battle of Tilly-sur-Seule was raging in the background as they conferred.) Selwyn noted that casualties in Second Army since the landing totalled 17,656. Further 'review' conferences (as they were known) were held on 7 July and 28 July (Selwyn's 40th birthday) at 0930 hours. On 28 July Dempsey spoke of Second Army's main task being to draw on to itself the maximum German strength, particularly the armoured, and then weaken it.[77] For the whole of July time did not allow for letters to be sent, but by 17 August when the Main HQ was at Tracy Bocage, Selwyn took stock of the situation both in letters home and for Second Army Records. For the latter he suffered no censorship restrictions and noted:

Second Army has been opposed by very considerable numbers of enemy formations including the bulk of his armour.

The country on our sector has been very close and difficult – and has greatly favoured defence –

The constant attacks with limited objectives which Second Army has made have achieved a threefold purpose:

(a) they have kept the initiative firmly with us

(b) they have forced the enemy to plug the holes as they have shown signs of appearing, and put his reserves with the line just as he was labouring to build them up.

(c) They have inflicted heavy casualties upon him.

Selwyn justly summed up the progress as 'a major success'.

We have broken through in a part of the front where progress has been made for sometime: the enemy defences were well organised and there were minefields to be traversed which were deeper than any yet experienced on our front.[78]

The Army Commander's conference on 19 June concerned the EPSOM operation. The task of the EPSOM plan, as it related to

Second Army, centred on the capture of Caen, itself part of a general plan to establish 30 Corps, 8 Corps and 1 Corps in the Aunay Sur Odon–Conde Sur Noireau, Thury Harcourt–Bretteville and Vimont–Troarn and Dives sectors respectively. Selwyn noted in the minutes that he prepared for Dempsey, 'As the support of the attack by the RAF is of primary importance the operation may be postponed if weather precludes fighter bombers taking part. It will NOT be postponed if medium bombers cannot take part.'[79] The enveloping operation of EPSOM did not bring early success. EPSOM gave way to CHARNWOOD and CHARNWOOD to GOODWOOD, Caen falling into Allied hands on 19 July. The aim of GOODWOOD was to entice the weight of the German Panzer Divisions on to Second Army's front so as to relieve the pressure in the First American Army sector, and although by 19 July not all the village objectives had been seized, the wider objective had been accomplished. However, many reverses lay ahead, not least the failure to close the Falaise Gap in August. 'I remember after the battle of the Falaise Gap driving through, up the main road, and the retreating Germans had been caught in the crossfire of the artillery, Americans and British, and the corpses were being piled up. And I've never seen a sort of sight with human life extinct in that number of people at the same time.'[80] It was a far cry from the young German pilot in a Suffolk field four years earlier. In the fields it seemed as though there had been an early harvest. On closer inspection the advancing troops saw that the stooks were not of corn, but of corpses. Selwyn experienced nothing like it until he entered Belsen.

When time permitted he sent censored 'little despatches' (as he called them) to his parents and elder sister in the Wirral. 'Everyone is well satisfied with the course of events', he wrote on 17 August. 'The troops have been fighting extremely well on Second Army front and putting paid to a lot of Huns. The Germans are definitely reeling and if we can keep on blow after blow he will be knocked out in Western Europe by winter.'[81] He was still optimistic that the war would be over by October. From 28 August to 4 September the 11th Armoured Division covered 250 miles in 6 days from Vernon, north west of Paris, to the heart of Belgium. In his caravan Selwyn's 'empire' updated the flags on the various maps as the information came in from radio and telephone. 'I had an interesting tea party the other day,' he wrote at this time, 'the other three persons present being Monty, Dempsey and Harry Crerar who commands the Canadian Army. The four of us sorted out the War together and fixed it all up!! Monty was wearing his grey sweater, black beret and corduroy trousers, and was in good heart. He was very amusing about Churchill who had just been paying him a visit. Monty in spite of his teetotal principles had to give him a whisky and soda, and was obviously proud of the fact that he had some to give.'[82] At the end of September Maurice Chilton was away. 'I have been acting for him – a role which I would not have foretold for myself 5 years ago. I shall not be sorry when it is all over – there is never any relaxation of the strain – and the knowledge that any mistake you make may cost men's lives is burdensome. Also we are fighting some very complicated battles; however a price must be paid, I suppose, for making military history.'[83] This was a laconic description of one of the three great planning operations with which Selwyn was intimately concerned at an executive level.* Operation MARKET GARDEN, the battle for Arnhem, 17–25 September 1944, was Selwyn's first experience of working with Brigadier H. E. ('Pete') Pyman, who was to succeed Chilton as Chief of Staff Second Army on 23 January 1945. But they had been contemporaries at Fettes and had known each other for a long time. (Their closest co-operation was to come in March 1945 with Operation PLUNDER – '21 Army Group will now cross the River Rhine'.)[84] MARKET GARDEN, which came at the end of an advance of 500 miles in just seven weeks, was Selwyn's highest executive responsibility to date. The problems of liaising air support with the artillery were a logistical nightmare and Selwyn was the main Second Army link with the 82nd US Airborne Division and with General William Simpson, commander of 9th US Army. Anglo-American relationships at this critical stage of the war were far from harmonious and Selwyn considered it vital that they should be smoothed. In this he played his part. In 1971, when Pete Pyman was preparing his autobiography *Call to Arms*, Selwyn helped with the researches for both MARKET GARDEN and PLUNDER. 'My general recollection of the Arnhem operation', he wrote to Pyman on 5 May 1971, 'was the folly of having the air control of one part of the operation in England, i.e. the droppings and supply from the air, & the control of the tactical ground support air force in Belgium. I remember you (at least I think it was you) appealing to me for air attack upon ground targets and my having to answer that we had been ordered out of the air for the next x hours because of flying in from England.'[85] Over PLUNDER he reminded Pyman that Dempsey had an instinctive sense of precisely what different types of armour could do and of how (jointly) they had begun their planning study for the crossing of the Rhine after the Ardennes Battle (the Battle of the Bulge) on 30 January 1945.[86]

'I suppose the papers have been full of the Airborne operation', he

---

* COSSAC in 1943, MARKET GARDEN in 1944 and PLUNDER in 1945.

wrote home at the beginning of October 1944. 'The operation was one full of risks and was in the main brilliantly successful . . . I went up the other day and saw the big bridge which we captured over the main stream of the Rhine at Nijmegen – the Germans were shelling it hard at the time so I did not stay long!'[87] But the Low Countries were not an ideal place for a winter campaign (Selwyn felt that Marlborough had much better ideas about winter quarters) and hopes that the war would be over by the end of 1944 were now clearly unrealistic. By January 1945, though, Selwyn felt the goal was in sight. 'Unless the Hun wins some great victory over the Russians in the next few days, I think he cannot possibly continue the war for more than another 3 months', he wrote home. 'We are just finishing off a neat little Second Army operation, clearing up the Salient between the ROER and the MAAS.'[88] In February he received the CBE Military division and noted of the New Year's Honours, 'Lloyd George's Earldom came as a great surprise – I wonder how Megan will like being Lady Megan. It is a good job that Gwilym is the younger son and his career will not be affected. I am surprised that the old man accepted it, but I suppose he felt he could not face another election at his age.'[89] As Lloyd George bowed out of electioneering, so Selwyn prepared to enter the fray again after a sixteen-year interval.

On 14 October 1944 Selwyn had received, out of the blue, a letter from Albert Buckley of the Wirral Conservative Association. In this Buckley told him that Alan Graham was not standing again for the Wirral and that many people thought, 'you would be just the man for this constituency.' Roland Marshall had suggested to Selwyn before the war that he should stand as a Conservative. Now the opportunity to do so was being presented to him on his home ground, even though, as Buckley cautioned, 'there will probably be a good many names to be considered'.[90] Selwyn had voted for Clayton (the Conservative National candidate) in 1931 and for Graham in 1935, so in his formal letter of application to be put on the list for Parliamentary candidate wrote, 'I have however for the last ten years considered myself as a Conservative, and was about to take a more active part when war broke out.'[91] In any case the line between Conservative and certain brands of Liberalism (particularly John Simon's National Liberals) was a very thin one and by no means the divergence of a later generation. David Maxwell Fyfe acted as Selwyn's referee and on 4 December Selwyn heard that he had been put on the short list.

The selection meeting was fixed for 13 January 1945. Selwyn was given a week's leave to attend and decided (wisely in the event) to set off four days before the meeting. On 9 January there was a blizzard and no aircraft were flying and he hoped to go on a motor torpedo boat from Ostend to Dover. He left Neerpelt early, getting to Brussels at lunchtime, checking in at 21 Army Group Headquarters to get documentation for the boat. Ten miles from Brussels the gasket in the car blew. A military driver then took him to Ostend, but as it was dark and snowing he lost his way, at one stage the signs that loomed up were to Dunkirk, still at that time in German hands. (Selwyn said that at that stage he had visions of being put before a very different selection committee.) Eventually they reached Ostend. On 10 January there was a four-hour wait for despatches before the boat could sail. The seas were very rough and the boat was late arriving at Dover, by which time the last London trains had gone. Selwyn hitched a lift and put up at the Euston hotel in the midst of a V2 raid. On 12 January he reached the Wirral. 'That journey was a sort of allegorical story of a politician's life', recalled Selwyn. 'The political weather is usually bad. One is continually frustrated. Some- times one gets on the wrong road. It takes a long time to achieve anything. There are dangers and pitfalls all the time. The enemy is intelligent and resourceful.'[92] As Buckley had warned, there were many others in the field for one of the safest Conservative seats in the country. Selwyn's main opponent was Sir John Smyth, VC, who later recalled:

> To my great surprise I was short-listed for the Wirral in Cheshire . . . I was told afterwards by one of the Wirral selection committee that my final adoption had hinged on my answer to one question: Would I take a house there and live in the constituency? Had I merely answered 'Yes' the seat was mine.[93]

By such margins are political destinies decided. Dr Lloyd recorded the final outcome in his diary for 13 January: 'Selwyn appeared before Conservative Committee & made 5 minute speech to Executive & 30 minute speech to about 100 members . . . He was unanimously adopted as candidate for Wirral.'[94] In this manner did Selwyn secure the nomination for the seat which was to sustain him in Parliament for the next 31 years. His good fortune in entering Parliament in 1945 at the time of the greatest Labour landslide gave him a five-year start over the majority of his Conservative contemporaries.

With the nomination for the Wirral constituency safely secured Selwyn returned to Neerpelt to prepare for the last major operation of the campaign, the crossing of the Rhine. Selwyn organised the logistics of the sector from Wesel to Emmerich and then the crossing by 12 British Corps on 23–25 March. He studied the area of assault in very great detail, leaving records regarding the flood plain of the river, the flood banks, the approaches to the banks, the average level of water and other information necessary to the engineering tasks.[95] Three days before the crossing he wrote a 'round robin' letter to his sister Dorice for all the family. 'We have had a hectic few days preparatory to the Battle of the Rhine, but it has gone off most successfully. These airborne operations are most difficult and tricky to organise – this is my third – and I get a good many more grey hairs each time . . . Let us hope it really is the beginning of the end. The Siegfried Line was a big snag now a thing of the past as I look out of my caravan window at it – the Rhine was the next major problem, and that too is v. nearly a thing of the past. What the next obstacle is I don't quite know.'[96] He felt that if the water-level in the Rhine behaved itself, then it would mean, 'war over by end of May, if not before, & General Election about August or September, and back at the Bar for the Autumn Assizes . . . I really don't think it will be far out.'[97] The sense of the ending of a great adventure was at hand. On 8 April he wrote home: 'The trees and bushes are just beginning to show signs of life . . . Everything has gone extremely well since I last wrote and our soldiers have made some sensational advances – it has gone quicker than we ever dared to hope and the Germans' power to resist is becoming negligible . . . Some further news for you. They have made me a Brigadier!!!!'[98]

Two memories of his last weeks in Germany were to stay with Selwyn always. On 15 April Belsen Concentration Camp was liberated by 8 Corps. As the allied forces approached Lüneburg Heath, curious messages were picked up about a belt of typhoid, many of the German prisoners of war were chattering about it. At Main HQ it was decided that a party should be sent ahead into the countryside to find out what it was all about. They stumbled upon Belsen. Selwyn went in with Dempsey and Alan Moorehead. Moorehead told Selwyn it was a story he could never write but Selwyn told him it was one he must write. There were 10,000 unburied corpses and (as Selwyn remembered) no smell because the corpses were bone with nothing to putrify. In the next few days a further 17,000 inmates died. Selwyn never spoke much of this searing experience, though those who went into the camp with him recalled that the most appalling thing was the way in which the animal level had replaced the human. Nobody, man, woman or child, made the slightest attempt to seek privacy for the basic functions. Latrines were practically non-existent and those that there were consisted of a single pole over unscreened trenches. Excreta trickled down from the upper bunks on to those too weak to move from the lower ones. In a Foreign Affairs debate on 11 February 1960 Selwyn made a brief reference to his experience. 'I myself, if I might mention a personal thing, went into Belsen within a few hours of it being uncovered by the Second British Army. I saw the conditions there, the huts with the dead, the dying and those just living. That was a sight and experience I shall never forget to the end of my life.'[99]

Shortly afterwards he stopped by a Red Cross van in which there were 15 new born babies. 'In a way it was the new generation. There they were all squalling their heads off looking very healthy and happy. One cannot help thinking of all the good fellows who have been killed.'[100] The contrast with Belsen, where the gutters were filled with the rotting dead and men had come to the gutters to die using the kerbstones as headrests, where livers, kidneys and hearts were knifed out of the recently dead and the Commandant was quite unashamed, was profound. The last great task of Dempsey's Second Army was organising food, water, medical supplies and treatment for the mutilated thousands.

Selwyn's second memory was his most bizarre experience of the entire war. Dempsey had received the surrender of Hamburg on 3 May ('A *very* satisfactory morning'),[101] the day Main HQ was established at Lüneburg. VE day was on 8 May and though Second Army did not cease to exist as a Headquarters in the Field until 23 June 1945, as a parliamentary candidate Selwyn was granted early demobilisation to fight the General Election which was to be on 5 July. On 23 May (his last day in Germany) Selwyn was dining at Tac HQ with Dempsey. Dempsey and Pyman had an understanding that they did not bother each other after the last meal of the day, so it was clearly something out of the ordinary when Dempsey received a call during this meal to say that Pyman wanted to speak to him. Himmler had been captured and wished to speak to the Second Army Commander. 'Good. Good night', was Dempsey's response. Shortly afterwards news came through that Himmler had committed suicide. Dempsey reluctantly came to the telephone again. 'What is the matter with you tonight, Chief of Staff?' Pyman reported that Himmler had committed suicide. 'Good. Good night', said Dempsey, putting down the telephone. But Selwyn was despatched to investigate on behalf of the Army Commander.[102]

It transpired that Himmler had run into a British patrol near Bremervorde. Not realising the identity of their prisoner (Himmler had shaved off his moustache, wore no pince-nez and was wearing a plain white shirt), the patrol took him to spend the night under guard in a house nearby. On the afternoon of 23 May Himmler was taken to the Westertimke Internment Camp of 30 Corps, where he disclosed his identity and said he would speak only with the Army Commander. Colonel 'Spud' Murphy (GS1) and Lt-Colonel Michael Osborn (G

Ops), together with Lt-Colonel Stapleton were despatched from Second Army HQ by Pete Pyman to investigate. When they arrived at 9.45 p.m. Colonel Murphy ordered Himmler's two companions to be taken to an adjoining room and a complete set of clothes to be brought for Himmler. When Himmler was told that he would be forcibly stripped and changed he muttered, 'Dann ist Schluss', fearing that he would be put in British uniform for propaganda purposes. When Himmler had been dressed he was taken by car with Stapleton in the back, 'Spud' Murphy driving and Michael Osborn navigating, to a nearby house where the military police and doctors were. Himmler asked if it was true that Admiral Friedeburg had committed suicide. Otherwise he said little, except grunting 'Rechts' and 'Links' when it became clear that the driver was getting lost on the local unlit roads. On arrival at the Medical Unit, Himmler still insisted that he would speak only with the Army Commander, which is when the first call was put through to Dempsey. At 11 p.m. Captain C. J. Wells, Medical Officer i/c Rear HQ began his medical inspection of Himmler. After completing an examination of the trunk and limbs, he proceeded to examine Himmler's mouth and teeth. On pulling the cheeks aside he momentarily caught sight of a small object with a blue tip lying in the sulcus between his left cheek and lower jaw. At once Captain Wells tried to sweep this object out of Himmler's mouth but was unable to prevent Himmler biting on it. A strong smell of potassium cyanide was immediately recognised. Himmler collapsed at 11.04 p.m. and though his jaws were forced open and his mouth swabbed out with water and artificial respiration attempted, it was soon clear that the suicide had been successful. At this point the second phone call was put through to Dempsey. When the news reached the Mess that Selwyn had set off to identify the body, the gramophone was playing *My Blue Heaven*. The song was soon changed to *My Blue Himmler*.[103]

The first dead German Selwyn had seen had been the young pilot in the crashed aircraft in the Suffolk field. Then his emotions, not hardened by five years of total war, had been ones of sympathy. The last dead German he saw was Heinrich Himmler, not that at first he believed it was Himmler. Selwyn went to the villa where this dead body lay on the bare boards. 'Is that Himmler?', he asked. A Corporal put his big army boot under the head and lifted it up. *Rigor mortis* had not yet set in and all the double chins fell into place, so Selwyn realised it was in fact Himmler. Then the Corporal took his boot away and the head fell back with a dull thud on the floor, a sound that Selwyn said stayed with him for the rest of his life. There goes a man, he later recalled, who was responsible for the deaths of millions and millions of people. Two grave-diggers were at once despatched and under supervision of Colonel Murphy they 'buried him darkly at dead of night', on Lüneburg Heath in an unmarked grave, so that he would never be the focus of German 'martyr' feelings. The next day Selwyn set back for England.

Selwyn's period of military service, from its humble beginnings on a TA camp in the summer of 1939 to his position as Deputy Chief of Staff, Brigadier Second Army, was a microcosm of his entire career. With no tradition of professional military service in the family (though his father had been a volunteer in the First World War) he had risen from Adjutant to Brigadier in the space of a few short years. He had made friendships that were to last the rest of his life and came into close contact with two men of contrasting genius, Montgomery and Dempsey. ('I had a telephone conversation with Monty yesterday in which he called me "Selwyn"', he wrote home in 1944. 'I have not yet reached the stage of calling him Bernard – no doubt that will come in time.'[104] It did.) Of the three men who had the deepest influence on Selwyn's life – Miles Dempsey, Anthony Eden and Harold Macmillan – Dempsey was the only one whose influence was wholly beneficial. At one stage Selwyn thought of writing Dempsey's life, and although circumstances did not allow him to undertake such a major task, he was instrumental with John Prideaux and Geoffrey Hardy-Roberts in preserving Dempsey's papers and war diaries for the Public Record Office, negotiating with Simonds & Co., Dempsey's solicitors, on the transfer of the archive to the public domain. He was also instrumental in placing a memorial Second Army window in Christ Church, Portsdown in 1947, from where the great adventure had begun. For his part Dempsey did not forget what he owed his staff officers. 'Make a good maiden speech', he wrote to Selwyn on 11 July. 'I shall look forward to reading it. Thank you once again for all you did for Second Army – and for me. It was a very great deal, and I will never forget it. Good luck, Yours ever, Miles Dempsey.'

Selwyn believed that Dempsey was the most underrated of the British field commanders of the Second World War. When Dempsey died in June 1969 Selwyn wrote a tribute to his former chief which *The Times* published as a supplement to its obituary. After recalling that Dempsey died almost twenty-five years to the hour after the airborne troops under his command began to drop near the crossings over the River Orne in Normandy, Selwyn continued:

> He was a great commander and a remarkable man. That this was not more widely realized was solely due to his modesty. He disliked

publicity. He shrank from anything that seemed like self-advertisement. He would not tolerate any notion of flamboyant anniversaries of his Army's achievements.

He was an outstanding commander. I crossed the Channel with him on D-day in the destroyer *Impulsive*. He was calm, fresh, fit and confident. He was ashore on D plus one, and wherever he went he inspired confidence and was a most welcome visitor to any harassed commander of a subordinate formation. Time and again he realized the tactical opportunity and saw that it was exploited. But his experience in the First World War, particularly at Passchendaele, had made him determined to have no unnecessary casualties. His career and life and philosophy were epitomized by the word integrity, and, coupled with it, an almost excessive humility. Of nothing in my life am I prouder than that I served under him during great events and that he was my friend.[105]

5

Member for the Wirral

Negotiations on the timing of the 1945 General Election took place against the background of a shared assumption that Churchill and the Conservatives would be returned to power. With the aid of hindsight many later claimed to have read the Labour landslide in the psephological tea leaves, but only Aneurin Bevan, R. A. Butler, the Duke of Devonshire and Emanuel Shinwell (Selwyn's pair for 26 years) actually predicted the outcome in advance. King George VI gave a truer reflection of public opinion when he wrote in his diary that the result was, 'a great surprise to one and all.'[1] The great war-time coalition came to an end on 28 May – 'The light of history will shine on all your helmets', declared Churchill at a farewell dinner at which he distributed specially struck medallions – and the Conservatives prepared, somewhat complacently, for the election on 5 July. During the war the American Ambassador, John Winant had told R. A. Butler that the Conservatives would have a fight on their hands and that there were many historical precedents for radical governments being returned when peace came. Butler warned Churchill of the unprepared state of the Conservative Party machine and was roundly rebuked by Lord Beaverbrook for being a foolish young man. If he spoke like that there would be no place for him in the next government, to which Butler replied that if he did not speak like that then there would be no next Conservative government.[2]

The Wirral constituency organisation, in common with many other Conservative ones in largely rural areas, was in a run-down state after the war, particularly as many wives, on whom the Conservatives had traditionally depended for much voluntary unpaid party work, no longer had the domestic help which in more spacious pre-war days had enabled them to give freely of their time. Their husbands were still away at the war and the demands of the family came first. These problems were exacerbated in the Wirral because of the geographical nature of the constituency and the difficulties in obtaining petrol. Although eventually Selwyn was to see the constituency reduced from a sprawling peninsula which embraced the boundaries of Birkenhead, the working-class area of Ellesmere Port and the northern borders of Cheshire, in 1945 the Wirral had an electorate of 110,570 – the largest in Britain. That the party organisation was not entirely subsumed was largely owing to the efforts of Mrs Egerton Macdona, of Hilbre House, West Kirby. Mrs Macdona, who had known Selwyn from his boyhood, was to become a significant influence in his adult life. The Macdonas were a prominent Anglo-Irish family, who had been established in the Wirral for eighty years. In 1866 Mrs Macdona's father-in-law, John Cumming Macdona, had supervised the building of Hilbre House, a white-walled mansion with Gothic decorations, overlooking the Dee estuary. Here he specialized in breeding St Bernard dogs, the most famous being Tell, Champion Rough Coat of England, painted by Landseer in 1869 and commemorated in stained glass in Hilbre House. Like Dr Grimesby Roylott in Arthur Conan Doyle's *The Speckled Band*, John Cumming Macdona allowed all manner of beasts to wander in the extensive grounds. When Tell died in January 1871 he erected over the dog's grave a commemorative folly, Tell's Tower, which was used as a sea mark by passing vessels. Originally a native of Liverpool Mrs Macdona had lived for some years in Hilbre House with her husband Egerton, who was to die in 1948. Born in 1865, the year that Wilkes Booth assassinated Lincoln, Mrs Macdona lived until 1969, the year that men first landed on the moon, active to the end as Chairman and President of the Wirral Conservative Association or Chairman of the West Kirby Women's Committee (a post she had held since 1918) and a tireless worker for many Wirral charities. Selwyn, however, was under no illusions about the potential for friction with such a strong-willed personality if he became Wirral's MP, instrumental though Mrs Macdona was in pushing for his nomination as candidate. Towards the end of the war one of his mother's charities overlapped with one of Mrs Macdona's. 'I am sorry that you have had to compete with Mrs. Macdona', Selwyn wrote to his mother from Neerpelt on 4 March 1945. 'She is really quite a nice old thing* but whatever you do, don't get drawn into her web. Say that your health won't stand it, or that you are a Communist.'[3] Although Selwyn's initial response to Mrs Macdona's political presence in West Kirby was one of cautious wariness he soon came to realise that she represented a substantial corpus of opinion in the large rambling constituency and gradually

---

* Mrs Macdona was to live for another 24 years.

their political association became one of mutual trust. She became an assiduous despatcher of congratulations telegrams at appropriate moments in his career. On her death in 1969 she bequeathed Hilbre House to Selwyn – a bequest of which Selwyn had fifteen years' notice as she promised it to him in her 90th year – because she wanted the house to retain its links with Wirral Conservatism.

Selwyn was formally adopted as Conservative candidate for the Wirral on 16 June, beginning to campaign in earnest with his agent, Mr Bert Gill, in the week of 18 June. Since 1918 the constituency had only once failed to return a Conservative, in December 1923 when the Liberal had won with a 7.2 per cent majority of the votes cast. This did not mean that Selwyn entered the campaign in a complacent or over-confident mood. Trygve Lie, the Norwegian Foreign Minister, warned Anthony Eden on 23 May of the leftward tendency among the armed forces and this very much coincided with Selwyn's own impressions among both officers and other ranks in Second Army. Initially the contest was to be four-cornered but the *Birkenhead Advertiser and Wallasey Guardian* reported the withdrawal of the Commonweath candidate on 2 June. On the same day Selwyn gave his first interview. 'I think it will be a stiff battle, but I am quite convinced that the country will not change Mr Churchill at the present time.'[4] Privately he was not so confident of the overall result. He regretted the ending of the Coalition government which he felt should have continued until the defeat of Japan, the task of nursing the world back to health and normal conditions should have been started by all parties.

When nominations closed Selwyn was opposed by Miss A. L. Bulley (Labour), who was well known in local government circles in Bebington and Ellesmere Port, and by Brigadier Eric Dorman Smith (Liberal), who had served as Deputy Chief of Staff to Auchinleck in the Western Desert and then (more briefly) under Montgomery. The Press made much of the contest between the two Brigadiers, the Tory-turned-Liberal Dorman Smith against the Liberal-turned-Tory Selwyn Lloyd. Dorman Smith's slogan was, 'Vote for the man of two wars'.[5] Selwyn had not wanted to campaign as Brigadier Lloyd, but Conservative policy was against the dropping of military rank in election addresses. Selwyn's first meetings were in Ellesmere Port, Hoylake and Heswall. Until 1945 the Wirral had had nine divisions and though one division was to be given its own representation in the post-war redistribution, the constituency was extremely diverse and demanding with its huge electorate. When Selwyn campaigned for electoral reform in the late 1960s he always regarded the unevenness of electorates as being indefensible. (Attlee's constituency in 1945,

Limehouse, had fewer than 20,000 voters). Selwyn spoke on both foreign issues, advocating a rebuilding of the League of Nations in a new format, and domestic ones, saying there was a need to mobilise to build houses as in war there had been the drive to build aircraft and tanks.[6] He warned (an interesting pre-echo of his time on the Beveridge Broadcasting Committee) against 'A State Monopoly which would have no one to control it.'[7] He emphasised that political idealism (in 1945 over 10 million people voted Conservative) was not confined to the left. On 15 June Selwyn had written to the *West Kirby Advertiser* explaining why he had left the Liberal Party. In 1929 the Liberals had put the Labour Party in and would do so again. (At the end of his life the Labour government of James Callaghan was sustained for a while by a Lib-Lab pact). In 1931, together with the late S. R. Dodds, Liberal MP for the Wirral 1923–4, he had supported the (National) Conservative candidate Sir Christopher Clayton and, in 1935, had voted for Clayton's successor, Captain Alan Graham. That principle of National Unity had been adhered to by the Conservatives. But most important of all, 'The fiscal issue of Free Trade versus Protection which so long constituted a real division between Liberals and Conservatives no longer figures as a matter of acute political controversy.'[8] Over the previous fifteen years he had become a free enterprise Conservative with an anti-monopolist stance. He was always clear what he was against and this aversion to monopoly had its roots in the nineteenth-century free trade Liberalism of the Nonconformist voter.

The Conservative majority over Labour in 1935 had been 25,816 in a straight fight. The fact that Wirral was clearly a safe Conservative seat meant that, 'the fight was more agreeable than in some places. There was very little bitterness, and the Labour tide did not flow as strongly as elsewhere.'[9] What bitterness there was (and Selwyn, remembering the unpleasantness with Remer in Macclesfield in 1929, appealed at a women's meeting in Heswall for an absence of mud-slinging and personal abuse)[10] centred on the Conservative–Liberal clash rather than the Conservative–Labour one. On 30 June, the Saturday before polling, there were reports of systematic tearing down of Liberal posters and the Liberal loud speaker van was stoned. The one thing that worried Selwyn on the eve of his national political career was whether his parents would be able to bear the hurtful things that would inevitably be said of him, not so much at Westminster but by his old Liberal Nonconformist colleagues many of whom were family friends.[11] In fact Dr Lloyd accompanied his son throughout the campaign, keeping a record of the various meetings. On 25 June he noted:

Big squash at Council school, W.K. S spoke to full house &
many cd not get in. Questions about means test. S v tired
too many people around him on stage. S has seven meetings
today.

But the campaign had its lighter moments. In a meeting before
500 people at Neston Town Hall on 29 June an elderly lady got up at
question time and said, 'What's the good of listening to a lot of
futile questions. If the candidate was good enough for General
Montgomery he's good enough for Wirral.'[12] On 30 June as the
campaign drew to its close Selwyn shook hands with over 1,000
people in Ellesmere Port, returning with a streaming cold which kept
him in bed on the Sunday before polling.

Thursday 5 July 1945, one of the great watersheds of modern
British politics, was in the Wirral a day of glorious weather, which led
to an exceptionally high poll. Large numbers of servicemen's proxies
found that they were not able to vote as the registers were incomplete. 'It's a put up job', said one man. 'They knew which way we'd
vote.'[13] At Grove Street Booth, four servicemen arrived to vote, but
only one was registered. One young man and his wife cycled from
Rhyl to vote and one elderly lady arrived at her polling station and
asked loudly, 'Where can I vote for Brigadier Lloyd?'[14] Selwyn
returned home to the Rushes at 10.30 p.m. (the polls closed at 9 p.m.
in those days) well pleased with the day's work. Bert Gill had no
doubts as to his eventual success. Owing to the large number of
servicemen's postal votes, counting was delayed until 26 July. The
waiting was tedious, but Dr Lloyd noted in his diary on 21 July, 'Sel
not worrying.'[15] Selwyn took his parents and Rachel (Ronnie had not
yet been demobilised) to the Lake District for five days as he was the
only one with access to petrol. He was confident of victory at the
forthcoming count and to keep abreast of his next boss (Selwyn was
always a great one for keeping abreast of developments) he spent the
time reading Churchill's Life of Marlborough, a work which spanned
his own military and political preoccupations of 1945. On Wednesday
25 July Selwyn and his younger sister Rachel went to the Hulme Hall,
Port Sunlight to inspect and check the proxy votes of the servicemen.
The count started in earnest on the Thursday morning, with J.
Wilson, Town Clerk and Returning Officer presiding, and the result
was ready for 1 p.m., all candidates having been present during the
count. Although the Conservative vote had been reduced some 25
per cent since the straight fight with Labour in 1935, Selwyn polled
one of the highest Conservative votes in the country in 1945. The
figures were:

14 Selwyn Lloyd, K.C., 16 May 1947.

15 Selwyn and Alexander visiting Commonwealth troops in Korea during their round-the-world trip, June 1952: Major-General A.J.H. Cassels points out the front line.

16 The opening meeting of the 7th session of the United Nations General Assembly, 14 October 1952: on the front row, left, is Selwyn, next to Gladwyn Jebb; second right is Gromyko, brooding.

Lloyd, Brig. J. S. B. (Conservative)   42,544
Bulley, Miss A. L. (Labour)   25,919
Dorman Smith, Brig. E. (Liberal)   14,302
Majority   16,625

Within two days of his 41st birthday Selwyn had won one of the safest Conservative seats in the country, a seat that was to return him uninterruptedly to Parliament for the next 31 years.

In his victory speech, Selwyn said that he had won, first, because the majority of the electors in the Wirral desired that Mr Churchill should continue to be the national leader; second, because he had advocated the progressive programme of the present Conservative Party; and third, because the electorate showed a preference for a local man. For the rest of the day, and throughout 27 July, Selwyn toured all parts of the constituency, thanking his supporters, and taking with him his twelve-year-old nephew, John Shone. Although the years at Cambridge and in the Army had long drawn him away from the strict Methodism of his parents, the old shibboleths remained. 'What's that you're drinking, Uncle Sel?', asked John Shone as the celebrations continued in each division. 'Just coloured water, Johnny', replied Selwyn.[16]

The result in the Wirral was very much against the national trend, which gave the Labour Party a landslide victory with a majority of 147 seats. Dr Lloyd recorded on 27 July:

Labour majority. 390 to Cons 193 seats. The country & foreign states astounded at treatment of Churchill the outstanding man of the 2nd Great War. He resigns PMship. Americans shocked. Attlee to form government. Selwyn's success all the more remarkable as there has been such a left wing swing & there are many Labour & Socialists in the Wirral constituency.[17]

Although Selwyn was a local man with a distinguished war record and had proved an industrious candidate who responded intelligently to questions, Sir John Smyth or any other Conservative candidate would have swept to victory. The northern part of the constituency had suffered war damage, yet this was minor compared with the devastation in other parts of the country. The middle class in the Wirral had not had extensive contact with evacuees (that coming together of different social groups described by Evelyn Waugh in *Put Out More Flags*) as the proximity of the Liverpool docks had made the area unsuitable for widespread billeting. As a result it had been partially isolated from social trends elsewhere and the Socialist message, never strong in such dormitory areas as Heswall and

Neston, even found Ellesmere Port, which in Alan Graham's day had been very much the Achilles' heel of the constituency for the Conservatives, less fruitful ground with a considerable measure of working-class apathy. In the true Disraelian manner Selwyn set out to cultivate the working men's association in 'the Port' (as he always called it), a process which at the end of his career was to lead to his being granted the Freedom of the Borough. On 28 July Selwyn celebrated his birthday, the first at home for six years, and then set off for London on 31 July to be sworn in as Wirral's MP. After the worlds of the law and the army, he was now to enter on his third career, that of politician.

Selwyn took the oath on Friday 3 August. Brigadiers sworn in that day included Otho Prior-Palmer, Toby Low, Antony Head, Fitzroy Maclean, Ralph Rayner, Frank Medlicott and Selwyn Lloyd – Hon. and gallant members as the Speaker addressed them. Much has been made of the Tory Brigadiers who entered Parliament in 1945, but to speak of a military group of MPs in that Parliament is misleading, for so many members of that time on both sides of the house were inevitably ex-servicemen. What was clear was that the Conservative band (at whom Hugh Dalton was to jibe, 'We'll reduce all the Tory Brigadiers to the ranks, when the Red Revolution comes')[18] were a group of proved competence and reliability of whom the party managers had great expectations. The Parliament that assembled to hear the King's Speech on 15 August 1945 was a very different one from that elected ten years earlier. When the Conservatives, a depleted band of 209 members at the final count, took their seats on the opposition benches the first thing that many of the older members noticed was that the Speaker appeared to them to be sitting in the 'wrong' place. For Selwyn he was just glad to be there at all. 'I succeeded in fighting my way into the House of Lords without a ticket by crowding in on the tail of the Cabinet, and just got into the Chamber, and could see the King and Queen intermittently by standing on my toes, and could just hear the King, but could not really see who else was there', he wrote home. 'Just seen Megan – she sends her remembrances to you.'[19] The once proud Liberal Party that Megan's father had led (albeit from 1926–31 when its palmy days were over) had been reduced to a sad rump of 12 members. Even the Lloyd Georges were to desert the ship, Gwilym joining the Conservative government in 1951, while Megan, having been defeated at Anglesey in 1951 as a Liberal, threw in her lot with Labour in 1955, becoming MP for Carmarthen after a fiercely fought by-election in February 1957.

The 1945 Parliament was a wonderful period of opportunity for the articulate and ambitious Tory backbencher. The Whips wanted people to speak. In Government there is a far greater restriction on the freedom to 'sound off' on a great variety of subjects. Then the Whips only wanted the spokesman to appear, and it was very difficult for a younger man to get himself established as a speaker (which made Iain Macleod's achievement in a famous Health debate in 1952 the more remarkable). In Government the Whips have a tendency to tell people to sit down; in the 1945 parliament the Conservative Whips were urging everyone to have a go. Another opportunity that came Selwyn's way was that the leaders of the party were not 'tucked away in government' and thus inaccessible. They were around, in the corridors, in the smoking room, at lunch and were approachable. This was an immense advantage for new MPs like Selwyn. They could get to know their leaders and, more important, the leaders could get to know them, their strengths, their special interests, their potential. Eden with his Foreign Affairs Committees, Rab Butler with the Charters and Oliver Stanley as a genial overlord all had their contact with Selwyn in this first year (both Eden and Butler were to seek Selwyn's services when the Conservatives returned to power in October 1951). Also of value to Selwyn for when he was Leader of the House and then Speaker, his years in opposition gave him an insight into the life and needs of ordinary backbenchers. In the life of any politician the years out of office can be as formative an influence as the years in power. This was particularly so with Selwyn, both from 1945–51 and, later, from 1962–3.

He began to pick up the threads of his legal career – his first case since 1939 was on 14 August before Judge Fraser Harrison at Salford – and decided to take the House of Commons slowly.[20] At first, therefore, he was the epitome of the lawyer-politician. A lawyer takes other people's cases, arguing not for himself but for his client. A politician on the other hand argues his own case, he must speak for himself. Selwyn did not find this transition easy at first and when he adjusted it was a lawyer's success that he experienced rather than a politician's. He settled to a conscientious and varied pattern of constituency and party work and fostered cross-party friendships, many of them with North-West links. Bessie Braddock, Sidney Silverman (his pre-war legal colleague) and Harold Wilson shared many a Liverpool train journey and political gossip in these years. Selwyn found fulfilling political friendships across the floor of the House and supported Sidney Silverman in his campaign against capital punishment, a very independent line for a newly elected Conservative MP to take in the 1945 Parliament. Although Selwyn was granted a largely free rein by the Conservative Whips to consolidate his legal interests, particularly as they developed in London, the centre of gravity was shifting more in his career to the political. There were many opportunities in opposition for the ambitious and hard working MP and Selwyn took them all. He became, for instance, Chairman of the Parliamentary Committee of the Institute of Taxation and built a reputation as an MP knowledgeable in financial and taxation matters. 'It was a pretty exhausting routine', he remembered. 'In Court on Monday and Tuesday, to London Tuesday evening, Wednesday and Thursday in the House of Commons, back by the midnight train on Thursday, in court on Friday, opinions and pleadings most of Saturday and Sunday.'[21]

Social life too was more hectic than in the Wirral. In London he lived in a flat in Bill Aitken's house in Eccleston Square, an interim arrangement which lasted until Selwyn married in 1951, by which time Bill Aitken was MP for Bury St Edmunds and a parliamentary colleague as well as one of Selwyn's oldest Conservative contacts from pre-war days. Selwyn became an honorary member of the Aitken family, an important thread in his life to the end. VJ Day on 2 September was a splendid landmark which Selwyn celebrated in style with Toby Low, Douglas Dodds-Parker and Jack Robinson (later Lord Martonmere). He became more relaxed, less buttoned-up, and there was a greater ease in his legal style. One day in court at this time he listened to an indictment read out by Bill Graham, the clerk, which went on for some twenty minutes. Selwyn handed a note to his junior, Richard Bingham. 'Well done, Bill', it read. 'Have a pint of ink on me.'[22] But he was intense in preparation, largely because in many respects he did not like litigation.

Selwyn made his maiden speech on 12 February 1946 on the Trades Disputes and Trade Union Bill.[23] He broke convention in two ways when he rose to speak at 7.59 p.m. He spoke not on his own constituency and on a contentious issue. 'It may well be considered both stupid and arrogant for a new Member to attempt to make his maiden speech on so controversial a subject.' But, warming to his theme, he said that it was clear that the leaders of the TUC had demanded their pound of flesh, declaring that on the Labour side there had been, 'what has amounted to an attempted complete justification of the general strike'. Remembering his own part in 1926 he summed up by saying that, 'the people will be ready to smash another general strike just as they did that of 1926'. He ended his peroration by quoting Isabella's words from *Measure for Measure*:

> O, it is excellent
> To have a giant's strength! But it is tyrannous
> To use it like a giant.

'That', he said, 'is the essence of good democratic government.'

He sat down at 8.18 p.m. and was congratulated by Mrs Viant (MP for Willesden West). Although lacking the impact of such famous maiden speeches as F. E. Smith's (inevitably), or the wit of Iain Macleod's onslaught on Aneurin Bevan in the Health debate in 1952, Selwyn's speech nevertheless made quite a stir at Westminster. When speaking from a prepared text he was an effective Parliamentary (and later Conference) Speaker. But despite the training of the Union, the 25 Club in Liverpool and the Northern Circuit he was rarely at ease with the cut and thrust of Parliamentary intervention. Nevertheless after one speech by Selwyn in 1946 Sir John Simon told Toby Low that he had heard a future Foreign Secretary.[24] There was one amusing aftermath of Selwyn's maiden speech and his first contact with Harold Macmillan. As Selwyn recalled in his self-deprecatory manner, 'There were about 10 people in the Chamber. Harold Macmillan was on duty on the front Opposition bench. After my speech he wrote me a charming note – I have it still – in generous and flattering terms. Unfortunately for its effect on me, he addressed it to Brigadier A. R. W. Low, but of course in those days of the 1945 Parliament one Brigadier was as good as another.'[25]

By March 1947 Selwyn decided to apply for silk. His main referee was Mr Justice Lynskey (of Lynskey tribunal fame).[26] On 16 May 1947 Selwyn became one of the new KCs. (His father was particularly proud of him at that time and took to running up a flag at the Rushes when Selwyn was in residence.) Selwyn's delight at becoming a KC was somewhat tempered by the following letter he received from Hartley Shawcross, his old colleague on the Northern Circuit:

My dear Peter, My very best wishes on the silk gown. When I got mine I did not know whether it marked the end of the beginning or the beginning of the end. I know now all right – but I must not discourage you. Yours ever, Hartley Shawcross.[27]

In the next twelve months Selwyn found that he was more tied than he had been as a Junior. His practice was entirely on the Northern Circuit. 'I was lucky enough to get quite a lot of work straight away but whereas as a junior I could slip off to London and if one of my cases came unexpectedly into the assize list, rely on my leader to cover me, once I was myself a K.C. the clients naturally expected me to be there ready and waiting all the time.'[28] The time was rapidly approaching when he would have to decide whether he was to be a full-time lawyer who dabbled in politics or primarily a politician. He discussed this with his father. In the law there was now a certain guaranteed ceiling, but politics remained the great uncertainty (and no clear prospect of a Conservative government for some years). Nevertheless he chose politics and made it known that he would now go on the Northern Circuit only if specially employed, so that he could concentrate on the House of Commons. This meant a considerable financial sacrifice unless he could build up a London practice and this dip in his income is shown clearly in these years. Whereas in the financial year 1946–7 he earned £4,485 7s. 10d. (of which barrister's fees amounted to £3,231 7s. 7d.), in 1947–8 he earned £3,140 13s. 7d. (of which the legal proportion was £1,888 13s. 10d.), with further drops in the years up to 1951 when he became a Minister.*[29]

Political activity filled more and more of his time. He dined at the political clubs. On 20 October 1947 he found himself next to Stanley Baldwin at the Carlton Club. Baldwin talked freely to him of the Abdication crisis, telling Selwyn that the great delay came over the replies from New Zealand in response to the proposal that the King should enter into a morganatic marriage. 'They could not find out who Mrs. Simpson was. Then the Prime Minister of New Zealand wanted to know what Mrs. Simpson would be called if not H.R.H. When he was told, "Her Grace the Duchess of Windsor", he answered, "and quite enough too!" Baldwin much enjoyed telling this story.'[30] In the 1948 session Selwyn took a prominent part in Parliament (though he found time because of his interest in the theatre to take on a Directorship of the Liverpool Playhouse). He spoke on a number of important matters and wound up on behalf of the Opposition the debates in the House of Commons on the Liverpool Cotton Market (a perennial 'local' interest since the time in February 1947 that he had spoken against the proposal to abolish the Liverpool Cotton Exchange and to substitute for it bulk buying of raw cotton by the Government), the third reading of the Finance Bill and the second day's debate on the second reading of the Steel Bill. He also initiated a debate on Hyderabad, in which Attlee and Churchill spoke. He was joint Secretary of the Conservative Parliamentary Committee on Financial Policy and a member of the Standing Committee dealing with the Iron and Steel Bill. He was also a member of the Estimates Committee and of Lord Uthwatt's Committee on Leasehold Reform.[31]

* An MP's salary was £600 in 1945. From 1946 it was £1,000, together with free travel to the constituency.

Although Selwyn had no desire to become a 'one issue' MP he nevertheless did feel it necessary to specialise and he decided to concentrate on finance. In debates on the Finance Bill there is no time-limit, Standing Orders limiting debate do not apply, so for an Opposition member this gives wider opportunity. Accordingly Selwyn began to take part in the work of the Finance Committee of the Conservative Parliamentary Party and to help over the drafting of amendments and by speaking on more technical matters. As joint Secretary he came increasingly into contact with Oliver Stanley, the Chairman of the Finance Committee. Selwyn learned many of his earliest political lessons from Stanley who was very much, though informally, the number three in the party after Churchill and Eden. The most intelligent of men, possessor of the historic Derby name, very rich, yet with no strong personal ambition, he had that indecisiveness of will that sprang essentially from the intellectual's ability to see both sides of a case and wielded immense influence in the party. A respected President of the first post-war Tory conference, Stanley was a man of great jocularity who tilted at the Labour government well and was popular within the party because of it. Churchill thought the world of him. 'That's Stanley', he would say approvingly to the young hopefuls, taking them aside, 'a good man, watch him.'[32]

Selwyn was one of the new recruits who did watch. He described Stanley as one of the most charming and likeable people he had ever known. 'He used to tell me quite a lot about what went on', Selwyn recalled. 'He had one habit which I soon discovered. When he was Chairman of a meeting he used to sit with crossed legs. If he disliked the speaker or disagreed strongly with what he was saying, he would move his foot violently up and down. I used in my capacity as Secretary to sit beside him and watch with delight his foot beginning to move when certain colleagues who considered their views important were addressing the meeting – not the slightest indication by expression or by word of mouth from the Chairman but a vigorous movement of the foot under the table.'[33] On 1 June 1948 Selwyn appeared with Stanley on the Finance Bill and became (together with Anthony Nutting) something of a Stanley protégé. On 22 July he saw Robert Shone* of the Iron and Steel Federation at Steel House to concert plans for the autumn sessions on the Iron and Steel Bill and told him that one of his earliest lessons in politics was never to underestimate the Stanleys.[34]

Apart from Oliver Stanley, whose death in 1950 was a grievous

* In 1962 Selwyn appointed Robert Shone the first Director-General of the National Economic Development Council.

blow to the Party, another figure Selwyn worked with in these years of opposition was Rab Butler, and though never a member of the Tory Reform Committee, Selwyn was seen as being on the liberal wing of the party, especially on domestic matters. (Later, though he retained this reputation, he was considered as being a more right-wing figure on foreign affairs). For the Conservative Party the immediate post-war years were ones of great rebuilding in the three crucial areas of finance (overhauled by David Maxwell Fyfe in his 1948 Report into the Party), organisation (in the hands of the avuncular and popular Party Chairman, Lord Woolton) and philosophy. The central figure in policy making was Rab Butler, who had taken over the Chairmanship of the Conservative Research Department at Churchill's request in November 1945. How far this reformulation of Conservative thinking – the Charters, a succession of new Tamworth Manifestos – has been a question of some academic argument, but all admit Butler as the central figure.[35] He gathered round him sympathetic lieutenants – David Clarke as Director, Michael Fraser (later Lord Fraser of Kilmorack) Director from 1951–64 and Deputy Chairman of the Party from 1964–75, together with the famous trio of the 1950 intake, Iain Macleod, Reginald Maudling and Enoch Powell – and as the 1950 Election neared, the Research Department assumed a greater importance and was an effective block to any Labour claims that the Tories had no policies. Selwyn began to work with Butler on the manifesto for the 1950 Election and was later to assume an even more central role in the preparation of policy statements for the October 1951 Election. He had considerable empathy with Rab Butler's progressive attitudes, particularly over the issue of capital punishment.

On 7 July 1948 Selwyn noted with regret in his diary, 'Criminal Justice Bill amendment – Lords struck out of the Criminal Justice Bill the clause which would have abolished capital punishment for murder for the next five years.'[36] The issue of capital punishment was to be significant both for Selwyn's future Cabinet postings and for his relationship with his constituency, one of the few instances in which he 'led' rather than 'represented' opinion in the Wirral.* As a lawyer Selwyn had appeared in many capital cases and not always for the defence. On 1 November 1948, for instance, he was to appear for the prosecution in the case of Rex v. Gilbert Peter Rothwell who was charged with murdering a Mr George Walker at Leigh. But the memories of the case at Carlisle Assizes in 1939 made him a consistent

---

* Walter Bagehot wrote that one of the functions of the House of Commons was to teach (*The English Constitution*, 1867, Chapter IV).

opponent of capital punishment, a stance which in the Conservative Party of the 1940s was seen by some as one of foolhardy independence. The difficulties that Rab Butler faced at party conferences in the late 1950s on law and order issues while Home Secretary were similar to those faced by Selwyn in the Wirral for siding with Labour figures such as Sidney Silverman. Yet for Selwyn it was always an issue of principle, not party politics. In the autumn of 1948 Selwyn prepared a private memorandum, *The Suspension of the Death Penalty*, which he used as the basis for replies to constituents who had corresponded with him criticising his stance on capital punishment. (One of the things his Wirral constituents soon came to take for granted was that all letters were promptly answered, often by return of post.) Selwyn wrote in this memorandum:

> Since the vote on the death penalty, I have been asked by a number of my supporters for my reasons for voting as I did in favour of suspension. The case for the retention of the death penalty is put forward on four main grounds. (1) its deterrent effect (2) its severity is mitigated under the present system by reprieve in any case of doubt or extenuating circumstances (3) its abolition would mean the loosing upon society after a term of imprisonment of all convicted murderers not found to be insane (4) its abolition would discourage the police at a time of increased lawlessness.
>
> These are weighty arguments. I was led to reject them not by 'sentiment' or 'sympathy with woolly headed Socialists' (as has been suggested to me) but by my experience of the criminal law and murder trials over the past 20 years.

Selwyn then proceeded to deal with the four arguments in favour of capital punishment, avoiding the ambiguities of which Rab Butler sometimes stood accused. (At one of those dreary fringe evening meetings at a Conservative conference in the late 1950s a seminar was held for delegates on capital punishment and the views of Butler as Home Secretary were eagerly awaited. At the end of the evening, Douglas Glover, who was in the chair, thanked all those who had taken part, Mr X for having put the case against capital punishment so well, Mr Y for having put the case for it so well, and then without any conscious sense of irony concluded by thanking Rab Butler for having put the case for both sides so well.) Selwyn was an out and out abolitionist and he was unrepentant about it. On deterrence he believed that life imprisonment (and by life imprisonment he meant life imprisonment, not automatic release after ten or twelve years) was as great a deterrent as capital punishment. With regard to the reprieve system, Selwyn knew from experience at the Carlisle Assizes that mistakes were possible (and this was before Timothy Evans was granted a posthumous pardon for a murder subsequently proved to have been committed by John Christie at 10 Rillington Place). 'The finality of the death penalty makes subsequent re-examination or release impossible.' He also doubted whether the 'old lag' with a long sentence in prospect would be more likely to carry a gun to shoot his way out of a crime. But these were negative reasons and he preferred to concentrate on positives.

> I believe that at present juries are deterred by the death penalty from finding verdicts according to the evidence. I believe that criminals guilty of murder have been found guilty but insane or guilty of manslaughter or not guilty because of the reluctance of juries to be responsible for the hanging of a fellow citizen. With the death penalty in operation, a murderer has a better chance of acquittal.
>
> Then there is a class of murderers who are exhibitionists who love the drama of the contest in which their stake is the supreme one of life itself.* This feeling is pandered to by the wide publicity, morbid interest and mob hysteria aroused by the murder trial and the gruesome details of the hanging. Such persons (acknowledged by those who have studied the matter to exist) will be less inclined to murder if the consequence is life imprisonment.'

Selwyn believed that it was right and proper that such a matter should not be a party one for the Whips but a free vote according to conscience.

> 'Accordingly having weighed up the arguments to the best of my ability and drawn upon my own experience of murder trials and the criminal law, I came to the conclusion that if I were conscientiously to vote in favour of what I believed to be right and in the best interests of law and order, I must vote in favour of suspension, however distasteful it might be to differ from the majority of my friends and to vote with many whose views on most other matters I abhor. I feel that the electors in Wirral would have nothing but contempt for a Member who having come to a conclusion particularly in a matter left to a free vote, had not the courage to vote as he thought right.'[37]

Selwyn's views on capital punishment became well known. There was no ambivalence. This was effectively to put him out of the

---

* As was to be the case with the Glasgow trial of the murderer Manuel who dismissed his counsel to assume his own defence.

running for the post of Home Secretary (a Cabinet job for which he would have been well qualified). When Macmillan sacked Selwyn as Chancellor of the Exchequer in July 1962 there was no question of his being moved sideways to the Home Office. In October 1963 when Lord Home became Prime Minister he initially offered Selwyn the Home Secretaryship. One of Selwyn's reasons for preferring the post of Lord Privy Seal and Leader of the House of Commons was that he did not wish to have the responsibility for the prerogative of mercy. The corridors of the Home Office, as Herbert Morrison used to remark, were paved with dynamite enough.[38]

Selwyn's first official dealings with the Home Office came in the autumn of 1948 when the Home Secretary, Chuter Ede, invited him to allow his name to be submitted to King George VI as Recorder of Wigan, an appointment which was confirmed on 24 September. 'Ede told me yesterday that they have appointed me Recorder of Wigan to succeed Gorman who has got Liverpool', he wrote home next day. '(About £200 a year, I think, and not much work, but keep that under your hat.)'[39] Congratulations came in from many sides. (Mrs Macdona wrote, 'Doesn't it show how clever we were at our Selection Committee in 1945 in spotting a "winner"!')[40] One correspondent, obviously believing that a Recorder of Wigan should have a wife, wrote in Limerick form:

> All hail, new Recorder of Wigan,
> Since we know that the stipend's a big 'un.
>> Will you mope, a lone seer,
>> At the end of your pier,
> Or will you get married to Megan?[41]

Megan Lloyd George was about to reappear in Selwyn's life, though not in the manner the correspondent hoped, when both were appointed to membership of the Broadcasting Committee in 1949.*

Selwyn was sworn in with ancient ceremonial as Recorder of Wigan on 18 October 1948. *The Wigan Observer* reported that William Court Gulley MP, Recorder of Wigan from 1886 to 1895, was subsequently elected Speaker of the House of Commons.[42] Few could have predicted in October 1948 how history was to repeat itself. Selwyn delighted in the historical associations of the post. His principal legal responsibility as borough magistrate was the holding of court of Quarter sessions, and he forged links with Wigan (a Mayoral delegation was to attend his wedding in 1951, complete with chains and regalia) similar to those with Macclesfield in 1929. He adopted

* See Chapter 6.

Wigan Grammar School and added it to the list of those schools at which he gave out prizes (a growing task in these years). At the school's Speech Day on 23 November 1949 he explained to the boys that a Recorder was a judge, principally in criminal matters, 'therefore I must be careful how I say I hope to see many of you again'.[43]

Apart from the Wigan Recordership these years leading up to the 1950 Election saw a continued diminution of his legal activities and an increasing involvement in the round of overseas Parliamentary delegations. He was a delegate to the Council of Europe and also attended the conference of the inter-Parliamentary union in Stockholm. In August 1949 he went to Austria as a member of a Parliamentary delegation. 'We met the Austrian Chancellor and most of his Cabinet and the leading politicians and civil servants of the two provinces. In addition we spent a considerable amount of time with the British officers and civilians employed on the Allied Control Commission and with the British occupying forces', noted Selwyn on 23 August. He visited the internment camp at Wolfsberg, in which nearly four thousand leading Nazis were confined awaiting trial. Owing to the location of the camp and the difficulty in providing guards, only about one tenth of the internees went out to work. The remainder spent their days behind the barbed wire, former industrialists, technicians and administrators of the Nazi regime in Austria. 'They looked bitter, hard faced and quite unrepentant.'[44] In December 1949 as Secretary of the Conservative Finance Committee he went on an export mission to Africa, sailing from Liverpool to Las Palmas where he saw plans for a £2.25m dock scheme. He also visited the West African Mills Ltd, the only plant in the Gold Coast for processing cocoa. Selwyn saw big possibilities for marketing modern British machinery in Accra and Lagos during his tour.

As in his Cambridge days he was conscious of moving in circles very different from those in the Wirral. He began to be invited to country house weekends and holidays by Michael Astor and John Morrison. 'Just a line to tell you of the very high society in which I have been moving', he wrote home on 10 May 1949 after lunching at the Spanish Embassy with Princess Alice of Athlone.[45] He became a stalwart of the Parliamentary Golfing Society at Walton Heath, winning the Parliamentary Handicap in 1950, no mean feat when golfers of the calibre of P.B. ('Laddy') Lucas – another close friend from these years – were in the field.[46] The camaraderie of the Conservatives in those days was also strengthened by the feeling that the years of political austerity would shortly be at an end. They hunted in a pack and the game was afoot. On 6 April 1949 the fragile peace between the two sides, the Labour Party fractious and tired, the Conservatives office-hungry (as they had been before the First World War under Bonar Law) was broken by one of the most spectacular rows the Commons had seen for many years, an incident to which Selwyn referred in 1972 when he was criticised as Speaker for his handling of Bernadette Devlin's attack on Reginald Maudling.*

'We had a first class row last night', he wrote home to his parents. 'Strachey was making a very bad speech when Martin Lindsay called him an ex-Fascist – that infuriated the Socialists – Paton described it as a lying accusation – Hogg lost his temper with the Deputy Speaker because he would not make Paton withdraw. Strachey's last words were drowned in hubbub. After the question was put, there were nearly some free fights.' Bessie Braddock kept up a chant of 'Hooligans' throughout as MPs milled on to the floor of the chamber. 'Waldron Smithers who was well away tried to push into the middle of the scrum and shoved Lady Davidson out of the way so she turned on him – he told her to shut her b—— mouth, so that was a private Conservative row. Eddie Winterton said it was quite like old times when the Irish Nationalists were still here. Altogether a good time was had by all.'[47]

As the first post-war Parliament drew to its close Selwyn counted himself fortunate in the way that his back-bench years had worked out. The first piece of good fortune of which he was very conscious was that Patrick Buchan-Hepburn (a crucial figure in the episode of Selwyn's first ministerial appointment), who was then Conservative Deputy Chief Whip, sat for a Liverpool constituency, East Toxteth (he switched to Beckenham in 1950). By the time that he became Chief Whip in 1948 Buchan-Hepburn had already spotted Selwyn as a future minister. He was well-disposed towards Selwyn from the start because of the Liverpool association (one effect of the North-West association was that Selwyn frequently accompanied Buchan-Hepburn on train journeys to Liverpool and chance threw them together, rather as Selwyn's friendship with Michael Ramsey first grew out of a shared train journey.) Buchan-Hepburn put Selwyn on the Leasehold Reform Committee, dealing with the law of Landlord and Tenant, and generally encouraged his career. In a diminished Parliamentary party the younger, more active figures, particularly those few with safe parliamentary seats, were the recipients of whatever crumbs of patronage an Opposition Whip could give in those years, with the promise of better to follow.

The most significant piece of patronage that was steered in Selwyn's direction by Buchan-Hepburn concerned the Broadcasting

---

* See Chapter 15.

Committee that was being set up under Lord Radcliffe. On 14 May 1949 Selwyn wrote to his parents (from Rab Butler's house in Essex where he was staying for the weekend), 'I expect you have heard of the BBC job for me which was given out on Thursday. I am glad Megan is also on it. They have also asked me to wind up for our side on the second reading of the Finance Bill on Wednesday, which means rather a sweat, but I suppose I ought to feel honoured. I won my income tax case on Wednesday.'[48] Several strands of Selwyn's past and future career come together in this typically low-key letter – the memories of Criccieth days, now to be revived with Megan Lloyd George on the Broadcasting Committee, the quiet but steady background hum of the legal profession, his growing involvement with significant opinion formers in the Conservative Party, and the range and industry of his work. So far Selwyn had been, in national terms, 'the relatively unknown Conservative member for the Wirral'[49] (though Grace Wyndham Goldie regarded him as, 'an influential Conservative').[50] His membership of the Broadcasting Committee, initially under the chairmanship of Lord Radcliffe, but subsequently under Lord Beveridge, after which it took its name, was to transform that. With the publication of Selwyn's dissenting minority report in 1951 his name was to become more widely known and the repercussions of that minority report were to have profound effects upon the development of broadcasting policy and the cultural atmosphere of the 1950s and 1960s. It is to Selwyn Lloyd's membership of that Committee and the work he did on it in the two years leading up to 1951 that we must now turn.

6

'*The Father of Commercial Television*'

The Broadcasting Committee of 1949 – the fourth such inquiry into broadcasting policy – was announced by Herbert Morrison, the Lord President of the Council, in conjunction with Wilfred Paling, the Postmaster-General, on 12 May of that year. Its terms of reference were, 'to consider the constitution, control, finance and other general aspects of the sound and television broadcasting services of the United Kingdom (excluding those aspects of the overseas services for which the BBC are not responsible) and to advise on the conditions under which these services and wire broadcasting should be conducted after the 31st December 1951.'[1] Though the Committee was commissioned by a Labour government, its recommendations were to be considered by the Conservative administration elected in October 1951 and it proved impossible for that Labour government at the fag-end of its time to take up many of the issues raised by the members of the Committee.

The original Chairman, Sir Cyril Radcliffe, Deputy Chairman of the BBC's General Advisory Council, was unable to take up his duties owing to his appointment as a Lord of Appeal-in-Ordinary on 27 May. Though Selwyn Lloyd missed this opportunity of serving with Lord Radcliffe (as he became) in 1949 their paths were to cross in 1967 when they served as two of the three Privy Councillors in the 'D'-Notice Inquiry of that year. In looking for a replacement for Lord Radcliffe, the Labour Government turned, almost inevitably after the impact of the Report on Social Insurance and Allied Services of November 1942, to the 69-year-old Lord Beveridge, whose appointment was announced on 21 June. Beveridge was one of the principal prophets of the New Jerusalem the Labour Government was elected to create in 1945, but also a man, 'whose righteousness went hand in hand with authoritarian arrogance and skill at manipulating the press', which made him 'the Field Marshal Montgomery of social welfare'.[2] As Selwyn was a man who admired the Dempsey way of doing things, rather than the Montgomery, Beveridge's appointment was to sow the seeds of potential disagreement with the least malleable member of his Committee, and in the end outright dissociation by Selwyn from Beveridge's vision of future broadcasting policy. Had Radcliffe, one of the outstanding pre-war figures from the Chancery Bar, remained Chairman things could have turned out very differently as Selwyn had an inbuilt regard for his fellow legal practitioners, particularly those of such distinction as Radcliffe.

By the time Beveridge's appointment was made known the die was already cast (though not without some difficulty) as regards the membership of the Committee. Great efforts had been made by Herbert Morrison to include people of the highest calibre in what was clearly going to be – with the recommencement of the television service after the war years – a vitally important governmental inquiry. The original list of names mooted included Lord Halifax, former Foreign Secretary and war time Ambassador in Washington, the historian G. M. Trevelyan, and figures as diverse and distinguished as Rab Butler, Oliver Franks and Julian Huxley, the criteria being (as Herbert Morrison explained in Parliament on 24 May 1949) to have, 'a Committee not of specialists but rather of persons of broad approach and a capacity for balanced judgment.'[3] Indeed the government deliberately sought committee members who could give an independent, objective view, though by including Selwyn Lloyd in the list they did not perhaps get what they bargained for. The final list of committee members, in which Selwyn was the MP 'representative' of the Conservative Party, was largely composed of people whose national reputations were yet to be made.

Selwyn owed his place on the committee to Lord Woolton, Chairman of the Conservative Party, and to Patrick Buchan-Hepburn, the Conservative Chief Whip, who nominated him after consultation with senior figures in the party. The fact that Rab Butler had been a possibility – though unavailable because of his heavy involvement with the Conservative Research Department and the series of policy Charters – and that Selwyn was increasingly coming into Rab's orbit were two of the reasons he was nominated. The Conservative Party managers put forward Selwyn as their nominee at a meeting with Morrison in the Lord President's office on 14 April 1949. On the initial list of October 1948 there had been no Conservative member and Patrick Buchan-Hepburn had made sure this was altered. The Committee contained a diverse cross-section of what later became known as 'the great and the good'. To Selwyn's delight the MP 'representative' of the Liberal Party was Megan Lloyd George.

Joseph Reeves, Co-operative Labour MP, and his parliamentary colleague Ernest Davies represented the government side. Other figures included the Headmaster of Winchester, W. F. Oakeshott; A. L. Binns, the Director of Education for Lancashire (a north-west connection for Selwyn); the Earl of Elgin, and the figure with whom Selwyn was to work most closely during the two years of the inquiry, Mary Stocks, the Principal of Westfield College. But it was clear from the start that Beveridge intended the Committee to bear his name in no formal sense and that he saw himself as being more than *primus inter pares*.

In accordance with the three preceding Broadcasting Inquiries – the Sykes Committee of 1923, the Crawford Committee of 1925 and the Ullswater Committee of 1935 – the Beveridge Committee held its meetings in private (though not without vociferous protests from the right-wing Conservative MP, Sir Waldron Smithers, a perpetual thorn in the side of the Committee, who saw reds behind every crystal set). They met on 62 occasions over the next two years, on 42 of which they took oral evidence, in addition to interviews and inquiries carried out by sub-committees and individual members. The final report was signed on 15 December 1950 by all members except Selwyn Lloyd, who produced his own minority report. * The incoming Conservative administration first considered the Committee's recommendations (and Selwyn's alternative proposals) at a Cabinet meeting on 8 April 1952.[4] Senior figures in the BBC always considered the delay caused by Sir William Haley in arguing *ad infinitum* over the regional governors for Northern Ireland, Scotland and Wales was the crucial reason that prevented the outgoing Labour government from having the whole issue signed and sealed before the Election of October 1951.[5] Thus there was no legislatory corollary to the Committee and, therefore, by the chance of politics it was left to Selwyn's party to implement, reject or amend the Committee's findings.

The organisation into which the Beveridge Committee inquired was at a crucial transitional stage. Its terms of reference were to consider 'the sound and television broadcasting services', an accurate reflection of the priority given by the Government in 1949 to sound broadcasting, though the most important ramifications of the Report (and specifically Selwyn's Minority Report) were to be in the field of television, then the Cinderella. Few foresaw the rapid expansion of the television service after 1952. One of the persistent myths about television in the 1950s was that its popularity was established by the

* Reprinted in Appendix A.

Coronation broadcast of 2 June 1953, whereas it was the television coverage of King George VI's funeral on 15 February 1952, watched in countless shared 'front rooms' that sparked off the mass-purchasing of sets *in time for* 2 June 1953. The upper and middle classes were initially more resistant to television and when later in the 1950s they too succumbed, it was usually explained as being for the children to watch the nature programmes – excuse by Zoo Quest out of George Cansdale. Before the days of the Beveridge Committee neither Selwyn nor his parents had a television receiver (as sets were quaintly called in the 1940s) at the Rushes, though this was soon rectified and Selwyn was loaned a 12-inch set in London for the period of his Beveridge Committee membership. Selwyn, however, was always very keen on the 'wireless' (though his long-standing enthusiasm for the cinema, especially adventure films and Westerns, made his conversion to television very swift) and he had 'a 4 valve little Ferranti with quite a nice tone'.[6]

The British Broadcasting Corporation into which Beveridge and his colleagues inquired had originally been called the British Broadcasting Company, a confederation of some 200 manufacturers and shareholders, including the six main radio manufacturers. From the start the relationship between the Government of the day and the British Broadcasting Company was one of potential friction, as the newly-founded company fought to maintain its independence and editorial control. But the fact remained that the Government, in the person of the Postmaster-General (Neville Chamberlain from 31 October 1922, Sir William Joynson-Hicks from 7 March 1923) had power to control telegraphs and to withhold a licence to broadcast (the ultimate Damoclean sword) if the Company was considered to be lacking in impartiality. The first licence to broadcast was granted by Neville Chamberlain on 18 January 1923, though a proposal that the King's Speech should be broadcast from the State Opening of Parliament was not welcomed by Chamberlain as he felt that this would be used as a precedent for broadcasting Commons debates, 'a prospect which makes one shudder'.[7] John Reith ('that Wuthering Height', as Churchill called him) had been appointed General Manager of the Company on 14 December and his presence was to hover over the BBC (both Company and Corporation) for the rest of his life, even though he retired as Director-General in 1938. The evidence he submitted to the Beveridge Committee between April and June 1950, both in person and on paper, was a crucial factor in turning Selwyn against the idea of the BBC monopoly.

Reith was a member of the original Sykes Committee of 1923, which arose out of the financial difficulties of the British Broadcasting

Company, and one of the results of that inquiry was the extension of the licence to 31 December 1926 and the recommendation that 'the control of such a potential power over public opinion and the life of the nation ought to remain within the state'.[8] But the underlying tension was on policy, not finance, and the deadlock that existed between Reith and Joynson-Hicks on the interpretation of the Company's role. Sykes's own opinion was that Reith 'was always trying to create a monopoly',[9] and the report when published on 1 October 1923 bore all the hallmarks of Reith's influence, advocating as it did greater freedom over broadcasting conditions, the abolition of the system of royalties on wireless sets, and staunchly setting itself against advertising on the grounds that this would lead to a debasement of standards. (Reith was later to liken the start of independent television to the arrival of bubonic plague.) The second major inquiry, the Crawford Committee of 1926, was a far more substantial affair and led to the establishment of the British Broadcasting Corporation under Royal Charter. This time Reith was not a member of the Committee, as he had been for the Sykes inquiry, but in many respects his influence was stronger in that he appeared before the Committee on several occasions to give evidence. His firm belief that the BBC should be a monopoly based on the principle of public service was accepted by the Crawford Committee when it reported on 5 March 1926, rejecting as it did the 'United States system of uncontrolled transmission and reception', and confirming the idea that the BBC should be a monopoly, 'controlled by a single authority'.[10] The Government accepted the Crawford recommendations on 14 July 1926 and the newly titled British Broadcasting Corporation was given its Royal Charter on 20 December 1926. Reith became the first Director-General on New Year's Day 1927. Under the terms of the Charter the BBC's licence was to run for ten years and it was out of the ten-yearly cycle of renewal that the Ullswater and Beveridge inquiries arose.

The 1936 inquiry was headed by the 80-year-old Lord Ullswater, a former Speaker of the House of Commons (and Selwyn's guest at the Suffolk HQ on 5 May 1940),* and was a great vindication of the BBC as constituted under Reith. The ten-year licence was renewed with enthusiasm. For the first time television rated a separate mention. The Crawford Committee had established the licence fee system based on households possessing radio sets and the independence of the BBC as a corporation within the overall control of the state; the Ullswater Committee saw no need for any major changes in the

* See page 73.

future organisation of broadcasting. The pressure for change came about after the war and was, in part, a response to the wartime experience, which had led to a far greater concentration of the BBC's resources as an agent of State policy. Social conditions were changing also. The Americanisation of British tastes during the war led to an impatience in some quarters with the BBC's staid 'Aunty' image. The 1936 Charter was due to expire in 1946 and in the midst of other pressing questions the War Cabinet did find time to consider the future role of the BBC. A Cabinet meeting on 27 January 1944 considered the Charter of the BBC which Clement Attlee, the Lord President of the Council, said would be coming up for renewal in two years time. The Minister of Information, Brendan Bracken, also said at this Cabinet meeting that, owing to the great developments in the field of broadcasting, the Charter of the BBC would be out of date and he agreed that there was need for a proper inquiry, under an independent Chairman, to look into the whole question of broadcasting policy.[11] Initially a committee of ministers under the chairmanship of Lord Woolton, then Minister of Reconstruction, was to make recommendations but little came of this before the end of the war and the subsequent election of the Labour Government in July 1945. The new Lord President of the Council was Herbert Morrison and he said at a Cabinet meeting on 17 December 1945 that there 'need not be any enquiry by any independent Committee . . . and that the BBC should continue to be the sole authority licensed to broadcast in the United Kingdom for the further period of ten years from the 1st January 1947.'[12] But a head of steam was now building up in Parliament for a fully fledged Committee (on the lines of the Ullswater Committee in 1935) to be established and on 18 February 1946 Attlee answered a supplementary question (from Mr Butcher MP) as to whether or not an independent investigation should be held into broadcasting policy before the BBC charter was renewed and a motion (sponsored by Churchill and leading members of the Conservative, Liberal and National Liberal parties and independent MPs such as Sir Alan Herbert) was put down, 'That the question of the renewal, with or without amendment of the Charter of the BBC be referred to a Joint Select Committee of both houses.' Attlee, therefore, conceded in Cabinet on 21 June 1946 that, 'the demand for a Joint Select Committee must be treated seriously.'[13] The feeling was widespread, especially on the Conservative benches, that, in wartime conditions, the BBC had become an instrument of government. The pressure for some kind of inquiry was becoming irresistible.

A further staging-post on the way to Beveridge came five days after Attlee's statement to Cabinet with the publication of a letter in *The*

Times on 26 June from Reith's successor as Director-General, Sir
Frederick Ogilvie. This was headed: FUTURE OF THE BBC MONOPOLY
AND ITS DANGERS − SIR F. OGILVIE'S VIEWS. The letter articulated a
growing feeling that the BBC monopoly should no longer be sacro-
sanct and was the most forceful counterblast to the Reithian view that
monopoly was not only desirable on practical grounds but also on
ethical ones.[14] 'Freedom is choice', wrote Ogilvie. 'And monopoly of
broadcasting is inevitably the negation of freedom, no matter how
efficiently it is run, or how wise and kindly the boards or committees
in charge of it. It denies freedom of choice to listeners . . . The
dangers of monopoly have long been recognized in the film industry
and the Press and the theatre, and active steps have been taken to
prevent it. In tolerating monopoly of broadcasting we are alone
among the democratic countries of the world.' He concluded by
saying that the present issue was not the patient and admirable BBC,
'The issue is the broadcasting system itself, and well-wishers of the
Government must hope that it will be very willing to institute a full
and open inquiry into it.'[15] In July 1946 the Government issued a
White Paper on *Broadcasting Policy*.[16] A Committee would be set up
to inquire into long-term policy and out of this promise was born the
Radcliffe, later Beveridge, Committee. As a compromise the BBC
would have a five-year extension of its Charter (from 1 January 1947).
The confidence felt by the BBC at the time of the Ullswater inquiry
had now evaporated and as a contemporary headline in the *News
Chronicle* put it, there was a 'Question Mark over the BBC'. Lord
Simon of Wythenshawe, the Chairman of the BBC, Sir William
Haley, Director-General since 1944, and Lord Reith* prepared their
defences to the expected criticisms.

    Nearly three years elapsed before the White Paper on Broad-
casting Policy and the first meeting of the Beveridge Committee. As
the BBC's charter expired on 31 December 1951 (and the first
post-war Labour Government's by July 1950) time was of the essence
if future broadcasting decisions were to be made before any General
Election. Attlee was returned to office by a narrow margin in the
General Election of February 1950 and although Beveridge reported
in December of that year Attlee was removed from office in October
1951. Few members of the Beveridge Committee, when it first met at
2.45 p.m. in the Council Chamber at Church House, Westminster, on
Friday 24 June 1949 (least of all Selwyn Lloyd) would have forecast
that their one dissenting member would be a member of the new
administration which had to implement it.

---

* He had been raised to the peerage in 1940.

Beveridge proved an exacting and conscientious Chairman. The timetable of investigation was meticulously planned. The original plan was that meetings should take place on successive Thursdays and Fridays once a month, though this timetable was interrupted by the General Election of February 1950. The Committee invited letters from listeners (the BBC's audience was still primarily understood to be of listeners rather than viewers) and was inundated with distinctly crankish correspondence, one parent criticising Bing Crosby records on the grounds that they were a bad influence on her 19-year-old Army son. Written and oral evidence to the Committee also showed a wide divergence of views. From the outset Beveridge realised that the question of the BBC's future monopoly would be a central theme. 'In regard to all proposals to break up the present Public Service monopoly, we shall have to consider', he submitted at an early meeting, 'not only the physical difficulties of competition, but what advantages can be claimed for it.'[17] Selwyn's conversion, alone among the members of the Committee, to the ending of monopoly was a gradual process. 'I started off very well disposed towards the continuation of the Monopoly', he later recalled to Phillip White-head. 'I had no preconceived notions at all.'[18] The doubts soon began to creep in as he considered the evidence.

From October 1949 until April 1950 the Committee listened to the oral evidence of a wide variety of witnesses. From May to July 1950 they discussed this oral evidence and drafted the main body of the Report that summer. In the autumn of 1950 the pace of work increased as meetings were held, first at Church House, Westminster, and then at 1 Chester Street, on two successive days at fortnightly intervals for the completion of the Report. One early memorandum received by the Committee was from the Listeners' Association which urged the Broadcasting Committee to take the necessary steps to break the existing monopoly enjoyed by the BBC.[19] 'Commercial Television would be welcomed by the Listener. It would bring him something new and bright, something to relieve him from the stale-ness of the sound programmes, something which the BBC, with its limited resources, can never hope to establish throughout the country.' This was one of the few submissions at this time to realise that the true potential of television. Other witnesses also questioned the monopoly. Not surprisingly the Radio and Television Retailers Association submitted a memorandum advocating the ending of monopoly.[20] Sir Waldron Smithers had been pressing divisional Conservative Organisations for three years to strengthen their arm against monopolies and he was soon bombarding the Committee with his views.[21] Geoffrey Crowther thought it was very strange, 'that this question (of monopoly) has never had a proper public airing.'[22] But the arguments in favour of the status quo were advanced with equal firmness. The Labour Party were convinced, 'that competition between a public corporation and commercial radio stations is not the kind of competition that would best serve broadcasting in Great Britain.'[23] As with so many submissions the main concentration was on the future of radio. Preliminary oral evidence on behalf of the BBC was given to the Committee by Lord Simon of Wythenshawe and Sir William Haley on Thursday 13 October 1949, so even before the main BBC's submissions in defence of the monopoly between April and June 1950, Beveridge said in Committee (on 3 January 1950) that he felt that there was little prospect in the near future of a change in the system.[24]

The BBC's main case against competition was contained in their submission, Monopoly and Competition in Broadcasting, in April 1950.[25] Their main arguments against a system of competitive broadcasting were that it would lead to a lessening of responsibility, a lowering of standards, an elimination of the rights of minorities, a failure to serve educational and cultural purposes, a likelihood of making listeners more passive citizens and a wasteful expenditure of technical resources, money and manpower. These arguments were powerfully marshalled but they paled into insignificance compared with the moment on 19 April 1950 when Lord Reith (veteran of all inquiries since the time of Sykes) gave evidence before the Committee. If Churchill's life in May 1940 had been but a preparation for his moment of destiny, so could Lord Reith's previous career be seen as a preparation for this moment. Reith defended the monopoly in all its ramifications. For instance he felt that the BBC's being a monopoly employer was not important as staff had the right of appeal to the Director-General. In cross-examination Selwyn asked Reith about the Public Relations Department. Selwyn's overriding impression of this day was of the undesirable autonomy of the BBC and of the power vested in the office of Director-General. Reith spoke again to the Committee in June and on 21 June 1950 submitted 'with respect' his opinion on monopoly. This submission was the seminal moment for Selwyn.

Reith wrote: 'It was the brute force of monopoly that enabled the BBC to become what it did; and to do what it did; that made possible a policy in which moral responsibility – moral in the broadest way; intellectual and ethical – ranked high. If there is to be competition it will be of cheapness not of goodness. There is no reality in the moral disadvantages and dangers of monopoly as applied to Broadcasting, it is in fact a potent incentive.'[26] Selwyn made several critical points to

the Committee arising out of Reith's evidence, but it was the revealing phrase, 'the brute force of monopoly', that worried him most.
Selwyn told the Committee that in his view the BBC's efficiency and
sense of public duty were impressive but that its size and power were
rather terrifying. He did not think it would be fair to describe the
BBC as being smug, but he felt that the breaking up of the centralised
organisation was so important that it would be worthwhile accepting a
certain loss of overall efficiency to achieve it. The present licence
system he felt should be maintained permanently but it would be
desirable to consider whether some sponsoring should be permitted
in television. He felt that the BBC should publish more informative
reports and that the possibility of sponsorship for sound broadcasting should be further considered as it might prove an incentive to the
BBC. As a final point he felt that the Governors should be paid more
and give more of their time to the BBC.[27] 'I got more and more
worried about there being so much power in the hands of one man or
a group of people, and when Lord Reith talked about the brute force
of monopoly I thought it was wrong.'[28] This was not just in single
aspects of programmes, but over the musical programmes, the
theatre programmes, all the way through he felt that it was just one
authority deciding what should be done, and who should do it. There
was an unhealthy lack of competition. Competition between the
Light programme or whatever another programme might be called
was not in his mind *real* competition and he became increasingly
sceptical about the so-called advantages of corporatism in the BBC's
structure. His objections to monopoly were on the grounds of (a) its
size and unwieldiness (b) the hindrance of development (c) the fact
that there was only one employer (d) the excessive power vested in
one authority and (e) the restriction of cultural choice.[29] The 'brute
force of monopoly' was brutish in the wrong way.

Discussing the reasons for his Minority Report with Reith's biographer Andrew Boyle in 1971, Selwyn said that he went against
monopoly because of two impressions. 'What mainly put me off was
the appalling evidence of Reith – and the rolling eyes of William
Haley.'[30] He was also increasingly appalled not only by Reith's
evidence, but by Beveridge's manner of taking evidence. When, for
instance, the Controller of the Third Programme, Harman
Grisewood, gave evidence, Beveridge cross-examined him at length
as to why Beveridge, a Wordsworthian, had not been asked for a
contribution to the Wordsworth centenary celebrations. 'It was',
recalled Grisewood, 'the most prolonged exhibition of pique and
vanity which I have ever witnessed.'[31] Grisewood's impression was
that there was now a serious threat to the BBC monopoly.[32]

Two of Selwyn's dicta, both from Fettes days, were, 'Do your prep' and 'This is a serious matter.' As the future of the BBC was clearly a serious matter, he now did his prep and this showed in the coherence with which he marshalled his arguments in the Minority Report. As Selwyn was a loner on the Committee on this issue he felt it incumbent upon himself to find out the facts at first-hand. He worked assiduously at the arduous and time-consuming committee work, of which he had already had experience in the Hoylake UDC, at Ashley Gardens and latterly at Westminster, but wanted to visit the BBC and some foreign broadcasting stations. At his own request he paid a day long visit to the BBC on 6 June 1950.

The Committee was told on Friday 2 June 1950 that Selwyn Lloyd would be devoting the whole of Tuesday 6 June after 2.30 p.m. to a visit to the BBC, which could go on *ad lib* for the rest of the day and evening. Selwyn made it clear that what he was looking for was a 'hard travelling tour', with the object of sensing the atmosphere and that he would require a 'bear leader'. This guide was M. C. Farquharson, the Head of the Secretariat, who in his report to the Director-General on 8 June noted that he had given Selwyn Lloyd 'a non-stop tour of inspection on Tuesday from 2.15 p.m.–11.25 p.m., in the course of which we visited Broadcasting House, Alexandra Palace, Bush House and Egton House.' He met the head of Home programmes, the chief of European services and head of News service. 'My own impression', reported Farquharson to Sir William Haley, 'was that Mr Lloyd learnt a great deal about the BBC from these three senior people especially.'[33] What Selwyn learnt was put to good subsequent use and he spent the afternoon and evening ferreting his way into many corners of BBC life in a manner which made the senior staff wary about his later intentions. Selwyn's reputation as an anti-monopolist had preceded him and the staff did the best they could to please him, calculating that this was the most effective way of disarming his criticisms. Farquharson reported to Haley:

He started the day with 2 obsessions,
  (1) Why really did we object to the idea of sponsored programmes 'suitably controlled'?
  (2) The BBC is a monster, i.e. too powerful.
I had a lot of talk with him on these two points.

Haley replied to Maurice Farquharson with a note (initialled 9/6) 'Many thanks. I hope you demonsterized us!'[34]

The hope was in vain. Selwyn's visit confirmed his worst fears. He thought the BBC was too large and essentially too complacent.

Competition would do everybody a lot of good. On 15 June Selwyn attended with other members of the Committee a meeting at the BBC at 10 a.m., 'when each member of the Committee had to explain views on Beveridge's fundamental points; quite a strain after no sleep at all.'[35] (Selwyn had been involved in the all night debate on the Finance Bill.) He again stressed that he felt that the size and power of the BBC were terrifying. Considerable apprehension was now felt in the BBC at the prospect of Selwyn's final report. On 20 July, for instance, Selwyn noted in his diary:

> BBC Committee in morning – discussed U.S. tour. Lunch with George Barnes: BBC's antipathy to the Beveridge Committee – my remark to Simon about this monster has gone round the whole staff.[36]

Selwyn had met George Barnes, Director of Talks, with other senior BBC staff on his visit of 6 June, but his lunch with Barnes on 20 July was one of his most valuable meetings. He found out what the BBC thought of him and through that their fears and weaknesses.

George Barnes was to be of great help to Selwyn in other ways too, for Selwyn's second piece of independent fact-finding was even more ambitious. It was agreed at the 44th meeting of the Committee on 12 July 1950 that Selwyn Lloyd and Mrs Stocks should visit Canada and the United States in the early part of September. (This was a second overseas visit connected with the broadcasting inquiry, for when Selwyn had been to Lagos in 1949 Beveridge had asked him, in a letter of 25 November, to keep a weather eye open for any broadcasting details that might be of interest to the Committee, even though he was primarily on a parliamentary trade delegation. 'It occurs to me to ask you while you are in West Africa to take note of anything in connexion with broadcasting there which is likely to assist our Committee.')[37] As it was known that Selwyn was particularly interested in seeing the possibilities of local broadcasting on his American tour, George Barnes suggested to him in a letter of 25 July, 'Why not go to Syracuse or Rochester on the American side of the Lake, both of which are towns with small universities or colleges and where there is certain to be some interesting local broadcasting, much more easily accessible than in a big city like Detroit.'[38] Barnes's real influence on the future of the BBC monopoly, though, was an indirect one: in October 1950 he was appointed to the new post of Director of Television by Sir William Haley, to the intense disappointment of Norman Collins who promptly resigned from the BBC on 13 October to become the predominant driving force for independence television.

In his evidence to the Beveridge Committee Collins had said that television was a, 'profoundly different medium from sound broadcasting', which he believed it would ultimately replace.[39] He envisaged himself in the vanguard of that change. If Norman Collins had been appointed Director of BBC Television in October 1950 he would have been the internal pioneer and the campaign for independent television would have lost one of its most forceful and determined advocates. The passing over of Norman Collins was thus a most significant staging-post in the ultimate adoption of the recommendations of Selwyn's Minority Report.

As Selwyn prepared to go to the United States he received a letter from Oliver Stanley, thanking him for all his efforts on the Finance Bill in what was proving to be a most exhausting summer. A month after the Lloyd/Stocks transatlantic visit, two more Beveridge Committee members, Lord Elgin and Alderman Reeves, also went to the USA, examining the evidence of the first sortie before embarking on their own fact-finding mission. These visits caused great interest in the Press on both sides of the Atlantic. They had arisen out of a suggestion made by Lord Simon, who had visited broadcasting stations in America in the autumn of 1948, and who thought it would be of benefit to the Committee to compare the British and American patterns. In the evidence he had given to the Committee on 13 October 1949, together with Sir William Haley, Lord Simon had pointed out that the Australian Broadcasting Commission, which had to compete with private broadcasting organisations, was slowly being strangled. He remained of the firm belief that the case for a public service monopoly of broadcasting rested on the fact that a public corporation enjoying such a monopoly had a responsibility for maintaining certain standards. It was subject to continual criticism from the public, Parliament, the Press and informed opinion, and so must be impartial and maintain the highest standards. Competition, believed both Simon and Haley, would be simply for the largest number of listeners, and the more passive the better.[40] Simon hoped that the vulgarity of the commercial stations in America, and their subservience to advertisers, would alert Selwyn to the dangers of breaking the monopoly.

Continuing the policy of killing with kindness, the BBC assisted in the preparation of a full itinerary for Selwyn and Mrs Stocks, suggesting contacts in America that might be useful. Sir Ian Jacob, then Director of Overseas Services, was particularly helpful, emphasising to Mr N. Luke, the BBC's representative in New York, that Selwyn and Mrs Stocks wished to travel incognito. 'They have said that they do not want anyone to be informed of their projected visit, or of their arrival, as they particularly do not want to be caught up with invitations & interviews with radio magnates. They want to arrive as private individuals & spend time listening in their hotel.'[41] Simon also hoped, Dogberry like, that the comparisons would be 'odorous' and that the BBC would emerge as the exemplar. In that hope he was to be disappointed. Selwyn's American visit, like the visit to the BBC itself on 6 June, confirmed him in the belief that the monopoly must be ended.

Only the British Committee system could have thrown up such unlikely pairings as the Earl of Elgin and the Co-operative Labour MP Alderman Joseph Reeves on the one hand, and Selwyn Lloyd and Mary Stocks on the other. The incompatibility of Selwyn and Mrs Stocks, the distinguished Principal of Westfield College, though masked by perfect courtesy on both sides, stemmed from many sources. Not least was the difference in political outlook. 'Our political views were of course wide apart', recalled Mrs Stocks. 'I had a built-in addiction to a public service as such. Selwyn Lloyd's addiction was to private enterprise. And my impression is that our approach to the whole problem of broadcasting was rather different. I was primarily interested in programmes, the end product of broadcasting. He was primarily interested in organisation. Therefore, though he tended to take a dim view of the innumerable sponsored programmes which we dutifully sat through, he nevertheless returned to England with a favourable view of some form, though not necessarily the precise form encountered in the United States, of competitive commercial broadcasting.'[42] Another incompatibility was in social outlook and standards of dress. Selwyn was a rather formal bachelor of 46, whose wardrobe reflected the professional habits of his father's generation. Mary Stocks affected the more casual approach of the liberal intelligentsia and reminded Selwyn of his former housemaster, K. P. Wilson, whom he had once described as a '15th rate ploughboy'.* 'Mrs Stocks is rather like a female K.P.', he wrote home to his parents from the Hotel New Weston in New York on 30 August 1950. 'She does not care a hoot about dress, talks at the top of her voice and is a typical headmistress.'[43] There was also the unspoken embarrassment Selwyn felt, particularly in the more constrained atmosphere of the 1950s, of accompanying a married lady. There was a difficult scene when they embarked on the *Empress of Canada* on 15 August. 'They managed to find me a cabin to myself on D deck, a two berth cabin which the ticket holders failed to claim, and also one for Mrs Stocks right at the last minute for which I was very

* See p. 17.

glad otherwise I should have felt uncomfortable', he wrote home on 17 August.[44]

It was with some relief that he was able to plead pressure of parliamentary business in mid-September and fly home separately, leaving Mrs Stocks to travel on the *Queen Mary*. Though their views on social, political and broadcasting matters did tend to diverge, leading to what was later called creative tension, there was a surprising degree of unanimity and shared assumptions. Both felt that the government was potentially afraid of Beveridge and were aware also that Beveridge had a built-in grievance against the BBC, stemming from the failure to consult him over the Wordsworth centenary. (Many Tories were delighted to 'ignore' Beveridge. Selwyn wondered whether they would have ignored Radcliffe.) Both saw that Beveridge had a liberal mistrust of monopoly, but Beveridge's difficulty, for a man who believed in a paternalistic 'sweetness and light' form of public broadcasting, was how to reconcile that with the inevitable commercial sponsorship. Mary Stocks believed it was not possible. Selwyn, with greater optimism, was prepared to try (although by the time of the Pilkington Report in 1962 he was willing to admit that the two aims were incompatible).

In Canada they had a meeting with the Montreal Chamber of Commerce on 22 August and a tour of the Canadian Broadcasting Corporation. Their visit to Ottawa later in the week coincided with a rail strike. Selwyn wrote home:

> The Deputy High Commissioner gave an informal dinner for us, about a dozen there, the Chairman and the General Manager of the Canadian Broadcasting Corporation, a man from their Foreign Office, a prominent member of the Order of the Daughters of the Empire who sat next to me and never drew breath. On Friday we visited a number of people interested in radio, went over a small private station, saw a Trade Union leader, spent the afternoon with the officials of the C.B.C. and went to a dinner by the Chairman.

Selwyn's one moment of relaxation – from broadcasting and Mrs Stocks – was a round of golf at the Royal Ottawa Golf Club. 'We played with the large sized ball', he told his father. 'It definitely does not go as far.'[45]

They travelled on to America via Niagara Falls. Selwyn then took every opportunity to visit local radio stations, including one at Ashtabula, Ohio, a rural community with a radio service independent of the big networks. They also visited a small local broadcasting station at Silver Springs, where a radio programme composed of local news items, gramophone records and advertisements was being broadcast. For Mrs Stocks, with her interest in the end-product, this was a programme not worth putting on the air. Selwyn, with his interest in the organisation and free enterprise, was much encouraged that a young man with a war gratuity and individual drive was able to make a financial success of his project. The first week of September was spent in New York, much of it on the 18th floor of the Hotel New Weston where Selwyn listened to interminable programmes from the various stations and met BBC personnel (including Mr Luke) at the BBC's offices, which were conveniently situated on the 35th floor of his hotel. Before going on to Washington Selwyn visited Long Island. 'It will be a pleasant change and rest from Mrs S, who is beginning to get slightly on my nerves, as I am sure I am on hers!!', he wrote home.[46] After a further week in Washington, going over much of the same ground, he was glad to fly home.

'A most interesting, if exhausting trip', he wrote to Haley on 18 September, in thanking him for BBC co-operation on the American side, arrangements which were not to go so smoothly for Lord Elgin and James Reeves.[47] He told Haley that he particularly liked the 'competition to produce good programmes', which he found in America, not exactly what Haley had been hoping to hear. In a final interview in America Selwyn had refused to commit himself as to whether he thought sponsorship was desirable. His response was to be for Beveridge, not the media. He wrote at once to Beveridge on his return to Britain:

> Personally I am still in difficulty on the issue of monopoly. I do not dispute that the BBC is probably very well run and does excellent work, nor do I fail to appreciate the practical difficulties, technical and economic, in enduring competition. I agree that it may be possible to contrive very real safeguards to prevent abuse of the monopoly. Nevertheless, I find great difficulty in agreeing to the principle of a perpetual monopoly of a single Corporation in the provision of information, education, or entertainment by a particular medium. I feel that at any reasonable cost we must break the monopoly, the potential dangers of which are terrifying. The fact that it may take time to develop the private system is not a sufficient objection. The crux of the matter probably lies in the answer to the question whether the great British public will object to advertisements on the air even if there is also a non-advertisement public service programme available.[48]

Selwyn now prepared a substantial memorandum *Broadcasting in the USA* (dated 28 September 1950) which was both a fuller version of his letter to Beveridge and a 'dry run' for the Minority Report.[49] In this he admitted that there was much that seemed bad or unaccept-able in American broadcasting, but that many of the sweeping allegations made against it were not well founded. He believed that the defects in the American system primarily derived from the fact that there was no public service network. 'It is often said that the effect of sponsoring has been to drive anything worthwhile off the air during the best listening hours. This is quite untrue so far as New York is concerned.' But the advertisements left much to be desired. 'Much of the advertisement matter is boring, repetitive and rather offensive to British ears. There seems to be too much of it, it comes at too frequent intervals, and it spoils enjoyment of otherwise good items.' However, Selwyn felt that the British pattern would not be the same. 'In Great Britain we do our lobbying more discreetly', he wrote in a separate submission to the Committee.[50] 'I would not willingly agree to British listeners being subjected to the full blast of US radio advertisement. On the other hand, I should not think it impossible to devise rules which would make it more tolerable. Nevertheless, advertising matter is a price to be paid, and must be faced as such.' The advantages of the American system he felt were manifold. Above all there was a great variety of programmes. Listeners had access to the very best people in the entertainment world and also to a very great variety of information and comment on public affairs. He was very impressed by the large number of small private stations. 'The small local stations can be used to promote community spirit and local interest, to encourage local talent and enterprises, and to perform the function of the local newspaper in Britain, but rather more attractively.' (Selwyn was very pleased by the expansion of local radio in Britain in the 1970s and in particular Radio Merseyside to whom he gave his last interview.) The one inescapable conclusion from the American system was that, despite the crudity of some of the advertising material, the monopoly of the BBC should be ended. In a further submission, which was discussed by the Committee between 23 and 27 October, Selwyn put four questions directly to Beveridge:

1 Is a monopoly theoretically defensible in the field of provision of information, education and entertainment by this medium?
2 In order to avoid the dangers or defects of monopoly, would it be right to accept a rather lower standard (but probably not a *much* lower standard) than that given by a well run monopoly?
3 Is it practicable to provide another system which will put an end to the monopoly either in such a way as to preserve or improve broadcasting standards, or in such a way that the price to be paid will not be too high?

4 Which of the following variants from monopoly is most worthy
of study?
(a) autonomous regions within a BBC framework
(b) system of competing national corporations
(c) a system of competing networks financially supported by
revenue from sponsors, a general overall control being
exercised by a public control board
(d) a combination of public service and private broadcasting

Faced by these choices Selwyn was firmly of the belief that a
combination of public service and private broadcasting, if technically
practicable, was the right answer. The advantages in such an arrangement would, he argued, be manifold:

i while giving the BBC the power to preserve all that is best in
its programmes, it would have to compete by excellence* of
its programmes for listeners.
ii it would not be within the power of a single body to decide
what the British people *must* listen to.
iii the listener would have a chance of greater variety, of more
original programmes and of hearing the great figures in the
entertainment world.
iv there would be more than one employer for those who earn
their living by broadcasting.
v the dangers inherent in this monopoly would be avoided.[51]

Selwyn also considered the disadvantages of breaking the monopoly. First, there would be inevitable confusion during the transition.
'No monopoly will ever be broken up without that.' Second, there
would be 'a certain amount of advertisement matter in the programme.' Selwyn faced up to this squarely from the start, unlike the
Conservative MP for Worthing, Otho Prior-Palmer who said when
the Television Bill of 1954 was about to go on the statue book, 'Well
that's all right then, as long as there isn't any advertising.'[52] Third,
this could lead to the influence of advertisers in the programme
content. This was a point picked up at once by one of the most
persistent critics of the breaking of the monopoly, Christopher
Mayhew, who wrote in his polemical pamphlet *Dear Viewer*, 'The
apparent aim is to give pleasure: the real aim is to sell toothpaste.'[53]
On balance Selwyn was confident that the US failings could be
minimised. 'After our trip to Canada and the States I am not nearly so

---

* In retrospect it is easy to see this as the weak point of the argument. Competition
is for popularity, in relation to which conventional notions of 'excellence' might
appear rather remote.

frightened of Gresham's Law* as I expected to be or as the BBC appear to be.' To illustrate the point about advertising Selwyn cited his experience of travelling on the London Underground on 21 September. On the panels opposite him which he could not help reading were listed remedies for constipation, spots and catarrh. 'I do not like being reminded of constipation, ugly spots or catarrh. But I was not conscious of any resentment against the Passenger Transport Board or the advertiser.'[54]

At the meeting of the Committee on 23 October Selwyn amplified these views. He said that he had altered his opinion on the subject of the monopoly since his visit to the USA and Canada where he had seen the great scope for local stations offered by VHF broadcasting. He had previously believed that these developments would not be practicable for a considerable number of years, but he now believed it would be possible at once to set up in this country a system of many VHF stations.[55] These points, and the points in his Memorandum, were fully discussed by the Committee, but when it became clear to Selwyn that he was not carrying the rest of the Committee with him he determined to produce his own Minority Report. His contributions to the Committee discussions now became increasingly independent. At the 48th meeting on 24 October 1950 he said that the subsidy to TV from sound licence revenue was only tolerable if improvements in the sound broadcasting service, particularly in the remote areas, were made in parallel with the extension of the television service. (The Holme Moss transmitter which brought TV to substantial parts of the north of England was not opened until 12 October 1951.) At the 55th meeting on 15 November 1950 he said he believed that sponsorship as well as advertising should be permitted and he intended to put in a dissenting note. At the 60th meeting on 7 December 1950 he formally announced that he would not be signing the main report. He did not agree with the methods proposed to safeguard against the dangers of monopoly. At the 62nd and final meeting of the Committee on 15 December 1950 Selwyn said that his Minority Report, written in a week, while agreeing with many points in the main report, disagreed on the fundamental question of monopoly, and suggested the setting up of alternative broadcasting. In such a manner did the process begin which ended with the decision for independent television, a decision described by Grace Wyndham Goldie as, 'the most momentous in the history of British broadcasting.'[56] At this stage Selwyn agreed not to say anything beyond the statement released to the Press, even though this might place him in some embarrassment. Selwyn's Minority

---

* That the good, in the long run, will inescapably be driven out by the bad.

Report, like the main Report, was dated 15 December 1950. The formal signing of both Reports was on 16 December, an occasion on which the members of the Committee gave Beveridge 'a leather case for papers', as a memento.[57] The inquiry was over, but the controversies were about to begin.

The main body of the Report had a hundred recommendations, Beveridge actually holding back the two volumes which originally contained 99 recommendations until they could be rounded-up to a hundred. Lord Simon's initial response in reading the massive report was that the question mark over the BBC's monopoly had been removed. In this he was not alone, but he was mistaken. Selwyn Lloyd's Minority Report was 'destined to become the most influential part of the Beveridge Report',[58] and in the words of Asa Briggs, the historian of the BBC, 'the real dynamite'.[59] Yet that was not how it was seen at first. In a considered response to Beveridge (the Report was submitted to Parliament on 18 January 1951) the *Spectator* in a leading article headed 'BBC for ever' prophesied that, 'the quiet protest of Mr Selwyn Lloyd's minority report', would be drowned.[60] The *New Statesman* concluded, 'No Revolution at the BBC'.[61] But those who thought the BBC's monopoly safe discounted two factors. First, the Conservatives set up a Committee on Broadcasting on 26 February 1951 under Ralph Assheton (Selwyn's pre-war friend from Clitheroe) to consider and make recommendations regarding the Party's policy on broadcasting services, in view of the expiry of the BBC Charter at the end of the year. Apart from Selwyn, the Committee contained impatient Young Turks such as Ian Orr-Ewing, John Profumo and John Rodgers. The second factor was that by October a Conservative, not a Labour government, would be deciding future broadcasting policy.

Gradually these two factors blended together. At the first meeting of the Committee on 28 February 1951 it was clear that a substantial body of Conservative opinion was against the monopoly. In particular Kenneth Pickthorn, John Profumo and John Rodgers were convinced that competition would produce a better service for the listening and (significantly) viewing public. Duncan Sandys was also against the monopoly but alone doubted whether it was feasible to break it. Geoffrey Lloyd was one of the few who was for the monopoly, as was Brendan Bracken, though he was not a regular attender. Selwyn had raised a standard and though he could not in the long-term fight under that standard himself, because by the time battle was joined he had other responsibilities as Minister of State at the Foreign Office, the younger back-bench members of the Broadcasting Committee, particularly John Profumo, kept him in touch with the latest developments in the struggle.

The battle for independent television (Norman Collins had correctly predicted that television rather than radio would be the medium of the future) was not fought on party lines. The battle was essentially between the Old Guard and the Young Turks. In an interesting precursor of the contested election for the Chancellorship of Oxford University in 1960, when the establishment candidate, Oliver Franks, was defeated by an even more establishment candidate, Harold Macmillan, the defeat of the BBC monopoly was a case of one establishment being defeated by another. On one side were such figures as the Foreign Secretary, Anthony Eden, Lord de La Warr (as Postmaster-General the Minister in charge of Broadcasting), Lord Salisbury and Lord Halifax, the Archbishop of Canterbury and Lady Violet Bonham Carter. Churchill's position was cautiously ambivalent. Though regarding commercial television as a 'peep-show', the more he considered the matter in the light of the 1951 Election slogan of 'Set the people free', the more he felt that the monopoly must go. Reith's entry into the debate on the side of the BBC proved a mixed blessing. However, there was a distinct movement of opinion in the Conservative party away from the paternalistic attitude to broadcasting of the older, landed element. The younger Conservatives, particularly the 'Class of 1950', were anxious to see some denationalisation. Apart from steel, broadcasting seemed the most promising area. This dash for freedom was most important. There was a sense of frustration among many younger Conservatives, particularly when they discovered that politics was, after all, the art of the possible. If the frontiers of nationalisation could not be rolled back then the BBC's monopoly was at least one area where the people could be set free. The younger, non-landed Tories wanted to bring in some private enterprise and it was in the area of broadcasting that they were to have their most spectacular success, born out of the frustration about the slowness of removing other restrictions. Selwyn was the one who set the ball rolling.

Two important debates took place on the future of broadcasting during the last months of the Labour government. The first was in the Commons on 19 July 1951, the second in the Lords on 25 July. Selwyn Lloyd took a prominent part in the first of these debates, which was opened by Patrick Gordon Walker, the Commonwealth Relations Secretary. The mood of the Commons at this time, even before the defeat of the Labour government, was far more responsive to Selwyn's case than was the Lords. Indeed it was a sign of Selwyn's influence on the issue of monopoly that Gordon Walker devoted most of his speech to the Minority Report, which he said stemmed, 'rather from an objection to monopoly than a positive desire for commercial or sponsored programmes'. He came down firmly on the side of those who believed that television should be arranged under 'the single Charter and the single Corporation.'[62] In his speech Selwyn referred specifically to his dislike of the American radio advertising pattern. 'I think the advertising system could probably make a very good code of rules for itself, although I quite agree it would have to be supervised.'[63] He did not want the debate to be about the merits and demerits of the American system and made it quite clear that he wanted to maintain a public service of broadcasting which did not exist in America. He again stressed the importance of local broadcasting.

'We had a tremendous Debate all yesterday on the BBC, and I spoke for 31 minutes, attacking the monopoly of the BBC', he wrote home on 20 July 1951. 'I got quite a lot of support, principally from people on my own side, but also from a few of the Socialists. I have been spending all day today working at the Conservative Research Department with R. A. Butler, and I am going down this evening to Halstead* . . . to stay the weekend. I am going to try to get up to Manchester next week, to do a manslaughter case at the Manchester Assizes.'[64] In the midst of the preparation of the 1951 Election Manifesto and his legal work, Selwyn nevertheless realised that success in the campaign for commercial television would be immeasurably helped by favourable speeches in the Lords debate on 25 July where the prevailing tone would be one of opposition. Rather like the Under Secretaries who rebelled against the Conservative leadership at the famous Carlton Club meeting of October 1922 (where the decision was taken to break with Lloyd George and fight the forthcoming election as an independent party) Selwyn wanted some senior support to prevent the Conservative establishment leading the party in a direction in which many younger members did not wish to go. Accordingly he wrote an important letter to Lord Woolton on 20 July setting out his position:

As you no doubt know, we had a Debate last night in the Commons on the BBC.

My views are not those of the Shadow Cabinet, and therefore I cannot expect you to put them forward in the Lords, the difference between the two points of view being that the Shadow Cabinet are in favour of a continuance of a BBC monopoly for a number of

* Rab Butler's Essex home was at Halstead at that time.

years, reserving the right to review the monopoly at the end of the period. I believe that unless a decision is taken to break the monopoly within a short space of time – i.e. at the most, the next 18 months – it will be very difficult ever to do it. The simplest way of breaking it would be to transfer to another Corporation the responsibility for developing broadcasting under the V.H.F. system.

The disadvantages of the monopoly are, I am sure, already well known to you: size, conservatism in the worst sense of the term, one employer, and power concentrated in too few hands. We do not have a monopoly of the Press, the Theatre, book-publishers, etc., and it seems to me quite wrong to leave the power to say what should or should not go on the air or the screen to a single body of people. I believe that the rank and file of the Party are much more strongly against the continuance of the monopoly than the Front Bench.

I do not want to worry you with too long a letter. My Minority Report was, however, only ten pages in length (201 to 210 in the Beveridge Report), and if you could find time to read it, you will see my point of view, and practical suggestions rather more adequately expressed than they can be in a letter.[65]

Not only did Woolton read the Minority Report, but he was so impressed by it that he took on board many of the ideas that Selwyn expressed and actively encouraged him in his campaign. He was an important ally from the ranks of the Old Guard.

Arguably Selwyn never left a more important legacy than his Minority Report. Its tone of quiet yet forceful reasonableness, based on sound, practical first-hand evidence allied to the remorseless logic of a lawyer-politician made the document the standard under which the Young Turks fought. No polemic on the other side of the argument had the same intellectual coherence. Selwyn called un-equivocally for commercial radio and television to be established in Britain. He rehearsed the Evils of Monopoly, laying particular stress on the dangers in a monopoly for workers with only one employer. (Reith's argument about the right of appeal to the Director-General cut no ice at all.) In fact the influence of Reith lay heavy over the Minority Report, as did Beveridge, two autocratic figures against whom Selwyn vigorously reacted. In the most closely argued passage of the Minority Report (Paragraphs 7–12) Selwyn recalled how Lord Reith 'gloried in the power of the BBC'. This was the 'appalling evidence' of June 1950. 'I am afraid that [the] dangers [of monopoly] in regard to this medium of expression are both insidious and

insufficiently appreciated by the public.' In bringing this to the
attention of the public, he continued, 'I am not attracted by the idea
of compulsory uplift achieved by "the brute force of monopoly" to
use Lord Reith's phrase. If people are to be trusted with the franchise, surely they should be able to decide for themselves whether
they want to be educated or entertained in the evening.' He believed
that, 'the BBC should remain to set the standards, and with the duty
of providing the News, Education and Overseas Services, and that
the Corporation should be given adequate financial resources . . . In
due course one or more other Companies or Corporations could be
licensed to provide the alternative television programmes which
sooner or later the public will certainly demand, and which are now
technically feasible.' Monopoly was an evil (he chose the word
deliberately). 'The evil lies in the system, the control by a monopoly
of this great medium of expression. It involves the concentration of
great power in the hands of a few men and women, and the tendency
to create a uniform pattern of thought and culture.'[66]

The Report was in tune with a growing mood. As Asa Briggs has
noted, 'Selwyn Lloyd's prognostications were suited to the time. The
year 1951, the year of the Festival of Britain, marked the climax of the
age of austerity and the shift to a new era of affluence.'[67] As John
Corner wrote in a perceptive article in the *Listener* in 1985, 'Its
arguments are a telling instance of the vivacious directness and
plausibility of market reasoning when put up against expansively
conceived liberal aspirations disinclined to contest too openly matters
of basic political principle.'[68] The White Paper on Broadcasting
Policy in July 1951 (the Attlee government's last say in the matter)
certainly had no such inclination, stating that the best interests would
be served with the continuance of the BBC, 'substantially on the same
basis'.[69] The General Election of October 1951 altered the para-
meters. The influence of the Conservative Broadcasting Committee
was first seen in the White Paper of May 1952.[70] At Cabinet on 12
May 1952, when this White Paper was being finalised, the so-called
'Trojan Horse' clause made its first recorded appearance and as the
Cabinet minutes state, 'The present government have come to the
conclusion that in the expanding field of television provision *should*
be made to permit some element of competition.'[71] This was taken
further in the second White Paper on TV Policy in November 1953,
which stated, 'Many of the fears lately expressed as to the Government's Policy arise from a misconception of the form competitive
broadcasting might take in this country.'[72] A crucial figure, both in
Cabinet and Cabinet committees, had been Lord Woolton. 'The
present system lends itself unduly to wrongful interference by an

unscrupulous government', he had submitted in a memorandum to his Cabinet colleagues. 'A licence for television transmission should be given to at least one private enterprise organisation', he wrote, 'arrived at on the basis of political compromise within our own party.'[73] The way was being paved for a second corporation as a full competitor with the BBC.

Although by this time Selwyn was fully committed to his work in the Foreign Office, he prepared on 15 March 1953 a draft letter for those who wrote to him about commercial television (rather in the manner of the 1948 memorandum to his correspondents on capital punishment). The key passage ran:

> The Government stand firm on the principle that there should be an element of competition in the television service. I strongly support this view. It seems to me to permit this medium of expression and thought to remain in the hands of a public monopoly might in time endanger the freedom of our whole society. I believe that there must be an element of competition and diversity and I hope that in due course we shall develop certainly as much choice as there is in the popular Press at the present time.
>
> With regard to sponsoring, I appreciate the disadvantages and risks involved. I would certainly be opposed to sponsoring if it were to be in substitution for the BBC.[74]

The defenders of the monopoly concentrated on these disadvantages, especially the dangers of Americanisation. In this area of the debate, J. Fred Muggs holds an honoured and special place. J. Fred Muggs was a chimpanzee who appeared on American breakfast television. In June 1953 his appearances were dovetailed with the Coronation ceremonies from Westminster Abbey and J. Fred Muggs became the symbol of what might happen in Britain if commercial broadcasting was given its head. Christopher Mayhew, a coordinating member of Lady Violet Bonham Carter's National Television Council, appeared in a debate at the Oxford Union against the principal advocate for ITV, Norman Collins. Mayhew hired a chimpanzee which he took down to the debate, with the result that he was able to pour ridicule on the United States TV companies. He never had an easier debating victory, but the decision was not going to be taken at the Oxford Union.

Selwyn consulted closely with Norman Collins. 'Dinner with Norman Collins', he wrote in his diary for 7 January 1954. They agreed on three points to put to Lord de la Warr, the Postmaster-General, in the run-up to the Television Bill:

    i immediate decision as to frequencies for proposed transmit-
      ters, so that radio manufacturers can begin to make new sets
      twin tuned.
   ii language in the Bill wide enough to enable the new Corpor-
      ation to let each transmitter to only one programme produc-
      ing company.
  iii safeguards to be prescribed – sustaining time to be a per-
      centage of total, and that part of the programme must be
      subcontracted.

He reckoned that it would need someone to risk 10 million
pounds to get an adequate programme going. I am doubtful about
the government scheme. It can only work if the above decisions are
taken.[75]

Selwyn continued to lobby discreetly in the right quarters. He sent
a particularly detailed memorandum to the Lord Privy Seal, Harry
Crookshank. In this he rehearsed many of the arguments of the
Minority Report (and as always when writing to people about broadcasting, suggesting that the recipient should read pages 201–10 of the
Beveridge Report), but moved on to the more practical details as to
how the monopoly could be broken. VHF and UHF wavelengths had
completely changed the situation. (Although the decision in the end
was for commercial television only, Selwyn would have liked to have
had commercial radio as well.) Sound broadcasting had its measure of
variety – Home, Light and Third programmes, plus regional vari-
ations – but there was no equivalent diversity in television. (In a
debate in the House of Commons in June 1963 on the second ITV
channel in the wake of the Pilkington Report Selwyn argued the same
point, 'I want as many channels as possible as quickly as possible . . .
One of the great dangers about this medium which I have always felt
. . . (is) that a single channel or a single programme can have too
much power.')[76] Inevitably the fact of TV advertising had to be faced.
Without extra income there could be no choice and as there was a
limit to the licence fee ceiling, commercial television was the only way
to achieve the necessary variety. 'These proposals may seem complicated', concluded Selwyn, 'they illustrate the practical difficulties of
breaking a monopoly.'[77]

Events now moved swiftly and the Independent Television
Authority was set up by the Television Act on 4 August 1954. The two
ideas of spot advertisements rather than sponsoring and the ITA as a
public regulatory body were absolutely decisive in undercutting
opposition. The first programmes were transmitted on 22 September
1955. A crucial change in the social history of the country had taken

place. Many preconceptions had gone out of the window after the war. One of them was the belief in a paternalistic public broadcasting corporation on the Reithian lines of the pre-war BBC. Historically it fell to Selwyn Lloyd to articulate that sense of social unease with the status quo, associated in the public mind with dinner-jacketed announcers. In an article published in 1965 in *TV Times* Selwyn looked back on his time on the Beveridge Committee:

> I was in a minority of one on the Beveridge Committee. But among the rank and file of the Conservative Party in the House of Commons, I believe that my views commanded overwhelming support. There was also some support for them in the Labour Party. In the circumstances, was it surprising that the majority view prevailed, even though powerful members of the Establishment supported the BBC's case? If, as has been alleged, some M.Ps. connected with advertising or electronics were more active than others, those connections lessened rather than increased their influence on this issue in the House of Commons. In fact the creation of independent television was the victory of the majority over some highly placed, very powerful and extremely respectable pressure groups.[78]

Indeed a sign of Selwyn's objective detachment from the commercial possibilities of ITV is that he was one of the few people advocating independent broadcasting who did not make any money out of it himself.

The Television Act of 1954 established independent television for an initial period of ten years (on the lines of Ullswater in pre-war days for the BBC). The inevitable corollary was the need for another major broadcasting inquiry, the Pilkington Report of 1962, which was so heavily critical of ITV. Selwyn's open-mindedness shows in that he was so much in sympathy with the Pilkington findings. In the debate in the House of Commons in June 1963 he openly admitted that, 'the present position where there is only one provider of advertising time . . . is not what I had in mind.'[79] Nor did he foresee how the commercial ethos was to lead to what J. B. Priestley termed *Admass*, a centralised and materialistic view of society. One of the subsidiary effects of his Minority Report was that it made the BBC prepare its response to Pilkington with far greater thoroughness than it had to Beveridge. There were no Reith 'own goals' when Sir Hugh Greene gave evidence. Maurice Farquharson, who remembered Selwyn's critical visit of 6 June 1950, marshalled the evidence very strongly, so that Pilkington was an almost embarrassing vindication of the BBC.[80]

The Beveridge Report was the most significant of all the broadcast-ing inquiries and Selwyn Lloyd's Minority Report the most influential part of it. Not only did it articulate the feelings of post-war Conserva-tive thinking in 'setting the people free', but it was not written in committee prose. Its arguments for competition and a more pluralis-tic society were cogently expressed. Christopher Mayhew's *Dear Viewer* and Mark Chapman Walker's *Free Speech – why not free switch?* (from opposite sides of the argument) were on a much broader polemical level. The Minority Report, as it had to be, was far deeper in its intellectual arguments and was all the more persuasive for being pro-competition and not anti-BBC. It challenged the opponents of commercial television to set out arguments of com-mensurate weight *for* the BBC monopoly. Selwyn underestimated the pervasive influence of American advertising patterns, the squeez-ing of the allowed quota into the peak time hours rather than across the day, the trimming of programmes (particularly drama) to suit the timings, and what Vance Packard was to call the 'hidden' persuader, especially in sports programmes, where the effects were to be felt even in the BBC's output. This was because he had the confidence of the liberal democrat that there would be proper controls and volun-tary restraint through fair-minded figures of high moral purpose, though the whole thrust of his argument, perhaps paradoxically, was anti-centralisation. Perhaps this was to take too high a view of human nature, particularly for one in whom in so many other areas (from travel arrangements to the outcomes of General Elections) the pessimistic strain ran strong. Selwyn always preferred the idea of sponsorship rather than the 'spot' advertising that later became the established financial pattern. But even J. Fred Muggs was a price worth paying if it ended the monopoly. When Sir Hugh Greene was in Chicago on BBC business in 1953 the American broadcasters still remembered Selwyn Lloyd's visit and the forcefulness with which he argued against monopoly. His mind was quite made up and he was determined that 'the brute force' should be ended.[81] The fact that the Labour Party believed in statism helped him in his case. Herbert Morrison's view, expressed both to the War Cabinet and the post-war Labour Cabinet in discussions on broadcasting policy, was that if the monopoly of the BBC went it would be an encroachment into the corporate state. For the younger Conservatives this sharpened the thrust of the argument: it became free enterprise versus centralism; the market economy or the planned economy.

Selwyn transcended many of the broader elements of the debate that followed. Labour and Conservative responses tended to concen-trate on one of three levels – the political arguments, the economic arguments or the cultural ones. The strength of Selwyn's contribution was that he took all three into consideration. He was not interested in one to the exclusion of the others. Primarily he thought of the economic arguments and in some respects was wary of the political implications. Perhaps he was least convincing on the cultural side (he never had aesthetic sensibility), not only at the time, but in retrospect. Once the monopoly had been broken by political action economic advantages would be inevitable, with an increase in employment. On the cultural side he had too high a faith in the system of safeguards. In the end Gresham's Law was not so easily discarded. He was willing to acknowledge this. Towards the end of his life he said that the great disappointments of his life were the failure of *We Can Conquer Unemployment* in 1929, the failure to establish a viable centre party in the 1930s and the outcome of independent television.[82]

So the BBC monopoly ended, and on 22 September the first images were transmitted on Independent Television from the celebratory Guildhall banquet, the statues of Gog and Magog being thought in some viewers' minds to represent the BBC and ITV. What had first been mooted in Selwyn Lloyd's Minority Report in December 1950 had, after a fierce parliamentary battle, become reality. Selwyn Lloyd is often called 'the father of commercial television'. Strictly speaking, that title, if it belongs to anyone, belongs to Norman Collins. Selwyn was more a benevolent godfather. Above all else though he was the prophet of commercial television, the one who had seen the way ahead and who had proclaimed it out loud. As a result he was a prophet who was not without honour in his own party.

7

On the Ladder

The final stages of the Beveridge Report coincided with the aftermath of one General Election and the beginnings of another. An election was due by the summer of 1950, but there were many in the Labour Party – notably Cripps, Dalton and Bevan – who felt that a much earlier election should have been called and that Attlee should have combined the devaluation of September 1949 with an appeal to the country for a fresh mandate. (It was during this period that the political wags said that if Cabinet minutes were to give a true account of the Labour government they should conclude, 'Also present was the ghost of 1931'.) The date chosen was a curious compromise between autumn and summer expectations. The Parliament elected in 1945 was dissolved on 10 January 1950 and Attlee announced Polling Day as 23 February.

The principal Labour figures of the 1950 campaign – Attlee, Bevin and Morrison – had been in continuous office for almost a decade and after the high expectations of the New Jerusalem of the immediate post-war years and the hard reality of continuing austerity, the administration not unnaturally had a care-worn look about it. Bevin and Cripps were dying men and, with the economy in difficulties, Attlee's leadership under scrutiny and the Parliamentary Labour Party disenchanted and ill-disciplined, Conservative hopes of gaining outright victory at the polls, particularly after the Maxwell Fyfe Report of 1948 and Rab Butler's policy reforms, seemed on the surface to be no fanciful pipe-dream. The austerity of the immediate post-war years, unavoidable though much of it was with the necessary concentration on export markets, meant that not only the Parliamentary Labour Party was disenchanted. Rationing, controls (Harold Wilson's 'bonfire' as President of the Board of Trade was on 5 November 1948), that strange tinned fish from South Africa called 'snoek' (even the ubiquitous wartime 'Woolton Pie' had been more appetising), fuel shortages, the black market, the bitter winter of 1947 – all these were laid at the door of Socialism (with slogans such as 'Starve with Strachey and Shiver with Shinwell') by the frustrated middle classes, deprived of their pre-war status and financial security. But their hopes for an outright Conservative victory were not to be realised. The Labour government had the cushion of its landslide victory of 1945 and even a 3 per cent swing to the Conservatives was not sufficient to return Churchill to Downing Street at the first attempt. Labour won 315 seats, the Conservatives 298 and the Liberals a mere 9. (Just before the 1955 Election even Megan Lloyd George left the Liberals and joined Labour;[1] her brother Gwilym was already fighting in the Conservative interest and was to be in Churchill's 1951 government. So ended Criccieth Liberalism.) Churchill called for one more heave in the next election which was shortly expected.

Selwyn Lloyd faced two new opponents in the Wirral in a constituency reduced from a voting strength of over 110,000 to a more manageable 59,000. The campaign was uneventful, only the closeness of the national result at the end bringing some excitement. Dr Lloyd, now in benign old age, sat in for the count and saw his son's majority, thanks to a sharply reduced Labour vote, only marginally down on the 1945 figure. The result was:

Lloyd, J. S. B. (Conservative)	29,232
Kelly, Lt-Col. H. A. (Labour)	15,993
Banks, T. M. (Liberal)	6,018
Majority	13,239

The Brigadier label was all that had been lost.

Selwyn received telegrams from the Leas School and on 27 February from Winston Churchill. In a letter of 28 February he confided to a constituent, 'I was . . . rather disappointed that we did not pull it off nationally.'[2] But there were compensations. His friend Hennie Oakeshott (later one of Selwyn's Parliamentary Private Secretaries) was returned at neighbouring Bebington and the Conservative intake – the famous Class of 1950, which Nye Bevan said was the most notable Conservative vintage in history – buckled down to the task of accomplishing what Churchill demanded.

The Conservative Party of 1950 was a very different creature from that of 1945. The Maxwell Fyfe recommendations of 1948 (the next main inquiry into the state of the Conservative Party organisation was to be conducted by Selwyn in 1962–3) prepared the way for a broadening of the social intake of future MPs by limiting the amount of money a constituency could expect from its sitting member or its candidate.* Under Rab Butler the Conservative Research Department had poured forth a stream of new policy statements, of which the Industrial Charter of 1947 was the first extensive Conservative response to post-war political conditions, emphasising the role of private enterprise while at the same time accepting at least some of the aspects of Labour's *dirigisme*. The 1950 Manifesto had been based on the Research Department's *The Right Road for Britain*, published in July 1949, and during the summer recess of 1950 many of the new intake prepared another influential Conservative Political Centre booklet, *One Nation*, which became the Disraelian name, not just of a manifesto statement, but of a whole political group.[3] Though not a member of that group, Selwyn was very much in tune with their aims and aspirations and was one of only two MPs already in the House (the other was Lord Dunglass) to go out of his way to be friendly and welcoming to many of the newcomers, especially the more retiring ones.[4] At the Blackpool Conference (12–14 October 1950) the One Nation group had a significant influence on social policy and were instrumental in the adoption of the resolution to aim for a house-building programme of 300,000 homes a year. Selwyn spoke on Leasehold Reform at the 1950 Conference and was seen as both a 'coming' man, and by virtue of his membership of the House since 1945, quite an 'established' one, a potent combination. An indication of Selwyn's position in the political world at this time can be gleaned from a confidential BBC report. The BBC were always conscious of the need to bring in new faces (and voices) for its various current affairs programmes and staff were sent to the Party conferences specifically to report on possible recruits. Three days after the Conservative Conference Selwyn's 'profile' went into the files:

SELWYN LLOYD, CBE, KC, MP for Wirral. He spoke brilliantly – crowding a number of well marshalled facts into a very short time. He has a nice sense of humour & never approached pomposity. He is extremely lively & would make an excellent speaker either scripted or unscripted. He would be useful when legal background was needed because he could hold the legal point of view without slowing down a discussion.[5]

At this time there was growing unrest in the BBC at the domination by Robert Boothby and Michael Foot of the influential programme *In the News*. George Barnes, whose appointment as Director of TV had sparked off Norman Collins's resignation from the BBC, asked

* A sum not in excess of £50 pa from an MP and not in excess of £25 pa from a candidate.

Michael Balkwill of the news department how many times Boothby and Foot had appeared between 6 October 1950 and 19 January 1951. It transpired that Foot had appeared 13 times and Boothby 10, no other MP appearing more than 4 times. Barnes believed that representatives of the 'main core of opinion' in the two major parties should be included and out of this request (and the earlier BBC report on file), Selwyn first appeared on the programme on 20 April 1951, a dramatic political week that witnessed Ernest Bevin's death, Hugh Gaitskell's only Budget and the subsequent resignations of Nye Bevan and Harold Wilson. Television, however, was never Selwyn's *métier*. He was no more successful now than later when he was both more experienced and more exposed as a government spokesman. 'It is a business that needs a lot of practice', he admitted in a letter of 22 April 1951.[6] In Parliament he was more successful. Patrick Buchan-Hepburn, as we have seen, had put Selwyn on the Conservative Leasehold Reform Committee (Selwyn's special responsibility was the law dealing with landlord and tenant) in which capacity he spoke from the Opposition front bench on the Leasehold Property Bill, the *Evening Standard* noting that he was the first Conservative back-bencher in that Parliament to receive such an honour.[7] His old friend Hartley Shawcross had moved the Second Reading of the Leasehold Property (Temporary Provisions Bill) and in his reply Selwyn – flanked by Anthony Eden and Reginald Manningham-Buller – said that the law of landlord and tenant was in a hopelessly unsatisfactory condition. Nothing was doing more to produce slums than the Rent Restriction Acts. He concluded by saying that the only compensation was that Attlee's government would not be in office during the 1950s. The *Daily Despatch* reported, 'Mr Lloyd dealt with a complex and complicated section of the law with clarity, and he dealt with the government with courage.'[8] All this was witnessed at first-hand by Eden, who within the year was to have Selwyn as his right-hand man at the Foreign Office.

Also in December 1950 Selwyn began important contacts with the Alliance (later Sun Alliance) Assurance Company when he became a director, an association that was to be renewed during the years in Opposition in the 1960s. He became a member of the Brigands, a golfing and dining club that included parliamentary friends such as Toby Low, Gwilym Lloyd George, P. B. Lucas, John Tilney, an old pre-war friend from 25 Club days who became MP for Wavertree, and elder statesmen such as Lord Balfour of Inchrye and Viscount Simon, with whom Selwyn had played golf at the Gogs in far-off Cambridge Liberal days. Yet there was a rootlessness at the centre. Bill Aitken was about to leave Eccleston Square, where Selwyn had his flat, and Selwyn was conscious of the difficulties facing a bachelor MP, particularly in a large and socially demanding constituency. At the age of 47 he now took one of the central decisions of his life. For over two years his secretary at Westminster had been Elizabeth Marshall, known as Bae, the daughter of Roland Marshall. Selwyn had known Bae since pre-war days and the two years at the end of the Attlee government had seen them drawing closer together. (One of Selwyn's colleagues of the time remembers the dusty conditions in Westminister Hall where in the midst of rebuilding work Selwyn always ensured that Bae had a good packing-case on which to sit when transcribing parliamentary business.) Thus he stumbled, as it were, into marriage and although there was pleasure in the constituency in the linking of the Lloyd and Marshall families, there were also those who had their doubts, notably Selwyn's younger sister, Rachel, who counselled him until the engagement that it was not irrevocable, and Bae's mother who was convinced – rightly as it turned out – that a man of Selwyn's age and temperament could never make her daughter happy. Bae was half Selwyn's age and some of Selwyn's own reserve is seen in the letter he wrote to his parents on 28 November 1950:

> Well the die is cast and the fatal announcement will see the light of day on Thursday morning, I trust in the Times and Telegraph. I feel like someone shivering on the brink of a very cold bath, however I expect it will be warmer in the water . . . It is a great adventure but we know one another pretty well and I think that all should be well. Much love, think of me and pray for me!![9]

The engagement was widely noticed in the national Press and messages of congratulation came in from all sides. Lord Beveridge, with doubtful relevance, sent him a copy of a book he had written on India, but the letter that touched Selwyn most was the one from Bill McKerrow, briefly Eileen's husband, who had remained a brother-in-law for life. The wedding took place on 29 March 1951 at St Andrew's Church, West Kirby, conducted by the Rev. Eric Fairfax Robson. On the marriage certificate Selwyn was described as King's Counsel. It was a cold, snowy day but a big social occasion in the Wirral nevertheless, with crowds lining the roads around the church. John Tilney, MP for Wavertree, was best man. One of the telegrams he read out said: 'You've always wanted a change of government. Now you've got it.' At the reception one of the guests said to Selwyn, 'You've got a beautiful bride.' 'Yes', he replied, 'and I've got a beautiful wedding cake too.'[10]

The honeymoon was spent motoring in Southern France. 'We have

hired a ridiculous little French Renault motor car, just like a peram-
bulator, and toddle about in it', Selwyn wrote home. 'Yesterday we
went to St Raphael and one day soon we shall get to Nice and
Monaco.'[11] On his return Selwyn was again given front-bench responsibilities. 'They have asked me to wind up on the Second Reading
Debate on the Finance Bill next Tuesday . . . It is rather a bore, but
on the other hand we must not refuse opportunities when they arise',
he noted on 4 May. On the same day, in an interesting foretaste of the
issues that would be awaiting him in the autumn, Selwyn recorded, 'I
went to listen to a Director of the Anglo-Persian [Oil Company]
talking about the situation in Persia. It does not seem to be too good
and the Anglo-Persian people could have been very much cleverer
than they have been.' One diversion from the increasingly hectic
parliamentary scene was the opening that week of the Festival of
Britain, a commemoration of the centenary of the Great Exhibition
of 1851, and a statement of social purpose – an indication of the
brave new world that lay beyond austerity. Selwyn's attitude to the
Festival, like that of many Conservatives, was cautious. 'Today E and
I have been to the opening of the South Bank exhibition of the
Festival of Britain to see the King and Queen open it. The King
looked rather haggard. It is difficult to say whether the Exhibition
itself will be a success or not . . . We did not go into the Festival Hall.
Oliver Lyttelton said that the concert there last night was a great
success and that Rule Britannia brought down the house and even
Bevan who was just behind him sang it vigorously. On balance, I
think the Festival is fairly good, but not good enough to make a lot of
fuss about and certainly not good enough to spend £10m pounds
on.'[12]

After Selwyn's marriage it became clear that the Rushes, the old
family home in Stanley Road, was too big for his parents, so the
Lloyds moved to 32 Queen's Road, Hoylake, where, after the death
of Dr Lloyd in 1954, they were to be joined by Miss Wright as
companion-housekeeper to Mrs Lloyd. Selwyn settled in his London
residence at 26 Chester Street as the 'grand' years began to unfold and
32 Queen's Road became his constituency base. In the Wirral he was
always conscious of being on parade and though throughout the 1950s
and early 1960s Selwyn stayed in this solid Edwardian corner-
terraced red-brick house when on constituency business, even preparing some of his Foreign Office speeches (and later his Budget
notes) in the small bay-windowed study on the first floor with its view
over a quiet crossroads, he was aware of the dangers of being
continually on his own parliamentary doorstep. Nevertheless,
scrambler telephones were installed in the small downstairs hall and

Selwyn successfully gave the impression (to Anthony Sampson, for instance, in *The Anatomy of Britain**) of living simply in a red-brick semi-detached world. 'Until you have seen York Cottage, you will never understand my father', said the Duke of Windsor to Harold Nicolson when Nicolson was researching the life of King George V.[13] The same was only partly true of Selwyn Lloyd and 32 Queen's Road, but it was a concept that Selwyn did nothing to dispel, though in reality things were different. Queen's Road remained Selwyn's family home and the centre of gravity in the constituency.

In the summer of 1951 Rab Butler called Selwyn into the team preparing the Manifesto statement *Britain Strong and Free*, initially for the autumn conference at Scarborough, though by the time the document was at the printers these plans had been overtaken by Attlee's announcement of a General Election on 25 October. Much of the work on the policy details of this document had been formulated in the 1949 statement *The Right Road for Britain* (the basis of the 1950 Manifesto *This is the Road*). Rab Butler sought to broaden the representation on the Manifesto Committee, hence Selwyn's involvement, together with Antony Head (who worked on defence matters) and Anthony Nutting (overseas policy). Under Rab Butler's general guidance, drafting of the document *Britain Strong and Free* was in the hands of this small committee of MPs (with Selwyn in the chair, a considerable feather in his cap) drawn from the newly constituted Advisory Committee on Policy. As it was expected that Selwyn would be appointed to an economic portfolio in the event of a Conservative victory, he concentrated on this aspect. Detailed drafting was in the hands of Selwyn, Michael Fraser, whose appointment to succeed David Clarke as Director of the Research Department was announced on 28 June 1951, and Peter Goldman. Churchill's personal manifesto for the 1951 Election was then based on this document.[14] In a letter to Selwyn on 10 May 1951 Rab Butler outlined the kind of help he expected in the run-up to the election. 'Unless events cause me to change my mind, I consider that we should work towards providing a guidance statement of Policy by the end of July for a possible or probable Party Conference in October. If an Election supervenes we can switch our tactics and consider the different form which an Election manifesto may take.'[15] A strict timetable was drawn up (by the third week in May Selwyn was distributing drafts to Anthony Eden, Oliver Lyttelton, Harold Macmillan, David Maxwell Fyfe, Harry Crookshank and Lord Salisbury). Rab Butler used Selwyn very much as his eyes and ears at this stage. Meetings of the

* Anthony Sampson, *Anatomy of Britain*, 1962, p. 288.

Advisory Committee on Policy continued and this body approved in principle a second draft on 31 July.[16] Further work was undertaken during the recess. In August during a walking holiday at Parracombe Selwyn made additions both on economic and defence policy. On the subject of present economic difficulties he minuted, 'The trick is to keep wages down.'[17] On 30 August 1951 Selwyn sent a draft of *Britain Strong and Free* (the title had been suggested by David Clarke) to the Party Chairman, Lord Woolton, commenting, 'I feel that the principal criticism to be made of it is that it is too long & in places too stodgy.'[18] The final draft, in which Selwyn again took a major part, was ready two days before Attlee dissolved Parliament on 5 October. Rab Butler was delighted with Selwyn's industry. 'I have only to thank you very much now for an intensely hard interlude in which you have been most helpful.'[19] Any doubts that Selwyn would be a member of the new administration were removed by his work on the policy statements throughout 1951. With the publication of the Beveridge Report as well he was now very much a coming man. Not only had he assisted in the formulation of policy but he had performed the function of integrating the Parliamentary Party with the policy process as Oliver Poole had done over the production of *The Right Road for Britain*.[20] The work may have seemed, in Rab Butler's words, an interlude, but it was the prelude to thirteen years of Conservative government, and Selwyn was to be on the front bench for twelve of those years.

The 1951 General Election campaign provided the one extra heave that Churchill had demanded. Unusually for a British election, foreign affairs played a large role, and as in 1950 there was a close finish, with the Conservatives winning 321 seats, the Labour Party (though with a higher popular vote) 298 seats and the Liberals reduced to a 'taxi-cab' of 6 seats. The Liberals did not contest the Wirral and Selwyn increased his majority in a straight fight. The figures were:

Lloyd, J. S. B. (Conservative)	32,631
Chrimes, R. B. (Labour)	17,392
Majority	15,239

'Tory victory in Gen Election. Thank God!!', wrote Dr Lloyd in his diary.[21] With this victory much attention was now concentrated on Churchill's new administration. In the higher reaches there were to be some surprises, with Rab Butler, not Oliver Lyttelton, whose city associations militated against him, as Chancellor of the Exchequer, and with Walter Monckton rather than David Maxwell Fyfe at the Ministry of Labour because Churchill, with his small majority, wanted a diplomat to handle the unions. One of the crucial (and at the time unregarded) appointments was of Harold Macmillan at Housing with the opportunity of fulfilling the commitment to build 300,000 houses a year. But the possibility of such jobs did not involve Selwyn Lloyd, Hugh Fraser and other friends successfully returning to London from their north-west constituencies on the weekend of 27 October, where they were house guests of Michael Astor at Bruern Abbey. Their prospects, if any, lay in the next rung of government posts. It was, therefore, a rather anxious group of younger MPs who gathered for dinner that Saturday evening in the hospitable environs of Bruern. As the dinner progressed it became clear that Selwyn and Hugh Fraser had left their telephone number of the evening with Downing Street in case the Prime Minister or Patrick Buchan-Hepburn, the Chief Whip, needed to get in touch. As time passed the anxieties grew. Eventually, well after nine, the telephone rang. The butler came in to tell an attentive audience that there was a telephone call from Mr Churchill and could he please speak to Mr Hugh Fraser. With difficulty, Hugh Fraser tried to look not too pleased at the way the Fates had smiled on him and Selwyn was considerably chastened. A few moments later Hugh Fraser returned somewhat crestfallen. The call was from *Randolph* Churchill who was spending the evening ringing up colleagues as a practical joke.[22]

On Monday 29 October Selwyn received an invitation to call on Churchill at Chartwell. (Downing Street had tried to contact him at his Chambers at 1 Temple Gardens.) He had been 'much-sought-after'.[23] Selwyn half expected some job connected with the Board of Trade or Finance, as he had been Secretary of the Conservative Finance Committee, but rather feared that it might be a Law Office, possibly the Solicitor-Generalship, which he was determined to refuse as he considered it a political cul-de-sac. 'To become Attorney-General seemed to me, perhaps wrongly, to be a different matter. He is the head of the profession and although I didn't want it, I was doubtful whether it was possible to refuse it.'[24] Instead he found himself in a 'home and away' swop with John Boyd-Carpenter (a Foreign Office Shadow in Opposition), who became Financial Secretary to the Treasury, while Selwyn was appointed Minister of State. Churchill liked to see as many of his ministers as possible on appointment so the process tended to spread over three to four days. The first batch of ministers were summoned to Churchill's London home, 28 Hyde Park Gate. More junior ministers, such as Selwyn, were summoned to Chartwell. At this key moment in his life, Selwyn's car failed him and in some desperation he rang his old friend Glanvill Benn at Benn publishers to explain the situation. Glanvill Benn at once despatched a Benn car with Falconer, his driver, to take Selwyn to Chartwell. The house was full of private and political secretaries and other bidden ministers. The timetable was running late and Selwyn was ushered into the library for a while to watch three fish tanks bubbling away. Patrick Buchan-Hepburn was there and from time to time Selwyn became aware of the presence of Rab Butler, Harry Crookshank and James Stuart, newly appointed to the Scottish Office.[25] Eventually he was summoned into Churchill's presence. Churchill, dressed in his blue siren suit, said that they had not seen much of one another in the past, except occasionally during stages of the Finance Bill, but that he had heard good reports from everyone. (Selwyn vaguely suspected that Churchill had mistaken him for somebody else, possibly Geoffrey Lloyd, who was to become Minister for Fuel and Power.[26] However, there was no mistake on the offer, because Patrick Buchan-Hepburn, the king-maker at this second rank had been closely involved.) Churchill said that Anthony Eden had asked for Selwyn at the Foreign Office and, therefore, he was being offered the post of Minister of State. Would he take it? 'When I heard the words "Foreign Office"', Selwyn wrote home on 31 October, 'the proverbial feather would have demolished me.'[27] Churchill spoke about the seriousness of the world situation, the difficulties of the new Government and the wide scope offered by this position. Selwyn's reply grew in the telling. 'But sir, I think there must be some mistake, I've never been to a foreign country, I don't speak any foreign languages, I don't like foreigners.' 'Young man', replied Churchill, 'these all seem to me to be positive advantages.'[28] In this manner Selwyn was appointed to his first government post. He was congratulated by Buchan-Hepburn, Crookshank and Stuart and then, with Falconer navigating (they had to stop in Whitehall to ask a policeman the way to the Foreign Office), Selwyn set off to meet his new master. His route to the Foreign Office post was a politically tortuous one as well.

Anthony Eden's real protégé was Anthony Nutting and his preferred Minister of State, but Nutting was nearly sixteen years Selwyn's junior and would clearly have to work his way up first through an Under-Secretaryship (as happened). This left a vacuum. The 1951 government list was almost complete when Selwyn's name came in, late on, as Buchan-Hepburn's idea. This rather discomfited Butler who wanted Selwyn at the Treasury, but pleased Churchill who believed in the benefits of switching over Shadow ministers when they came to government office so they would approach things in a fresh manner. There was a last-minute suggestion (involving Selwyn) that there was a need for legal brains in legal posts, but Churchill said,

'Can't Walter [Monckton] deal with all that?'[29] Without Nutting, Eden had to look elsewhere. Selwyn then became his choice. Robert Rhodes James paints a bleak picture of this appointment. 'He [Lloyd] was grossly overpromoted and out of his sphere. Eden had had little to do with Lloyd's appointment, and indeed hardly knew him.'[30] This was not strictly true. In October 1951 foreign policy was still run largely on a bi-partisan approach. It did not actually matter whether the Minister of State had a foreign affairs background, no more than that the Minister of Transport should have a working knowledge of the internal combustion engine. What mattered was the executive capacity to make decisions from a series of options and recommendations presented by highly professional and knowledgeable officials and this administrative ability was widely acknowledged to be one of Selwyn's proven *fortes*. Eden certainly regarded Selwyn as his choice. When Selwyn was preparing his book on Suez (the gestation period was over many years) he discussed most of the issues with Eden, then Earl of Avon. Eden was very concerned about the self-effacing story that Selwyn put about concerning his appointment as Minister of State. 'You mentioned that you were going to describe your short-comings for the F.O. as you put them to Winston', Eden wrote on 13 October 1962. 'I see no objection to that, but please do not overdo it to the point of making me seem half-witted in having chosen you for the job, because I was not, you know.'[31] Patrick Buchan-Hepburn's memory on this latter point was very clear. On 20 January 1957, after Selwyn had been retained as Foreign Secretary by Macmillan, Buchan-Hepburn wrote a letter of congratulation. 'I seem to remember being cross in November 1951 when I was told Anthony Eden had demanded you for the Foreign Office when Winston & I had been working on a plan for you to be Financial Secretary. I wonder how all that would have worked out by now? Probably not so well.'[32] The important thing for Selwyn's career was that, partly by chance, partly by the choice of his superiors, his first ministerial experience was to be in the Foreign Office and this was to condition his later attitudes as ministers often (and Selwyn was no exception) become imbued with the ethos of the department in which they first serve or have influence.

There was a sense of surprise in the Foreign Office at Selwyn's appointment, but not of misgiving. He arrived with the reputation of being something of a political staff-officer who would adapt well to the type of work he would now find in his new responsibilities. 'I was shown up to my room, which seemed enormous, met my new Private Secretary Michael Hadow, and was then taken to the Foreign Secretary's room where Eden was having a conference with officials about the U.N.O. meeting in Paris. His room was of magnificent proportions, but still with the rather strange decor approved by Palmerston, and the portrait of George III over the mantelpiece. *Little did I think that I later would occupy this room in my own right for four years and seven months.* Eden greeted me very pleasantly, said how glad he was that I had agreed to come to him, and explained his reason for asking me.'[33] As Anthony Nutting, the new Under-Secretary, had experience of foreign affairs, Eden now wanted someone in between who had no previous connection with the Foreign Service and no preconceived notions on foreign affairs. On Tuesday 30 October Selwyn was sworn in as a member of the Privy Council, Dr Lloyd noting in his diary of his son, 'He has shaken hands & kissed the hand of the King (Geo VI) on being made a Privy Councillor. He is surprised & very pleased. His elderly parents are pleased also.'[34] Two things that pleased Selwyn in particular were that Fettes was given a half holiday and that he had a letter of congratulation from General Sir Kenneth Anderson, his first Chief at Second Army.[35]

As Minister of State, Selwyn was following in distinguished footsteps. His two immediate predecessors had been Hector McNeil and Kenneth Younger, both among the brightest and best of their Labour generation. Kenneth Younger, who had met Selwyn during the war when on Montgomery's staff, was a Bevanite Wykehamist who had the Brave New World feeling that only the Left could win the peace. He was the lively young cub to the old polar bear of a Foreign Secretary, Ernest Bevin, and when Bevin had been away at the Colombo Conference in January 1950, and latterly with illness, Younger had been acting Foreign Secretary. He would have been a far more appropriate Foreign Secretary than Herbert Morrison (who succeeded Bevin in March 1951) but Attlee fought shy of the kind of appointment that had brought Eden to the Foreign Office in 1935, and was to bring David Owen there in 1976 (both at the age of 38), believing that a senior figure was needed. The Office adored Kenneth, especially the old Tory lady typist from Clapham.[36] With typical courtesy (though doubtful constitutional propriety) he stayed behind after the election to help Selwyn in a half-hour changeover talk in the Minister of State's room. Kenneth Younger then took his leave of a somewhat tearful office. Selwyn did not get off to a good start, owing to ignorance of Foreign Office ways. The lady typist from Clapham (Selwyn met everyone in the office at his own request) came out chattering with rage because Selwyn had asked her how she had voted in the election. He got off on the wrong foot with his private secretaries too by asking them what they thought of Kenneth

Younger. This was not the best way to deal with civil servants, but was a sign of political naïvety as his real intention was to find out how he should operate in what were for him uncharted waters. After this awkward start relations improved and the office warmed to him, not because he was the brisk Tory Brigadier (on the first day he mentioned that he was very proud of his military decorations) who was going to clean up sloppy Socialist influence, but because he was so straight and honest and not a political schemer. Also he soon learned that his favoured kind of humour (the bantering, almost aggressive type that demanded response in kind) was not to Foreign Office taste. Selwyn's insecurity was often masked by nervous brusqueness (the remark about his wedding cake for instance) and this innate characteristic had already manifested itself pre-war and in Second Army days when the camaraderie in a world of fear and tension was one of rapid give-and-take humour. In that world of febrile intensity there was not time for the niceties. The flippancy came, not because the soldiers did not care, but because they cared too much. This kind of ragging humour matched the mood of the 1940s, but many of the senior Foreign Office people did not like it and Selwyn took time to adjust. But he settled into the job because he was in the same mould as Kenneth Younger, methodical, efficient and hard-working. As Kenneth Younger was a Minister of State who had made his reputation at the San Francisco Conference in 1945, so Selwyn was to make his mark at United Nations meetings in Paris and New York. The office appreciated the way that Selwyn wanted to hear the truth, however unpalatable, encouraging and admiring officials who spoke their mind. He was never in the business of scoring points off the Labour Opposition. He proved a good team man, administratively sound and an expert master of a brief. He told his staff that there was no point in a Minister of State unless he took on tasks for his master. Selwyn soon proved himself the sort of subordinate with whom senior ministers could feel comfortable. He was reliable and did not alarm with displays of brilliance. There was no need for a senior minister to be looking over his shoulder. If loyalty was the Tories' secret weapon, it was Selwyn's open one.

After seeing Eden for a further briefing on his first day in office, Selwyn asked Michael Hadow what he did next. He was told they were leaving for Paris on Saturday (3 November). 'Good', replied Selwyn, 'I've never been there before.' He wanted to know if he could take his wife and when it was clear that this would be possible he asked how long they would be there. When told that it would be the best part of three months his face fell. 'They want me out of the way', he said. The next day he wrote to tell his parents of developments:

I have spent the last 24 hours reading feverishly and meeting some of the leading officials. I have to go to Paris on Saturday. Eden comes for about a week, and then I am left in charge of the British delegation at the United Nations meetings. These meetings may go on for a couple of months, so I am afraid that I shall not see you again for some time to come.[37]

Discussions with Eden focused his mind on the legacy of the Labour Party in foreign affairs. Selwyn felt that they had left a good legacy on such things as Marshall Aid, Bevin deserving much of the credit for that. The robustness of the attitude to the Berlin situation and the subsequent Air Lift Selwyn also attributed to Bevin's firm direction. The credit side also contained NATO, resistance to aggression in Korea, a firm line with the USSR and reconciliation with Germany and Italy. On the debit side most of the problems lay in the Middle East. He felt the British had stayed too long in Cairo and that 'we had made a mess of Palestine'. In Iran (Eden's initial concern) there were the problems consequent upon Mossadeq's nationalisation of the Anglo-Iranian Oil Company.

The main agenda that faced the new team included the UN, a Korean armistice, disarmament talks (Selwyn's main responsibility), preparing for the end of occupied status in Germany, the Bonn agreement and German rearmament. In the Middle East there was the whole question of the Suez base – 100,000 troops were tied up there – the move towards Sudanese independence (over which Selwyn was to be deeply occupied), the nuclear deterrent and Indo-China. There was plenty to keep the Government occupied and on 31 October the *News Chronicle* stated that it was clear that Churchill took foreign affairs seriously from the quality of people appointed to the task, not only Eden and Selwyn Lloyd, but also Lord Salisbury who was expected to have some overseeing role in foreign affairs.

The trip to Paris took shape. On 29 October Eden wrote to Churchill about the arrangements for the UN delegation. 'Chief delegates, apart from myself, will be the Minister of State, Sir Gladwyn Jebb & a Law Officer.'[38] In practice, this meant that Selwyn was the acting head of the delegation, though he was very glad to be able to draw on the experience of Sir Gladwyn Jebb, the United Kingdom's permanent representative at the United Nations since 1950. Selwyn flew to Paris on 4 November for the opening of the sixth session of the General Assembly. 'Here I am comfortably installed in Paris', wrote Selwyn to his parents from his suite in the Hotel Bristol. 'I still cannot quite believe that I am not dreaming it!!!'[39] The next day

he had his first conference in the office with other members of the
delegation ('As I know precious little about any of it, it will not be
unfunny')[40] before meeting some of the foreign delegates with whom
he would be dealing, not only in the next three months, but in many
cases over the next three years. These included Andrei Vyshinsky for
the Russians, Jules Moch for the French and Philip Jessup for the
United States. Selwyn noted down his impressions of those he met.
Of Vyshinsky he wrote:

> Although he led his country's delegation, I do not think that
> Vyshinsky counted for much in the Soviet hierarchy. He was
> regarded by them as a competent mouthpiece. I doubt whether he
> had any discretion about the substance of what he had to say. He
> often seemed worried; perhaps this was not surprising while Stalin
> was still alive. He spoke at interminable length, for four and a half
> hours on one occasion, and usually for not less than two hours. He
> could be offensive in debate, but was always courteous in private.
> When dealing with him, however, I could never forget his role as a
> public prosecutor. He seemed to have cold and cruel eyes.[41]

For his part Vyshinsky came to regard Selwyn as potentially a very
difficult opponent and once was reported as saying that he had never
had a harder capitalist nut to crack than Selwyn Lloyd.[42]

During the first week of the Paris General Assembly each country
made its speech in the general debate. Eden was to speak for Britain
on Monday 12 November, so Selwyn's task was to produce ideas and
drafts for that speech, one night staying up until 2 a.m. (fortified by
neat whisky) working in his suite at the Hotel Bristol with Evelyn
Shuckburgh, Eden's principal private secretary.[43] When Eden gave
his speech, much of it was taken up by rebuttal of Vyshinsky's fierce
polemic of the previous Wednesday.[44] This taught Selwyn two things
about international diplomacy, which he never forgot. First, many
hours will be fruitlessly spent on work that has to be jettisoned in the
light of developments; and second, Eden's great success at the
Conference caused much jealousy and resentment among the American delegation, notably when the British view on a Korean cease-fire
won the day. In Eden's absence it was formally ratified that Selwyn
was head of the delegation, but he shared with Gladwyn Jebb
responsibility for the political committee.[45] 'There is a lot of social
activity, and an endless round of meetings', Selwyn wrote home on 20
November. 'Foreign Affairs seem to be one mass of insoluble problems. At the moment it is very difficult to get at grips with anything,
but that no doubt is the novelty.'[46] Selwyn's task, both in and out of
conference, was greatly eased by the arrival of his Parliamentary

Private Secretary, David Ormsby-Gore (later Lord Harlech), who supplied a sophistication rather wanting in Selwyn, particularly on the representational side.[47] In these months in Paris in 1951–2 Selwyn became known for two things – the early hours at which he summoned his secretariat and (under instructions from the Treasury) his ruthless pursuit of economy. The delegation, which in previous years had totalled 110, was now held at 70, and weekly expenses were reduced by the (then) significant figure of £160. Although much of this advantage was lost on the occasion of Eden's visits (a weekend visit in December consumed £350 of the quarterly entertainment allowance of £2,000),[48] Selwyn was still known to Jacob Malik (later Soviet Ambassador to Britain) as 'Slasher Lloyd'. He was punctilious about paying all Bae's expenses and despatched sharp notes to Eden, as on 6 December when he wrote, 'I was disappointed to learn that in spite of your approval of my efforts to effect a 10% reduction in the costs of our delegation here the Ministry of Labour have found it necessary to ask that the names of two high level advisers from their department should be added to our delegation list.'[49]

But Selwyn's main sparring was with Vyshinsky, whose deliberate obstructiveness annoyed him considerably. As a newcomer to the United Nations he was merely having to come to terms with what was familiar to the old hands. Vyshinsky's career as a prosecutor had left him touchy, even cringing and subservient (as with Bulganin and Khrushchev when they were Vice-Premier and First Secretary respectively), but on the podium at the United Nations all inhibitions left him. Selwyn's first key-note speech was on 22 November. 'I have seen with my own eyes something of war and its by-products', he said. 'I loathe and detest war and the thought of war. My country has sacrificed countless lives and much wealth in two world wars. In Britain, as in Russia, we know what war means.'[50] In a speech six days later he made no attempt to hide his disappointment at the lack of progress. 'We have not hesitated to bring forward important modifications to plans which we have put forward in the past. Here really is the main cause for my disappointment at the Soviet delegate's speech. For in it I can find no trace that Mr Vyshinsky has even listened to what is new, let alone realised how we have moved forward.'[51] On 21 December Selwyn managed to discomfit Vyshinsky (and greatly amuse the Polish delegation) by his recounting of a 'Russian' proverb. Cabot Lodge, the American delegate, had made a helpful speech on disarmament with specific proposals. This was followed by a 45-minute harangue from Vyshinsky, full of sound and fury. Selwyn said in his reply that there was a Russian proverb to the effect that the cow that makes the most noise gives the least milk.

Vyshinsky, quivering with rage, said there was no such Russian proverb. He felt that Selwyn was the victim of a practical joke if he believed it to be Russian. Selwyn looked at his notes with pre-arranged care and came to his peroration:

'He says that I was a victim of a practical joke when I quoted as a Russian proverb the saying that the cow which makes much noise yields little milk. Well, I must say to Mr Vyshinsky how sorry I am for describing the proverb as a Russian one. It is, of course, Polish and I am surprised that Mr Vyshinsky – of all people – failed to recognise it. I will give it to him in Polish if he likes and if he will accept my bad pronunciation . . . (Selwyn then gave the "Polish version") . . . Perhaps the trouble is, Mr Vyshinsky, that Polish cows behave very differently from Russian ones – a dangerous deviation which I am sure you will now take rapid steps to correct in the interests of Slav solidarity.' And then with the kind of shift of tone of which the Cambridge Union and the 25 Club would have approved he concluded, 'Mr Vyshinsky in his speech used a phrase of which I took particular notice. He talked about countries marching to victory under the Communist banner. Well, they are not going to march over us or our allies, and let us have no mistake or misunderstanding about that. As that fact becomes increasingly clear to the East then I believe the hopes of peace become brighter.'[52] As the old year drew to its close it was agreed that Selwyn had made an impressive début. Selwyn gained a further insight into Vyshinsky's character when he attended a gala performance at the Paris Opera with the Vyshinskys. 'Sat in the President's box, all very grand', he wrote home. 'And for half the performance I sat in the front row beside Madame Vyshinsky. She looks as though she has been through it and wears a red wig.'[53]

After a fleeting visit to the Wirral for Christmas with Bae, Selwyn returned to Paris for the last four weeks of the Assembly. Things had not changed. Vyshinsky began the New Year with a speech lasting 2½ hours, shortly after which Selwyn said at an Anglo-American Press lunch that the principal attribute a UN delegate needed to bring to the debates was the Patience of Job, adding that the speeches of some delegates reminded him of the story of Bernard Shaw who, after listening to a string quartet, was told it had been playing for 12 years. 'Only 12 years', he replied, 'I thought we had been here much longer.'[54] Of much greater interest to Selwyn was his first extended meeting with Eisenhower. Eight years earlier Selwyn had been in Fort Southwick, wondering whether Eisenhower had taken the right decision to launch the D-Day invasion. Now he was lunching and negotiating with him. 'I went down to see General Eisenhower at his headquarters yesterday for lunch and arrived in the middle of a hail-storm which lifted the roof off one of the buildings of his headquarters', he wrote home on 18 January 1952. 'He was in very good form, looked very well and was very affable. He has a 22 oz. golf club which he uses purely for swinging purposes to loosen his shoulders. He swings it in his office while dictating letters. His handicap is 16 and he seems very keen.'[55] At the beginning of February Selwyn and Bae left Paris. It had been a bitter four weeks with the skies heavy with snow. 'We are really not sorry to leave Paris – the central heating is too hot and the food is too rich – we are both longing for some badly cooked English cabbage', he wrote home on Monday 4 February, the day of their departure.[56] So ended Selwyn's first experience of high international diplomacy.

Although little progress was made over disarmament, the months in Paris were politically important for Selwyn on two counts. First it gave him the opportunity to appear on a wider stage with world figures such as Eisenhower and Vyshinsky. He made his mark in a new circle. But he also made his mark with Eden, who came increasingly to trust his judgment and respect his industry. Although neither man was to know it, the next two years were to see prolonged absences of Eden from the Foreign Office. Selwyn had established himself in Paris as the safe pair of hands who could carry on and fill the vacuum. But it was not only for culinary reasons that he was glad to return home. When Michael Hadow had first told him in October that he would be away for some three months he felt that he was being shunted away. In fact, he referred specifically to this feeling in what was his first speech as Minister of State in the Commons during the Foreign Affairs debate on Tuesday 5 February when he gave the House details of the United Nations meetings in Paris. He rose at 9.30 p.m. and spoke of his three months of exile and hard labour. 'I longed for the atmosphere of this House with its interruptions and shorter speeches', he said. 'We have made great efforts to impress the Soviet *bloc* with the peaceful intentions of this country and to establish some kind of common ground with them, in spite of their constant and abusive rebuffs.'[57] After Selwyn's speech the House adjourned at 10.21 p.m. It was the last speech delivered by a government minister during the reign of King George VI.

On the morning of Wednesday 6 February Selwyn was working in the Minister of State's room at the Foreign Office when a telephone call reached Michael Hadow to say that the King had died in his sleep at Sandringham and that a Privy Councillors' meeting was to be held at Buckingham Palace in half an hour. The news was totally unexpected and no driver could be found to take Selwyn to the Palace.

Eventually a driver was located but by the time Selwyn arrived at the Palace the meeting had started and Selwyn was not admitted. This distressed him very much (he felt he was missing a piece of history) and the hitch contributed to his general sense of unease about most travel arrangements.* But he did go on to the Accession Council at St James's Palace and on 11 February attended the service in Westminster Hall when the coffin of the late King was received. 'The three Queens stopped just opposite where I was', he wrote home that day. 'They were clad in deep black with black veils. Queen Mary walked all the way up Westminster Hall . . . I felt very sorry for the Duke of Edinburgh who had Queen Mary, the Queen Mother and Queen Elizabeth to look after . . . He looked as if he felt that anything might happen to any of them at any time. However in fact they all played their parts with great dignity and composure. It was a very dignified piece of ceremonial, but Westminster Hall was bitterly cold and I should think there would be one or two incipient pneumonias further developed by tomorrow.' The cold was Selwyn's lasting impression of the funeral at Windsor four days later. 'No heating of any sort and everyone was frozen', he wrote, adding, 'The Foreign Royalties, etc as usual looked a pretty mixed lot.'[58] The death of King George VI at the age of 56 touched Selwyn very much. Since his first meeting with the King at a wartime investiture he had met him on occasions connected with his work at the Foreign Office and had found the King both informed and sympathetic. His sudden death, the return of the young Queen from Kenya and the sombre ceremonial that pervaded London touched his sense of history.

Selwyn was very conscious after his return from Paris that he must not neglect constituency business in the midst of his increasing government commitments. (The day before the King's funeral Selwyn attended his first Economic Policy Committee of the Cabinet.)[59] 'I'll have a word', was his usual expression to his assistant private secretary, James Reeve, at this time when a Wirral problem arose. Injustice and any form of local bureaucracy always stirred him into action. 'Is that fair?' was another of his phrases. He often did the unexpected, keeping his staff on their toes, and would follow through seemingly mundane problems until they were solved. David Ormsby-Gore, quiet and unobtrusive, was his link with back-bench opinion; Michael Hadow and James Reeve kept him in touch with Eden and

---

* 'You are going just 5 miles an hour too fast for my liking', he would say as a passenger. When travelling he saw England in terms of constituencies, not counties, pointing out whose constituency they were now entering – and what the majority had been at the last election.

Nutting at 'the other end of the corridor'. Geographically, the Minister of State's room is down towards the old India Office part of the building. When Gerald Reading became an additional Minister of State in November 1953 (the instigation coming from Selwyn), Selwyn and he built a good working relationship, whereas at the other nucleus of the Secretary of State's room it tended to be Eden and Nutting who 'had a word'. Selwyn was cautious. He never fired off missives regarding other departments – unlike Harold Macmillan at Housing, who frequently had his say on Foreign Office matters, as on 19 March 1953 when he submitted a memorandum *The European Defence Community and European Unity*, which Selwyn then had to deal with.[60] Selwyn soon learned – when attending Cabinet as Minister of State – that Foreign Affairs was a subject on which most ministers had a view. This was not the case with matters such as Housing or Transport. Selwyn was tidy in his dress, but not tidy in his papers, which were strewn around in a seemingly haphazard fashion. But he knew where everything was and was reluctant to throw anything out. He could be sentimental. When his old watch broke he remarked to James Reeve, 'And to think that this saw me all through the war.' And so he settled to the tripartite routine of the constituency, the House and the Foreign Office.

In the summer of 1952 the new Minister of Defence, Field Marshal Alexander (Churchill had initially reappointed himself to the post he had held during the war), was planning to visit the Korean battle-fields, one of the few political initiatives of his largely unhappy spell at the Ministry of Defence. As the mission was political rather than military Alexander felt that Selwyn, who had experience of both worlds, would be a useful companion. He wrote to General Mark Clark, the Commander-in-Chief of the United Nations forces in Korea, on 1 June 1952: 'I am hoping, if this is agreeable to you, to be accompanied by Selwyn Lloyd, Minister of State at the Foreign Office. He is an old friend of mine and I should much like to have the benefit of his advice and experience.'[61] There were three main aims behind their visit. First, they were going to see the British troops, second to impress upon Syngman Rhee, puppet ruler of the South, that popular support in the democracies would wane unless he behaved with higher respect for democratic practices, and third, to see if they could help in any way with the Panmunjom Armistice talks which were at a delicate stage.[62] They left London on 6 June, Selwyn accompanied by his new private secretary, Tony Duff, on a journey of 25,000 miles in 19 days. 'The plane Atlanta is the one (an Argonaut) which brought Queen to and from E Africa at the time of the King's death', noted Selwyn in the diary he kept of the visit.[63] En route they had talks with Nehru in Delhi, their first staging-post, and in Hong Kong with the Governor, Sir Alexander Grantham, both on Chinese economic pressure on the colony and on the Formosa Straits. Alexander and Selwyn Lloyd (no less than Mrs Stocks and Selwyn Lloyd) were an unlikely combination as they traversed the globe. Alexander, the legendary Field Marshal, with his urbane grace and perfect charm, was a reluctant politician and, like many military figures before and since, had not found it easy to move from the casque to the cushion. Selwyn, on the other hand, was now primarily a politician but found all his old interest in military matters reawakened and was fascinated by his visits to the front line and Mark Clark's headquarters. They were welcomed by Mark Clark and guards of honour on 10 June, before moving on to Tokyo on 11 June, where they had an audience of the Emperor. Selwyn jotted down his impressions:

> Meeting Mikado – Imperial Palace burnt down in air-raid during war – He now lives in what were offices – went into waiting room – Emperor came in very cordial shook hands for a long time – asked after Royal Family – asked A then me questioned in turn – Egypt-Sudan etc – I asked him whether he had been to Korea – he said no – other questions he said he was not sufficiently informed – he has a nervous twitch – cannot keep still.

Their audience was for an hour, the three men alone. 'Impression of rather pathetic and faded grandeur', recorded Selwyn, 'but he did not lack dignity.'[64]

The next day (12 June) the two men lunched alone with Mark Clark before flying on to Korea. Here they saw Commonwealth troops in the front line and the prisoner of war camp at Kojě ('rather a Belsenic appearance about the notorious camp 76 which the US troops had to assault', noted Selwyn)[65] before flying by helicopter to get a view of No Man's Land and the Chinese positions. After leaving Kojě Island they saw several million dollars' worth of ammunition blown up at a dump, the most expensive Field Marshal's salute he had ever received, as Selwyn remarked to Alexander.[66] On 16 June Alexander and Selwyn returned to Pusan where they met Syngman Rhee, 'whose age was never known, whether he was 90 or 95'. For a man who had locked up nineteen members of the Korean Opposition in a bus for eighteen hours (Alexander politely told Rhee, 'You know, Mr Churchill wouldn't approve of that') he was 'very frightened of committing himself to anything after I had asked a few questions', recorded Selwyn, 'to all of which he replied, "how can you expect me to answer?"' Rhee was absolutely inscrutable and when he offered Alexander and Selwyn a cup of tea Selwyn felt that, 'it might be full of some other liquid, but anyhow one took one's courage in one's hands and drank it.' Selwyn's impression was that despite his methods Rhee was in fact a great patriot, utterly unscrupulous and ruthless as a Dictator, but he believed in the independence of South Korea and he fought for it. Selwyn summed up his visit: 'The Koreans were much more likeable than I expected – they are obviously a turbulent and quarrelsome people . . . it is a tragedy that they cannot be a British protectorate for 25 years.'[67] On Tuesday 17 June before they left Korea, Selwyn, although privately critical of the British officials, feeling that many of them did not carry enough weight for the job, addressed the Embassy staff and spoke about the importance of their work in the context of foreign policy. The next day they flew to Canada, a home-coming for Alexander who had only recently relinquished the role of Governor-General. They dined at Government House, Ottawa, on 19 June and had four days of talks with representatives of the Canadian Government and the Canadian Chiefs of Staff, before travelling on to Washington on 23 June. In both Canada and America they gave their impressions of the current Korean situation and ended their round of talks by seeing President Truman ('He is obviously delighted at the thought of being out of office after the next election', recorded Selwyn)[68] at the White House on the morning of 24 June. The world tour ended with an overnight flight to Heathrow. Selwyn was met by Bae and Anthony Nutting, 'who whisked me off to the House of Commons to answer Parliamentary questions on Korea.'[69] On 1 July Selwyn wound up for the government in the debate on Korea. The whole experience consolidated Selwyn's position in the Foreign Office team. He broadcast on 8 July about the tour. 'By invading South Korea the Communist bloc threw down a challenge to the free world. Our only hope of peace for the long run lay in accepting that challenge promptly. The action of the United Nations led by the United States may well have prevented World War III.'[70] The tour boosted his self-confidence and he now felt that he had some first-hand experience of an important area of Foreign Office responsibility.

This was a happy time for Selwyn. Bae was expecting their first child and he was more at home with his political responsibilities. August looked as though it might be a quiet month. Instead it proved to be the first time that Selwyn was acting Foreign Secretary, an experience repeated many times in the next two years. 'Our principal excitement has been Eden's engagement', Selwyn wrote home on 13 August. 'He told me about it on Monday, and asked whether I was ready for a shock. I expected to be told that he or I were to leave the Foreign Office! . . . I am very glad for his sake – it will make all the difference to his life . . . One byproduct of the operation is that I will be in charge of the Foreign Office while he is on his honeymoon in Portugal.'[71] As Eden's engagement to Clarissa Churchill had been kept secret for some time, many people in Eden's social circle (Selwyn was one of the guests at the stag-party) began to wonder what they had said about Eden in front of Clarissa during the past few months. 'We have been feverishly racking our brains to think whether we said anything we should not have said, because of course we did not expect anything of this nature', wrote Selwyn.[72] In fact with Selwyn it was very much the reverse. When he had been a house guest at Petworth earlier in the year, a house party at which Clarissa Churchill had also been present, Selwyn had been very shocked by the uncomplimentary manner in which dinner conversation had turned to Eden, his master. The only person who did not join in the general denigration (at a time when figures like Randolph Churchill were referring to 'Jerk Eden') was Selwyn, who loyally stood up for him. Others present at Petworth that weekend now set about an embarrassed recovering of the traces.[73]

While the Edens were on their honeymoon Selwyn was thrown into frequent contact with Churchill. 'I have had a very busy time since I last wrote', Selwyn reported on 26 August. 'I went down to Chartwell on Sunday to have lunch with the Prime Minister. He was in bed when I got there, smoking a cigar and correcting the proofs of his book* . . . He was reviling the Foreign Office for being too long-winded in all its telegrams and reports and said that they should use monosyllables where possible, and anyhow be very much shorter. Just after that he remarked that there had been a substantial increase in the temperature that morning, so I said that if he practised what he preached, instead of using a long phrase like that he should have said it was warmer. "Ah, the spoken words are but the exhalations of the moment. I was referring to written words which last for ever." '[74] On 7 September Eden was back and in full charge, a relief for Selwyn as Bae's child, expected in August, had still not arrived. But on Tuesday 16 September, while he was hosting a reception at Carlton Gardens, Bae gave birth to a daughter, Joanna, at the Middlesex Hospital. One of the first telegrams of congratulation was from Winston and Clementine Churchill. The arrival of Joanna brought a new dimension into Selwyn's life. From the start he doted on his infant daughter and later in the 1950s (after his separation and divorce) Joanna filled a great vacuum. As the newspaper photograph establishes the public persona more than the columns of Hansard so the image of Selwyn

---

* *A History of the English–Speaking Peoples.*

and his young daughter, on the windswept tarmac of Heathrow Airport, was the one fixed in the political consciousness and it contributed to his aura of kindly vulnerability.

Shortly after the birth of Joanna, Selwyn was on his travels again, this time to the seventh session of the United Nations in New York. Travel and lengthy absences from home and Parliament were an inescapable part of the job. Small incidents from time to time leavened the political round and Selwyn was always prepared to smile at himself, as on the occasion in a NAAFI hut in the Middle East, miles from anywhere, when the officer in charge mistook Selwyn for the ENSA touring manager and began to make the appropriate noises.[75]

At the United Nations Selwyn crossed swords again with Vyshinsky – though privately he felt that the vitriol was 'a routine affair with no surprises'[76] – and became involved in negotiations over the Korean issue. 'We have been having our debate in the first Committee on Korea and as I expect you read, I spoke there on Thursday afternoon', he wrote home. 'Acheson spoke for two and three quarter hours, Vyshinsky for 3½ hours. My effort for 1 hr was therefore a comparatively minor one.' It was, though, a speech now based on first-hand knowledge and was the more effective by virtue of its relative brevity and informed reasoning. Selwyn acted as a conciliator between the Americans and Krishna Menon's Indian delegation. 'It has been a matter of keeping the Americans from denouncing the Indian plan.' On Tuesday 2 December he recorded, 'We passed the Indian Resolution on Korea last night by 53 votes to 5 – a great triumph for the U.K. delegation. If it leads to an armistice well and good, if it does not, we at least have done our best.'[77] But Selwyn remembered two other things about this time. It was after the vote on the Indian plan that Dean Acheson warned Selwyn, 'It does not pay to win victories over your friends.'[78] Also the American Presidential Election in November had cast a blight over the whole of the United Nations business that autumn and Selwyn found that people were, 'rather marking time'. Both he recalled in even more dramatic circumstances at the time of the next Presidential Election in November 1956 at the height of the Suez crisis. Symptomatic of this period of almost political moratorium was the luncheon he and Gladwyn Jebb had attended with the Russian delegation at which the talk was of 'the precise form of trouser that Gromkyo should wear at the Coronation.'[79] Before returning to England for Christmas (with Joanna as the focus of the festivities in the Wirral) Selwyn appeared live on American TV and was gratified to be regarded as one who did good by stealth and blushed to find it fame. After the 1945 San

Francisco Conference Eden was regarded as the man who had made the United Nations; after the seventh General Assembly his deputy was increasingly regarded as the man whom the United Nations had made.

The New Year began with the problems of Egypt and the Sudan very much to the fore. The Sudan was one of the many factors in the background of the Suez crisis and a constant source of friction between Britain and Egypt despite the Condominium of 1899 which settled a dual control over the Sudan. In October 1951 this agreement had been abrogated by Nahas Pasha, the Prime Minister of Egypt, who declared Farouk King of both Egypt and the Sudan. The question of Sudanese self-determination (and Britain's relationship with Egypt) had exercised Eden throughout 1952. Britain had 100,000 troops in the Suez base, guarding a mass of stores, not in Selwyn's opinion, 'a very suitable occupation for 100,000 people.' The possible withdrawal of British troops from the Canal Zone had been discussed in Cabinet, at Eden's request, as early as 31 March 1952.[80] In a Cabinet Defence Committee on 2 July 1952 Selwyn had warned that if the present Egyptian government remained in power, he foresaw 'a marked deterioration in our relations with Egypt and further outbreaks of trouble sooner or later'.[81] At a full Cabinet meeting on Thursday 24 July Selwyn reported on the *coup d'état* that had overthrown King Farouk and placed General Neguib in power in Egypt. He told the Cabinet that the coup 'aimed at the introduction of a revolutionary anti-capitalist regime.'[82] Two days later Eden warned the Cabinet that, 'an ill disposed Egyptian Government might at any time try to restrict or stop traffic going through the Suez Canal.'[83] Of one thing Eden was certain. The new Egyptian government was not going, 'to bounce the Sudanese into a union which was not to their liking.'[84] Patient diplomacy by Eden led to a signing of an agreement between Egypt and Britain on the future of the Sudan in Cairo on 12 February 1953. This gave the Sudanese self-government for a period of three years, at the end of which they would decide on full independence. For the next two months Selwyn's main task at the Foreign Office was in dealing with the aftermath of this agreement, a period which ended with his statement to the House of Commons on 2 April after his visit to the Sudan.[85] After the signing of the agreement (but not before, Selwyn always maintained the constitutional proprieties) Selwyn wrote to his father from the Foreign Office on 13 February:

We have had an extremely busy time this week with the final stages of the negotiations over the Sudan and the visit of the French

Ministers. I am sure that on balance the Sudan Agreement was a wise one to make. We have promised them independence again and again, and once one has done that it is futile to try and outstay one's welcome. By taking this bold step now I think we have a chance of retaining the goodwill of the Sudanese. It is rather interesting to know that in Calcutta, for example, the British population is now bigger and more business is done than at the time we ruled India. I went and had an audience with the Queen yesterday, and I enclose a copy of the Court Circular from The Times. I saw her alone . . . We talked about all the complications of the various kinds of uniform for the Coronation; about the flood damage which she had been visiting in Norfolk; about the christening which she had been to the day before of her Private Secretary's child. I told her that Joanna was being christened in the Crypt today. She then asked about the United Nations and we had a talk about what happened in New York. She talked about Mr. Eden's health.[86]

It was during President Tito's visit to London in March 1953 (a visit in which Selwyn was deeply involved) that Eden's state of health had first been commented upon in public. Eden's appearance was haggard and Tito was not the only one to express concern. His absences in 1953 were to have considerable political implications for Selwyn. Despite feeling far from well Eden flew to Washington on 4 March. Just before he left he heard of Stalin's illness – a stroke which was to prove fatal. Selwyn was, therefore, once more the acting head of the Foreign Office at a time of some delicacy following Stalin's death on 9 March. 'Eden's absence in some ways makes things easier because I don't have to worry what he is up to!', he wrote to his parents on 6 March. 'On the other hand there is an awful lot of paper.'[87] The boxes continued to arrive, even on Sundays. After Tito's visit and Eden's return from Washington Selwyn paid a visit to the Sudan from 21–27 March. He was pessimistic about Egyptian intentions towards the recently signed agreement. 'I do not think there is anyone who believes that Egypt will try to honour the agreement in good faith.'[88] In the Sudan Selwyn met the leaders of the various parties in an attempt to assess the current state of Egyptian and Sudanese nationalism. He found that Egyptian propaganda was being picked up on Sudanese radio and that anti-British feeling was running high. In these circumstances Selwyn was convinced that Britain had taken the right course in signing the agreement in February. 'Some have called this appeasement', he wrote later. 'I think that it was recognition of the facts.'[89] On his return he advised Eden that eventual

Sudanese independence was a political inevitability. In retrospect the most interesting part of the tour came, not in the Sudan, but in Cairo on 28 March. On that day Selwyn saw both Neguib and Colonel Nasser. Selwyn's first impressions of Nasser were favourable. He felt that he was informed and interested on many issues, not least on the Suez Base situation. But he was not taken in by outward Egyptian appearances. At the Cabinet meeting on 18 April 1953 Selwyn submitted a memorandum on the Sudan warning that Egyptian intentions were 'strictly dishonourable'.[90] Selwyn was now attending Cabinet meetings on a regular basis following Eden's (unsuccessful) gall-bladder operation on 12 April and the Foreign Secretary's recuperation at Chequers before a further operation in Boston in June. For Selwyn this was a vital period of political consolidation, the Westminster equivalent of stepping in at short notice to sing for the indisposed star tenor. (In fact between Wednesday 20 February 1952 and Wednesday 30 March 1955 Selwyn attended a total of 91 Cabinet meetings, before entering the Cabinet as Minister of Defence in his own right on 7 April 1955, a prolonged political apprenticeship extremely rare in the post-war period.)

During Eden's absence, Churchill became the titular head of the Foreign Office, but the day-to-day business was conducted by Selwyn.[91] As Selwyn wrote in a letter, 'The PM is in theory in charge of the Foreign Office, but does not do any of the detailed work.'[92] Lord Swinton, who knew Churchill's moods well, advised Selwyn to stand up for himself when faced by Churchill's intransigence. As Selwyn recalled of this period, 'On one or two occasions Winston was less than civil: then there came the time when I said that I had to make a speech at some international meeting, and I wanted Cabinet authority for what I wanted to say. Winston grumbled away opposite me. Why did I have to say anything at all? Anyhow what I proposed to say did not seem to him to make much sense. Although he had fallen into my trap I did have a slight shivering down my spine. I felt I was out of my class, competing in a league well above my own. However, I said as boldly as I could, "Prime Minster on an occasion like this, it would be quite impossible, indeed humiliating, for a representative of Her Majesty's government to remain silent. As for what I propose to say, it is an exact quotation from the speech which you yourself made on such and such a date." There was silence. We passed on to the next business. After that encounter, I got on well with Winston.'[93]

The most important event of this interim period was Churchill's speech on Foreign Affairs on 11 May in which he called for a summit between the leading powers. In the post-Stalinist era it seemed that *détente* could be placed on the political agenda. This was in flagrant defiance of Eden's known views and so annoyed Lord Salisbury (who at last had his overseeing role in Foreign Affairs) that resignations nearly followed. Selwyn was placed in a position of some delicacy, for on this issue he felt that Churchill's instincts were right. This led to a certain cooling of the relationship between himself and Eden, whose parting shot to Selwyn before departing for his operation in Boston was, 'Don't appease that Russian bear too much in my absence.'[94] Also Selwyn had worked closely with Churchill on the speech. In the week before the Foreign Affairs debate he had written to his parents that Churchill was 'in very good form, not at all difficult to deal with except when he has a brain wave and then it is not easy to divert him on to the right line again. We are getting to know one another quite well.'[95] In a long memorandum Selwyn had outlined possible topics for inclusion in Churchill's speech. These were:

1 A report on the NATO Council Meeting in Paris
2 A declaration of Britain's attitude towards Europe and the EDC
3 Our position in relation to the developments since Stalin's death
4 Possibly something on the Middle East
5 Possibly something on SE Asia[96]

Of these it was the third point for which the speech was remembered. On the morning of 11 May Selwyn went to see Churchill in his bedroom to work on the final draft of the speech. Churchill was 'in his full bedroom regalia – a bucket in which to flick the ash from his cigar – the cigar with a kind of strap round it to prevent it from disintegrating – rubber arrangement for his elbows so that they could rest comfortably upon his bed table – a whisky and soda.'[97] Selwyn's close involvement with Churchill at this time (he used to take Foreign Office telegrams to him late at night and while Churchill was engrossed in the business that had come in Selwyn used to read the next morning's papers newly delivered to the Prime Minister, thus saving himself an hour in the morning)[98] gave him a clear insight into the brittle, suspicious relationship that had grown up between Churchill and Eden. He described this retrospectively as follows:

When Anthony was about, he and Winston had continual arguments. I heard something of this from both sides. Egypt was the first bone of contention, in the end Winston gave way. On Summitry, Winston got his way, in the sense of floating the idea. On Europe, I did not follow the argument closely enough – I do not think Winston liked E.D.C. although much more favourable to

Strasbourg than Anthony. The most painful incident between them
to which I was a party was when Anthony was in Geneva for the
Indo-China conference. W & he had been [in] agreement about
holding off the US & Dulles from intervention to try to save Dien
Din Phow [sic]. Then at one stage, Winston wanted to make a
statement in the House in answer to a question, I think. I told him
that I thought A. would prefer him not to. He said he did not care
and would make it. I sent a copy to A. I then had A on the phone
from Geneva furious. I must stop the old man ruining everything. I
told W. He was furious. I could ring up and tell A he was PM and
would make the statement. I got A on the line, the line nearly
fused. I then said to A, I can do no more. I am connecting you to No
10 where W is, you must speak to him yourself. I went over to see W
later. He was in the little drawing room upstairs – furious – he
gave me a glass of brandy – and then stalked up and down the room
saying that A was the most selfish man he had ever known –
thought only of himself, had to do everything himself, was a prima
donna, and quite impossible to work with, etc., etc. As the storm
blew itself out, it transpired that W had truncated his statement to
please Anthony.[99]

Selwyn was very conscious of being caught between mighty op-
posites, especially as he had to maintain the momentum on issues
such as the future of the Canal Base in Eden's continued absence.
'We have always had serious doubts of Egyptian capacity now or in
the future to maintain the base; and the general attitude of the
Egyptians has not been such as to inspire confidence in their willingness to do so', he wrote to Churchill on 22 May. 'If we could get
effective American support for the principle of British command and
control in the essential installations the Egyptians may hesitate to
push matters to extremes. As this is really a matter of military
commonsense, it might be a good idea for some United States soldier
to be told all about it. General Robertson will be here for the
Coronation. I wonder whether it would be a good idea to suggest that
General Hull (the U.S. officer who was to go to Cairo) should come
over, ostensibly for the Coronation, but really to talk to
Robertson.'[100] Owing to Eden's illness Selwyn took a prominent part
in the meeting of the Commonwealth Prime Ministers that was timed
to coincide with the week of Coronation festivities.

In 1937 Selwyn had been master-minding the Coronation festivities
for the Hoylake Urban District Council; in 1953 he was prominent in
the ceremonies on the government's behalf. 'It has certainly been a
remarkable week', he wrote home on Sunday 7 June, during a pause

in the seemingly endless round of celebrations and meetings. 'We were up about 6 a.m. on Coronation Day, left here in all our finery about 7.20 and got into our seats at the Abbey about ten to eight. We were in the 4th row of the balcony above the peers looking straight down on the throne on which the Queen received homage towards the end. So we had an excellent view of all the processions.'[101] Attending the Queen throughout the long ceremonial, as Bishop of Durham, was Michael Ramsey. Selwyn and he had both gone a long way since Magdalene.

The second week of Coronation celebrations began with the world première of Benjamin Britten's specially commissioned opera *Gloriana*. Its cool reception from a largely non-musical audience is part of operatic history. Selwyn, who was no aesthete, contributed his mite. 'In the evening we went to the Covent Garden opera – everyone was there – we had quite good seats with a very good view of the Royal Box. The Queen looked lovely, but I expect you saw it on television', he wrote to his parents. 'The opera itself was only fairly good – a lot of noise and a rather unpleasant part of Queen Elizabeth's I's life, when she sentenced Essex to death, forming the plot.'[102] So protracted was the evening that a meeting of ministers called to Downing Street by Churchill did not end until 3 a.m. More to Selwyn's taste that summer was the reception he attended on 7 July to meet the returning members of the successful Everest expedition.

During Eden's extended absence that summer relationships with Number 10 became very fraught as the strains of non-stop activity began to be felt, even by Churchill. When Eden was undergoing his operation in Boston shortly after the Coronation, Selwyn continued to control the day-to-day affairs of the Foreign Office, but missives arrived daily from across the road. A typical one read, 'I have frequently noticed in Foreign Office telegrams the use of the word "prepared" when what is meant is "willing". In my experience the Foreign Office is often willing but never prepared.'[103] Unlike Eden, Selwyn and his team were unused to this kind of interference. (Eden gave Selwyn a very free hand as Minister of State.) But they soon came to expect the memoranda with the shaky initials WSC in red ink at the bottom. Selwyn's team – headed by Tony Duff – was of course smaller than Eden's and lacked the seniority of a Secretary of State's team. Also in 1953 Selwyn's assistant private secretary, James Reeve, was moved to the post of second secretary at the British Embassy in Washington and Selwyn had to interview various candidates for the vacancy, an interview which left a lasting impression on Reeve's eventual successor, John Leahy.

'Do you really want to be my private secretary?' asked Selwyn of the enthusiastic junior candidate in front of him in the Minister of State's room. After a disconcerting and momentary silence Selwyn continued, 'I can't think why, I certainly wouldn't want the job myself!'[104]

Life in the office after the Coronation was a strange mixture of the idiosyncratic and the conscientious. Selwyn instituted a system of bell signals, one ring for Tony Duff and two for John Leahy. Often in his impatience to get Tony Duff repeated rings would produce John Leahy, much to Selwyn's annoyance. His handwriting was notoriously illegible, so much so that at times Selwyn could not read it himself. 'It's not my job to read my handwriting,' he would say to John Leahy, 'that's what you're paid for.'[105] Yet even though the desk was in a cluttered state, Selwyn had the lawyer's gift for getting to the heart of the relevant document, a fact his staff soon learned as they did his various nicknames for colleagues. (Gladwyn Jebb was always The Deb, and most private secretaries at No 10 were dubbed Sir Horace, after the notorious Sir Horace Wilson of pre-war Chamberlain days.)[106]

At the end of June, Churchill was entertaining the Italian Prime Minister, de Gasperi, in London and on 23 June a dinner was held at Downing Street for the Italian delegation. During the course of the evening, Churchill was taken ill and it was clear to his staff that he had had a stroke. The next morning Churchill took a Cabinet, but was unable to answer questions in the House in the afternoon. On 25 June he was driven secretly to Chartwell and was not expected to last the weekend. The extent of Churchill's illness was disguised from all but a restricted inner circle. Selwyn had sent a top secret minute to Churchill on Sudan and on 28 June received a reply from John Colville, saying that Churchill was 'not now in a position' to deal with this suggestion and instructing him to 'consult Lord Salisbury in respect of any action which you and he think appropriate and desirable'.[107] Although it was made clear on Churchill's behalf that the Minister of State would be 'responsible for the day to day conduct of the Foreign Office', Lord Salisbury became the titular head of the office in the absence of both Churchill and Eden.[108] Selwyn was intensely disappointed that he had been denied the outward recognition of the inner reality and had to be personally reassured by Churchill (who astonished his doctors by the speed of his recovery) that he was very much the Number One Minister of State when Lord Reading became an additional Minister of State on 11 November 1953. Selwyn, who got on well with Reading personally, was nevertheless touchy and somewhat insecure about his status vis-à-vis the Marquess, as had been seen when Reading was an Under-Secretary in the Foreign Office. At a formal dinner given at Number 10, Lady Churchill had made the arrangements for the seating plan at the top table. Selwyn, as Minister of State, found himself at the far end of one of the subsidiary prongs, in the company of Christopher Soames and John Colville. It was a convivial evening of relaxed gossip and a relief at being spared diplomatic conversation with foreign dignitaries. But it was clear that Selwyn was not entirely happy with the arrange-ments. Next morning he rang John Colville at Number 10 to ask if it was the Prime Minister's wish that the order of precedence should be changed. Why had the Under-Secretary at the Foreign Office been placed on Lady Churchill's left and Selwyn, as Minister of State, banished to outer darkness? It was explained politely that Lady Churchill had placed the Marquess of Reading on her left purely as a matter of social precedence. Selwyn was still not happy. Later in the morning he put through another call. Did that mean that all the embassies were going to have to change? It would make a big difference if Under-Secretaries came before the Minister of State. Would Colville ask the Prime Minister if this was his wish? Only when Colville tactfully pointed out to Selwyn that if such a question was put Selwyn would no longer be Minister of State by 6 p.m. did he desist from further inquiries.[109] This was the insecure side of Selwyn, despite his growing experience. He was not, however, the only one with such insecurities. On his return to London at the end of September Eden could reasonably have expected some indication from Churchill as to when he might be retiring from office. Nothing materialised, and Eden became increasingly philosophical about the situation, as Selwyn noted in his diary on 5 January 1954:

> Eden discussed personal problems. There have lately been rumours that W.S.C. wanted at last to go. He said something to that effect just before Christmas. He was very disappointed with Bermuda and quite ill there. The family are reputed to have urged him to go. Rab and Harold had indicated the same to Anthony. Pitblado, however, at No. 10 had said to Evelyn Shuckburgh that the prospect had receded during the last day or two. Anthony said to me that he had ceased to worry about the future, and events could develop without his interference. He did, however, want me to know that if he did form a Government, I would certainly be in the Cabinet.[110]

Churchill showed no signs of wanting to retire in 1954, even though Harold Macmillan had told him directly in July that he ought to go. Part of the reluctance stemmed from Churchill's growing belief that Eden had not the capacity for the Premiership.[111] And then there was

Eden's uncertain health. At one Cabinet during Eden's absence Churchill had said to the Minister of Agriculture, Thomas Dugdale, 'I'm very worried about this myxomatosis. You don't think there's any chance of Anthony catching it?'[112] Indeed when Churchill called Eden and Butler to the Cabinet room in March 1955 to tell them of his retirement, he at first motioned Butler to sit at his right hand before swiftly correcting the slip.[113] The general air of unease communicated itself to Selwyn, who stood to gain as much as most in any government reshuffle. At a party at the Austrian Embassy on 11 December 1953 Selwyn had asked Clarissa Eden if she could press for him to be included in the Cabinet (hence Eden's reassurance to Selwyn on 5 January 1954).[114] Even for a casual remark at a social gathering this was an extraordinarily naïve thing for Selwyn to have done but symptomatic of the air of frustration felt in a period of standstill. (Nobody was to know at that stage that the Conservatives were to be in office for another decade.)

Eden was away at the Berlin Conference of the four occupying powers in January and February 1954 and Selwyn once more held the fort at home, attending Cabinet on a regular basis. His draft papers (particularly one suggesting some form of 'arbitration' over the Canal Base issue)[115] did not escape Eden's gimlet eyes and the lines buzzed with corrective telegrams.[116] 'I shall not be sorry when Eden & Nutting come back. It is rather difficult to act as a go-between [between] Winston & Eden.'[117] The old suspicions in Eden that Selwyn was coming too much under the influence of Number 10 surfaced (as they had done at the time of Churchill's speech on *détente*). These feelings communicated themselves to Eden's secretariat and when Eden flew back to London on 19 February 1954, Evelyn Shuckburgh noted in his diary, 'Selwyn Lloyd, true to form, is not going to be in town when we get home'.[118] In fact Selwyn had a long-standing engagement in his Wirral constituency for that day (a Friday) and wrote independently in his diary, 'Anthony came back from the Berlin Conference this day; I was unfortunately not able to meet him, but Lord Salisbury and Sir Ivone Kirkpatrick went to the Airport to welcome him.'[119] Waiting for Eden on his return was a long letter from Selwyn in which he expressed his doubts about his suitability to represent Britain at the forthcoming opening of the Sudanese Parliament. 'Do you think I am senior enough?', asked Selwyn.[120] In his own hand Eden added, 'Nobody could do this so well, & I certainly think that you should go, & so does the PM. It could be a most useful visit. We will have a word about it.'[121] This talk, which embraced a general discussion of the foreign situation, took place on Sunday evening (21 February) at Carlton Gardens.

Eden was all charm and assured Selwyn of his indispensability. Accordingly Selwyn left London Airport on 27 February with his private secretary Tony Duff for what was to be the most dramatic of his missions as Minister of State. During the flight there were confused reports as to whether Neguib had been ousted in Egypt and, even if not, there was considerable doubt as to whether he would now risk coming to Khartoum for the opening of the Sudanese Parliament. On arrival Selwyn went to the Governor-General's residence (which was on the site where General Gordon had been murdered). The next day not only had Neguib arrived but also a belligerent crowd of his supporters. They were pushed back by the police, but in the ensuing fight the British commandant of the police was killed, and there were other casualties. Selwyn showed great calm throughout this riot, walking on an inner balcony with Neguib and Tony Duff. The only moment of anxiety was when it looked as though the crowd were coming in over the garden wall and would storm the residence from the back. By this time Neguib had joined Selwyn in a room where all the spears which had been captured at Omdurman were displayed and Selwyn told Neguib that if one of the Ansar sect broke through he might recognise grandpa's spear and come upstairs and use it.[122] Selwyn added that duplicating General Gordon's end on an Anglo-Egyptian basis would cement the relationship between the two countries.[123] Neguib was rather bemused by both of these observations. As he always seemed to be grinning it was not clear whether he thought them appropriate or not. Selwyn stayed on in the Sudan in the aftermath of these tragic events for further talks with Sudanese officials and representatives of the British community. On his return to London he gave full reports to the Cabinet and to the Queen Mother at an audience at Clarence House ('She was interested in the Sudan as she and the late King had stayed there').[124]

Selwyn's time as Minister of State was coming to its end. The Suez Canal Base agreement was signed on 27 July 1954, the inevitable ingredient (said the dissentient 'Suez group' of Conservative MPs) for the disasters that were to unfold almost two years to the day. The last months of Selwyn's first spell at the Foreign Office were concerned with the Persian oil settlement (the great Middle Eastern problem inherited by Eden in October 1951) and the beginnings of the Cyprus question, in which Selwyn was to be deeply involved before the decade was out. On the Persian question, the authority of the Shah had been re-established in August 1953 and the oil industry was brought under the control of an international organisation in which Britain held a 40 per cent share stake. Oil was once more available to the West and on 5 August Selwyn noted in his diary, 'I gave a Press

Conference to announce the Persian oil settlement.'[125] Twelve days later Selwyn was holding a meeting on Cyprus when a telephone message was received from his elder sister Dorice. His father had died in his 90th year. One of the first messages of condolence he received was from President Eisenhower, whom he now knew not only on a political basis, but from personal meetings at the John Barry Ryan home at Newport, Rhode Island. After the recess Selwyn was a rather lonely and sombre figure. His mother was alone at 32 Queen's Road and there were the first signs that all was not well with his own marriage.

Following the Party Conference at Blackpool in October Churchill conducted a limited reshuffle of his administration. The main changes involved David Maxwell Fyfe leaving the Home Office and Welsh Affairs for the Woolsack (he was succeeded by Gwilym Lloyd George) and Harold Macmillan moving from Housing and Local Government to Defence. Duncan Sandys was promoted from Supply to the Ministry of Housing and Local Government and the jigsaw was completed by Selwyn filling the vacancy at the Ministry of Supply, the first time he had headed his own department.

Selwyn's time at the Foreign Office as Minister of State from October 1951 to October 1954 can be seen in retrospect as one of the most rewarding and happy periods in his political career. It was a good time to come into government. There was the freshness and vigour of a new administration coming to office (a similar sense of excitement at the start of the 1964 Labour Government is communicated by Tony Benn in his diaries, *Out of the Wilderness*) and the job that Selwyn was asked to do was one that suited his temperament and his administrative talent. He served a master for whom he had, particularly in the first two years, great political sympathy, but even when their views differed Selwyn still retained great respect, though not as has often been thought, undue deference. That friendship was to deepen in the years after Eden's retirement. Eden had given him his opportunity and Selwyn had taken it. He particularly valued the chance it had been to serve with Churchill. Though Churchill at first had regarded him as 'that most dangerous of men – the clever fool',[126] he soon came to revise that opinion. On 15 July 1954 John Colville wrote to Selwyn, 'Since second-hand compliments are best, I thought I might tell you that the P.M. was so impressed by the excellence of your speech last night that he dilated on its merits while we were having a 11 p.m. – 1.0 a.m. Bezique game to an extent which was positively disturbing to the game.'[127]

So Selwyn left the Foreign Office, albeit temporarily, with some regrets. He never came to terms with the essential insecurity of the political process. Three years had been a long time in one post, but over the next two years he seemed (certainly to the despatcher of telegrams at the Leas School) constantly on the move. The significance of the Ministry of Supply was that it moved him out of the orbit of one master, Eden, into the orbit of another and eventually even more significant one, Macmillan, behind whom he now took his place on the political escalator. On Thursday 21 October 1954 Selwyn Lloyd attended the Swearing-in Ceremony in the Lord President's room at the House of Lords and took up office as Minister of Supply.

8

His Master's Voice?

The Ministry of Supply had begun in July 1939 as a ramshackle organisation in which an inventive and industrious civil servant (such as Oliver Franks) could profitably run his own hare. Within two years it was an organised ministry with immense responsibilities for the war effort and for civilian provision, comprising the War Production Department, hived off from the old Board of Trade, and control over raw materials needed for both military and civilian purposes. After the war this centralisation ended and the old departments reasserted themselves, and although there were important agencies such as the Steel Board which came under the Ministry of Supply, the centralist days were over. Indeed there was a move in 1951 to abolish the department altogether (and it was wound up in 1957). When Selwyn became Minister of Supply in October 1954 he was moving from a junior position in a big field to a senior position in a contracting field. Nevertheless Eden (who had tried to get him the Ministry of Transport)[1] urged Selwyn to accept the post. Rab Butler told Selwyn that Churchill was very pleased with the rather courtly terms of Selwyn's acceptance of the offer.[2] Situated in the Shell Mex Building in the Strand, the Ministry of Supply was a nuts and bolts department, dealing with practical issues such as Ordnance Factories, Harwell and Defence funding, and was the kind of department to which Selwyn was suited, arguably more so than the Foreign Office or the Treasury which had a tendency to deal with more generalised concepts. However, the quality of service at the Foreign Office was so good that Selwyn at first missed the likes of Michael Hadow and Tony Duff until he came to realise that E. G. Cass (his principal private secretary and formerly secretary to Attlee and Churchill at Number 10) was of the highest calibre and no 'Sir Horace'. (Throughout his career Selwyn was very fortunate in his private secretaries and the list includes some of the most distinguished civil servants of their generation.)

Selwyn's predecessor at Supply had been Duncan Sandys which (as one civil servant cryptically commented) meant that Selwyn Lloyd was very popular on arrival.[3] The senior officials soon found that the new Minister was a man who knew what he was talking about in defence terms and this was valuable at a time when the issue of the Hunter and Swift aircraft was to the fore. Selwyn started the day early at Shell Mex House, well briefed and energetic. He had no senior figure looking over his shoulder. The Ministry gave him executive responsibility over a domestic industrial field, an important widening of experience, and from 1954 Selwyn never laboured under the disadvantage of having served exclusively in the field of foreign affairs (like Eden). His civil servants remember him as being conscientious, intelligent and loyal. Duncan Sandys had worked unnecessarily long hours, which at times had driven the staff to distraction with the constant attention to the most pettifogging detail. Selwyn cut a swathe through all this and got the measure of a brief very quickly. The Ministry of Supply was a technical department and Selwyn felt he would need six months to learn what it was all about. On 17 December 1954 he wrote to Richard Casey, Minister for External Affairs in Australia, with his impressions of his new post. 'I am finding my new department very different, very large and very bewildering. I am afraid it is obviously going to take months for me to play myself in. I am the sponsoring Minister for iron and steel, engineering, electronics and aircraft manufacture. In addition to that I have a lot of the functions of the Ministry of Aircraft Production during the war and of the old Ministry of Supply organisation before the war. It is an enormous field but one of fascinating interest.'[4] With his Second Army background he was very conscious of the security aspects of his job (one could never imagine Selwyn leaving a bundle of official papers in Prunier's), when travelling by train he reserved the whole compartment and pulled the blinds down. ('So they can't see what we are getting up to with our women', he used to joke to the secretaries.)[5] Yet he was nicely informal on official visits. When on a tour of the RAF Ordnance Factory at Nottingham he was due to be picked up by car to go on to the Rolls-Royce factory at Derby. Lord Hives, the chairman of Rolls-Royce, had sent a chauffeur with a new automatic model to Nottingham. As Selwyn so much admired this shining motor, the chauffeur asked if Selwyn would like to try it. Not only did he try it but he drove it all the way to Derby without batting an eyelid. Supply may not have been a glamorous department but it was an important cog in the government machine. The staff appreciated the way that Selwyn regarded it as being important in its own right and was never perceived as being a bird of passage waiting for something better to turn up (which was particularly true of his successor, Reginald Maudling). He worked long but, unlike Duncan Sandys, sensible hours. As he soon became aware that the shortage of scientists, engineers and technologists had blighted Britain's industrial performance in the post-war age, he proselytised on their behalf, particularly when visiting schools. When he was principal guest at Fettes Founder's Day in June 1955 he stressed this in his speech, hoping that many sixth formers would consider careers in those fields. The last time he had appeared on that platform, he said, he had been a weaver.[6]

Selwyn went to Shell Mex House for the first time on the morning of 22 October 1954 to meet James Helmore, the Permanent Secretary, and Cyril Musgrave, the Deputy Permanent Secretary. His first working day (25 October) was a good indication of the range of his new responsibilities. In the morning he held a meeting with James Helmore and other officials to discuss the future of the Comet aircraft (two of which had been lost in mysterious circumstances in January and April 1954) and the prospects for the de Havilland firm, 'neither of which', he recorded in his diary, 'looks very bright'.[7] He attended his first Cabinet meeting as Minister of Supply that day to discuss issues arising from the European Coal and Steel community.[8] Later that week he attended a meeting of the Defence Review Committee (the difficulty of Supply was traditionally in its relationship with the Service Ministries) and was soon involved in questions of defence procurement economies, the Admiralty seeking savings of £3½m (a first introduction to the delicate balancing acts he would himself have to perform at both Defence and the Treasury). Selwyn was particularly concerned about the effect of these cuts on unemployment in Northern Ireland. In November he attended the motor-cycle show at Earls Court and studied film on atomic tests in Australia.

At the end of November Churchill celebrated his eightieth birthday and Selwyn attended (and contributed to) the presentation of the Graham Sutherland portrait of the Prime Minister, 'a remarkable example of modern art', as Churchill dubbed it. In the furore which followed, most Conservative MPs were interested not so much in the merits or demerits of Sutherland's doomed portrait (it was shortly to be destroyed on the orders of Lady Churchill)[9] but on whether Churchill would now gracefully retire and allow Eden a clear run into the next election due before October 1956. Selwyn was always of the firm belief that Churchill overstayed his welcome. It was time, he felt, for a clean break with the past. But the year ended with Churchill still at the helm.

The year 1954 had been an important transitional one for Selwyn. He had consolidated his political reputation, but there had been sadnesses too, notably the death of his father. His marriage, sadly, was moving to separation. It was also the year in which he began his long association with the Ensesa family and their growing holiday complex on the Spanish coast near S'Agaro. For some years Selwyn and Bae, with their friends Toby and Leo O'Brien had travelled to Spain. Toby O'Brien, a public relations consultant, had been commissioned by the Spanish to investigate tourist possibilities and export facilities, and it was on one such visit in June 1954 that Selwyn first met the Ensesas. From the time of that first visit until his death hardly a year passed without a visit to the Ensesa's hotel on the spur above the bay. It became a latter-day Aix-les-Bains. Selwyn was known by the local community as 'El Ministro', taking part in local customs such as skittles and 'cheese swinging' in which he took on the local expert 'El Maestro' in this exotic Spanish pastime. He also indulged in one of his main relaxations, swimming, on more than one occasion setting off with a pilot boat and swimming for a mile or more round the bay itself. In the difficult years that lay ahead S'Agaro was to become an even more important part of his life.

The early months of 1955 saw Selwyn working closely with Harold Macmillan for the first time. On 9 February the Ministry of Defence and the Ministry of Supply combined in the publication of a White Paper *The Supply of Military Aircraft*.[10] This paper took into account the volatile military situation following the outbreak of the Korean War and the need to re-equip the RAF for any emergencies after 1957. With Viscount de L'Isle, the Air Minister, Selwyn visited the Ministry of Supply establishment at Boscombe Down in the aftermath of the publication of the White Paper. Selwyn worked hard at these administrative aspects of his job and was regarded as an efficient Minister. A Cabinet minute of 22 February 1955 recorded that, 'In discussion there was general support for the recommendations put forward by the Minister of Supply.'[11] He began to be more assured in his parliamentary performances too. Richard Crossman, never less than an exacting critic, noted in his diary for 3 March 1955:

Selwyn Lloyd, as Minister of Supply, was replying to the accusations about aircraft production made by Woodrow (Wyatt) the night before, and within half an hour he had turned the debate into a vote of censure on the Opposition, with Arthur Henderson, George Strauss and Shinwell bobbing up to defend themselves and ask for approbation for what they had done.[12]

Selwyn attended his last Cabinet in Churchill's administration on 30 March when he reported on the series of one day strikes at Renfrew Airport.[13] With a newspaper strike (and a threatened rail strike) this was a time of industrial difficulty Eden was determined to resolve as speedily as possible as he prepared to enter his belated inheritance. On 5 April Selwyn was called to a meeting in the Cabinet Room at 10 Downing Street where Churchill bade farewell to the non-Cabinet members of the government. From there he was called to see Eden to hear about his new responsibilities.

Eden had promised Selwyn in January 1954 that he would be in the Cabinet, a promise handsomely upheld when he appointed Selwyn to the post of Minister of Defence (always in Tory eyes a psychologically important post) to replace Harold Macmillan who had become the new Foreign Secretary. In any successful politician's career there is the crucial promotion and for Selwyn it came on 7 April 1955 as he moved from the relatively humdrum area of Supply to the exposed heights of Defence. Eden conducted only a limited reshuffle of the Cabinet he had inherited from Churchill (the big reshuffle came in December 1955) and it largely centred on the chain of events occasioned by his own departure from the Foreign Office. Arguably this was the first mistake of his Premiership and he should have embarked on a more radical reconstruction immediately to avoid any accusations that his government was merely a continuation of Churchill's. There was certainly much disappointment in the junior ranks of the party. Nine days after becoming Prime Minister Eden announced that a General Election would be held on 26 May. This was a very brave and, in the outcome, politically successful decision. Eden had waited so long for the Premiership and although the Conservatives went into the election (in less volatile days) with a 4 per cent lead in the opinion polls, there was no guarantee of victory and had things gone wrong Eden would have taken from Bonar Law the unenviable title of the shortest serving Prime Minister of the century. For a man who had been trained to win the political Derby from 1938 to have fallen as soon as he came out of the electoral starting gate in 1955 would have been a consummation perhaps even more devastating than the one that eventually overtook him in January 1957. Although Rab Butler's Budget on 19 April (6*d.* off income tax among other measures) helped the Tory campaign, Selwyn was not confident about the outcome. 'I am not at all sure about the result', he wrote to Richard Casey in Australia on 6 May, the day he was adopted in the Wirral. 'The whole thing hangs on such very small margins. The Labour Party have put a lot of specious bribes like higher public assistance rates, free teeth and spectacles, etc. Whether the electorate will see through it is not clear. Also, as you so well know, any Government which has been in office does create a number of small irritations with it.' Looking to the future, Selwyn continued: 'If we do get back and I keep this job, I am looking forward to a very happy and interesting time. Having worked for three years with Anthony Eden I think I understand how his mind works. My six months at the Ministry of Supply have given me a considerable insight into the armament producing side of things and during those six months I got on very well with Harold Macmillan.' But Selwyn was under no illusions about the tasks of reorganisation that would be necessary if the Minister of Defence was to have the requisite executive control. 'The task of the Minister of Defence in this country is a very difficult one. He is really a planner and co-ordinator. He has no executive power. He is not even Chairman of the Defence Committee. The Prime Minister is that. But time will reveal its real scope.'[14]

Election or not Selwyn was Minister of Defence and was never more glad that, whatever might happen nationally, at least the Wirral was a safe seat. Before moving to the Ministry of Defence (then in Storey's Gate) he had preliminary talks with his new principal private secretary, W. N. Hanna, and met the rest of his Private Office staff on 12 April. Selwyn was at the Ministry of Defence in a transitional period, at a time when the Service Chiefs had direct access to the Prime Minister. (The First Lord of the Admiralty was commonly known as the Last Lord of the Admiralty.) Its three broad functions were (1) allocating available resources between the three services (2) settling the question of any general administration of a common policy for the three services (3) the administration of the inter-service organisation. The second of these responsibilities entailed liaison with the Ministry of Supply, as did the civilian aspects of the job on research and development. In both of these areas he had already worked with Harold Macmillan.[15] One of the most important political factors in gaining the confidence of the Chiefs of Staff was that the Defence Minister should be a confidant of the Prime Minister. Selwyn passed this test. However, by the nature of the command chain (and the presence of three independent Service Ministries) things tended to be hedged round with compromise, and the later federated structure adopted under Mountbatten by the Wilson government was something which Selwyn anticipated and of which he approved.

On Wednesday 4 May Selwyn took the chair at his first meeting of the Standing Committee of Service Ministers. 'We discussed a mixed bag of topics', he noted in his diary, 'ranging from education allowances for the children of Service parents to the desirability of providing a "grace and favour" residence near London for a senior retired

officer. The education allowance is a very difficult one, on which the
Treasury have been holding out on the Services for some years.'[16] On
5 May he lunched with Montgomery at the House of Lords to discuss
defence matters. Ten years before to the day both had been on
Lüneburg Heath. Now, in a reversal of roles, Selwyn found that he
was the pursued whose ear was sought. He became the recipient of a
succession of letters from Montgomery. ('Thank God you are safely
back in the Ministry of Defence', Montgomery wrote after the
election. 'If at any time I can lend a hand, do not hesitate to summon
me for a talk.')[17]

The Election itself was one of the quietest and dullest of the
century. Selwyn's main contribution was in giving an election broadcast on radio at 9.15 p.m. on 18 May. (During his visit to the BBC he
met Gilbert Harding again, for the first time since Cambridge Union
days.) His brief was to speak on foreign policy and he gave a review of
the developments in that field over the previous four years, mention-
ing in particular the work done on disarmament at the United
Nations.[18]

On Election day Selwyn toured the constituency with Bae. 'Things
seem to be going very well', he wrote in his diary.[19] Nationally the
Conservatives improved on their 1951 position, winning 344 seats
against the Labour Party's 277. The Liberal Party, under whose
banner Selwyn had fought in the 1920s, was now reduced to a mere 6
seats. In the Wirral too Selwyn increased his majority, the result
being:

J. S. B. Lloyd (Conservative)	33,027
R. B. Chrimes (Labour)	15,976
Majority	17,051

On the day the results were announced (27 May) Selwyn attended
his one hundredth Cabinet meeting. All seemed set fair for the next
five years.

Eden retained his Cabinet *en bloc*, admitting to Robert Carr that
he ought to have moved Rab Butler from the Treasury but that after
Sidney Butler's death (in December 1954) he flinched from the
decision because it would have been an additional blow for Rab.[20]
For his part Selwyn now looked forward to 'a number of years in a
congenial department',[21] a desire which surfaced again in the summer
of 1960 when he asked Macmillan for a guarantee that he would have
some years in the Treasury as the price for going there, a promise
Macmillan rashly gave. Yet within eight months he was moved to the
Foreign Office. His short tenure of the Ministry of Defence was,

therefore, an unusual blend of the inconsequential and the significant. It was insignificant in defence and military terms because his time in office did not coincide with the key period (January–March) which saw the preparation of the Annual Defence White Paper, or with the defence debate in February. In the 1955 debate Harold Macmillan had thought Selwyn – then still at Supply – had spoken 'with remarkable skill'.[22] The timetable for the 1956 White Paper was not unlike that of a Budget. In the late part of the year the department began to mull over the issues for the annual review; the review itself was written in January and February before going to the Defence Committee of the Cabinet for consideration, before the annual two-day defence debate. Thus April to December, the period of Selwyn's tenure, almost exactly coincided with what was in relative terms a lull. Yet it was a significant time for two reasons. It established him as a front-rank minister (and there are even those who believed that Eden intended to have him as Foreign Secretary all along and was using Defence as the necessary halfway house so that Selwyn could attain the necessary patina of seniority) and it was one of the first examples of his ability to get *une idée en marche*. For an old Free-Trade Liberal Selwyn was quite a centralist at heart. He believed in the five-year forward plan (an idea which surfaced again at the Treasury) and took the first steps on long-term planning of defence expenditure. He also considered the whole question of the future of National Service and took the first steps (against considerable opposition) towards defence unification by appointing a fourth member of the Chiefs of Staff Committee (Marshal of the Royal Air Force Sir William Dickson). On 21 November 1955, Selwyn wrote to General Ismay, Secretary General of NATO:

> I am glad that you feel that the idea of a Chairman of the Chiefs of Staff Committee is well worth a trial . . . I think the new arrangement will take some of the load off the other three Chiefs of Staff and be a great help to me.
>
> The more difficult matter is the relationship of the Minister of Defence with the three Service Ministers, and pressure is growing here for a change. I am rather trying to avoid that issue – at all events for a few months – until Dickson has settled in and the next lot of Service Estimates are over.[23]

Yet Selwyn established a good relationship with the three service Ministers, de L'Isle at the Air Ministry, J. P. L. Thomas (later Viscount Cilcennin) at the Admiralty, and Antony Head at the War Office. He had worked with de L'Isle at Supply and knew J. P. L. Thomas well from the days with Eden, Thomas being one of Eden's closest political and personal associates. He also managed to be firm, yet tactful, with the Service Chiefs, not the easiest of tasks when they included such towering personalities as Lord Mountbatten and Field Marshal Sir Gerald Templer. After his relatively quiet profile at Supply Selwyn found himself drawn more into the representational side of things, not something he always found to his liking, quite apart from the time consumed, noting in his diary for 2 June that at the Royal Tournament, 'having to take the salute after each item . . . proved something of a bore'.[24] As a result he held discussions with his principal officials at the Commons rather than at Storey's Gate, something which did not go down too well with the department who had been accustomed to meeting their political chief at the Ministry. As at the Foreign Office it took Selwyn some time to adjust to the new personnel, though one of his principal officials had happy recollections of him as a Minister and a human being, always friendly and good to work with, and with a strong sense of the comic, an alleviating advantage in the severe administrative world of defence.[25]

W. N. Hanna, who served four successive Defence Ministers – Alexander, Macmillan, Selwyn Lloyd and Walter Monckton – came from an Admiralty background and was private secretary in 1952 because on the rota basis that operated at the time it was the Admiralty's turn to provide one. Of the four Ministers Selwyn was by far the most demanding in time, not because he was inconsiderate, but because he worked so hard. 'What's this?', he would bark as more paper came in. 'What am I supposed to do with this?' When Selwyn moved on to the Foreign Office, Walter Monckton gave the staff the impression of being more friendly as he put his arm round people's shoulders when going down corridors, but this was misleading, he was so short-sighted he needed to. Selwyn was more open and frank. When he first moved to Storey's Gate he sold his full-bottomed wig to a Liverpool lawyer, saying to Hanna as he packed it up, 'I shan't be wanting this again'. Hanna wondered if he might be wanting it again if he went to the Woolsack. Selwyn at once discounted this as a possibility, because of his Methodist background. Later the prospect of the Woolsack appealed to him more and he regretted that he had disposed of the wig.* He was less decisive than Harold Macmillan, but he was seen as a man who cared about the problems with which he was dealing, as in his attempt to get the Treasury to accept the principle of boarding-school allowances for all ranks, and not just officers.

---

* For the story of how he acquired Hartley Shawcross's wig when Speaker see ch. 15.

In the Cabinet minutes this issue is referred to as *Armed Forces: Education Grants.*[26] In practice this meant a boarding-school allowance for the children of officers stationed abroad. Selwyn surveyed for Cabinet the options facing an officer posted overseas. He could take the children with him; he could set up a home in Britain for his wife, which he concluded, 'is not conducive to a contented or efficient service'; he could place the child or children with relatives; and finally, there was boarding-school. 'This is usually the most satisfactory solution, but the financial burden imposed is beyond the means of the average Service officer.' Selwyn, therefore, proposed a tax-free grant of £75 p.a. (amounting to an annual charge to the Treasury of £3–4m). He believed the grant should not be decided on a basis of rank but should be available to non-officers and their families also. Indeed he believed there was a case for making even more money available for this second category. From his own experience Selwyn was a firm believer in the efficacy of the boarding-school system, particularly for those whose professions (the Diplomatic service was one of which he had direct knowledge) led to frequent overseas postings. But he found the ear of the Treasury unbending.

His other major initiative was more in tune with Treasury thinking, the thorny question of the future of National Service, the need being to balance defence requirements with whatever economic resources were available. Selwyn proposed at a Cabinet meeting on 22 September 1955 (incidentally the day that independent television started and thus a time of celebration for Selwyn) that the total strength of the armed forces should be reduced to 700,000 by 31 March 1958. There were two methods by which this could be achieved; first, a period of National Service with a higher age for call up in the future, or second, a formal reduction of the period of National Service for all to 21 months. He felt that the first alternative was preferable on military grounds, but that the second was on political grounds. In any case he felt the obligations of part-time service should be substantially reduced. It was arranged that Eden should make a statement on the future of National Service at the Party Conference in Bournemouth in October, while in the meantime Selwyn would prepare a White Paper on the issue. By April 1957 the government took the decision to end National Service completely in 1960, a decision in which Selwyn was involved in his capacity as Foreign Secretary.[27]

Other issues in which Selwyn was involved – the future of the Simonstown Naval Base in South Africa, Aden, constitutional advance in Cyprus (on which he worked with the Colonial Secretary, Alan Lennox-Boyd, an increasingly close political associate at this time), and the possibility of a Guided Weapons Training Range in the

Hebrides – were at a more interim stage. Cyprus, in particular, was to be one of his major concerns when Foreign Secretary. On 14 November 1955 Selwyn paid a sentimental journey to the Staff College at Camberley, where he had studied in 1939, little realising that it was to be one of his last commitments as Defence Minister. He told the students that the problems of defence came largely from the transitional stage of political organisation and technological change. The impact of science on defence was greater than ever before, with scientific development proceeding at an unprecedented pace. It was no longer possible to plan year by year and a longer-term view needed to be taken (a theme that was to recur at the Treasury). He predicted that all three services would soon be needing guided missiles in one form or another.[28] He hoped to be present to see through some of these vast changes, but by Christmas he was in another job.

The curious, and from the political point of view, strangely unsatis-factory Cabinet reshuffle Eden conducted on 20 December 1955 had its origins in two otherwise unconnected events. Rab Butler had been at the Treasury for four gruelling years. The Opposition had seen the Budget of April 1955 as an electioneering one and the so-called 'Pots and Pans' Budget of October 1955 (which dampened consumer spending by increases in purchase tax) and the financial difficulties that coincided with it occasioned much belated gloating on the Labour benches. At a time when four years of expansion were coming to a close and the glitter of his Chancellorship no longer had the same lustre (1955 had been a year of industrial unrest and a weakening pound) Butler had a world-weary look. An emergency Budget itself was a very unusual occurrence before the more frequent fiscal statements of the 1970s. Clearly Butler needed a change of portfolio and it would have been better for him had this change taken place when Eden became Prime Minister, notwithstanding his sad personal circumstances of the time. The second element in the chain of events concerned Eden's somewhat prickly relationship with Harold Macmillan. Macmillan's inventive independence (he had even de-spatched foreign policy memoranda while at Housing) was not to Eden's liking. With his long experience of Foreign Affairs, Eden psychologically resented another man dominating his 'preserve'. If Macmillan could be persuaded (and it took some persuasion) to move to the Treasury it would thus solve two problems. Eden first mooted this change with Macmillan as early as 23 September, telling him that Selwyn Lloyd would succeed him as Foreign Secretary if he moved. Macmillan was both disappointed and astonished, asking Buchan-Hepburn, the Chief Whip, 'if the Prime Minister's purpose was really to get back control of the Foreign Office',[29] exactly the thought that struck Selwyn when he was offered the job.

A subsidiary factor in Eden's calculations was the election of Hugh Gaitskell to succeed Clement Attlee as Labour Leader on 14 December, a week before the reshuffle. The somewhat elderly Labour team was thus given a new and more youthful look and Selwyn was the main beneficiary of this background element to the reshuffle. As an ironic corollary he was the main victim of the same reasoning in July 1962. Selwyn was not at all happy with the prospect of the move, noting retrospectively:

> It was not a change which I wholeheartedly welcomed. True it was promotion on the grand scale. But I had only been in the Cabinet for eight months, and I believe that the Foreign Secretary ought to be one of the three or four senior members of the party and in the Cabinet. Edward Grey, Curzon, Austen Chamberlain, Halifax are obvious examples and Douglas-Home and Callaghan more recently.
>
> However Eden did not agree, perhaps because he himself was appointed Foreign Secretary in 1935 after only five months in the Cabinet and when he was comparatively junior in the ministerial hierarchy. I also knew that human nature being what it is, my rapid promotion would not find favour with my ministerial colleagues in and out of Cabinet.[30]

But Eden's will prevailed (as it usually did at that time) and Selwyn became Foreign Secretary. At this time Selwyn's passport was due for replacement. He looked in amazement at the Curzonian inscription on the inside cover of the old book: *Her Britannic Majesty's Principal Secretary of State for Foreign Affairs Requests and Requires*, and pencilled alongside: *Me!*

Selwyn Lloyd's appointment as Foreign Secretary was a climacteric of his career. He was acutely aware of the jealousies that would be occasioned and also of the muttering campaign that would say he was merely Eden's poodle. He mentioned this specifically to his friends, but admitted that the Foreign Office is not something one turns down lightly. 'I was sorry to have to go', he wrote to Lord Carrington, his Parliamentary Secretary at the Ministry of Defence on 28 December 1955. 'I should have much preferred to stay on to finish off the work on the Defence Programme which we had begun together. However, I had to do what I was told.'[31] Selwyn had now been 'away' from Eden for over a year. It has often been said that Selwyn was appointed to this high post because Eden wanted a more malleable Foreign

Secretary.[32] Truth, as Oscar Wilde noted, is rarely simple. Though Selwyn was clearly not as forceful (or calculating) a political figure as Harold Macmillan, Eden valued him for other characteristics. Selwyn was a minister with whom he felt comfortable. They had worked together closely for three years and Selwyn had direct personal experience of the leading foreign ministers of the world powers and the external affairs ministers of the Commonwealth countries (Richard Casey in Australia in particular). He had had practical experience of diplomatic negotiation, especially over the Sudan and disarmament. Moreover, the latter part of Selwyn's time as Minister of State had not all been a case of Eden dictating the line. As has been seen, considerable tensions arose in 1953 and 1954, first over Churchill and détente and then while Eden was away in Berlin. What Eden remembered was Selwyn's reliable efficiency. In a Cabinet not short of prima donnas this was a considerable asset. 'What matters really', recalled Selwyn, 'is whether the Prime Minister and the Foreign Minister have complete confidence in one another, whether they trust one another and they know that nothing will be done behind the other's back.'[33] Eden had cause to remember this more than most. He had lacked that basic rapport with Neville Chamberlain in 1937–8 ('No word has reached the Foreign Office and I am still Foreign Secretary', he had complained to Chamberlain at the time of his resignation in February 1938)[34] and the history of the relationship between Number 10 and the Foreign Office is littered with suspicions and doubts. Eden knew that Selwyn would be expeditious in dealing with the business of the office, that he would not waste time on unnecessary factors. He also knew that when an issue came up which Selwyn thought was important he would say so. Macmillan conceived the Foreign Secretary as being a sun among the planets; Selwyn knew that the Foreign Secretary was but one of the planets that revolved around the sun, but was not the sun itself. This suited Eden. It also suited Selwyn. People would say that he was His Master's Voice. Let them say.

Selwyn Lloyd was Foreign Secretary, as he himself carefully noted, for 4 years, 7 months and 7 days.[35] The prospect of this junior Cabinet minister in a senior post was not one that commended itself to Selwyn's contemporaries. As he had anticipated there was much jealous muttering, for he was the first of the political generation of 1945 to achieve one of the 'great' offices of state. Not even Peter Thorneycroft, who had first entered the House in 1938, had yet achieved that. The implication was that, at the age of 51, time was on his side and that one day he could even be a contender for the leadership itself, a point not missed in many of the letters of congratulation that now poured in. As Patrick Devlin (now a Justice of the High Court) wrote on 21 December:

> Dear Selwyn,
> I cannot go on writing like this every six months. I shall make a new rule. When you become Prime Minister I shall take judicial notice of it: but until then – Garter, O.M.'s & the like – shall go unrewarded.[36]

Selwyn was particularly pleased to receive a generous letter from Attlee, 'Congratulations on a well deserved promotion to perhaps the most important post in the Government.'[37] Not everyone was so encouraging. The opinion among many was similar to that voiced by Hugh Dalton in February 1951 when Attlee had mooted Sir Hartley Shawcross for the post. 'I declared violently against this; no lawyers at the F.O.! Remember Simon.'[38]

Selwyn's tenure of the Foreign Office can be divided into three clear phases – pre-Suez, Suez and post-Suez, though this third phase as Macmillan's Foreign Secretary could arguably be sub-divided into the period before February 1958 (the time of Selwyn's offered resignation) and afterwards. He became Foreign Secretary at a moment of great transition in Britain's international position. Suez was the event that made this transition abundantly clear, not perhaps so much in the world at large where many perceptive commentators could already see what was happening (Dean Acheson's comment, 'Great Britain has lost an Empire and has not yet found a role', was to sum up that feeling in 1962)[39] but in a more important sense in Britain itself. This transition was seen in particularly sharp focus during Selwyn's first twelve months in King Charles Street. In December 1955 Britain still had a large colonial empire (with bases in Aden, Singapore and in Simonstown) and there seemed to be great scope for independent manoeuvre. By December 1956 that ability was being called into question. Selwyn's subsequent task as Foreign Secretary, unlike Curzon's or even Bevin's, was essentially a *reactive* one. He was thus Foreign Secretary at a difficult period, Suez apart. What the Foreign Office likes above all is a Secretary of State who can make his will prevail in Cabinet, which is why Bevin was so popular. Yet Bevin was really the last of a breed and though Eden had this ability it was only intermittently. By Selwyn's time the Foreign Office was no longer one of Curzonian detachment. The Office had to adjust to this and the old hands did not like it, with the result that some of the overspill of resentment flooded in Selwyn's direction.

In his time as Foreign Secretary Selwyn had experience of two Permanent Under-Secretaries, Sir Ivone Kirkpatrick (until 1957) and

Sir Frederick (Derick) Hoyer Millar (later Lord Inchyra). Before that as Minister of State he had worked with Sir William Strang. When Strang retired as Permanent Under-Secretary in November 1953 Selwyn had written to him from New York:

> It is impossible for me to express adequately my appreciation of your kindness during the past two years. Ministers must be exceedingly tiresome people, particularly when they are new, ignorant and self-opinionated. Your wisdom and tactful guidance really have been wonderful.[40]

Selwyn's affinity with Strang was never recaptured with his successor as Permanent Under-Secretary, Sir Ivone Kirkpatrick, who treated Selwyn with barely disguised disdain, sending emissaries on many matters and preferring to deal with Eden in Number 10. At the end relations were severely strained and it was only when Derick Hoyer Millar became Permanent Under-Secretary that a fruitful working relationship was re-established.

As the Foreign Secretary's principal private secretary, Selwyn was served by Pat Hancock, Denis Laskey and Ian Samuel. Although in the final analysis the Foreign Secretary's success will not depend on getting on with his private secretary (Bevin did not get on particularly well with Frank Roberts for instance) it clearly helps if mutual trust can be established. This did not materialise with Pat Hancock. The insouciant Wykehamist style was not to Selwyn's liking and for his part Hancock could not take Selwyn's staccato schoolboyish humour. There were some difficult moments and it was a relief on both sides when Pat Hancock became Head of the Western Department of the Foreign Office early in 1956 and later Ambassador in Israel.[41] As a result of this unsatisfactory start Selwyn was determined to get on with Denis Laskey and this became one of the most important partnerships of his career. When Laskey was moved to the Rome Embassy in October 1959 Selwyn inscribed a photograph to 'the perfect private secretary' not as a mere politeness.[42] After the October 1959 Election Ian Samuel became Selwyn's private secretary and the relationship, though of shorter duration than that with Denis Laskey, was happy and fruitful. When Selwyn left for the Treasury in July 1960 he sent Ian Samuel a particularly gracious letter, saying how well aware he was of the success Samuel had had in linking the political side of his work with the Office side.

From the beginning of January 1956 Donald Logan (who was to accompany Selwyn on the most secret of the Suez missions) was the Number 2 secretary, and the team was completed by John Graham and R. J. Langridge. As Foreign Secretary Selwyn was very conscious of the various hierarchies and he wanted to understand the structure: how the first room was the headquarters of a particular department, the second room housed the assistant head and the third room (where no Eden trod) the desk officer of the day. He tried to keep in touch with all levels of the Office, even those beyond the 'third room' and used to ask the lady typists, 'Are you happy in your work?', a stock phrase which became a Foreign Office in-joke in the late 1950s.

There was a great divergence of opinion about Selwyn himself. Those, like Pat Hancock, who had worked with Macmillan tended to look back with regret to past glories. Selwyn was aware of these feelings and in May 1956 at a weekend at the home of his old Second Army friend, Geoffrey Hardy-Roberts in Fittleworth, asked John Graham, who had worked with Macmillan, why it was that certain elements did not like him. He learned that his manner grated. From then on he worked hard to counter criticisms of his brusqueness, but the period of induction was not easy.

Selwyn's day often began with an informal meeting at 8.15 at his official residence, 1 Carlton Gardens, and he aimed to be in the Foreign Office by 10 a.m. by then having read his overnight boxes. Meetings followed all day unless he had a commitment in the House of Commons. He tried to make time in the early evening (particularly with his marriage under increasing strain) to see his daughter Joanna before bed. The Office appreciated how swiftly Selwyn took on board the instinctive truth that where other departments administrate the Foreign Office negotiates. He knew from the time of his first contribution to Cabinet, a substantial document on German War Criminals, suggesting a 4-power judicial board to review the sentences of figures such as Hess and Doenitz, that his job would primarily be one of reaction before action.[43] One problem that Selwyn had not foreseen was how the majority of those around the Cabinet table saw themselves as being 'licensed' to pronounce on Foreign Affairs, whereas not everybody set themselves up as experts on mundane matters. Selwyn was thus assailed on two sides in Cabinet, by the accepted expert on Foreign Affairs, Eden; and by those who were senior to him, though not in one of the three 'great' offices. As a result he remained something of a loner in Cabinet, one of his few associates being Alan Lennox-Boyd, the Colonial Secretary. He soon learned the value of patience. Unlike Eden, who in a Churchillian sense wanted action not only this day but every day, Selwyn knew that in foreign affairs six weeks is a short time. (Later when Julian Amery was involved in the Cyprus negotiations for five months in 1960 it did not worry Selwyn. What mattered was that it should come out all right in the end.)

He set a great store by good relationships with his opposite numbers from other countries, building a considerable friendship with Maurice Couve de Murville and establishing good relationships with figures as diverse as Joseph Luns, Paul-Henri Spaak and the Egyptian foreign minister, Dr Fawzi (although the fact that Selwyn got on with Fawzi did not endear him to Eden as the Suez crisis unfolded). He had a quality of looking for the good in people rather than the bad, always seeking out the human and the humane in those he met, though this was countered by his irritating habit of being a tease with the home-team, with remarks such as, 'Good for Nutting', and, 'You're a deb, Sir Gladwyn Jebb'. He could appear grumpy and unappreciative, calling for a particular document which a junior official would prepare with great care. In dealing with the matter Selwyn would then put searching questions. To the official his work appeared to be little appreciated and the Secretary of State's attitude cold and demanding. Yet many days later Selwyn would suddenly refer to the work when talking with his private secretaries and praise it. Of this the junior would rarely hear directly and as a result Selwyn's reputation was higher with senior officials. To the juniors he appeared aloof, a pattern repeated at the Treasury. Yet he showed the patience of Job over the telegrams and over Eden's continued attention to them.

Selwyn enjoyed the historical associations of the high-ceilinged room overlooking St James's Park, from where, by the large central window, Sir Edward Grey had made his celebrated remark in August 1914 about the lamps going out all over Europe. He knew that one day, on the walls of the private office next door, his photograph would hang in the company of Curzon, Austen Chamberlain and Bevin. Not so much to his liking was the endless round of representational work and he soon developed a code with his private secretaries of scratching his right ear when he wanted to be 'rescued' at social gatherings. He could be very sharp if the signal was not acted upon promptly.

Politically the Foreign Office scene in 1956 was a quieter European and South-East Asia situation, the latter largely owing to Eden's success at Geneva, but a more volatile Middle-Eastern situation, fuelled by a resurgence of Arab nationalism and (as Selwyn knew only too well from his experience of the Sudan) virulent anti-British propaganda. Eden's legacy included the South-East Asia Treaty Organisation (SEATO). More important in the crises that were shortly to unfold was the Central Treaty Organisation (CENTO), a product of the Baghdad Pact signed by Iraq and Turkey on 24

17 Selwyn and Bae setting off for the Coronation of Queen Elizabeth II on the morning of 2 June 1953.

18 Dr John Wesley Lloyd in benign old age.

19 Minister of Defence, 7 April 1955.

20 Measuring up the new Foreign Secretary, December 1955.

February 1955, to which the United Kingdom, Pakistan and Iran later acceded. A permanent ministerial council was established and the first meeting was held in Baghdad a month before Selwyn became Foreign Secretary. Nasser's hatred of this 'northern tier' alliance was high on the agenda when Selwyn made his first overseas trip as Foreign Secretary in the company of Eden, sailing to the United States and Canada on the *Queen Elizabeth* on 25 January. MIG fighters and other Russian military equipment were being supplied to Cairo under the terms of an arms agreement Nasser had signed with Czechoslovakia in September 1955. The volatility of the Middle East had been emphasised by the New Year rioting in Jordan and Nasser's continued anti-Western stance. Although Eisenhower received his guests with courtesy and even warmth, Selwyn thought the talks disappointing and that they only underlined what he regarded as the danger of having highly publicised meetings between heads of state where high expectations were often so cruelly dashed. His Foreign Secretaryship was to end with such a disappointment, the Paris summit in 1960 in the wake of the U2 spy-plane episode.* Although no such disaster befell these talks Eden could not persuade Dulles to membership of the Baghdad Pact and little tangible emerged.

In retrospect the most interesting item was waning American enthusiasm for the Aswan High Dam project, Nasser's grand scheme for controllable irrigation using Nile waters, an essential element in Egypt's push towards industrialisation. If America withdrew financial aid the political domino effect could be incalculable. Eden was more satisfied with these talks than Selwyn as was clear in the Cabinet meeting held in the Prime Minister's room at the House of Commons on 9 February when Eden and Selwyn reported to their Cabinet colleagues. Eden said that in the Middle East the United States government had seen the most urgent need as giving their full support to the Baghdad Pact and to compose the differences between the Arab states and Israel. Selwyn said that he was surprised to find the United States taking such a strong line over Israel despite the importance of the Jewish vote in an election year.[44] The American election was to return to haunt the British government many times before November.

Despite the inconsequential outcome to the meetings, Selwyn had enjoyed the relaxed Atlantic crossing with Eden and the opportunity it afforded for wide-ranging conversation. He much regretted the demise of the ocean liners. Aeroplanes were a mixed blessing, and not only because the return flight from Ottawa had been dogged by

* See Chapter 10.

problems. 'There was a lot of publicity in the papers about our flight
from Ottawa but it really was not as exciting as it sounded', he wrote
to his sister Dorice on 11 February. 'Joanna is full of beans and
growing fast. I bought her a giant panda of large dimensions at
Washington which has been a great success.'[45]

On his return from Washington Selwyn moved into the Foreign
Secretary's official residence, 1 Carlton Gardens. Two days later (on
22 February) he made a statement in the House of Commons about
the interview which Burgess and Maclean (who had defected to
Russia in May 1951) had given in Moscow to selected representatives
of the British and Soviet Press. He was authorised to disclose the
limited connection which Burgess had had with the Security Service
during the war. (For some time one of the stories circulating in the
Office has been that the uncertainties of current Soviet policy had
been due to a struggle for power which was going on in the Kremlin
between Burgess and Maclean!)[46] The forthcoming visit of the
Russian leaders Bulganin and Khrushchev, on which Eden set great
store, had exercised the Cabinet from January, particularly in the
light of the anti-British statements made by the two men in Burma
and India, but Eden felt that on balance the invitation should remain
open. For the next two months Selwyn dealt with many of the
arrangements for this visit. But before B and K (as the British Press
dubbed them) came to England, Selwyn had his first major solo
overseas trip.

At the Cabinet meeting on 22 February Selwyn said that in the
course of his Middle-Eastern tour en route to the SEATO meeting in
Karachi (a tour planned to last from 29 February to 15 March) he
would be meeting Nasser in Cairo. Subject to the Cabinet's views, he
proposed to take a firm line in his discussions with Nasser about the
tone of Egyptian propaganda in the Middle East, and to make plain to
Egypt the advantages of a friendlier relationship with the United
Kingdom. It was not to be expected that, if Egypt showed such
hostility towards us, we should continue to give her financial assistance towards the construction of the Aswan High Dam. He intended
to make it clear that Egypt could not expect further help from Britain
unless she changed her policy. The Cabinet felt that no decision could
be taken on this without prior consultation with the United States
government. Selwyn said that at this stage he would not be specific
about the consequences which would follow if the Egyptians failed to
modify their policy towards us.[47] On 27 February before his departure Selwyn spoke in the Foreign Affairs debate. His main aim, he
told the House, apart from maintaining peace, was to seek a solution
to the Arab-Israeli dispute and to point out the dangers of too close a

political embrace with Russia for those uncommitted Middle East states that cared for their freedom. On 28 February, the day before he flew to the Middle East, Selwyn drew the Cabinet's attention to telegrams from HM Ambassador in Amman, reporting that the Government of Jordan had asked Britain for an assurance of military assistance in the light of recent events and the possibility of an attack by Israel on Syria. Selwyn's reply was that if Israel attacked an Arab state other than Jordan the United Kingdom government would not be under any obligation to render military assistance to Jordan under the terms of the Anglo-Jordan treaty. He stressed that he would be wanting to uphold the Baghdad Pact and proposed to decline hospitality in Jerusalem lest it be taken to imply that the United Kingdom government recognised it as Israel's capital.[48]

Selwyn was met in Cairo by the Egyptian Foreign Minister, Dr Fawzi, a man in whose company he was to spend so many hours before 1956 was over. Although Selwyn felt he was a 'smooth and rather slippery customer', nevertheless he thought they would be able to do business.[49] During the afternoon of 1 March Selwyn and Dr Fawzi had wide-ranging discussions, centring at first on the Baghdad Pact before moving on to Soviet influence in the Middle East and the Aswan High Dam project, which Selwyn told Fawzi that he hoped would go through. The centre-piece of Selwyn's visit to Cairo was the dinner that evening with Nasser. Apart from Nasser and Selwyn, four others sat down at table – Fawzi and Hakim Amer (the Egyptian commander) on the one side, and Humphrey Trevelyan (British Ambassador in Cairo) and Harold Caccia (the Deputy Under-Secretary of State at the Foreign Office) on the other. The political leaders had talks before dinner, but it was agreed that the discussion of Anglo-Egyptian problems would wait until after the dinner. 'I fully understand,' said Selwyn to Nasser. 'Perhaps instead you can tell us how you rose from being an Egyptian army major to being ruler of your fatherland.' This proved an inspiration. From the soup through to the dessert and beyond, Nasser unfolded his complete life-history to the fascinated British party, his origins, his methods and his aims. They felt it to be the equivalent of hearing Hitler dilate upon *Mein Kampf* without omitting any embarrassing footnotes. It brought home to the British party the kind of man with whom they were dealing, far more accurately than could have been gleaned from official sources. Nasser told the British (in front of a silent Fawzi) that first of all one gets rid of the King (a necessary prelude to getting rid of the British), then one puts in a front man, Neguib, which in its turn is only a prelude to his eventual removal. All that then remained was to get ride of the front man, assume power and cover one's flanks. As

Selwyn said to his officials after the dinner, 'we now know exactly the kind of man we are dealing with'.[50]

Before the dinner Selwyn had given Nasser his word that Great Britain would renew the moratorium on the Baghdad Pact if Nasser would calm the propaganda attacks.[51] What Selwyn did not know as he went in to dinner was that in Jordan King Hussein had summarily dismissed Glubb Pasha, the British Commander of the Arab Legion. When he left the dinner to return to the Embassy Humphrey Trevelyan showed Selwyn the message stating that Glubb had been dismissed. Selwyn was both angry and despondent as he was sure that Nasser had known what was going on. Selwyn at once got in touch with London. Eden's first reaction was that Selwyn should fly on to Jordan to reason with Hussein. Selwyn wisely countered this suggestion by pointing out that the peremptory nature of Glubb's dismissal would probably mean that he would have left Jordan before the Foreign Secretary could arrive, which would mean 'a further humiliation'.[52] He continued with his original plans.

Before he left Cairo Selwyn had his second meeting with Nasser, on 2 March. Nasser congratulated Britain, in the person of its Foreign Secretary, for having arranged the dismissal of Glubb as a means of improving relations between Britain and Egypt. This observation would have been unconvincing at the best of times. In the light of recent developments Selwyn, who had had only two hours sleep, found it outrageous and left Nasser in no doubt about his feelings. Later at the height of the Suez crisis, when Selwyn was in New York, he was found by one of his aides in a darkened hotel room watching a passionate speech by Nasser on the television. 'And this is the man we could not match', he said with almost reluctant admiration.[53]

When the British party (led by Selwyn and Caccia) reached Bahrain later on 2 March the motorcade was stoned by an angry mob. As further demonstrations were expected on the return journey to the airport Selwyn delayed his departure until 1.30 a.m. by which time the streets were no longer lined with anti-British demonstrators. The next day (3 March) Selwyn wrote to Eden giving his impressions of the Egyptian visit. He stressed the mutual suspicion that existed between Britain and Egypt, describing the Glubb incident as 'a body line ball in the middle of the innings.' As for Nasser he felt 'he was fatter and more self-confident than when I last saw him in 1953 . . . Fawzi too seemed more sure of himself.'[54] The visit gave both sides new insights: the British into Nasser's character and the Egyptians into the strength of the hand that they could play. 'Many important developments stemmed from the tragedy of Selwyn Lloyd's mission', wrote Mohammed Heikal later, 'but probably the most important was that he personally but in all innocence started the chain of events which led to Nasser's decision to nationalize the Suez Canal.'[55]

The rest of the tour was less eventful. Selwyn stayed at New Delhi with Nehru and talked with Dulles in Karachi about the latest Middle East developments. On his return to London Selwyn reported to Cabinet at its morning meeting on 21 March. He told his colleagues he was satisfied that Nasser was unwilling to work with the Western powers or to co-operate in the task of securing peace in the Middle East. Nasser was aiming at leadership of the Arab world and in order to secure it he was willing to accept the aid of the Russians, both politically and economically. He felt that Britain should seek in-creased support for the Baghdad Pact and above all America should be persuaded to join. He felt that Britain should seek to draw Iraq and Jordan more closely together and should try to detach Saudi Arabia from Egypt by making plain to King Saud the nature of Nasser's ambitions. He concluded by stating that there were possibilities of action aimed more directly at Egypt to counter Egyptian subversion in the Sudan and the Persian Gulf. He men-tioned specifically the withholding of military supplies, the with-drawal of financial support for the Aswan Dam, the reduction of United States economic aid and the blocking of the sterling balances. But he emphasised that the first task was to seek Anglo-American agreement on a general re-alignment of policy towards Egypt.[56]

Selwyn also believed that it was vital that the Opposition should be kept in touch with developments and to that end he had a meeting with Gaitskell, the Labour leader, at the Foreign Office on 11 April. Gaitskell found that 'it was quite clear that they [the Government] have got so fed up with Nasser and Egypt generally, that they are now being driven into accepting our position on arms for Israel.'[57] Much of the conversation, though, centred on the forthcoming visit of Bulganin and Khrushchev, Gaitskell telling Selwyn that the Opposition 'had no intention of asking for a debate on the Middle East until after the visit of the Soviet leaders.' Selwyn told him, on Privy Councillor terms, that military planning was taking place between the United States and Great Britain, though Gaitskell warned Selwyn (with absolute prescience) that, 'in his view the Americans were hopeless and he thought in an election year there was not the slightest chance of the Americans taking any action, whatever the extent of the emergency'.

Surprisingly, as he was not overfond of Wykehamists, Selwyn built up a useful and frank relationship with Gaitskell, even discussing Shadow Cabinet personalities in some detail at this meeting. Selwyn asked if the Shadow Foreign Secretary, Alfred Robens, objected to the fact that the Foreign Secretary was seeing Gaitskell and not himself. Gaitskell said that he believed that when Attlee had been Leader of the Opposition he had always been seen by the Prime Minister. 'I said that that was not so and that the present Prime Minister, when Foreign Secretary, used to see Mr Attlee from time to time and that I indeed, as Minister of State, had seen him more than once when the Foreign Secretary was away. He thought that I should see Robens occasionally in order to avoid hurting his feelings, but felt that on the whole, although he had confidence in Robens's discretion, I should not necessarily tell him as much as I would tell Mr Gaitskell himself. He said that the trouble about Robens was not that he was indiscreet, but that he really did not know very much about these matters.'[58] They arranged to meet again from time to time for confidential talks.

For his part Gaitskell never underestimated Selwyn. Later in the year he very much agreed with the views of Jean Chauvel, French Ambassador in London, 1955–62, noting in his diary: 'I drew him [Chauvel] out a bit on his views on Eden and Selwyn Lloyd. He said that they thought Eden was very nervous; on the other hand they had a considerable opinion of Selwyn Lloyd, or rather Chauvel had. He saw him a lot, he thought he was clear-headed, knew his own mind and was very balanced. He takes everything into account, he said, including the internal position here.'[59] From this Gaitskell deduced that Selwyn knew that over Suez, 'the Government would be in some difficulty in going to war because of the position of the Labour Party.'[60]

Selwyn now had to turn his mind to the visit of Bulganin and Khrushchev. The invitation had been made at the Geneva Conference in 1955 and the visit was one on which Eden pinned great hopes for the lowering of East-West tension. The Russians arrived at Portsmouth on 18 April and stayed for a week. A full programme of diplomatic, social and political meetings had been arranged for them. There was a collective sigh of relief from the diplomatic and political community when the Russian guests departed on 27 April, for the visit had been attended by more than its fair share of potential, and in some cases actual embarrassment. A full agenda had been prepared by the Foreign Office, centring first on Anglo-Soviet relations, but also taking in the European situation, the Middle East, the Far East and Disarmament. Selwyn had taken a prominent part in preparing this agenda and Eden was relieved when the Russians, who had made many detailed objections to the programme, had no criticisms of the actual agenda. The talks took place informally at Claridge's, where the Russian delegation was staying, more formally at the Cabinet table in 10 Downing Street ('See how well trained we are, we file in like horses into their stalls', Khrushchev remarked)[61] and, 'least inhibited' of all in Eden's opinion, at a Chequers weekend.[62] It was not, however, for the private and official talks that the visit established itself in the political consciousness, but for the number of contretemps, rows, demonstrations and, finally, the major diplomatic incident of the disappearance of Commander Crabb, a naval frogman, at Portsmouth and the later discovery of a decapitated body. The most notorious event was the public row that broke out at the dinner the Labour leaders gave for the Russians which culminated in a slanging match between George Brown and Khrushchev, who said that if he lived in Great Britain he would vote Conservative. (In 1959 when he accompanied Macmillan to Moscow, Selwyn reminded Khrushchev of this incident and, with a British General Election in the offing, asked Khrushchev at dinner through the interpreter, 'Now if you were a British voter would you still vote Conservative?' 'Of course,' replied Khrushchev, 'it was Bulganin who was Labour and look where he is now.')[63] Selwyn was involved in another, although less serious, embarrassment when he accompanied the Russians to Harwell and Oxford and questions were asked about Russian moves towards free trade unions. In Oxford undergraduates sang 'Poor old Joe' and a woman spat at Khrushchev.

Potentially the most embarrassing episode arose at the luncheon that Selwyn, as Foreign Secretary, gave for Bulganin and Khrushchev at 1 Carlton Gardens on 25 April 1956 following a morning of discussions at Number 10. Selwyn was extraordinarily nervous and had a premonition that something would go wrong with this function. The shadow of Eden as Foreign Secretary still hung over him and he was fearful of anything upsetting the Prime Minister about the arrangements. Members of the Office, plus relevant officials, including the Soviet and British Ambassadors, attended. The pre-lunch gathering got off to a confused start when Selwyn introduced his Parliamentary Private Secretary, Lord Lambton, to Khrushchev as a 'shooting' Lord. When this was translated Khrushchev looked at Lord Lambton with some surprise and not a little sympathy, asking his interpreter to retranslate. When this was done Khrushchev nodded his head and shook hands with an expressionless face, believing (as it later transpired) that Lambton was under sentence of death and shortly to be shot. Although this greatly amused the Foreign Office staff as the story circulated, Selwyn feigned not to have heard and remained aloof from the atmosphere of genial confusion. But the Russian translator was soon to be matched by his English counterpart, a junior official called in at the last moment to deputise for an indisposed colleague. Lunch was at an E-shaped table, the normal mahogany and Louis XV walnut chairs having been displaced to accommodate the larger number of guests. Selwyn was flanked at the top table by Bulganin and Khrushchev, who were placed next to other Foreign Office grandees. Lesser mortals sat along the projecting arms of the table.

Lunch itself was a fairly bland affair, enlivened by the provision of much vodka, which one of those present remembers as being rather like offering whisky to Scotsmen. Loyal toasts followed and the speechmaking began. Selwyn made an anodyne speech in a rather faltering manner, clearly discomfited by having to pause every two or three sentences to allow the inexperienced interpreter to repeat his remarks to a largely uninterested Russian leadership. Once Selwyn had got into the rhythm of pausing to give the young interpreter time to translate, he remarked that he found it rather convenient to make a speech one sentence at a time as it gave him time to think what he was going to say next. From his seated position Khrushchev quickly retorted that it was an even cleverer idea to employ an interpreter who stuttered.[64] Selwyn went through the usual politeness, the kind of representational stance at which he had now had five years' worth of ministerial experience, before coming on to the crux of his speech, one area of paramount importance which he hoped would be clearly understood. The Russians must realise that Britain was prepared to defend the Middle East by force if necessary, a No 10 dictum which had not pleased the Foreign Office when they had advance warning that it was to be included in Selwyn's speech. But if the Russians were angered by this forthright declaration they showed no sign of it and Selwyn sat down without having caused the slightest change of expression on the faces of either of the Russian leaders. Khrushchev's was a short speech and ended with the hope that better times lay ahead. There were clearly no hard feelings, for Bulganin concluded the proceedings with a prepared speech in which he spoke about 'this very pleasant occasion' and 'such a friendly reception'.[65]

Considering the difficulties which had attended the visit, Bulganin and Khrushchev were very patient guests. The one undoubted success was the tour of Holyrood House in Edinburgh, which the Russians thought was some Siberian outpost where the peasants (in actual fact senior members of the General Assembly of the Church of Scotland) were being well looked after.[66] But Khrushchev found Selwyn a compatible host. 'I have every confidence in Lloyd' (he always called him Lloyd) he said.[67] 'I would much rather deal with the Conservatives', he said to the Labour delegation of Gaitskell and Bevan in Moscow in 1959. 'I always could get on very well with

Selwyn Lloyd.'[68] Selwyn accompanied the Russians to Portsmouth as they prepared to set sail from Britain on 27 April. By that time the disappearance of Commander Crabb was filling the newspapers. With the dismissal of Glubb, the stoning of the Foreign Secretary in Bahrain and now the Crabb episode, the year had begun inauspiciously for the Eden government. But these were only the prelude to even greater problems.

For Selwyn the early summer of 1956 was very much a case of the lull before the storm. After the visit of the Russians he was confined to his bed for a week with bronchitis before the NATO meeting in Paris. He attended the Second Army Service at Christ Church, Portsdown in June. Also in June he flew to Sweden to join the Royal Party in *Britannia* as Minister in attendance on the Queen, the first of many such tours. Before he flew to Sweden Captain Waterhouse of the Suez group of Conservative MPs let Selwyn know of the reservations his wing of the Party had about the withdrawal from the Canal Base, due to be completed on 14 June. On his return from Sweden he had talks with the Libyan Prime Minister and later hosted visits by the Foreign Ministers of West Germany, Canada and Italy. Neither did Selwyn neglect his constituency work. In many ways the higher he rose in the ministerial ranks the more assiduous he became in cultivating grass-roots support and in June 1956 he fulfilled many Wirral commitments, receiving deputations from the Birkenhead Society and attending garden fêtes and party functions at Heswall, Neston and West Kirby. At the end of the month the Commonwealth Prime Ministers' Conference was due to be held in London, to be followed by the State Visit of the King of Iraq. The opening meeting of the Commonwealth Prime Ministers' Conference was at 3 p.m. on 27 June. This occupied Selwyn until 6 July, not only with issues such as Britain's nuclear role but also with the beginnings of closer links with Europe, Macmillan (now Chancellor of the Exchequer) advocating a European Free Trade Area.

Selwyn was now approaching his 52nd birthday and had been Foreign Secretary for six months. They had been months of political consolidation (the meetings with Nasser in March had been well handled in difficult circumstances) and he was beginning to take a more active part in Cabinet discussions, particularly on 21 March. But it was a difficult time for him personally. Bae had been involved in a serious car accident at the end of 1955 and after surgery was recuperating in Sussex. There was a tacit acceptance on both sides that the marriage was now over. This placed Selwyn in an isolated domestic situation as the great crisis of his career was about to unfold. 'Poor Selwyn Lloyd, who two years ago was a pleasant, coming young man, looked harassed and bedraggled', wrote Richard Crossman in his diary on 25 June 1956 of a Labour Party meeting with the Foreign Secretary over Israel. 'Apparently he has had some domestic disaster, with his wife in a car smash.'[69] The private lives of public figures are now remorselessly examined, but this was not so cruelly done in the 1950s, although Selwyn was to suffer some unwelcome attention from the Press in 1957 during his divorce. His widowed mother came from time to time to stay at 1 Carlton Gardens, but the domestic arrangements devolved upon Nanny Watson. Dependable, homely and comfortable, Nanny Watson's calming influence was of inestimable benefit to Selwyn in the summer of 1956. Following the divorce Selwyn and Bae were to evolve an understanding relationship – which lasted to the end of Selwyn's life – as he recognised when he wrote privately in his diary: 'I had a marriage which because of disparity of age did not succeed, but after it failed I remained on terms of genuine friendship with my former wife.'[70] This helped to ensure the stability of Joanna's upbringing, her parents' main concern being that she should have as settled a life as possible. A family holiday had been booked at Seaview in the Isle of Wight for Joanna and Nanny Watson, with Donald Logan on hand in case business affairs arose. A black labrador puppy was purchased. It was a sign of the innocence of those days that the British Foreign Secretary could actually christen such a dog Sambo without criticism. In the next six years Sambo was a constant domestic companion and was the cause of one poignant political moment.*

Despite Richard Crossman's gloomy picture, Selwyn's standing in the Eden Cabinet in June 1956 was high. If there were daggers in men's smiles Selwyn did not notice them for he was too busy with the work in hand. Eden was impressed ('clear, firm and consistent', he wrote)[71] and although Rab Butler had drifted apart from Selwyn and no longer had such a high opinion of him, perhaps seeing him as a possible rival, Butler himself was at something of a political crossroads in his own career. Among the Cabinet Selwyn got on well with Alan Lennox-Boyd and Lord Home, Colonial and Commonwealth Secretaries respectively. Derick Heathcoat Amory, a similarly rather lonely figure in Cabinet, with local roots but no strong national or party following, was a kindred spirit also. Kilmuir, one of his earliest legal contacts, was Lord Chancellor and Gwilym Lloyd George, Home Secretary, was a link with Criccieth days. So he had his friends but remained obstinately outside the central core of the Cabinet's power base. The question mark that hung over him was how far he

---

* See Chapter 12.

could be considered a malleable, compliant figure ('only an office boy to Eden', as Crossman wrote in his diary)[72] who was merely His Master's Voice?

It is a question of some complexity to which there is no easy answer. In the three years from October 1951 Selwyn Lloyd had moved steadily up the ministerial ladder by performing competently and loyally in subordinate positions, the political staff officer *par excellence*. Not surprisingly he had deferred a good deal to Eden's greater experience in Foreign Affairs, admitting to Michael Astor at Bruern that he had been charmed by Eden, but in this he was not alone. But, unusually for a Minister of State, and largely owing to the successive illnesses that had beset both Eden and Churchill, he had been given considerable independent executive autonomy. Some of those who worked with him at the time, particularly John Leahy, believe that Selwyn had a desire to make his personality felt and that to describe him as being compliant probably did him less than justice.[73] Although the question as to whether he would be independent did not arise so much in departments such as Supply and Defence, Selwyn's greatest apprehension on being offered the Foreign Office in December 1955 was that he would be regarded as Eden's poodle. 'It was frequently said by my detractors that I was a biddable Minister, a compliant servant of the political master of the moment', wrote Selwyn in his draft memoirs. 'I do not think that was true. I frequently held independent views, for example in my attitude to broadcasting and the death penalty. I had taken an independent line in discussions over disarmament, in my behaviour towards the Americans over the Korean armistice, over the future of the Sudan, German war criminals and conscription.'[74] Although Selwyn would clearly be intending to portray himself in the best light it is an impressive catalogue of what might be termed 'dissenting views'. At this stage of his career the charge that he was merely His Master's Voice is largely an unproven one. As yet there had been no major collision of purpose, no issue on which he had felt impelled to protest vigorously or on which in the last resort he had wished to resign. That loyalty was now to be severely tested in the months that lay ahead.

9

Suez

Selwyn Lloyd once said that being Foreign Secretary was like playing a round of golf at Hoylake with the wind against you at every hole. Never did the wind blow more strongly against him than over the Suez crisis. As Foreign Secretary he was in the eye of the storm and his vantage-point was unique. His role varied as events unfolded; sometimes he was conciliator, sometimes negotiator, at other times the government spokesman fending off the Opposition's questions, but mainly, as he privately admitted in another golfing metaphor, a political niblick to get his Party out of bad lies. Selwyn never fully revealed the part he played over Suez and was always defensive about 'exactly what happened'. Critics said that he was defensive with good cause, but Selwyn was unrepentant. The agreements reached at Sèvres in the third week of October 1956, for instance, were secret. Selwyn's definition of a secret was not something that you only told one person at a time. As a result his narrative of the crisis, *Suez 1956, A Personal Account*, published posthumously is only a partial lifting of the skirt. Although it was a book embarked upon towards the end of Eden's life, it was one about which both men had talked for the better part of twenty years. In his biography of Anthony Eden Dr David Carlton writes:

> Towards the end of his life he had to face still more anxiety when Lloyd expressed his intention to produce a volume on Suez based on privileged access to official documents. This cannot have been particularly welcome to Avon but he could not prevent it. He did not live to see the work appear.[1]

In fact Eden always knew that one day Selwyn would publish his recollections of Suez, either as part of his memoirs or (as happened) as a self-contained book. It was tacitly understood (Selwyn was seven years Eden's junior) that in the normal course of events these recollections would not be published in Eden's lifetime. What they did not anticipate was that they would not be published in Selwyn's lifetime either. They had detailed talks about the book in the last year of Eden's life. 'Thank you for our talk last night and for your visit here', Eden wrote (in the last letter he ever sent Selwyn) from Alvediston on 11 August 1976.[2] Their talks had centred on the legal aspects of Nasser's action and the judgment of the Lord Chancellor, Lord Kilmuir. In his reply Selwyn wrote:

> It would be a help to me to have the quotation which you read out to me giving David's judgment about the legality of Nasser's action in seizing the Canal. I will try to avoid using it, but it will be useful to have it, if only to refer to and tell other people to look for it. I will not do that unless I am hard pressed.[3]

In addition to their discussions Selwyn sent drafts of the various chapters of *Suez 1956* to Eden for comment and proofs were actually flown out to Hobe Sound, Florida, where Eden was staying with the Averell Harrimans during his last illness in the winter of 1976. However, his letters to Eden show that, whatever Eden's apprehensions may have been, Selwyn reserved the right to give his account one day, as fair and complete as he could make it.

Another figure Selwyn consulted during the writing of the book was the constitutional historian Lord Blake. The advice he received was that there was no point in writing such a book unless it was candid, because he was in a unique position to give the British point of view. As Nigel Fisher wrote in *The Tory Leaders* in 1977. 'There are probably no official papers on Suez in existence in Britain except those in Lord Selwyn Lloyd's private files and he is almost certainly the only British statesman alive today who knows exactly what happened.'[4] Nevertheless the shadow of Eden's presence lay heavy over Selwyn's shoulder as he wrote.

A full history of the Suez crisis would fill many volumes. The bibliography of it, as Robert Rhodes James has noted, 'seems likely to rival that on Gallipoli'.[5] The account which follows, based on the first reading of Selwyn Lloyd's private papers, does not seek to give a comprehensive history of the origins, developments and repercussions of Suez, but to detail his part in the crisis from the summer of 1956 until the resignation of Eden in January 1957 and thus to complement the many accounts which have been, and will continue to be, published about the political events which split the nation that long hot summer.

In his papers Selwyn kept a file which he rather melodramatically called SUEZANA VERY SECRET.[6] Before the publication of *Suez 1956* Selwyn had already contributed, although anonymously, to many of the accounts published in his lifetime, making major contributions to Terence Robertson's *Crisis: the inside story of the Suez conspiracy* (1965) and Hugh Thomas's *The Suez Affair* (1966). His usual conditions were that he must not be quoted in the books (or identified by numbered notes) and that the authors should not mention in private conversation that he had spoken to them. What the authors did not know in many cases was that, although they did not speak about his contributions, Selwyn spoke about them to Eden. For after Eden's resignation in January 1957 Selwyn and he arrived at an understanding. This was to the effect that when either of them was approached by a *bona fide* historian seeking information about Suez neither would respond to such an inquiry until he had agreed with the other what he was going to say. This was not on the time-honoured principle of Lord Melbourne in Cabinet that, 'it is not much matter what we say, but mind, we must all say *the same*', but to ensure that no wedge would be driven between them by a published account.

One of the most interesting sections in Selwyn's papers on Suez is that devoted to his private correspondence with Eden, particularly in the air mail letters Eden sent from the RMS *Rangitata* en route to New Zealand in January 1957 (which exist only in Selwyn's file). In these letters, some written only days after the crisis, Eden unburdens himself, with humour and without rancour, of his innermost thoughts to the man to whom he felt closest at that time and who, in the remaining twenty years of Eden's life, was never to let him down and would become closer still. When the historians started to approach them for primary material it was thus inevitable that the two would consult over their response. Some historians they would not see at all. Some Eden recommended to Selwyn (especially the 'transatlantic' historians), others vice versa. In 1958 a weekend meeting was held at Eden's Wiltshire home. A partial account of this meeting was released at the Public Record Office in 1987 and received extensive attention in the Press, largely because of Eden's sour comments about Peter Thorneycroft. An even franker version exists in Selwyn's papers. This shows that Selwyn felt that until Eden died he was bound by friendship to reveal only as much as Eden wished to be revealed. As a result the first revelations of Sèvres were to come from French and Israeli, rather than British sources. (As early as 31 October 1956 the Conservative MP William Yates was to mention in the House of Commons that he had heard of some kind of clandestine conspiracy.) It was independently confirmed to me by many of those party to the inner secrets of Suez that Moshe Dayan's account was substantially the most accurate. Thus by the time that Selwyn came to write his side of the story events had rather overtaken him. There was no point in writing *Suez 1956* (certainly he did not do it for financial reasons) unless it added materially to the historical record, as Lord Blake shrewdly told Selwyn. Yet Selwyn had a unique piece of the jigsaw in his possession. But it was not only his respect for Eden that inhibited him. In 1967 Sir Anthony Nutting, Selwyn's successor as Minister of State, had published *No End of a Lesson*. Although he profoundly disagreed with many of Nutting's conclusions (and also thought it a premature work) in a strangely resigned manner Selwyn recognised Nutting's book, with its flair and frankness, as one that surpassed anything he would be able to add. It was left to Donald Logan Selwyn's assistant private secretary at the time of Suez, who was the only British representative at all the meetings in France in the week beginning 22 October 1956, to give the fullest version of British involvement thirty years later.[7]

Selwyn's involvement with the problems of Egypt – what Napoleon had called the most important country because it lay at the crossroads of Africa, Asia and Europe – began when he was appointed Minister of State in October 1951. Until Sudanese independence in 1954 this had been only one of many responsibilities – disarmament work at the United Nations filled much of his time – but the Suez Base agreement of July 1954, the prelude to the withdrawal of British troops from the Canal Zone, marked a new phase in the history of Anglo-Egyptian relations and by the time Nasser nationalised the Suez Canal on 26 July 1956 Selwyn, as Foreign Secretary, was at the centre of a difficult network of relationships, where his recognised characteristics of industry and application were to be tested to the full. It is in an examination of how he conducted himself in these relationships that a greater understanding of his career and personality can be appreciated.

The controversial Suez Base agreement of July 1954 had led to considerable schism in the Conservative Party between those such as Alexander (Defence Minister) and Head (Secretary of State for War), who believed that the nuclear age had made the Suez base redundant, and the Suez group, led by Charles Waterhouse, who saw the agreement as a dangerous sell out. When Churchill was asked to come and speak at a 1922 Committee meeting which promised to be particularly critical he replied, 'I'm not sure I'm on our side.'[8] Selwyn too was one of the doubters. 'I felt that we probably had to go in the long-run, but I would have preferred a much slower process.'[9] So when the crisis broke in July 1956 there was a feeling in certain quarters of the Conservative Party that Eden had brought the problem upon himself by the withdrawal of 1954.

The subsequent two years had inevitably heightened Selwyn's awareness of the divisions within his own party and he was always conscious of the difficulties of reconciling those divisions. He hoped that there would be a conciliatory understanding and he proved approachable as Foreign Secretary, stretching his timetable to accommodate representations from Charles Waterhouse (in the midst of a long afternoon with Krishna Menon) as well as listening to grass-roots opinion whenever possible. His application in this area of internal Party division was to be superseded however by the industry required as intermediary between Eden and the American Secretary of State, John Foster Dulles. Selwyn was always aware of the debt he owed Eden as his mentor and of Eden's reputation and experience in Foreign Affairs. As the crisis unfolded he soon became aware of Eden's impatience with Nasser, his conviction that force would be necessary and indeed eagerness to proceed with it. This was to undermine much of Selwyn's careful work with Dulles, for he shared the desire of Dulles to avoid force, yet had to play his part in preparing the policy of the Prime Minister. So as Dulles dealt with Selwyn Lloyd with the object of keeping the peaceful options open, so Selwyn exploited Dulles's proposals to the full with Eden. This can be seen in his work both before and at the 18-power conference in August, over the Suez Canal Users' Association but above all at the United Nations in October. The frustration he felt as his talks with the Egyptian Foreign Minister Fawzi (with whom he established a real rapport) were aborted in October was compounded by his bitter disappointment at being made the instrument of the Sèvres plan. The three men had met together for the first time when Eden and Selwyn had visited Washington in January for talks. In their discussions on Egypt on 30 January Eden had wondered how long Britain could continue to co-operate with Nasser. Dulles, for his part, promised support, though Selwyn regretted it was only 'moral support',[10] over the Baghdad Pact. On Tuesday 31 January Selwyn had had his first long tête-à-tête with Dulles, mainly about South-East Asia and strengthening SEATO. In the next few months Selwyn's relationship with Dulles was to be a crucial factor in the unfolding crisis. They were men of similar background, lawyers, Nonconformists, and both had an eye for detail. It has sometimes been conjectured that they were soon at loggerheads. This was not the case. While never ruling out force explicitly, Dulles produced a succession of ideas which kept the prospect of a peaceful solution on the table. The difficulty was to be that, although Dulles took the lead in private, he was increasingly unwilling to do so in public. Selwyn appreciated Dulles's skills and when Dulles realised that Selwyn was not a man to be browbeaten by a stronger personality they struck up a good working pattern. 'Foster, you're a corporation lawyer, and anything you put to me I've got to see that the signatures are all around the document', Selwyn said to Dulles early on over Suez. Dulles respected this, even when he did not agree with what the British government were doing. There was an unexpected amount of laughter. 'We had really quite a lot of fun together', Selwyn recalled. 'I ended up by liking him.'[11]

There were others whom Selwyn liked also, though many disparate personalities were involved. Selwyn was aware that Macmillan, his predecessor as Foreign Secretary was a very different political character with wider social contacts, a following in the Party and distinct views on Foreign Affairs. Anthony Nutting too was from a different age group with an idealistic personality and a close working knowledge of the Foreign Office and Eden's methods. Nutting's subsequent resignation saddened Selwyn greatly, but he was unable to prevent it. By the time of Eden's resignation political circumstances were to draw Selwyn even more into Macmillan's orbit, but before the crisis was resolved he was closer to the lawyer politicians – Kilmuir and Monckton – making important contributions himself on legal points to the meetings of the Egypt Committee. Lennox-Boyd, too, 'was a staunch and helpful colleague';[12] Butler, who was ill for much of the time with a mysterious virus, was to confide many of his doubts to Selwyn privately. Selwyn was thus caught in the middle of a complex web of conflicting interests and different viewpoints, essentially impossible to reconcile, and his role in the events that were now to unfold should be seen against that background.

After the Commonwealth Prime Ministers' Conference in late June, the only major commitment Selwyn had in his diary before the proposed summer holiday in the Isle of Wight was the State Visit of the King of Iraq in July. The week of 16 July therefore had an end of term feel about it. Eden was tired and beginning to look forward to his holiday in Malta.[13] On Monday 16 July Selwyn undertook a ceremonial duty that meant a lot to him, travelling by helicopter with Winthrop Aldrich, the American Ambassador, for the dedication of the United States war cemetery at Cambridge. Many of the 3,811 American dead who were buried there had been on the invasion of Normandy in 1944. That evening Selwyn attended the State Banquet for the King of Iraq. But the week was to be remembered for other reasons. At the Cabinet meeting at 10.30 a.m. on Tuesday 17 July Selwyn reported on the impending withdrawal of American aid for the financing of the Aswan High Dam, the civil engineering project costing some $1,300 million which Nasser had persuaded the United States, Britain and the World Bank to support to the tune of $270 million, Britain's contribution being $14 million. The loans were dependent on Egypt's ability to raise a further $900 million through a properly managed economy. The seeds of Dulles's dissatisfaction with this arrangement, which led to a policy of letting the loan 'wither on the vine', was Nasser's recognition of Communist China in May, the presence of the Russian Foreign Minister Shepilov in Cairo at a time of ostentatious celebration in June of British withdrawal from the Canal zone and the use of Egyptian crop revenues for the purchase of Czechoslovakian arms. Eden's distrust of the project was even deeper and Selwyn's first six months at the Foreign Office had coincided with a period of questioning of the viability of such a financial commitment. As early as April 1956 the United States and Britain had agreed to let the offer languish, Eden's view being that Britain could not afford such a commitment and that any available finance should go to British allies rather than to Nasser. In America Congress was not in favour of the administration helping Nasser either. The visit of Shepilov to Cairo at the end of June seemed, on both sides of the Atlantic, to be a preliminary to the announcement of Soviet aid. In his statement to Cabinet Selwyn said that the United States government was likely to share the British view that the offer should be withdrawn. He intended to circulate a memorandum to the Cabinet on the best means of presenting such a decision to the Egyptian government. It would probably be best, he said, to indicate to the Egyptians that, in view of their commitments for expenditure on armaments and military installations, the two governments had been forced to the conclusion that the financing of the Dam, even with the assistance which had been proposed, would be beyond Egypt's resources. In what was a serious underestimate of the effects of such a statement Selwyn concluded by telling Cabinet that this might well lead to a deterioration in our relations with Egypt with serious consequences for our trade.[14] How right he was.

On 19 July Dulles informed the Egyptian Ambassador in Washington, Ahmad Hussein, that the Americans were withdrawing their offer of financial help for the Aswan High Dam. In *Suez 1956* Selwyn wrote, 'Makins, the British Ambassador, was informed one hour before the meeting.'[15] The chronology of events was more interesting. Sir Roger Makins had first discussed the possibility of American withdrawal of the offer on 13 July. On Tuesday 17 July (the day of Selwyn's statement to Cabinet) Makins had a further meeting with Dulles. Of this meeting Makins wrote:

My recollection is that the Egyptian Ambassador returned to the U.S.A. and stated on arrival that he was going to accept the offer; that Dulles told me that morning that, for congressional reasons, he would feel obliged to tell the Ambassador in the next couple of days that the offer was withdrawn; that he regretted the short notice, but the announcement could be in line with the agreed policy that the offer should 'wither on the vine'.

I reported this conversation immediately to the Foreign Office, and there was plenty of time (forty-eight hours, I think) to provoke some reaction and to send some instructions. I was surprised to get none, as I rather expected some expostulation from Selwyn or Anthony Eden at the abruptness of the decision, or some comment on what should be said. Nor do I recall any message following the announcement complaining of Dulles's action.[16]

Dulles's action was not ill received in London because it was the essential preliminary to British withdrawal on 20 July (a decision Selwyn was authorised to announce that day by Cabinet).[17] It suited the United Kingdom government to go along with the United States and thus there was no response to the first warning telegram by Makins. The joint withdrawal of aid by America and Britain was then the action that provoked Nasser's nationalisation of the Suez Canal on 26 July.

The week of 23 July began with no hint of the storm that was about to break. On the Monday Selwyn attended a dinner for the touring Australian cricket team, the day on which Nasser was hastening his plans for the take over of the Canal. On Tuesday 24 July, the day that Nasser virulently attacked the United States, Selwyn was attending a reception at (of all places) the Egyptian Embassy. On the Wednesday, he lunched with Nuri-es-Said, the Prime Minister of Iraq, at 10 Downing Street and dined in the evening with Lady Waverley. It was the week of his 52nd birthday and he was looking ahead to the recess. The events of Thursday 26 July were to alter all that. 'It is the custom on the stage', wrote Charles Dickens, 'to present the tragic and the comic scenes, in as regular alternation, as the layers of red and white in a side of streaky bacon.'[18] Such a juxtaposition was certainly a feature of the first day of the Suez crisis for Selwyn.

On 26 July Selwyn was in a tetchy mood. His labrador, Sambo, was ill and had to be taken to the vet. Coincidentally in his post that morning Selwyn received a letter from the Tail Waggers' Club of Great Britain asking him if he would like to register his new pet as a member. Selwyn talked about this with Donald Logan and arranged to send off a subscription. (In due course he received a membership card certifying that, 'Sambo, the True Friend of the Rt. Hon. Mr. J. Selwyn Lloyd of 1 Carlton Gardens', had been registered, 'as Tail Wagger 1000082').[19] Shortly afterwards news came through that the Swedish liner *Andrea Doria*, on which Selwyn had booked a cruise, had sunk after a collision off New York the previous evening. And then to complete the battalion of sorrows Selwyn's housekeeper at 1 Carlton Gardens was admitted to hospital, hence the catering difficulties Selwyn experienced on the evening of Sunday 29 July during the visit for talks of Robert Murphy, United States Deputy Under-Secretary of State, and Christian Pineau, a problem solved by dining at the Carlton Club.[20] Selwyn's first meeting of the day was at 10.30 a.m. on a proposed Middle East tour, followed by a Cabinet at 11 (at which he reported that the Soviet Union had offered to supply arms to Jordan without payment).[21] At 12.45 he lunched with American Press correspondents, saw the French Ambassador, M. Chauvel, at 3.30 regarding a visit by his opposite number, M. Christian Pineau, before attending to constituency business with his secretary, Helen Snow, at 4. He attended an At Home given by Lord Cilcennin, the First Lord of the Admiralty, at 6.30 before changing into white tie and tails for the banquet at 10 Downing Street for King Feisal of Iraq at 8.15.[22] Other minor meetings filled any available gaps in this timetable. But the political day was yet to begin.

While the senior members of the British government entertained the King of Iraq in the upstairs State Dining Room, an all-male dinner of tails and decorations, news came towards 10 p.m. that Nasser had nationalised the Suez Canal. Eden sent immediate instructions to summon the French Ambassador, the American Chargé-d'Affaires, and the Chiefs of Staff. Hugh Gaitskell, who had been attending the banquet in his capacity as Leader of the Opposition, heard the news of the nationalisation some 45 minutes after Eden had first been informed. 'I want you to know – and I think the Opposition should know as well – what Nasser has done tonight', Eden told Gaitskell.[23] Eden's first thought was that the matter should be taken to the Security Council of the United Nations. 'Supposing Nasser doesn't take any notice?', asked Gaitskell. Selwyn, who was standing near by, said, 'Well, I suppose in that case the old-fashioned ultimatum will be necessary.' Gaitskell again stressed, as he had done to Selwyn in their talk on 11 April, that the Americans must be brought in.[24] Towards midnight five members of the Cabinet (Eden, Salisbury, Kilmuir, Home and Selwyn Lloyd), the two foreign diplomats, and the Chiefs of Staff, Mountbatten, Templer, and Dermot Boyle (who had actually been at the dinner), gathered in the Cabinet room. The main decision to emerge from this meeting was that concerted action should be taken by the United States, French and British governments. Selwyn took Andrew Foster, the American Chargé-d'Affaires, aside and said that he felt that the only solution to the problem would be a Western Consortium taking the Canal over, by force if necessary.[25] When this was reported back to Eisenhower, Robert Murphy was quickly despatched across the Atlantic to find out which way the wind was blowing. The meeting broke up at 2 a.m. with the Chiefs of Staff being instructed to prepare plans for a possible invasion of Egypt, work on which they began some seven hours later.[26]

Later that morning (Friday 27 July) Selwyn's office cancelled his engagements. Parliament met at 11 a.m. Eden made a statement and was encouraged by Hugh Gaitskell's deploring what he called 'a totally unjustifiable step by the Egyptian government'.[27] (In May 1957 Nye Bevan was to say of Nasser's action, 'If the sending of one's police and soldiers into the darkness of the night to seize somebody else's property is nationalisation, Ali Baba used the wrong terminology'.)[28] The first Cabinet meeting of the Suez Crisis was held at 11.20 a.m. in Eden's room in the House of Commons. Eden briefly recapitulated on the events of the previous evening for ministers (such as Harold Macmillan) who had not been present. He put the central issue in unequivocal terms. 'The fundamental question before the Cabinet, however, was whether they were prepared in the last resort to pursue their objective by the threat or even the use of force, and whether they were ready, in default of assistance from the United States and France, to take military action alone.'[29] It was decided that the Foreign Office should consider what should be done about advising the 15,000 or so British subjects in Egypt, but the most important consequence of this Cabinet meeting was the formation ('for putting our policy into effect')[30] of the Egypt Committee to deal with military contingencies and initially consisting of Eden, Selwyn Lloyd, Lord Salisbury, Harold Macmillan, Lord Home and Walter Monckton, though other ministers attended as the occasion arose. So began what was for Selwyn a period of intense activity which he later likened to the Ashley Gardens planning days of Second Army in 1944. Rab Butler, in effect Deputy Prime Minister, was ill at Stanstead and not included formally in the Egypt Committee, though he later took to turning up to some of the meetings and actually chaired that held on 8 October.[31] Although there had been such War Committees before (in 1855 during the Crimean War) and were to be again (during the Falklands conflict of 1982) the Egypt Committee of 1956 was of special constitutional significance and was, whatever Eden may have subsequently claimed, where the executive power lay. 'The detailed negotiations of the next few months lay with this group, though on key matters of arrangement with the French and through them with the Israelis, the Prime Minister acted with the Foreign Secretary or on his own', wrote J. P. Mackintosh.[32] 'The interest of this episode is that it illustrates how, in time of pressure of events and when international negotiations are involved, the actual planning of action and taking of decisions is removed from the Cabinet to a Committee of those most concerned and then, at special moments of stress or delicate negotiation, to one or two ministers or even to the Prime Minister alone.'[33] Three members of the Committee were lawyers (Kilmuir, Monckton and Selwyn Lloyd) and a division arose between these three, who concerned themselves with matters of legality, and Harold Macmillan who in a more pragmatic manner wanted to know what they were going to do about Nasser. Butler, when he attended, fell uneasily between these two groups. When asked for advice at the Egypt Committee Selwyn often took up the legal aspects which were at the heart of the problem. He did not take initiatives for the simple reason that he still hoped for a negotiated settlement. He proved adept at seeing the logistical difficulties of the proposed military build-up and was, for instance, particularly concerned about the speed of the convoys from Malta being dictated by the slowest ship, an echo of Second Army. He also offered much advice on transport and on loading tables in a manner reminiscent of Overlord planning. Eden's inability to delegate meant that he involved himself far too much in these military matters (arguably the same was true of Selwyn, though he saw himself as filling a vacuum) when he should have been concentrating on political details. The role for which Selwyn's character best fitted him in the ensuing crisis, would have been that of a political liaison officer with the Chiefs of Staff. The role that he was actually given (by turns secret negotiator and public relations spokesman) was one totally unsuited to his honest inarticulacy. It is hard to imagine any member of Eden's Cabinet more unsuited to be sent on a clandestine mission to Sèvres, yet it was the hand that fate dealt him.

The first meeting of the Egypt Committee was at 7 p.m. on Friday 27 July and was attended by Eden, Macmillan, Selwyn Lloyd, Monckton, and Harold Watkinson (the Minister of Transport).[34] (Between 27 July and 9 November there were 42 meetings of this Committee, all but five of which Selwyn attended. During those five meetings he was at the United Nations.) They met to consider in the first instance the financial questions, but soon moved on to the role of the naval forces and the position of British employees in the Suez Canal Company. Macmillan very much took the initiative at this meeting. Selwyn was invited to ask the United States government to consider whether they could not advise their ship-owners to arrange for their dues for transit through the Canal to be paid, for the time being, elsewhere than in Egypt. He was also invited to concert with the governments of the United States and France an agreed policy to be followed by ship-owners in the event of Egypt's requiring payment of transit dues on the spot. As regards British employees of the Suez Canal Company decisions were left to individuals in Egypt. At the third Egypt Committee meeting on 30 July Selwyn reported that in his consultations with the representatives of the United States and French governments there had been strong support for the proposal to call a conference of maritime powers. Selwyn arranged to see representatives of the Baghdad Pact countries that afternoon.[35] From the start Selwyn believed it was necessary to mobilise international public opinion and thought that the best way to do so would be to assemble a conference of those powers with an interest in the Canal, a proposal he discussed with Murphy and Pineau before 'Foster flew in' on 31 July.[36] It was during this visit to London that Dulles made the remark that a way had to be found to make Nasser disgorge. Although this did not amount to a specific assurance of any military backing from the United States in the event of Anglo-French military intervention, the remark did give comfort to the British government, still in a state of stunned shock over what had happened. Selwyn noted in his record, 'In view of Dulles's robust view that Nasser must be made to disgorge his ill gotten gain, we did not despair of him.'[37] It was to prove a costly miscalculation. Selwyn, together with Abba Eban, Israel's Permanent Representative at the United Nations, always hoped that Dulles would be the agent for a salvaging operation, but as the Presidential Election neared it was increasingly Eisenhower who, in American parlance, called the shots.

The main outcome of Dulles's visit was the first London Conference (16–23 August). If a conference of interested parties was to be held, Dulles had firm views both on its composition and venue. Dulles would have preferred the Conference to have been held in Geneva, or at least not in Paris or London. He would also have liked to have had the Soviets invited.[38] At a meeting at 5 p.m. on 1 August Selwyn proposed to the Americans, in the person of Murphy, a deal on some of these points, which proved to be acceptable. He was prepared to defer to Dulles's wish to invite the Soviet Union, albeit reluctantly, if in return the United States government would agree to the kind of communiqué that Britain would like to issue and also help to ensure that the conference took place as soon as possible and concluded its efforts satisfactorily and quickly.[39] Preparations for this first London

Conference on the future of the Canal went ahead and the next fourteen days were to be among the busiest of the whole crisis for Selwyn. He understood the political reality that the Conference would in fact be directed by Dulles and was happy that this should be so, as he knew American co-operation was vital. (The Conference in August 1956 is in fact one of the best examples in Selwyn's career of the precept to which he always held, namely that there is no limit to what can be achieved in life, as long as people do not mind who takes the credit.) On 2 August reservists were called up and the Egypt Committee considered (and endorsed) the first plans submitted by the Chiefs of Staff for 'Action against Egypt'. Selwyn was already finding himself in a diplomatically exposed position. On the one hand Harold Macmillan (at the Egypt Committee meeting on 2 August) brought up the possibility of Israel's attacking Egypt as, 'it would be helpful if Egypt were faced with the possibility of a war on two fronts'.[40] On the other hand the International Conference was now very much Selwyn's 'baby' and to be looking into the question of Israeli involvement (as he was asked to do with the Chiefs of Staff) and at the same time continue preparations for the Conference in an atmosphere of military preparation led to contradictions which he did his best to play down. In a conversation with the French Ambassador on 3 August, for instance, Selwyn called for co-ordination of the guidance which the British and French governments would give the Press. He said that the British were anxious to create the best possible atmosphere for the London Conference and to this end would ensure that the British Press did not play up the military precautions which were being taken. He made it clear to the French Ambassador that any move to have French troops on standby in Malta before the Conference had ended, either in success or failure, could only prejudice the hopes for a satisfactory conclusion. Over the next few days he saw the Ambassadors of Italy and Sweden, and the Indian High Commissioner. He broadcast about the crisis on 14 August, a talk reprinted in the *Listener*. Again he stressed the importance of United States' involvement and the fact that Nasser was a military dictator. The eight parties to the 1888 Convention had all been invited to the Conference, which he hoped would contribute to the lessening of tension.[41] The day before the Conference opened he saw the leaders of the various delegations as they assembled in London. To several he developed arguments showing why safeguards for freedom of transit were not enough. He emphasised to the Pakistan Foreign Minister that there were three kinds of pressure that could be brought to bear on Egypt – international opinion, economic or other sanctions, and finally force. With the Netherlands Foreign Minister he discussed the withholding of Canal dues from the Egyptian government.[42]

Just before the Conference opened there were two important developments. On 14 August Eden and Selwyn met the Labour leaders, a meeting at which they told Eden they were opposed to the use of force, a view later communicated to the Cabinet at 11.30 that morning. Robert Menzies, the Australian Prime Minister, attended this Cabinet and stressed the need to educate public opinion about the wider implications of the crisis. Selwyn, for his part, saw it as his role to educate the Cabinet about the background to the Conference which was about to open. He stressed his hope that Dulles would introduce a resolution proposing the establishment of an international authority to be responsible for the control and operation of the Canal. Talk of military preparations he left to Eden.[43] Selwyn genuinely regarded the Conference as 'a good chance of pulling off a major diplomatic success'.[44]

Dulles, now in London for the Conference, was doubtful about the validity of British chairmanship of the meetings, but agreed with the arrangement after Selwyn told him that Indian support had been secured from Krishna Menon on the grounds that the United Kingdom was the host country, although at the outset the Soviet delegate hinted that it might be better if the chair were occupied by the representative of a country less closely concerned with the crisis. These negotiations were typical of the procedural difficulties that occupied Selwyn as Secretary of State over the next two months. His job, which involved stamina and patience, was a delicate balancing act. On 10 August, for instance, he had a difficult meeting with the British directors of the Suez Canal Company, including Lord Hankey (Secretary to the Cabinet 1916–38) who felt that he had a right to a seat at the Conference. Hankey felt that Selwyn was most rude and 'determined not to listen', preferring an international settlement of the dispute.[45] After a fleeting visit to Joanna and Nanny Watson at the Seaview Hotel, Isle of Wight on 11–12 August (where a Suez Canal was built in a desultory fashion on the beach), Selwyn embarked on the most intense period of his life since Second Army days at Ashley Gardens.

The Conference opened at 11 a.m. on 16 August, when Selwyn was elected Chairman. A second meeting was held at 3 p.m. and in the evening Selwyn hosted a dinner at Lancaster House. The next seven days were crammed with meetings, lunches and receptions. A typical day, which gives some flavour of the hectic pace, was Monday 20 August. Selwyn had morning meetings with the Ambassadors and Foreign Ministers of Argentina, Spain and the Baghdad Pact countries (squeezing in an Egypt Committee meeting at 11.30 at Number 10), he lunched with the Ethiopian, Iranian and New Zealand Foreign Ministers at 1 Carlton Gardens, held a tripartite ministerial meeting at 2.30, chaired the 3.30 session of the Conference before attending a dinner for all the Suez delegates at Number 10, itself the prelude to an evening reception from 10 p.m. onwards.[46] His chairmanship of the Conference was redolent of the impartial objectivity of a High Court Judge, just the kind of stance that was needed. He was quite happy for Dulles to take the initiative. At Cabinet on 21 August he reported on the United States proposals for the future control of the Canal and felt that Dulles, the corporation lawyer, was proceeding on the right lines by laying so much emphasis on the 1888 Convention. It seemed that 18 of the 22 countries represented would support the statement of principles tabled by the United States delegation. What was needed was a clear idea of the response needed if this statement was rejected by Egypt.[47] The first London Conference ended on 23 August and the Menzies mission to Cairo (fatally undermined by Eisenhower's unconditional rejection of the use of force at a Press Conference on 4 September) received a blunt rejection of the 18-power proposals from Nasser. Selwyn was greatly depressed, though not surprised, by this development. But as one door closed, so another opened.

One of Selwyn's important contacts at this time was Allen Dulles (John Foster Dulles's brother) of the CIA. After the ending of the first London Conference, but before the rejection of the Menzies mission proposals, Selwyn dined at Carlton Gardens with Allen Dulles and Patrick Reilly, then Minister in Paris and temporarily replacing Patrick Dean (who was on leave) as Deputy Under-Secretary in the Foreign Office. There is no record of this dinner in the Foreign Office archives. During the long discussions that evening it became clear to Reilly that Selwyn was trying to make Dulles understand that if the 18-power proposals were rejected then military intervention by the British should be regarded as a very serious possibility, an idea Allen Dulles for his part did not acknowledge had been mooted. Shortly afterwards, during the first weekend of September when John Foster Dulles was staying at his retreat at Duck Island, Lake Ontario, he produced his Suez Canal Users' Association plan, which according to Robert Murphy, was simply a device to forestall military intervention by the French and the British. Not for the first time Selwyn had been the indirect cause of activity in others.

Following the first London Conference, Suez increasingly proved to be a Number 10 operation rather than a Foreign Office one. The feeling in the Office at the time was that they were not 'up with the game' and that Anthony 'over the road' was making all the running.[48] This situation was far from being without precedent in the stormy history of relations between the Foreign Office and Number 10. The Chanak crisis of October 1922 and the differences that arose regarding the European dictators in February 1938 had both been occasions on which the Foreign Office had been placed in a position of some ambiguity. In October 1922 a seemingly omniscient Prime Minister (Lloyd George) had been forced from office; in February 1938 the Foreign Secretary (ironically Eden himself) had volunteered his resignation. There were to be many parallels with these two situations in the next five months before the crisis was resolved.

Divisions among Cabinet ministers were now becoming more marked, albeit backstage. Walter Monckton had a savage outburst at the Egypt Committee meeting on 24 August, one not recorded in the minutes, but which occasioned a great flurry of inter-ministerial correspondence. Selwyn continued to place his hopes in a negotiated settlement, but was aware of the contradictions in the British position. At the Egypt Committee meeting held at Number 10 at 6 p.m. on 27 August Selwyn discussed taking the whole matter to the Security Council. 'The main difficulty', he warned, 'would be to correlate an appeal to the Security Council with the present timetable of military preparation.' He was shortly to attend a regular NATO meeting in Paris and he wanted NATO to be informed of the latest situation. He was bound to be questioned by the Press and wanted authority, 'to put into proper perspective the precautionary measures we were taking'.[49] But the plans themselves were changing. 'Musketeer' (the military operation which centred on an assault on Alexandria) gave way in the first week of September to 'Musketeer Revise' (an attack on Port Said). At the same time Dulles came up with the SCUA proposals, a mutual help organisation which would deny Nasser Canal revenues, but which Selwyn feared would prove unworkable unless it was given 'teeth'. Selwyn flew to Paris on the morning of Wednesday 5 September with Paul-Henri Spaak, the Belgian Foreign Minister, for the NATO meeting. At 11.45 a.m. he had a private meeting with Pineau during which Pineau declared himself to be dubious about the Security Council option. Would not matters, he asked, be protracted until it was too late to take military action. (Musketeer Revise was a practicable option only until the end of October.) Later that evening Selwyn had further talks with Mollet and Pineau at which it was agreed that if Menzies had not received a favourable answer from Nasser by the end of the week (the Menzies mission was currently in Cairo) then the British and the French would go to the Security Council of the United Nations, so Selwyn's view prevailed. However, on 7 September Selwyn was warned by Lester Pearson that neither Canada nor the United States would allow the United Nations to be used merely as a cover for war. On 9 September Nasser formally rejected the 18-power proposals communicated by the Menzies mission and the next, and potentially more dangerous, phase of the Suez crisis had begun.[50]

Between 8–10 September Selwyn exchanged a series of telegrams with Sir Roger Makins, the British Ambassador in Washington, emphasising the need for haste. Every day Nasser strengthened his position and the Prime Minister must be able to announce the setting up of the Suez Canal Users' Association in the House of Commons otherwise Britain would have to go to the Security Council. Makins reported that Dulles had said that he had never seen the President more worried about anything.[51] At the Cabinet meeting on Tuesday 11 September (of which Selwyn later recorded there was the 'clearest possible indication of intention to use force')[52] Selwyn reported that the Menzies mission to Cairo had at least produced a clear-cut result in that the Egyptian government had flatly rejected the proposals for international control of the Canal. There were now, Selwyn outlined, three possible courses of action. First, military action at once; second, the government could call on the United Nations to make Egypt restore the rights of the 1888 Convention; or third, Britain could adopt the United States' plan of establishing an organisation to enable the principal users of the Canal to exercise their rights under the 1888 Convention. Selwyn warned that if this third option were to be adopted it would require the co-operation of the Egyptian authorities. But it would have two great advantages in that it would involve the United States in action designed to enforce the rights of the users of the Canal, and it would deprive the Egyptian government of more than 80 per cent of the transit dues for passage through the Canal. The Egypt Committee (and it must be remembered that the majority of the Cabinet were only brought up to date on Egypt Committee deliberations by such discussions in Cabinet itself) had decided at their meeting on 10 September to go forward with this plan if the United States government were willing that their intention to participate in it should be publicly announced in the forthcoming debate (on 11 and 12 September) in the House of Commons.[53]

At the Egypt Committee on 12 September Selwyn said that as it had been decided to announce that afternoon the proposal to form an association of user countries to operate the Canal, it was essential that no delay should occur in bringing this association into being. He therefore proposed to arrange forthwith for further consultations on the details of the plan between the Americans, the French and the

British, to be followed by a meeting of representatives of the 18 nations which had endorsed the London proposals. Dulles's plan, whatever its fate, would now precede a British appeal to the United Nations. It was one of the great turning points of the crisis. Selwyn was not the only one on the British side who feared that SCUA might prove unworkable. In a press conference on 11 September Eisenhower had given his most unequivocal statement to date on United States' refusal to be drawn into the use of force against Egypt. Selwyn was in receipt at this time of telegrams from Makins in Washington reporting that Eisenhower was now less confident about his re-election in November.[54] But events had moved on, seemingly out of British government control. And how resolute was American support?

The second London Conference opened on Wednesday 19 September, with Selwyn Lloyd elected Chairman. In his opening address he argued for international control over the Canal. Dulles outlined his proposals for a Suez Canal Users' Association in a speech which Selwyn regarded as the best he ever heard him make.[55] Selwyn now hoped that the failure of the SCUA proposals (followed by an appeal to the Security Council of the United Nations) would be tantamount to an endorsement by America of the right of Britain to use force, even if they themselves did not become directly involved. Douglas Dillon, American Ambassador to Paris, had pointed out to Dulles at the outset of the crisis that in his view Great Britain and France would be pretty well forced to take physical action against Nasser unless they were assured by the Americans that strong economic pressure would be promptly brought to bear on the Egyptian leader, thus ensuring his downfall in the long run by means other than war. The difficulty was to lie, not in any duplicity by Dulles, but in that he tended to improvise in foreign policy. SCUA, for instance, was thought up almost on the spur of the moment to meet the strong British demand for economic pressure (and to forestall military intervention), but was then gradually modified as events unfolded. Dulles never really let the British and the French know where they stood and Selwyn was not alone in mistaking the shadow for the substance.

In private talks during this second London Conference Dulles made it plain to the Foreign Secretary that he was deeply disturbed by the manner in which Nasser was winning the propaganda battle.[56] The SCUA negotiations were likely to be protracted and for his part, therefore, Selwyn was in favour of an immediate appeal to the United Nations to reaffirm the right of free navigation through the Suez Canal so that a preliminary meeting could be held (hopefully on

Monday 1 October). Dulles, however, wanted to see SCUA established before an appeal to the United Nations.[57] Dulles was also
concerned that if military action against Egypt failed this would
strengthen Nasser's position, a fear that was to be fully justified by
subsequent events. 'I have always thought that the most damning
criticism of us was that we misjudged the United States reaction',
Selwyn later admitted. 'We did not realise the gap in thinking
between Eisenhower and Dulles.'[58] His personal opinion of Dulles,
however, remained unchanged. 'My opinion will surprise many
people. He had virtues which are well known – incorruptibility,
courage and a belief in Western values, an appreciation of the horrors
of totalitarian states. He had defects which are well known. He could
not begin a negotiation about the line to be pursued without an escape
clause. He was devious. He would say one thing and do another. But
believe it or not I liked him. We got on very well together. Whenever
I was in close contact with him and could influence him from day to
day, things did not go too badly.'[59] Selwyn cited the SCUA Conference and subsequent meetings at the Security Council as occasions on
which Dulles understood the pressures on the British and 'genuinely
tried to make up to us.'[60] Out of these private discussions with Dulles
came the appeal on 23 September to the President of the Security
Council about navigation rights and, interviewed on BBC television's
Panorama the following evening, Selwyn stressed that force would
only be used as a last resort.

   At Cabinet on the morning of Wednesday 26 September Selwyn
informed his colleagues of the inconsequential outcome of the second
London Conference.[61] Although the Security Council arranged the
same day for the British appeal to be placed on the agenda for 5
October, Eden's impatience with the turn of events was plain and the
Cabinet turned to the discussions that the Prime Minister and the
Foreign Secretary were to have in Paris with M. Mollet and M.
Pineau. Later that afternoon Eden and Selwyn Lloyd flew to Paris,
where for a period of over an hour they had talks with their French
counterparts unaccompanied by any advisers or even interpreters.
The exclusion of the British Ambassador, Sir Gladwyn Jebb, from
these talks was his first inkling that something secret was afoot, a
feeling confirmed when no record of what passed was ever conveyed
to him. The British delegation dined at the Quai d'Orsay at 8.30 p.m.
and during the evening the Chancellor of the Exchequer, Harold
Macmillan, who was in America at an IMF meeting, reported (omin-
ously as Selwyn thought) that Eisenhower was 'very anxious to win
his election.'[62] The implications of this on United States involvement
in any British or French use of force ought to have been clear to all

concerned from this point – they were to Selwyn – yet for Pineau (if not at this stage Mollet) force by the end of October was of the highest priority.[63] Further talks followed on the morning of 27 September and after lunch with Mollet Eden and Selwyn Lloyd left for Le Bourget airport. Selwyn cancelled a proposed visit to the theatre that evening with Sir Geoffrey and Lady Hardy-Roberts because of his preparation for the third London Conference due to open at 11 a.m. on 1 October, even though it was not a conference he was to attend for long. At 8.30 p.m. that day Selwyn flew to New York. He was to be out of the country until the morning of 16 October, but it was to be his period of greatest autonomy during the whole Suez crisis.

On arrival in New York on 2 October for the Security Council debates Selwyn made it plain that the 18-power proposals were the only existing acceptable basis for negotiation. He was prepared for one final effort, though he was not prepared to negotiate with the Egyptians about finding an alternative basis. In other words Britain would not have a negotiation about a negotiation. Dag Hammarskjöld, Secretary-General of the United Nations, also thought, however, that talks with Fawzi, the Egyptian Foreign Minister, might be fruitful. These talks, Selwyn's most positive contribution to a settlement, led to the so-called Six Principles and it is one of the greatest ironies of the crisis that just at the moment at which these showed some prospect of providing the basis for negotiation Selwyn should have been unceremoniously summoned back to London by Eden to embark on a totally different course, such was the tussle of interests.

Selwyn told Hammarskjöld that he was in favour of the Security Council's going into secret session after the opening round of speeches and of an adjournment for two days after the first secret session. This, he felt, would create an opportunity for examining the possibility of a settlement in private talks with the Egyptians. It would, above all, show that the British and the French were being reasonable. Pineau did not dissent when the idea was put to him at a meeting on 4 October. Dulles too went along with the idea on 5 October. It was at this time that it seemed to both the French and the British delegates that Dulles was moving towards a position where he did not rule out the possibility of force as a last resort. Selwyn emphasised that the Security Council meetings should not drag on in an open-ended way as there was an urgent need for a decision. It was, for instance, adopted at his suggestion that the Council should dispense with consecutive translation of prepared speeches, thus halving the time of the General Debate. In a conversation with Dulles on 7 October Selwyn referred to reports that were emerging of Anglo-American differences and asked that he should be told what

they were so he could have some opportunity of dealing with them.
Dulles became very emollient after this approach, denying that the
Americans had any plans behind the British backs. This was true in
that the Americans had no plan at all apart from keeping matters on
as calm a level as possible until Eisenhower was safely back in the
White House. When Krishna Menon arrived in New York on 9
October he got in touch immediately with Selwyn. Shortly afterwards
Selwyn had his first extended meeting with Fawzi, whom he had met
in March when in Cairo. Selwyn found that Fawzi too wished to
proceed by negotiation. Fawzi felt that the presence of Menon and
others on the sidelines would complicate the issue, but was quite
happy to talk directly with Selwyn. After the public meeting of the
Security Council on the morning of 9 October, there was a meeting in
Pineau's room, at which Selwyn was present with Dr Fawzi. Fawzi
emerged from this meeting to tell an expectant group of journalists
that they had discussed the procedure for the afternoon's private
session. He then made as if to leave the building but rejoined the
meeting in the President of the Council's room by another entrance.
Selwyn urged the others on the Security Council to listen to what he
called Dr Fawzi's 'interesting ideas'. He was certainly prepared to
listen and over the next three days (10–12 October) had further
private talks with Fawzi. Selwyn worked hard at these negotiations.
In reply to his telegrams sent to the Egypt Committee on 10 October
Eden had endorsed Selwyn's 'handling of the very difficult situation'
but, 'in view of the importance of keeping firmly in line with the
French during these discussions', the Minutes of the Egypt Committee continued, 'the Foreign Secretary should be advised to ensure
that Monsieur Pineau was present at all future meetings with Dr.
Fawzi.'[64] By 13 October Selwyn believed that Fawzi was prepared to
accept seven points. These were:

a with regard to the 1888 Convention, Egypt was willing to leave
   it either as it was, or with additional adherents or to become
   party to a new convention
b he accepted that the operation of the Canal should be
   insulated from the politics of any one government
c Egypt was prepared to recognise the Suez Canal Users'
   Association
d Egypt was prepared to enter into an agreement on fixed tolls
e Egypt would be prepared to set aside an agreed percentage of
   the revenue of the Canal for its development
f procedures to deal with SCUA disagreements
g recruitment of non-Egyptian personnel to serve the Canal
   authority[65]

21 The visit of Bulganin (left) and Khrushchev, 19 April 1956. Despite the smiles it was a visit fraught with unforeseen difficulties.

22 John Foster Dulles and Selwyn during the Suez crisis. 'I ended up by liking him,' recalled Selwyn.

23 Talking over old times with his former chief: Selwyn with Eden at Broadchalke, Wiltshire, 30 May 1958.

With minor emendations these points became the basis for the Six Principles.[66] Selwyn now felt that distinct progress was being made. Together with Pineau he pressed Fawzi on the means of ensuring that the proposed system of co-operation would be effective in safeguarding the interests of the users. Fawzi proved amenable on this also. It was at this stage that Selwyn became gravely concerned by Pineau's attitude. He thought Pineau seemed determined to prevent any concrete agreement. Was there something he knew that Selwyn did not? On 13 October Pineau left New York. Fawzi thought that Pineau had been 'very louche – less arrogant but more mysterious.'[67] French intentions were shortly to be revealed in the most dramatic of circumstances. In the last few days left to him in New York Selwyn worked further to get agreement with Fawzi. After Pineau's departure success seemed even closer. Nevertheless Selwyn warned the Egypt Committee against exaggerated optimism (rightly as it transpired) and said that there were still wide gaps between Egypt and Great Britain. He wrote down his recollections of those days:

> We did agree upon six principles, but there was no agreement about how to implement them – in fact I doubt really whether on one of them the Egyptian government did really accept the idea that the Canal should be insulated from the politics of any one country – I don't think Colonel Nasser really accepted that ever. But the initiative was left with the Egyptians – that they were to start negotiations again when they were ready and they had proposals for implementing these principles, and of course they made no suggestion for re-convening the talks after the Israeli attack had taken place.[68]

During Selwyn's absence in New York the Conservative Party Conference had taken place at Llandudno (11–13 October) and both Eden and Anthony Nutting, deputising for Lord Salisbury, had made belligerent speeches, so much so that on 15 October the Egyptian Foreign Minister, Dr Fawzi, complained about Eden's saying that although force was the last resort it 'cannot be excluded'.[69] Had Fawzi known what was also happening on 13 October elsewhere he might have complained even more. For on that day Sir Gladwyn Jebb reported to Sir Ivone Kirkpatrick evidence that up to 95 French Mystères aircraft had recently been sent to Israel, perhaps with French pilots, information which he included in a letter of the same date to Anthony Nutting, who was acting for Selwyn in his absence.

Events now moved swiftly. Following the Conservative Party Conference Eden was at Chequers where he was visited – in conditions of great secrecy – by the acting French Foreign Minister,

M. Gazier, together with General Maurice Challe, a deputy Chief of Staff of the French Air Force. Despite his wish to accompany Gazier and Challe, the British Ambassador, Sir Gladwyn Jebb, was not invited, but it was explained that the French Ambassador would not be invited either as M. Gazier wanted to convey a message from M. Mollet and to see Eden alone. At this Chequers meeting the French outlined to Eden and Anthony Nutting what became known as The Plan. The Israelis were to be invited to launch an attack on Egypt across the Sinai Peninsula. When most of Sinai had been captured the British and French should then order both the Israelis and the Egyptians to withdraw their troops from the Suez Canal area. The British and French could then send an invasion force to the Canal to separate the combatants and thus safeguard their rights of free navigation. Nutting was horrified by this scenario which was like a bolt from the blue. In the previous three days Eden and Selwyn had been in constant telegraphic communication and it had seemed to Nutting that Eden was accepting the inevitability of a diplomatic solution. (On 14 October, the day of the French visit to Chequers, Eden had sent Selwyn a further message of congratulation on his efforts.)[70] But the French suggestion altered everything. It was at this point that the rug was pulled from underneath Selwyn and all his efforts in New York set to naught. As Jebb was anxious that Eden should be in possession of the evidence regarding the Mystères aircraft before seeing Gazier, he sent him a personal telegram. If anything, this telegram strengthened Eden's resolve to topple Nasser as it showed him the seriousness of French intentions. When Anthony Nutting, dismayed by Eden's willingness to keep this plan on the agenda, attempted a stalling operation (Eden had promised a response to the French plan by the next day) by saying that nothing could be decided while the Foreign Secretary was in New York, Eden promptly telephoned New York to recall Selwyn. With some difficulty (the international operator asked Selwyn of 10 Downing Street, 'Say, is that a hotel?')[71] the two made contact and Selwyn was summarily recalled to London. This was from Selwyn's point of view the most frustrating development. For over a fortnight he had worked unceasingly with Fawzi to frame some basis for a negotiated settlement and was now on the very brink of success with the Six Principles, which he described as 'a good natured preamble to a missing treaty.'[72] Though he had had his differences with Hammarskjöld about exactly what had been decided at the tripartite meetings between Pineau, Fawzi and himself, he was due to meet the Secretary-General again on Monday 15 October and so asked Eden for a day's respite. The Foreign Secretary was told he was required as soon as possible. In the event a compromise was reached whereby Selwyn returned on the overnight flight on Monday 15 October, seeing Hammarskjöld at 10 a.m. New York time, Krishna Menon at 12.30 p.m. and taking off for London at 5 p.m. Before leaving New York Selwyn had entertained Commonwealth Ambassadors and delegates to lunch. 'Fawzi might come back with a practical offer in the near future,' he told them, 'but meanwhile it's all a question of for whom the canal tolls.'[73]

Selwyn arrived at Heathrow at 11.15 a.m. British time on Tuesday 16 October and drove at once to Downing Street to meet Eden. At this stage he knew nothing of the plan. The next few hours – he was to take off with Eden for Paris at 4 p.m. – were to be among the most difficult of his career. Two people sought his ear at once, Nutting and Eden, though for very different reasons. Despite the effects of the overnight flight, Selwyn arrived in Downing Street in ebullient mood. He told Nutting, who met him first, that he had 'clinched it'[74] by getting what he believed to be a reasonable deal with Fawzi over the Six Principles. What Nutting now told him was that such a settlement was no longer on the agenda. Selwyn had believed that the deal was not everything that was wanted, but it was a workable compromise, 'admittedly one under which Nasser would have had to give up a good deal but he would have kept the canal nationalised and received the revenues on terms no more onerous than those on which he after- wards got loans from the World Bank.'[75] Selwyn's mood changed when Nutting brought him up to date with the Challe/Gazier plan. He told Nutting that he was 'absolutely right', and that they must have 'nothing to do with this.'[76]

At this stage, however, Eden moved to isolate Selwyn from Nutting's influence. Selwyn joined other Ministers in the Cabinet room, where 'a general discussion of a rather indeterminate nature'[77] was taking place, indeterminate because of Selwyn's absence. If Eden was to carry The Plan then he would need to carry Selwyn with him. Nothing was decided at the meeting, at the end of which Eden asked Selwyn to remain behind. Over lunch Eden gave Selwyn the outlines of the French proposals. The two politicians had worked closely together now for over ten years and Eden knew his man. Though Selwyn was initially hostile to The Plan and told Eden so, all Eden's persuasiveness was brought to bear on his jet-lagged Foreign Secre- tary. Although Nutting contacted Selwyn on the telephone before he left for Paris with Eden, it was too late. 'Eden had clearly used the lunch to devastating effect', Nutting later wrote, 'for Lloyd not only seemed prepared to acquiesce in the French plan, but now took the line that his agreement with Fawzi would never hold.'[78] Nutting was deeply aggrieved by the turn of events. When Hugh Thomas was preparing his book *The Suez Affair*, Nutting told him that Selwyn had been 'brainwashed' by Eden. Hugh Thomas toned this down to read, 'Exhausted after his flight and weeks of incessant work, he was swept along by Eden.'[79] Eden had the political instinct to realise that if he was to make a case for British involvement in the French plan then he would first have to persuade his Foreign Secretary of its viability and this would be best done by isolating him from the one man who was in a position to argue with equal force the opposite case, namely Anthony Nutting. In retrospect, Eden's lunch with Selwyn *à deux* at Number 10 on 16 October was one of the most important pre-emptive strikes of the whole crisis.

Meanwhile in France Maurice Bourgès-Maunoury, the French Defence Minister, was vague and evasive about the Chequers meeting when questioned by Jebb, though he told him at lunch on 16 October that Anthony Nutting was expected in Paris with a reply to M. Gazier's message. Decisions on The Plan were clearly imminent, the urgency of the situation being underlined by the fact that it was not Nutting who came to Paris on 16 October, but Eden with a jet-lagged Selwyn Lloyd.

Eden and Selwyn Lloyd were met at the airport by Jebb and in the car on the way to the Embassy the Ambassador asked Eden if he had received the telegram about the Mystères aircraft. In a rather embarrassed way Eden said that, 'somebody had told him about it'. The matter was never raised again. Jebb then told Eden that further exclusion of the Ambassadors from the talks was a bad precedent. Eden's only reply was, 'It must be à quatre – those are our instructions.' Accompanying the Prime Minister's party was Guy Millard, Eden's private secretary. Before leaving the Embassy for the talks Eden said to Millard, 'Don't forget the piece of paper for M. Mollet.' A sheet of typescript was then placed in the box. After dining with Mollet and Pineau, Eden and Selwyn Lloyd had two hours of private talks as the French had insisted. The Ambassadors and other officials waited in an ante-room, the prevailing feeling at that time being that force would not be used owing to the adverse effect on sterling. But they were wrong. Events were now approaching the moment when, like the launching of some great ocean liner, they became irreversible.

Although Nutting considered Selwyn a 'lost cause' at this stage, the Foreign Secretary continued to express his doubts at, and after this meeting, though Eden was now persuaded that Musketeer Revise (with D-Day fixed for 29 October) was the last opportunity before winter set in of having an invasion at all. The truth was that in the face of French determination to press ahead, Selwyn's views counted for very little. At the talks Selwyn continued to press for a settlement on the basis not of international management but of international control through restrictions on increases in tolls, with disputes being referred to an independent body. Mollet and Pineau both said that such an arrangement would be quite unsatisfactory. The French expressed a trenchant view of Dulles and SCUA. They said that Dulles had double-crossed the British. SCUA was to stop Britain going to the Security Council. After that Dulles had no desire to make SCUA work. The talks then turned to the consequences of an Israeli attack on Egypt. Mollet said that repeated threats had been made by the Egyptians to exterminate the Israelis and the State of Israel. In those circumstances if Israel attacked first there was quite an argument for maintaining it was in self-defence. Eden said that he was worried about the consequences of an Israeli attack on Jordan when Britain would be bound to go to Jordan's help. The idea was then reiterated by Mollet that it might be possible for the Western Powers to intervene to stop fighting in the area of the Canal. It was thought improbable that the United States would be willing to join such action, particularly during the course of an election campaign. Mollet then asked directly that if there were hostilities in the area of the Canal, would Great Britain intervene? Although more worried by the prospect of an attack by Israel on Jordan, Eden affirmed that they would.[80]

Selwyn returned to London with Eden on Wednesday 17 October. At the Egypt Committee that afternoon Selwyn made a brief report on the Security Council's discussion of the Suez dispute. He pointed out that after the proceedings in the Security Council had ended Fawzi had remained in New York for further talks with Hammarskjöld.[81] What he did not point out was that Fawzi's influence on future policy was likely to be limited – in truth an accurate description of his own position. Selwyn rightly described 18 October as 'an important day'.[82] Jebb had a meeting at the Foreign Office with Sir Ivone Kirkpatrick in which he protested about the continued exclusion of the Ambassador from the talks and wanted to know what all the secrecy was about. Although Sir Ivone Kirkpatrick personally felt that the Ambassador should be told what was afoot he said that he would have to clear this with the Secretary of State and let Jebb know the result. Selwyn Lloyd was already in receipt of a manuscript letter from Jebb which said that if as Ambassador he continued to be kept in the dark then he would have to consider his position.[83] Further talks that day left Selwyn in no doubt as to the unease felt in certain other quarters. In the waiting lobby outside the Cabinet room that morning Selwyn had buttonholed Rab Butler, a crucial figure in the unfolding internecine Conservative battles and one who, because of illness, had been absent from many recent Cabinets. Butler recorded of their talk before Cabinet, 'Selwyn Lloyd seemed anxious about my own reaction.'[84] This anxiety was not so much about the substance of recent talks but of Selwyn's involvement in them at all. The old insecurities in Selwyn, never far below the surface, were emerging once more. Another dissentient voice was heard by Selwyn when he lunched that day at Brooks's with Walter Monckton, who had been moved (at his own request) from the Ministry of Defence to the less exposed position of Paymaster General. He had told Eden of his wish to resign as early as 24 September and his formal letter confirming this wish was written on 11 October. Ostensibly Monckton's resignation was on grounds of ill health, though this hardly accorded with his retention of Cabinet office as Paymaster General. Selwyn noted caustically that Monckton was 'privy to all the early decisions, including the decision to use force and did not oppose them.'[85] Selwyn and Monckton discussed the morning's developments at Cabinet. Eden had concluded this meeting by saying that the Cabinet should be aware that while Britain continued to seek an agreement of the Suez dispute in pursuance of the Resolution of the Security Council, it was possible that the issue might be brought more rapidly to a head as a result of military action by Israel against Egypt.[86] Selwyn knew that this was an equivocal statement of the position (there are those who think that he should have resigned at this point) but still hoped that the operation of the Canal should be insulated from the politics of any one country.[87] During the afternoon of 18 October telegrams sent by Sir Humphrey Trevelyan, Britain's Ambassador in Cairo, confirmed that Nasser was not going to compromise on that specific point. Sir Pierson Dixon also sent Selwyn telegrams, bringing him up to date on the talks that Fawzi had had with Hammarskjöld, but the time for talks was running out, though Selwyn still hoped for a peaceful settlement.

On Friday 19 October Selwyn had a private meeting with Rab Butler at 1 Carlton Gardens at 9.30 a.m. He brought Butler more fully into the picture regarding the previous 36 hours and the visit to Paris. Both men then adjourned to 10 Downing Street for a day of talks broken only by luncheon (which Selwyn took at Buckingham Palace, a long-standing engagement). At 2.45 when the talks resumed they centred first on the results of the Jordan General Election which were likely to show a clear anti-Western majority, but soon moved to the subject of Selwyn's visit to the Wirral on constituency business over the weekend. Selwyn was due to speak at the half-yearly meeting of the North-Western Area Conservative Council at the Crane Theatre, Liverpool, at 2.30 p.m. on Saturday 20 October. The BBC and representatives of the national Press were to be present, so Eden decided that Selwyn's speech would be a statement of the government's position. Butler's private secretary at the Lord Privy Seal's Office, Ian Bancroft, sent a circular to the private secretaries of all ministers. 'You should be aware that the Foreign Secretary, in a speech at Liverpool tomorrow, 20th October, will deal extensively with the Suez problem and full use should be made of the points he brings out.'[88] Although Selwyn was going to the Wirral on party business (apart from the speech in Liverpool he was opening a new Conservative Club extension at Ellesmere Port),[89] he took with him his assistant private secretary, Donald Logan, to handle any official communications which might come in over the weekend. Donald Logan was thus to become, in an entirely fortuitous manner, the central British witness of the events of the next six days. Among Selwyn's secretariat, Denis Laskey and John Graham were both married and, out of consideration for their family commitments, Selwyn tended to take Logan, at that time a bachelor, on weekend Foreign Office visits. A further consideration that weekend was that John Graham's first child was expected at any time – a daughter was born on Sunday 21 October – so he was unavailable. An interesting footnote to the Suez story is that when Selwyn returned to London on that Sunday John Graham asked if he might have the day off on Monday 29 October to fetch his wife home from hospital. The answer *in advance* from Selwyn was, 'Well, it's going to be such a hectic and busy day nobody will miss you.' 29 October was of course the day Israel launched its attack on Egypt.

So it was that Selwyn and Donald Logan caught the 4.55 p.m. train from Euston, arriving in Liverpool at 8.22. They travelled first to 32 Queen's Road, Hoylake, where Selwyn had his Foreign Office scrambler telephone, before going to stay with Selwyn's sister and brother-in-law, Dorice and Howard Shone, at Stanmore in Meols Drive. Also at Stanmore that night was Selwyn's nephew, Patrick Shone, who had put off going to a meeting of the 25 Club in Liverpool as he wanted to see JSBL, as Selwyn was colloquially known in the family. After all the travelling and stress of recent weeks a quiet dinner with family and friends was a welcome tonic for Selwyn. On Saturday 20 October Selwyn had two appointments – the speech to the North-Western Area Conservative Council after lunch and then the 7 p.m. opening of the Conservative Club extension in Westminster Road, Ellesmere Port. But the day was not to work out like that. In the morning Selwyn received a call from Eden on the unscrambled line at Stanmore, a sign not of the routine nature of the call but of its

extreme urgency. As Patrick Shone noted in his diary for that day,
'JSBL had his secretary Donald Logan with him and he seemed to
spend nearly the entire morning on the telephone to Whitehall.'[90]
(On 1 November Donald Logan was to write to Howard Shone about
how they had monopolised the telephone during their recent visit and
letting him know that the Foreign Office would be paying for all the
calls.)[91] Eden had heard that the Israelis were expected in Paris
shortly to discuss plans for the invasion of Egypt and was warning
Selwyn that he would be required to represent Britain at these secret
talks. So with Donald Logan remaining behind at Stanmore (to take
any further messages emanating from Downing Street) Selwyn set off
to fulfil the first of his obligations, the speech to the North-Western
Area Conservative Association, through a Liverpool already filling
up with football traffic. He began by telling his audience (and an
unusually large number of Press reporters) that he wanted to say
something about the proceedings in the Security Council and he gave
a bland, but accurate, account of developments in New York. The
second half of the speech contained the passages to which Ian
Bancroft had directed ministers' attention. 'Our objective is an
effective means of securing that this great international waterway
shall not be under the unrestricted control of one Government. As we
have said from the beginning, that is the principle on which we are not
prepared to compromise.'[92] The speech was Selwyn's, but the words
were those of Anthony Eden and a résumé of the government's
position. Selwyn returned to Stanmore to find that Howard and
Patrick Shone were out on the golf-course so he walked out to
accompany them in over the finishing holes. After tea and a change of
clothes he set off for the Ellesmere Port Conservative Club. A curtain
had been set up on the stage and arrangements made for a platform
party. 'I don't want to be up there,' said Selwyn, 'I want to be down
here with you.' For a couple of hours the problems of Suez were
pushed to the back of his mind. He returned to Stanmore at 9.30 p.m.
where his other brother-in-law, Ronnie Clayton, was waiting to drive
him and Donald Logan back to Liverpool to catch the overnight train
to London. So Selwyn came to what he later described as *The Plan for
which I did not care.*[93]

Selwyn found Eden in a state of some agitation when he called on
him at Chequers on Sunday 21 October. The arrival of the Israelis in
Paris was imminent and Selwyn would have to travel incognito to a
villa at Sèvres in conditions of the utmost secrecy. It was decided that
it would be put out that he had a cold and was indisposed, the irony
being that he actually did have a sinus problem that weekend. As
Donald Logan had been with Selwyn in the Wirral Eden felt that

there would be less chance of covering arrangements being discovered if Logan in fact drove Selwyn to the airport on Monday in his own private car so that no official driver would know that the indisposition story was untrue, or the destination of the Secretary of State. While Donald Logan prepared for the next day's journey at his London home, Eden brought Selwyn up to date with developments over the weekend. 'The Israeli leaders were coming to Paris on the following day', wrote Selwyn later, 'and it was important, the French thought, that we should be represented there as well.'[94] So it came about that the head of the ostensibly pro-Arab Foreign Office was singled out to meet David Ben-Gurion, the Prime Minister of Israel. Selwyn was there to represent Britain, which made him a first-hand witness of what transpired. But the real reason for his mission was a more subtle one. 'Eden's decision to single out Lloyd to meet Ben-Gurion was a move of some shrewdness. For it tied the hitherto hesitant Foreign Secretary closely into the plan just at the point when it was becoming an outright conspiracy', writes Dr David Carlton in his biography of Eden. 'Clearly if Lloyd would do this, there was unlikely to be any sticking point for him. Hence Eden could thereafter count on the loyalty of at least one senior colleague.'[95] Selwyn had not looked so many moves ahead on the chess board, but after the visit to Sèvres he was committed.

Despite his supposed indisposition Selwyn reached the Foreign Office early on the morning of Monday 22 October, wearing as a concession to anonymity a rather old and battered mackintosh. He would have been far less conspicuous in more normal attire. In certain circles the 'old mackintosh' became one of the received legends of the Sèvres expedition, so much so that when Selwyn later arrived that autumn at a dinner at Pamela Berry's in an old coat, his hostess addressed the garment teasingly, 'Mackintosh, mackintosh, where have you been?'[96] In Selwyn's Foreign Office records for that day all his engagements are deleted and a note substituted in Donald Logan's hand, 'A day, marked among other things, by a nearly fatal car accident – for which my driving was not responsible.'[97] In Selwyn's own diary for the day there is but one entry, 'SL's journey'.[98] For a man who was normally so punctilious about keeping written records this entry in itself speaks volumes about his inner feelings. Donald Logan arrived at the Foreign Office at 10 a.m. and with a 'Well, I'm off' to his colleagues in the Private Office drove Selwyn to Hendon airport where an RAF plane was waiting to take the two men to the Villacoublay military airfield outside Paris. On the way to the airport Selwyn put Logan (who knew nothing beyond the fact that they were heading for Villacoublay) in the picture. There were no

papers, no brief. Selwyn stated baldly that they were going to meet
French and Israeli ministers to discuss military action against Egypt.
After a flight made longer by landing difficulties, the two men
eventually reached Villacoublay where they were met by a French
officer who drove them at some speed to their destination, a villa in
the rue Emanuel Girot belonging to the Bonnier de la Chapelles
family, and which had been used by Maurice Bourgès-Maunoury
(now the French Defence Minister) as a Resistance base during the
war. En route to the villa Selwyn's car was nearly hit by a much larger
car emerging across their path from a side road. The first thought of
both Selwyn and Donald Logan was not about their narrow escape
but about the political consequences that would have followed the
revelation of their whereabouts. The two men arrived at the villa in
the early evening, and were thus at Sèvres far longer than has been
appreciated in some accounts.

Selwyn and Donald Logan were met first by the French delegation,
Mollet, Pineau and Bourgès-Maunoury. Also present, in the second
rank of the French hierarchy, but significantly higher than Logan on
the British side, were Abel Thomas of the French Ministry of
Defence, and for a while, General Challe. The Israelis also had a
two-tier delegation, consisting of David Ben-Gurion, General Moshe
Dayan (the Chief of Staff) and Shimon Peres (Director-General of
the Ministry of Defence) with Mordechai Bar-On (head of Dayan's
staff). In the presence of two Prime Ministers, a Foreign Minister and
various military leaders, it could be fairly claimed that Britain was
under-represented. Selwyn accompanied only by Donald Logan, at
that stage a relatively junior official in the Foreign Office, felt
exposed and isolated in a far from welcoming atmosphere. Selwyn
liked to ponder issues (disarmament in the early 1950s, Cyprus later
in the decade), not to give instant judgments and decisions. Sèvres
was palpably going to be a meeting which needed a quick resolution.
At first the French delegation alone met Selwyn and Donald Logan
and brought the British up to date on the discussions that had already
taken place. Pineau said that the Israelis were going to attack Egypt
but only if the British and the French guaranteed air support. Selwyn
said that he did not have the executive authority to give such
guarantees. Only Eden could satisfy them on that point. Selwyn then
went with Donald Logan and the French into a room which contained
a largish dining-room table. 'My first impression was of a roomful of
utterly exhausted people, mostly asleep', wrote Selwyn. 'One young
man* was snoring loudly in an armchair. Ben-Gurion himself looked

---

* This was Mordechai Bar-On.

far from well.'[99] Eleven people gathered round the table and Donald
Logan was surprised to find himself swept up into such a gathering.
Sir John Colville has recorded that Lord Moran, Churchill's doctor,
was under the erroneous impression that he was often present when
history was made, commenting, 'Lord Moran was never present
when history was made, though he was quite often invited to
luncheon afterwards.'[100] Donald Logan, on the other hand, was now
afforded a place at the table itself.

Although Selwyn had now discarded his mackintosh, Bourgès-
Maunoury has gone on record as saying that the Foreign Secretary
was wearing a false moustache.[101] Time dulls the accuracy of recollection. As Selwyn came into the presence of the Israeli delegation, in an
aside to relieve the tension (typical of the kind of staccato humour
that the urbane Foreign Office had found it so hard to accommodate)
Selwyn joked, 'I ought to have had a false moustache.' This remark
was met with embarrassed silence. As the meeting began (the discussions were in English to the relief of the English pair) the true purpose
of the tripartite discussions became clear. Ben-Gurion initially took
the lead and proposed that the three governments should concert
their policies so as to form a grand alliance for the whole Middle East.
As it was only eight years since Britain had abandoned the mandate in
Palestine, and as the Foreign Office had close links with Arab states
strongly opposed to Israel (notably treaty obligations to Jordan),
such a federated approach posed insuperable practical problems.
Selwyn moved the discussions on to a more particular level. He said
that he had come to talk about the actions the three governments
would take in the event of an Israeli attack on Egypt, pointing out that
little more than a week earlier he had been close to an agreement at
the United Nations with Dr Fawzi on the Six Principles. This was
emphatically not what the meeting wanted to hear, but Selwyn
warned that the United Nations would be opposed to any military
action. The Israelis soon made it clear that the question to be settled
was not *if* the British were going to bomb Egyptian airfields, but
when. Although Selwyn pointed out that public opinion in Britain,
certain Commonwealth countries and Scandinavia (information
gleaned at the United Nations) would be opposed to military action,
Ben-Gurion did not hold back. Israeli cities would be vulnerable to
air strikes from Egypt as soon as an Israeli attack was launched. It was
imperative, therefore, that the British should 'take out' the Egyptian
air fields as soon as possible. Forty-eight hours after the initial Israeli
attack was too long a delay. Selwyn pointed out, however, that an
almost immediate strike would undermine any pretence that there
had been no foreknowledge of Israeli intentions. Forty-eight hours,

therefore, was the earliest possible time after the Israeli strike for a plausible attack. Under pressure (particularly from Dayan) Selwyn conceded that a compromise of thirty-six hours might be possible, but only in the event of what would be perceived as a real act of war, not a small-scale raid – but all this was something on which Eden would have to decide.

After an hour there was a tacitly arranged break when the delegations retired to talk privately. Selwyn, who was very embarrassed by what was unfolding, asked Donald Logan (who had recently returned from a posting in Kuwait) what he thought of it all. Logan said that if it was going to happen it was important to get it over quickly, then the Arabs might come to accept it and might be secretly pleased if Nasser was toppled. Selwyn remained worried about the implications of any attack on Jordan as, under treaty obligations, they would have to come to the defence of that country if it were attacked by Israel. The meeting then resumed but soon degenerated into circling around the two issues of principle and timing. Selwyn was more concerned about the principles, the others about the timings, but for Selwyn the whole concept was unpalatable. The talks had reached an impasse. Dinner was then served, the table dominated by an enormous fish from which the various delegates took pieces. Selwyn remained very quiet throughout the meal. Conversation was stilted and awkward. Ben-Gurion discussed with Donald Logan the role of a private secretary. If Eden had been present the conversation would never have taken such a mundane course, but would probably have moved on to painting or literature (anything but The Plan), and it was indicative of the fraught atmosphere that the conversation was not more expansive. The situation was too serious for frivolous talk, but it was not the time for the kind of conversation that did develop. After the fish had been disposed of the talks began again, but merely went over the same ground. Towards midnight Selwyn said he would have to consult Eden and he left with Logan for Villacoublay airport. As Selwyn flew off into the foggy night (his plane was the last to get out) he remembered that two days earlier he had been opening the Conservative Club extension in Ellesmere Port. It seemed a lifetime away.

The next day the newspapers were full, not for once of Suez, but of the Hungarian uprising. For Eden and Selwyn, however, even that tragic event had to take second place. On his return at 2 a.m. Selwyn had telephoned Eden, telling him that Ben-Gurion had been very truculent.[102] He gave a full report to a group of senior ministers (not an official Egypt Committee meeting) at 10 a.m. and then to the

Cabinet at 11. Under Item 6 of this Cabinet Eden recalled that when the Cabinet had last discussed the Suez situation on 18 October, there had been reason to believe that the issue might be brought to a head as a result of military action by Israel against Egypt. Eden, reflecting Selwyn's account of events at Sèvres, then said that it now seemed unlikely that the Israelis would launch a full-scale attack against Egypt. This was not so much deception of the Cabinet as wishful thinking on Selwyn's part, who now said that he would not exclude the possibility that we might be able to reach, by negotiations with the Egyptians, a settlement which would give us the substance of our demand for effective international supervision of the Canal. He did point out, however, that there were three serious objections to a policy of seeking a settlement by negotiation. First, it now seemed clear that the French government would not give their full co-operation in such a policy. Second, it was evident that some relaxation of our military preparations would have to be made and to that extent we should weaken our negotiating position. Finally, Selwyn said that he saw no prospect of reaching such a settlement as would diminish Nasser's influence throughout the Middle East. Eden then warned the Cabinet that grave decisions would have to be taken by the Cabinet in the course of the next few days.[103]

Donald Logan was despatched back to Paris to explain to Pineau that a definite response from the Cabinet would not be possible at this stage. Travel difficulties delayed Logan's arrival at the Quai d'Orsay, by which time Pineau was set to travel to London to see Eden in person. Logan returned with him, glad of the dark at London Airport which allowed him to merge with the official welcoming party, headed by Denis Laskey. Pineau dined with Selwyn at 1 Carlton Gardens at 7.30 p.m. when the conversation of the previous evening was continued. Eden joined the two Foreign Ministers at Carlton Gardens after dinner. Pineau outlined Dayan's plan to Eden, necessarily giving it a more positive slant than Selwyn had done. At this meeting Eden decided to accept it. Selwyn was a bystander in his own home and for the record wrote to Pineau later that night:

> It must be clear, in view of what we said yesterday, that the United Kingdom has not asked the Israeli Government to undertake any action whatever. We merely asked ourselves what our reactions would be in the event that certain events transpire.[104]

There was further discussion about the action to be taken if Israel attacked the Canal Zone. Selwyn recorded, 'It was thought that we might serve notice on the parties to stop and withdraw a certain distance from the Canal and threaten them with military intervention by France and Britain if this was not done.'[105] Further talks at Sèvres were inevitable, but Selwyn was determined that he would never return to that villa. His first absence had been accounted for by the false story of an indisposition. As he had been seen in London on 23 October in an official capacity he could not now claim a second indisposition without arousing undue suspicions. Also he was due to record a broadcast to mark United Nations Day (24 October) at 12.30 p.m. on the morrow and to answer parliamentary questions at 2.30 p.m. After that he was to meet Gladwyn Jebb, the Ambassador in Paris, a follow-up to the fraught events of 16 October when Jebb was excluded from the discussions in Paris. Only the last of these engagements was postponable. The build-up of public commitments, culminating in a farewell function to be given at the Royal Festival Hall by the English Speaking Union for General Al Gruenther (a particular friend of Selwyn from Ministry of Defence days), the retiring Supreme Allied Commander in Europe, had to be attended to. So at this stage Patrick Dean, Assistant Under-Secretary at the Foreign Office, was deputed to represent the British government.

Selwyn's first engagement on 24 October was thus at 10 a.m. with Patrick Dean. Dean had just come from a meeting with Eden at which he had been instructed to go to Paris to represent the Government at further Anglo-French talks in the wake of the first Sèvres meeting on Monday 22 October. The Permanent Under-Secretary, Sir Ivone Kirkpatrick, had reiterated that it was Dean's duty to do as instructed, but that first he should report to the Secretary of State. At this meeting Selwyn gave Dean details of Monday's talks and told him that Donald Logan would be accompanying him. As on the Monday, Logan was to drive a senior figure incognito in his private car to Hendon Airport. When the two officials arrived in Paris Patrick Dean handed Pineau the letter which Selwyn had penned the previous evening, in which Selwyn emphasised that Britain had not asked the Israelis to take pre-emptive action.[106] Later that morning Eden held a Cabinet which Selwyn attended and at which ministers were informed of the results of the consultations held with Pineau the previous evening. From this it was clear that the French preferred that any military action against Egypt should be based on grounds which concerned the United Kingdom as well as France. While the French favoured early military action they were unable to find sufficient reasons for undertaking it at the present time. If it were taken, the first objective would be to obtain control over the Suez Canal by landing an Anglo-French force after a preliminary air bombardment designed to eliminate the Egyptian air force. The second objective would be to secure the downfall of Colonel Nasser's régime in Egypt.

Eden stressed that such measures would have to be quick and effective because of the way it would unite the Arab world in support of Egypt.[107]

Following this Cabinet Selwyn recorded his annual United Nations Day broadcast for the BBC (a legacy of his Minister of State days) and after lunch answered parliamentary questions, none of which touched the substantive issue of the previous 48 hours for the simple reason that the Sèvres meetings were – and for some years were to remain – secret. Nevertheless it was a hurdle that Selwyn was glad to clear. A more difficult meeting awaited him in his room at the House of Commons with Gladwyn Jebb, the understandably aggrieved Ambassador in Paris, in the presence of Sir Ivone Kirkpatrick.

'Kirk tells me that you are very angry with me for keeping you in the dark', began Selwyn. Jebb did not deny this. Selwyn then said that though this would be breaking all his undertakings he was prepared to tell the Ambassador something about what had happened during the secret talks. This information was couched in very general terms, with Selwyn conceding that the talks concerned the Israelis but saying that he did not feel he could enlarge on that. Honour was satisfied and the meeting ended. A short meeting of ministers followed at 4 p.m. in Eden's room at the House of Commons after which Selwyn (paired from 5.30 p.m.) went to the Royal Festival Hall for the English Speaking Union farewell to General Gruenther. While his United Nations Day broadcast was going out at 9.15 p.m. Selwyn was dining with Geoffrey Hardy-Roberts, a rare moment of respite in this fullest of days, for at 11 p.m. Selwyn was at 10 Downing Street (together with other members of the Egypt Committee, plus Lord Mountbatten, the First Sea Lord) to hear Patrick Dean's report on the further Paris talks.

The news that Dean brought horrified Eden. The talks themselves had gone according to plan – there was no longer any arguing about the timing of the bombing – so Logan and Dean presumed that Pineau had now received satisfactory assurances from Eden. The Israelis intended to undertake military action in the region of the Mitla Pass (as well as at Sharm al-Shaikh on the Straits of Tiran) to safeguard passage to the port of Aqaba. A recapitulation of the week's discussions followed, after which the French produced three copies of a plain, typed document (alongside Chamberlain's Munich agreement one of the most celebrated diplomatic papers of the century) summarising the agreement whereby the Israelis would launch their attack on 29 October. Ben-Gurion had pressed for tripartite signature of what became known as the Treaty of Sèvres, though the British were to refer to it correctly as a Protocol, a record of conversation. Dean asked Logan for his advice about signing as he (Dean) had not been present at the earlier meeting. As the document was an accurate summary of what had been discussed Logan felt that as long as it was signed *ad referendum* there could be no objections and that indeed Eden would welcome a precise résumé of the meeting. However, when Dean produced the document for Eden on his return to London it became clear that Eden wanted no written record. He despatched Logan and Dean on an (unsuccessful) mission to Paris to ensure the destruction of the French and the Israeli copy. It was too late. The Israeli copy had been taken by Ben-Gurion. The French copy too had survived and from it Pineau was to publish an abbreviated text of the Protocol of Sèvres in 1976. But copy or no copy, for the British Cabinet the moment of decision had now arrived. The full details of The Plan would be revealed at Cabinet on the morrow, 25 October, ironically St Crispin's Day. Those that outlived that day would indeed remember it, but not as on an earlier occasion with advantages.

At the Cabinet at 10 a.m. on 25 October Eden gave a full outline of what was proposed if Israel launched a full-scale military operation against Egypt. The Prime Minister left no doubt that, 'if one or both governments failed to undertake within twelve hours to comply with these requirements (a cease fire and a 10-mile withdrawal from the Canal Zone), British and French forces would intervene to enforce compliance.' Eden continued, 'We must face the risk that we should be accused of collusion with Israel.' As Foreign Secretary Selwyn backed the line that Eden had taken, almost like a junior barrister summing-up the case made by leading counsel before the jury retired. He said that there 'seemed to be little prospect of any other early opportunity for bringing this issue to a head', which was hardly a rallying call to Agincourt. It was time for the jury to declare. Significantly, Lord Salisbury (the only figure of sufficient seniority to act as a political counter-weight to Eden) was absent through illness. Butler did not demur (had he done so Iain Macleod would have been his ally), neither did Monckton; only Derick Heathcoat Amory (a junior figure as Minister of Agriculture) spoke out on the issue of the effect such a manoeuvre would have on Anglo-American relations and on Britain's standing at the United Nations. After discussion the Cabinet agreed 'in principle' with the course of action outlined by Eden.[108] The Cabinet minutes make it clear that four days before the Israelis attacked Egypt ministers decided upon their course of action and though the details of the Sèvres negotiations were not revealed the substantive matter was placed before Cabinet. The Cabinet, as the minutes show, was not united but such is the doctrine of collective responsibility once the doubts had been aired and this plan adopted it was incumbent upon those in that Cabinet either to work for it or to resign. No resignations ensued. In the next twenty years there was a great deal of hindsight, but that was a bandwagon aboard which Selwyn never climbed, despite the fact that he was in a unique position to blow the gaff on the whole operation (a point made to him by many correspondents on his retirement as Speaker in 1976). Despite his doubts, particularly over the military logistics, he had stood by Eden at the Cabinet of 25 October, and for better or worse he stood by him until Eden died, and indeed until his own death. He had no time for those who were wise after the event, but he respected, even if he disagreed with, those who were wise before the event.

One of his closest parliamentary colleagues – Anthony Nutting – was among that number. On his return from Sèvres Selwyn was saddened to hear that Nutting was intending to resign. He arranged to lunch with Nutting in what was to prove a vain attempt to make him change his mind. At this lunch Nutting told Selwyn that he was resigning for three reasons (the intention was not to be made public until 5 November); first, because what Great Britain intended to do contravened the agreement that he had signed with Nasser in 1954; second, because Britain was acting contrary to the spirit of the Tripartite Declaration, and third, because Britain was breaking the United Nations Charter.[109] Selwyn later recalled his counter arguments. 'When Tony Nutting told me he could not go along with what was happening and must resign, I told him about my views on Ministerial responsibility and loyalty between colleagues. I said that if one became a Minister, one lost some sovereignty – one no longer had the freedom to flounce out if one disagreed with one's colleagues. That was part of the system. It would not work otherwise.'[110] But Nutting was not to be deflected, despite Selwyn's warning that if he resigned he might bring down the government, and with his departure became the Duff Cooper of Suez. His political fate was harder though than that of Duff Cooper after Munich; there was no Ministry of Information or Paris Embassy under a later administration. Nutting resigned not only his post as Minister of State, but also (and Selwyn found this both unnecessary and incomprehensible) his parliamentary seat. But the virulence of the feeling against him in certain quarters of the Conservative Party never abated. With the publication of *No End of a Lesson*, Nutting's account of Suez, in 1967 it flared anew.[111] Those who thought they could involve Selwyn in personal attacks on his former Minister of State had much mistaken their man. Nutting and Selwyn had had a professional disagreement, but there was no animus. Nutting, whose greatest regret in writing *No End of a Lesson* was that it reflected badly on Selwyn, was to send Selwyn one of the most generous of letters after the Night of the Long Knives in 1962, and Selwyn for his part was to speak for Nutting in his campaign at Oldham in the General Election of 1964. Nor was there a personal break with Jakie Astor, one of Selwyn's former Parliamentary Private Secretaries. On 7 December, when the dust had (partially) settled, Jakie Astor wrote to Selwyn; 'A line from a dissenter from H.M.G.'s action to say that I find you have been almost the only Minister who has personally come well out of the confusion.'[112]

The focus of activity (though the Egypt Committee meetings continued unabated)* now shifted to Israel. The Israeli reserves were mobilised and on Sunday 28 October the Israeli Cabinet took the decision to attack Egypt next day. That Sunday evening Gladwyn Jebb had a meeting with Selwyn in his upstairs flat at 1 Carlton Gardens. The Italian Ambassador was present briefly but after his departure Selwyn told Jebb that, 'it was fixed up for tomorrow'. Though he spoke in general terms the Foreign Secretary made it perfectly clear that the Israelis were about to attack Egypt. (Two days earlier Jebb had written to Sir Ivone Kirkpatrick asking for private coded messages to be sent on the Permanent Under-Secretary's responsibility, with such letters to be burned on receipt, so that the Ambassador would not be placed in the position of stressing the importance of continued negotiations while D-day might only be a matter of hours away.) Jebb at once inquired whether the Americans knew about this development. Selwyn admitted that 'they knew absolutely nothing', at which point Jebb indicated surprise and concern. Even the Permanent Under-Secretary, Kirkpatrick, had 'only been brought fully into the picture', within the last few days. As events unfolded Selwyn was to be in receipt of further strongly worded letters from Jebb about his continued exclusion. When Eden declared in the House of Commons on 20 December that he had no foreknowledge of the Israeli offensive,[114] Jebb wrote to Selwyn the next day pointing out that in the light of what he had been told at his two meetings with the Secretary of State on 24 and 28 October either he himself knew something which the Prime Minister did not know, or the Prime Minister was not telling the truth. On 3 January 1957 (in what was to be Eden's last week as Prime Minister) Selwyn wrote rather apologetically to Jebb from the Foreign Office, thanking him for his various letters. 'I should like to talk to you about them some time. When will you next be over here?'[115] There were some things that were never to be committed to paper.

* Selwyn attended four Egypt Committee meetings on 25 and 26 October.[113]

News of the Israeli attack was received during a dinner given at Number 10 for the Norwegian Prime Minister. Interrupted meals in Downing Street feature often in the Suez story, but unlike the interruption on 26 July this one was expected. Eden told the Cabinet of the Israeli invasion on the morning of 30 October, the day Mollet and Pineau arrived in London as a prelude to the Anglo-French ultimatum. As British ships sailed from Malta that day Selwyn wrote in a letter to Patrick Devlin, 'Things get more and more complicated.'[116] The American Ambassador, Winthrop Aldrich, saw Selwyn on the morning of 30 October, but received only cautious replies regarding the British response to the Israeli action. Selwyn said that he would be in a position to tell Aldrich further details at 4.45 p.m. after the British and the French had co-ordinated their action. In the event Selwyn had to be in the House of Commons during the afternoon and Aldrich was seen by Sir Ivone Kirkpatrick. This episode was to have a particularly damaging effect on the British government's relationship with both Eisenhower and Dulles, who heard of the Anglo-French ultimatum at first through press agency reports. Matters were further complicated at this crucial stage since the Washington Embassy was without a British Ambassador at the time, following Sir Roger Makins's return to England to take up his post as Joint Head of the Treasury. Makins's successor, Harold (later Lord) Caccia, was en route to America by sea, so arrangements were in the capable hands of John (later Sir John) Coulson, the British Chargé d'Affaires. In Cabinet at 12.30 p.m. on 31 October the decision to declare the ultimatum was endorsed. Selwyn advised the Cabinet that he would hold in readiness, for immediate issue if the need arose, a warning to the Syrian government that any Egyptian aircraft which were allowed to use Syrian airfields would be liable to be attacked.[117] Later that day Nutting formally resigned and two other Foreign Office ministers came very close to resignation also, being deeply concerned about not having been told what was afoot. As events unfolded many of the younger officials also wanted to resign, but refrained for understandable financial reasons and growing family commitments.[118]

Ever since Eden's statement (at 4.30 p.m. on 30 October) about the Anglo-French ultimatum, the House of Commons had been like a bear garden. The political temperature had risen to heights matched only by the Constitutional Crisis of 1911 and the Munich debates of 1938. The Speaker suspended the House for the first time since 1924, a far cry from Selwyn's own later experience as Speaker. At 9.37 p.m. on 31 October Selwyn, never entirely at ease as a parliamentary performer, rose in the House of Commons to make what in retrospect

was his most controversial public utterance on Suez. Amid rising
hubbub he declared, 'It is quite wrong to state that Israel was incited
to this action by Her Majesty's Government. There was no prior
agreement between us about it.'[119] In Selwyn's own copy of Hansard
(now in the library at Fettes College) this passage is underlined in
pencil. It was a statement made with a lawyer's attention to detail.
The first sentence was completely true. Her Majesty's Government
had never incited Israel to her action. As Pineau recalled after the
Sèvres talks, 'We've brought the British round from complete misunderstanding to partial misunderstanding.'[120] The second sentence
is more ambiguous and the lawyers would have a field day deciding
whether the word 'it' referred to the incitement or the action. But
whatever the ambiguities (and in retrospect as the secrets of Sèvres
were revealed they were considerable) Selwyn's withers were completely unwrung. He took a straightforward, old-fashioned view,
redolent of his Nonconformist upbringing, of what was agreed at
Sèvres. If a government had undertaken secret agreements (however
controversial those agreements might have been) then it was not the
part of a government servant to reveal those agreements. In Selwyn's
book, 'lying through one's teeth' in the House of Commons (as the
critics put it) was, in the circumstances, actually an honourable rather
than a dishonourable action. Not only did he mark this sentence in his
own copy of Hansard, but he continually returned to it in private
conversation and letters. In his diary on 17 January 1968 (after the
first flush of the ten-year 'revelations' by Nutting, Hugh Thomas and
others) Selwyn summed up his attitude to this speech:

> If I thought it would save British lives, protect British property and
> serve British interests to conceal part of the facts from Parliament,
> I would not hesitate for a moment to do so, particularly when active
> hostilities were taking place or there was an inflammatory situ-
> ation. That is my general attitude to this business of a Prime
> Minister or a Foreign Secretary telling all the facts to the House of
> Commons.[121]

Sèvres was to remain secret. Eden's miscalculation was in believing
that this could be so in perpetuity, but he never had cause to complain
that Selwyn was the man to break the British confidences.

On Thursday 1 November, Nasser proclaimed martial law and
general mobilisation in Egypt. Across the Atlantic the United
Nations went into emergency session to debate the situation caused
by the Israeli invasion. Dulles tabled ('with a heavy heart') a resolution urging a cease-fire and the withdrawal of the invading forces,
which provoked a British veto. Some thirty-six hours later Dulles was

removed from the political arena when he was rushed to hospital for an operation for cancer. At the Foreign Office on 1 November Selwyn was informed that French aircraft operating from Israeli airfields had joint forces marking, that the French cruiser *Georges Leygues* had shelled Refah on 31 October in direct support of Israeli operations there and that French naval staff had asked for the British destroyer *Gazelle*, under the command of Admiral Grantham, to proceed through the Enterprise Channel to assist the Israelis after their operation in the desert, a request the British had not granted. A telegram was sent to Mollet from the Foreign Office via Eden. 'Actions of this sort, which cannot possibly remain secret, are extremely embarrassing. I hope you will agree that in our common interest they must be discontinued. Nothing could do more harm to our role as peacemaker than to be identified in this way with one of the two parties.' Anthony Eden added in his own distinctive hand in red ink, 'I am sure that you will share this view.'[122] The telegram was despatched to Mollet at 8.29 p.m. The next day Jebb was able to report from Paris that the French had agreed to discontinue actions of these kinds.

Selwyn attended two Cabinets on Friday 2 November. At the meeting held at 4.30 p.m. (records for which are closed until 2007) Selwyn stated that, 'we could not hope to avoid serious difficulties with the Arab states for more than a very short time longer, certainly not for as long as it would take us to complete an opposed occupation of Egypt.' For his part Eden spoke about the conditions which would need to obtain for a United Nations force to become the peace-keeping force between the combatants.[123] At the meeting at 9.30 p.m. Selwyn reported on the problem of continued export of arms to Israel. He had also been asked by the British Petroleum Company whether they should divert a cargo of aviation spirit, which was at present lying in a port in the South of France consigned to Israel. Such details were soon to be subsumed in the wider political and military developments which were to unfold over the coming weekend. Sunday 4 November was, as Selwyn recalled, 'one of the most dramatic days in the whole period of the Suez crisis'.[124] Not only did he spend virtually the whole day at 10 Downing Street, first of all in private discussions with Eden and then in a succession of Egypt Committees, followed by a full Cabinet at 6.30 p.m. (at which the decision to invade Egypt was finally taken), but these meetings were held against the background noise of the huge anti-Government demonstrations in Trafalgar Square. In his talk with a tired Eden before the first Egypt Committee meeting Selwyn stressed that to call off the operation now would lead to 'dreadful' consequences, an interesting pre-echo of Churchill's later statement that he would never have dared to start the operation but once having started it he would never have dared to have stopped. Following this talk Selwyn rang up Jebb in Paris and asked him to arrange for a further visit by M. Pineau, accompanied by M. Bourgès-Maunoury, and on this occasion with Jebb to travel also. The Egypt Committee met at 12.30 p.m. Selwyn reported that the United States had not pressed to a vote their resolution in the General Assembly of the United Nations, but that resolutions had been put forward by Canada and by a group of Afro-Asian states, the former inviting the Secretary-General to prepare within 48 hours a plan for the constitution of a United Nations force to secure the cessation of hostilities.[125] Selwyn advised that the British government should respond initially to Canada and not to the Afro-Asian bloc. Clearly he would soon have to put the government's case at the United Nations, and he warned his colleagues of the possibility of oil sanctions against Britain and France. At the second Egypt Committee meeting at 3.30 p.m. Selwyn said that the British Ambassador in Baghdad had reported that unless the United Kingdom quickly took some overt action in condemnation of Israeli aggression against Egypt then the British position in Iraq would become untenable. This raised the question of whether further military operations were justified if both Israel and Egypt agreed to a cease-fire. Final decisions were left to the full Cabinet which met at 6.30 p.m. At this crucial Cabinet Eden invited each of his colleagues (eighteen of whom were present) to indicate his view on three possible courses. These were for the initial phase of the Anglo-French action to continue, a suspension of the parachute landings for 24 hours, or a deferment of further military action indefinitely. As the minutes record, 'the preponderant opinion in the Cabinet was in favour of the first course.' Two ministers (Salisbury and Buchan-Hepburn) 'were inclined to favour the third course, but they made it clear that if a majority of the Cabinet favoured a different course, they would support it.' The most clearly dissenting minister was Walter Monckton, the Paymaster General, who 'said that he remained in favour of suspending further military action indefinitely and that if this course did not commend itself to his colleagues he must reserve his position.' So the Cabinet settled on the first course. Selwyn was with the twelve who favoured that course, Butler, Kilmuir and Heathcoat Amory (the most reluctant buccaneer of them all) had favoured the second course. But the collective will of Cabinet was clear.[126]

The events of the next few days belong properly to military history rather than to a biography of the British Foreign Secretary. Against a background of the American presidential election, the British parachute drop took place at first light on 5 November, the day on which Selwyn was given a stormy reception in the House of Commons when making a statement, first on the Russian invasion of Hungary and then on Suez. A sherry party at 10 Downing Street at 6.30 p.m. to mark the Queen's Speech the next day coincided with the announcement of Nutting's resignation, the final incongruous touch on a dreadful day. At this low point Selwyn was encouraged by the receipt of a letter from Sir Gladwyn Jebb in Paris about the attitude of Doug Dillon. 'The American Ambassador is not in the least dismayed or put out by the action which we and the French took without consulting his government', Jebb reported on 5 November. 'Indeed he thinks it was inevitable that we should take some such action, primarily as a result of the lamentable policy pursued by his own Secretary of State.'[127] So the divisions were not only on the British side.

On 6 November Eden called a Cabinet meeting in his room at the House of Commons at the unusually early hour of 9.45 a.m. The presence of Marshal of the Royal Air Force, Sir William Dickson, Chairman of the Chiefs of Staff Committee, indicated to ministers that decisions of a crucial military nature were imminent. The pace of events was now quickening. Eden told ministers that he had been speaking to Pierson Dixon on the telephone from New York and that Dixon had reported a very critical situation in the Assembly. Pierson Dixon had told him that there was a concerted effort being made, with the Americans taking part, to draft a resolution which would impose economic sanctions on the British and the French if they did not agree to an immediate cease-fire. Eden said that he was convinced that some such resolution would be agreed and would be put to the vote later that day. Such was the strength of the emotions aroused that Dixon felt it would be carried by a near unanimous vote. As the United Kingdom representative Dixon had asked for instructions. This news was a grave shock to ministers and Harold Macmillan, the Chancellor of the Exchequer, who had been told by the American Treasury Secretary, George Humphrey, that no more economic assistance would be forthcoming until after a cease-fire, said that this was a very serious development because if the United States voted for the resolution they would be bound to honour it and consequences would have a critical effect on Britain's ability to weather our economic difficulties. With the British forces in possession of Port Said and having advanced twenty-three miles to El Cap, a cease-fire was announced for 5 p.m. The Suez expedition had been brought to a halt within twenty-four hours of its launch and in the most humiliating circumstances. That night there was a dinner to mark the State Opening of Parliament. Selwyn absented himself.[128]

The final phase of the Suez crisis saw the centre of attention turning increasingly to the United Nations. The political ramifications of a blocked canal, an invaded Egypt and a United Nations peace force would occupy Selwyn for the rest of 1956. In the new administration from January 1957 he would have a prominent part to play in the process of rebuilding the relationship between Britain and America. The General Assembly passed a resolution on 7 November calling for the withdrawal of the Anglo-French forces and those of the invading Israelis. At the Egypt Committee held at 10 Downing Street at 3 p.m. that day Selwyn said that he had discussed the situation by telephone with Sir Pierson Dixon in New York. Selwyn had told Dixon that in a situation of considerable complexity with several available alternative courses of action he should make it clear that Britain was not prepared to withdraw the Anglo-French force until it could be succeeded by an international force which Britain accepted as competent to fulfil the purposes they had had in view.[129] Before his departure for New York, Selwyn had discussed with Eden a replacement for Nutting and the choice had fallen on Commander Allan Noble, a former parliamentary private secretary to Eden. Noble was to attend the Egypt Committee meetings on Selwyn's behalf. Remembrance Sunday (always an important day for Selwyn) fell in 1956 on 11 November itself, the exact anniversary of the end of the First World War. After attending the service at the Cenotaph, Selwyn flew to New York. 'Arrived safely after quite a good flight', he wrote to Eden once in New York. 'I gather the situation is thawing between the U.S. and ourselves and I shall continue to try to drive into their heads that the Anglo-French forces in Port Said are the only effective bargaining counter for either the United Nations or the Americans with the Egyptians and the Russians.'[130]

The 11th session of the United Nations General Assembly began on Monday 12 November and memories of Selwyn's first visit to the equivalent meeting in Paris in the now far off days of November 1951 came flooding back. Selwyn was to stay in New York until the evening of 27 November. It was a period of disillusionment, culminating in his offer of resignation on return to Britain. After weeks in the divided and over-heated world of Westminster Selwyn now also experienced the hostile atmosphere of the wider political world. He met the various Commonwealth leaders, dining alone with Richard Casey on 12 November. One unexpected and unwelcome development from Selwyn's point of view was Hammarskjöld's visit to Cairo for talks with Nasser. 'The Secretary-General's departure for Cairo is awkward from the point of view of my personal movements', Selwyn wrote to Eden on 14 November. 'I think I ought to be here when he returns because that is when the Assembly is almost certain to take up the Egyptian question again and the clamour for the immediate withdrawal from Port Said will renew itself.'[131] With the departure of Hammarskjöld, who was to be away until Monday 19 November, Selwyn decided to visit Washington, staying with Harold Caccia at the Embassy on 17 and 18 November.[132] He did not hold out much hope of being able to see Eisenhower when forty Foreign Ministers were in the United States. The main motive of his visit was to see Dulles. On 18 November Selwyn went with Harold Caccia and Herbert Hoover, the United States' Assistant Secretary of State, to visit Dulles at the Bethesda Naval Hospital. They were among the first visitors Dulles had been allowed after his operation and they were told by a hospital nurse not to stay longer than twenty minutes. When his visitors came forward into the room Dulles reached out and shook Selwyn's hand, saying, 'Selwyn, when you started, why didn't you go through with it?'[133] As Selwyn wrote in his Suez file, 'To put it mildly I was shattered by Dulles's question. One explanation was that he was trying to be maliciously funny. I do not believe that. I think that it showed that he had already realised what a mess he and the President between them had made of the situation.' Selwyn wondered what the best remark might be in the circumstances and settled for, 'Well, Foster, if you had so much as winked perhaps we might have,' at which Dulles turned away and said, 'Oh, I couldn't possibly have done that.'[134] Both Selwyn and Caccia thought that Dulles was serious in his question. If so, it underlined the depth of misunderstanding between Britain and her American allies.

Selwyn returned to New York on the evening of Sunday 18 November, after a fruitful meeting with Bedell Smith, Under-Secretary of State, whom Selwyn regarded as Britain's true friend in a largely hostile and questioning environment, but Bedell Smith told him that Eisenhower was the only American whose views really counted. The early part of the week was taken up with further talks with Hammarskjöld on the clearance of the Canal before Selwyn made his speech to the General Assembly on Friday 23 November, his most public act of the Suez period – the same day that Eden flew to Jamaica to recuperate at Ian Fleming's remote house, Goldeneye. Selwyn had been informed on 19 November that Eden would be giving up the reins temporarily on medical advice. 'By all means telephone me if you want to', Eden had cabled.[135] But it was clear that the Eden premiership was coming to an end in a welter of recrimination, tears and sadness. The Egypt Committee had been disbanded after forty-six meetings, the last chaired by Butler. Selwyn was now at one remove from the intense jockeying for the succession that was occurring in London.

In his speech (reprinted at some length in his Suez book)[136] Selwyn made the offer on behalf of the British government to withdraw the British forces from Egypt as soon as a United Nations emergency force was ready to take over; in essence the acceptance of an Argentine resolution. In the course of the speech he said that Britain had 'stopped a small war from spreading into a larger war.' This theme was to recur in the next few weeks with increasing frequency until 'putting out the bushfire' became Selwyn's *leitmotiv*. The speech was received with attention and some applause, though there were some delegates who wished to press for a vote. A vitriolic attack by Krishna Menon[137] was largely counter-productive, but on an amendment of Paul-Henri Spaak, 23 voted in favour, 37 against with 18 abstentions. An unamended resolution was carried by 63 votes to 5.[138] On the evening of 27 November Selwyn flew home to join his increasingly beleaguered colleagues. He was now ready to step down.

At the Cabinet meeting held at Number 10 on Wednesday 28 November at 4.30 p.m. Rab Butler, who was presiding, welcomed Selwyn back from New York. Selwyn reported that the atmosphere in the United Nations had shown some improvement in the last few days, but it was clear that the Assembly would continue to debate the Suez situation at intervals and would maintain their pressure for the early withdrawal of the Anglo-French forces. He pointed out that economic considerations were now even more important than political ones. Britain could probably sustain her position in the United Nations for three or four weeks, but, far from gaining anything by deferring a withdrawal of the Anglo-French forces (which could be completed within the next fortnight), would thereby risk losing the good will of public opinion.[139] Selwyn then offered his resignation as Foreign Secretary (an offer not recorded in the Cabinet Minutes). Later Lord Hinchingbrooke, one of the Suez group of Conservative MPs, was to say that if Selwyn was a man of honour he should have resigned. This speech, Selwyn recalled, 'wounded me in view of the fact that at the first Cabinet meeting after my return from the United States I had said that I thought the best thing was to have a scapegoat and I was willing to resign. The others all said no, it would break the Government, make things infinitely worse for the party, and implied that it would be a dishonourable act, of gross disloyalty to those who had backed the policy which I as Foreign Secretary had advocated. In

"... But, above all, Heaven preserve me from my friends!"

this they were right, and I knew that it was out of the question for me to defect then.'[140]

The next day, Thursday 29 November, Selwyn made a general statement on the Middle East in the House at 3.30 p.m. (with no hints of the terrible storms that were to break when he next spoke on the following Monday) and addressed the 1922 Committee of Conservative backbenchers at 6, recapitulating on his time at the United Nations. He did not speak on the withdrawal which was now widely seen as inevitable. That statement was to come on 3 December. This last act of the Suez drama was personally the most painful time of all for Selwyn. Eden was still in Jamaica and, as many of the cartoons of the time show, Selwyn was thrown to the political lions. In the absence of Eden it would have been more politically astute of Butler to have made the statement of withdrawal himself as the acting head of the government, but it was decided otherwise, a miscalculation by Butler in the light of the later events. At the Cabinet at 11.30 a.m. on

Monday 3 December the draft statement on withdrawal was considered paragraph by paragraph. Even then there were loose ends
and ambiguities. Regarding the resumption of negotiations on the
future administration of the Canal, Selwyn said that it had not yet
been possible to reach agreement on the question whether the
statement should include mention of the principles set out in the
18-power resolution adopted by the London conference in August
and so it was decided that this matter must be left to the discretion of
the Foreign Secretary.[141] Selwyn was going to have to face the music
alone.

Selwyn made his statement on the withdrawal of the British troops
to a deeply hostile, divided and raucous house. One of the memories
of that afternoon is of Rab Butler, Selwyn and Harold Macmillan
coming along a corridor in the House of Commons, the two taller men
flanking Selwyn, almost as though he was a prisoner in handcuffs
being taken to the cells, though it was intended as a gesture of
solidarity.[142] Selwyn announced that the British forces would be
withdrawn, the precise timetable to be decided by General Keightley
and the Commander of the United Nations Emergency Force, Lt-
Gen. Burns. Whether as a desire that mutton should be dressed as
lamb, or by political miscalculation after the months of strain, Selwyn
unwisely elaborated on this statement claiming that the success of the
invasion had been such that they could now withdraw safely. Even
Nye Bevan, who was later to describe Selwyn as the monkey to
Eden's organ grinder, seemed lost for words, 'I feel I would be a bully
if I proceeded further.' Nye Bevan was a great destructive orator but
he needed counter invective to be at his best and he found Selwyn a
curiously flaccid and unsatisfying opponent. Although Bevan heaped
public humiliation on Selwyn for 'sounding the bugle of advance to
cover his retreat', deeper criticism within the Conservative ranks was
directed at Butler for not making the statement. This omission was
arguably the final straw that decided the succession in January.[143]

That night Selwyn dined with Michael Astor. Looking back over
the whole sorry year he admitted that it was a mistake to have been so
charmed by Eden. The Cabinet and the Commons waited on developments from Jamaica. Selwyn opened the Suez debate on 5
December. After the chastening experience of 3 December he kept
himself low in the water. The return of the red-blooded, almost
nineteenth-century fervour, the continual baying, had left him
bruised, but unlike some he was to weather the storm. Bevan was
again his most perceptive critic, picking at once on the weakest part of
the argument. 'The Right Hon. and learned gentleman gave the
House the impression that at no time had he ever warned Israel

against attacking Egypt.'[144] That evening Selwyn spoke to the
Foreign Affairs Committee of the Conservative Party. He admitted
that what had been done was 'not a pleasant decision'. He said that he
would not have associated himself with it if he had thought a
practicable alternative existed. 'The question is would you rather see
the end of the sterling area than this? The moral is that we have got to
organise ourselves economically.'[145] The post mortems were already
beginning. Edward Boyle, who had resigned as Economic Secretary
to the Treasury on 6 November, was quite clear as to what had
happened, as the Labour MP Patrick Gordon Walker recorded in his
diary:

> I met Boyle in New Palace Yard after the debate on Suez about a
> week ago. He told me that the reasons for the abandonment of the
> operation were:
>   1 Macmillan's realization of the run on gold.
>   2 Selwyn Lloyd's realization that the Baghdad Pact was break-
>   ing up.
>   <u>These two changed sides together.</u>
>   3 A united Cabinet (with Heathcoat Amory & Monckton) had
>   only been achieved by accepting the operation alone to restore
>   the peace. The Israeli acceptance of the cease-fire – & thus
>   the achievement of the ostensible object of separating the
>   combatants – made it impossible to go on with a united
>   Cabinet.[146]

At this low point in Selwyn's political career matters were also
coming to a head regarding his marriage. He wrote privately to his
solicitor, regarding the forthcoming divorce case, on 8 December: 'I
have to go to Paris tomorrow and will not be back till the end of the
week. I plan to go up North for a week about the 21st of December. I
think that we should plan to meet again either between the 17th and
21st or after the 28th December.'[147] Selwyn again offered resignation, to take effect at an appropriate time prior to the public
divorce proceedings, lest it be a political embarrassment, but this was
not considered necessary by his colleagues.

Eden returned from Jamaica, ostensibly restored to health, on 14
December, but to a political situation which was far from healthy. On
20 December he gave to the Commons his denial of any foreknowledge of the Israeli intention to attack Egypt. Selwyn in his turn now
succumbed to the physical pressures of the past few months and was
intermittently absent in the last fortnight of 1956, though he was able
to attend Joanna's nativity play on 18 December. He spent Christmas
quietly in the Wirral. On 27 December the clearance operation by the

United Nations forces began, but it was to be months before the Canal was operational again.

In the first week of 1957 Eisenhower adumbrated what became known as the 'Eisenhower Doctrine', a response to what he regarded as growing Soviet influence in the Middle East, to many British eyes a question of too little, too late, recommending as it did the use of American forces to defend any Middle Eastern state threatened by any state controlled by international Communism. It was to be a time of general rebuilding. In Cabinet on 8 January Selwyn said that the time was now ripe for a fresh initiative towards a closer association between the United Kingdom and Europe, a major theme of the incoming administration. Wednesday 9 January began with no indications of the drama that would be unfolding before the end of the day, though it was known that Eden had been staying overnight at Sandringham. As the Cabinet assembled at 5 p.m. only Salisbury, Kilmuir, Macmillan and Butler knew that Eden was about to resign. Selwyn may have been Foreign Secretary and Eden's closest political ally in the previous six months, but he was given no advance warning of his chief's departure. Eden read a prepared statement to the Cabinet, saying that he was sorry to have to inform his colleagues that he was unable to continue in office. His resignation would carry with it the resignation of the whole administration and ministers should regard their offices as at the disposal of his successor.[148] A chapter in British political history had come to an end.

The shadow of Suez lay long over the rest of Selwyn's life and he never succeeded in exorcising its spirit. When he died in May 1978 nearly all the newspaper headlines referred to the 'Man of Suez'.[149] His political epitaph was 'The Man who survived Suez'. He had lived with this for twenty-two years and although he would have preferred to have been remembered for his Minority Report on the Beveridge Committee inquiry into broadcasting and (later) for the founding of the National Economic Development Council,* this was not the way of the political world.

Selwyn's response to Suez can be considered under three headings. First, he amassed as much documentary evidence as he could against the time when he would set his own account on the record. Second, he became the source of information himself for responsible historians. Finally, he published *Suez 1956*, his account of the crisis, which appeared in the summer of 1978.

After Eden's resignation in January 1957 his fair-weather friends

---

* See Chapter 11.

melted away but Selwyn was not among that number. Eden wrote the first of many air mail letters to Selwyn from the RMS *Rangitata* (on which he was sailing to New Zealand) on 27 January, in which he thanked Selwyn for 'all your kindnesses in these last and very melancholy days.' Eden continued:

> As you can imagine I have thought much about them here, & though I wish more & more that some other course had been possible, on all personal & political grounds (selfishly of course), I just cannot pretend to myself that I think it was . . . I have only one prayer, that you will support the Israelis in their demand for freedom of passage for all commerce in the gulf of Aqaba . . . Meanwhile this incredible US administration seems to think the only 2 powers in the world worth courting are Nasser & Ibn Saud.* I cannot help thinking the American people will have had enough of this before long. Provided always we stand by what we have done & maintain that it was right. I feel far more strongly about this than I did in 1938. It was just† an open question then, I thought, whether appeasement might succeed. Now it cannot possibly . . . Sorry for all this lecture, but when I heard after sailing that Boyle was back still proclaiming that he was right to resign, I did not like it. Forgive & keep to yourself please.
>
> Clarissa & I had a small bet anonymously on a horse in one of our ship's games. I couldn't resist it. 'No policy' by Eisenhower out of Dulles, & it won! I swear I had nothing to do with the christening – or anything else.[150]

When Eden returned to Wiltshire and an uncertain financial retirement he often invited Selwyn over, first to Broadchalke and later to Alvediston (when Joanna was at Sherborne Girls' School in the 1960s Selwyn took to inviting himself for lunch in Wiltshire on the way down and was always welcomed with open arms) to discuss details of his own volume of memoirs, *Full Circle*, and he later reciprocated when Selwyn was preparing his own account of 1956. Eden helped Selwyn in other ways over the garnering of information. For instance, on 24 April 1967 Selwyn wrote to Kathleen Hill, Churchill's former secretary and then the Curator at Chequers:

> This is to make a very private request to you with the authority of Lord Avon.‡ Could you let me have a list of the people who came as guests to Chequers during the month of October, 1956. I assume

---

* King of Saudi Arabia.
† The word 'just' was added as an afterthought in the letter.
‡ The title Eden took on retirement.

the Visitors' Book for that period is still intact. I wonder whether you have any other private record.

The reply confirmed what Selwyn was looking for, namely that Albert Gazier visited Chequers on Sunday 14 October. 'The signature is indecipherable', wrote Mrs Hill, 'but may be that of a foreign lady who came to tea with Monsieur Gazier.'[151] This signature was not that of a foreign lady, but was the clumsily deleted signature of General Challe. As Lord Wilson of Rievaulx wrote in his memoirs, *The Making of a Prime Minister*:

> On the critical Sunday the guests were listed, but strangely a civil servant's name was included, contrary to the usual practice. It seemed to me that a name had been scratched out by a sharp instrument, such as a razor blade, and the official's name written in over it.[152]

Further examination by Harold Wilson with a magnifying glass in the Long Gallery revealed that this was in fact the case and that the original name was that of General Challe. All such information Selwyn filed away, from correspondence, from conversation with Eden and other colleagues (particularly Alan Lennox-Boyd, Colonial Secretary at the time of Suez) and as the book took shape from his own papers in the Foreign Office, to which he was allowed privileged access. As late as 18 June 1977 he had a meeting with Sir William Dickson, who had attended many of the crucial Cabinets, and who told Selwyn that the Chiefs of Staff knew that the United States had broken the French codes and knew of all the military operations that were planned.[153] Even Selwyn found in his researches that Suez was a jig-saw for which there were always more pieces.

The second area in which Selwyn contributed to the post-Suez story was in the help he gave to historians. This process was anticipated in two meetings Selwyn had with Eden in Wiltshire, the first on 30 May 1958 and the second on 11 September 1966. Selwyn's meeting with Eden at Broadchalke in May 1958 was a very relaxed occasion, Selwyn in benign mood and glad to talk over old times with his former chief. The *Daily Express* got wind of the meeting and snapped Eden, in casual clothes, and Selwyn in smart double breasted suit, striding through the Wiltshire lanes. During their talk Eden told Selwyn that he thought that the British case over Suez was largely going by default, something he intended to deal with in the volume of memoirs he was then researching. Both of them agreed that they should talk to historians on a discreet and anonymous basis so as to disseminate information on the crisis for the record. Eden promised Selwyn that when he had written his book he would show it to Selwyn and Harold Macmillan (a significant pairing) and did not think that Selwyn would have anything to complain about in it. He told Selwyn, for instance, that he had given him full credit for his efforts to prevent him agreeing to the Users' Association, an error Eden deeply regretted.[154]

Selwyn then brought up the question of his own resignation, which had first been offered on 28 November, while Rab Butler was acting head of government and Anthony Eden had been in Jamaica. 'I told him that I thought we would all have been in a much stronger position if I had been allowed to carry out my intention to resign at the end of November 1956. I came back from New York having failed to persuade the Americans to do a deal over our withdrawal from Port Said. Eden said that he thought that was the moment when we all should have resigned. Unfortunately, he had been ill. He added that he himself had thought that a more appropriate moment for my resignation would have been after Bermuda when we had apparently handed over to the United States authority to settle with the Egyptians on the best terms possible for the reopening of the Canal. Finally he returned to the question of Suez and the public presentation of the rightness of our case. He begged me to impress upon our colleagues that they under-estimated the degree of popular support for our action and the extent to which the public now realised that we had been right. Nasser had been saved by the Americans after Suez. The next thing had been the expropriation by the Indonesians of the Dutch; the Yemen was next on the list, then had come the Lebanon and so it would go on. It all stemmed from condoning the original illegality of the Egyptians in nationalizing the Canal.'[155]

Following this 1958 meeting with Eden Selwyn began to collate material in his *Suezana* file. From this he refreshed his memory before speaking to historians. One of the first to benefit was Terence Robertson, author of *Crisis: The Inside Story of the Suez Conspiracy*, published in 1965. The following summer – the tenth anniversary of Suez – saw a renewal of interest in the crisis. All the old controversies were raised by the proposal to hold a debate in Parliament. Eden stated publicly that such a debate would serve no useful purpose and would merely revive a controversy upon which the country was deeply divided. There were other developments also. Nutting was known to be preparing his account (published as *No End of a Lesson* in 1967) and Macmillan's multi-volume memoirs were now nearing the mid 1950s. Although *Riding the Storm*, Macmillan's account of 1956–9, was not to be published until 1971, Selwyn felt that he should have another meeting with Eden about the requests for interviews which were still coming in. The most significant of these came in a

letter of 18 July 1966 from Hugh Thomas, Professor of History at
Reading University, who was researching a series of articles at the
instigation of the *Sunday Times*. (These articles were to be the basis
of *The Suez Affair*, first published in 1967). Selwyn had his first
meeting with Thomas on 2 August 1966, his final one on 5 February
1967. He was surprisingly frank, even ebullient during these occasional meetings, emphasising that Eden was not the autocratic figure
he was commonly supposed to be. Selwyn commented in detail on
Thomas's drafts and *Sunday Times* articles and in a constructive
manner. Of Eden he wrote:

> He did a greal deal of consulting, certainly of his senior colleagues.
> If, for example, Butler disagreed at any phase, he had plenty of
> chance of saying so. In the second place, I don't think that you
> bring out sufficiently clearly that our primary objective throughout
> was a peaceful settlement, admittedly one under which Nasser
> would have had to give up a good deal but he would have kept the
> canal nationalised and received the revenues on terms no more
> onerous than those on which he afterwards got loans from the
> World Bank. I get the impression from your article that from the
> 26th of July we were all longing to have a physical smack at Nasser.
> That really is not true. Eden, Head and I had had too much trouble
> over the Suez base to want to go back to a physical presence in
> Egypt other than that agreed under the 1954 agreement. This
> applied to the August Conference, the acceptance of SCUA, and
> to the final reference of the Security Council. If a peaceful settle-
> ment was not possible, then the use of force would be justified.[156]

Following the first of these meetings with Hugh Thomas, Selwyn
wrote to Eden on 17 August 1966 to set out the agenda for their talk
about the action they should take if there was a debate when
Parliament resumed:

> The matters which I suggested we ought to be thinking about are:
>   i if there is a debate, should it be preceded by a statement from
>   you? If so, what should you say?
> ii should I speak and if so, what should I say? What should be
>   the attitude of the Opposition Front bench?
> iii what should our attitude be to an enquiry (a) in the debate (b)
>   if the Government sets one up?
> There is Nutting's book to be considered and Harold
> Macmillan's.[157]

Selwyn was not entirely reassured by this second 'summit' with
Eden, feeling that with Eden now in the Lords, he would have to bear

the brunt of any parliamentary debate in the Commons. He returned to this question at his next meeting with Hugh Thomas, asking him for his advice on what attitude he should adopt if (as seemed likely) there was a debate on Suez when Parliament reassembled. Hugh Thomas managed to allay some of Selwyn's fears. (The Labour MP Richard Crossman, for instance, had told Hugh Thomas that impeachment, or some such process, would never wash, because everyone liked Selwyn Lloyd.) In a letter of 20 September he gave his considered advice:

I think that whatever you do you should not forget that sooner or later Nutting's book will appear and that eventually the period will be dealt with in other memoirs . . . There might be more in the idea of an inquiry on the model of the Gallipoli expedition than originally met your eye; as you pointed out, that inquiry was limited to military matters (a fact that Michael Foot has apparently forgotten) . . . On the other hand you could surely use this opportunity to make a very long speech, carefully checked with your ex-colleagues such as Lord Avon and Harold Macmillan for facts, which could give a full and complete account of the origins and development of the crisis, facing all the accusations and doubtless admitting some mistakes and errors of judgment (though attributing these to the pressures under which you were working) and making a broad and generous appeal for public sympathy and magnanimity. It would be a great parliamentary occasion in the course of which you could redress the balance of evidence hitherto dominated by *ex parte* accounts by Israelis and Frenchmen . . . you told me that the truth lay halfway between Eden's speech of 20 December 1956 (no foreknowledge but suspicions) and Pineau (a treaty); declaration of intent, in fact.[158]

As there was no debate Selwyn had no immediate opportunity to follow this advice. A speech on the lines suggested by Hugh Thomas would indeed have been 'a great parliamentary occasion', outstripping in importance even such great defensive speeches as that made by Lloyd George in the Maurice Debate on 8 May 1918. But it was not to be. 'I do not think I am the person to make the sort of statement you envisage yet', Selwyn wrote. 'Nor would it be easy to draft!!'[159] When Hugh Thomas began his researches he did so with no sympathy for the Eden-Lloyd actions; by the time he had finished what was one of the most skilful early reconstructions of Suez (which was reprinted substantially unchanged for the 30th anniversary) he had far greater empathy for Selwyn and his dilemmas. Selwyn stressed that there were times in politics when issues did not fall into clear divisions of black and white; Sèvres, he said, was the prime example in his career. Their final meeting on 5 February 1967 before the book was 'put to bed' was a relaxed social occasion over lunch at Selwyn's Oxfordshire home for Hugh Thomas and his wife (Gladwyn Jebb's daughter). Selwyn raised no objections to any of the criticisms implicit in Hugh Thomas's account, writing in his teasing manner afterwards, 'I am bound to say that there is still a great deal in your narrative and your conclusion with which I profoundly disagree. Nevertheless I believe that you have tried to be fair and to discount your own prejudices – as you are a dangerous leftist, so I am told, that is saying a great deal!!'[160]

In the same year that Hugh Thomas published *The Suez Affair*, Nutting's *No End of a Lesson* also appeared. Although 11 years separated the publication of Nutting's book from Selwyn's *Suez 1956*, it was the appearance of *No End of a Lesson* that ensured that one day Selwyn would put his record before the public. Selwyn never fell into the trap of regarding Nutting's book as being a bad case of sour grapes. 'As a result of it', he wrote in his Suez file, 'we have to face a number of important issues. I will try to set them out and deal with them.' This process was in essence the first structural draft of *Suez 1956*. The most important of these issues was the extent to which the Foreign Secretary should be expected to make a full disclosure to the House of all that is going on in his department. (The clear parallel, which Selwyn did not draw, was Stafford Cripps's denial of the intent to devalue before devaluation in September 1949.) 'I believe it to be quite impossible. Sir Edward Grey certainly did not – Mr Ernest Bevin certainly did not.' The Foreign Secretary was the Minister, 'to whom the Secret Service reports. He discusses these matters only with the Prime Minister of the day. He has also to consider the effect of what he says upon British lives and interests overseas. Of course this raises difficulties for the Foreign Secretary of the day – he cannot approve or deny allegation. Mr Nutting has not accused me of telling an untruth to the House of Commons – but of deceiving it by suppressing the full story. Whatever I said to the House was not said in a personal capacity – it was said as an act of State, with the authority of the Prime Minister of the day. I would not have had the slightest hesitation in concealing the truth from the House of Commons if I thought it was in the national interest.' If it was secret who was he to divulge it? 'On October 31st British troops were already in action. There were many British troops scattered throughout the Middle East, and valuable British property. In December the process of withdrawal was not complete.' As a result he was unrepentant about his role. 'I have no sense of guilt about the events of 1956.

Whatever was done then, was done in what was genuinely believed to be the national interest.'[161]

After twenty years of reflection Selwyn began work in earnest on *Suez 1956* after he had retired from the Speakership on 3 February 1976. It was his main retirement occupation. Selwyn came to authorship late, publishing his book on the Speakership in 1976, but he never lived to see his Suez book in print. Although *Suez 1956* was the first 'official' admission from the British side that Sèvres had ever taken place, after the publication of the memoirs of Dayan and Pineau (both of which had appeared in 1976), it confirmed rather than revealed. It received a muted press. 'He has done his best at the very end of his life to justify British policy', wrote Humphrey Trevelyan in his review in *The Times*, 'but I fear that he does not convince.'[162] This was a not untypical reaction. In private the Suez critics were even harsher. 'I thought his published Suez apologia pathetic,' wrote Nigel Nicolson, one of the most outspoken of them.[163] Yet it was a book Selwyn felt he had to write, almost as a form of personal therapy. On 11 October 1977 he wrote to Alan Lennox-Boyd, 'I feel that I *must* write the book. Our story has not been told, and I have a lot of good stuff about Nasser and his ambitions up to 26th July, but the tricky bit is obviously October 16–29.'[164] 'Collusion' loomed large too in the extensive correspondence he had with Lord Home about the book, Selwyn writing on 6 December 1977, 'I suppose that at sometime I must say something about collusion – collusion implies something dishonourable and we were all honourable men!'[165] He consulted widely during his researches, receiving much help from Antony Head, who had been Minister of Defence during the latter stages of the crisis. The Chiefs of Staff were unfailingly helpful. Selwyn was even advised by one senior official that although there was still an embargo on Suez intelligence reports he could consult *The Aeroplane* of 9 November 1956, which gave an accurate estimate of RAF strength.[166] Sir William Dickson gave him advice over General Keightley's despatches, which he said were essential reading. In many respects the military side awakened all his old interest in the profession of arms. The political events of October–December 1956 Selwyn described as 'a gruelling test', both in the living and in the retelling. 'Coupled with private troubles, they took their toll . . . I bitterly resented criticism of the Foreign Office or myself on the ground that we were just messenger boys.'[167]

Even before he had the recollections of former colleagues to hand Selwyn had embarked on months of research among his official papers at the Foreign and Commonwealth Office library. Under the rules governing privileged access, no researcher could be sent in on a minister's behalf, and not even Rab Butler had been allowed access to Selwyn's papers when he had been writing *The Art of the Possible*. At this stage, with the book progressing chapter by chapter with House of Lords paper tagging the top of each pile, Sir Donald Logan had come to help Selwyn one last time. By March 1978 it was apparent to those close to Selwyn that he could no longer concentrate on the job in hand or marshal the voluminous evidence in the right chronological order. As in Foreign Office days papers were scattered around, the two differences being that, unlike the 1950s, the papers were in Selwyn's small Gray's Inn flat and he could no longer pinpoint what he wanted as he checked his first draft against the official records. He could not spend long on the task, ten minutes to a quarter of an hour and he had had enough. The book, though, was nearly finished and he was determined to see it through. Only the final compilation remained. So the papers were taken to Donald Logan's house in Thurloe Street where all was laid out in order on the big dining table and chronology restored. 'It was, I believe, characteristic of Selwyn that he was frequently unable to maintain to the end of a project the very strong concentration which he always gave to it at the beginning', recalled Donald Logan. 'This was not for any lack of will or energy but rather that he liked to handle himself the detail as well as the structure of any work in hand and so the burden became a very personal one. Though the signs of his illness were visible from about the end of 1977 until his death, he maintained his determination that the book should be his work alone. He was often unable at this time to sleep and quickly tired even in the company of his closest friends. It became increasingly difficult for him to keep papers in order and of course the awareness of it made him depressed.'[168]

Despite these difficulties, *Suez 1956*, though an uneven book, was the way Selwyn saw it and a contribution to the historical record. Criticism can be directed not on its historical accuracy – it remains one of the best narratives of the crisis – but on the conclusions drawn from the material. His loyalty to Eden comes out, perhaps overmuch. The weakest part of his book remains his defence of collusion. His argument boils down to the fact that in collusion motive is everything. Since in our contacts with the Israelis our motives were good, then *ergo* there was no collusion. He was franker in his Suez records. 'I have always thought collusion a red herring – I did not mislead the House of Commons – I certainly did not tell them the whole story – but I said that we had not instigated the Israeli attack and there was no agreement between us and the French to do so. That was true. On the other hand for a government not to have discussed with possible friends against probably enemies would be irresponsible.'[169] Privately Selwyn felt that the lesson of Suez in general was that it was 'bedevilled throughout by lack of a clear political aim. This resulted from Conferences, tripartite meetings, U.N. debates.' From Army experience Selwyn felt, 'Military action cannot be successful if it is kept continuously hanging on a string.' He also believed that the military were never told enough 'for them to realise possible need for a quick operation.' But then Selwyn admitted, 'I had always my own doubts as to whether it was desirable to have an outright military success because supposing we had reoccupied Egypt what would we have done with it?'[170] This, rather than collusion, was the central unanswered question.

In the light of Selwyn's book, Douglas Jay felt that it was more a case of 'confusion' than 'collusion'.[171] A fuller defence was given by Robert Blake in an essay on Eden's premiership:

> There must have been a great deal of *suppressio veri* – principally of course in connection with the charge of 'collusion'. No one of sense will regard such falsehoods in a particularly serious light. The motive was the honourable one of averting further trouble in the Middle East, and this was a serious consideration for many years after the event. The conferment in 1971 upon Selwyn Lloyd of the Speakership, the greatest honour which the House of Commons can give, showed that politicians on both sides recognised the dilemma in which he found himself, and did not in retrospect count his conduct against him.[172]

By any standards Suez was a watershed in Britain's post-war history. The actions initiated by Eden had four main aims. First, to secure the Suez Canal. Second and consequentially, to ensure continuity of oil supplies. Third, to shatter Nasser. Fourth, to keep the Russians out of the Middle East. The results of the crisis were that the Suez Canal was blocked, oil supplies were interrupted, Nasser's position was strengthened and the way was left open for Russian intrusion into the Middle East. Had Eden died (as he nearly did) on the operating table in 1953, his historical reputation would have been entirely different. As it is, his name will always be associated with Suez, rather in the manner (and just as disproportionately) that Neville Chamberlain's name is linked with Munich. The main victors, if such a word can be applied, were the Israelis and (paradoxically) the Egyptians. In personal terms Nasser became the acknowledged leader of Arab nationalism. The main losers were the British and the French. Apart from Eden, whose career ended in obloquy, the main British losers were Butler, whose ambiguity was to cost him dear in the forthcoming leadership struggle, and perhaps the greatest loser of all, Anthony Nutting, whose parliamentary career was over just at the moment when it could have expected to have fulfilled all the hopes placed in him by Eden. The main domestic political consequence was that the Conservatives lost the intellectual vote, psychologically far more important than its numerical strength might suggest, for a generation.

The main British beneficiaries in political terms were Macmillan, in that the Suez crisis was a decisive factor in bringing him to Number 10, and, such is the curious turn of fate, Selwyn Lloyd. In the ordinary course of events Eden would have reshuffled his Cabinet in 1958–9, prior to an election in the spring of 1960. Not only is it doubtful whether Selwyn would have been retained at the Foreign Office, but it is even more unlikely that Eden would have given him the Treasury. But for Macmillan, one head on a charger was enough, and he did not wish, nor could he at that stage feel able, to go against that section of the Conservative Party that was pro-Eden on Suez. 'What did you expect?' said Churchill when his doctor, Lord Moran, told him that Selwyn had been retained as Foreign Secretary. 'Lloyd stands for the position of the nation in this dispute.'[173] The events of the latter half of 1956 ensured that whoever's head was on the charger it would not be Selwyn Lloyd's. The great survivor lived on to fight another day.

10

Macmillan's Foreign Secretary

Selwyn Lloyd returned to the Foreign Office in January 1957, said the political wags, through a long arch of raised eyebrows. It was one of many surprises that month, of which the first two were the timing of Eden's resignation and the emergence of Macmillan as the new Premier. Yet Eden's resignation, despite its suddenness on 9 January, had the air of inevitability and it is doubtful if he could have long survived the ferment of discontent that was building within Conservative ranks whatever the advice of his doctors. The general expectation was that Rab Butler would be summoned to the Palace, only Randolph Churchill, tipped off by Beaverbrook, correctly predicting in the *Evening Standard* that the choice would fall on Macmillan. The most inaccurate prophecy came in the *Daily Worker*. Its main story for 10 January ran:

> EDEN QUITS   –   NEW PREMIER TODAY
> Selwyn Lloyd the hottest
> tip
> There was a strong belief among Tory M.Ps. that the Cabinet had agreed on Mr. Selwyn Lloyd in the belief that neither of the other two candidates would be acceptable to the back benchers.[1]

Its only correct supposition was that the Cabinet had been consulted, because on 9 January initial soundings were taken by Lord Kilmuir, the Lord Chancellor, and Lord Salisbury, the Lord President of the Council, as to the succession, which was clearly between Macmillan and Butler. Kilmuir and Salisbury interviewed each member of the Cabinet, apart from the two contenders, in the neighbouring Privy Council Office after Cabinet. Eden, like Bonar Law in May 1923, was in no fit condition to take charge of difficult and potentially controversial soundings, and neither Kilmuir nor Salisbury, by virtue of their membership of the Lords, was a contender for the post. Yet both, like the 4th Marquess of Salisbury (father of the Lord President) and Balfour in 1923, were elder statesmen whose advice might be sought by the Monarch. Salisbury was brusque and to the point. 'Well, which is it,' he asked, 'Wab or Hawold?' Only Buchan-Hepburn declared for Wab. The overwhelming majority favoured Macmillan. Selwyn, however, was not among their number. Alone among the Cabinet he objected to the soundings being taken by two peers (although constitutionally it was not clear how else the Cabinet, whose views mattered, were to be canvassed quickly) and declared no preference. Later he was to tell Rab of this decision, writing in his diary:

> 7 Sep 1962 Rab came to dinner. I told him that at the famous Cabinet vote on the Prime Ministership, I had not voted, as I did not think it was the right way (in fact, I told Salisbury and Kilmuir that I was sure it had to be either Rab or Harold, that I was not prepared to choose between them, but would serve either if asked to – as Suez Foreign Secretary I felt that I was too close to it all to do more.)[2]

Selwyn was not to take such a detached line at the next change of leadership.

The Cabinet was not the only section of the party to be consulted. The Chief Whip, Edward Heath; the Chairman of the Party, Oliver Poole, and the Chairman of the 1922 Committee of Conservative backbenchers, John Morrison (later Lord Margadale), were all asked for soundings. By the morning of 10 January these views had been telephoned to Salisbury and Kilmuir. There was a groundswell of opinion among backbenchers for Macmillan, and there was a small minority who were implacably opposed to Butler at any price. The combination of these two factors secured the decision for Macmillan. Many Conservatives were away that week at the Council of Europe meeting at Strasbourg. They were canvassed also and Julian Amery, Macmillan's son-in-law, was telephoned while at breakfast at Strasbourg that morning and told that the decision was to be for Macmillan, who was then forewarned by Amery that he was going to be asked to form an administration.[3] At 2 p.m. on 10 January Macmillan was received in audience by the Queen and appointed Prime Minister and First Lord of the Treasury. Butler's reaction was endearingly enigmatic. 'After all', he said, 'it's not every man who *nearly* becomes Prime Minister of England.'[4]

In forming his administration, Macmillan faced a situation of some delicacy. Salisbury was at once reappointed Lord President of the

Council and Leader of the House of Lords (though this was not to last in the long term). But the core of the problem centred on Butler's position. In May 1923 when Curzon was passed over in favour of Baldwin he retained his position as Foreign Secretary and was seen (at least in his own eyes) as the acknowledged Number 2. Things were not so clear-cut in January 1957. Butler had served four years at the Treasury from 1951, before a period in the non-departmental job of Lord Privy Seal away from the main stream of the three great offices of state. He now wanted to return to the centre and the Foreign Office was his preferred portfolio. Butler saw Macmillan twice on 10 January, a sign of the difficulty there was in resolving the situation. Selwyn's secretaries watched the comings and goings and were mistakenly convinced that Selwyn's days in King Charles Street were numbered. Macmillan felt that 'one head on a charger should be enough.'[5] Selwyn noted in his diary: 'I had little doubt that he would ask me to stay on when he became Prime Minister. He did so, saying that with Eden gone and Head going, I had to stay at the F.O., otherwise it would seem like a repudiation of the policy'.[6] Macmillan's refusal to give the Foreign Office to Butler was the underlining of that determination. There were also less positive reasons for reappointing Selwyn. Macmillan, as a 'hawk' on Suez, felt there was no telling what uncomfortable beans he might spill if liberated from office, a fundamental misreading of Selwyn's character. With some reluctance Butler became Home Secretary and Leader of the House, in addition to holding the post of Lord Privy Seal, an uneasy alliance of three-fold responsibility.

Selwyn was summoned to Downing Street at 11 a.m. on Friday 11 January. After the prolonged and difficult discussions with Butler, Macmillan now moved more quickly. Simply and without preamble he asked Selwyn if he would stay at the Foreign Office. Selwyn agreed at once. 'You don't look very happy about it', said Macmillan. 'Oh yes', replied Selwyn, 'I'm just composing a face of disappointment for the newspaper reporters outside.' Selwyn's relations with the Press had deteriorated sharply during the latter part of 1956 and he was now preparing to enjoy a joke at their expense. He came out of Number 10 to run the gauntlet of the waiting Press men. 'Will you be remaining as Foreign Secretary?' he was asked. 'Ah, time will tell', he replied. To his great delight successive editions of the evening papers were delivered to the Foreign Office during the day forecasting a change of Foreign Secretary. 'A thoughtful Mr Selwyn Lloyd leaves the Premier's House', ran the story in the *Evening Standard* under a picture which proved the point. 'Few Tories would be now surprised if he lost the Foreign Office.'[7] (Officials at the Foreign Office were

"WHY, SELWYN DIDN'T EVEN BOTHER TO GET UP!"

convinced that Selwyn's demeanour meant they were to get a new master.)

The new Cabinet was announced on Monday 14 January. Peter Thorneycroft moved to the Treasury (an appointment, like Lord Salisbury's, that was to end in resignation), David Eccles succeeding him at the Board of Trade. Selwyn's former departments of Supply and Defence were filled by Aubrey Jones and Duncan Sandys respectively. Lord Hailsham entered the Cabinet as Minister of Education, a Cabinet career that was to span thirty years. Harold Watkinson (Transport and Civil Aviation), Jack Maclay (Scottish Office) and Dr Charles Hill (Chancellor of the Duchy of Lancaster) became Cabinet ministers for the first time. Their careers were not to be so long and, like Selwyn, they were to be victims of the Night of the Long Knives.* Though four senior ministers – Gwilym Lloyd George, Walter Monckton, Patrick Buchan-Hepburn (had his support for Rab leaked?) and James Stuart – went to the Lords, the general impression was of musical chairs rather than wholesale butchery (though Macmillan was to make amends in this latter area). The *Daily Mirror* published a Vicky cartoon on 16 January after the changes had been dissected by the pundits. Harold Macmillan at the piano accompanies Lord Salisbury in Fun and Party Games, as an undignified musical chairs ensues. Selwyn, arms folded, sits impassively on his chair. The caption reads, 'Why, Selwyn didn't even bother to get up!'[8]

Hopes for the new administration were not high, least of all with Macmillan, who warned the Queen that it might not last six weeks, a

---

* See Chapter 12.

fact of which the Queen reminded him when he retired six years later. There was a 'caretaker' feel about the political atmosphere, but to the disappointment of the Labour Opposition the fall-out from Suez was unexpectedly light and even contributed to the Conservative determination to rally round the new leader. Before he left for New Zealand, Eden wrote to Selwyn from Chequers on 16 January:

> I have now underlined on two separate occasions to Harold how very high I rate your work. With every month that passed you clearly had a firmer & more confident grip of all your vexing topics. I hope that you will feel able to stay, because I am sure that time will vindicate our policies & raise your stature to lead the party in the future. I am more sure that we were right than I was in 1938.[9]

So Selwyn embarked on the third great professional relationship of his career. It was the most dramatic of them all.

Selwyn's political bonds with Harold Macmillan were very complex and never as secure as Selwyn believed. Macmillan had experience of worlds foreign to Selwyn – Minister Resident in North Africa, A.D.C. to the Governor General of Canada, Duke's son-in-law (and as Rab Butler was fond of pointing out, crofter's grandson when that seemed more appropriate), family business, quite apart from having a completely different sensibility. Where Macmillan would relax with a Jane Austen, with Selwyn it would be a Georgette Heyer. Macmillan liked to meet intellectual figures, to ruminate over the late-night whisky upon grand designs and lofty concepts, yet underneath the insouciance, particularly when about to embark on an important speech, he was a bag of nerves. As a result Selwyn's steadiness (more unflappable than the much vaunted unflappability of Macmillan)* complemented Macmillan's edginess very well, particularly over the visit to Moscow in February 1959, where (not for the first time) Selwyn played the Bonar Law to Macmillan's Lloyd George. They dovetailed in other ways. Selwyn was a man for the minutiae of policy (as has been seen at Supply and Defence), whereas Macmillan, particularly as Prime Minister, painted with a broader brush. Clearly Selwyn lacked the urbanity of Macmillan, his subtle sense of analogy or metaphor. On 11 January, when Prime Minister for over a day, Macmillan was dining with Sir Oliver Franks and dilating enthusiastically upon his new job. He compared it to the excitement of owning a new car. One turned the key and the engine started smoothly, one tried the brakes and the steering and found they were reliable, the seats were comfortable, one could control

---

* A French interpreter once translated 'unflappability' as 'Macmillanisme'.

everything. Selwyn would never have spoken in this way, rather of the hard work that lay ahead and the heavy responsibilities. For all their friendship over the next five years, Macmillan and Selwyn Lloyd were creatures of different worlds.

Eden and Macmillan were prima donnas in their own distinctive ways; the fact that Selwyn was not rather suited both men. Eden could treat his inferiors with boisterous rudeness, slamming down the telephone, but the next day he would ring back and apologise, and there were few who were not won back. Had Macmillan acted like that (and it was not his style) Selwyn would not have been charmed so easily, even though Eden was at times impossible. But the essential difference in style between the two Prime Ministers was that Macmillan could delegate, whereas Eden could not. Selwyn's versatility was his ability to adapt and be valued under both systems. For the first time, under Macmillan, Selwyn became a 'real' Foreign Secretary. Macmillan deeply regretted his short tenure of the Foreign Office – he was intensely interested in foreign affairs – but gave a much freer hand than Eden did to his Cabinet Ministers, and did not fuss them. He expected ministers to have the ability to know when they should consult him and kept a detached but percipient eye. Under Macmillan, therefore, Selwyn began the third and most fruitful period of his tenure of the Foreign Office. As Selwyn noted, he was Foreign Secretary for '4 years, 7 months, 7 days',[10] and the majority of that period was under Macmillan. 'There was hardly a day when I was not in touch with him', wrote Selwyn. 'If I was overseas, by telegram; if the House was in recess by telephone; more usually by seeing him at No. 10. We would transact whatever Foreign Office business there was. Like most of his predecessors (Baldwin and Attlee were exceptions) he had the urge to communicate personally as frequently as possible with other Heads of Government. He would send us a draft. My officials would examine it with me. Our hair would occasionally stand on end. We would alter the draft. My job was then to convince him that our amendments flowed from his own ideas.'[11]

In personal matters Macmillan showed great kindness towards Selwyn, particularly over the difficult domestic conditions with the impending divorce. This was never more appreciated by Selwyn than over the question of Chequers. Under the Chequers Acts of 1917 and 1921 the Prime Minister can allow a nominated senior Cabinet colleague the use of his official country residence in the event of his not requiring it himself. Macmillan never formally relinquished the right to use the house as, under the various Acts of Parliament, he would not then have been able to claim it back in the course of that Parliament, but he made early arrangements for Selwyn to have free access to guest rooms.[12] So Selwyn became, in effect, the tenant of Chequers from 1957, though Macmillan characteristically under-played his kindness by saying that it was all because 'Lady Dorothy didn't like weeding other people's gardens'.[13] Selwyn loved Chequers, as did his family (not to mention Sambo). He had nursery tea parties in the White Parlour with friends such as P. B. ('Laddy') Lucas and his family. His more formal meetings were held in the Old Drawing Room on the first floor. His own bedroom was 'Number 3' – the Blue Room – where he kept overnight things for five years. However pleasant this privilege was on a domestic level (and Selwyn of course adored the historical associations – was this paved garden where Ramsay Macdonald had posed with Joan, was this the dining room where Churchill had heard of the attack on Pearl Harbour, above all was this the house where Lloyd George had stayed when he was not at Brynawelon?), its political benefits were more doubtful. It conditioned Selwyn into thinking he was more secure than he was. In January 1957 he seemed the great man's favourite, but 'the great man down, you mark his favourite flies.'[14] If anything happened to disturb the sense of political equanimity then more than a job would be at stake. (Selwyn had been planning a family Christmas at Chequers in 1962, but that was before his dismissal.)

When Macmillan came to Chequers from Birch Grove it was almost as though he were the guest in Selwyn's country house – Chequers was a leasehold yet Selwyn mistakenly assumed it was some kind of freehold – and there was an edge to the relationship that Selwyn's antennae did not detect. On the evening of 17 June 1962 Macmillan was sitting in the Great Hall with Selwyn, Iain Macleod (then Chairman of the Party) and Michael Fraser (Director of the Con-servative Research Department), to mull over economic policy and the National Incomes Commission. Selwyn had seemed very tired, but he perked up a bit after dinner. Suddenly he pointed out to the Prime Minister from the depths of an arm chair that Macmillan was now in the unusual, if not unique, position of being in the undiluted presence of three Old Fettesians. It took some little time to get the point across and then Macmillan's response was to grunt in an uninterested manner.*

One of the problems facing Selwyn in the early months of 1957 was that morale in the Foreign Office was at a low ebb. As Selwyn cared for the welfare of the Office and took a great personal interest in

---

* When I spoke to Harold Macmillan about Selwyn's career he asked me where Selwyn 'came from'. When reminded that it was the Wirral, he gestured with his right hand, 'That's up there, isn't it, juts out?' and then after an interminable pause *sotto voce*, 'Funny place to come from.'

people, particularly those who were relatively junior, he worked hard to restore confidence. Unlike Sir John Simon in the 1930s, who golfed on Saturday mornings and then came into the office in the afternoons, Selwyn was considerate of his staff and organised his Saturdays the other way round. This did have one incidental disadvantage for a junior minister at the weekend as lunchtime approached, for then Selwyn would ring up on the inter-connecting telephone and suggest a luncheon followed by a cinema matinée. As Selwyn's taste was for the latest Western this was not a weekend chore that found much favour with the staff and various deflecting ploys were attempted, usually with little success. One Saturday Selwyn was told that he would be accompanied to the cinema only if the choice was Laurence Olivier's recently released film version of Shakespeare's *Richard III*. 'That's all right', said Selwyn, after a moment's reflection, 'there's a battle.'[15] Saturday evenings were a lonely time for Selwyn too, dominated by telegrams and red boxes. A niece remembers staying at 1 Carlton Gardens for the weekend and leaving Selwyn behind in a huge room, surrounded by despatches, as she went out to the theatre with her husband.

His staff found him the kind of Foreign Secretary who was pre-pared to listen. On one occasion an expert laid down the law on Cyprus, telling the story from A to Z. Selwyn did not take umbrage as Eden would have done. He was always glad to hear the views of those who knew what they were talking about and had the requisite background knowledge that would help him. His European coun-terparts – figures like Dr Joseph Luns of Holland and Couve de Murville of France – found him courteous, but tenacious in de-fending the British point of view, with a good grasp of international affairs. He got on well with figures like Archie Ross, Assistant Under-Secretary from 1956, and Michael Wilford, who joined his secretarial team in 1959. There were changes in the parliamentary team also and one area of difficulty remained the House of Commons where Suez acrimonies resurfaced in debates. Selwyn's speeches, particularly when he had to depart from the chosen text, were not always convincing and after the departure of Nutting and the arrival of Douglas Dodds-Parker it was felt that the government point of view needed stronger emphasis. In January 1957 David Ormsby-Gore (later Lord Harlech) replaced Reading as a Minister of State and Ian Harvey became an Under Secretary. Selwyn had never got on particularly well with Douglas Dodds-Parker, their differences in-cluding the question of the Sudan (where Dodds-Parker had served with distinction in the 1930s).[16] Ormsby-Gore had been his Par-liamentary Private Secretary, and Ian Harvey, an old Fettesian, had been active in the lobby for commercial television in the early 1950s. In 1958 Brooks Richards was drafted in as an assistant private secretary to help with speeches. Selwyn, however, was never fluent in the House of Commons and was more at home in informal discussion, as behind the scenes at the Foreign Ministers' Conference at Geneva in 1959 where Selwyn had a marked success.

In Cabinet Selwyn never sheltered behind excuses. Some Foreign Secretaries would say that the House would not stand for a certain measure, meaning in effect that the Secretary of State was not prepared for the hassle of getting it through. Selwyn developed his thinking in close association with his Cabinet colleagues and Macmillan recorded that he was 'fertile in ideas and resourceful in proposing solutions to tangled and baffled [*sic*] difficulties'.[17] Yet there was a sense of reserve in the Office. With his principal private secretary Denis Laskey and with Donald Logan, who was particularly kind and helpful to Selwyn over his personal difficulties, there was complete harmony. But some officials remembered him as the man who had been in the inner Cabinet during Suez and who had not taken the Office fully into his confidence. Also the Office had to come to accept a slightly diminished role, particularly as the Treasury began to increase in importance. With Lord Home at the Commonwealth Relations Office Selwyn forged close inter-departmental links, but the independent expansiveness of Curzonian days had gone for ever.

One thing that had not diminished was the Foreign Secretary's work load. He had a continuous round of dinners and receptions to attend, speeches to make, and visits abroad. He was Minister in attendance on the Queen and the Duke of Edinburgh during the State Visit to Portugal in February. 'The Portugal visit was a great success', he wrote to his mother on 25 February.[18] The most important of these trips was to Bermuda from 21–24 March, the first stage in rebuilding the Anglo-American relationship. Eisenhower, re-elected as American President in November 1956, had mooted such a meeting less than a fortnight after Macmillan had become Prime Minister; only the timing and the venue were in doubt. After consultation with the French, an Anglo-American conference was fixed for Bermuda. The British Party consisted of Macmillan (accompanied by Norman Brook and Freddie Bishop) and Selwyn (with Patrick Dean and John Graham), plus a formidable retinue of back-up staff. Eisenhower flew in with Dulles and attendant FBI men. It was a grand occasion and the whole island seemed *en fête*, the only discontented person being the golf professional at the Mid Ocean Golf-Club (Eisenhower's headquarters), where the shop had to close.[19]

Macmillan and Eisenhower greeted each other like long lost

friends. In North Africa during the war Eisenhower had leant very heavily on Macmillan for political advice whenever Roosevelt had mooted some new policy. The Bermuda Conference re-established that relationship. At first Selwyn played a subsidiary role, largely being a 'pair' for Dulles and he felt rather isolated as Macmillan and Eisenhower sat long into the night reminiscing about the war. For his part Selwyn preferred the early morning swims with Dulles and John Graham, various security men hovering with snorkels. Towards the end of the visit, however, Macmillan succumbed to a heavy cold and Selwyn moved more into the foreground, particularly in the preparation of a down-to-earth Protocol on such matters as the British Defence contribution to Europe and the nuclear deterrent. But the success of the Conference was not to be measured by the political agreements; its success was psychological in that it marked the beginning of a new start in Anglo-American affairs and in this Selwyn played his part. He remembered it as 'a conference which improved our co-operation in a notable manner.'[20]

Macmillan and Selwyn returned from Bermuda to find Lord Salisbury on the verge of resignation over the release of Archbishop Makarios from detention in the Seychelles, a decision announced by the government on 28 March. When Macmillan had been Foreign Secretary the question of Cyprus had moved to the front of the political agenda, only temporarily being overshadowed by the Suez crisis. As the process of decolonisation began the government had been agreeable to self-government for the Cypriots, but as the Cypriots in addition wanted self-determination in the form of union with Greece (Enosis), and as this was unacceptable to the Turks, what had seemed an internal British colonial matter soon escalated into a situation of considerable international tension. The 1955 Conference convened by Macmillan had been set against a background of terrorism by the Greek Cypriot organisation EOKA and anti-British propaganda co-ordinated by Makarios, who was exiled to the Seychelles in March 1956. On the eve of his departure for Bermuda Macmillan had been told by the new Governor General of Cyprus, Field Marshal Sir John Harding, that EOKA were distributing leaflets to the effect that if Makarios were released they would call off their campaign of violence, a situation which resembled in strikingly pessimistic form the Kilmainham Treaty of April 1882 when Gladstone agreed to the release of Charles Stuart Parnell, leader of the Irish Nationalists, from jail in the vain hope that he would be able to control the campaign of terrorist violence in Ireland. The decision to release Makarios was taken in Bermuda by Macmillan, after consultation with Selwyn. Salisbury's resignation

was announced on 29 March. A Conservative government without a
Cecil seemed a contradiction in terms, but not a dog barked and
Salisbury's resignation was a nine day wonder. Its main effect was to
strengthen Macmillan's hold over his Cabinet, as Selwyn noted in a
perceptive memorandum later:

> What then should be the assessment of Harold Macmillan?
>
> I think that he believed in the Presidential form of Government.
> He modelled himself upon an American President, with subordi-
> nates, not colleagues. He could be close to some, and treat them as
> intimate and trusted friends, just as Eisenhower was close to Foster
> Dulles and George Humphrey. But most of his Ministers he would
> talk about as though they were junior officers in a unit which he
> commanded. He welcomed Lord Salisbury's resignation in 1957
> because it removed the only member of the Cabinet who was a
> contemporary and his equal in experience and authority. He
> regarded the Cabinet as an instrument for him to play upon, a body
> to be moulded to his will and it was entertaining to watch him
> handle with infinite pains the obstinate or the uncertain. Very
> rarely did he fail to get his own way, but by determined and subtle
> persuasion.
>
> His belief in the Presidential system did not complicate my
> relations with him when I was Foreign Secretary. The head of the
> government had to send messages to other heads of government.
> He was always extremely good about accepting advice as to their
> contents.[21]

On the day of Salisbury's resignation the first convoy of ships since
October 1956 entered the Suez Canal and on 15 May petrol rationing
ended, coincidentally the day of the big Suez Debate in the House of
Commons. In this the Labour Opposition concentrated their attack
on Selwyn over the question of collusion. Selwyn replied:

> The House, of course, will bear in mind the consideration – I am
> afraid the inevitable fact – that a great deal of the activity of any
> Government in negotiations with other Governments must necess-
> arily be confidential. I should like nothing better than to lay before
> the House a full record of our negotiations and representations
> during the past four months, but if there is to be any value in
> confidential discussions they must be confidential.[22]

The government's future hung on the outcome of the debate and
Macmillan was prepared for defeat. When the House divided there
were 14 abstentions on the Tory side. For Selwyn the saddest aspect
of the debate was that it led to the resignation of Lord Lambton,

who had worked so closely with him as his Parliamentary Private Secretary. 'Tony Lambton's defection was a cruel blow', he noted. But as with the resignation of Nutting some months earlier Selwyn had the maturity to separate professional differences from personal ones. He wrote to Lambton on 31 May 1957:

> As you know your resignation was a bitter blow to me but that must be forgotten. The purpose of this note is to tell you how grateful I am for your care and attention and many kindnesses during the 2½ years we were together, as the Americans would say, 'through the Ministries of Supply, Defence and the Foreign Office'.[23]

Despite their disagreements at this time (which led to Macmillan's remark about 'A Middle Class Lawyer from Liverpool') Selwyn kept in touch and spent Christmas with the Lambtons in 1957.

Lord Lambton was not the only one in a resigning mood. Selwyn now asked Macmillan to accept his own resignation for personal reasons. He had filed for divorce on 14 March 1957 and this was beginning to attract attention in the Press.[24] In the *Evening Standard* on 21 May 1957 Randolph Churchill wrote an article entitled, 'Who will be the next Foreign Secretary?'[25] On 21 June Selwyn was granted a decree nisi in front of Mr Justice Collingwood. Macmillan refused to countenance Selwyn's resignation because of the divorce and he agreed to soldier on. But it was a low point. Always lonely and reserved he now became broody and introspective. Like Bonar Law, who threw himself into work after he had been widowed, Selwyn now maintained a crushing schedule of engagements and beavered long hours at his boxes. He was philosophical, though, about this (first major) reverse. Although subsequently there were those who thought of 'suitable' people to whom Selwyn might be introduced, privately he said that having made one mistake over marriage he was not going to make another. But with Bae Selwyn travelled to see Joanna in her various school plays (later Joanna studied at the Central School of Drama) and made every effort to compensate for the breakdown of the marriage.[26] Selwyn spent his summer holidays at his Spanish bolthole of S'Agaro with the Ensesas and their family. On 3 September 1957 he wrote in his diary, 'I was so depressed yesterday at the prospect of returning to England.'[27]

The problems that faced him in this third spell at the Foreign Office were seemingly intractable. In addition to Cyprus, a perennial theme until 1960, there were the questions of disarmament (one of the areas in which Macmillan gave him considerable autonomy), the strengthening of the alliance in Europe, particularly over the integration of

Germany into the comity of Western European nations. Indeed closer economic union with Europe loomed large as an issue, particularly after the meeting of the Six Nations* at Messina in June 1955, when proposals were considered for a European Economic Community. As a former Defence Minister he had observed the abortive attempt to form a European Defence Community and was conscious of the logistical and political difficulties in establishing such organisations. He believed for instance that the European Free Trade Association (established at Stockholm on 20 November 1959, with Britain as a founder member) would need to establish working arrangements with the European Economic Community if it was to be fully effective. Selwyn, in short, was a hesitant European.

Even so he knew that links with Europe should complement rather than replace links with America, as he noted in a later memorandum on 'Relations with U.S.A.':

> The P.M. is regarded as being dominated by the purpose of preserving the Anglo/U.S. Alliance and special relationship. That has certainly been true during the Eisenhower period. But this has been the kernel of Foreign Office Policy. It was Winston's policy and Eden's (even over Suez Eden really believed that the U.S. would be benevolently neutral). The F.O. have been loyal to the Anglo/U.S. relationship to such an extent that I have had from time to time to try to impress the importance of renaissant Europe.[28]

The Anglo-American relationship was put to the test, and not found wanting, over successive crises in Oman (in July 1957) and in the Levant (in August), though Selwyn's main concerns that summer were in other areas. In June he had travelled to the Baghdad Pact meeting in Karachi, accompanied by the Chief of the Imperial General Staff, Field Marshal Sir Gerald Templer, for talks which led to an increase in planning staff rather than major reorganisation. On 1 July Selwyn spoke on disarmament at the Commonwealth Prime Ministers' Meeting in London against the background of Britain's first thermo-nuclear explosions in May and the Aldermaston marches. The year 1957 was filled with meetings and was one of diplomatic rehabilitation, in which Selwyn's role was varied and extensive. For the sixth time in seven consecutive years he was present at the general Debate of the United Nations (and was in attendance on the Queen during her visit to America that autumn). In December he accompanied Macmillan to the NATO meeting in

* Belgium, France, West Germany, Italy, Luxembourg and The Netherlands.

Paris, which was notable for agreements on American bases in Europe. On 4 October the Russians had launched a satellite into earth orbit; with this in mind Selwyn summed up his year by saying that the Foreign Secretary was a form of 'human sputnik'.[29]

Selwyn always believed that it was when the skies were seemingly at their clearest that the thunderbolts fell. After the traumas of the Suez debates, the routine two-day debate on Foreign Affairs beginning in the House on 19 February 1958 did not appear in advance to be an unduly difficult political hurdle for the Foreign Secretary to clear. In the event it was to prove one of Selwyn's most humiliating failures. Macmillan and Selwyn Lloyd were billed as the main government speakers, while Gaitskell and Bevan were due to speak for the Opposition. Macmillan and Gaitskell both opened with statesman-like speeches, in Macmillan's case tinged with his own idiosyncratic humour. Bevan, who appeared to be speaking more to his own side rather than to the House in general, embarked on a tortuous explanation of what he had meant by his speech at the Labour Party Conference the previous October at Brighton when he had said that unilateral renunciation of nuclear weapons would mean sending the British Foreign Secretary, 'naked into the conference chamber'.[30] As Macmillan noted in his memoirs: 'The Foreign Secretary, who followed, contented himself with delivering the somewhat formal speech which he had already prepared; a more agile Parliamentarian would have torn Bevan to pieces.'[31] As a result of Selwyn's disappointing performance – which led to some demands for his resignation – Macmillan decided to wind up for the government on the second day. As the entire Treasury front bench team (of Peter Thorneycroft, Nigel Birch and Enoch Powell) had resigned on 6 January, Macmillan, however much he regretted Selwyn's undoubted failure in this debate, could not afford another major resignation and Selwyn knew this.

Nevertheless he had two days of agonised talks with Macmillan about his future. Despite Macmillan's reassurances, Selwyn determined formally to offer his resignation, 'a tactical move on my part, so that I could say that I was not clinging to office', he later recorded.[32] The letter of resignation was sent to 10 Downing Street at 8 p.m. on 24 February and handed to John Wyndham, the Prime Minister's private secretary. Macmillan commented as he opened it, 'If it's his resignation, I'm not accepting it.' In the letter Selwyn wrote: 'You will remember that I wished to resign at the end of November 1956 and that there was a subsequent occasion when for private reasons I asked you to consider my resignation. Now I feel that I must press it again.'[33] Macmillan refused and on 27 February

Selwyn agreed to continue. He had already written on 25 February to Thomas Harley, an old Liverpool friend, 'It has been tough going here the last few days, but I intend to hang on.'[34] This offer of resignation was something of a turning point in Selwyn's post-Suez spell as Foreign Secretary. The combination of the Treasury resignations and his own failure in the Foreign Affairs Debate perversely strengthened his position. His response to the situation had also shown a sharpening awareness of the importance of political strategy, employed for once in his own defence.

By the spring of 1958 Selwyn was half way through his tenure of the Foreign Office. His attention was largely focused on two problems that were to continue up to and beyond the 1959 General Election: Cyprus and nuclear tests. In addition the Middle East problems were perennial. May brought a full-scale crisis in the Lebanon with the possibility of Lebanon's being forced into the United Arab Republic and with Nasser further asserting himself. President Camille Chamoun, who was pro-Western, appealed to Britain and America in the face of this threat from the United Arab Republic of Egypt, Syria and the Yemen. Selwyn flew to Washington for talks with Dulles and although he was to make an unfortunate private remark about the Americans allowing Communists to take over Lebanon (a remark which caused Hammerskjöld to leave his own dining table when hosting a dinner)[35] he co-ordinated Anglo-American responses with Dulles. The subsequent landing of American troops at Beirut by the US Sixth Fleet and two British paratroop battalions in Jordan in response to King Hussein's request for help showed that it was not only Britain that had learned from the Bermuda Conference of the importance of a co-ordinated stand. Selwyn was further gratified by America's overtures to the Baghdad Pact. The tragic events of July 1958 in the Middle East culminated in the assassination of King Feisal of Iraq (who had been dining at 10 Downing Street the night of the nationalisation of the Suez Canal), together with the Crown Prince and Nuri Pasha. While in America seeing Dulles, Selwyn attended a special meeting of the General Assembly which dealt with the situation arising out of the murders in Iraq and the landing of troops in the Lebanon and Jordan. Later he was to meet Dr Fawzi, their first contact since October 1956. Selwyn said that they should try to improve Anglo-Egyptian relations after a bad patch. Fawzi 'assured me that he too wanted to see friendly relations restored between us', recorded Selwyn.[36] He told Fawzi that a step could be made if anti-British propaganda were to be moderated, and Fawzi did not deny it was happening.

By the end of August the Far East had moved to the top of the foreign policy agenda with the delicate question of the Formosa straits. For Selwyn (and particularly Macmillan) the importance of this crisis, which arose out of the Communist government in mainland China attacking the island of Quemoy (held, like Formosa, by the US supported nationalist forces of Chiang Kai-shek), was in avoiding any strain on the recently rebuilt Anglo-American relationship. It was Britain's turn to warn of 'brinkmanship', though publicly supporting the American stance. In a difficult situation Selwyn was a calming influence.

During the summer of 1958 Selwyn had informal (and often lengthy) talks with Churchill about the world scene, believing that this could only help his understanding of complex issues. Of one of them he wrote in his diary:

I had an hour's conversation with Winston last night. He looked rather better and was in good form, but very deaf. He talked about Suez. He confirmed the remark that he would not have been brave enough to go in, but if he had gone in, he would not have been brave enough to come out. He said he thought we ought to have pushed on and taken Cairo.

He spoke about Anthony's book and said he hoped he would stick to the chronological order; it would be a mistake for him to bring out the bit about Suez too soon. He said that he had found Anthony rather better in himself but somewhat frail when he had stayed at Chartwell the weekend before last. He did not see, however, why he [Eden] should not stand for Parliament at the next Election. He then said with a chuckle, 'And if the Tories lose, there will then be three Conservative ex-Prime Ministers sitting on the Opposition Front Bench.' He added, 'I have every intention of doing that.'

He said he never understood the reason for our leaving the Sudan. It had been too complicated for him. He asked me whether I still worked in the big room in the Foreign Office. The first time he went there was when he went to see Lord Salisbury to get permission from him to go as a correspondent on some military expedition. He spoke about de Gaulle. He said it was untrue to say that he had no sense of humour. He had a sense of humour which was not always very apparent.

He talked about President Truman and said that he had been an absolutely first-class President. It was a pity, however, that he was faced with his responsibilities with so little training. If he had had more experience, he would never have agreed to American troops abandoning so much of Europe to the Russians.[37]

Experience was certainly Selwyn's trump card in his last two years as Foreign Secretary. By the autumn of 1958 he was gaining in self-confidence and was recognised as a thread of continuity in Macmillan's government. Though not renowned as a Conference speaker, he had a great triumph at Blackpool in October 1958. 'The explanation of the ovation is two-fold', explained *The Times* on 11 October. 'First, the Conference wanted to show gratitude for the unsparing work the Foreign Secretary has done in the most thankless of political offices. Secondly, in this time of fair weather they wanted to rid themselves of guilt feelings about the coolness with which they treated him in the past.'[38] This experience was much appreciated as the long-running Cyprus negotiations came to their head in the late 1950s.

In the autumn of 1957 Sir Hugh Foot (later Lord Caradon) had succeeded Field Marshal Harding as Governor of Cyprus. This was another example of Selwyn's past catching up with him. His friendship with Foot stemmed from Cambridge days and the West Country Liberal Land Campaigns. As Hugh Foot wrote of their later association over Cyprus:

> Selwyn Lloyd was an old friend . . . It was a great help through so many anxious times to be able to speak to him without reservation – and without undue respect. I was impressed by his thoroughness and his mastery of detail. I was dealing with Cyprus alone. He, as Foreign Secretary was being closely informed of all the crises of the world. But I believe that he knew all the complicated Cyprus documents better than I did. He brought a barrister's grasp to the Cyprus case. I remember chiding him once with taking too much of the detailed work on himself; he replied that in negotiation you must never allow the other side the advantage of knowing more than you do yourself.[39]

Selwyn made two notable contributions to the eventual Cyprus settlement on 1 July 1960 (his last month as Foreign Secretary). In December 1958 at a NATO Ministerial Council Selwyn negotiated with Evangelos Averoff, the Greek Foreign Minister, and Fatin Zorlu, his Turkish counterpart, the 'sovereign bases' concept which was to prove so vital in the final agreement. Then he gave Julian Amery, Under-Secretary at the Colonial Office, every encouragement and backing in 1960, when negotiations lasted some five months. Selwyn knew that after five years final agreement could not be reached overnight and that questions of the size of the British sovereign bases should not be confused with the main issue of the concept of them. The sovereign bases in Cyprus showed Selwyn at his patient best. When he retired as Speaker in February 1976 Selwyn received a letter from Julian Amery. On Cyprus he wrote:

> If I achieved anything at all – and the Sovereign Base Areas are still there – it was because of the unwavering support you gave me from start to finish and, scarcely less important though more technical, the speed with which you acted on my different recommendations.[40]

Selwyn showed his appreciation of political sensibilities in other ways during this period. On 17 February 1959 the plane bringing Adnan Menderes, the Turkish Prime Minister, to the Cyprus Conference crashed at Gatwick Airport with many fatalities. Miraculously Menderes was not among them as he was in the middle part of the plane which had withstood the impact. When Selwyn received news that the plane had crashed he kept it to himself until his talks with Averoff and Zorlu were over. Afterwards Selwyn, who could be an apprehensive traveller, asked his staff to book (usually without success as diplomatic seats were provided at the front) what he always referred to as 'the Menderes seat'.[41]

The negotiations dragged on into 1960. Selwyn's diary gives a flavour of the difficulties. On 16 January he wrote:

> Cyprus conference very difficult – a plethora of advice and advisers – the task of completing the agreement was hopeless from the word go – we made progress – time will show how much.
>
> Makarios civil – many personal interviews with him – untrustworthy not so much from deliberate dishonesty as from instability.

Sunday 24 January was 'A long day – devoted entirely to Cyprus'. The following week was crucial. 'On Cyprus we have fought our way line by line. On Wed (27 January) after a morning meeting we sat from 4 to 10.30 without a pause for food. Julian Amery has been v. helpful.'[42] On Monday 1 February Selwyn made a statement in the House but he still believed it was touch and go as to whether there would be a settlement. By the second week of February, however, the basis of an agreement had been negotiated in that Cyprus would become an independent republic with Britain having sovereignty over its military bases. This successful outcome, together with his renewed association with Hugh Foot, was one of the high points of Selwyn's tenure of the Foreign Office.

By the time the Cyprus question was settled the Conservatives had been returned to power at the General Election held in October 1959. The prospect of an Election had concentrated the political minds on both sides of the House and has generally been considered one of the main motives for Macmillan's visit to Moscow in February 1959. Though no party leader is willingly going to throw over the opportunity of appearing on the world stage with an Election in the offing, the truth of the matter was more complex. There were genuine fears in the West that the situation over Berlin (in November 1958 the Russians had demanded the withdrawal of Western forces within a period of six months) was the focus for a dangerous escalation of international tension. Anything that might defuse such tension was worth attempting. Although Selwyn was normally sceptical about the value of summit meetings ('Summiting is an occupational weakness of any incumbent of No. 10, with the notable exceptions of Baldwin and Attlee', he wrote. 'Since the war, Winston was the principal advocate. Eden disapproved when Foreign Secretary, but not when P.M.')[43] in this instance he spoke to Macmillan in December 1958, after Khrushchev's ultimatum, about the possible benefits of such a visit. 'I had always been very impressed by what I had been told in Yugoslavia in 1957/58 that Mr. K was the man for us. He believed in peaceful co-existence.'[44] Accordingly Selwyn suggested to Macmillan that the main reason for making a visit was 'the fact that the West was in hopeless disarray over Berlin . . . if nothing was done before May (when the ultimatum expired) . . . I really wondered whether with Foster Dulles's illness we could have preserved any sort of common front.'[45] Macmillan too was conscious of the dangers (from his experience at the Summit Conference in Geneva in 1955) of public expectations being disappointed by the turn of events. If they were successful, as the 1959 visit to Moscow undoubtedly was, the summits were hailed as imaginative exercises; if they failed, as in Paris in 1960, there was no hiding place. Even though the Foreign Office was sceptical, on 22 January 1959 Macmillan made a preliminary inquiry through the British Ambassador in Moscow, Sir Patrick Reilly, about the desirability of a visit. A formal request was put through Mr Gromyko two days later. After some delays and difficulties the visit was announced on 5 February. Before leaving for Moscow on 21 February Macmillan hosted a series of briefings at Chequers, attended by Selwyn and Sir Patrick Reilly. In an informal atmosphere a mass of paper work was despatched. As these meetings ended news arrived of Dulles's final and fatal illness, news which was received with genuine sadness by Macmillan and Selwyn.

Outwardly the visit to Moscow was one of relaxed conviviality, but was not without its excursions and alarms. The part Selwyn played in saving the visit during its more difficult moments has not been documented. In matters of public relations Macmillan was an

undoubted master, wearing a white Finnish fur hat, which not only
added to his physical stature at the airport, but which became the
chief visual memory of the trip. Macmillan found that the Russian for
'Good day' was phonetically the equivalent of 'Double gin' and was
thus a phrase which served a useful dual purpose at Anglo-Russian
gatherings. On the social side the Russian hosts made every effort to
please and impress their British visitors. Apart from the obligatory
visit to the Bolshoi, an exhibition of modern French pictures was
organised at the Hermitage, many of which had never been shown
before because they were at variance with Socialist realism. The
atmosphere was reminiscent of Turgenev and Pushkin, with troikas in
the snow, clay pigeon shooting from the dachas and holes cut in the
ice so that officials could fish. Before the visit, however, the Foreign
Office had arranged a conference warning of the security aspects and
it was not entirely a surprise to Selwyn's staff to find that a special tent
had been set up in Sir Patrick Reilly's study at the Embassy, within
which confidential discussions could take place against a background
recording of taped cocktail party noise and the sound, as one typist
remembers, of rushing water. One of Selwyn's staff noticed how
different this Foreign Office world was from the Party Conference at
Blackpool the previous October. There Selwyn had been on home
territory and there was a great deal of north country conviviality
which contrasted with the more formal and staid Foreign Office
ambience. Selwyn noticed many revealing details about the closed
nature of Russian society on this visit. In Leningrad, for instance, the
people who had come to cheer the British visitors were shepherded
back to buses in side streets to be driven away once the show was
over.

If the social side ran relatively smoothly the same could not be said
of the political. There were difficult moments. Sir Patrick Reilly
wrote on 8 March:

> Mr. K. frankly behaved abominably. But to his credit he seems to
> have realised it and at the end he made up for it. The PM and the
> Foreign Secretary handled the whole thing brilliantly. I knew the
> PM would of course. It was all the more remarkable, however,
> since he was so tired and unwell much of the time, and the
> programme was gruelling. What I did not expect was that Lloyd
> would be so good. He was quite first class and they make an
> admirable team and obviously get on splendidly. Such a contrast
> with the days when I saw him (Lloyd) working with Eden.[46]

Later Selwyn was to tell Sir Patrick Reilly how worried he had been
about Macmillan's physical condition at the outset of the trip.

The low point of the visit came on 24 February when Khrushchev made a virulent speech about the capitalist system, Britain and her allies. Macmillan and Selwyn were visiting a nuclear research station at Dubna on the Volga, north of Moscow, when the speech was made and reports were fleeting and contradictory. Selwyn had an important talk with Gromyko at this stage in which he warned that mutual cordiality could not disguise the seriousness of the situation and he spoke of having, 'a sense of impending calamity'. Though true, this did not go down well with Gromyko. That evening a social gathering at the British Embassy in Moscow went ahead as though nothing untoward had happened, Khrushchev engaging in lighthearted discussions with Selwyn about wines and whisky. For his part Selwyn reminded Khrushchev of his visit to London in 1956 and of his comment at the notorious Labour Party dinner that if he lived in Britain he would vote Conservative. 'Was this still the case?', asked Selwyn. Khrushchev replied that it was. Bulganin was the one who was going to vote Labour and look where that had got him.[47] On the morning of 25 February Macmillan and Selwyn walked in the snow-strewn grounds of their government dacha with their advisers. Despite his reputation for unflappability this was one of the occasions when Macmillan was very worried indeed and without the support of both Selwyn and Sir Patrick Reilly at this critical stage might well have called off the visit. Remembering Vyshinsky at the United Nations Selwyn stressed the nature of Russian bravura and encouraged Macmillan to stay the course, warning of the alternatives. Khrushchev continued to be difficult. On 26 February came the 'tooth-ache' insult when Khrushchev announced that he would not be accompanying his visitors to Kiev the following day (there had been acrimonious words about Selwyn's 'dangerous imagination' and about guns firing at Suez) as he had to have a filling. Macmillan politely (and with considerable patience in the circumstances) said merely that he would be sorry to miss Khrushchev's company on the next day and hoped that he would soon be feeling better. Selwyn (an occasion when his humour struck a happy chord) said that Khrushchev's dentist must have used a British drill. The meeting broke up with Khrushchev smiling broadly.

When Macmillan and Selwyn returned to London at the beginning of March there was a sense of relief that, though the eleven days of the visit had not been incident free, they could have been much worse, and there was now a basis for future understanding, particularly over the vexed question of Berlin, which the communiqué, largely prepared by Selwyn and Gromyko, did not shirk. The Moscow trip was an important moment of emancipation in Selwyn's tenure of the

Foreign Office. Macmillan gained important diplomatic and electoral credit for his efforts at a time of great uncertainty. Privately he told Selwyn that without his support (especially his suggestion that in response to Khrushchev's toothache Macmillan should have a diplomatic cold and stay in his dacha for two days to allow breathing time) the summit would have been a failure. Sir Patrick Reilly was much impressed by Macmillan's performance, but he also noted:

> Selwyn Lloyd's performance was in its different way equally remarkable. He was the ideal second: always at hand but careful to leave the limelight to the Prime Minister: solicitous and anxious to lighten his burden: ready to take on all the disagreeable jobs, like the tough talking needed with Kuznetsov, the First Deputy Foreign Minister, and with Gromyko: always sensible, calm and a steadying influence during the bad times of the visit. Its ultimate success owed a great deal to his part in it. I am very glad after so many years to record my admiration for a man, who, at that time at least; was much underrated.[48]

On his return from Moscow Selwyn continued as the human sputnik, visiting Paris and Bonn to report to de Gaulle and Adenauer, before flying to Ottawa to brief Diefenbaker on the talks and thence on to Washington to see Eisenhower and the dying Dulles. When Dulles died on 24 May, Selwyn wrote at once to his widow. Less than a month later Selwyn's mother died, on 22 June, and one of the first letters he received was from Mrs John Foster Dulles. Messages, including ones from the Queen and from Eisenhower, came to him from around the world. After his mother's death Selwyn kept 32 Queen's Road as a constituency base, with Miss Wright presiding as housekeeper, but there was a certain Wirral retrenchment, particularly in financial matters. 'Mount Pleasant' was finally sold and Selwyn's political ties in London led to a moving of the centre of gravity of his life southwards, a process which was to be underlined when he leased a house at Preston Crowmarsh in Oxfordshire in the early 1960s, as a country retreat, after he had lost Chequers. On behalf of the family Selwyn arranged for a memorial window to his parents to be placed in the Westbourne Road Methodist Church. 'We would, of course, prefer a window which could be seen from the old family pew at the back of the Church on the right hand side as one enters it', he wrote to the Rev. Dr W. Lawson Jones on 7 July.[49] The window was dedicated the following year.

The summer of 1959 was dominated for Selwyn, not by the run up to the General Election, widely expected that autumn, but by the

Foreign Ministers' Conference at Geneva. This was the penultimate summit that Selwyn attended as Foreign Secretary and one during which he was neither accompanied nor overshadowed by Macmillan. The British delegation was headed by Selwyn (with Antony Acland, his new assistant private secretary, in attendance) and was housed in a villa on the shores of Lake Geneva. Like some latterday Paris Peace Conference (and the Geneva Conference of 1959 was very pre-war in atmosphere with its expansiveness and lengthy time scale), there was a 'Big Four' of Gromyko, Christian Herter, the new American Secretary of State following Dulles's death, Couve de Murville, and Selwyn. On the Western side Selwyn was the unquestioned leader and by saving the Conference from collapse made it possible for Eisenhower to issue his invitation to Khrushchev, which was a major step in avoiding further confrontation over Berlin. Also with Selwyn in the British delegation was Sir Patrick Reilly, who helped with the drafts of many of the speeches. Sir Patrick later recorded, 'By this time Lloyd was a master of the subject matter of the Conference and in negotiation, especially in the informal discussions over meals, his touch was consistently excellent.' It was all very different from those far off hesitant days in Paris in November 1951. 'However unproductive in concrete results,' wrote Sir Patrick, 'this Conference may well be considered the finest achievement of his years as Foreign Secretary.'[50]

The Conference had its lighter moments. The proximity of the Lake gave Selwyn many opportunities for swimming, which he did with Sergeant Thompson, his detective, swimming along at a safe covering distance and once being unable to alert Selwyn to the fact that a wasp had alighted on his head, owing to the ear plugs that Selwyn used, and being dissuaded from attempting a William Tell act by Antony Acland. Swimming was now Selwyn's main relaxation and Couve de Murville arrived one afternoon unexpectedly to find the British delegation on the lawn of their villa in bathing robes, reviving themselves with whisky, and Selwyn always remembered Couve's eyebrows going up. As the Russians insisted that the East Germans be represented at the conference table an impasse arose at the outset about the placing of the tables. Selwyn said to Gromyko, 'What about having the East German delegation alongside us but at a separate table? We will sit at this table and then he will have a little table by himself and we will be that far apart.' Gromyko, who was not without a sense of humour, said, 'No: *that* far apart.' Two inches was all that separated the delegation, but it was enough to save face. As Macmillan gratefully recorded in his diary, 'Largely owing to Selwyn's initial efforts, the Conference has at last got started.'[51] After a break for the delegates to attend Dulles's funeral in Washington the negotiations started again.

It was at this moment that one of the most bizarre episodes in Selwyn's career occurred. On 1 June 1959 *The Times* began its main news story:

PRIME MINISTER'S PLANS
FOR MR. SELWYN LLOYD

EASING STRAIN OF OFFICE

POSSIBLE TRANSFER STILL
SEVERAL MONTHS AHEAD

The story from the paper's political correspondent concluded by saying that Macmillan had taken Selwyn aside and told him that at the Foreign Office in these troubled times 'enough is enough'.[52] In Geneva, where the Russians saw *The Times* as a British equivalent of *Pravda*, the story had considerable impact. Back in London Randolph Churchill colourfully claimed that it was Rab Butler's way of removing Selwyn from his path. Macmillan reassured a disturbed Selwyn (privately Macmillan was furious with Sir William Haley, the Editor of *The Times*, for allowing such a story and Selwyn even wondered if it was delayed revenge for his Minority Broadcasting Report) and the incident blew over. In the end it was the prestige of *The Times* that suffered most.

GOODNESS, A MERE PAPER DART WON'T SINK HIM!

24 HM the Queen accompanied by her Foreign Secretary and the Duke of Norfolk in 1958.

25 The 1959 General Election: Selwyn and his agent Bert Gill on nomination day in the Wirral constituency.

26 Selwyn and his daughter Joanna with Sambo, July 1960.

The main purpose of the Conference was for the Foreign Ministers to prepare the ground for a full summit, so its purpose was fulfilled when it was announced in August that Khrushchev was to visit Eisenhower in Washington. In late July Selwyn had made a great rearguard action to save the Geneva Conference, acting as go-between between Herter and Gromyko. He persuaded Herter to support an appeal to Eisenhower to call a summit, not later than 1 September. Herter was willing to do this as long as Gromyko gave a satisfactory statement on Berlin. On 27 July Selwyn made great efforts to persuade Gromyko to some form of conciliatory statement on Berlin, part of the private, informal series of negotiations that had emerged as the preferred diplomatic process. Sensing that Gromyko was responsive to the direct approach, Selwyn was not averse to some gentle cajoling when he thought it appropriate. There was a lunch at Couve de Murville's villa, with Herter and Gromyko, during which Selwyn said that he could see a party in a boat on the lake, one of whom was wearing a red jersey. He pointed out that the red-jerseyed rower was rocking the boat and not pulling his weight. In the last days of the Conference, which ended on 11 August, Selwyn entertained Gromyko several times at his villa. The subsequent Washington summit owed much to his unobtrusive efforts.

Once the Conference was over Selwyn only had a brief respite before he flew to New York to make a speech on disarmament at the General Assembly. It was while he was in America that he heard from Macmillan that the General Election was to be on 8 October. Preparations for this had been underway ever since Macmillan succeeded to the Premiership in January 1957. As Foreign Secretary Selwyn had no role in the preparation of the Manifesto, *The Next Five Years*, which was published on 11 September, though Macmillan had sent the first draft of the Foreign Affairs section to Selwyn at Geneva. 'Such is his wonderful activity', wrote Macmillan of Selwyn to the secretary of the Steering Committee on the Manifesto, Michael Fraser, 'that I would not be at all surprised if he were to do a draft in Geneva.'[53]

A launching pad for Macmillan's campaign was Eisenhower's visit to London in late August. 'President Eisenhower had a wonderful welcome last night', Selwyn wrote to José Ensesa in S'Agaro on 28 August. 'I have never seen the London crowds so happy and express-ive. I am off to Chequers this evening for talks between him and the Prime Minister.'[54] Despite the buoyant position of the economy and the healthy standing of the Conservatives in the public opinion polls (Colman, Prentis and Varley had conducted an advertising campaign costing £½m since June 1957) Selwyn was his usual pessimistic self about the outcome. 'The result, I think, is very uncertain', he wrote to a constituent on 6 October.[55] He campaigned vigorously, usually in the wake of Robens, the shadow Foreign Secretary, visiting places as diverse as York, a particularly successful meeting, Barnstaple and Woolwich. He also made the Conservatives' national television broadcast on 19 September.[56]

In the Wirral Selwyn's opponent was Councillor F. W. Venables from Ellesmere Port in a straight fight with Labour. Selwyn's misreading of the national political mood was largely owing to his prolonged absences from Britain since 1956. Indeed he attended no joint forums with Venables during the campaign (he was away in America when the Election was announced and when in Britain was engaged as a speaker in marginal constituencies rather than in the Wirral, one of the safest Conservative seats in the country). In the course of one evening Selwyn was called 'murderer' and 'darling', though as he recorded, 'not by the same person'.[57] The turning point of the national campaign came on 28 September with Hugh Gaitskell's pledge in Newcastle that, 'there will be no increase in the standard or other rates of income tax under the Labour Government so long as normal peacetime conditions continue.'[58] Selwyn returned to the Wirral for polling day. In a letter to his niece Barbara Stileman he described how the family had watched the results coming in at 32 Queen's Road, pointing out that at 6 a.m. 'I was still up watching the television at Queen's Road. But the rest of the family had fallen out at about between 1 and 2.'[59] The count in the Wirral in those days did not begin until the Friday morning, by which time Gaitskell had conceded. Selwyn had said to Venables before the results were known nationally, 'In politics it is always necessary to remember it is possible to lose as well as to win', and he had been greatly touched by the dignity of Gaitskell in defeat, bayed round by chanting opponents at Leeds substituting 'Hugh Gaitskell' for 'Tom Dooley' in a popular ballad of the time that they were singing with vindictive glee, a scene shown on television first with the indoor count and then on the balcony outside.[60]

Selwyn experienced no such worries. When the figures were announced he had his biggest ever majority. In an electorate of 71,025 the figures were:

Lloyd, J. S. B. (Conservative)	39,807
Venables, F. W. (Labour)	18,805
Majority	21,002

As he continued in his letter to his niece, 'We did quite well in the Wirral, considering all the new development that is going on around

Ellesmere Port. They polled very heavily there and our people were rather depressed. But in the event a lot of them must have voted for me, which was surprising.'[61] Nationally the Conservatives won 365 seats and the Labour Party 258. The overall majority was 100, the figure Gaitskell predicted ('We've lost by a hundred seats') on hearing the results of the archetypal Billericay result at 9.55 p.m. 'I will be quite frank', wrote Selwyn to a constituent on 28 October, 'and say that I was very surprised at the size of our majority and at the same time very thankful.'[62]

When Macmillan had formed his first administration in 1957 Selwyn was the third figure he appointed. It was a sign of his enhanced status in the party (Macmillan at this stage even considered Selwyn a possible successor) that Selwyn was the first figure to be appointed. 'That he was tired, not only with the burden of office but by the long and wearisome negotiations in which he had been involved, I was well aware; and I had it in mind that I might be able to make a change in the following summer', Macmillan recorded in his memoirs.[63] Derick Amory, the reluctant Chancellor, had already intimated that he wished to retire to his business and Scouting interests in Devon in due course, and in Macmillan's mind Selwyn was the obvious successor. Much speculation centred on the possibility of Butler's moving to the Foreign Office (*The Economist* had twice advocated such a move) but Butler no longer had the zest for foreign affairs and was genuinely immersed and satisfied at the Home Office. Nevertheless Macmillan (possibly with some sense of residual guilt for the events of January 1957) wanted to enhance Butler's standing and made him Chairman of the Party, though this was not a vital post in the aftermath of a successful election campaign. The more interesting changes came lower down the Cabinet rankings. Iain Macleod continued his rise when he was appointed Colonial Secretary, a department in which he was to make the greatest historic impact since Joseph Chamberlain, though at the cost of alienating the right wing of the party. Maudling was promoted to the Board of Trade. Anthony Barber, another future Chancellor, became Economic Secretary. Selwyn's position in the top echelons of the party was confirmed.

On 1 November 1959 Selwyn began to keep a very detailed political diary which he continued until the aftermath of the Night of the Long Knives in July 1962. It is a perceptive and informed account of the political scene with some very shrewd and indiscreet, though never malicious, comments on his contemporaries. To give a preliminary flavour of this important document, here is its opening entry:

First some reflections on the new Government. To what extent is it a seething mass of the ambitious and the jealous? I should say not at all – the PM is very tired after his Election effort, but I have urged him several times to do what Anthony Eden did not do in 1955, and that is have a real rest – he is at Chequers for 4 days and hopes to get away 20–30 Nov. He is tired but happy – he said to me when about to make his speech on the Q's speech, 'Thank God it is the last time I shall do this in a new Parliament.' I wonder. Health will be the answer. He will have to take great care to survive, but he has a wonderful capacity for recuperation.

Rab is very happy after his marriage.* His ego is very satisfied with being Chairman of the Party as well as Leader of House and Home Secretary. There are some very important Home Office Bills coming along – Betting & Gaming etc. He should be busy and at his best. His position as Crown Prince is, I think, impregnable, but there are some who say not.

Derry Amory seems content to go on, although there have been threats of only one more Budget.† David Eccles is put out to be sent back to Education, Reggie Maudling delighted with the B of T, Iain Macleod, if he is not to get the F.O. or Exchequer v. happy with the Colonies, apparently, although he is deeper than some of the colleagues. Duncan Sandys gets the nasty jobs to do, and, taking a long view, wisely makes the best of them.‡ Harold Watkinson is v. pleased with Defence.

Selwyn then turned to his own position.

Of one's own position, the usual drip of denigration – e.g. Mr. Massingham in the Observer – 'his great asset to the PM is that when he is dropped, no one will notice his departure.' Reggie Paget in H of C last Thursday – 'there has been no Foreign Secretary since Macmillan in 1955.' Massingham – 'he is of no significance in the party or with the public.' Does all this worry one? Of course it does – perhaps irritate rather than worry is the word.

It was a good General Election from a personal point of view – excellent meetings – Cleckheaton, York, Barnstaple, Bideford, Woolwich etc. Considerable praise for the T.V.s. etc.

---

* On 21 October Butler had married Mollie Courtauld, the widow of August Courtauld.

† Selwyn did not know of Amory's talks with Macmillan.

‡ Duncan Sandys was given the task of winding up the Ministry of Supply and starting the new Aviation Ministry.

Selwyn also considered Macmillan's performance at this time:

The P.M. is a master of acquiring ideas – this is a good thing – he persuades himself they are his own – also a good thing – a small example – in the Stockholm negotiations,* I suggested to him using the Swedes as intermediaries. I spoke very strongly in Committee of Cabinet and in Cabinet on importance of driving Stockholm through – time against us – & U.S., the Six etc. I spoke much more strongly than anyone else, and helped to dispose of hesitations of colleagues. The penny has dropped. The P.M. is agog to drive it through. I bet his diary will say that this was all his doing.† A large, more important example, the visit to Moscow, which I began suggesting to him in the autumn of last year, and then evermore after K's ultimatum about Berlin, as something which had to be done before a General Election, not to influence it but because failure to make it would be made much of by the Opposition. From Xmas onwards I was pressing it as the only way to keep the Western front intact until the April NATO meeting.[64]

Selwyn's one miscalculation concerned Derick Amory. Three days later Amory came to see him in the Foreign Office. Selwyn recorded with surprise and dismay:

4 Nov After my official talk with Derry Amory, he said he wanted to have a serious personal talk with me. He was going to resign within a matter of 'months' – he felt that I ought to succeed him – he wanted to talk seriously about this.
    What do I do?[66]

Shortly after the 1959 Election Selwyn met Eden at Chequers, a reunion that had been arranged for Eden to dine with Adenauer, Chancellor of the Federal Republic of Germany, who was on a visit to Britain. Eden, who was feeling rather out of things, was grateful to Selwyn and Macmillan for the invitation. After Adenauer had left, the three men sat over a drink in the Great Hall and the talk turned to the domestic situation and Eden's great theme of 'the property owning democracy'. Selwyn said what a great difference the recent profit sharing scheme had made to the political thinking of employees. Eden warmed to this and said that he hoped that profit sharing would become one of the Conservative themes during the

* The meeting in October & November 1959 which led to EFTA.
† 'Maudling in particular had been through a long and frustrating period of negotiation. I had charged him with the task of trying to obtain European agreement upon an Industrial Free Trade Area to cover all the countries.'[65]

new administration. At this, as Selwyn recorded in his diary, 'Harold walked across the Hall at Chequers to the drinks table and said, "That would not suit the publishers at all." '[67] They also talked about the first volume of Eden's memoirs which were now in proof stage. Selwyn agreed to verify various details for Eden, particularly over October 1956.

'Thank you for your letter', he wrote to Eden on 14 November. 'I am delighted to hear we will meet next Thursday. In the meantime I will try to check on any records that I have as to our movements on the day in question.'[68] The next Thursday Selwyn recorded in his diary:

> *Thursday Nov 19* Anthony Eden came for lunch looking frail but fairly well – he had had no fever for 3 weeks. Talk with him afterwards about Suez – agreed a wording for the sentences in his book about Oct 16 1956.*

That evening at a dinner at the Dorchester for the Anglo-German Conference of Editors Selwyn found himself sitting next to Donald Tyerman of *The Economist*. 'He had admired my tenacity, I had beaten Eden 3½ years,† I must now beat Bevin 5½ years.‡ He would have preferred a swop after the Election between Amory and myself to get some freshness. Rab had told him in 1957 that he wanted the Foreign Secretaryship then – he is bitterly disappointed at being passed over for PM and thought he would not get it unless he did Foreign S. Tyerman said that it had been a brilliant stroke of Harold's to keep me on. T. had seen Rab the other day and asked him whether he still wanted it. Rab had said not now, 'but I don't want any of the others to get it', meaning his likely competitors, Iain Macleod etc. Tyerman said I was in a very strong position, but he did not know who could succeed me. I said "Heath".'[69]

As 1959, an eventful and exhausting year, drew to its close, the papers began their retrospectives. Crossbencher in the *Sunday Express* on 22 November 'forecast Derry Amory's retirement – and the "durable" Mr Lloyd as his successor, because by then Harold M. will be diverting his attention to home politics again and will want someone to fetch and carry!' The Labour Party, in the wake of its third successive electoral defeat, was conducting a fairly public inquest into its failings and its possible future direction. 'The Labour

---

* *Full Circle*, p. 510, the paragraph beginning, 'The Foreign Secretary and I flew to Paris on October 16th to see M. Mollet and M. Pineau.'

   † In his third and final spell as Foreign Secretary.

   ‡ Not what *The Economist* had advocated in its articles on 21 September 1957 and 5 April 1958.

inquest has proceeded with much vigour', Selwyn noted on 4 December. 'They profess to be a party of high ideals and noble purposes. Individually they exhibit nothing but envy, hatred, malice and all uncharitableness . . . Mrs Castle said the voters were "suckers" to have voted Conservative – an odd word to use – never have the voters shown more clearly that they are not suckers. Labour offered them 10/- a week pensions + retirement benefits + lower rents + reduction in sizes of classes + no Eleven Plus + free teeth spectacles & prescriptions + no increase in income tax + a better roads programme etc etc . . . One could add the feeling of distaste for a party which consistently takes an anti-British line. The inquest has revealed a much deeper split on the question of nationalisation than one could have hoped for.'

After being on the defensive at the hands of Bevan for so long Selwyn was pleased to get in a retaliatory thrust at a dinner at the Italian Embassy. 'I said to Bevan that I had let him off in the House when he talked about my modesty. I had in mind (which was not true because I only thought of it then) to say that I found it strange that Bevan should talk about modesty when he had some difficulty at Blackpool in deciding whether he was the Son, the Father or the Holy Ghost. (He had talked about Gaitskell, B. Castle & himself as the Trinity, but he did not know which he was.) Bevan was not at all pleased.'

The year came to an end with Selwyn at the apex of his political standing. He was securely placed in one of the great offices of state, with the prospect of moving to another. Only on the personal side was the loneliness apparent. His mother had died and though he had a house in the Wirral it was not a home. On New Year's Eve he recorded his final entry for the year:

31 Dec 1959 I have nobody back to see New Year in.[70]

The New Year though was to be one of the most important of his political career.

During January 1960 (while the Cyprus conference was proceeding on its tortuous and difficult course) Selwyn dined privately with Rab Butler (18 January) and with Derick Amory (23 January). Both of them poured out their private thoughts on the political scene to Selwyn.

Dined with Rab Butler – an extraordinary conversation – kind about Harold Macmillan – very critical of Anthony Eden's dishonesty in his memoirs particularly about Churchill's retirement* –

* *Full Circle*, p. 265, 'No two men have ever changed guard more smoothly.'

critical of Derry Amory for having no power of decision – critical
of Macleod for his scheming and playing up to the Press – criticism
of Marples for pinching credit for what Rab at Home Office had
done preparing for some Bill – suggested Exchequer or Leading
House for me – said Harold might make Duncan Sandys Foreign
Secretary because he is always fascinated by cads.[71]

Apart from showing remarkable prescience in that Butler suggested for Selwyn the two government posts that he was next to fill the
conversation is also another pointer to why Butler failed to inspire
confidence in the party (there could be no friendship between the
top five men in a Cabinet, Lloyd George said) and was to be denied
the succession in 1963.

Derick Amory returned to the subject of his retirement when he
dined with Selwyn on the Saturday of the same week:

> he is determined to go out next summer – will stay on as Paymaster
> General or Commonwealth Secretary but loathes H of C – wants
> me either to stay on, or go to Treasury if too exhausted by F.O.
> Talked about money for Cyprus – the next Budget – the Railways.
> Quite a dilemma is building up for the summer. If my chest goes on
> as it is, I will not be a candidate for anything.[72]

Selwyn had suffered intermittently from poor health since December 1956 (particularly over teeth) and despite his care to take decent
holidays at S'Agaro had felt under the weather for some time. He had
always been something of a hypochondriac because of the family
medical background.

Eden's memoirs were serialised in *The Times* in January 1960.
Despite the help Selwyn had given over various episodes he was not
impressed by the finished result:

> *Monday Feb 1*
>   Anthony Eden's Suez memoirs finished in The Times today – I
> was asked at a Commonwealth Press Conference whether I
> approved – I said that I thought it was a bit soon, but he had been
> so attacked and abused that the fault lay with his traducers for the
> book coming out now. I do not think that they have been a great
> success. They could have done more harm, but I wait to read the
> whole book in its final form.

The first week of February was marked by one of Macmillan's most
important speeches. On 2 February Macmillan reached Cape Town
on his tour of South Africa, staying with the Prime Minister, Dr
Verwoerd. The next day he spoke of 'the wind of change' that was

blowing through the Continent. 'Harold made a courageous speech in Cape Town', noted Selwyn in his diary on 4 February. 'He quoted my bit at the UN in September on our aim of non racial societies.'[73] On his return from Africa Macmillan was uncertain of the prospects for the Paris summit (due to start on 16 May), as Khrushchev's speeches had become increasingly belligerent. Macmillan was determined that the Paris Conference should be a success. It was the theme of the post-election period and many Conservative MPs believe that the public failure of that summit was the moment when the Macmillan premiership began to lose its sense of direction. (There were others who believed that Selwyn's appointment as Chancellor of the Exchequer in the wake of that failure consolidated and compounded those doubts.)[74]

Selwyn was saddened to hear of the final illness that now gripped his old adversary Aneurin Bevan and he wrote a generous and kindly letter to Jennie Lee. When he heard that Bevan was making a great fight of his battle against cancer, he noted in his diary, 'Doctors had been impressed by 3 things – his guts, his charm, and his hatred of Gaitskell – no doubt it was the last that kept him alive.'[75]

Two days later on 11 February Selwyn made his emotional reference to Belsen in a speech in the House.* Churchill came up to congratulate him. Selwyn was frank in his response. 'I felt more mastery of the House than ever before (not saying much!)', he noted in his diary. 'Winston said in the lobby, "you have improved very much in your speaking." I told him my trouble had been in being promoted by him too early.'[76] In March Selwyn travelled to Washington where he met Richard Nixon, with whom he had a long talk about the forthcoming American election. 'Nixon seemed to think that if there was no recession, he should beat everyone except Kennedy – about him, he seemed doubtful.'[77] A meeting of the CENTO Council at Tehran, followed by the NATO Council at Istanbul, occupied Selwyn from 28 April – 3 May. In these last months of his Foreign Secretaryship he was very much helped by his new principal private secretary, Ian Samuel, who had replaced Denis Laskey (who had become a Minister in the British Embassy in Rome) after the October 1959 Election. Selwyn used Samuel very much as a sounding board and was also very supportive and helpful to his new secretary. On 25 February 1960, for instance, there was a visit by the President of Peru, which involved a luncheon at 1 Carlton Gardens. Ian Samuel found himself seated next to the Shadow Foreign Secretary, George Brown, and the conversation turned to a recent unfavourable ruling on

* See page 91–2.

widows' pensions. George Brown heatedly said that it was all wrong:
£100m on a battleship would go straight through, but 10*s*. for a
widow's pension was blocked. Ian Samuel inquired what the overall
cost of the pension arrangement was, knowing that the figures were
not £100m v. 10*s*. At this George Brown lost his temper. 'I know you,
just a Tory, wait till the Labour Government comes in.' (By this time
people were looking agitatedly towards George Brown's end of the
table.) 'We'll send you to somewhere nobody wants to go – I know,
we'll send you to Peru!' Ian Samuel was very concerned at the way the
conversation had become heated, but afterwards Selwyn could not
have been more reassuring. 'Don't worry, George Brown is always
like that', he said. 'And the one thing you have to remember is that
he's a patriot and that's what matters.' This was Selwyn too. He was a
patriot and tolerant, and he always saw the good side in others. At a
weekend gathering at Chequers (12–14 March 1960) Selwyn confided
to Ian Samuel that his one great unfulfilled ambition was to be Lord
Chancellor, while admitting with typical modesty that in the final
analysis he did not consider himself a good enough lawyer for the
post, a judgment he was to revise when Reginald Manningham-
Buller went to the Woolsack on 13 July 1962.

Selwyn's last major commitment as Foreign Secretary was the long
awaited Paris summit (for which Moscow and Geneva had been such
important preludes) which was due to open on 16 May. The news that
an American U2 spy plane had been shot down over Russia and the
pilot, Gary Powers, captured alive was announced by Khrushchev on
5 May. From that moment the Paris summit was under a cloud that
was never to lift. Suddenly all the hopes that the Western powers (and
in particular Macmillan) had for the success of the summit were
dashed. Selwyn and Macmillan both spoke in the Foreign Affairs
debate in the Commons which was dominated by the U2 episode.
Selwyn wrote in his diary:

> The debate went quite well but the House is a strange place – I
> irritated them by saying that the U2 incident would shake people
> out of their complacency about the Summit. They thought that in
> some way I was getting at the Opposition – quite unintentional.
> Harold wound up very well.[78]

Nevertheless it was with considerable apprehension that Selwyn
(attended by Ian Samuel) flew to Paris on 14 May. Despite the U2
episode there was a festive atmosphere in Paris and a house-party
atmosphere at the British Embassy where Gladwyn Jebb dispensed
sophisticated and generous hospitality. (To mark the hoped-for
accord Jebb had bought cases of rare claret at auction, which, to

general disappointment, were left unopened as the proceedings turned into a wake.) On arrival Selwyn went straight into a working lunch at the Embassy and a meeting with his opposite numbers, US Secretary of State Christian Herter, Couve de Murville and Heinrich von Brentano, the West German Foreign Minister. They concentrated on the issues of Berlin and nuclear tests, Selwyn noting, 'We made some progress and are not too far apart.'[79] In the evening there was a more relaxed dinner ('after a short talk, mainly on disarmament, we played bridge – I won $6!')[80] Also at this dinner was Livingston Merchant of the US State Department. Selwyn stressed that in his opinion Eisenhower should have 'a long confessional talk' with Khrushchev as 'confession is good for the soul'.[81] The next five days were among the most dispiriting of Selwyn's career. The difficulties did not all stem from Khrushchev. The French were always conscious that the British were more willing to negotiate with the Russians in the new situation than they (the French) were. The French were in Selwyn's eyes the intransigent partners in conference. Macmillan was really anxious to get some form of compromise, but the French did not want to compromise their rights in Berlin.[82] On Sunday 15 May de Gaulle told Macmillan that Khrushchev intended to wrest an apology from the United States for their 'act of aggression', punishment for the wrong doers and a promise never to do it again. At 4.30 p.m. Khrushchev came to the Embassy and Macmillan asked for reasonableness. Eisenhower, de Gaulle and Macmillan met, with their Foreign Ministers, at 6.30, but as Selwyn noted, 'nothing much transpired.'[83] The events of Monday 16 May are best described in Selwyn's words:

> Harold went to breakfast with Ike – I joined them about 10. They have drawn up a statement for the President to make, stating that the overflights had been discontinued and would not be resumed.
>
> We went on to the Élysée for the 11 a.m. meeting with the Russians. It was tense. K. asked to speak first, then rose to his feet & made a tough speech . . . Ike made his reply with dignity. Harold and de Gaulle appealed for reason, de Gaulle saying that he could not understand all this fuss about overflying – the Soviet satellite passed through French air space 18 times a day.
>
> K. relaxed a little, stopped getting up to speak and made a joke or two about Sputniks, but stuck to his terms. We broke up about 2.30 p.m.[84]

In the evening Macmillan made one last despairing visit to Khrushchev at the Soviet Embassy. Selwyn and Gladwyn Jebb were left behind. Selwyn was furious and said to Freddie Bishop and Philip de

Zulueta (Macmillan's secretaries in attendance), 'This is government by private secretary', to which came the reply, 'Well, the only alternative is government by politician.'[85] For Jebb this exclusion was an experience he had had before (in October 1956), for Selwyn it was a new one and he noted in his diary:

> I tried to stop him seeing K that night, but Harold was rather incited by the Private Secretaries to do it. In fact he was too tired, and in any case we wanted time. However he went (without me which annoyed me!) and had a civil talk but made no impression. It looked as if the Summit was dead although one could not be quite certain whether the Russians were bluffing.[86]

On Tuesday 17 May the three Western Heads of Government, plus their Foreign Ministers, met at the Élysée and it was decided that de Gaulle should in writing summon a meeting of the main delegates at 3 p.m. Khrushchev did not come. The summit was effectively over. Wednesday 18 May was a mournful day. The British party asked Khrushchev and the Russians to come round and say goodbye and a group gathered at the Embassy as though it were a dentist's waiting room. At one moment of pause in the desultory conversation Selwyn turned to Ian Samuel and said in a stage whisper, 'This is the moment when Gladwyn will tell us the vintage of the claret.'[87]

The failure of the Paris summit was a grievous blow to Macmillan's hopes for détente and a sad conclusion to Selwyn's 4½ years in King Charles Street, though Selwyn took little executive part in the summit, reduced as he was to following on in Macmillan's wake, 'making the occasional bleating noise'.[88] Selwyn pleaded despairingly with Herter to ask Eisenhower to say he was sorry for the U2 episode, but Herter said that in all honesty Eisenhower could not. The British party flew back to London on 19 May. When the dust settled Macmillan had a rethink about the future. He had been blown off course by events outside his control. The new 'theme' that was to emerge was entry into Europe. But before that could be set in motion it was time for the Cabinet reshuffle following Amory's retirement from politics. In this reshuffle Selwyn was to be the central figure. When Selwyn spoke on 25 July in the House of Commons Harold Wilson, the Shadow Chancellor of the Exchequer, said, 'I was not clear whether he was making his last speech as Foreign Secretary or his first speech as Chancellor.'[89] Two days later Selwyn was appointed Chancellor of the Exchequer.

Selwyn's departure from the Foreign Office was a time of surprising emotion. The Diplomatic Corps presented him with four silver candlesticks dated 1764 ('Perfectly delightful and if I had been asked to name a present, I would have put them at the top of the list', Selwyn confided to his diary. 'It was an extremely handsome gesture.')[90] Selwyn gave a farewell party (a less mournful one than Ernest Bevin had given in March 1951).

> I then went to the lift to go, but somewhat mysteriously was told that I was to go down the main staircase. When I got there, Derek Hoyer Millar was there with a large crowd, and gave 3 cheers, which again reduced me to the point of tears; I left very moved, and after what I was told was a unique send off, with a loving memory.[91]

It was not only Selwyn who was surprised by this very un-Foreign Office-like tribute. The enduring memory of those present is that when Derek Hoyer Millar called for three cheers so astonished were they that the cheers petered out after two. So Selwyn went down the great staircase past the bust of Ernest Bevin and made his way to the Treasury. E. M. Forster could only muster two cheers for democracy. Should the Foreign Office have managed a third for Selwyn Lloyd?

Selwyn's position among the post-war Foreign Secretaries is difficult to assess for two reasons. First, he was Foreign Secretary at a time when Britain was having to adjust to the fact that she was no longer a front-rank nation capable of independent action on a world stage. He cannot, therefore, be directly compared with Bevin, the colossus of Foreign Secretaries since 1945.[92] Second, his spell at the Foreign Office fell into three highly contrasted periods (pre-Suez, Suez and post-Suez) which made continuity difficult. Moreover, he had to adjust to two dominating and highly contrasting personalities as Prime Minister. In the pre-Suez days he was finding his feet as 'a junior Cabinet Minister holding a senior post'.[93] He was well aware of the anomalies and difficulties implicit in such a position. During the Suez crisis he was swept along by events (and a Prime Minister) over which he had little or no control. Only in the final period from 1957–60 did he approach a position of independent autonomy. Though he was never in a position to dictate to Cabinet (Eden was the last Foreign Secretary to be able to do that) he did manage some notable achievements – at Geneva in 1959 and over difficult negotiations on such issues as the Formosan straits and, above all, Cyprus. Nevertheless, there is great divergence of view about his ultimate historical standing. One very senior Foreign Office figure who worked closely with Selwyn (and who liked him personally) dryly commented that his place in the post-war pantheon of Foreign Secretaries was 'above Herbert Morrison' (of whom the saying was, 'Ernie Bevin didn't know how to pronounce the names of the places either, but at least he knew where they were'). He had fierce critics. 'I did not admire him. I found his attitude during the Suez crisis weak and mendacious', wrote Nigel Nicolson. 'I remember that when Dag Hammarskjöld came to London, and there was a reception in Lancaster House, Selwyn introduced me to him with the words, "This is Nigel Nicolson, who had the audacity to say that we were wrong about Suez", jocularly but I remember the contemptuous look that Hammarskjöld gave him.'[94] But there is another side to the coin. Jakie Astor, like Nigel Nicolson a Suez 'rebel', paid warm tribute to Selwyn, as we have seen, even at the moment of their greatest political divergence. Selwyn was an acquired taste. He could be brusque and rude, yet he could be considerate in matters of personal relationships. When Peter Hope became Head of the News Department Selwyn was very appreciative of his work. 'I'm glad the papers gave such and such a good coverage', he would say when things went well. 'I'm sorry I gave you such a bad brief', he would say if things went wrong. One day at the Paris Embassy as the party progressed from the Boudoir Violet via the Salon Carmélite to the Grand Salon Vert Selwyn noticed Antony Acland bringing up the rear. He came back through the great rooms of the Embassy and ensured that his new secretary was properly introduced. When Ian Harvey resigned on 24 November 1958 following a personal scandal Selwyn was told only when he arrived at the office after 9. Yet the news had been received at the Foreign Office at 6.30 a.m. 'You should have wakened me up and told me at once', he said. He was responsive to the staff and their place in the hierarchy. When Denis Laskey left the Office in October 1959 to go to the Embassy in Rome it was clear that Selwyn knew the changes twelve deep. Most Foreign Secretaries would not have known beyond the first two or three. Those who worked with him over a long period came to appreciate his qualities. Sir William Hayter, Deputy Under-Secretary of State from 1957 to 1958, was one such person. In January 1958 he went with Selwyn to Ankara for a Baghdad Pact Council. 'It was during this meeting that I revised my opinion of him. It had not been easy to take him seriously as Foreign Secretary when Eden was Prime Minister, since at that time all foreign policy was run from No. 10, and when I returned to the Foreign Office I found, in daily contact with Selwyn Lloyd, that his teasing, leg-pulling, bullying manner was not sympathetic. But living with him for some days at close quarters in the Ankara Embassy I suddenly realized that I liked him and even respected him and that he was really a very able Minister.'[95] The final judgment may well be that, though he was below Bevin and Eden in achievement, he was very much in the next rung of Foreign Secretaries.

II

Chancellor of the Exchequer

The important Cabinet reshuffle in July 1960 was prompted by Derick Heathcoat Amory's retirement as Chancellor of the Exchequer. Amory had warned Macmillan before the 1959 General Election that he wished to step down and had only been persuaded with difficulty to stay on until the summer. With the failure of the Paris summit and the parliamentary recess ahead, Macmillan decided that the moment had come to accede to Amory's wishes. Unlike the occasion in January 1958 when Peter Thorneycroft and the Treasury team had resigned *en bloc* Macmillan had had ample time to reflect on the succession and he concluded that Selwyn Lloyd was the Cabinet minister of requisite seniority who should be considered for the post. Macmillan felt that entry into Europe was the most painless way of making the British economy more competitive, while at the same time less vulnerable both economically and in terms of defence. For this he required a Chancellor with an international overview and one of his subsequent disappointments with Selwyn's performance was that his Chancellor became enmeshed in a Treasury web of domestic economic controversies. Indeed both men came to regret the move.

The possibility that he might become Chancellor of the Exchequer had been in Selwyn's mind ever since his dinner with Amory in January. Speculation had been rife in the Press throughout the spring, Selwyn noting in his diary for Sunday 22 May:

Sunday Express – I am to stay in Foreign Office – a reverse for me on the journey to No 10.
Observer – Lloyd sick of his desk etc – must stay on to obey His Master's Voice.
Sunday Times – The Exchequer awaits Lloyd but is the timing right?
The Economist – Is it right to give the Exchequer to a worthy but weary Foreign Secretary?[1]

On Monday 23 May Amory dined with Selwyn again. He repeated that he intended to go and his wish that Selwyn should succeed him, though he now doubted whether Macmillan could spare Selwyn from the Foreign Office. Selwyn wrote in his diary that night:

His choice as his successor has been myself. Harold has now said that he cannot go on without me – availability day & night – quickness – 4½ years of working together – understanding how to present issues etc. In the circumstances Derry says that it is my duty to continue where I am if I physically can. Possible choices for Chancellor. Eccles – judgment not reliable – Maudling – disappointing and not yet mature – Macleod otherwise engaged – Sandys too slow and unpredictable – Brooke – reliable, sound, experienced – therefore Brooke gets it. Rather depressing survey of the material coming up.[2]

The next day Selwyn had a long talk with Macmillan about the future direction of the Administration, in the course of which (to tempt Selwyn to fall in with his wishes?) Macmillan dangled the prospect of Selwyn's eventually leading the party if he became Chancellor now, stressing, 'it was very important from my point of view because if ever I was to lead the party, I must have experience away from Foreign Affairs'.[3] The conversation was extremely wide-ranging with Selwyn being used as a sounding board for Macmillan's ruminations:

Tuesday May 24
Talk to Harold – a very different picture – I shall have what I want. He does not wish to disturb the balance of the Cabinet –

First echelon	himself,
	Rab,
	myself,
	Amory, who is to go
2nd echelon	Sandys ⎱ both prewar members
	Brooke ⎰
3rd echelon	Maudling
	Eccles
	Heath
	Macleod
	Watkinson
Not to be considered for various reasons	
	Maclay
	Hare
	Mills
	Hill
	? Marples

and because they are in the Lords
>Kilmuir
>Hailsham

If I go to the Exchequer
>could Home do F.S.
>Butler could not work with him –

If I stay, who does Exchequer?
>v. disappointed in Maudling
>Brooke would just be a Treasury spokesman.

He wants someone with original ideas.

He said he was sure that Butler could not lead the party – he would not hand over to him. I was at the perfect age – I ought to go to the Exchequer in my own interest – the race for the leadership was very open – It would be hell for him.

Two years ago he had told the Queen that if he was killed in an aircraft accident, she should send for Alec Home for advice, not Bobbety* – and his own advice would be Derry Amory. Her Majesty had now sent him back his letter.

There was plenty of time to think it all over . . .

Did I think Alec could do F.S.?

I said that for purely physical reasons I did not think so, and the burden on Harold himself would be too great.

He seemed to envisage the possibility of his fighting another Election. I said that we would be getting tired of him about 1970.[4]

Several revealing factors emerge from this diary entry. First, it is the kind of conversation that Macmillan ought to have been having with the acknowledged Number Two in the government, Rab Butler (were it not for the fact that Macmillan's relationship with him precluded such discussion), whereas the actual conversation with Selwyn shows – three years before the question of the succession arose – Macmillan's determination that Butler should not become Prime Minister. Secondly, it reveals how close Selwyn was to Macmillan in the aftermath of the Paris summit, so much so that Macmillan is even encouraging Selwyn to consider himself in the running as a potential successor. The listing of the third echelon of the Cabinet is also significant in that it contained the names of Maudling (at that time a 'disappointment'), Heath and Macleod, who were brought on as potential successors in the 1962 reshuffle when Selwyn had fallen by the wayside. The strangest comment of all is that Macmillan wanted as Chancellor 'someone with original ideas', and was considering Selwyn for the post. 'If I did not accept, he would

---

* Lord Salisbury.

offer the Treasury to Henry Brooke', Selwyn recorded in a fuller memorandum on these talks,[5] yet Brooke was the man who 'would just be a Treasury spokesman.' Selwyn agreed to think over the options and to meet again at the beginning of the following week.

'Saw Harold at No. 10', wrote Selwyn in his diary for Monday 30 May. 'He wants me to go to the Treasury – Alec to F.O.'[6] So now the die was cast, as far as Macmillan was concerned, and the ball was in Selwyn's court. Even then most of their conversation centred on the suitability of Alec Home as Selwyn's successor. 'I said that that could only work if there was another Foreign Office minister in the Cabinet – I think there is a lot to be said for Foreign S. in the Lords, but he must have a senior Minister as No. 2 – to take weight off PM and also to help with foreign representations. We agreed to think it all over after Whit.'[7]

On Friday 10 June Selwyn went down to Fittleworth to stay with the Hardy-Roberts. Macmillan was also weekending in Sussex (at nearby Petworth with John Wyndham) and on the Saturday Selwyn drove over for lunch. During the afternoon Macmillan and Selwyn discussed the Cabinet reshuffle for three hours. The first question was the Exchequer. Selwyn agreed to become Chancellor, subject to four conditions – that he could stay on in 1 Carlton Gardens (Downing Street was about to undergo a major reconstruction and Macmillan had to move to Admiralty House for three years), that he could keep Sergeant Wren as his principal detective, that he could take Antony Acland with him as private secretary and – the most audacious of constitutional suggestions and one that showed how much he was in Macmillan's confidence at the time – that he should be granted a three to four year spell at the Treasury to get public expenditure under control and to bring to fruition any long term plans that he and his advisers thought desirable. Macmillan gave him his word at Petworth that afternoon that he would not be prematurely removed from the Treasury where he could expect to stay until the next election. It was a promise that Macmillan came to rue and which helps to explain the hesitant touch he showed two years later in the run-up to the Night of the Long Knives. Indeed, although Selwyn stayed on at 1 Carlton Gardens until 1961, in the longer term of his four conditions only one (that Sergeant Wren should remain with him) was fulfilled. While 11 Downing Street was being renovated he was given a rather gloomy government flat in Buckingham Gate and it was in the domestic arrangements here that his visitors became aware of how much he lacked a hostess. Although Butler was allowed to take Ian Bancroft with him when he became Lord Privy Seal, Selwyn had to adapt to the established Treasury secretariat. In retrospect, it is astonishing that Macmillan should have agreed to the fourth request. Yet his hands were tied. Apart from Brooke (and Macmillan admitted that he was very much a second choice) there were really no other figures available. So Selwyn, *force majeure*, got his way. With that promise and with the tenure of Chequers his false sense of security was complete. Chequers was a 'grand' address and Selwyn loved the place dearly, but it induced a sense of political somnolence.

Macmillan had been frank with Selwyn and now Selwyn was equally frank in return. 'I told him he was wrong if he expected any originality. I had v. orthodox ideas about taxation and public expenditure, and knew nothing about the City.' Selwyn knew that his métier was as the staff officer. The seeds of Macmillan's disenchantment were already sown, but the fault did not lie with Selwyn. As it was now tacitly assumed that Selwyn would be Chancellor, the two men discussed the further consequential changes. 'Long talks about other jobs – Would Erroll* do for the 2nd FO Minister?'[8] Eventually it was decided that Edward Heath would undertake this responsibility as Lord Privy Seal. The reshuffle was announced on 27 July. Macmillan ensured that a wedge was not driven between the various wings of the party, and just as Stanley Baldwin had given Austen Chamberlain office in October 1924 to end a political rift so two of the former Treasury team returned to the fold (Peter Thorneycroft as Minister of Aviation and Enoch Powell as Minister of Health). In the event the greatest Press attention – with rather unoriginal references to Caligula and horses – would be paid to the appointment of Lord Home as Foreign Secretary. Selwyn therefore began his spell at the Treasury away from the full glare of publicity, something which suited him well. All this lay some weeks ahead, however. On 11 June Selwyn returned in the evening to the Hardy-Roberts at Fittleworth. 'Do you know whom you are speaking to?', he asked his host in the doorway of the Mill House. 'You are speaking to the next Chancellor of the Exchequer', adding, tongue-in-cheek, 'Why me? This moderate man.' Just over two years later his tenure of the Exchequer which began at Fittleworth was to end while staying with the same hosts in the same house.

One of Selwyn's thoughts was of Criccieth and the charades at Brynawelon with the Lloyd Georges. Who would have believed that in those games of cricket were a past and a future Chancellor? Macmillan had overcome Selwyn's doubts by persuasively pointing out that in the first post-war Parliament he had been in the shadow Treasury team and it had been more of a surprise that he had first

* Frederick Erroll, then Minister of State at the Department of Trade.

gone to the Foreign Office. Nevertheless Selwyn later came to believe that he had bought the stock when it was overvalued. 'With hindsight, I realize that I was foolish not to go into the state of the economy more thoroughly before accepting. It is a mistake for a Minister who has been concerned with Foreign Affairs and Defence for many years to go straight into the office of Chancellor of the Exchequer. I had not been able to prepare myself sufficiently. I had been very much occupied by the abortive Summit Meeting in Paris, and in endeavouring to sustain Macmillan in his grievous disappointment. The result was that in July when I became Chancellor it took quite a time for me to bring myself up to date. I was described as being very much on the defensive with the financial correspondents and experts. This was not surprising because frequently I did not know how qualified they were to offer the advice which they gave in no uncertain fashion and moment.' For the time being the summer of 1960 was golden. Eleven days after their meeting at Petworth (with the government changes still in cold storage) Harold Macmillan, as the newly elected Chancellor of Oxford University, presided at his first Encaenia. Among the honorary graduands he had nominated was Selwyn, whose place in the procession was alongside the Archbishop of York. 'I walked into the Sheldonian with Michael Ramsey – an odd quirk – we sat for the same scholarship exam, went up the same term and had rooms next door to one another', Selwyn wrote in his diary on 22 June. 'Lunch at All Souls – Harold having telephone calls all the time about the Bank Rate.'[9] It was the only cloud in an otherwise perfect day, which ended with a Gaudy at Christ Church.

Selwyn was now at the crossroads of his political career. After the Treasury it seemed there were only two possibilities – Number 10 or retirement. The day after the degree ceremony at Oxford Bank Rate was raised to 6 per cent. 'I did not want to have to do it myself', wrote Selwyn, 'and also the greater evil is inflation.' The post-election euphoria was already giving way to a more sober realisation of the economic facts of life. Selwyn had a month to contemplate these facts as he began to wind up his activities at the Foreign Office. His diary at this time is full of self-doubt ('I know what they will all say – PM intends to assume control of the Treasury'), but there was little Press controversy when his appointment was announced on 27 July. Lord Home's move to the Foreign Office drew all the headlines. 'There is a furious controversy going on', wrote Selwyn. 'Comment on my own translation was rather lost in the row about Home.'[10]

The next day was Selwyn's 56th birthday, 'a memorable day', as he noted in his diary. The Queen's secretary, Sir Michael (later Lord)

Adeane, rang to make arrangements for an audience at the Palace, as Selwyn had been Foreign Secretary for over 4½ years. The Queen received Selwyn that morning before the Privy Council. 'She was very nice, as always, said what fun we had had on the various State visits. We talked of Portugal and the beards.'*[11] From this audience Selwyn went to his first Cabinet as Chancellor, 'noting my place has been changed – from David Kilmuir's right to his left. As a creature of habit, if one has sat in one place for 4½ years, why change? My first reaction was an odd amount of annoyance.'[12] At 3.15 he visited the Royal Mint. This ceremonial side of his new job, speaking at Guild-hall or the Mansion House, Selwyn loved and though there were not many occasions on which the Chancellor could don his black and gold robes they appeared when possible. His first substantive meeting was on 29 July with Sir Frank Lee (the Head of the Treasury), Edward Boyle and Anthony Barber (Financial Secretaries), Sir Thomas Padmore (Head of Home Finance), Sir Robert Hall (the Government's Chief Economic Adviser), Sir Alexander Johnston (Head of the Inland Revenue) and Lord Cobbold (the Governor of the Bank of England). Selwyn was soon aware of the intellectual calibre of his advisers and of the different ways of the Treasury after his long period at the Foreign Office. During his first week he asked his private secretary David Hubback to come for a business meeting at 10 p.m. It was quietly pointed out to him that there was no need for the Treasury to work to that kind of timetable. Selwyn found differences in other ways too. At the Foreign Office he needed lots of stamina because of all the travelling involved. At the Treasury he needed the stamina because of all the internal battles with his Cabinet colleagues. At the Foreign Office it had been a seven-day week reading the telegrams and despatches, but unless there was a particu-lar crisis Selwyn did not find that he had to take day-to-day decisions, rather putting forward suggestions for an approach, moulding opin-ion towards a particular course. (As Chancellor of the Exchequer he handled with discretion and sympathy the case of an Ambassador who was £20,000 out of pocket after subsidising the costs of his Embassy.) At the Treasury he found that the office hours were shorter, the weekends freer (he used Chequers more than ever before) and that the paper work was not so sustained. On the other

---

* In February 1957, the Duke of Edinburgh joined the State Visit to Portugal after a lengthy tour of Antarctica, where he had grown a beard. For the Duke's private arrival at Lisbon Airport, the Royal Party (including Selwyn as Minister in attend-ance) had sported false beards. The subsequent hilarity was long remembered in Royal circles, particularly as it had succeeded 'in cheering up poor Selwyn'. (Private information).

hand, he might have three battles a day on the expenditure side. Out of this came, from 9 October 1961, the appointment as Chief Secretary to the Treasury of Henry Brooke who handled this expenditure side so that the Chancellor did not have to spend his whole time negotiating with his colleagues but could think more of the general economic direction of the country. Macmillan had found the job of Foreign Secretary like editing a daily newspaper, that of Chancellor like a weekly or even monthly journal.[13] From his first day Selwyn saw himself as the daily editor. One of Amory's themes as Chancellor had been to cut down on tax evasion and Selwyn entered Great George Street understanding that this was now 'read'. He was determined to be a reforming Chancellor and many of his officials (contrary to later received opinion) regarded him as having the potential to fulfil that aim had he not been sacked in July 1962. 'We must have a sense of purpose', was one of Selwyn's oft-repeated phrases that first summer. Unlike his move to Defence, which came at precisely the wrong moment in the cyclical process, Selwyn's move to the Treasury was fortunate in its timing. Amory's Budget measures were being absorbed into the system and July saw the first meetings of the Budget Committee and the first national income forecasts with the preliminary Exchequer Prospects Table. During the recess he was able to acquaint himself with the brief before his first public commitment at the September meeting of the International Monetary Fund in Vienna.

It soon became clear to the Treasury team that in Selwyn Lloyd there was a progressive Tory Chancellor trying to get out. Neddy, the regulators, planning – these were all things that a Labour figure might have been expected to embrace. After the 1959 Election a marked sea-change came over the political scene in that there was a move towards a more *dirigiste* society, a move in which Selwyn Lloyd was caught up. A degree of interventionism in economic policy was once more in fashion (the French Commissariat du Plan was an influence here) and the concept of the corporate state could be seen with the National Economic Development Council, the National Incomes Commission, the pay pause and the guiding light. In the early 1960s there was not only a change of direction and emphasis in economic thinking but also in four key positions. Apart from the Chancellor, the Permanent Secretary to the Treasury, the Governor of the Bank of England and the Government's Chief Economic Adviser were all to change between 1960 and 1962 and this led to what Samuel Brittan has called 'The Great Reappraisal', a process in which he identified Sir Frank Lee (who had become Permanent Secretary on 1 January 1960) and Selwyn Lloyd as the two key figures.[14] Selwyn established a very fruitful relationship with Lee from the start. There was an informal frankness about their dealings as though they were determined to stick a pin into the atmosphere of official business. On one occasion Frank Lee prepared an exhaustive paper on the promotional prospects of key Treasury personnel. After reading it with great interest Selwyn said, 'I wish you could do a note like that for me about all the members of the Cabinet.'[15] Lee was noted for his ability at managing good personal relationships (he sent Selwyn one of the warmest letters after the events of July 1962) and it was significant that he was away ill at Much Hadham for the greater part of 1962 when Selwyn was running into political difficulties. He stressed the importance of competition in economic management at a time when the trend (as seen with the Radcliffe Committee of 1957 and the Plowden Report of 1961) was towards the concept of planning.

After Frank Lee's heart attack in Paris in 1961 Selwyn leant heavily for advice on Thomas Padmore, the Head of the Home Section of the Treasury. Thomas Padmore had first met Selwyn in a House of Commons Economic Committee in the post-war Parliament when he was much impressed by Selwyn's leadership (with Peter Thorneycroft) of the Opposition committee members. He was not surprised that their paths crossed again. Selwyn assimilated the points that Padmore put to him. He was never the kind of Chancellor who made up his mind by arguing with his advisers. He listened to the arguments and counter-arguments and asked questions in an unaggressive manner. As a result his advisers liked him, not because he did what they wanted him to do but because he made up his mind in a fair and impartial manner. He gained the reputation of being a thinking Chancellor who did not take as gospel what had been said because it had been said by an expert, but because he had been persuaded. On Home Policy Finance questions he also established good working relationships with Otto Clarke, Samuel Goldman and Peter Vinter, who was a leading figure in the creation of Neddy. Otto Clarke, a guiding influence over the Plowden Report, and one of the legendary post-war Treasury figures, rated Selwyn highly, telling Thomas Padmore that in his opinion Selwyn was one of the best post-war Chancellors.[16]

On overseas finance Selwyn was greatly helped by Sir Denis Rickett. (After Suez Rickett had been in charge of the negotiations with the Egyptians about the unfreezing of their number one account at the Bank of England for the return of appropriated British assets in Egypt, though Selwyn's separate negotiations with Fawzi on the same matter had not always been appreciated by the Treasury.) Rickett found Selwyn a reticent figure, who was surprisingly diffident about what he could do, particularly over the question of the overseas balances where there was a conflict between Treasury caution and the political desire for expansion. In Amory's time Macmillan had been prone to saying, 'What use is the Treasury? I have to do all the work.' Selwyn soon found himself caught up in the battle between the Stocktonian Keynesians on the one hand and Treasury orthodoxy on the other.

When Selwyn became Chancellor his first thought was that he wished to reduce the burden of taxation. The Inland Revenue, then based at Somerset House and headed by Sir Alexander Johnston, found him a very open-minded Chancellor and were pleased by his willingness to listen and by his ability to take independent decisions, notably over the raising of the surtax exemption ceiling in the 1961 Budget. Nevertheless he remained an anxious Chancellor – 'How's the patient?', he would ask of the exchange rate – and he was not naturally at home in the conceptual world of the Treasury, despite the quality of the help and advice he received. Throughout his career Selwyn had had the good fortune to work with some of the brightest figures in Whitehall, particularly with his private secretaries, a line which included Michael Hadow, Antony Duff, Denis Laskey, Donald Logan, John Graham, Antony Acland and Ian Samuel. His team at Great George Street was in this tradition – David Hubback, Tom Caulcott (from September 1961) and Colin Peterson, all of whom took their turn in sustaining Selwyn at Chequers, where he tended to 'over-provide' (as was true of his innovation of the third Deputy when he was Speaker),* though part of this was because he enjoyed social companionship. In many ways he was closest to Colin Peterson, who was responsible for parliamentary questions and constituency correspondence. Selwyn was very anxious about parliamentary questions and at 4.30 on the eve of questions he would assemble the full muster of the Treasury mandarins – Frank Lee, Tom Padmore, Denis Rickett and William Armstrong – to pore over the minutiae of supplementaries. For the mandarins this was very small beer and unnecessary in that Selwyn coped perfectly well with questions. Another disconcerting factor was Selwyn's excessive reliance at these meetings on William Armstrong, whom he much admired. 'What do *you* think, William?', would always be his overriding concern, irrespective of whether the matter under discussion was Armstrong's province or not. On the parliamentary level he was well served by Edward Boyle and Anthony Barber ('The heavenly twins'

---

* See Chapter 15.

as he called them) and by Hennie Oakeshott, as Parliamentary Private Secretary. Barber was a particular protégé.

In July 1960 Lord Cobbold was coming to the end of his period of office as Governor of the Bank of England. Macmillan and Selwyn had many discussions about his successor. Sir Oliver Franks was their favoured candidate, though this plan fell through. Later Selwyn was to invite Franks to be one of the founder members of the NEDC. Selwyn was not the only Chancellor to defer to the patrician figure of Cobbold, who had been Governor of the Bank since 1949, and whose influence was akin to that of Montagu Norman in pre-war days. Selwyn felt more comfortable with Lord Cromer, who became Governor on 1 July 1961, though some believe that he deferred too much to Cromer, especially over the July measures of 1961. But this was a false impression not dispelled by Selwyn's sense of social diffidence in Cromer's presence. The inner circle knew that there was no division of opinion between the Chancellor's advisers in the Treasury and the Bank in July 1961. Another long-standing servant in Whitehall, Robert Hall, retired as Chief Economic Adviser in 1961. From Hall came the impetus for a 'guiding light' on pay increases. He was succeeded by Alec Cairncross ('I like your wee Scotsman', said Macmillan to Selwyn when Cairncross's appointment was under consideration)[17] and Selwyn wasted no time in seeking Cairncross's help. 'I had hardly set foot in the Treasury when the Chancellor sent for me', wrote Cairncross in his diary for 17 June 1961. 'He was in braces, smoking Turkish cigarettes, and surrounded by papers.' Yet Macmillan stressed to Selwyn that a Chancellor had to break away from his Treasury advisers, telling him that the Treasury would never have come up with a plan as audacious as Premium Bonds (though they were in fact the brainchild of Edmund Compton), which Macmillan introduced in his only Budget in 1956. Macmillan encouraged him to go his own way. It was only when he did and electoral considerations obtruded that Macmillan moved to wrest back control. Selwyn's sacking was partly because of his independence. By comparison with Macmillan there was none of the lively banter of discussion documents, no *First Thoughts from a Treasury Window*, such as Macmillan had written on arrival in Great George Street (a document which was irreverently known in Whitehall as *What the Butler never saw*). Selwyn was glad to have economic advice, but where the political decisions were concerned he preferred to trust his own intuition. Where Selwyn may not have had original ideas (though he did at certain key moments), he was nevertheless the cause of activity in others. In that sense he was an effective political leader of the Treasury and was never over-reached or dominated by his advisers. It was pointed out in Whitehall that, 'a subtler person would have seen more difficulties and snags and not accomplished as much, so curious are the workings of human chemistry.'[18]

Selwyn's time at the Treasury lay under the shadow of the recurring balance of payments crises of 1955, 1958 and later, in 1961. He appreciated that this was because Britain's cost structure and efficiency were out of line with those of her major industrial competitors. As Chancellor therefore he had three priorities. He wanted the Treasury to plan ahead and gain some measure of long-term funding; he needed restraint of wage costs for economic (if not political) purposes; and finally, he wanted the bright people to have the opportunity of putting forward views. Plowden, the pay pause and Neddy were the offspring of these priorities.

Between 1958 and 1960 the United Kingdom had enjoyed a period of relative price stability, resulting firstly from a fall in the price of imports before 1958 and a fall in food prices after that. Amory had reduced the burden of direct taxation in the 1959 Budget, something which Selwyn was determined to continue. During the run up to his Chancellorship the level of investment was maintained and at 1958 prices rose £289m (or 8.3 per cent) between 1957 and 1959.[19] On the other hand there was a rise in consumer spending of £586m (or 3.7 per cent), but as there was a considerable degree of surplus capacity in the economy all this was achieved without undue inflationary pressure. The balance of payments situation was less satisfactory. Although in 1958 there had been a surplus of £202m, by 1959 this had become a deficit of £405m.[20] 'I do not think you have given me a very tranquil assignment', Selwyn wrote to Macmillan on 4 August, 'but I will do my best'.[21] Although the autumn was quite a honeymoon period, Selwyn soon realised that economically he had come in at the turnover point at the wrong end of a boom. Reviewing 1960, he found that in the first quarter United Kingdom exports increased 17 per cent over the same period in 1959, but that world exports had increased 26 per cent. In the second quarter the figures were 7 per cent to 16 per cent, and in the third quarter 4 per cent to 14 per cent.[22] Production targets had to be improved. At the second meeting of the NEDC in May 1962 he insisted upon a 4 per cent growth target ('Mr Selwyn Lloyd's greatest personal achievement as Chancellor', wrote Samuel Brittan)[23] and had wanted to aim for 5 per cent. The tension between the opposing claims of growth and caution was at the heart of Selwyn's Chancellorship.

'At the end of the first real week of work at the Treasury, it is apparent how different all this is from the F.O.', he wrote in his diary on 4 September. 'Probably one is still suffering from reaction; after being taught for 4½ years to meet any shock – for example this week the Jordan Prime Minister has been assassinated, and Mr K has announced his intention of leading the Soviet delegation to the U.N. I have felt very flat and rather bored – but Joanna has been away too. The most important business has been that of coal prices. The NCB deficit will be £51m next year. They wanted immediate approval to raise prices to bring in £61m.'[24] After much toing and froing a small increase was agreed. The next shadow on the horizon was University grants. Strikes, threatened or actual, were a constant worry. No sooner had a possible power strike been settled in August than an unofficial shipping strike threatened a prolonged interruption of the export market, but this lasted only twelve days. A railway strike failed to materialise, although there was a minor administrative strike in the London docks in September. In this new field of industrial relations Selwyn worked closely with John Hare (later Lord Blakenham), who was to become one of his doughtiest champions in and out of Cabinet and a close personal friend. Selwyn believed that there must be dialogue between government and unions and in this belief was the seed of Neddy.

On Monday 12 September Selwyn met his Budget Committee – Frank Lee, Robert Hall, Alexander Johnston and William Armstrong (who was to succeed Lee as Head of the Treasury in 1962). Selwyn made five points. He wanted the 1961 Budget to be as little concerned with 'tidying up' as possible. He did not wish its theme to be 'anti-evasion' (Amory's battle). Substantive positive themes were what mattered and he listed three – incentives to effort (including questions of surtax – husbands' and wives' taxation – the old query whether a capital gains tax is the price for a surtax reform and what could be done for the lower income groups); how to increase exports (was it through alterations in purchase tax, export councils, better credit facilities, expenditure overseas or Trade fairs?); and how to restrict consumption that fuelled imports. Selwyn recorded in his diary 'A good discussion – Armstrong said that it was the best with any Chancellor (he has served Rab, Harold, Peter & Derry) that he has known. Lee said much the same.'[25] This encouraging start did much to boost Selwyn's confidence though his spirits were a little dashed when he looked in at the Economic Planning Board to ask Nigel Birch about the recent TUC Conference in the Isle of Man. 'I asked Birch what the weather had been like at Douglas during the T.U.C. Conference – he said that it had been bloody awful, but a damned sight better than anything else.'[26] The next day (13 September) Selwyn had his first meeting with the TUC, led by Sir Vincent

Tewson and George Woodcock. In the light of later developments this was a meeting of considerable psychological importance on both sides. The Treasury wanted to keep Selwyn on a fairly tight rein. 'The Treasury brief was that I should appear friendly, sincere and well intentioned and avoid any discussion of substance', Selwyn wrote in his diary. But he was more outgoing and found the TUC responsive. 'They had much to contribute. *Daily Herald* said afterwards that I pleased them.'[27]

Another body that Selwyn (eventually) pleased was the Board of the National Theatre. Although it was not appreciated at the time, this was to prove one of his most important legacies as Chancellor. 'Lunch with Oliver Poole to meet the *Financial Times*', wrote Selwyn in his diary on 14 September. 'Drogheda very polite, I think perhaps because I hold the money bags and he is very keen on the National Theatre – he has always been a little off hand before.' Throughout his first autumn at the Treasury Selwyn found himself in frequent briefings about the proposed National Theatre building on the South Bank, an important delegation on 9 December consisting of Sir Kenneth Clark, his old colleague Lord Chandos (formerly Oliver Lyttelton and after whom one of the three auditoriums in the new National Theatre was eventually to be named) and Peter Hall, at that time director of the Royal Shakespeare Company but destined to be Lord Olivier's successor as director of the National Theatre. Selwyn proved himself stubborn to be wooed and on 21 March 1961 initially said that any available money would go to regional theatres rather than the National.[28] During the spring of 1961 intense negotiations followed between the interested parties, Lord Cottesloe (after whom the third auditorium in the new building was to be named) of the London County Council devising with Selwyn on 9 June 1961 a scheme whereby the LCC offered the South Bank site and £1.3m, with the government providing £1m, a scheme announced on 12 July.[29] By the time these plans came to fruition Selwyn was no longer Chancellor, but the National Theatre had not forgotten his part. On 3 November 1969 Selwyn attended the ceremonial cement pouring on the South Bank and although the National Theatre was not to move into its new home until 1976 it was established under the auspices of the Old Vic on 22 October 1963 with a production of *Hamlet*, starring Peter O'Toole. Selwyn was the guest of honour at this first night, Lord Chandos having written on 19 September with tickets. 'They are a miniscule tribute to the only man in two hundred years who has had the guts (and at a difficult time) to back the National Theatre.' Peter Hall also wrote to Selwyn saying that without him they would not be there.[30] Selwyn has often been called 'the father of commercial television'; he played an important role in establishing the National Theatre also.

Selwyn's first months as Chancellor saw a continuation of the honeymoon period. 'Very pleasant reception at the Party Conference in Scarborough, and at the Bankers' Dinner, an adequate speech in the House of Commons, pleasant meetings with City people, lunches etc.', Selwyn noted.[31] At a lunch at Claridges on 22 September Selwyn had a long talk with Harold Wilson, the Shadow Chancellor. 'I gave him a lift back. On the way he said that he was in two minds whether or not to stand for the Deputy Leadership of the Labour Party. He was afraid that George Brown would stand against him and win . . . He had always got on very well with Derry Amory. He used to agree with him how long the Finance Bill should take, and promised to carry out that programme provided he, Harold Wilson, could decide when to stop each night. He hoped I would make the same arrangement.'[32] Bank Rate was reduced to 5½ per cent in October and a further cut on 8 December brought the rate down to 5 per cent. At Cabinet on 29 November Selwyn had warned that prices were likely to rise with consequential demands for higher wages. It was agreed that employers should be encouraged to resist any unjustified demands. Selwyn departed for Christmas (which he spent with the Ormsby-Gores) in fairly buoyant mood. The rise in home demand had slowed down considerably and though pressure on the labour side had not yet diminished the United Kingdom's position with the IMF had strengthened to £127m and investment was rising satisfactorily.

Selwyn saw the main problem of 1961 as inflation, particularly for its effect on the export market. He met George Woodcock, General Secretary of the TUC, and Frank Cousins, Secretary of the Transport and General Workers' Union, on 12 January 1961 to discuss the level of wage increases, and shortly afterwards met the Federation of British Industries. Selwyn did not see why he should not meet both delegations in a joint forum and, following his talks with John Hare on Labour relations, and these two meetings in January 1961, he conceived the idea of what was later to be the National Economic Development Council, the major institutional legacy of his Chancellorship. Before he could pursue this idea Selwyn found himself in the midst of a balance of payments crisis, following the revaluation of the German Mark in the first week of March. 'That put the cat among the pigeons: we had only a few hours warning. We lost £50m. in one day. The Basle agreement between the Central Banks saved us', wrote Selwyn in his diary. The total loss for the week of 6 March was £170m. 'I cannot think that all this flurry is really a good way for the Western

world to manage its affairs', Selwyn wrote to Mr Dillon of the
American Treasury on 10 March, 'but we are resolved to weather the
storm.'[33] The meeting of Central Bank governors in Basle on 13
March, arranged before the revaluation of the German Mark, agreed
on means of accommodating speculative flow of funds with an IMF
safety net if required. This was hardly the best background for
Selwyn's first Budget. On the same day as the Basle agreement he
wrote in his diary, 'I am now in the throes of semi-final decisions
about the Budget. We have at least a clear £50 million of extra
taxation. We have to fight out surtax and profits tax.'[34] The German
situation had led Macmillan and Selwyn to have a mini-economic
summit at Chequers the previous weekend and the Press had fastened
on to this as evidence that Macmillan was now running the Treasury.
Selwyn was furious. At such moments he did assert himself and on 16
March sent the following letter to Macmillan:

> I get the feeling that those who conduct your public relations think
> that it strengthens your position for it to be thought that you are
> controlling and directing in minute detail every aspect of Govern-
> ment effort. I may be wrong about this feeling. If I am wrong I do
> not understand why more is not done to deflate the Press stories,
> i.e. about this weekend. Any idea that it was a meeting to discuss
> the Budget was laughable.
>
> If I am right about this feeling that it is thought important to
> 'boost' the Prime Minister I suspect that it is the worst possible
> tactics. The idea that you are now preparing the Budget . . . does
> not in my view enhance your prestige. Whether you are in fact
> doing it is quite a different matter. But the build up of your
> colleagues is a fact more important for you, provided of course you
> trust them. On the general issue your prestige is so high and the
> smooth working relations with your ministers so good that it is not
> helpful to portray the image of 'Mac Winston' trying to do every-
> thing himself.
>
> One expects the malicious Press to do this, because their purpose
> is to damage you. I may be quite unjust, but I think they get some
> help in their purpose perhaps unintentionally from Admiralty
> House.[35]

Macmillan made no written reply to this letter, but they discussed
the issues in it on 17 March, and Macmillan was notably emollient
towards Selwyn in the run-up to the Budget.

Although Budgets are traditionally held on Tuesdays, Selwyn
believed that Monday was a far better day and both his Budgets were
delivered on Mondays. This allowed a Cabinet meeting on Saturday

morning, a visit to Windsor to see the Queen on Saturday evening (he stayed for dinner on the 1961 visit), a rest on Sunday, and then Monday for Budget day itself – the Speech, the Finance Committee and TV and sound broadcasting. The 1961 Budget was thus fixed for Monday 17 April. From 'semi-final' decisions Selwyn now moved with his advisers to the broad outline shape of what he hoped would be a reforming Budget. His advisers found him surprisingly independent ('Tax E launched on me this morning by Frank Lee I will not have if I can help it'),[36] nowhere more so than in the surtax exemption level. The two revenue departments of the Treasury met Selwyn with proposals for easing the burden of a tax instituted by Lloyd George in 1909 (when income tax was 1s. 2d. in the £) on incomes in excess of £2,000. They believed that the level of exemption could be raised to £3,000, but Selwyn told them that this was nothing like enough ('What I want to do is to do this job properly')[37] and said they must think again. With great reservations (the Treasury felt he would 'never get away with it') a scheme was prepared at Selwyn's insistence for raising the starting point to £4,000. Even then by applying the income tax allowance of two ninths on earned income up to £4,000, the effective starting point became £5,000. The advisers were not against his action, but they were in awe of his boldness and waited for the political fall-out. It never came and Frank Lee and William Armstrong, authors of key passages in the 1961 Budget, bowed before Selwyn's judgment. A full Cabinet discussion on control of public expenditure was held on 28 March. It was calculated that public expenditure in 1961–2 would amount to £10,450m. Growth rate was forecast at 2.9 per cent with a wages increase of 5 per cent set against an inflation rate of 2.7 per cent. The Plowden Report (to be published in June 1961) was also on the agenda and Selwyn recommended the longer-scale planning of government expenditure. (As Minister of Defence in 1955 he had been horrified at the absence of long term financial planning and had an (unpublished) expenditure plan ready when he moved to the Foreign Office.) Nationalised industries, for instance, must pay their way (the genesis of the notorious Beeching axe on British Rail in 1962). At the beginning of April he went to Chequers for five days with his Treasury advisers (Douglas Wass he found particularly helpful) to put the finishing touches to his speech. He gave details to the Cabinet at 10 a.m. on Saturday 15 April (no revolt as there would be in 1962), travelling to Windsor in the afternoon to see the Queen, dining there after his audience (unlike 1962 when he was to be dealing with the aftermath of the Cabinet revolt). It was all very relaxed. On Sunday there were the usual pre-Budget photographs (Selwyn walking with Joanna in the Chequers countryside accompanied by Sambo and Mrs Hill's dog Nicky) before Budget Day itself on the Monday.

With 11 Downing Street undergoing its major reconstruction, Selwyn paraded the famous battered Budget box from the steps of the Treasury before leaving for the House. He lunched quietly with Hennie Oakeshott, recording in his diary:

> My Budget drink was brandy and water. I tasted it so many times in my room before going into the Chamber, to see that the mixture was right, that Hennie got very alarmed about my possible inso- briety. The speech went well – 90 minutes – everyone most kind – tax reorganisation (although rather thin) went well – the regulator – surtax – TV advertising. Immediately after the Budget, Finance Committee upstairs. Then TV and a sound broadcast. What a day![38]

The substantive part of that day began when Selwyn rose to speak at 3.33 p.m.[39] After a gracious reference to Churchill, who was sitting in his customary seat below the gangway and 'who presented his first Budget thirty-six years ago', Selwyn began his review of the nation's finances. He declared that the purpose of his Budget was to restrain the rise in personal consumption, which was why he was so encour- aged by the record of National Savings. The broad effect of the Budget must be counter-inflationary. Its main features were two new regulators, which allowed the government to vary taxes by 10 per cent without recourse to a Budget. ('Either way?', intervened Hugh Gaitskell. 'Either way', replied the Chancellor.) The first referred to all the main Customs and Excise Revenue duties and to Purchase Tax.* The second regulator, should it be needed, would apply to the employers' share of the National Insurance stamp with a limit of four shillings a week per employee (the payroll tax). At this point Selwyn paused to refresh himself in the traditional manner and, turning to Sir Gordon Touche, Chairman of the Ways and Means Committee who was in the chair, said, 'For every gallon that you drink, Sir Gordon, the revenue benefits to the tune of £10 10s.' Selwyn then concisely covered the main changes – on surtax levels (the relief of £83 was postdated to January 1963), profits tax up 2½ per cent, motor vehicle tax up to £15, and 2d. on fuel oil per gallon. One of the surprises in the package was a 10 per cent tax on television advertising revenue.

---

* The 10 per cent was, of course, a 10 per cent variation on the percentage of the current rate, not a 10 per cent change in the tax itself. The regulator was an example of Selwyn's willingness to try new ideas, the 'Premium Bond' factor.

27 and 28 Macmillan's diplomatic round: (above) with Selwyn Lloyd in
Russia, 27 February 1959; (below) leaving Buckingham Palace
with President Kennedy, 5 June 1961.

29 Selwyn Lloyd receiving an honorary degree at Oxford, 22 June 1960, with Harry Crookshank (left) and Lord Home. It was Harold Macmillan's first Encaenia as Chancellor of the University.

30 Selwyn Lloyd with John and Valerie Profumo at Stratford-upon-Avon, 1961.

'Because of my minority report as a member of the Beveridge Committee on Broadcasting, I feel that I have a certain personal responsibility for the introduction of commercial television. If I may mix up my metaphor, I am sure that those concerned with the payment of the duty will not mind too much being bitten by the hand which originally fed them.' He ended by stating that there would be no capital gains tax. In all he budgeted for an overall deficit of £69m with a surplus above the line of £506m (in practice the deficit was £211m over the year). There was a shift from monetary to fiscal measures, and of the burden of taxation from individuals to companies. Overall the Budget was neutral as regards demand. After a friendly reception at the Finance Committee Selwyn prepared for his various broadcasts. On television that night he said, 'I have set out to restrain the growth of personal spending here at home – for two reasons – if there is too much spending we shall have the old situation which used to be described as too many people and too much money chasing too few goods . . . Mr Gladstone a hundred years ago was responsible for expenditure of 69 million pounds in the fiscal year. I am responsible for over 6,000 million pounds.'[40]

There was considerable interest in the first Budget of a new Chancellor. Although the Labour Party criticised the raising of the surtax exemption level, the Budget was well received in Fleet Street. *The Times* called it 'an imaginative and important general plan'[41] and the *Financial Times* declared, 'The elements of a really first-class economic policy now exist'.[42] The most ringing endorsement came, improbably, from the *Guardian*. 'Mr. Lloyd's first Budget marks a radical departure in British economic policy. Its starting point is a bold programme of tax reforms far surpassing anything attempted by any other Conservative Chancellor since the war . . . Politically the first consequence of this radical Budget may have to be an equally radical revision of the hitherto accepted assessment of Mr Lloyd himself.' Norman Shrapnel, the paper's political correspondent, went even further. 'Gone was the harassed, tentative Mr Lloyd we knew of old. The drab and ill-used Foreign Secretary has been re-born rehatched, on this sunny April day, into a most perky Chancellor, full of life and assurance and even plumage.'[43] But it was the end of the honeymoon period.

Pressure on sterling continued through the summer, Selwyn reporting to the Cabinet on 6 June of particularly heavy selling. The unofficial dock strike in May had led to a substantial widening in that month's trade gap. There was a loss of £100m in the reserves with rumours of a revaluation of the Swiss franc in the second week of June. On 15 June Selwyn met the Governor of the Bank of England to discuss the state of the economy, reporting to Cabinet the next day. Regulators could not be used until the Finance Bill was completed at the end of July, but restraint on wage demands was essential. In a statement to the House on 21 June Selwyn said that the government would take what action was necessary to preserve the improvement in the balance of visible trade. This was followed the next day by a tough speech to the British Chamber of Commerce, though in Cabinet on 30 June Selwyn ruled out the idea of import controls. On 1 July Cromer succeeded Cobbold as Governor of the Bank of England. Never did any incoming Governor have such a baptism. July 1961 was *the* crisis month, a depressing continuation of the seemingly endless three-year cycle of a balance of payments crisis ending in a deflationary package. The question was, how deflationary was deflationary?

The overall trade gap in June had been £80m. Incomes were running at an average increase of close on 8 per cent with output and productivity up only 3 per cent. It is against this background that the 'July measures' (announced by Selwyn in the Commons on 25 July) should be seen and as part of a series of recurring crises. Selwyn saw the crisis measures as phase one of a two-part operation. It was not sufficient to curb wages (and thus demand). The important thing was then to find ways of increasing co-operation between both sides of industry and fixing on some agreed target for growth. The July package (the first attempt at an incomes policy) was in four main sections. On the fiscal side Selwyn employed the new regulator by raising indirect taxes, coupled with a cut in public expenditure, a measure urged by the IMF. As Macmillan recorded in his diary two days before the Chancellor's statement, 'If we are to get our "drawings" from the International Monetary Fund, we shall have to make – or pretend to make – large savings on Government Expenditure.'[44] The second section of the package saw Bank Rate raised to 7 per cent, together with a calling in of Special Deposits and a credit squeeze. Third, controls were introduced on private investment outside the sterling area and incentives established for the investing in Britain of profits made by British firms overseas. The measure which caused the biggest headlines (and with hindsight proved to be the beginning of the end for Selwyn politically, however justified economically) was the introduction of the 'pay pause' in the public sector with the hope (always a vain one) that where the public sector led the private sector might follow. The 'little Budget', as it came to be known, was deeply resented, particularly among groups of public workers such as nurses and teachers, who had little industrial muscle (unlike the electricity workers who breached the pay pause in

November) and for whom there was a broad measure of public sympathy. Yet the Treasury and the Bank of England had wanted the deflationary package to be even more severe. Frank Lee, however, congratulated Selwyn on the substance, balance and firmness of his statement in a letter on 26 July. He felt confident that the measures would meet the immediate crisis, but warned that new ground could only be gained if the government stood firm on the wages front.[45] With the Conservative Party in edgy mid-term mood, this was to prove the real sticking point.

After the July measures Selwyn turned his thoughts once more to the concept of bringing together government, trades unions and industry in some tripartite national forum as the necessary follow-up. He envisaged a joint examination of the economic prospects of the country, stretching five or more years into the future, with both sides of industry sharing with government the task of relating plans to the available resources. On 8 August Selwyn invited both sides of industry to join with him in such a forum. The invitation was treated with considerable scepticism by the trades unions, who feared it was a backdoor method of imposing an incomes policy, and by several members of the Cabinet, Selwyn receiving backing only from John Hare, the Minister of Labour, and Lord Hailsham, Minister for Science. John Hare, in particular, supported Selwyn during the Cabinet discussions which came to a conclusion at a stormy meeting on 21 September, at which considerable doubts were expressed about the remit and standing of Selwyn's proposed tripartite body. If ministers were members of this body could the Government dissociate itself from the Council's conclusions and reject its advice? In the end Macmillan's covert support tipped the balance and on 23 September 1961 Selwyn sent a formal letter to the Trades Union Congress, the Federation of British Industries, the British Employers' Confederation, the Association of British Chambers of Commerce and the National Union of Manufacturers.*

Response was mixed. In 1962 the Unions were very cagey about joining the NEDC although their self-esteem demanded that they should be accorded influence. In 1987, just after the 25th anniversary celebrations of Neddy (as the body was soon dubbed), the Chancellor of the Exchequer, Nigel Lawson, announced a scaling down of the number of regular tripartite meetings. This was met by a chorus of Union protest, which told a great deal about the reduced status of the Union movement after a quarter of a century. In 1962 they came grudgingly into Neddy, but it was only one iron in the fire; in 1987 it

* See Appendix B.

was one of the few formal avenues left for involvement, however
peripheral. Neddy, like its instigator, was one of the great survivors
and did not go the way of such statutory bodies as the Prices and
Incomes Commission. Despite this response Selwyn believed that the
adversarial approach got the country nowhere and he persisted in
protracted negotiations with George Woodcock. Indeed the appointment of Sir Robert Shone as the first Director General had been
announced on 18 December 1961 before the Unions had formally
agreed to co-operate. The crucial meeting between George Woodcock and Selwyn took place on the evening of 11 January 1962.
Woodcock was very frank, but not in the way that might have been
expected, as Selwyn recorded in his diary:

> He began with a curious statement about the wages pause. He said
> that I would get no credit from 'history', the 'clever boys' including
> himself would still say how badly matters had been handled, but in
> fact I had by the wages pause performed a great public service, I
> really had concentrated public attention upon incomes policy. It
> had not successfully been done before. He had told the T.U.C.
> this. He then repeated his thesis that the T.U.C. were impotent and
> that I must not expect any help from them.[46]

Selwyn stressed that nevertheless he would like to try. For him
TUC involvement was more important than the precise terms (to
Woodcock's surprise.) It was then Selwyn's turn to be surprised as
Woodcock proved to be an enthusiast for the concept. First, it would
give the TUC an important bridgehead (the alternative was a place on
the sidelines); and second it would direct the TUC's attention away
from internecine arguments over nuclear disarmament and concen-
trate it more properly on economic matters.[47] For Woodcock, how-
ever, the important point was that the NEDC should not be part of
the Treasury machine (if it was he would not be able to persuade the
TUC to join). Selwyn accepted this change of emphasis. At the end of
February the TUC formally agreed to participate in Neddy and on 1
March Selwyn invited George Woodcock to be a member of the
Council.[48]

Although Neddy was intended as a tripartite organisation, Selwyn
was very keen that it should contain 'independent' figures from other
fields, especially the academic. He sent personal invitations to figures
such as Oliver Franks, previously Ambassador in Washington and
Provost of Worcester College, Oxford and then Chairman of Lloyds
Bank, and Professor Henry Phelps Brown of the London School of
Economics. They were to add weight and distinction to the deliberations, which took place in what could be described as a guarded but

friendly atmosphere. When, at the eleventh hour, the TUC had decided to come in there was a general willingness to 'give it a go'. Selwyn was aware that the idea was an experiment, even a daring innovation that could fail completely. Even if he could not turn the lock he was willing to hold the key. In the early meetings (and Selwyn chaired only three meetings before his sacking in July 1962) he impressed upon all participants that for too long Britain's economic problems had been viewed from a sectarian angle, and that he did not exempt government from this charge, and that he wished things to be looked at from a national angle, because the problems were everybody's problems and by helping, even if in a small way, to solve them they would in fact be gaining sectarian advantage. His hopes were only partially fulfilled. Neddy was perceived by many as a 'talking shop', a sweetener, a substitute for action. It also suffered, especially in the early stages, from Treasury suspicion. Neddy was never a rival focus of economic control (unlike the Department of Economic Affairs from 1964–9) but the Treasury felt that it might weaken their influence. Selwyn certainly wished to be availed of more views than the Treasury view, but it was a battle the Treasury never had to fight. When the battle did come – with the DEA – it was a battle the Treasury won hands down.

When Selwyn decided to establish Neddy he was at once on the look out for a possible director. In the summer of 1961 he first sounded out Sir Robert Shone of the Iron and Steel Board over a Sunday lunchtime drink, but made it clear that this was in no sense an implied offer. At that stage two other strong possibilities were Norman Kipping of the FBI and Len Murray of the TUC. What tipped the balance in favour of Robert Shone was that he was politically impartial. He was nonetheless politically aware and very much in favour of the kind of cross-fertilisation of ideas that Selwyn sought. Robert Shone drew Selwyn's attention to the French Commissariat du Plan and early in 1962 a team of Treasury planners visited their French counterparts to see what might be learned. The visit was an eye-opener. They found a sense of urgency totally absent in Britain. The whole railway infra-structure had been rebuilt, for instance, because of the war-time damage. The atmosphere was different. At that time the Treasury seemed incapable of putting on a good meal for visitors. In France the British team found that their meetings with senior officials at the Ministre du Finance had stately lunches at which the waiters wore white gloves. Somehow this detail – the white gloves, so different from the infamous chipped white cups of Dover – brought home how ramshackle and complacent much British thinking was. Selwyn took all this information on board when the team returned. He believed there was a need for something better for Britain, a breaking away from the old idea that the world owed Britain a living and that the country could compete by standing still.

While Selwyn had been appointing the first Director General of Neddy and wooing the TUC the economic discussion in Cabinet had centred on how to move from Phase 1 of an Incomes Policy to Phase 2, the so-called 'guiding light'. On 7 December the Cabinet decided on 2½ per cent (a figure announced in February 1962). Selwyn looked back on 1961 with some relief. Bank Rate had fallen to 6½ per cent on 5 October and then to 6 per cent on 2 November. The pressure of demand was declining, personal spending fell and the increase in incomes was slowing down. But against this prices continued to rise, as did Government current expenditure. Macmillan had carried out a limited reshuffle of the Cabinet in October, Iain Macleod becoming Leader of the House and Chairman of the Party. In his diary Selwyn reflected on the political atmosphere:

> Rab deeply wounded about removal from Leadership of House and Chairmanship of Party. Not a good word to say for Macleod. Alec Home goes from strength to strength – also Ted Heath. Macleod not very scrutable – much happier than before, but a strange character – a mixture of deepness, cleverness and a certain sort of simplicity. Marples has been disappointing over railway wages – he was always the one to say that we must have a show-down, but now he is mesmerized by Beeching and says that the railwaymen ought to get large increases. Beeching is an able but obstinate man.[49]

Sir Robert Shone became the first Director-General of the NEDC on 1 January 1962. On his shoulders rested much of the responsibility for its success. The headquarters were initially at 1 Bridge Street, but there was neither personnel nor even blotting paper. An office had to be equipped in the only available premises (the later move to Millbank Tower was seen by many as a good example of Parkinson's second law)* on the corner of Bridge Street. Sir Robert Shone then invited the economist Sir Donald MacDougall (over a drink at the Reform Club) to become Economic Director and later secured T. C. Fraser of the Wool Industry as Industrial Director. MacDougall was a great advocate of the expansion of demand, which dovetailed well with Shone's view of the importance of reforming the supply side,

---

* C. Northcote Parkinson's second law states that institutions move into grand new buildings at the moment of their decline.

after which he felt growth would come. MacDougall also proved useful at recruiting younger economists.

The first meeting of the NEDC took place at 4 p.m. on Wednesday 7 March at 1 Bridge Street, with Selwyn Lloyd in the chair. A photograph was taken which hangs to this day in the Council Chamber at Millbank Tower. Nineteen other members of the Council were present, including John Hare and Frederick Erroll (now President of the Board of Trade) from the government side; George Woodcock and Frank Cousins from the trades unions; industrialists such as Dr Beeching and independent members such as Sir Oliver Franks and Professor Henry Phelps Brown. Selwyn welcomed members to the first meeting. He was particularly glad that all invitations to serve on the Council had been accepted and he hoped that its establishment would come to be regarded as a major step in Britain's economic history. He defined the tasks of the Council as threefold:

(a) To examine the economic performance of the nation with particular concern for plans for the future in both the private and the public sectors in industry.
(b) To consider together what are the obstacles to quicker growth, what can be done to improve efficiency, and whether the best use is being made of our resources.
(c) To seek agreement upon ways of improving economic performance, competitive power and efficiency, in other words to increase the rate of sound growth.[50]

A paper submitted by the Treasury was then considered. The Council established at once that in future papers should stem from them or be overseen by the Director General. Selwyn laid down that all issues could be raised, except for devaluation. This was necessary, but it was limiting as it meant that the one thing that many members of Neddy, including the Director General, felt was necessary to improve Britain's competitiveness could not be raised as an issue. The balance of payments and the overvalued pound were the two time bombs ticking away in the background. How far would growth prove the panacea? 4 per cent (an over-confident figure) was the target, though it was never achieved. In Neddy there were three conflicting views as to how this could be attained – the view of the indicative planners, that of the purposive planners (which Selwyn and Robert Shone favoured), and that of the imperative planners (a stance which would not be acceptable in peace-time conditions, certainly not to an old free trade Liberal like Selwyn). So the word went out: let us be purposive in preparing policies. Out of this quest came a whole series of policy statements, the so-called Green Books (independent inquiries into investment, productivity and quantitative matters) and the Orange Books (such as the influential *Conditions favourable to faster growth*, published in 1963) which actually set out policies. 'Little Neddies' sprouted to consider particular issues. Mobility of labour, taxation policy, regional policy and income restraint all came under scrutiny. Meetings were planned on a monthly basis (Selwyn preferred mornings followed by a relaxed lunch). They were brisk, cheerful and (apart from one occasion when George Woodcock questioned the status of the independent members) friendly. This may not have been a steady drive towards definable goals, but it was an important psychological safety valve. When Selwyn set out on the road of Neddy he was not sure where it might lead, but he was convinced that the journey would be interesting and in the end worthwhile. His confidence was not misplaced.

On Sunday 4 March Selwyn dined with Macmillan to discuss his budget proposals. They were 'accepted without demur'.[51] Macmillan soon moved on to another topic:

> Talks about the future. He will have to decide six months before next election whether he will continue as PM or not – that means March 63 if election is autumn 63, or Oct 63 if Election in May 64. If he is going to resign he must give his successor a chance. He would have to reconstruct the Government with people who were going to continue after the election – win or lose. Several would want to go – Charles Hill – Ernest Marples – Harold Watkinson – Jack Maclay – perhaps Alec Home – perhaps Hailsham – certainly Mills. He thought Eccles would probably go this July. He thought Thorneycroft might go. Soames, Hare, Brooke, self, Heath, Maudling, Erroll, Sandys would stay on. Kilmuir would do what was wanted – he might stay on as Lord President. Butler would not stay on unless PM or prospect of it. I said, 'What about myself?' He said, 'You would have to stay on if PM.' I said that I was not sure I wanted this. He talked again about his advice to the Queen to ask Home and Kilmuir for advice as to his successor. He was very good. He did not propose to write his memoirs unless he was bankrupt.[52]

Four days after this remarkable conversation Bank Rate fell to 5½ per cent. On 22 March it fell to 5 per cent. Bank Rate was not the only thing to fall in March 1962. Because of the pay pause the Government's popularity had gone into decline and this was shown in spectacular fashion by the disastrous Orpington by-election of 14 March 1962 when a 14,000 Conservative majority was converted into a Liberal one of over 8,000. The financial disenchantment of the middle classes (put in sharp focus by Giles Cooper's play *Everything in the Garden*, which opened in May 1962) was very much in Selwyn's mind as he prepared his second (and last) Budget. He was the man in the political spotlight. On 2 April a full length profile was broadcast on the BBC programme *Panorama*. With the Budget a week away the programme wondered whether the Chancellor had a Puritan belief that winning popularity for his programme was not part of his duty.[53] Selwyn certainly saw his Budget as part of a continuing series. As a result he planned a largely neutral, holding Budget. He had no inkling of the furore that was to erupt at the pre-Budget Cabinet on Saturday 7 April. The main point at issue was the abolition of Schedule A (the Party Conference at Scarborough in October 1960 had passed a motion calling for the ending of this tax on privately owned houses so resented by the owner-occupier), but there was also concern about the political presentation. Selwyn wrote in his diary:

At the Cabinet on Sat 7 April, strong criticisms were made of my proposals. Hailsham said the Budget was unsaleable. Eccles said that the 'economic balance' was right but the methods were wrong, and others joined in. Not one of those whom I had consulted supported it. Rab, Maudling, Erroll, Macleod, Hill who knew what was in it, kept quiet – a lot of talk about Schedule A – I promised to reconsider.

I had lunch at the US Embassy and on my way back looked in at No 10. I saw Harold and Rab. They were disposed to leave it to me. Rab said Harold thinks that you are very upset about this morning. I told him you are not!! I told Rab that he was absolutely right . . . Next morning, after thinking it over, I came to the conclusion that I would not hold to Schedule A against the party's wishes. If therefore I was in any case going to lose, say at the end of July, it was much better to make a virtue of necessity and yield now. I did realise that the legal complications were considerable and we might satisfy only a proportion of householders but I felt that it could be done and therefore I should not oppose the collective wisdom of my colleagues.[54]

Selwyn then went to the Treasury after seeing Macmillan. He was in a considerable state of depression. The pre-emptive strike of the *fait accompli* that Chancellors are traditionally supposed to enjoy had been denied him and he was in no doubt that his standing had been damaged. 'We've got to do something else', he told his secretary Tom Caulcott. It was an unprecedented defeat for a Chancellor on the eve of a Budget and the pre-printed Budget Red Book (available in the vote office after the Chancellor has sat down) proved on the Monday to be only a partial summary of the proposals. Selwyn decided that he should announce his intention to abolish Schedule A (at a cost to the Exchequer of £60m in a full year), a change introduced by his successor, Reginald Maudling, in 1963. From the Treasury Selwyn travelled to Windsor for an audience of the Queen at 6.30 p.m., but because of the changes that needed to be incorporated into his speech returned to Chequers for dinner. He was acutely aware of how much the party expected him to lift their electoral fortunes; but he was even more aware of how important it was to get the economy on a sound footing.

Selwyn rose to deliver his second Budget at 3.32 p.m. on 9 April. He began by emphasising the importance of the NEDC and continued by stating his intention to abolish Schedule A.[55] But the atmosphere was very different from the previous year and his 'joke' about brandy duty fell flat. The most important innovation was a short-term capital gains tax, an acorn by 1970s standards. Differential purchase tax rates were consolidated at 10 per cent. Overall he budgeted for an above the line surplus of £443m in a revenue of £6,807m. This compared with an actual surplus above the line in 1962–3 of £410m, as against the £506m for which he had budgeted the previous April. It was a long, complex and rather dull Budget with little to fix itself in the public consciousness. That was until Selwyn came to an innocuous tax, 15 per cent on confectionery, ice-cream and soft drinks yielding £30m in 1962 and £50m in a full year (not an insignificant sum when the deficit for 1961–2 had been £211m and the expected deficit in the next financial year was £74m). 'As the father of a small daughter I expect some trouble on the home front myself', he said. It was not only on the home front. Sixteen girls at a primary school at St Anne's, Lancashire sent Selwyn a letter. 'It's not fair. You probably ate as many sweets and lollipops as we do, when you were a little boy.'[56] Selwyn was aware that his Budget had failed to make much impact, or at least only in areas he could well have done without. (His sister Rachel wrote from Hoylake the next day, 'My dear Sel, Well, well! Taxing the poor children's pocket money!!')[57] He wrote in his diary that night:

It was pretty complicated but they listened well –
only one moment of uncertainty after sweets announcement – I had a reference to Joanna, 'as the father of a small daughter, I expect [some] trouble on the home front' – I was going to say, 'Last year she got mumps during the Budget, I don't know what it will be this year', but the House had got a little nasty and I did not risk it.[58]

Press comment was mixed, the popular papers concentrating on the sweets tax, the financial journals regretting that there was no reference to export incentives, increased private investment, or any easing of credit controls. The next Sunday William Rees-Mogg headed his account, 'Mr. Lloyd's last Budget.'[59]

Selwyn could have been forgiven for thinking that his post as Chancellor was secure when he received the following letter from Harold Macmillan:

Dear Selwyn,

That was the best speech I have ever heard from you both in manner & matter.

The general character of the Budget had to be firm – a sound base for expansion. But you got the note of tempered and reasonable optimism wh. was needed.

You managed the Purchase Tax changes very skilfully indeed. Your colleagues were too apprehensive. The scale of Reform was put across admirably.

The last minute change was right – I'm sure of that.

Well done.

You must be tired, but happy.

Yours ever, Harold.[60]

Two days later, on 11 April, Macmillan wrote telling Selwyn that he should 'study possibilities for next year's Budget on the assumption that the economic situation allows an expansionist Budget and substantial reductions of taxation. Do not leave it too late. As easy to study them now as after Christmas.'[61] By that time Selwyn would no longer be Chancellor. With Macmillan's encouragement now, though, Selwyn began to plan out the next year's timetable. Bank Rate fell further to 4½ per cent on 26 April. Things seemed set fair. But the political going was getting increasingly tough, with further by-election reverses to come and, like Peter Thorneycroft before him, Selwyn was to find that in such a situation he no longer retained Macmillan's unequivocal support.

12

The Night of the Long Knives

Selwyn Lloyd lunched with Harold Macmillan on 12 April, the fourth day of the Budget debate. In his Commons speech that evening he found himself once more on the defensive over what was now widely dubbed the 'pocket money' tax. 'A great deal will come from the expensive confectionery consumed by adults', he said.[1] His discussion with Macmillan was more substantive, centring on the White Paper on Incomes Policy* Selwyn had presented to Parliament on 2 February, outlining the 'guiding light' of 2½ per cent agreed in Cabinet in December 1961. In this White Paper Selwyn had stressed that the only justification for increased wages was increased productivity, although exceptions could be made for more exacting or onerous work, or if there had been a removal of restrictive practices. There was a hint that increases might be justified if 'a build up of manpower in one industry relatively to another is plainly necessary'.[2]

For Macmillan this was no substitute for the introduction of a proper incomes policy. He was frankly impatient. What about those groups of workers – Macmillan specified nurses, probation workers and university teachers – the nature of whose work largely precluded them from increased productivity? These groups should be revalued to permit increases much larger than the guiding light allowed. Any increases would not be cost of living adjustments, but major reassessments of the economic and social value of certain employments. There was a feeling in the Party that the Chancellor had boxed himself in on issues such as nurses' pay and was not showing the political acumen to extricate himself.

Selwyn Lloyd's Chancellorship was to founder, not on the by-election rocks of Orpington, or on a sweets tax, not even on the White Paper of February 1962 and his subsequent failure to establish a

---

* *Incomes Policy: the next step*, Cmnd 1626, HMSO, 1962.

formal incomes policy but on the series of cumulative political difficulties that arose for the government at the time. Macmillan's impatience was seen in the fact that he had private talks with Sir Laurence Helsby, Permanent Secretary at the Ministry of Labour, over the formation of the National Incomes Commission which was announced in July. The Council on Prices, Productivity and Incomes (the 'Three Wise Men') had not been a conspicuous success in 1957 and Macmillan was determined to learn from experience. The rift in economic thinking between Macmillan and his Chancellor became ever sharper. They lunched together again on 25 May and dined at Admiralty House on 7 June. 'We talked all the time about my third year and my third Budget', recorded Selwyn.[3] On 22 June Macmillan sent Selwyn a minute saying that too much had been made of the danger of inflation.[4] Selwyn's Nonconformist upbringing told him otherwise. An expansionist Prime Minister ('If in doubt, reflate', was how the Treasury saw Macmillan)[5] sought now to persuade a mon-etarist Chancellor. On 4 July Selwyn underlined his disagreements in a letter to Macmillan:

> For the first time since the war there is in general an absence of inflation in the world today, and normal disciplines on prices through international competition have begun to assert themselves. We do not want to see the development of a general deflationary movement, nor would we wish to take action that would create a return to the inflationary conditions of the early post-war era.[6]

The boundaries were thus drawn on clear-cut lines. Between April and July 1962 Macmillan showed himself primarily to be concerned with the political consequences of his Chancellor's policies, whereas Selwyn continued to be preoccupied by the economic consequences. As the General Election moved ever nearer, there could only be one winner of that particular battle.

By-elections continued to give a clear indication of the Government's unpopularity. In the middle of April Macmillan was particularly dismayed by the poor showing of the Conservative candidate at Derby, who was pushed into third place with only half the 1959 vote. In a major speech at the Cutler's Feast in Sheffield on 30 April Selwyn said that firm budgetary policy was essential if there was to be any relaxation on the monetary side. If there was a need to stimulate demand, plenty of instruments now existed. In the light of Macmillan's letter of 11 April and their subsequent discussions the use of the word 'if' showed either courageous independence or political foolhardiness. Nevertheless Macmillan was 'charming' about this

speech, as he was about a subsequent one Selwyn delivered to a
conference of Women Conservatives at the Albert Hall on 23 May.
More significant was the fact that Macmillan's speech to the same
audience praised all his senior colleagues with the exception of
Selwyn.[7] After his speech at the Cutler's Feast Selwyn turned his
attention to the second meeting of the NEDC. In Cabinet on 3 May
there was a review of the economic situation. Macmillan again
pressed for expansion. But at the meeting of the NEDC on 9 May
Selwyn returned to the question of obstacles to economic growth. In
discussion the Council accepted that 'growth depended largely on
technical invention and technological change'.[8] For Selwyn this was
the only way to wage increases in real terms. The Council accepted
Selwyn's desire to explore the possibilities of a 4 per cent growth rate,
which was now his talisman. The principle of the 'guiding light'
received its severest blow to date on 12 May, when the dockers
received a settlement of 9 per cent. The debate on nurses' pay two
days later was thus particularly difficult for Selwyn. At this time
Selwyn began what some of his Treasury officials called 'grizzling',
unfocused complaints about the advice he was getting. This 'grizzling' communicated itself to Macmillan in the general atmosphere in
Cabinet and was a contributory factor in the Prime Minister's growing
unease with his Chancellor.

On 28 May Wall Street suffered its sharpest fall since October 1929.
Further transatlantic troubles came with the Canadian financial crisis
in June. In consultation with the Bank of England and the Chancellor
Macmillan arranged a loan of $100m. While Selwyn was involved in
the third meeting of the NEDC on 6 June (and the arrangements for
the fourth meeting on 18 July), Macmillan was much occupied with
the genesis of the National Incomes Commission ('Nicky' as it was
to be dubbed). Macmillan was increasingly immersing himself in
the details of financial management. Selwyn did not detect the
significance of this shift of emphasis. There was no respite
from by-election tribulation, with reverses for the Government at
Middlesbrough and West Lothian. Selwyn spent the last weekend of
June at Chequers. Though he was not to know it at the time it was to
be his final stay. The countdown to the Night of the Long Knives had
begun.

Macmillan lunched with Rab Butler on 21 June. Their discussion
concerned the position of the Chancellor of the Exchequer, 'an
immense human and political problem', as Macmillan recorded in his
diary.[9] The seeds of doubt which had been in Macmillan's mind since
the publication of the White Paper on Incomes Policy in February

now began to take root. Butler's doubts about Selwyn's performance as Chancellor reinforced Macmillan's inner conviction that, however painful it would be personally, he would be forced to make a change at the Treasury. On 6 July Macmillan and Butler had got to the stage of considering the qualifications of Reginald Maudling for Chancellor. As Colonial Secretary Maudling was due to go to Kenya on 10 July, but before he departed Macmillan confirmed what he had said to him earlier, that 'he would like him to come back on the Economic front again.'[10] On Monday 9 July Conservative Central Office reported to Iain Macleod, the Chairman of the Party, the predicted loss of the Conservative deposit at the Leicester North-East by-election, a Labour marginal being contested that week.* The next day Macmillan met Butler and Macleod to discuss possible government changes. Macleod brought the bad prognostication which he confirmed by letter on 11 July, of the Leicester North-East by-election. He urged that government changes should be made before the recess, advice confirmed by the Chief Whip, Martin Redmayne.[11] On the same day that Macmillan received Macleod's letter Selwyn sent the Prime Minister his last memorandum as Chancellor. After discussing long-term interest rates (down to 6.25 per cent at the end of June) he emphasised that the Government 'should maintain firmly the present anti-inflationary policies.'[12] Selwyn was unaware of the dispositions that had been made since Macmillan's lunch with Butler on 21 June. Macmillan's resolve to sack his Chancellor had hardened, if not the resolve to tell him. On 8 July Macmillan had written in his diary that he was sure it was right to make a change at the Treasury.[13] An appointment was made with the Chancellor's principal private secretary, David Hubback, for Selwyn to see the Prime Minister at 6 p.m. on Thursday 12 July at Admiralty House. Even then Macmillan seemed to flinch from the task that lay ahead – making an irrevocable break with one of his most senior colleagues. In his diary he referred to 'forewarning' the Chancellor.[14] But his hand was to be forced. What tipped the balance from forewarning to outright dismissal was not the Leicester North-East by-election (which in itself would probably have prolonged rather than shortened Selwyn's tenure of Great George Street, lest Macmillan be accused of over-reacting to outside events), but a curious episode that occurred at a luncheon given by Lord Rothermere at Warwick House on Wednesday 11 July.

One of the guests was Rab Butler. In conversation with his host, who was the proprietor of the *Daily Mail*, Butler leaked details of

---

* Although the Conservatives saved their deposit their candidate came a poor third and their overall share of the vote fell from 48.1 per cent in the 1959 General Election to 24.2 per cent.

Macmillan's long-term intentions. The front page of the *Daily Mail* next morning contained a story by the paper's political correspondent, Walter Terry, headlined MAC'S MASTER PLAN. Terry predicted that Butler, Lloyd and Macleod would be involved in an autumn* Cabinet reshuffle, when 'Mr. Lloyd may find himself in the House of Lords, as Lord Chancellor in place of Viscount Kilmuir'.[15] The article convinced Macmillan that he must move at once to end the speculation. The speed with which he now moved was one of the most uncharacteristic errors of Macmillan's Premiership. The meeting to 'forewarn' Selwyn (as the first stage in what Macmillan hoped would be a smooth transition to a career in the City) became the moment for his immediate dismissal. Looking through the Chancellor's diary for Thursday 12 July Tom Caulcott asked David Hubback why there was a 6 p.m. appointment with the Prime Minister. It seemed rather unusual. Hubback (who was the only person in the Treasury to know the real reason) was non-committal. Caulcott guessed what was afoot. 'Is it?' he asked. Hubback nodded.

Selwyn Lloyd had no inkling that Thursday 12 July 1962 was to prove such a dramatic day. Yet 'it was on the 12th of July that my house of cards collapsed.'[16] A Cabinet meeting had been called at Admiralty House for 10.30 a.m. Selwyn took a prominent part in the discussions. He had seen the various Employers' Organisations about the proposed National Incomes Commission on 5 July and he now reported on their reactions. There was then a full discussion on the proposals to be brought forward in the forthcoming debate on the Economic situation. The National Incomes Commission was the principal topic of discussion. Selwyn explained what had happened the previous week at the British Employers' Confederation, outlining his intentions in the next round of discussions the following week. As Selwyn recorded, 'I got no hint of any change in the wind.'[17] Towards the end of the discussion Selwyn referred to the reports in the morning's papers. Macmillan remarked that each department appeared to have its own Press service. 'I said to the Cabinet that I had no previous knowledge of any statements and they had appeared without my authority. Their origin was a meeting between Tony Barber and the Lobby, Tony acting as Deputy to Charles Hill. I said I was angry because the headline seemed much too complacent. The material itself had mostly been said before but there were misleading headlines such as 'Increased consumption' when the text merely said there was a possibility of increased consumption. I made it very clear that I did not share that complacency particularly with regard to what

* Such was the intention on 11 July.

might happen internationally in 1963.' As no record of this statement appeared in the Cabinet minutes Selwyn wrote a formal letter to the Cabinet Secretary Sir Norman Brook on 31 July 1962 to have them amended.

As the Cabinet broke up Selwyn went over to Macmillan and said that he thought he had a very good candidate for the Chairmanship of the NIC, Lord Justice Sellers. As Kilmuir had also worked with Fred Sellers in Liverpool before the war Selwyn had already sought his view and Kilmuir 'thoroughly approved'. Selwyn said that he had not himself seen Sellers for some time. 'Would the PM mind if I sounded him out on a purely personal basis? The PM did appear a little distrait but said yes, he thought it would be a good idea if I had a talk to Sellers.' Selwyn then lunched at Buck's with John Hare and Oliver Poole. At 4.30 he was due to meet the Governor of the Bank of England, together with Frank Lee and Denis Rickett to discuss the repayment of the IMF drawing (the United Kingdom had been granted credits of £714m on 4 August 1961 in the wake of the July measures) and was preparing for this meeting when David Hubback came in at 4.15. He said that Tim Bligh, the Prime Minister's principal private secretary, wished to see Selwyn urgently on a personal matter. Selwyn recorded that Bligh 'was ashen pale, stammering more than usual. He said he had come without the Prime Minister's agreement to warn me that my talk with the PM at 6.00 p.m., which had been fixed for some time on the topic of repayment of our debt to the I.M.F. was not going to be confined to that subject. He said that we had always been good friends and because of that friendship it would not be fair for him to let me go to the meeting thinking I was going to talk about the I.M.F. I said, "Does that mean he is going to talk to me about the Reshuffle?", concerning which the papers had been speculating that morning. He said, "Yes". He was grey in the face and stammering badly. I said, "Does that mean that the PM wants me to go?" He said "Yes". I thanked him very much for his friendly action in coming to see me and he left.' Selwyn then went into his meeting with Lord Cromer, the Governor of the Bank of England, about the repayment of the drawing. 'We agreed that it would be repaid. I told Hubback to draft a written minute for me to take to the PM at six. I asked Cromer and Lee to stay behind and told them the news. They were amazed and I think distressed. They both said they had not the slightest idea of anything like this being possible.' Selwyn was then driven to Admiralty House for his meeting with Macmillan.

The two men met in the small study at Admiralty House. 'I took out of my bag the papers about the I.M.F. drawing. He said, "Oh must we really talk about that tonight?" I said, "Yes". There was a decision to repay the I.M.F. which had to be made that night. I handed him the papers with the minute on top. He read them carefully and looked up and said, "I agree". I wrote, "The PM agrees", on the minute.

'He then said that I had told him some time ago that there might come a time that after a career in sections i.e. the Bar, the Army and the House of Commons, I might like to go into the City for the final decade of my life. I said, "Does that mean you want me to go?" He said, "I am in great difficulty. I could go myself leaving Butler in charge. He would not last six months. Secondly we could go on as we are but never has a government had so low a measure of political support in the country. Thirdly I could reconstruct in a radical fashion." And that he intended to do.

'I asked who else was to go. He said, "Kilmuir and Mills for certain." He had not yet decided upon the others.' Selwyn's reaction, totally unexpected by Macmillan, to the news of his dismissal had a profound effect upon the next phase of the reshuffle. Selwyn's account continues:

I said that we had frequently talked before about a government reconstruction at some stage but did not this sudden move savour of panic? He said that the situation was desperate and something had to be done quickly. I said that I thought it was wrong psychology to do it at this moment. I thought that if he intended a radical reconstruction he had much better wait until October. He said that the situation was too desperate for that. I said, 'Do you not think that they will say it is "the old man" who ought to go?' He said, 'Maybe'. I asked him when he wanted it announced. He said he wanted it out by 7 p.m. the next day. He referred to the Press leaks.

Macmillan then came on to the question of a peerage. To his considerable discomfiture and surprise, Selwyn said that he had no intention of giving up his constituents in the Wirral. He would stay in the House of Commons and support the financial policies he had established. Macmillan had anticipated one of two reactions, a quiet retreat to the City or a disgruntled one to the cave of Adullam. During their talk Macmillan had emphasised that there was 'a conspiracy against him.'[18] What saddened Selwyn was that it became clear that Macmillan felt that his Chancellor was in some way part of it. This was as great a misreading of Selwyn's past behaviour (and character) as it was of his future conduct. Neither the City nor the Adullamites beckoned. What Macmillan got was loyal support from a former colleague who remained a member of the House of

Commons. This threw his calculations completely. 'We had some desultory conversation about living accommodation and an exchange of letters. He came to the head of the stairs and said "Goodbye" in obvious distress.' Selwyn returned to the Treasury at 6.40 p.m. In his disappointment he thought of the political difficulties that Macmillan would now face. 'So we parted after 5½ years of close association, in which I had received many kindnesses at his hands. He had allowed me to use Chequers, shown sympathy in my domestic troubles and been very thoughtful for the comfort and convenience of myself and my daughter. I was sad for him as well as for myself, because I thought he was damaging his own position, perhaps beyond repair.' It was an accurate prognosis.

The first thing Selwyn did on returning to the Treasury was to ring Martin Redmayne, the Chief Whip, and asked him to come over as soon as possible. He then rang John Hare with the news. 'I asked whether any of the other Treasury ministers were in. I was told they were in but the Chief Secretary (Henry Brooke) had been asked to go to Admiralty House.' Selwyn saw Frank Lee and recounted his interview. The atmosphere in the Treasury was very tense. When Redmayne arrived shortly after 7 p.m. he said that he was sorry. Selwyn said, 'How am I to take this, it seems crazy, what was all the hurry about, I do not think it will be popular with the parliamentary party.' Redmayne was obviously both distressed and uncomfortable. 'He said that he hoped I would take it in my customary big hearted way. He did not think the change would be so unpopular with the parliamentary party; there had been considerable criticism of me for indecisiveness. I said it was a pity I had not heard that earlier.' At 7.30 Henry Brooke arrived back from his interview with Macmillan. He said that politics was a strange business. He himself had been offered the Home Office, but was upset by the turn of events. For a moment Selwyn wondered whether Rab Butler too was out. On such a night anything seemed possible.

Selwyn then went back to his flat at Buckingham Gate to change before a dinner for the French Ambassador at 8.30 p.m. Ironically, this was to be at Lord Rothermere's Warwick House, where Rab Butler had started the hare on Wednesday lunchtime. Selwyn sat next to Lady Shawcross, but was not very forthcoming in his conversation. His old friend and former legal colleague Lord Shawcross asked him privately at an opportune moment whether he was feeling all right. Selwyn was renowned among his pre-war friends for his impish humour and love of a practical joke. Therefore, when Selwyn told Shawcross that he had just been dismissed as Chancellor of the Exchequer he was not believed and it took some moments to convince

Shawcross that this was no joke, but the reality. After dinner Selwyn asked to be excused from going upstairs to join the ladies, for word had come that John Hare and Duncan Sandys had arrived and were waiting to see him in a small room on the ground floor. Selwyn told Sandys what had happened, adding that he thought it was a shocking way to treat an old colleague, and very bad tactics. Sensing that Selwyn might say something that he might later regret John Hare broke off the conversation and drove Selwyn home. They then had nearly two hours discussion on whether Hare should resign in protest. 'In the heat of the moment I was rather in favour of it', recorded Selwyn. Hare said that he would discuss it with his wife and also with Alec Home. He left the flat at 1.30 a.m. It was now Friday 13 July.

Later that morning Hare rang to say that he had decided not to resign but that he would try to secure an undertaking from the Prime Minister not to change the financial policies. Selwyn said that he entirely agreed and that he must forget everything said the previous evening. After breakfast Selwyn went to the Treasury and rang up Nigel Birch. He came straightaway and Edward Boyle joined their discussions. Nigel Birch said, 'You must fight this, he must not be allowed to get away with it; you have a lot of support for your policies within the party. You must write a letter and insist on it being published.' To Birch's relief Selwyn confirmed that he had already told Macmillan that he wanted an exchange of letters. When Birch himself had resigned in the 'little local difficulty' of 6 January 1958, Macmillan had not wanted to publish his letter and only agreed to do so after Birch had threatened to send it to the papers himself. They then started to draft a letter. The first version contained a sentence saying that Selwyn had been conscious over the last few weeks of a measure of disagreement between himself and his colleagues. Birch believed it was important to stress this. After Birch had gone, Edward Boyle and Selwyn produced the final version, which Macmillan felt 'rather stiff'.[19] This read as follows:

Dear Prime Minister,
    You have told me that you would like me to resign and this I willingly do.
    I realise that the policies with which I have been associated have been unpopular. On the other hand I believe that they have been right and have had a considerable measure of success. In my view our currency is stronger and our economic prospects on a firmer basis than for some time, and we are in a better position to face any difficulties which may come.
    I am also glad to have been associated with certain new depar-

tures, such as the development of an incomes policy and the creation of the National Economic Development Council. My primary aim has been to strengthen the country's competitive power and lay the foundation for sound growth.

I know that you are well aware of my concern that these policies should be continued, and also of my anxiety that the growth of public expenditure, so much of it highly desirable in itself, should not outstrip our resources.

I am very grateful to you for the many personal kindnesses which you have shown me.

Yours ever,
Selwyn.

A more trenchant letter had already been sent by hand to *The Times* by Nigel Birch. It appeared prominently on 14 July:

Sir,

For the second time the Prime Minister has got rid of a Chancellor of the Exchequer who tried to get expenditure under control. Once is more than enough.

Yours truly,
Nigel Birch.[20]

Selwyn lunched with Edward Boyle at the Turf Club. Boyle was generous in his comfort of Selwyn. 'He said repeatedly that the last two years at the Treasury had been the most imaginative of any two since the war. Surtax, regulator, incomes policy, NEDC, new forms of control of public expenditure, Treasury reorganisation, company taxation, public accounts etc.' As the news of his sacking was to be officially released at 7 p.m., after lunch Selwyn began the melancholy task of informing those closest to him as he did not wish his family to see the television bulletins unprepared. He rang his elder sister Dorice at Hoylake and she broke the news to other Wirral relatives. ('It's just like the Abdication all over again', said her husband Howard Shone to their youngest daughter when he met her that night at Lime Street Station with the placards full of the news.) Selwyn also rang Joe Harvey, the Chairman of the Wirral Conservative Party, who was to enter the story over the next few days, and told Hennie Oakeshott. Geoffrey Hardy-Roberts, Secretary-Superintendent of Middlesex Hospital, characteristically offered Selwyn immediate weekend sanctuary from the Press at Fittleworth. Selwyn had been due to speak for John Peyton in his Yeovil constituency that weekend. Martin Redmayne rang Peyton to tell him what was in the offing and asking if Central Office should provide another speaker as Selwyn was no longer in the government. Peyton declined Redmayne's offer. In the reshuffle Peyton was to become Parliamentary Under-Secretary at Power. ('You are on the way up', said Selwyn when congratulating him, 'and I am on the way down.') John Peyton was 'very distressed' at the sacking. He was not the only one. At 5 p.m. Tim Bligh rang up to say that, 'in his distress the evening before the PM had forgotten to offer me the CH, "would I like it?" I said I must think it over. He said he could give me about half an hour; the papers had to go to the Queen as soon as possible.'*

This was by no means the whole story. Overnight Macmillan had considered the new situation brought about by the unexpected refusal of Selwyn to go to the House of Lords. His original intention had been to dismiss Kilmuir, the Lord Chancellor, and Lord Mills, the Minister without Portfolio, in addition to Selwyn. But Kilmuir and Selwyn were the principals, a possible Liverpool Mafia. However, as he had said to Selwyn at Admiralty House, 'he had not yet decided upon the others'. The painful interview with Selwyn had made a deep impression on Macmillan, who under the calm insouciance of outward unflappability had always been a highly strung and nervous personality. Already he was feeling very self-conscious about the whole affair. In years to come there were at least three different versions of why he sacked Selwyn, all at odds with each other.[21] Guilt lay behind his next move. Overnight Macmillan had determined upon an even wider reconstruction of his government, politically a move that would have been better left until the new parliamentary session in the autumn, out of his desire to give Selwyn some company in the lifeboat. Although this decision arose out of his personal consideration for his departing Chancellor, politically it was the second grievous error of the week. For once he had started on the second series of interviews (with Harold Watkinson, the Minister of Defence) on the Friday morning it became clear that the fall of one domino led to another. By the evening of 13 July one third of the Cabinet of twenty-one had been dismissed, leading the Liberal MP Jeremy Thorpe to comment, 'Greater love hath no man than this, that he lay down his friends for his life.' Harold Watkinson, like Selwyn, was deeply shocked and hurt by his dismissal and as he departed to continue his business career (he became Group Managing Director of Schweppes) Macmillan mollified him by offering a Companionship of Honour, as he did to the departing Scottish Secretary, John Maclay.† As Kilmuir was granted an Earldom and

* The fact that 13 July was the first of that summer's Royal Garden parties complicated the timetable.

† Macmillan told Watkinson that he wanted to reduce the average age of the Cabinet, yet Watkinson's successor at the Ministry of Defence, Peter Thorneycroft, was an older man.

Mills a Viscountcy (like Watkinson), it would be the cause of wounding speculation if Selwyn had been excluded, especially as his refusal of a peerage could not be made public. Thus, at the last moment, Selwyn was added to the list of Companions of Honour. 'I wonder therefore whether the PM really forgot to offer me the CH', noted Selwyn in his diary on 30 July 1962 after he had heard the full story from Walter Monckton. Without being priggish, Selwyn felt that the Companionship of Honour was not the kind of decoration to be handed out as compensation to superannuated politicians (a point made forcefully on television that evening by John Freeman). He rightly associated it with figures distinguished in the worlds of music, literature and the sciences. (His Fettes contemporary Sir Michael Tippett, for instance, was to be awarded the C.H. in 1979.) But those whom he consulted, among them Hennie Oakeshott, John Hare and William Deedes, who was promoted to the Cabinet in place of Lord Mills, 'said that it was impossible for me to refuse'. Selwyn accepted their advice 'with some reluctance' and told Bligh, who confirmed that Selwyn's exchange of letters with Macmillan would be published in Saturday's papers.

As Selwyn knew that the Press would be swarming around after the 7 p.m. announcement (the BBC broke into the transmission of the final stages of the Open Golf Championship at Troon with the newsflash), he went to Geoffrey Hardy-Roberts's flat at the Middlesex Hospital shortly before 6. Ironically the Press had already laid siege to the Middlesex Hospital for news of Sir Winston Churchill, who had recently been admitted, and Geoffrey Hardy-Roberts could not set off to Sussex with Selwyn until the journalists had been given their evening bulletin about Churchill's progress. In the meantime Selwyn had broken the news to Joanna, whose reaction was, 'Thank goodness, no more photographs!' Selwyn heard the news bulletins at the Middlesex Hospital and left for Sussex at 8.30, arriving at the Mill House at Fittleworth with his host shortly after 10.

Although Selwyn had gone to ground, the Press Corps soon traced the scent. One newspaper rang up the Treasury to ask where the Chancellor was because his former wife had been involved in a car crash. As the evening wore on this was transposed into a rumour that Selwyn had been killed in a car crash. Toby O'Brien rang up Fittleworth asking for news as the *Daily Express* were wanting confirmation before they published. A reporter even rang Birch Grove, Macmillan's country house, to inquire whether Selwyn Lloyd was staying there for the weekend. 'You must be out of your mind', replied Lady Dorothy Macmillan, who had answered the telephone.[22] By Saturday morning the Press were hounding the

"Members of the crew! I have driven the ship on the rocks! For such shocking incompetence YOU'RE fired!"

Hardy-Roberts, even coming down the drive and asking, 'What is he going to have for dinner?' In return for being left in peace for the weekend Selwyn made a short statement and was photographed on the lawn holding a croquet mallet. 'So much for Joanna's reaction', he said.

The sackings were the biggest domestic political story for years. Hugh Gaitskell asked why the Prime Minister had stopped at seven. Yet the sensation was the extent of the changes in one fell swoop. (Mrs Thatcher was to remove far more members of her Cabinet, but as a gradual process.) Anthony Barber, Financial Secretary to the Treasury, was being driven in a taxi from Doncaster railway station to a constituency meeting when the 7 p.m. news came over the radio. The taxi went under three bridges in the space of a few hundred yards, but the dismissals, which Barber only partially heard as the radio 'faded' under each bridge, were still going strong after the third bridge. On arrival at his constituency meeting he had to ring the Treasury to find out if he was still in the government. Elsewhere in Yorkshire that Friday evening, Rab Butler was attending a reception at Sheffield University, of which he was Chancellor. 'I am so out of touch', he said to the Countess of Halifax, 'Do tell me what happened – who is in, who is out?'[23] Apart from Selwyn Lloyd, those out were Lord Kilmuir, Harold Watkinson, Dr Charles Hill, Lord Mills, Jack Maclay and David Eccles (who declined an offer of the Board of Trade). They were replaced respectively by Reginald Maudling, Sir Reginald Manningham-Buller (who became Lord Dilhorne), Peter Thorneycroft, Sir Keith Joseph, William Deedes, Michael Noble and

Sir Edward Boyle. Other consequential changes followed, of which the most significant was the departure of Rab Butler from the Home Office to the nebulous post of First Secretary of State, in effect a downgrading even though the Lobby was told it was the equivalent of Deputy Prime Minister, a post unknown to the Constitution, as King George VI had reminded Churchill on more than one occasion.

Selwyn was devastated by his sacking. As with the break-up of his marriage (the only other major reversal of his life) it was first and foremost a blow to his pride. Though he kept the hurt hidden in public 'I am so happy', he would joke, 'I no longer have to read *The Economist*.') in private it was something he never really came to terms with. He needed the therapy of sympathetic friends. Staying at Playford Hall, Ipswich, with Bill Aitken (whose son Jonathan had become Selwyn's private secretary on 1 July), he walked up and down the lawn for hours, with different members of the family taking turns in relay, like Admiral Hornblower pacing the deck. Irrespective of whether the decision for dismissal was justified (and it must not be forgotten that Macmillan carried the majority of the party with him on reflation in the uneasy post-Orpington atmosphere) few Cabinet ministers this century had been despatched in such a publicly humiliating manner.* (When relieved of the Woolsack Kilmuir complained that his cook would have had more notice. Macmillan pointed out that it was easier to get Lord Chancellors than cooks.)[24] The wound of the Night of the Long Knives never healed.

Metaphorically he did have a bad car smash on 13 July 1962 and however much he tried to put it out of mind he always came up to the political roundabouts with that extra bit of care from then on. There were those who thought he was a better man for the experience, less tense, more at terms with himself, the boil of ambition had been lanced and there was calm of mind. Although he was destined to have two more political careers (the comebacks of 1963 and 1971) it was never truly glad, confident morning again.

In his reactions to the sacking Selwyn was restrained to the point of excessive punctiliousness, a fact he later regretted. The shock and the speed were such that he was too stunned for a more considered response. The truth remains that, whatever the political expedience, however urgent the necessity, Harold Macmillan treated Selwyn in a most shameful and personally wounding manner. The man who was privy to all his counsels was unceremoniously and ungratefully

---

* The nearest parallel was Asquith's jettisoning of Haldane, his political ally for ten years, on 25 May 1915 when he formed his Coalition government.

despatched to an intended political oblivion. It was the unworthiest moment of Macmillan's entire Premiership.

On the morning of Sunday 15 July Anthony Eden rang Fittleworth to ask 'what on earth had happened.' He told Selwyn that he thought his letter to Macmillan had struck exactly the right tone, but that his statement to the Press on Saturday had been too effusive in its support of the Prime Minister. Eden said that he was due to speak to the Young Conservatives at Leamington Spa the following Saturday and would consider what to say about the July massacre. Before he rang off he gave Selwyn a valued piece of advice on which his former colleague acted. Eden said that when he had resigned as Foreign Secretary in February 1938 the first thing he had done was to seek a vote of confidence from his local constituency party as soon as possible and he advised Selwyn to do the same. Not only would the vote be a foregone conclusion, but it would put him in a much stronger position with regards to his eventual rehabilitation in politics. On Sunday Lord Woolton came to lunch at Fittleworth. He told Selwyn that he knew that something was in the wind, but he thought it involved Selwyn being moved to some other post. 'He said he was horrified at what had happened and how it had happened.' He stayed until 4 and was very kind and sympathetic to Selwyn. The next morning (16 July) Selwyn motored back to London. He was due to take leave of the Queen at 6.20 p.m. A rather mournful group of the dispossessed gathered that evening in an ante-room at Buckingham Palace. 'David Kilmuir, Harold Watkinson, Percy Mills and Jack Maclay were there too', Selwyn wrote in his diary. 'I had a word privately with Percy Mills. He said that he had been horrified at the way in which it had been done.' That evening Selwyn dined with David and Sylvia Kilmuir. 'They were both extremely angry.' The series of valedictory meals continued on Tuesday with for Selwyn the most touching gathering of all. Frank Lee had arranged a luncheon at the United Universities Club for the Treasury to bid farewell to their former political chief. Norman Brook, Denis Rickett, William Armstrong, Tom Padmore and David Hubback made up the party. 'Frank Lee made a very nice little speech at the end', Selwyn wrote in his diary. 'After lunch he drove me to the House of Commons.'

Selwyn knew that his first appearance in the Chamber after his sacking would be a delicate moment, but it was something he preferred to get over as soon as possible. The reaction was not the one he had expected. As he entered the Chamber at six minutes to three there were cheers from both sides of the House. When Macmillan came in at 3.10 there was 'no applause from our side, jeers from the Opposition'.[25] Although gratified by his own reception Selwyn was an old enough political hand by now to know that his inflated reception had been oblique criticism of Macmillan. The more the House boosted him, the more they were getting at the Prime Minister. 'The PM looked pale and ill', noted Selwyn. 'As he left after his questions he turned and looked for a moment at where I was sitting on the third bench below the gangway.'

In the Wirral meetings had been arranged for the evening of Thursday 19 July at the Parish Hall, West Kirby and at Ellesmere Port. Selwyn spent the next two days preparing his speech to his constituents. At the same time, Iain Macleod, the Chairman of the Party, was preparing a letter to be sent to all constituency parties. With great insensitivity, a copy of this duplicated communication was sent to Joe Harvey in the Wirral. 'The Prime Minister has just completed the reconstruction of the Government,' it began, 'and this is a good moment for me to write to constituency chairmen.' Joe Harvey replied, 'Having regard to the contents of your letter, you will probably appreciate that it is considered by me to be a most un-diplomatic letter received at an unfortunate time. In all the circum-stances it would appear to me that less annoyance would be caused in future were your letter not to remain on my files and it is therefore returned.' With Press reports circulating that Macmillan had referred to Selwyn as 'a little country notary', the mood in the constituency was very bitter.[26]

Selwyn spent the morning of 19 July completing his statement before travelling to the Wirral. He saw his sisters and their families in the afternoon before dining with Joe Harvey. Westbourne Road and the approaches to the Memorial Hall were almost impassable because of the television vans. Monitors had been set up outside for the overflow of people and it was with difficulty that the principals of the evening made their way to the platform. Selwyn, ever mindful of rehabilitation, was determined to burn no bridges and he spoke with restraint, never playing up to the gallery, much to the disappointment of the media who felt they had been put to a lot of expense and inconvenience for a very damp squib. Selwyn began by saying that it was a difficult occasion for him. 'Tonight I have come back to you, to many of you who have known me so long, in this Hall 400 yards from where I was born. It is important for a person in my present position to get his priorities right and I have thought a great deal about this since last Thursday evening.' He said that these priorities were the nation, the pound and the party. Only then could one consider oneself. 'In my two years as Chancellor I have been deeply interested in certain reforms and new departures, such as the five year forward planning of public expenditure; the creation, at my request, of the new post of Chief Secretary, "the regulator" to be used between Budgets and the creation of the National Economic Development Council.' After some relaxation and a decent rest he hoped to see more of all his constituents. He ended, 'No one likes to be asked to relinquish high office. It would be humbug to pretend otherwise.'[27] Many people in the body of the hall heard the acclamation with which Selwyn was greeted and then left to get a place at the other end of his constituency. When the West Kirby reception was duplicated at Ellesmere Port Selwyn knew how astute Eden's advice had been. One of the executive officers of the Wirral constituency party has recalled that evening:

> His constituents flocked to give him the vote of confidence which he asked for at a meeting held within days of his dismissal. The only reason ever adduced was a feeling on the Prime Minister's part that the Liverpool connection, Maxwell Fyfe as Lord Chancellor and Selwyn, was carrying too much weight in Cabinet, with perhaps a threat to the Prime Minister's position. Recrimination was totally absent from Selwyn's speech to the confidence meeting and for ever after. He must have been deeply hurt but never allowed it to show. His loyalty to the party and its leadership never wavered.[28]

As Selwyn had received a vote of confidence from his constituents, Macmillan was now forced into the same situation in Parliament where the Opposition had put down a motion of no confidence in the government to be debated on 26 July. After a good deal of thought Selwyn decided he must write a private line of good wishes to Macmillan before the debate. The letter read:

> My dear Harold,
>   I meant what I said in my published letter about your kindnesses to me – over Chequers, at the time of my personal troubles and in so many other ways. I am most grateful.
>   I also felt that I must, in view of our long and varied partnership send you just a line of good wishes before the debate.
>
> > Yours ever,
> > Selwyn.

Macmillan was deeply touched by this letter as Selwyn heard more fully when he lunched with Rab Butler on 31 October 1962. He recorded in his diary for that day:

> Butler said he knew I had written a letter to him. The Prime Minister had refused to show it to him on the grounds that it was personal but has said it was one of the nicest letters he has ever received.

Truly Selwyn believed that forgiveness was the best form of revenge.

On the way into the Chamber for the Debate Macmillan took Selwyn aside and had a word thanking him for the letter, 'and saying he would like to have a talk with me'. In the subsequent Debate the Government majority was 98 with not a single abstention. The next day (27 July) Selwyn received a letter from Macmillan inviting him to lunch at the Turf Club. Some of the surety of Macmillan's political touch had departed and Selwyn appreciated at once that it would be impossible for them to be seen meeting socially in a London club. What inferences would the Lobby draw? He therefore rang Tim Bligh and said that, though he would welcome a talk with Macmillan, it could not be at the Turf or any semi-public place. Bligh rang back and a meeting was fixed for Admiralty House at 6.30 p.m. on 1 August. Of all the episodes in the saga of the Night of the Long Knives, this was the strangest.

Tim Bligh met Selwyn in the entrance lobby to Admiralty House that evening. It was very different from their meeting in the Treasury on 12 July. To Selwyn's astonishment Bligh told him, 'He is spending all his time thinking of how to bring you back.'[29] Selwyn could hardly believe his ears and was sceptical. Bligh continued, 'He was depressed about the Common Market.' As this was an unexpected turn of events Selwyn was now more puzzled than embarrassed when he was ushered into the large drawing room at Admiralty House where Macmillan was waiting to receive him. There was a moment of silence as it was not clear who was to take the initiative. As Selwyn recorded, Macmillan then broke the silence:

He said that he had been very sorry about it all. I said that my regret was the damage that it had done to him. I could not understand why he had not discussed it with me beforehand. He said that he had made a mistake. He had been rushed. One day he would tell me the conspiracy against him which had forced his hand. I said that we had talked about everything else together. He had underestimated my loyalty. Did he think that I would lead a revolt against him? He said, 'No', but Butler had been plotting to divide the party on the Common Market, and bring him down. He realised that he had made a mess of it. He had meant to talk to me on 12th July about something which would happen this week or even after the House was up. His only anxiety was Europe. He would fight an election on that, perhaps lose, and then the Party and not the Queen would choose the next leader. That was important to me. I asked when he would do this. He said, 'Next autumn'. I said, '62' or '63'? He said

63. He asked about my arrangements. I told him about my holiday plans.

In that ruminative style which Macmillan so favoured in conversation (gaining much knowledge about other people by seeing their reactions to unexpected statements) the subject then turned to Suez, before Macmillan expanded further on the reshuffle.

He said that he had seen Eccles (on 13th July) who had been very frank and had said that he ought to be Chancellor. He knew about economics. Eccles had thought over the offer of another job for two hours and then turned it down. He (Macmillan) said that he would like another talk with me in October when I came back. I still had a part to play. He was deeply distressed, but my position was very strong.

Selwyn repeated that he was genuinely concerned at the harm Macmillan had done to his own reputation. He said that he had no desire to play the part of Strafford to Macmillan's King Charles I.

I added that I would not have minded the abattoir running with my blood if he had remedied what I thought was a fatal defect, the Chairman of the Party and the Leader of the House being one and the same person. He said that was being attended to, and he gave me the impression that there would be a change before the next session.

They parted with a pledge on Macmillan's part to keep in touch and Selwyn left Admiralty House unnoticed. The interview left a profound impression upon Selwyn and radically altered his perception of High Tory politics. 'I am afraid that my conclusion after the interview was one of his utter ruthlessness, and his determination to retain power by the sacrifice of even his closest friends. He was now concerned to conciliate me, because I had become a possible danger.'

So ended Selwyn's involvement in three of the most dramatic weeks in post-war British politics. The repercussions were yet to come.

Reactions to Selwyn's dismissal covered the whole gamut. 'Not a moment too soon', wrote Nigel Lawson, a future Chancellor, in the *Sunday Telegraph*. 'The Betrayal of Selwyn Lloyd', wrote Harold Wincott in the *Financial Times*. The day after the sackings *The Times* in a leader declared, 'More courageously than any other Tory Chancellor, with the exception of Mr Thorneycroft, he grasped the nettle of inflation.'[30] Those who approved of the changes (if not the manner) did so largely on political grounds; those who sympathised with Selwyn's fate tended to be the economists. In the days following his dismissal Selwyn was inundated with letters from political colleagues, civil servants, his family and the general public. Robert Hall, the Government's Chief Economic Adviser from 1953–61, wrote on 19 July:

> As you may know, I have thought for many years that the greatest weakness in our economic system was the lack of an incomes policy, and I tried to persuade every Chancellor of the Exchequer since Sir Stafford Cripps of this, though I am afraid without much practical result. I can only hope that I had some delayed effect, even though the policy was not adopted until I had left the Treasury! Anyway, it seems very ironic that just when the policy was taking hold, the Chief Architect should leave the team.[31]

Enoch Powell, who had resigned in January 1958 with Peter Thorneycroft and Nigel Birch, wrote from the Ministry of Health on 14 July:

> I want to thank you for your help to me during the two years I have been at Health. Without this, the long-term planning of the hospital & health services would not have been possible.
>
> This was only a part, of a small part, of the machinery of long-term financial control which you created & which I believe will be of lasting importance.
>
> How warmly I have agreed with your wages & expenditure policies, & tried to further them in my own department I think you know.
>
> All this cannot go for nothing.[32]

Letters came from both sides of the political spectrum and Selwyn was particularly cheered by messages of encouragement from James Callaghan and Robert Mellish, with whom he was to work closely in the 1970s, both inside and outside Parliament. Jakie Astor also wrote in warm terms:

> You have always shown courage. Even at the unhappy time of Suez, when we saw the situation differently, I always thought you acted with real courage and in good faith – very rare among politicians.[33]

Another figure from Suez days, Anthony Nutting, touched Selwyn with his letter:

> I know it is said that politics is a ruthless affair and there is no room for personal feelings: yet I can delay no longer in writing to tell you

how I feel about your leaving the Government. And I want you to know that I feel you have been abominably treated. After all that you have done in two of the toughest jobs in the land and at a time of recurring crisis from 1956 onwards, that you should have been dismissed by the man who, more than any other, shared with you the full responsibility for every policy you supported and initiated from Suez forward is nothing short of shameful.

As to your own conduct since you left the Treasury, I can only say that I have admired more than I can say your dignity and forbearance. You have gained immensely in stature as Harold has sadly, but deservedly, lost.[34]

In all Selwyn received 673 letters. Each one was filed, noted and personally acknowledged.[35] He did not receive only covert support. On Wednesday 18 July a rather embarrassed fourth meeting of the NEDC was held under the chairmanship of Reginald Maudling (who had already sent Selwyn a gracious letter).[36] There were references to Selwyn's sudden departure. A motion was passed (not merely in formal terms) thanking him for all he had done in setting up the Council and a letter was sent to him.[37] But the most public endorsement was yet to come. On Saturday 21 July Anthony Eden (now Lord Avon) spoke at the Young Conservative Rally at Leamington Spa. His remarks ('I feel that Mr Selwyn Lloyd has been harshly treated') received wide coverage in the weekend press. Two days later Eden wrote to Selwyn. 'I am glad that you feel that what I said was helpful. My references to you were certainly received with remarkable enthusiasm by a crowd sitting out of doors in a cold gale of wind.' In August Eden invited Selwyn to Fyfield Manor and they had a long talk. 'He was full of sympathy and listened to my account of events', Selwyn recorded. Eden said that he had heard of Rab's activities, commenting, 'He does not seem to realise that the antis and the pros sometimes meet.' Eden was sure that Butler could never win enough support to gain the succession to Macmillan. As for Macmillan's part Eden told Selwyn that he had heard that there had been a move to make Selwyn Home Secretary or Lord Chancellor in the reshuffle but that Macmillan had strongly resisted it, knowing that the Home Secretaryship was one of the most politically sensitive jobs in any government, requiring very nimble footwork. As for giving Selwyn the Lord Chancellorship, that would not have solved Macmillan's problem of how to bring on younger men. Selwyn's account of their talk ended, 'Eden said that he did not trust Macmillan and gave me one or two examples to show why, in particular at the time of Suez, Harold had gone behind his back to Winston to complain of military plans.'

31 The approach of Budget Day, April 1961.

32 The inaugural meeting of the National Economic Development Council, 7 March 1962, Selwyn Lloyd in the chair.

33 and 34 Calm after the storm: relaxing at S'Agaro, August 1962.

35 The jaunty cavalier: Selwyn attends a family wedding in the Wirral on 26 October 1963. Six days earlier he had returned to the Cabinet as Lord Privy Seal and Leader of the House of Commons.

The summer of 1962 was the time when Macmillan's Premiership began to drift off course. The reshuffle palpably failed to restore the government's fortunes. Deference was a vanishing commodity in the era of *Private Eye* and the satirical television programme *That was the week that was*. Peter Cook regaled audiences at a packed Fortune Theatre with his impersonation of Macmillan in *Beyond the Fringe* ('I spoke with the German Foreign Minister, Herr . . . Herr and there').[38] *Supermacbeth* was published on 31 July, starring Macmillan as Macbeth, Selwyn as Banquo ('Our fears in Banquo stick deep'), Maudling as Malcolm, Edward Boyle as Fleance, Randolph Churchill as the drunken Porter and Eden, Baldwin and Neville Chamberlain as the three apparitions.[39] When Selwyn read it he knew that the aptest parallel was:

> If it were done, when 'tis done, then 'twere well
> It were done quickly.

As the dust settled Selwyn began to pick up the pieces. He went to Buckingham Palace on 24 July to be invested with the Companionship of Honour. An equerry guided him in the drill and said, 'Then the Queen will give you the O.M.' Selwyn joked about this with the Queen and it covered any vestigial embarrassment. He wrote to Kathleen Hill with a cheque to distribute among the staff at Chequers. 'I have not yet got over the shock', replied Mrs Hill of his sudden departure on 7 August. 'I can hardly believe that I shall no longer have the pleasure of arranging for your weekend parties at Chequers.' The only secure tenant of Chequers was Sambo. He remained behind in the devoted care of Kathleen Hill and became the founder of a Chequers dynasty of puppies. Eventually he was buried by the North lawn. A fortnight after the Night of the Long Knives Macmillan held a Conservative forum to discuss pre-election strategy (Summer 1963 was very much an option at that time, an option removed by the Vassall tribunal and the Profumo affair). As Macmillan sat on the terrace in the cool of a July evening, expansively dilating upon the middle way ahead, other members of the entourage gradually became aware of the inquisitive presence of this black labrador dog, walking along the line of the assembled company vainly looking for his master. Those who were present have never forgotten the frisson that went through the gathering, nor the studied disregard with which Macmillan ignored the animal, knowing better than most what memories its presence evoked.

Selwyn decided that 'a bitter resentment against Macmillan would destroy my peace of mind.'[40] Forgiveness may have been the best form of revenge, but in the aftermath of a bitter day it also proved the best form of therapy. Nevertheless, as though to purge himself of the memories of 13 July, he wrote a final section to his record trying to assess Macmillan's motives. 'It is still impossible to do more than conjecture about Harold's motives and when he decided to do what. The evidence is insufficient and one cannot know whether people are consciously or unconsciously not telling the truth.' Gradually he pieced together from different sources the key moments. A year later he was still hearing titbits. His diary for 2 July 1963 reads:

> Lord Eccles said that Percy Mills told him after 13th July that the PM had told him in May that he intended to get rid of me and put Maudling in instead. If I would note the date when Maudling was added to the Economic Policy Committee that would reveal the time when the PM made up his mind.* He added that the things the PM said about Erroll when asking Eccles to take over the Board of Trade had to be heard to be believed. He just did not understand how the Prime Minister having spoken like that of a Minister could possibly keep him on.

This confirmed what Selwyn had heard from Frank Lee on 30 July 1962. 'He had no previous idea of any changes being made at the Treasury, but looking back and being wise after the event, he wondered whether when the PM at the beginning of May began to take a much greater interest in the economic policy that was the moment when he decided upon the change.' Rab Butler, who as a former Chancellor knew better than most the difficulties of balancing economic and political considerations, lunched with Selwyn on 31 October 1962. Butler told him:

> When he came back from Africa in June the Prime Minister had said he was having more to do at the Treasury than he liked. The Prime Minister mentioned the Group on Incomes Policy. Butler said that next time he walked past the Treasury he looked in on Tom Padmore and got the impression that I knew all about it and it was in fact being run by the Treasury with my approval.

Butler also talked about Macmillan's loneliness:

> He had said that he had missed me very much indeed. He said to Butler how fond he had been and how pained he had been having to do what he did . . . The Prime Minister had been very much aware of my magnanimity in the way I'd acted. Butler thought he would

---

* 28 May 1962.

be very anxious to re-open the lines of communication with me. He strongly advised me to make use of any opportunity to do so.

As he pieced together the evidence Selwyn searched back in his memory for indications. 'He had said some time before that I could not have Chequers for the last two weeks in July. Had that any significance?' What grieved Selwyn most was that Macmillan had never discussed his dissatisfactions with him. 'Why did he not tell me? 1 He did not like to. 2 He feared the consequence. 3 He feared a longer term development.'

He then recalled what Macmillan had said to him of his colleagues at various times and wondered what similar things might have been said about him.

What has he said about his colleagues?
Eden – this man cannot get on
Butler – round the bend
Macleod – not to be trusted
Maudling – no background*

Selwyn realised that, whatever Macmillan's original intentions may have been, the combination of Butler's indiscretion and the Leicester North-East by-election had forced his hand.

Looking back there were two signs to which I might have paid more importance. He asked me several times not to pay any attention to the Finance Bill, but to leave it to the others and myself to concentrate on planning. At the Albert Hall, in his speech to the women he praised all his senior colleagues except myself. When I complained mildly about another colleague beating the pistol on a Treasury matter, he was not sympathetic. When the Canadian trouble was on us, I noticed that after speaking to me on the phone (I suppose 4 or 5 times on the Sat and Sun) he always seemed to ring up the Governor of the Bank to confirm my advice, but the whole business was very technical and I did not take alarm.

Finally and most extraordinary of all, we both dined on 27 June with the Executive Committee of the World Methodist movement. The dinner ended at 9 p.m. It was at the National Liberal Club. He asked me to walk back with him to Admiralty House. We had a drink, and almost an hour's gossip together. Here surely was the chance to tell me? Eventually we played the grim farce of the week beginning July 9th, when he must, I suppose, have decided. He had

* Legal considerations preclude inclusion of Macmillan's descriptions of politicians still alive.

fixed the Thursday appointment at the end of the previous week. This would seem to indicate that he was working to a timed programme.

All kinds of suspicions crossed Selwyn's mind, especially over the National Incomes Commission.

As for NIC I saw the employers at 5 p.m. on Thursday 5th July. I was on TV at 6 p.m. the same day, and again at 4 p.m. of Wed 11 July. I reported fully the discussions of 5th July at a special meeting on Friday 6th July. Did he deliberately fix that meeting when it was known that I would be speaking in the House, moving the third Reading of the Finance Bill? If so, it did not come off, because I only spoke for 15 minutes and went to the meeting.

When it came to the exigence, however, despite the fact that Macmillan referred to Selwyn as 'my wise and sagacious counsellor' (particularly to the Queen) they differed fundamentally over the direction of economic policy as an election approached. Selwyn never had the searing experience of representing a constituency like Stockton in the 1930s. The view from the Hoylake Urban District Council was very different. Neither Selwyn Lloyd nor Peter Thorneycroft overlaid their economic thinking with the Stockton patina. Selwyn believed that Macmillan's biggest mistake was 'thinking unemployment a worse enemy than uncontrolled inflation'.[41] Selwyn's Nonconformist upbringing (what in the 1980s might be termed the Grantham factor) was very pronounced. Macmillan's treatment of Selwyn therefore mirrored the experience of Thorneycroft, whose influence with his Prime Minister declined in the latter part of 1957. The line of economic management that can be traced from Thorneycroft (and arguably Cripps in the late 1940s) through Selwyn to the years of the Thatcher experiment was not Macmillan's. Those who say that Selwyn was never Foreign Secretary in any meaningful sense could never say the same thing about his tenure of the Treasury. He was not sacked for being nothing; he was sacked for being that which Macmillan did not want.

Why was Selwyn not moved to another post? When Curzon had been removed from the Foreign Office in October 1924 by Stanley Baldwin he did at least receive the compensatory post of Lord President of the Council and there were many non-departmental jobs into which Selwyn could have been fitted. But accommodating Selwyn was not going to solve Macmillan's main problem when he was wanting to give the government a younger and fresher air. If Selwyn had been kept on it would have blocked promotion for one of the younger Turks. Macmillan was now making the decisive move in bringing to the fore the next generation (he had already passed over in his own mind the idea of Butler as a possible successor) and was to give Heath, Macleod and Maudling jobs of increasing prominence so that one of them might emerge as the natural replacement. Even more important was Macmillan's fear that the next election was lost anyway and that for the return of the Conservatives at the subsequent swing of the pendulum figures of Cabinet experience must be available. When Wilson became Prime Minister in October 1964 only he and Patrick Gordon Walker were survivors of the Attlee Cabinet. The Conservatives might be in Opposition for two full Parliaments or even longer. The Heaths, Macleods and Maudlings must be given the requisite experience to enable them to set down markers for the future. In these long-term calculations Selwyn clearly had no place.

After the Night of the Long Knives (though Rab Butler always called it The Massacre of Glencoe) a meeting between Macmillan and Selwyn Lloyd was fascinating to the informed onlooker. Macmillan tended to be effusive, uncharacteristically edgy; Selwyn was unusually calm, having come to outward terms with it all, thus making Macmillan's embarrassment the more noticeable. Selwyn very rarely spoke about the events of 1962 after the initial therapeutic outbursts. One night in 1976, however, he was entertaining an old bar colleague to a quiet supper when his guest told him strongly, in choice words, just what he thought of Macmillan's actions. Selwyn's only comment, before moving on to another subject, was, 'What you say is, if anything, an understatement.'[42]

The nature of Selwyn's sacking – some, continuing the *Macbeth* parallel, said that nothing in his Chancellorship became him like the leaving it – obscured the nature of his reforms and his long term reputation as Chancellor. He was an Auchinleck* of the Treasury as Alec Cairncross noted in his diary after a lunch with Tim Bligh on 29 August 1962:

> Tim said that the reasons for Selwyn's departure were in effect those in *The Times* leader the following morning. The P.M. had felt that Selwyn ought to have taken over on incomes policy instead of leaving it to him. When the N.I.C. proposal was being worked over, Selwyn was in on the Chequers discussion and could have insisted that he should handle the matter or, if he was opposed to the idea, fought it or if necessary resigned. The P.M. also felt that

---

* General Auchinleck, C.-in-C. Middle East, 1941–2.

S.L. was in the position of Auchinleck and had completed the operation he was appointed to carry out. According to Tim, the P.M. was not as physically tough as Winston or Attlee and was emotional about important decisions in a way they were not. He was an avid reader of the press and would be found in bed with newspapers strewn about him reading them for the second or even the third time. When he had to face his Cabinet reshuffle, he met with a hostile, critical reaction from S.L. that he hadn't altogether expected, and this made him rush through the other changes.[43]

Like Auchinleck then (and Strafford before that) Selwyn was 'hurried hence'. But many Treasury men look back to 1960–2 as the most reforming period since the Chancellorship of Sir Stafford Cripps. Although as Chancellor Selwyn never had a flaming sword or the national impact of Cripps, lacking what the grandees called 'bottom', the staff officer in him was well suited to the implementation of a series of institutional and policy reforms. He was the Chancellor who was never given the time (which he was promised on appointment) to put through those reforms. Unlike some post-war Chancellors he did not suffer from ingrained hubris. He liked to see his time at the Treasury as akin to that from 1927–9 when the Liberal Party Yellow Book was being prepared and a spirit of co-operation was abroad. He was monetarism with a human face. The City view of Selwyn (particularly after the Capital Gains Tax of 1962) was not particularly favourable, but Selwyn knew that the Square Mile did not speak with the authentic voice of England. On 20 July 1963 he was interested to receive a letter from the financial journalist and author Sam Brittan, who was researching material for his book *The Treasury under the Tories*, published in 1964. 'It seems to me', Brittan wrote, 'that two of the greatest advances made during your period at the Treasury were (a) the establishment of the N.E.D.C. and (b) the acceptance by the government for the first time of responsibility for an incomes policy. I know that you have always believed in a forward-look at Government expenditure and that you introduced the concept of a FIVE YEAR PLAN during your period at the Ministry of Defence.'[44] Selwyn was even more pleased when the book appeared and he kept a copy, transcribed in his own hand, of Brittan's summing up of 'his short reign':

1 The setting up of the National Economic Development Council, which made a new kind of long-term 'planning' respectable for the private sector.
2 Long-term forward looks for the Government's own spending plans along Plowden lines.

3 Acceptance by the Government – and later by the country – of at least the *idea* of an incomes policy.
4 The raising of the surtax starting point on earned income from £2000 to £5000.
5 The introduction of economic regulators giving the Chancellor power to vary tax between Budgets.
6 The reform of the archaic Budget Accounts.
7 A new policy towards the nationalized industries, which has completely transformed their morale, performance, and public standing.[45]

It is not therefore surprising that the view of many Treasury mandarins was that Selwyn as Chancellor was a man 'who builded better than he knew'.[46]

Many people expected Selwyn to quit politics after July 1962. The pickings of Mammon awaited. But they did not know their man. For Selwyn politics was always 'the best game in town', as Macmillan learned to his surprise when Selwyn refused to take a peerage. He had no wish for a full time City career, despite (as will be seen) many tempting offers. He promised himself that he would be back one day. He was not the only one to think there would be a return to the limelight. Following the Night of the Long Knives (as after all major political upheavals) the staff of Madame Tussaud's waxworks began a sifting of the fallen (Selwyn himself was made from a part of Sir Roy Welensky). Those whose careers are plainly over are consigned to melted oblivion, but there is a holding cupboard for others, reputed to be one of the most accurate political barometers in London. 'Put Mr. Selwyn Lloyd's head in a cupboard', said Monsieur Tussaud to his staff, 'we shall need it again.'[47] Nine years later it reappeared above the robes of Mr Speaker.

13

Rehabilitation

Selwyn Lloyd was not the first Cabinet minister to find that a spell in the political wilderness, however painful at the time, proved to be beneficial in the long run. The refreshing sabbatical of the business or academic world is not usually available to a Chancellor of the Exchequer and electoral defeats or dismissals are often terminating contracts. Selwyn, however, was to have both the refreshment and the return. He had been in high office without a break for close on eleven years. One consequence of this was that his finances were in very poor repair. In due course he moved to a smaller flat within the Buckingham Gate complex. Friends rallied round. Lord Robbins and Lord Cobbold advised him at a private lunch on 23 July not to act too quickly over directorships and to decide when the time came whether he wanted full time or part time work. Selwyn was gratified by the contract that was negotiated for him with the *Sunday Telegraph* (£5,000 for a series of articles). He never ceased to marvel at the fees that could be earned by well syndicated literary work. As a result he took great pains with these articles, striving for a view (especially over the Common Market), agonising over individual words, until they were characterised by a cautious blandness, 'aggressive' becoming 'abrasive' and eventually 'a little uncertain'. Selwyn could never have produced the explosive article that Iain Macleod wrote of the 1963 Tory leadership struggle for the *Spectator*. Most were drafted that summer while he was holidaying with the Ensesas at S'Agaro. The Ensesas had always been powerful members in Selwyn's arsenal of friendship. After July 1962 they were like a magic carpet for him and S'Agaro a more valued bolthole than ever before.

When the parliamentary session began in the autumn he seemed transformed, no longer weighed down by the worries of the world. 'He has got a new lease of life', wrote the Labour MP Richard Crossman in his diary. 'He's now happy, light-hearted, enjoying life on the back benches and, I would say, having a healthy influence there as well. I said, "How you have changed, Selwyn!" He said, "Well, there is nothing like being kicked out of your job (especially if you get a job too early, as I did in the Foreign Office) to make a man of you." [1] If he wished it though, another job was waiting for him. On 28 September 1962 Iain Macleod, as Chairman of the Party, wrote to ask Selwyn if he would undertake an inquiry into the organisation of the Conservative Party on the lines of the Maxwell Fyfe Report of 1948. 'I have a feeling that this sort of job, which requires very close knowledge of the Conservative Party, can best be done by one man rather than by a Committee, and I really believe that nobody could do it better than you.'[2] There were many politicians in Selwyn's position who would have consigned Macleod's letter to an early waste paper basket, but not Selwyn. If he remained in the Commons there was no point in playing the tented Achilles. Although it was magnanimous of Selwyn to undertake the seemingly humdrum task of investigating the Party organisation, there was an element of calculation in his decision. Selwyn appreciated that 'activities in a comparatively minor key'[3] would be the necessary prelude to his rehabilitation. With the help of Sir Michael Fraser, then Director of the Conservative Research Department, he assembled what the Press called his 'small secretariat', Ferdinand Mount, later head of the Prime Minister's Policy Unit in the early 1980s, and Diana Leishman (later Mrs John Kemp-Welch), Fraser's assistant secretary. Their task involved travel to the far corners of England and Wales (Scotland had its own separate organisation) in what turned out to be the worst winter since 1947, staying sometimes on their weekly forays with local party grandees like John Morrison, Chairman of the 1922 Committee, in Wiltshire, and Alan Lennox-Boyd in Cornwall; sometimes in small hotels. Despite the often bleak weather, the journeys were not without their amusing moments. One Saturday night, while Selwyn was waiting for a change of trains on Darlington station, a man approached out of the darkness. 'It is, isn't it?', he said, shaking Selwyn warmly by the hand. Selwyn did not demur, rather embarrassed by the attention he was getting, so the man continued. 'Wait till I get home and tell the wife', he exclaimed excitedly. 'I've always wanted to meet Duncan Sandys.' In his calmer mellowness such episodes entertained rather than annoyed Selwyn.

Other greetings were not so warm. Although Selwyn's inquiry was primarily an organisational one, the discontent (particularly in the North) was with policy and presentation. 'Feeling against Macmillan and Macleod as both Chairman and leader continues to accumulate', he wrote on 16 February 1963. 'The East Midlands were very strong

& I shall hear Yorkshire tomorrow.'[4] Selwyn was told that the
leader's reputation was sadly tarnished in the constituencies. The
Night of the Long Knives often came up in conversations, a situation
where Selwyn trod delicately, and after January 1963 a major topic
was the failure to get into Europe. A potential discontent, he became
the recipient of other people's dissatisfaction. He was assailed on
both sides, for from time to time he would receive notes from
Macmillan inquiring into the 'exact status' of his work. As he had
been commissioned by the Party Chairman, at such moments he
would hiss through his teeth in irritation. Nevertheless Selwyn enjoyed his contacts with the grass roots. The timetable of a typical day
can be seen in his visit with Ferdinand Mount to Huddersfield on 16
February 1963 ('an exhausting morning in Huddersfield', he wrote,
'leave again Friday afternoon for the Boyd Castle in Cornwall').[5]
They were staying with a party worker at Creskeld Hall, Arthington
outside Leeds overnight and were greeted in the morning at Huddersfield station by a brown-suited Alderman, who seemed to be
straight from the pages of J.B. Priestley. A frank meeting followed at
which the local president and the chairmen of the two constituency
parties (Huddersfield East and West) aired their grievances. At the
luncheon in Selwyn's honour a *Yorkshire Post* journalist openly
criticised government economic policy. Selwyn smiled agreeably but
refused to be drawn. In the afternoon he toured an area which had
seen MPs such as Victor Grayson and Philip Snowden. For Selwyn
this was just the kind of challenging constituency that the party (and
its agents) should cultivate: parliamentary majorities were not built
on safe seats alone. The abiding memory of the day was how Selwyn
relaxed in this world of solid business men and Yorkshire high teas, so
far removed from the Conservative Research Department and
Central Office. Local roots mattered. Provincial was never a term of
disparagement.

'I have found the Enquiry most interesting', he wrote to Macleod in
March 1963. 'I have visited every Area in England and Wales, & I
have met about 3,000 of our local Conservative leaders. I have had
many hundreds of memoranda and letters. Very many people have
taken immense care to put their views and suggestions to me, and I
have been deeply impressed by their enthusiasm and their devotion to
the party.'[6] He communicated privately to Macmillan, Macleod and
Redmayne some of the deep anxieties of the constituencies as the
General Election approached. 'I received a spate of criticism of the
arrangement whereby the Chairman of the Party was also the Leader
of the House of Commons', he told Macmillan, returning to one of
the points they had discussed at Admiralty House on 1 August 1962.[7]

(Lord Poole became Joint Chairman with Iain Macleod in April 1963, but Selwyn did not regard this as an ideal solution.) Selwyn had undertaken his task with great conscientiousness. His confidential correspondence with Macleod runs from September 1962 to April 1963 when he began to draft his report, in essence a final missive to the Party Chairman. One of the concerns was the marginal seat. On 20 March 1963 he told Macleod that too many speakers were being sent to safe seats and that the difficult areas were being neglected. 'There is an impression that Ministers are guided solely by the size of the audience and not its quality.'[8] He stressed from verbal evidence that the old race of voluntary worker was dying out. He wanted the Bow Group, with whom he dined on 15 January 1963, to be given their head and to become the 'Fabian' wing of the Conservative Party. He wrote a separate memorandum *Status & Financial Arrangements of Agents & Organisers* with sections on cars, housing, pay, career structure and proper contracts of employment. In the longer term Selwyn's most important recommendations in the Report concerned agents. Rab Butler had identified this weakness during his 1945 Election campaign in Essex, but little had been done. Agents, particularly in safe seats, tended to be retired officers who did not need a competitive salary owing to their service pensions. When this generation left politics the existing salaries were no longer good enough to attract younger figures. Selwyn had been fortunate in the Wirral, first with Bert Gill and then from the early 1960s with Gilbert Stephenson ('My first agent was Mr Bert Gill, let me introduce you to my second, Mr Gil Bert'), but his third agent, Peter Robinson, had been unable to take up an agency earlier in his career in Bolton because of family commitments. Selwyn stressed that if the party wanted a career structure for professional agents then it would have to be paid for. Good agents were needed in precisely those areas where the rewards were likely to be less attractive financially, Huddersfield for instance. A system was therefore devised whereby Central Office helped finance on a decreasing scale (100 per cent to 25 per cent over 3 years) local agencies in marginal seats to give an energetic agent time to build support.

The Report was published on 6 June 1963.* The day was to be remembered for other things. John Profumo, the Secretary of State for War, had resigned after admitting that he had lied to the House of Commons earlier about his association with Christine Keeler. Planned television appearances for Selwyn were cancelled (with profuse apologies by the Independent Television Authority),

---

* *The Selwyn Lloyd Report 1963* (Conservative Central Office).

never to be rearranged. Press coverage, if at all, was confined to the
innermost pages. Not many politicians would have taken such a
relaxed attitude to the culmination of nine months' hard work.
Selwyn's sadness was for John and Valerie Profumo, to whom he had
been and to whom he was to remain, a close friend. (John Profumo
read the first lesson at Selwyn's Memorial Service in Westminster
Abbey.) Selwyn did give a radio interview about the Report on the
BBC's 10 p.m. news, his interviewer saying that it seemed to be an
extremely frank Report 'full of worry and criticism'.[9] Selwyn had
intended it to be frank and the summary of recommendations covered
four pages. He believed there should be periodic changes in branch
officers, an increase in areas, increased representation on the National Executive for larger cities, special arrangements for 25–40 year
olds, the setting up of a Trade Union group, a third Vice Chairman to
be concerned solely with Local Government affairs, a branch to deal
with political ideas (he did not like the phrase 'political education' as
it smacked of Orwell's *Animal Farm*). He wanted a non-residential
'Swinton' College in London, increased subscriptions, less paper at
Central Office, more advertising and training in techniques of television presentation, better salaries for agents and more contact
between ministers and party workers. Although the Selwyn Lloyd
Report of 1963 was not as important historically as the Maxwell Fyfe
Report of 1948 (the coincidence that both reports were prepared by
Liverpool lawyers from the same chambers much appealed to
Selwyn) it came at a propitious time. The General Election was not
to be held until October 1964 (the Profumo affair effectively ruled out
1963 and thus prolonged rather than shortened the period of Conservative government) and there was time for some of the recommendations to be acted upon. The real harvest was to come later, in the
General Election of June 1970, particularly in the North West
marginal seats.

While travelling round the country in the winter of 1962–3 Selwyn
became conscious of the need for a base of his own outside London.
He had been looking in a desultory fashion in Oxfordshire when Sir
William Hayter, Warden of New College and former Ambassador
in Moscow, told him of a house in the village of Preston Crowmarsh
that was available for lease. 'I went to see the house at Preston
Crowmarsh', Selwyn wrote to the owner, Lady Jameson, on 29
January 1963. 'Although there was over six inches of snow and I could
not get a very good idea of the garden, I was very taken with the
house.'[10] Lower Farm House is a rambling whitewashed residence
with manageable grounds (Selwyn had a swimming pool at the back).

Its cosy homeliness appealed to Selwyn very much. Negotiations were amicably completed, though not without a touch of mischievousness on Selwyn's part. The house is in the flight path of nearby RAF Benson and when Selwyn and Lady Jameson made a joint visit there in March 1963 to finalise arrangements Selwyn made a preliminary inquiry of the RAF Commander at Benson, Group Captain O'Neill, as to whether flights would be taking place on the appointed day, letting slip that they would not be unwelcome. The point was taken. Unfortunately the RAF overdid things and as Harrier Jump jets skimmed the gables, Selwyn could keep a straight face no longer and confessed to Lady Jameson what he had done. 'I hope that you recovered from the aeroplanes', he wrote on 19 March, 'but I think it was only right that you should know the sort of life your unfortunate tenants will lead!'[11] Lower Farm House became a focus for many young members of the Oxford University Conservative Association. After a lifetime as a Cambridge man he now welcomed these links with 'the other place', speaking at meetings and giving generous hospitality to a new generation, figures such as Jonathan Aitken and William Waldegrave.

Selwyn was deeply saddened by Hugh Gaitskell's sudden and unexpected death on 18 January 1963. He followed the ensuing contest for the Labour leadership with great interest and though he appreciated George Brown's patriotism was in no doubt that Harold Wilson was the right choice. His association with Harold Wilson went back to the days of the 1945 Parliament. Apart from their countless shared train journeys back to their North-West constituencies, they had worked well together as Chancellor and Shadow Chancellor. Selwyn was under no illusions that Harold Wilson would prove a most formidable opponent when the contest was put to the electorate. Shorn of his front bench responsibilities, Selwyn became a far more relaxed parliamentary performer. He defended his 1962 Budget in a debate on 8 April, but admitted that he had recently tackled a Sunday newspaper quiz aimed at grading parliamentary potential. His marks were 61 per cent. The verdict was: 'Do not despair. You will make a charming backbencher, a pillar of your party. You will bask in the absent-minded smile of your leader.' He said that he no longer had the solid structure of the Despatch Box in front of him. 'Instead I have my friend Sir Gerald Nabarro.'[12] He relaxed in other ways too. Also in April he was an improbable guest at the 50th birthday celebrations for the political cartoonist Vicky, whose pen had caricatured him mercilessly over the years. He brought his own cartoon of Vicky as a devil with horns.[13] Financial worries were eased by his directorships of the Sun Alliance and the Rank Organisation. The latter company had its origins in the world of Methodism, but now enabled him to indulge his long standing enthusiasm for the cinema. He rarely missed a Royal Film Performance, though his favourite cinema remained the vicarious experience of John Wayne on television over an informal supper. Weekend meals at Lower Farm House, guests soon found, were adjusted to accommodate the schedules of *Radio Times*. In June 1963 his Beveridge past resurfaced when he had meetings with Reginald Bevins, the Postmaster General, over a proposed new television Bill. On the question of a second channel for the Independent Television Authority, Selwyn advised that 'safety lay in numbers as with newspapers' and pressed for expansion 'as quickly as possible'.[14] This was despite the fact that he agreed with the Pilkington Committee on Broadcasting which had reported adversely in 1962 on ITV's performance, one of the great disappointments of Selwyn's life.

Another disappointment came in June 1963 with the resignation of John Profumo. As one of his oldest friends Selwyn had been one of the Conservative MPs (and the only non-minister) to see Profumo privately in March when the Prime Minister had sought assurances as to his conduct after the Labour MP George Wigg had raised the matter in the House of Commons on grounds of security.* The fact that close friends of Profumo such as Sir John Hobson, the Attorney General, and Selwyn had seen and vouched for Profumo led Macmillan to back his War Secretary. Profumo's subsequent admission that he had lied to the House of Commons was a considerable personal sadness to Selwyn. As the Press began to crawl, as it were, along the frontier between truth and rumour with a hand lens, Selwyn became very anxious. In company with many other prominent figures, including members of the Royal family, he had had his portrait sketched by Stephen Ward, and he wondered how long it would be before he was accused of guilt by association. Together with de Gaulle's veto on Britain's application to join the Common Market on 29 January and the espionage charge brought against an Admiralty official, J. W. C. Vassall, which led to the resignation of Thomas Galbraith, a former Civil Lord of the Admiralty, because of ill-founded newspaper allegations from which he was exonerated by the Radcliffe Tribunal in April 1963, the Profumo affair completed a wretched six months for the Macmillan government. The one bright spot came in July with the improvement of many financial indicators.

* Christine Keeler, to whom Profumo had been introduced by Stephen Ward at a party at Cliveden, was alleged to have been involved at the same time with the Russian Assistant Naval Attaché, Ivanov.

Peter Walker, MP for Worcester since March 1961, made a speech pointing out that Selwyn deserved much of the credit:

> It is time that the nation realised the magnitude of the achievements attained during the two years that Mr Selwyn Lloyd was Chancellor of the Exchequer. There is an alarming tendency for persons to refer to the decisions taken during that period as decisions that resulted in a depression of the economy and to speak as though the two years of Mr Selwyn Lloyd's stewardship of the Treasury were typified by dull and dreary policies. The opposite is, in fact, true, for history will, I believe, judge that the period in which Mr Selwyn Lloyd controlled the Treasury was a period in which the Treasury embarked upon more exciting, important and original thinking than in any period since the Tories were returned in 1951.[15]

Though this broad brush assessment omitted consideration of the role played by Sir Frank Lee, it cheered Selwyn. Characteristically his first thought was of the damage it might do to the young backbencher. He wrote to Peter Walker, whom he had met on his West Country tour for the Conservative Report ('Let me introduce you to the best wine waiter in Droitwich', said Walker at one of the dinners), thanking him for the complimentary remarks especially as they would be of no political benefit to Walker personally, rather the reverse. On becoming Lord Privy Seal in October he asked for Peter Walker as his Parliamentary Private Secretary. This was a political relationship of mutual benefit. Peter Walker, like Brooks Richards in 1958–9, helped with the structure and pacing of Selwyn's speeches, and was himself set on the first rung of the ladder which led to Cabinet office. Selwyn became a godfather to the Walkers' eldest child, never forgetting a birthday or Christmas. Peter Walker for his part was the guiding spirit behind the presentation to Selwyn in June 1966 of a silver inkstand engraved with the names of his seven Parliamentary Private Secretaries (Jakie Astor, Robert Grosvenor, David Harlech, Tony Lambton, Charles Morrison, Hennie Oakeshott and Peter Walker) and inscribed: 'To Selwyn Lloyd, from his Parliamentary Private Secretaries, to whom he owes so much.'

Over the summer of 1963 Selwyn had faced a particularly difficult choice about the future direction of his career. As a former Chancellor of the Exchequer Selwyn had his price in the market place. After a change of government (especially when the Conservatives move into Opposition) there is a great scramble among the dispossessed ministers for appropriate directorships. Many friends, thinking his political

career was over (mistakenly in Selwyn's opinion), advised Selwyn to
take his pick of the plums before the crowd arrived. A firm and
tempting offer came from his old friend from pre-war Wirral days, Sir
John Nicholson, who would shortly be retiring from the Chairmanship of Martin's Bank, an important smaller clearing house.
Would Selwyn consider succeeding him as Chairman, after a transitional period on the board, in 1964 or 1965? Though Selwyn was
attracted, even flattered, by the offer, there was still the hurdle of
severing his links with the Commons and his Wirral constituency. He
gave the proposal careful thought and took advice from several
friends, notably Lord Woolton, all of whom advised him to take it.
He was not overburdened with money and there seemed little
prospect of further political advancement. Selwyn still held back. As
a decision neared, he wrote to Lord Woolton on 30 September:

> Since I spoke to you I have seen John Nicholson again and he has
> rather changed his tune. Instead of it being possible for me to stay
> on in the House of Commons if I wanted to for a year provided I
> took no part in the cut and thrust of party political strife, he now
> says that I would have to leave the House of Commons immediate-
> ly on my appointment, i.e. early 1965. That presents me with a very
> difficult decision as I am really a House of Commons man. I love it
> and my constituency, and would have much preferred to have
> continued in Parliament for as long as the latter wanted me and my
> health sufficed. I have got to give my answer by the end of
> October.[16]

Woolton's advice was direct. He should take up the offer, combining it perhaps with a seat in the Lords. But Selwyn was not to be
persuaded. A. J. Balfour always said that the only thing to expect in
politics was the unexpected and when Selwyn declined the Chairmanship of Martin's Bank he could not have anticipated how swiftly
things were to move in his favour. After the *annus horrendus* of 1962,
the gods now smiled more favourably. Within three weeks of receiving Woolton's letter, Selwyn was once more a Cabinet Minister.

He had had a fairly broad hint that he could be brought back in the
longer term when he had entertained Lord Aldington, Deputy
Chairman of the Conservative Party organisation, to dinner on 17
September. The conversation soon turned to the future leadership.
'With regard to the succession, he thought that Maudling, Heath and
Macleod were out. They were not yet sufficiently tried or experienced. He thought that Heath was deliberately playing it that way and
also Macleod. Maudling was the most arrogant of them, and still
thought that he was a candidate for the immediate vacancy. If those

three were eliminated, it left Butler and Hailsham. He thought that Hailsham had enormously improved and was much more balanced and ready to listen to advice than he had been. On the whole, however, he thought Butler was best, partly because of age – he would not be there very long, but principally because of his political skill. With regard to my future, he thought it quite likely that Butler or Hailsham would ask me to go back into the government, and he hoped I would plan my future in such a way that this would be possible if I were asked . . . Finally, he asked me whether my views on the death penalty would make it impossible for me to go to the Home Office. I said that I did not particularly want to go to the Home Office, but I thought whoever went there had to administer the law as it stands.'[17]

The political year traditionally opens with the Party Conferences. In 1963 the Conservatives met at Blackpool from 8–11 October. Little did the delegates realise as they gathered that they were to be participants in the most dramatic of all Party Conferences. As the 1963 President of the National Association of Conservative Clubs, Selwyn was billed to take a prominent part. It turned out to be more prominent than he had planned.

After much thought Macmillan decided (on 7 October, the eve of the Blackpool Conference) to lead the party into the next election.[18] He had lifted the Conservative Party from a lower point in 1957 and, in the absence of an agreed successor, saw no reason why, given good health, he should not do so again. But during the night of 7 October he was taken ill with prostate trouble. The condition had been partly diagnosed a year earlier. Now the crisis came at the worst possible moment. Dr King-Lewis (coincidentally Selwyn's doctor) attended Macmillan in the absence of his regular doctor. Despite Macmillan's condition he presided at a Cabinet meeting at 10 a.m., but by 9 p.m. was in King Edward VII Hospital for Officers. Plans to continue in office were abandoned (a decision Macmillan came to regret after the success of the subsequent operation), a decision announced by Lord Home as President of the National Association at the Party Conference at Blackpool on 10 October. Thus it was that Selwyn's speech that day to the Conference on his 1963 Inquiry, like the publication of the Report itself, was swept up in larger issues.

The Conservative Party Conference at Blackpool in October 1963 seemed to be enveloped in an atmosphere of gloom and despondency from the start. A young holidaymaker was drowned in the sea opposite the Imperial Hotel the day the delegates arrived and many who were present that week speak of the experience with loathing, of how they have never been able to visit the North West of England since and of how they could remember with particular vividness each hour of every day. Rab Butler, not surprisingly, always referred thereafter to the Imperial as 'that awful hotel.'[19] From the moment that Home read out Macmillan's letter to the delegates the potential candidates lost no opportunity of making their intentions known, some discreetly, though Lord Hailsham announced to an excited Conservative Political Centre meeting that he intended to renounce his title and seek election to the Commons. This exuberant act was to bring his challenge to an end almost before it had begun. His action would not have been possible had it not been for the Peerage Act 1963, which allowed members of the House of Lords to disclaim their titles. The second Viscount Stansgate, later Tony Benn, had fought a long and spirited battle to avoid elevation to the Upper House on the death of his father. A Joint Select Committee had recommended a Bill. Existing members of the Lords, as well as those succeeding to titles, were to be allowed to renounce their rank at the dissolution of a Parliament and thereafter under the government's proposals. The Lords, however, amended this Bill to make it operative from the moment of the Royal Assent on 31 July 1963. Without this amendment (to which the Commons raised no objection) neither Hailsham, nor later Home, could have been considered as candidates and by such a quirk of parliamentary behaviour was the powerful anti-Butler lobby given a further opportunity to deny Rab Butler the place he had coveted in vain for so long.

With the effective departure of Hailsham from the leadership contest (his cause had not been helped by the Americanised methods of Randolph Churchill, dispensing 'Q' buttons, like some medieval Pardoner) the names of four contenders emerged – Butler, Heath, Macleod and Maudling. The choice soon narrowed to Butler or Maudling, but there were many, faced with this choice, who decided to look elsewhere. Among them was Selwyn.

In the 1963 leadership crisis Selwyn played a crucial and largely unrecorded role. He was a pivotal figure in three ways. He was prominent among those who pressed Home to stand; he had influence with the rank and file delegates; and he had influence with Martin Redmayne, the Chief Whip. Selwyn watchers (and there were not many) knew that Alec Home would get it. (One such was Jonathan Aitken who told Randolph Churchill that Home was the certain choice in time for Randolph Churchill to lay off his bets. Subsequently Randolph Churchill presented Jonathan Aitken with a copy of his book *The Fight for the Tory Leadership*, inscribed 'To Jonathan Aitken, who saved my bacon.')

While the Lord Chancellor, Lord Dilhorne, began his informal soundings at Blackpool even before he had been invited by Macmillan to commence formal ones, soundings which he conducted, in the words of Rab Butler, 'like a large Clumber spaniel sniffing the bottoms of the hedgerows',[20] and Martin Redmayne began his canvass of MPs, Selwyn approached Home to see if he would stand. Other visitors to Home's hotel suite who urged him to allow his name to go forward were Lord Dilhorne, Duncan Sandys and John Hare. Sir William Anstruther-Gray, Sir Charles Mott-Radclyffe and Colonel Lancaster, all respected backbench MPs, also encouraged Home to enter the race. But Selwyn's advice was crucial in tipping the balance. On three separate occasions Selwyn advised Home that the Premiership was his for the asking. In a manner totally dissimilar to Randolph Churchill's, but all the more effective for it, Selwyn quietly spread the claims of Home. More than one MP can recall Selwyn in the corridors of the Imperial Hotel that week as fresh news broke, saying, 'I'll have to go and see Alec about this'. He compared notes with Martin Redmayne – by Friday 11 October the Chief Whip, the Lord Chancellor and the party's senior backbencher were all playing for Home – in an afternoon walk along the seafront. Here they were accosted by an old-age pensioner who told them that his Socialist household recognised in Home the qualities needed to lead the nation. This merely confirmed what the two men had already decided, Selwyn later recalling the pensioner as 'the gnarled voice of truth'.[21]

It was after this chance encounter that Selwyn paid his third and decisive visit to Home's suite. The question for Selwyn (considered responsive to grass roots feeling because of the 1963 Report) was not whether Home would be acceptable to the Party, but whether he could be brought to the water. (When one MP rang up Redmayne that afternoon and said that his view was 'Not for his Lordship', there was an awkward silence as Redmayne thought this was the anti-Home lobby underway, whereas the MP was against Hailsham, unaware at that stage that Home's name was even in the frame.)[22] Home came to the water and he drank. 'It was absolutely fascinating from start to finish', wrote Selwyn to Jonathan Aitken on 13 October. 'I did not get to bed until 4 a.m. most mornings, having been plied with free liquor until totally submerged (but still discreet). If Mac had not resigned it would have been a most successful conference for me, because no one spoke without a eulogy of Lloyd. Hogg, Macleod, Maudling, Chelmer, P. Goldman, P. Walker etc etc. But there was not time for it to catch on who shd. be the next leader *really*: Mac's resignation letter swept it all away. I had long talks with Poole, Home, the Treasurer,

J. Morrison, lunched with Rab . . . I go to Preston C. on Wed afternoon unless the Queen is asking my advice that day!!'[23] In case this should happen Selwyn consulted privately as many MPs as possible. He even rang up Anthony Nutting (the adopted candidate for Oldham) to see whom he favoured, adding at the end of the conversation, 'By the way, have you thought about me?' When the reply was a rather embarrassed negative, Selwyn said, 'Well, you should have. I'm 200–1 in the *Daily Express* this morning.'

On Saturday 12 October, the Homes lunched with the Butlers in the Imperial Hotel before Butler's keynote speech at 2 p.m. Home let Butler know that he intended to see his doctor in London the next week. The inference was clear and had a considerable psychological effect on Butler's performance at the subsequent closing rally. He always remembered the headline in one of the Sunday papers next morning: BUTLER FAILS TO ROUSE TORIES.[24] The remaining stages of the leadership battle were now fought out in London. On Sunday 13 October Redmayne began a systematic canvass of MPs. The next day Macmillan arranged for a four-way canvass of party views. The Lord Chancellor was to consult every member of the Cabinet, and together with Lord St Aldwyn, the Chief Whip in the Lords, was to see the independent Unionist peers; Redmayne was to consult the parliamentary party (both Dilhorne and Redmayne had anticipated the starting pistol); the joint Party Chairman, Lord Poole, was to seek the opinions of the party officers, through Lord Chelmer and Mrs Shepherd (Chairman of the Blackpool Conference). Conservative candidates and related Conservative bodies, such as the Women's National Advisory Committee, the Young Conservatives and the Trade Union Advisory Committee were to be consulted throughout the United Kingdom. Members of Parliament were asked three questions – their first choice for Prime Minister, their second choice and (most significant question of all) the names of anyone they would oppose.

On Monday 14 October Selwyn's week began with a visit to the Ministry of Aviation, where Hailsham's campaign headquarters had been established by Julian Amery, to explain in detail the various difficulties he saw over Hailsham's candidature. The next day he began to keep a detailed record of his part in the remaining drama. Home, Maudling, Macleod, Hailsham and Heath all visited Macmillan in hospital that Tuesday. After his visit, Home told Selwyn 'that he had come to the conclusion that he will accept if the Queen sends for him after all the consultations and it being apparent that most people want him.' Selwyn endorsed this decision. Home 'said that the opposition to Quintin in the Cabinet was: Heath, Powell, Boyle, Joseph. Sandys was strongly pressing Home to accept, and he thought that Soames, who was to be his next visitor, also wanted him to do so.' As the Prime Minister was to have some post-operative treatment which involved putting him out for a day or two it was unlikely that there would be a decision taken before the Saturday. At this point in the conversation the telephone rang. Lord Poole wanted to tell Selwyn that he was going to give up the Chairmanship of the Party and ask what Selwyn thought about taking on this task. Selwyn said that he would need time to consider all the implications. Later in the day Selwyn had his first meeting with Redmayne since Blackpool. 'I asked him whether the figures of Members of Parliament that Peter Walker had given me: 90 Hailsham, 60 Butler, 40 Home – represented the trend? He refused to be drawn except to the extent that those figures were not accurate. He said, however, that he thought that perhaps more important than the figures "For" were the people violently "Against", and I would be surprised how strong the opposition to Quintin was.' Selwyn went from this meeting to one with Hennie Oakeshott. His talk now centred not on the likelihood of Home being appointed Prime Minister, but on what job he (Selwyn) might expect in the new government.

> First, *Leadership of the House of Commons.* Hennie thought if Alec were chosen he would certainly offer this to Rab. He would have to mend his fences with Rab. He did not think Rab would go to the House of Lords, nor if he did would the Lords want him as Leader straight away. I doubted that.
> Second, *Home Secretary.*
> Third, *Commonwealth Secretary in the House of Commons.*
> Fourth, *Commonwealth Secretary in the House of Lords.*
> Fifth, *Chairman of the Party.*
> Hennie said that he hoped very much that I would consider the *Board of Trade.* It was an important Department which had suffered through not having sufficiently powerful Ministers in it. I said that the President of the Board of Trade was in Neddy, and I did not see how I could serve in Neddy under another Chairman after having started as Chairman myself. He thought there was something in that point.[25]

On Wednesday 16 October Macmillan received a further batch of Cabinet Ministers at the King Edward VII Hospital, including Thorneycroft, Boyle, Soames, Hare, Brooke, Joseph, and Sandys. Significantly Selwyn was also included in the day's visitors, being driven to the hospital by Diana Leishman in his battered old Mini, to pay his respects as he told waiting newsmen, but of course to confer about the succession. Selwyn had had many strange conversations with Macmillan over the years – the memories of 12 July and 1 August 1962 would never fade – but the talk he had with Macmillan that October morning surpassed them all.

'I went to see *Harold* at King Edward's Hospital for Officers. He looked drawn and yellow, but he revived as he talked. Obviously he liked talking. Soames had been before. He said that he was very glad to see me because of the great affection he had always had for me, and he thought I had an important role to play in these discussions.

'He had intended to announce at Blackpool his decision to continue to lead the Party. He was now finding that, difficult as it was to become Prime Minister, it was even more difficult to give up the position. His only desire was to help the Party to choose a successor. He was not a Hogg-ite or a Rab-ite or a Home-ite. His children were Hogg-ites, but he was not.'

Macmillan outlined to Selwyn the four-tier canvass of party opinion that was now underway. When these consultations were complete, 'he was going to be taken downstairs in his bed to a sort of boardroom', where he would see individually on the Thursday morning Dilhorne, Redmayne, Poole, Lord Chelmer and Mrs Shepherd, the last two representing the National Union. Then on the Thursday evening he was to see the Lord Chancellor, the Chief Whip and the joint party chairmen together.

'When he had got that kind of view, he would prepare a memorandum for the Queen. He might well want to see me again before he prepared that memorandum. The Queen had said that she would come and see him in hospital. He hoped that would be on Friday, when he would formally tender his resignation. It might be that it would continue until Saturday. The Queen would then, if she thought fit, take some opinions. He had it in mind to suggest to her that she should see me. It was important that it should not only be Lords, and anyhow people like Salisbury and Anthony Eden were not really in touch. He could not think of any other Member of the House of Commons who had my position. He thought it was all very bad luck on Rab, because had he [Macmillan] been run over by a car he assumed that the Queen would automatically have sent for Rab.'

The conversation now turned to Hailsham and Home. Macmillan remembered 'the anxious discussions about Quintin leading the House of Lords, but he had done that very well. He had been a very good First Lord of the Admiralty during Suez. Alec, on the other hand, had much to be said for him. The British liked a real aristocrat who could talk to ordinary people – people like the Duke of Devonshire, his father-in-law. We talked of the abuse that was thrown at Alec when he was made Foreign Secretary.'[26]

Selwyn made it clear that his own preference was for Home and he outlined some of the manoeuvres at Blackpool. After further historical ramblings through the intricacies of Lloyd George's splitting of the Liberal Party, Selwyn took his leave. When he came out of the hospital there was a sparkle in his eyes again and he insisted on driving to Preston Crowmarsh. He knew that he was on the verge of being recalled to office. Memories had been rekindled by his talk with Macmillan and he told Diana Leishman that he must dictate his Suez story before too long. As he drove towards the A40 (two circuits of the British Museum was the usual minimum before Selwyn reached a northbound road out of London) his secretary did her best to navigate junctions and remember the historic reminiscences of 1956 that now flowed freely. Selwyn was back in the game.

On the evening of Thursday 17 October Selwyn returned to London and went to see Home at 1 Carlton Gardens at 10. Martin Redmayne was already with the Foreign Secretary. During the afternoon the news had begun to leak out that the decision was for Home. No sooner had Selwyn arrived than the telephone calls began. The first call was taken by Home, as Selwyn recalled: 'Alec answered himself. The conversation began: "Is that you Reggie?" But it was Hailsham who "said that he thought it would be a disaster if Alec took the job and he would have to denounce him publicly."' At this point Selwyn took a telephone (he knew his way about Carlton Gardens) and warned that if Hailsham did this it would look like sour grapes. 'Macleod and Powell then came on, speaking from the same room, one by one saying that they were very much against his selection. They spoke to him, Alec said, politely but very firmly. The Chief Whip then spoke to Reggie Maudling who was less difficult but who said that he thought it was a mistake. There was some discussion as to whether Keith Joseph was now supporting Reggie Maudling.' Dilhorne then arrived. He assured Home that ten members of the Cabinet had indicated him as their first choice. Martin Redmayne added that 'by a narrow majority' Alec Home had received more votes from the Parliamentary Party than anyone else. Selwyn said that he understood that, although the constituencies preferred Hailsham, there was also strong support for Home. 'They agreed that this was so.' Home was discomfited by the way things were developing and in response to his wife's question, 'It looks rather smelly now, doesn't it?', replied, 'Well, I was quite prepared to come forward as the candidate to unify the Party, accepted by everyone; but if it is said that my coming forward would split the Party, that is a different proposition.' Dilhorne said it was just a group of disappointed over-ambitious colleagues and that 'Alec must pay no attention'.

Selwyn then drove Redmayne to Enoch Powell's house in South Eaton Place, where the famous 'midnight meeting', attended by Macleod, Maudling, Erroll and Aldington was taking place. Selwyn did not stay for this meeting, at which Redmayne was told that Macmillan must be informed of the feeling against Home. Macleod and Powell were convinced that Home had said at Cabinet on 7 October that, like Dilhorne, he was not a contender. When Selwyn returned to his flat he rang up Peter Walker and told him of developments. Walker's opinion was, 'that the very people who had stopped Hailsham getting it were now trying to use him to block Alec.'[27] But it was not to be. At 8.15 a.m. on Friday 18 October Macmillan's Parliamentary Private Secretary, Knox Cunningham, arrived at the King Edward VII Hospital, followed by Tim Bligh and the Chief Whip at 8.30. They told the Prime Minister of the overnight developments. Macmillan decided to proceed with his intention of resigning and during the morning Tim Bligh went to the Palace with the formal letter. A memorandum had been prepared for the Queen outlining the results of the four-way canvass of Party opinion, but while Bligh was at the Palace Macmillan and Knox Cunningham drafted an addendum to the original memorandum to include a report of the midnight meeting as told to them by the Chief Whip. Both documents were placed in an outsize white envelope which was handed to the Queen when she arrived at the hospital at 11.10 a.m. Macmillan met the Queen in the board room on the ground floor, putting on a white silk shirt for the audience, which lasted half an hour. When the Queen left the hospital she handed the gigantic envelope to her secretary, Sir Michael Adeane, who to Knox Cunningham seemed like Tenniel's drawing of the Frog Footman in a scene from *Alice in Wonderland*.[28]

Later that morning Selwyn was pleased to hear from Peter Walker that Hailsham 'had stated that he would not publicly denounce Alec and would serve him'. He rang Home to tell him. 'Thank you for some good news at last', was Home's response, before telling Selwyn that he understood that Macleod and Powell had been 'very stiff' with Redmayne. Selwyn then rang John Hare and 'told him to be up and doing and to sustain Alec.' But events were moving faster than even Home's supporters had envisaged. When Selwyn walked across to the Turf Club for lunch from his flat he got mixed up with the crowd of photographers who had just seen Home arrive at the Palace for his audience with the Queen. 'I had thought he was going in the afternoon', noted Selwyn. Home was asked to see if he could form an administration and although he did not at that stage formally kiss hands the invitation from the sovereign was to put him in the decisive position, as it had done in December 1905 when Sir Henry Campbell-Bannerman became Prime Minister despite the reservations of his three senior colleagues Asquith, Sir Edward Grey and Haldane. Home said that he would need time to consult his colleagues. As this meant the doubters Selwyn was not high on the list of those Home first saw when he returned to a Downing Street besieged by press and television. Selwyn went ahead with his plans to travel to Arundel for a dinner engagement, where he found the Duke of Norfolk 'very enthusiastic' about Home's appointment. As Selwyn pointed out that Home would be the only Prime Minister to have played first-class cricket this made the assembled company even more enthusiastic.

Selwyn was summoned to 10 Downing Street at 7.45 a.m. on Saturday 19 October, the early hour an indication of a long day for Home. Although Home was determined from the start to have Selwyn in his Cabinet, not because of his discreet but vital role in the succession crisis but because he was a solid representative of the rank and file of the party, there was considerable difficulty in finding the right square for him on the chessboard. The first suggestion was that he might become Home Secretary. This was eventually discounted, not because of the capital punishment issue, but because of the desire of Henry Brooke to continue in the post. 'Henry felt that his removal would be regarded as a sign that he had failed. I said that I thought a change there would be popular but I hated the idea of climbing on a dead man's horse.' The talk then turned to the Leadership of the House. 'Alec said he had already offered it to John Boyd-Carpenter, who had accepted it. Alec then said, "What about Minister without Portfolio, with some overriding interest like 'reform of Government' or something?"' Selwyn was too experienced a hand to be tempted by such a nebulous post, convinced that Rab's assumption of the post of First Secretary of State in July 1962 had been neither to Rab's benefit, nor the government's. 'I said that I thought those kind of appointments were never successful.' He also scotched any suggestion that he might become Chairman of the Party. 'I felt I had done all I could already. I couldn't bear the thought of another winter traipsing round the country.' They decided to wait on developments. Home had the more difficult interviews yet to come. Selwyn spent a quiet day at his flat, watching the news bulletins on television. At 10 p.m. Home spoke to him again on the telephone. Selwyn said that he had been thinking things over and felt that 'the Chairman of the Party must be in the House of Lords' and that 'the Leader of the House of Commons should not have a department', returning to the point he had twice underlined to Macmillan. His preference was still for the latter job and he 'was not particularly keen on the Home Office'. They agreed to speak again on the Sunday morning.[29]

At 10.30 p.m. the Chief Whip rang John Boyd-Carpenter.[30] Home was now beginning the delicate task of withdrawing the offer of the post of Leader of the House. This led to some difficulties (Home did not have the bluntness of Attlee's 'Well, untell him' during the 1945 Labour government), not least when Boyd-Carpenter stood aside for Selwyn on a second occasion over the contested Speakership in 1971.* Redmayne mooted the possibility of Boyd-Carpenter's leaving his post as Paymaster General and taking the Chairmanship of the Party with a seat in the Lords. Boyd-Carpenter said that he was not much attracted by this idea, but Redmayne said it was only an idea and 'not to lose any sleep over it'.[31] On Sunday 20 October Home attended matins at St James, Piccadilly before returning to the task of Cabinet making. Not having heard anything overnight Selwyn rang Downing Street at 12.30 p.m. Home was engaged, but rang back at 12.45 p.m. 'Would I be Lord Privy Seal? . . . He had not quite thought it all out but he had to start firming things up. I said "Certainly". He said it might be Chairman of the Party or some special job or Leading the House. I said "Yes".'[32] At 1.30 p.m. Home rang Boyd-Carpenter, who was at lunch. He opened by speaking of 'this problem of you and Selwyn'. In Boyd-Carpenter's words: 'This was the first reference I had heard to Selwyn Lloyd, who had been on the Back Benches since "the night of the long knives", or to the fact that he had anything to do with my appointment. He said that he was very sorry but Selwyn would not come back without the Leadership of the House.'[33] This was not strictly true, but Home had settled on the post for Selwyn. Boyd-Carpenter was offered the Ministry of Health to think over. Home then rang Selwyn again at 2.30 p.m. to make the formal offer of the posts of Lord Privy Seal and Leader of the House of Commons. Selwyn accepted and they agreed to meet at 10 Downing Street at 6 p.m. over a drink.[34] 'About 3.00 p.m. the Prime Minister rang again', wrote Boyd-Carpenter. 'He said, "It was all my fault", and that he was sorry. But he had to get Selwyn back.'[35] It was agreed that Boyd-Carpenter would stay at his Treasury post. The whole episode reveals the hidden tensions and adjustments that face a Prime Minister, even in filling the second echelon of Cabinet. 'You put a pistol to my head', said Balfour when offered the post of Foreign

* See Chapter 15.

Secretary by Lloyd George in December 1916. 'I must accept.' Unfortunately, as Asquith's biographers were to remark, there are never enough pistols to go round.

The Cabinet list was announced on the Sunday evening. Butler became Foreign Secretary, the post he had sought in 1957, and thus became only the second politician after Sir John Simon in modern times to have held all three major departments of state.* Henry Brooke remained at the Home Office and Maudling at the Treasury. To Selwyn's delight John Hare became Lord Blakenham and Chairman of the Party. Tony Barber became Minister of Health, both vacancies caused by the refusal of Macleod and Powell to serve in Home's Cabinet. When Selwyn had heard of their refusal he had spent part of the Sunday trying to persuade them to reconsider, but to no avail. Heath became the head of a considerably augmented Board of Trade.

Selwyn went to Downing Street in the evening. 'When Reggie Dilhorne came in we all agreed how much pleasanter a meeting it was than that at 10 p.m. on Thursday.' Home said that he was going to fight the Kinross and West Perthshire by-election, where the Conservative candidate George Younger (later Defence Minister in the 1980s) had stood aside, and that he was determined that Parliament should not meet until he was in the House of Commons. 'Only piece of gossip: Quintin had told Reggie that he would never speak to Iain Macleod again. Alec said that Enoch had told him he would very much like to join the Government, but felt himself pledged not to. In other words, it was quite obvious that he had promised Iain that if he stayed out he Enoch would also do so.'[36] A Privy Council was held at Buckingham Palace at 6 p.m. on Monday 21 October when the new ministers were sworn in, the ninth anniversary of Selwyn's being sworn in as Minister of Supply. 'The Lord Privy Seal's precedence† over Foreign Secretary delicately preserved by Rab walking in in front of me and my being sworn before him. The Queen full of smiles. Michael Adeane said that she had told him that she was very pleased that I was coming back.'[37] The Duke of Edinburgh, however, met Selwyn in the corridor with the remark, 'What, they haven't brought you back again, have they?'[38] Selwyn regarded this as the small change of political life. Better to have fought and lost, then never to have fought at all; better by far to have returned. On the way out of the Privy Council, Selwyn had a word with Rab Butler. 'He is very anxious that everyone should say that he has done the right thing.'[39]

---

* James Callaghan was the third.
† The Lord Privy Seal is seventh in order of precedence after the Royal Family.

So ended the 1963 leadership crisis which has many parallels with the contest fought out in 1911 when there were two well supported front runners, Austen Chamberlain and Walter Long (the equivalents of Rab Butler and Lord Hailsham) and in the deadlock that followed a totally dark horse emerged in the person of Bonar Law (Lord Home). When Lloyd George heard that Bonar Law had become Conservative leader he said, 'The fools have chosen their best man by accident.' With a General Election less than a year away, the question was very much whether the Conservatives had managed to do the same again.

Selwyn now embarked on what was to be one of the happiest years of his life, the only previous equivalent having been in 1922 as he waited to go up to Cambridge. On becoming Lord Privy Seal he wrote to his former Foreign Office secretary Archie Ross, 'I am glad to be back and feel rather like someone who has won a suit for wrongful dismissal!!!'[40] The office of Lord Privy Seal is one of those non-departmental posts ('Where is Lancaster? And what is a Duchy?', asked Churchill in 1915) that varies in importance depending on the Prime Minister's allocation of responsibility. In 1929 J. H. Thomas as Lord Privy Seal was charged with responsibilities for employment; in 1934 Eden had used it as a springboard for League of Nations affairs; in 1938 Sir John Anderson had been in charge of air raid preparations, while more recently Richard Stokes had co-ordinated the policy of the Home Information services. Selwyn had no specific remit, but was primarily Leader of the House, a post often combined with Lord Privy Seal.

The first task of the Leader of the House of Commons is to get through the parliamentary business of the government with the minimum of fuss and without annoying the Opposition into an obstructive stance. It proved a job, despite the initial reservations of some Conservatives ('How wrong we were', said one), for which he was well suited. As a lawyer he had always seen both sides of the question and the Leader of the House needs such open-mindedness. The second requirement of the job is to keep Parliament happy, mollify the unruly elements (a growing band at that time) and to be on good terms with the Opposition parties. The Leader of the House also needs to stand up for the rights of minority groups and be responsive to the welfare of backbenchers. As Leader of the House Selwyn had a good rapport with the ordinary member and proved a useful welfare officer over conditions of service. Although it was a barren period legislatively and there was an atmosphere of 'end of term' about the whole of Home's premiership, as in his legal days Selwyn was good 'in the corridor' in negotiating settlements of potential disputes. The only contentious (and in the end electorally damaging) measure was Resale Price Maintenance. The Leader of the House also needs to be something of an actor. As an orator Selwyn was clearly not in the category of Macleod, a recent predecessor in the post, nor did he have the ability to entrance the House with cryptic and ambiguous asides like Rab Butler. In his way this made him a better leader of the House in that members felt comfortable with him. Macleod was more centrist, more controversialist in style. This was not the persona required of the Leader of the House. Selwyn was the kind of Leader of the House who managed to persuade both the main parties that they ought to accept any reasonable conclusion from the Lawrence Committee which had been set up to deal with members' pay. The year he spent as Leader of the House 'sanitised' his reputation, helping to erase the bitterness, though not the memory, of Suez among the Opposition parties.

Parliament met on Thursday 24 October when Selwyn made a short business statement before the introduction of new members. The speech in which he established himself was on the Address on 19 November, the day on which he also answered Prime Minister's questions. In the month following his appointment as Selwyn's PPS, Peter Walker read all Selwyn's speeches of the previous fifteen years. One of the characteristics that he spotted was that they tended to be very 'explanatory' speeches, legalistic in style. Together Selwyn and Peter Walker worked at the technique of leavening the bread, leaving 'space' in the drafts to cope with interruptions. Peter Walker also advised Selwyn to be more combative when challenged. All this was to pay off on 19 November. Selwyn had never much enjoyed the parliamentary set piece, whether it was a statement on Suez or a Budget, and he had not looked forward to his first big test in his new role, but he took the advice to heart and in response to Fred Willey (Shadow Spokesman on Education) who criticised Selwyn over education funding in 1961–2 replied:

The suggestion was that I had unnecessarily and wantonly cut education. I, too, had to contend with pressures on the economy and with the problem of resources available; yet in 1961–1962 the amount of public money actually spent on all forms of education increased by £141 million, from £943 million to £1,084 million.

At this there was a concerted interruption from the Labour benches: 'Got the sack for it!' – to which Selwyn immediately retorted: 'Whatever may have happened, I am back again now', a reply greeted with acclamation on both sides of the House.[41] For the first time during a parliamentary speech he felt that people were with him and not against him. On the way out of the Chamber he turned to Peter Walker and said, 'When do we make another speech?' They were changed days. 'Enter a fresh Mr Selwyn Lloyd', reported *The Times* the next day. 'Not the gloomy Cassandra of the pay pause, or the sad forgotten figure on the third row beneath the gangway. Here was a jaunty cavalier of a party politician.'[42] He became an *habitué* of No 10, dining *en famille* with the Homes ('Menu: Haddock, Prunes and Rice Pudding. Elizabeth said if she had known I had been coming she would have had a grand lunch, but that was what Alec liked.').[43]

His work took him beyond the confines of Westminster. He had never lost touch with Michael Ramsey, but as Ramsey rose steadily through the Anglican hierarchy, becoming successively Archbishop of York and then the 100th Primate of All England, Selwyn saw more of him over religio-constitutional matters. In the early 1960s there was much talk of Anglo-Methodist union and Selwyn became involved in these talks. As Leader of the House Selwyn called in at Lambeth Palace from time to time to confer on this and other possible church legislation, telling Ramsey that he so much enjoyed his new job as it meant he could go out and meet people rather than being stuck in an office all day long.

It was a relaxed time. He got on well with his new driver, Bill Housden, who before the year was out would be driving for the new Prime Minister, Harold Wilson. He took up his Twickenham visits again, going to the Varsity match with Wavell Wakefield in December and the Home Internationals against Wales and Ireland in the New Year. He combined the Calcutta Cup match versus Scotland at Murrayfield with a lunch at Fettes with the headmaster, Dr I. D. McIntosh, with whom he discussed endowing a scholarship. He had never forgotten the difference that the Governors' scholarship had meant to him at Cambridge and he now wanted to give others the same opportunity. Selwyn's time as Lord Privy Seal, his only non-departmental Cabinet post, allowed him to ruminate on the whole structure of government, culminating in September 1964 on the eve of the General Election in a far-ranging memorandum he sent to Sir Alec Douglas Home on the current Cabinet system:

The weaknesses of the present system seem to me to be as follows:
  1 The Cabinet is far too big. It is frequently difficult to get a word in edgeways.
  2 Perhaps because of this the Cabinet is hardly informed about defence matters.
  3 The Cabinet Committee system is out of hand.[44]

Selwyn felt that the Economic Policy Committee did not stick to economics, the Home Affairs Committee had too wide a brief, and that as a result compromises arose. He recommended a Cabinet of twelve which would consist of the Prime Minister, the Lord Chancellor, the Lord President, the Foreign Secretary, the Chancellor of the Exchequer, the Lord Privy Seal, Home Secretary, Defence Secretary, Commonwealth Secretary, Trade and Industry, Education and Scotland. He felt that there were certain portfolios better contained in an outer ring (the view of Lloyd George in 1916, albeit in war) – Agriculture, Transport, Labour, Housing, Health, Power, Information, Public Building and the various 'Number Two' posts, such as the Chief Secretary to the Treasury. If a compromise led to a Cabinet of about 16, he felt that Agriculture, Transport, Labour or Housing could be upgraded. Returning to an old hobby horse, he stressed that the Party Chairman need not be in the Cabinet. But these issues were subsumed in the autumn Election campaign.

Old friends were falling by the wayside. Selwyn was saddened by the last and painful illness of Pete Pyman, his old Chief of Staff in 1945, and he made many visits to Millbank Military hospital that summer. A more personal bereavement was the death of Bill Aitken, a friend for over 30 years. Selwyn gave the address at the Memorial Service in Aitken's constituency in Bury St Edmunds and at St Margaret's, Westminster:

I first met Bill Aitken about 30 years ago staying for a weekend at the house of a mutual friend. What a weekend it was! Riding furiously before breakfast, going up in an aeroplane – the first time for me – dancing in the evening, being driven back at 80 miles an hour through Windsor Great Park . . . The next time I saw him was in 1945. He had served in the war as a pilot in the R.A.F., in Army Co-operation of the R.A.F., for which he always retained a deep loyalty. He showed the effects of his bad air crash in which he sustained serious multiple injuries about 2½ years before. At the General Election he had narrowly failed to win back for his Party the West Derbyshire division. He asked where I was going to live in London. I said I had no idea. With that friendliness which was so much in character he at once asked me to stay with him until I could find somewhere else. That stay lasted five years, and I got to know him very well.[45]

Selwyn now became in his turn a great help to the whole family in their bereavement. Bill Aitken's son, Jonathan, had already served as a private secretary for Selwyn intermittently from July 1962, Selwyn always joking that it was after a fortnight of Jonathan's speeches that Macmillan decided to sack him. Over the next three years Jonathan Aitken acted as private secretary, accompanying Selwyn (who had been appointed Shadow Commonwealth Secretary) on tours of New Zealand, Australia and – most significantly – Rhodesia in the wake of the unilateral declaration of independence by Ian Smith. The notice of Selwyn's life in the *Dictionary of National Biography* was to be written by Jonathan Aitken, by that time a member of the House of Commons himself.

Selwyn greatly encouraged Home in the run-up to the 1964 Election and suggested the riposte about 'the 14th Mr Wilson', which Home was to use effectively.* Home had given some six months' notice that the General Election would not be held until the autumn of 1964 to dampen down speculation and, of course, hoping to give the Conservatives a better chance of victory, thus following Walter Elliot's dictum that the best way to lose an election is to hold one. The advice he was receiving from Lord Blakenham and Sir Michael Fraser was that an early campaign was doomed to failure but that a later one offered some prospect of success, a forecast that proved to be remarkably accurate in the outcome. Indeed there were some who recommended that Home should wait until the last possible legal date early in November – a five year term beginning with the assembly of a Parliament not the General Election that created it – and if this advice had been followed the news of the fall from power in Russia of Khrushchev, which came as polling stations were closing on 15 October 1964, could well have tipped the balance in what was one of the closest elections of the century. Selwyn was an October man, though in a letter to Eden in June he confided, 'Our day with the public is over.'[46]

Parliament was dissolved on 15 September with Polling Day fixed for 15 October. Weeks before Selwyn had pencilled in opposite 15 October in his Desk Diary 'Election Day (according to newspapers)'.[47] He attended his adoption meeting at the Macdona Hall in West Kirby on 25 September and then set off on a wide-ranging tour of speaking engagements at Ipswich, Peterborough, York, Birmingham and the West Midlands (staying with the Peter Walkers) and finishing his campaign in Wales. On the last Monday of the campaign he gave a live television broadcast at 7 p.m. He was accompanied for

---

* In a speech in Manchester on 19 October 1963 Harold Wilson said, 'After half a century of democratic advance, the whole process had ground to a halt with a 14th Earl.' 'As far as the 14th Earl is concerned,' said Home in a television interview on 21 October 1963, 'I suppose Mr Wilson, when you come to think of it, is the 14th Mr Wilson.'

36 Welcoming the Prince of Wales to Speaker's House.

37 Selwyn listening to Black Rod from the Speaker's Chair, 1974.

38 Seventieth birthday party, Hilbre House, 28 July 1974.

39 A Garden Party at Hilbre House in aid of the Abbeyfield Society. Viola,
Duchess of Westminster, talking to Selwyn Lloyd and George Eustance,
September 1976.

much of the time by his personal assistant, Michael Howard, President of the Cambridge Union in 1962, who was just starting his pupillage after Cambridge and also learning the political ropes. In 1985 he was to be a member of the Government himself. For one who had been so pessimistic about the Conservative prospects five years earlier, Selwyn was by no means despondent about the October 1964 campaign, which turned out to be even more close run than that of February 1950. For the first time since the election Selwyn faced a three-cornered contest, though as usual the result was never in doubt. The figures were:

Lloyd, J. S. B. (Conservative)	32,084
Aspin Mrs. M. (Labour)	17,445
Williams, P. H. (Liberal)	14,574
Majority	14,639

As Selwyn prepared his vote of thanks he could not quite work out in time whether he had an overall majority as he intended to refer to that in his speech. He did, but it was a narrow one, reflecting the national trend away from the Conservatives, whose share of the total vote fell from 49.4 per cent in 1959 to 43.4 per cent. The outcome of the General Election was for so long uncertain that Home called a Cabinet on the afternoon of Friday 16 October to watch the final results and to consider whether he should carry on in the event that it should prove indecisive. The question was academic for the small group of ministers who were able to attend (Selwyn rang Home from the Wirral) as the Labour Party finally topped the 315 seat mark to gain an absolute, albeit narrow, majority. The final figures were Labour 317 seats, Conservatives 304 and Liberals 9. Selwyn was in Opposition for the first time since 1951. He wrote to Jonathan Aitken, who was on a debating tour in America, with news of the campaign. 'Billericay as usual was early on and when I heard that we had held it I really thought we were in again. I was pretty tired at the end of it, having visited 37 constituencies in the course of the campaign. Alec took his defeat with great dignity and although tired is in very good form. We have had a lot of to-ing and fro-ing about the Shadow Cabinet: I have maintained throughout that Butler must give up his hold on the Research Department, that means must be found of reconciling Maudling and Heath, that Macleod and Powell must be brought back and that Lloyd must have a large share in controlling the Opposition's tactics and morale.'[48]

It was no more than his due. His leadership of the House of Commons had been one of marked success, arguably the apogee of his parliamentary career. The House of Commons can be a very forgiving place and it certainly was with Selwyn from 1963–4. People felt instinctively that he had had a rough deal and they wanted to atone, especially as Macmillan's presence faded. Although there are those who would claim that nobody's finest political hour can come as Leader of the House of Commons, the twelve months from October 1963 were of particular importance in Selwyn's life and a turning point in people's perceptions of him. As Leader of the House Selwyn had laid the foundation for his later Speakership.

14

In Opposition

The General Election of 15 October 1964 brought to an end thirteen years of Conservative government. For nearly twelve of those years Selwyn Lloyd had been on the front bench and for seven years one of the inner core of Cabinet Ministers. Now the verdict of the electors had brought an enforced rest. Parliamentary life, after a long period of stable majorities, returned to the factious atmosphere of 1950–1. At a time of increasing bitterness Selwyn was glad to be paired with Emanuel Shinwell (his pair for 26 years overall) – two old hands who knew the ways of Westminster. Initially there was much bad feeling about the Smethwick result at the General Election when Patrick Gordon Walker, the Shadow Foreign Secretary, had been defeated in a campaign dominated by the racial issue. Difficulties of another kind awaited Wilson's government when Patrick Gordon Walker, nevertheless appointed Foreign Secretary despite having no seat in either House, lost the Leyton by-election on 21 January 1965 by 205 votes. The incoming Labour government made great political capital out of the £800m balance of payments deficit inherited from Maudling, imposing a 15 per cent surcharge on imports from 26 October. The new Chancellor of the Exchequer, James Callaghan, introduced a special Budget on 11 November and on Monday 23 November (not the normal day for such announcements) Bank Rate was raised by 2 per cent. Selwyn watched these events with wry detachment, but no satisfaction, writing to Jonathan Aitken in the United States on 24 November:

The political situation here is very interesting. The Government have made a mess of almost everything they have touched. Having talked of crisis throughout the Election campaign, they are now surprised that the foreigners have believed them. Their 15% surcharge on imports was introduced in about as bad a manner as

possible. They included on the original list all sorts of things which
are in fact raw materials for industries. They also failed to get any
support from foreigners beforehand and they have succeeded in
mortally offending all the members of EFTA and quite a lot of
other people. The Budget was no help to them, partly because they
put 6*d*. on petrol, only a fifth of which falls upon pleasure motorists
and the rest upon industry, distribution and transport generally.
And now with the 7% Bank Rate they have had to put on the
brakes with a vengeance. I have been reading with pleasure what
Mr Harold Wilson said of my 7% Bank Rate on July 26th, 1961.
Unfortunately, saying I told you so doesn't help the national
situation.[1]

Until July 1965 Selwyn acted as Shadow Leader of the House, but
he found it uncongenial work, 'talk and talk and talk . . . but no
power'.[2] He was appointed Chairman of the Conservative Policy
Group on immigration, producing in July 1965 a typically thorough
report which trod a delicate path through the minefields of a contentious issue, and was also a member of the Leader's Consultative
Committee investigating the procedures involved in choosing future
leaders of the Party. When Home told the 1922 Committee of
Conservative backbenchers on 5 November 1964 that there was to be
such a review, many felt that psychologically he was preparing the
way for his own eventual departure. If the Conservative MPs were
given a new electoral system then it would not be surprising for them
to be eager to give it a test drive, although it was clear from the outset
that the system would only be used at the next change of leadership.
That moment was to come much earlier than many MPs, especially
Selwyn, ever envisaged. On 14 April 1965 Selwyn wrote to Eden,
'There is still quite a lot of snarling about Alec but I don't think that
the potential successors are particularly distinguishing themselves. I
doubt myself whether the mood will change much for another twelve
months. Therefore I hope we do not have an early election.'[3] Selwyn
was therefore greatly relieved when Home announced on 26 June
1965 (in the wake of Conservative gains of 562 seats in the local
elections in May) that he intended to continue as leader. Tactically
Harold Wilson then made a move of great shrewdness when he ruled
out a General Election in 1965, which led to renewed speculation
about Home's long-term future as Conservative leader just at the
moment when it seemed to be settled in the short-term.

Many Conservatives, while privately respecting Home's integrity
(like Trollope's Plantagenet Palliser he was seen as 'a very noble
gentleman – such a one as justifies to the nation the seeming anomaly

of a hereditary peerage and of primogeniture'),[4] felt that he would never win an electoral battle against Harold Wilson, Sir Alec *v* Smart Alec as the pundits saw it. Selwyn was not of that number. A mere 900 votes in key marginals at the 1964 Election could have kept the Tories in power.* Home's leadership had not been a disadvantage at the recent local elections. When asked at this time why he thought the Conservatives would soon be back in power Selwyn told friends that as he was being invited to Pamela Berry's dinner parties again it was a sure indication. 'Why, it is only a month or two ago that I was pouring out drinks there for Mr and Mrs Tom Driberg.'[5] But local elections were not the same as General Elections and the crisis of confidence in Home's capacity to bring success on a national level reached a head on the weekend of 18 July 1965 with the publication of a thoughtful and reasoned article in the *Sunday Times* by William Rees-Mogg entitled, 'The right moment to change'. Home returned from the Hirsel, where he had been considering his position, on Monday 19 July. It was widely expected that he was close to a decision. A head of steam was now building up for a change (the Party Conference in the autumn was considered a particularly awkward hurdle) and Home had no desire to outstay his welcome. Selwyn had little confidence in the ability of the front runners, Reginald Maudling (whom he personally favoured if there was to be a change) and Edward Heath, to improve matters. The fact that Heath had recently improved his standing in the party with his performance as Shadow Chancellor over the Finance Bill also influenced Selwyn in cautioning Home against resigning.

It was to no avail. Home privately made the decision to go on Tuesday 20 July and by the time the Shadow Cabinet were informed on the Thursday the die was cast. The only two people Home did not tell until the decision was irrevocable were his wife and Selwyn. On Thursday 22 July Home sent Selwyn a message saying that he wanted to see him at 11.30 a.m. 'I then said to Susan† that I smelt a rat and thought that it must mean that Alec was giving up the leadership', Selwyn noted in his diary. 'When I got to his room in the House of Commons he said, "I am going to let you down. I have decided to chuck my hand in and give up the leadership."'[6] Selwyn was greatly saddened by this news and unsuccessfully pleaded with Home to reconsider. Home insisted that it was his final decision, the national opinion polls, the Press articles, the narrow division on the Executive

---

* The closest result was at Brighton Kemptown where the victorious Labour candidate had a majority of only 7 votes after several recounts.

† Susan Carter, Selwyn's secretary at Westminster.

of the 1922 Committee had all led him to believe that he must go. So for the second time in under two years the Conservatives were faced with a leadership contest at a time when there was no accepted heir apparent.

So much ink has been spilt over the leadership struggles within the Conservative Party in 1957 and 1963 that relatively little attention has been paid to that in July 1965, the first under an electoral system. The expectation at Westminster (and with the bookmakers) was that Reginald Maudling, the Shadow Foreign Secretary, would win. Although Selwyn was no longer the pivotal figure he had been in October 1963 (his continued support for Home, though showing commendable loyalty, also betrayed a lack of touch with current party thinking) he was to be closely involved in the ensuing struggle. The story begins with Home's appearance at the 1922 Committee on the evening of Thursday 22 July:

> At 6 o'clock the same day he came to the 1922 Committee looking terribly drawn and ill and made a moving little speech which was received with obvious sadness and sympathy. I then went into the Smoking Room, where several people said how unnecessary they thought it was.
>
> I then went to have a drink with Christopher Soames, who wanted to know whether I would be running for the leadership. I said I hadn't thought about it but didn't think it was likely. He felt very much that the bulk of the party did not want either Maudling or Heath and there should be a third candidate. I came back to the House of Commons and found Peter Hordern in the Smoking Room. We couldn't get a table and I went off to have dinner with him in some strange restaurant beyond Derry & Toms.
>
> We came back to the vote and afterwards I went along to Peter Thorneycroft's flat, where first of all Quintin Hogg, Julian Amery and Christopher Soames turned up. The thesis, as put forward by Quintin, was that 60% of the Party did not want either Maudling or Heath. Julian said the Home vote was looking for leadership. I said that I had no intention of standing, at all events on the first round, and thought it would be a great mistake for anyone else to. I thought a third candidate was only justified if there was something near to a dead heat and it looked as though a bitter conflict would ensue.[7]

The most significant part of this first diary entry on the 1965 Conservative leadership battle is Selwyn's statement that he had no intention of standing, '*at all events on the first round*'. Thus there was the tacit assumption that he had not ruled out the possibility of being drafted (after the manner of Bonar Law in November 1911) in the event of deadlock. As in 1975, however (when Heath was defeated by Margaret Thatcher), the issue was effectively to be settled at the first ballot. If Selwyn did not stand, this did not mean others of his generation would agree with Selwyn's view and stay on the sidelines:

> Peter Thorneycroft did not accept it and said that he was going to stand. When asked why, he said he thought he was a better man than either of the other two. He would, however, sleep on it. We left in due course and I went to the 400 with Christopher Soames and Willie Whitelaw to have bacon and eggs. I got home about half past two.[8]

Early on Friday 23 July Thorneycroft rang Selwyn and asked him to lunch. When he arrived at Westminster Susan Carter told him that the telephone had never stopped ringing with people asking what he thought, but above all trying to find out whether Selwyn intended to stand. Selwyn was now more concerned to prevent Thorneycroft from standing:

> I went to Peter's and he said that Julian and Christopher were also coming. I said that I had been thinking over his own position and I thought that he would make a great mistake if he stood. I did not think he would get more than a handful of votes and I begged him not to do it. Then Julian and Christopher arrived, followed by Quintin for whom an extra place was promptly set. Quintin had gone back to the House of Commons after our session the night before and romped about during the all-night sitting on the Judges' Remuneration Bill. I went out on to the balcony with Christopher and told him what I had said to Peter. He said that he thoroughly agreed. He had spoken to Harold Macmillan on the telephone that morning and Harold had said that he believed that the Party wanted one or other of Maudling or Heath. That was the type of person they wanted, the age they wanted and it was no use kicking against the pricks. It had to be one or the other. I said I agreed. We then went back to lunch where Peter stuck to his position that he thought he was better than either of them and he would probably stand. Quintin was rather silent. I had to leave to get down to Preston Crowmarsh. Peter came out to say goodbye and I told him again I thought he was making a most frightful mistake if he stood, certainly the first time.[9]

Ever since Macmillan had raised the possibility with him in 1960 – characteristically floating ideas before a colleague to gauge his reaction – Selwyn could have been excused for thinking of himself as a compromise Conservative leader, a Bonar Law who might emerge ahead of two more powerful and deadlocked rivals. A deeper sense of realism now prevailed on Selwyn's part, however, and in the event three candidates were nominated, Reginald Maudling, Edward Heath and Enoch Powell. The first ballot was fixed for 28 July. Public opinion polls showed 44 per cent favouring Maudling, 28 per cent Heath and only 3 per cent Powell. Opinion among Conservative MPs (the electorate that mattered) was much more closely divided between the two main contenders.

Selwyn spent the weekend at Preston Crowmarsh. On Sunday 25 July 'Anthony [Eden] and Clarissa came to lunch' but Eden's only comment on the succession was that he thought Home could have continued. He expressed no preference between Heath and Maudling. It was a busy day for Mrs Humphreys, Selwyn's house-keeper at Lower Farm House, as after the Avons had gone prep-arations were put in hand for the arrival of the Homes for tea and dinner. This time the conversation centred on the events of the week. 'Elizabeth was very angry that he had done it. She didn't think it at all necessary. I agreed with her. Alec was quite unmoved. We talked about the succession. He made it pretty clear that he himself was going to vote for Heath.'[10] Nominations closed on Monday 26 July and, as Selwyn noted, 'after the weekend it must have become clear to Peter Thorneycroft that there was no support for him and he announced that he was not standing.' The vote took place on 28 July (Selwyn's 61st birthday). 'I thought myself Maudling would lead Heath narrowly', wrote Selwyn. In fact it was to be the other way round and when the result was declared at 2.15 p.m. that day Heath had secured 150 votes, Maudling 133 (one of them Selwyn's) and Powell a mere 15. It was just an overall majority and though under the terms of the new rules Maudling could have gone on to a second ballot he 'withdrew gracefully and all was well'.[11]

With Sir Alec Douglas-Home's resignation of the post of Leader Selwyn's time as a figure of prominence within the Conservative Party came to an end. A new generation was moving into the positions of influence. Nevertheless he remained a member of the new Shadow Cabinet. Heath asked to see Selwyn at 10.30 a.m. on 4 August:

He asked me what I wanted to do. I said I would do whatever he wished. I had been against the leadership change for two principal reasons, one that I thought it would expose the Party to a charge of disloyalty, and secondly I thought there would be a bitter conflict for the succession. Owing to Alec's skill, the first had not happened, nor did I think it would, and he and Reggie had behaved so well that the second had not taken place.

Characteristically Selwyn did not mention the part he had played in discouraging Thorneycroft from standing.

I asked whether Reggie was going to do Foreign Affairs and he said no, he was going to be Deputy Leader. I said that in those circumstances I did not think there was any future as the Shadow Leader of the House. Alec had told me that had he had a reshuffle himself he might have asked me to take on Commonwealth Relations. This I would very much like to have done. I did not want to go to another department. However, I would quite understand if he didn't want me in the Shadow Cabinet. I would do everything I could to support him.[12]

Selwyn's preference for the Shadow Commonwealth portfolio was a natural one, arising out of his concern since the failure of the Common Market negotiations in January 1963 that steps must be taken to strengthen Commonwealth links. That evening, while at a cocktail party with the Victor Goodhews, Selwyn received a message that Heath wished to see him again. Heath told him that in the light of the political situation – a possible devaluation, the probability of an election within 12 months – he had decided to make no changes in the composition of the Shadow Cabinet but that there would be a general redistribution of portfolios. 'This did not mean that he might not later on ask some of the older ones to make way. He would like me to do Commonwealth Relations. That suggestion of course would involve no commitment if we won the Election and were to form a Government. I said I quite understood that and would be very pleased to do what he wanted.'[13] Selwyn was under no illusions about the implications of this conversation. He was an elder statesman figure who was being kept on in the short-term. After a General Election, win or lose, there would be no place for him. But his sights were no longer fixed on a place in a future Conservative Cabinet, unless it were the unlikely eventuality of the Lord Chancellorship. As a former Leader of the House of Commons his thoughts were already turning to the Speakership.[14]

After the 1964 Election Selwyn had been reappointed a non-executive director of the Rank Organisation. He had great respect for John Davis, the Chairman, and Rank for their part found Selwyn a good judge of the commercial possibilities of a film. John Davis liked people from different walks of life on the board and appreciated

Selwyn's insights into possible developments under a Labour government. Selwyn also renewed his ties with the Sun Alliance and London Insurance Ltd. He joined the English & Caledonian Investment Co. Ltd and later was to be taken on to the board of the construction company IDC Group Ltd by Howard Hicks. Selwyn had never been a man of independent wealth (one thing that annoyed him was repeated requests from much wealthier colleagues for contributions to worthy causes as for him charity was a process of doing, not donating) and these business links helped him maintain his London flat, his Hoylake constituency base and Preston Crowmarsh, increasingly the centre of his social activities. The autumn of 1965 was a relaxed, happy time. S'Agaro had worked its usual restorative power, Joanna was about to start at Sherborne School for Girls and, most memorably of all, Mrs Macdona, his stalwart supporter in the Wirral, had celebrated her 100th birthday on 4 September, an occasion which Selwyn ensured was marked by the traditional congratulatory telegram from Buckingham Palace. As Commonwealth Affairs spokesman for the Opposition he had a tour arranged for December, but before Selwyn could leave on this assignment white Rhodesia had declared UDI and the major non-domestic crisis of the first Wilson government was at hand.

Since the granting of independence to Nigeria in 1960 the retreat from colonisation had gathered pace, a process in which Selwyn had been involved with independence for Cyprus in 1961. It was in the early 1960s that the character of the new Commonwealth was established with Sierra Leone, Tanganyika, Jamaica, Trinidad, Uganda, Kenya, Zambia, Zanzibar, Malawi and Malta all being granted independence. In 1965 Gambia and Singapore were added to the list. The problems of Southern Rhodesia had been left to the end, largely because they were so intractable. A white population of 270,000 was determined that the winds of change, wherever else they might blow in Africa, would not disturb their political hegemony. The Rhodesian Front Party of Ian Smith won a massive victory when elections were held in May 1965, the culmination of a period which had seen the banning in 1964 of ZAPU (the Zimbabwe African People's Union) and ZANU (the Zimbabwe African National Union) by the Rhodesian Front, a visit to Rhodesia by the Commonwealth Secretary, Arthur (later Lord) Bottomley, in February 1965 which brought no progress and the issuing of a White Paper in April by the Rhodesian Government putting forward arguments for independence. The Rhodesian situation produced problems not only for the Labour Government, but also for the Conservative Opposition. Although the Labour Party was divided between those who wished to use force against Ian Smith if he declared UDI and those who favoured sanctions, the Conservative Party faced a three way split. On 17 October 1965 despite the official line being that the Conservatives should abstain (which the central body of the party did) on the issue of the imposition of oil sanctions and the blockading of the port of Beira in Mozambique, fifty right-wing Conservatives voted against sanctions while thirty-one figures on the left of the party, including one of Selwyn's Shadow Commonwealth team, Nigel Fisher, voted with the Wilson government. In November Ian Smith declared UDI.

This was the background to Selwyn's controversial tour in February 1966. By comparison the tour of New Zealand and Australia at the end of 1965 had been a social reunion with figures such as Robert Menzies and Richard Casey. On 10 December 1965 Selwyn had twice been recognised in Auckland, firstly on account of his Hawks Club tie from Cambridge days and then, as Jonathan Aitken wrote in his diary:

> Whilst standing in the street a man came up and said, 'I remember you, you were on the Hoylake Urban District Council a few years ago.' Selwyn, who was indeed on the Hoylake District Council, but has done one or two things since, was delighted to be recognised in this way in an Auckland street.[15]

The question of whether Selwyn should visit Rhodesia had been discussed by the Shadow Cabinet on 2 February 1966. In its favour Selwyn believed it would 'bring the Opposition into the game, copying Wilson's tactics in 64, it would please many of our supporters to feel that we were taking an initiative, it would comfort moderate White Rhodesians who feel abandoned. It would be an important point of contact with Smith, we might get credit, avoid trouble with Parliamentary Party.' On the other hand, he was keenly aware of the disadvantages – 'negotiating behind W's back, misinterpreted in other countries, incidents during visit?, anything that went wrong could be blamed on us by Govt.'[16] Selwyn had been briefed by Wilson on the position on 10 October 1965 after the breakdown of talks between the British government and the Rhodesian front and both he and Heath had met Ian Smith for talks the following day.[17] Pressure had been building up in the Conservative Party (although for different motives) for the Opposition to take some action. Although he was aware of the delicacy of the situation, Selwyn decided (with the backing of the Shadow Cabinet) that on balance it would be beneficial if he undertook a fact-finding mission. Arthur Bottomley immediately criticised Selwyn's action, returning to the attack in a speech on

12 February 1966 while Selwyn was still in Africa. 'I told Selwyn Lloyd before he went that I thought his visit was ill advised', he said. 'A Privy Councillor, Shadow Commonwealth Secretary, has been photographed being met officially at the Salisbury Airport by a member of the illegal Government. This sort of thing can only weaken Britain's position.'[18]

Selwyn had arrived in Salisbury at 10 p.m. on Monday 7 February, accompanied by Jonathan Aitken and John Chichester, a valued mainstay of Selwyn's secretariat in these years, their air tickets made out in the unlikely names of Messrs Bond, Loin and Groin.[19] They were met at the airport by the Minister of Information, P. K. Van Der Byl, and any thoughts the Smith regime may have had that the Shadow Commonweath Secretary was coming out to Rhodesia to offer comfort were soon removed.

> Van Der Byl was quick to offer Selwyn a government car, but since the Conservative Party doesn't recognise the Smith regime, we could hardly have Selwyn whistling around in one of the Smith regime's cars as soon as he arrived. Selwyn turned this down. P. K. Van Der Byl then said, 'You won't want to see anyone in detention, will you?' knowing perfectly well that Selwyn would, of course, want to see Nkomo and Sithole, and Selwyn said, 'I want to see everybody I can', at which point Van Der Byl stalked out of the airport lounge.[20]

Selwyn stayed at Meikles Hotel, from where he was in constant telecommunication with Edward Heath. As agreed in London, Selwyn was scrupulous in turning down any 'official' hospitality in Rhodesia. 'I have refused Dupont's invitation to what is clearly an official cocktail party tomorrow, but am lunching with him privately on Saturday', he telegraphed to Heath on 8 February.[21] His first call was a three hour visit to the Queen's representative, Sir Humphrey Gibbs, at Government House (all telephonic communication had been cut off since UDI). Selwyn was given a first-hand briefing on the situation, the most important point being that sanctions were not working, and if anything were stiffening the resolve of the white Rhodesians. In the next few days Selwyn saw 327 people, 60 of them Africans, and 6 ministers including Lardner Burke, the Justice Minister. He had 34 meetings on 8 February alone. On 9 February he had the first of three meetings with Ian Smith. This was the most substantive and yet for Selwyn the most depressing of all his meetings in Rhodesia.

Selwyn began with a request to visit Nkomo and Sithole. If this request was not granted back in England he would be accused of failing to take representative soundings while in Rhodesia. He received the impression that Smith would make the visit possible, though there might be difficulties with the security people. Selwyn pointed out that the Conservative Party's position on Rhodesia should not be gauged by the unrepresentative group of MPs who had visited Rhodesia so far. He further stressed that an insistence that any negotiations with Britain must start from the position that Rhodesia was independent was a recipe for stalemate. In that case the vast majority of Conservative MPs would in fact support Wilson's position. Smith insisted that he did not need 'recognition' as a prerequisite for talks and agreed that Selwyn might quote him on that on his return to Britain. After discussion of the possibility of negotiation through intermediaries and the position of Zambia, the talks moved on to sanctions. Although Smith felt in the short-term that Rhodesia could survive sanctions, he agreed with Selwyn that in the longer term they would lead to slow ruin. Smith discounted the use of force against him (not in this case a miscalculation like Nasser's in 1956) on the grounds that the British public would not tolerate it, and British troops would not actually attack Rhodesians. Selwyn urged Smith not to declare a republic. Smith said that Rhodesia was a very loyal country and he had no intention of so doing. Apart from anything else it would alienate countries like Australia and New Zealand, which he claimed were very sympathetic towards Rhodesia. At this point, after 45 minutes of general talk, Selwyn asked for a final session in private. This lasted a further 25 minutes, during which Smith said he wished to root out the more racialist members of the Rhodesian Front Party after independence had been settled and that he was prepared to make more concessions to get that independence.[22]

At further meetings with farmers, clergy, business men, shop-keepers, social workers and trade unionists Selwyn emphasised that a white minority could not for ever rule a black majority many times its size and that if the different races were to co-exist there must be an end to racial discrimination. At one 'tragic and sad meeting' with Rhodesian Front supporters 'Selwyn was almost weeping as he left the room.'[23] Obloquy was heaped on him from both sides of the political divide. The most difficult meeting (with a background of civil unrest reminiscent of his Middle East tours in the 1950s) was in Zambia on 16 February with President Kaunda. Seated in a bright red plastic chair, Kaunda harangued Selwyn about Conservative Party attitudes. Selwyn did his best to point out that fifty right-wing backbenchers did not constitute a majority in the Conservative Party.[24] Selwyn reported back to Heath the resentment in Black

African countries at the alleged pro-Smith line of the Conservative party, adding:

> Sanctions are biting, unemployment is increasing, there are definite signs of an exodus (of the white population) although this is only a trickle so far. Any idea that all this will be a quick process is illusory. The Governor and the High Commission are misinforming H.M.G. Although there will be a progressive decline in the economy it will be many months, perhaps years, before anything like an economic collapse will take place.

In conclusion, Selwyn felt that his visit was 'doing quite a lot of good out here in letting everyone of every sort and kind of opinion blow off steam.' How long his visit should continue was another matter. 'I am certain that we were right in the timing of my visit, but if Wilson is not going to have a general election, I should be disposed to let my stay drag on a bit.'[25]

Although a General Election was called shortly afterwards for 31 March 1966, it was the sense of stalemate that brought Selwyn's Rhodesia visit to its end. On his return he prepared a Confidential Report on the situation. He was intensely depressed by it. The Governor's position, as the Queen's representative, he found very sad, dishonoured as he was by the wealthy white people on whom sanctions were having little impact. Neither side could win. Therefore he felt there must be talks without prior conditions on either side. Yet his trip was of value. Back in London there were two irreconcilable views. At the extremes some said, 'Hang the traitors', others, 'Support our kith and kin'. Selwyn's visit brought the Conservative Party a deeper understanding of what the entrenched positions were. It led the way to a dialogue on very real problems, even preparing the way for the possibility of the talks on HMS *Tiger* in December 1966. The quality of advice being given to the Commonwealth Office was variable; Selwyn was the first figure of the appropriate seniority to apply himself directly to the problem and, as such, served as a bridge-builder with Wilson, Bottomley and George (later Lord) Thomson, Minister of State at the Foreign Office. But it was not the happiest of assignments on which to end his period as Shadow Commonwealth spokesman.

The General Election of 31 March 1966 vied with that of 26 May 1955 as the most uneventful of the century. The result was seen as a foregone conclusion, part two of the 1964 campaign, and it was a low-key contest. For the only time in his career, such was the swing to

Labour throughout the country, Selwyn failed to win an overall majority in the Wirral. The figures were:

Lloyd, J. S. B. (Conservative)	31,477
Hunt, D. U. (Labour)	21,624
Williams, P. H. (Liberal)	12,313
Majority	9,853

Nationally the Labour Party was returned with a majority of nearly a hundred, only the second occasion in its history that it had achieved power as distinct from office. It seemed that Harold Wilson was well on his way to making Labour 'the natural governing party'. Despite his defeat, Heath's position as Conservative leader was in no danger, but it was the end of the parliamentary road for many of his party. Selwyn had never been at ease in Heath's Shadow Cabinet and did not falter in his opinion that Maudling would have made a better leader. He did not wish to spend a full Parliament shadowing some uncongenial portfolio and had the political instinct to realise that Heath would probably not have wished him to continue in any case. He therefore wrote the following letter to Heath on 12 April:

My dear Ted,

As you have known for some time, I would prefer you not to consider me for a place in your new Shadow Cabinet.

According to the probabilities, we shall be in Opposition for the period of a normal Parliament. I feel that over the next four or five years I can help the Party better if I am freed from the routine duties of a Shadow Minister.

I want to be free to intervene in debates on a variety of topics outside the range of a single Department, and I can do that much more easily from the backbenches.

I also want to have time to consider problems of Party organisation, particularly in the North West, and of contact with sections of the electorate whose support we seem to have lost.[26]

In the last sentence of Selwyn's letter lay the eventual key to electoral success in 1970, the gains in that area tipping the balance to Conservative victory. Heath lunched at Preston Crowmarsh on 17 April and it was agreed that Selwyn would not be given another portfolio.

Selwyn was now able to devote more time to his growing concern for charitable organisations, one of the main threads of the last decade of his life. From 1964 he had been Chairman of the Advisory Council of Task Force, a London based organisation in which 12,000 young volunteers helped the old, the lonely and the physically handicapped. When the Young Volunteer Force Foundation grew out of Task Force in 1970 to extend such work on a national basis Selwyn became involved as Chairman. The list of his commitments was extensive. He was Patron of the Home Farm Trust, which provided lifelong care for the mentally handicapped, and of the Methodist Homes for the Aged. He was particularly active in the Wirral with the Wirral Associated Schools Project (WASP) and Wirral Action. He was President of the Abbeyfield Hoylake and West Kirby Society (in October 1971, 32 Queen's Road became the 500th Abbeyfield home in Britain), working with George Eustance, a former schoolmaster and now an assiduous worker in the Wirral in many social fields. The last Abbeyfield home he opened in Meols Drive, West Kirby was named Selwyn Lloyd House in December 1977. Such charitable concern was, like so many other aspects of his personality, the direct product of the example of his parents in childhood, so that there was a coming together of an Edwardian upbringing with the idealism of 1960s youth, 'Kennedy and all that', as one of his helpers put it.

His work brought him into contact with two energetic members of the younger generation, Anthony Steen, a barrister and later successor to John Tilney as MP for Wavertree, and Christopher Spence, director of the Young Volunteer Force Foundation and later founder of the London Lighthouse Hospice. Both had been guiding lights in the establishment of Task Force, the origins of which lay in a 'fundless, nameless and committeeless'[27] organisation that was concerned with youth club groups giving practical assistance to the elderly. What appealed to Selwyn was the combination of Self Help and the intermixing of the generations in supportive local communities. Selwyn, conscious of his waistline after years, as he put it, of dining for his country, joined enthusiastically in sponsored walks, and it was on one such walk that he first met Christopher Spence, who was to become his personal assistant when he was Speaker of the House of Commons.

The Young Volunteer Force Foundation was announced by Denis Howell, Under-Secretary at the Department of Education and Science, on 14 November 1967 with Selwyn Lloyd, Douglas Houghton and Jo Grimond as the three trustees. Despite the tripartite nature of this trusteeship, the Young Volunteer Force Foundation aroused some political suspicion. Lord Longford even felt it was a question of 'Blues under the bed' to capture the idealistic young. Other charitable organisations also felt that the three-year government grant would inevitably mean a reduction of the available 'cake' elsewhere. The three trustees ensured that the Young Volunteer

Force Foundation was depoliticised, though Selwyn delighted at the implied cocking of the snook at the official welfare state, mischievously enjoying the criticism of figures like Lord Longford. Selwyn's trusteeship came at just the right moment for him, giving a new direction and platform of responsibility when other doors were closing. The zest of the new generation appealed to him too and the student world in which he increasingly mixed was a nostalgic reminder of 17 Magdalene Street and the days when the world was young.

Another reminder of the past was the death of Megan Lloyd George on 14 May 1966. Selwyn was prominent among the public figures who paid tribute to her mercurial genius. Memories of Criccieth and Macclesfield were evoked, as they were in 1969 when he attended the Investiture of the Prince of Wales and when Olwen Carey Evans was created a DBE. Selwyn was one of the guests at the celebrations. 'I admired your father, I loved your mother and was very fond of Megan and Gwilym, and our paths crossed constantly', he wrote to Dame Olwen on 19 November. 'The warm friendship of your family has been a big element in my life.'[28] As the 25th anniversary of Lloyd George's death approached, Selwyn was the prime mover, together with the Liberal leader Jeremy Thorpe and the Secretary of State for Wales, George Thomas (later Viscount Tonypandy), in commissioning a memorial plaque designed by Clough Williams-Ellis in Welsh slate for Westminster Abbey. When the plaque was unveiled on 27 July 1970 Selwyn officially represented the Conservative Party, but it was an important part of his own past that he was representing also.[29]

The death of Mrs Macdona on 17 September 1969 at the age of 104 also removed from Selwyn's life one of its important influences. From the time that Mrs Macdona had been a major influence in the selection Committee that had chosen Selwyn as candidate for the Wirral division in 1945 her presence had been one of the threads running through his local constituency base. As promised some fourteen years earlier Mrs Macdona left Hilbre House to Selwyn in her will. Over the next eighteen months much of Selwyn's time was taken up with converting this handsome, but inevitably rather run down Victorian house with its castellations, dark panelling and stained glass memorial windows to champion St Bernard dogs into a modern, manageable residence. A swimming pool, of course, was a high priority, but so was security since the wide lawns ran down to the sea wall. Arthur and Marilyn Roberts, and later Sgt W. S. Golding, a retired police inspector, and his wife were engaged as resident housekeepers and both couples became loyal members of Selwyn's Wirral base. It was at this time too that, after an interim succession of

RAF couples from the nearby air base at Benson (one of whom had served, to Selwyn's mortification, brightly coloured cupcakes in their 'Co-op' wrapping to Lord Home one tea-time), Selwyn engaged Jill Pinsent (later Mrs Hugh Scurfield) as housekeeper at Lower Farm House. Jill Pinsent, with her daughter Sukie, was to be of the family until the end. Gardening and golf occupied his leisure time. As a gardener Selwyn worked with indiscriminate fervour, chopping and hacking with Gladstonian energy. In 1969 he was elected Captain of the Royal Liverpool Golf Club in its centenary year. The links at Hoylake had been part of his life since childhood and 1969 was a very special year of which a highlight was the staging of the Amateur Championship. In the final the eventual winner, Michael Bonallack, hooked a shot from the 4th tee and for a time it looked as though he would lose the hole. Even though he had not seen the teeshot Selwyn was able to walk straight to the spot where the ball would have landed.

Selwyn's gradual assumption of the role of elder statesman was emphasised during the years of the Labour governments by two official roles he was asked to undertake. In 1967 he became a member of the Committee of Privy Councillors on D-Notice Matters,* presided over by Lord Radcliffe (the original chairman of what became the Beveridge inquiry into broadcasting), together with Emanuel Shinwell. In 1969 he was a member of the Royal Commission on the Constitution under Lord Crowther. The D-Notice inquiry arose out of an article by Chapman Pincher, published in the *Daily Express* on 21 February, entitled 'Cable Vetting Sensation' and the allegation by the Prime Minister that the *Daily Express* had thus contravened a D-Notice concerning the examination of overseas telegrams. The Committee was appointed on 28 February and held its first meeting on 9 March, taking oral evidence throughout the rest of March and the early part of April. When the Committee reported in June† they assumed that their conclusion that there was no substance in the Prime Minister's allegations would, although unpalatable, be accepted by the government. Had the Committee realised that the government were going to reject their conclusion, with the publication of a White Paper,‡ they would have strengthened the language in

---

* A D-Notice is a request by the Joint Services, Press and Broadcasting Committee of the House of Commons to journalists to refrain from publishing matters concerning national security.

† *D-Notice Matters: Report of the Committee of Inquiry*, Cmnd 3309.

‡ *The D-Notice System: Presented to Parliament by the Prime Minister*, Cmnd 3312. ('Every dog is allowed one bite', said Harold Wilson on 2 March 1967, in what became known as the 'Dog Licence' speech.)

which their report was printed. In the debate on 22 June, Selwyn teasingly said, 'I did not particularly want to be a member of this Committee. It involved the Prime Minister describing me as an elder statesman and thereby ruining my chances of a modest position in the next administration. (Hon. Members: No.)'[30] Nevertheless Selwyn believed that the Committee's conclusions were right, as he told the House and later wrote in his diary on 3 January 1968:

> The D notice enquiry was great fun: Radcliffe was charming and Shinwell in this sort of situation if handled properly is good.
>
> We did not like Colonel Lohan* at all and on every issue of fact were reasonably certain that Chapman Pincher's version was to be preferred.
>
> What amazed us was the Government did not accept our report. It was mild, exonerated the Express from the deliberate breach, was not too unkind to Lohan or the Foreign Office, and made some modest recommendations for improvement in the system. Wilson turned us down. I cannot think why.[31]

The Royal Commission on the Constitution, set up on 15 April 1969, was a more substantial affair altogether. The first meeting (there were to be 163) was a fortnight later and public sessions were held in Edinburgh, Glasgow, Cardiff, Aberystwyth, Belfast, the Isle of Man and the Channel Islands. The Royal Commission was born out of the fear by the Labour Party of the advance of the Scottish Nationalists. The 'onlie begetter' was thus Mrs Winifred Ewing, the Scottish National Party victor at the Hamilton by-election on 2 November 1967. Harold Wilson wished to defuse the situation before the General Election, then expected in 1971. The Conservative victory in June 1970 rather took the steam out of the Commission, together with the untimely death of Lord Crowther. Though Selwyn gave up his membership of the Commission when he became Speaker – he was replaced by Sir David Renton in April 1971 – he was there during the operative part of the Commission. The London meetings were held in Kingsway, with weekend meetings at Trust House Hotels (Crowther as Chairman of Trust Houses was involved at the time with the – unsuccessful – attempt to fend off a take-over by Sir Charles Forte), and interim reports were issued on Northern Ireland and the working model for Stormont. The Commission also considered whether administrative devolution was satisfactory and whether legislative devolution, with its inevitable proliferation of policies should be contemplated. Selwyn worked conscientiously

* Secretary of the D-Notice Committee.

and enjoyed the companionship (one of his fellow Commission members was Douglas Houghton, a co-trustee of the Young Volunteer Force Foundation), but was never seduced into believing, like some members of the Commission, that it was anything but the shadow and not the substance of political power. Like the Public Schools Commission of 1966 it was essentially a political pigeonhole.

When the *Liverpool Echo* reported in a profile on 13 August 1968 that 'Selwyn Lloyd does seem slightly sad and solitary'[32] it was an accurate assessment. He continued to pay foreign visits – to Israel in 1967 and to South Africa in 1969 ('uncompromising talk with Vorster');[33] he became involved in campaigns for the Repeal of the new Selective Employment Tax (becoming Chairman of the Committee); he formed the North-West Industrialists' Council; Heath asked him to be Chairman of a Party Policy Group for the North-West Area ('I am the modern Lord Derby', he said, after completing 100 fund-raising meetings); he took up the cause of electoral reform, advocating a four-year term to Parliaments in a speech at Eastbourne in December 1968,[34] and he did much to help financially in the restoration of John Wesley's City Road Chapel. But he missed the cut and thrust of politics at the highest level as he wrote in his diary at the beginning of 1968:

> My activities are as follows:
>
> House of Commons – leading our side on the select Committee on Procedure – rather a bore – but helpful to Willie Whitelaw, and, with Crossman as Leader of the House, the consideration of the Reports is quite exciting. I am also still on the Select Committee on the Services of the House, and Chairman of the Sub Committee on Administration and accommodation.
>
> This is also rather a bore – I do it as a former leader of the House – and again to be helpful to W Whitelaw. To pretend that I only do these two jobs to help W.W. is pretty bogus – I also do them to keep in the swim of things, but whether it is worth the effort is another matter.
>
> Some say that they are too housemaidish jobs for an ex Foreign S & Chancellor of the E. Yes, but they are what a former Leader of the House should do, and that is the only job which I can see any possibility of my being offered if we win next time.[35]

However, at this time he did begin to talk over the possibility of two other posts with his friends. He felt that the Lord Chancellorship would lie between himself and Quintin Hogg if the Conservatives returned to power and as he believed that the office had become a Ministry of Justice demanding no outstanding up-to-the-minute legal knowledge there was no reason he should be disqualified. But realistically he felt that the 'other' Speakership was a greater possibility (part of the reason for his galley years on the Select Committee on the Services of the House and the like) and when he had lunched with Lord Gardiner and heard of the appallingly onerous duties of a present-day Lord Chancellor his thoughts increasingly turned to the Speakership of the House of Commons. He felt that a vigorous Speaker could carry out much necessary reform of parliamentary procedure. For the time being he kept his nose to the grindstone of North West Area constituency work. At times he wondered whether it was all worth it, but concluded that:

> the trouble with our party is that leaders are S.E. based (a) Heath, Maudling, Macleod, and (b) those with constituencies away from London are in fact Londoners, Joseph, Boyle . . . The only real provincials are Alec Douglas-Home & myself . . . therefore it is important that someone should make an effort.

He was also honest enough to face up to the realities:

> Am I exercising the influence I ought to be?
> The answer is probably a lesson – a backbencher however senior and experienced cannot do much.[36]

In January 1970 the Conservative Shadow Cabinet met for a weekend conference at the Selsdon Park Hotel in Croydon. Various advisers, though not Selwyn, were called in to give their opinions on policy in the run-up to the next General Election. At this time Selwyn said to Aubrey Jones, Chairman of the Prices and Incomes Board, that if he got the chance, 'Do impress upon Ted Heath the importance of an incomes policy because I don't think he's sound on it.' Although the Selsdon conference brought a commitment to end the new Selective Employment Tax, Selwyn was less happy about other proposals which signified a shift to the right in policy. 'Selsdon man' was not Wirral man.

The opportunity to put these new policies to the electorate came sooner than the Conservatives expected. On 18 May 1970, exuding confidence as he spoke to Hardiman Scott in the garden of 10 Downing Street, and buoyed up by the recent opinion polls, Harold Wilson explained his decision to call a General Election for 18 June. The resulting Conservative victory was the biggest electoral upset since Harry S. Truman had defeated Governor Dewey in the American Presidential Election in 1948. Selwyn Lloyd's pessimism, endemic at election times, was confounded. He increased his majority in the Wirral, the figures being:

Lloyd, J. S. B. (Conservative)	38,655
Paterson, R. G. (Labour)	22,197
Jones, Miss G. (Liberal)	9,276
Majority	16,458

Nationally the Conservatives gained 74 seats and there was a swing to them of 4.7 per cent, the only occasion since 1945 when a large majority for one Party has been turned into a workable majority for another in one General Election. Psephologists have never satisfactorily explained the unexpected result (England's defeat in the World Cup by West Germany the Sunday evening before polling, unfavourable trade figures at the beginning of the week, and the industrial holiday fortnights in many crucial northern constituencies have all been cited as contributory factors)[37] but one of the most significant contributions came with the ten victories in the North West, where Selwyn had worked so assiduously since he had left the Shadow Cabinet in April 1966. 'How pleased you must be with the North West', wrote Edward Heath to Selwyn on 24 June, 'so much due to you.'[38] Despite this mark of his leader's approval, Selwyn did not expect a job in the new administration (there was a far greater sense of continuity in the new Cabinet than at the changes of government in 1964, 1974 and 1979, fifteen of the seventeen members of the Consultative Committee of 1969–70 being appointed to Cabinet)[39] and was not overly disappointed when one was not offered.

Far more despondent was a colleague of whom Selwyn now saw a great deal, George Thomas, the former Labour Secretary of State for Wales. 'Overnight I lost 200 castles and a car', said George Thomas to Selwyn, as they shared a taxi in the early days of the Heath government. George Thomas had decided that this would be his last Parliament. 'It will be mine too', said Selwyn before offering a piece of shrewd advice. 'But don't tell anyone until the end of the Parliament, otherwise you will be politically dead.'[40] Little did either of them realise that the Parliament elected in June 1970 would not be their last and that in the course of the next decade they would become even closer colleagues and two of the best known of all Westminster figures to the wider and larger non-political public.

15

Mr Speaker

In July 1970 Selwyn Lloyd had been a Member of Parliament for twenty-five years. Together with others of the 1945 intake – John Boyd-Carpenter, Douglas Dodds-Parker, Vere Harvey, Harry Legge-Bourke and Ernest Marples – he attended a private dinner to mark this silver jubilee.[1] Of all the Conservatives who had first entered Parliament after the war, Selwyn had achieved the highest offices, but now as he sat down by the fire of memory with his contemporaries the senior positions in Heath's government were being filled by members of the famous class of 1950. Iain Macleod was the new Chancellor of the Exchequer and Reginald Maudling was Home Secretary, although there was no place for Enoch Powell after his 'River Tiber' speech to a Conservative Political Centre meeting in Birmingham on 21 April 1968. Selwyn's main interest in the Cabinet list was in the promotion of Anthony Barber (to Chancellor of the Duchy of Lancaster, with special responsibility for Europe) and Peter Walker (to the Ministry of Housing and Local Government). He had had his part in giving both men their opportunity and he had high hopes of them. Of his own prospects he was less sanguine. With Quintin Hogg (now re-ennobled as Lord Hailsham) on the Woolsack, everything hinged on Horace King's intentions as Speaker.

Politics, however, has a habit of throwing up the unexpected. In the week of the twenty-fifth anniversary of the 1945 General Election Iain Macleod suddenly died. From this grievous blow it could be argued that the Heath government, almost before it had started, never fully recovered. At the beginning of four of the stormiest years in post-war politics (which in economic terms were to prove even more contentious than when Selwyn was Chancellor) an experienced hand had been removed from the tiller. Not only did Macleod's untimely death leave a void in Cabinet, but the subsequent reshuffle (the first of two in 1970) upset the careful balance of the government.

Heath chose Barber to replace Macleod at the Treasury. Selwyn wrote to Barber at once. 'You know what it is to serve under a thoroughly unpopular Chancellor!' Selwyn said that, although he lamented the circumstances of Barber's appointment, he wished him the greatest success and hoped that he would remember the lessons of shrewd fiscal management he had learned in his earlier incarnation at the Treasury as one of the 'Heavenly Twins'.[2] In this he was to be disappointed. Selwyn watched more approvingly as Peter Walker became head of the new Environment Ministry and then in 1972 of Trade and Industry.

In the autumn of 1970 Horace King announced that he wished to step down as Speaker in January 1971 after a Commonwealth Speakers' Conference in India. Selwyn was mentioned as a possible successor in the *Sunday Express* before King's announcement and in the spring of 1970 Sir Vere Harvey, Chairman of the 1922 Committee, asked Selwyn if he would like to be Speaker. The Conservative victory at the General Election in June 1970 increased the probability that Selwyn would stand and would prove a strong, if not overwhelming candidate. Although he made the customary noises about it never having crossed his mind, the situation was not quite so straightforward. Selwyn was not an overly calculating politician, but in this case he was not entirely candid in his initial response. For some years now it had been a case of *respice finem*.* The truth is that Selwyn wanted to become Speaker very much. Unfortunately for Selwyn, Vere Harvey was not a dispenser of patronage but a conscientious sounder out of opinion. In March 1970 he put the same question to John Boyd-Carpenter. To both men it seemed like a tentative offer. After Horace King had decided to retire the Conservative Party managers had to face up to the fact that there were two potential Speakers waiting in the wings, neither of whom at that stage was aware of the approach to the other. The fact that Boyd-Carpenter had already stood down for Selwyn once in October 1963 over the Leadership of the House added to the delicacy of the situation. As it became known that Selwyn was a candidate there was an undercurrent of opposition. Although previous Speakers had from time to time been former Ministers (Sir Harry Hylton-Foster, King's predecessor, had gone straight from office as Solicitor-General to the Chair) there was a feeling in the House, vigorously expressed by the Liberal MP John Pardoe at the time of Selwyn's contested election, that a backbencher could best represent the interests of ordinary members. (In practice this was an unwarranted reservation about

* 'Look to the end.' Selwyn often employed such Latin tags.

Selwyn, who was as assiduous as Speaker in protecting the rights of minorities as he had been when he was Leader of the House.) Of more weight in the scales against him was the argument that he had held the highest offices and at times of acute controversy. The former Suez Foreign Secretary was not the same as an ex-Solicitor General. A third reservation was that he had not been Deputy Speaker or Chairman of the Ways and Means Committee as Horace King had been. But there were other qualities required for a Speaker. When Delane, the editor of *The Times*, was consulted by Palmerston on the essential qualifications for a Speaker he said they must include: 'imperturbable good temper, tact, patience and urbanity, a previous legal training, the possession of innate gentlemanly feelings which involuntarily command respect and deference, and personal dignity in voice and manner.' There were many who felt that Selwyn possessed exactly those qualities.[3]

The way to Speaker's House was not to be an easy one. On 23 June 1970 the Lord President of the Council, William Whitelaw, lunched with Boyd-Carpenter at the Carlton Club and put again, though in more official terms, Vere Harvey's original question. At a later meeting, having taken soundings among his friends, Boyd-Carpenter said that he had heard that Selwyn Lloyd was also in the running for the Speakership. Whitelaw told him that this was not the case. The lack of a wife (though this was not to be a disqualification in the case of George Thomas) would be a handicap and in any case Selwyn was about to be offered another post shortly which, if accepted, would clearly disqualify him. There the matter rested until Selwyn declined the post offered to him. After this everything was back in the melting pot again.[4] This post was the Washington Embassy. There were several precedents for such an offer to a former Foreign Secretary or Chancellor. In September 1919 Viscount Grey of Fallodon went on a special ambassadorial mission to Washington. In 1941 Lord Halifax became Ambassador in Washington at a crucial period in Anglo-American relations and was to enjoy an historic success. A more telling parallel was that in May 1923 when Stanley Baldwin offered Austen Chamberlain the Washington Embassy and there was a stormy meeting between the two men at Chequers. Austen Chamberlain was unwilling to go to Washington and so was Selwyn. In both cases a senior figure would have been removed from the front line of domestic politics. It was not a job with which Selwyn would have been at ease and, in any case, he felt it was properly a job for a career diplomat and not some kind of compensation at the end of a political career. With one of the more piquant ironies of recent years, Mrs Thatcher was to offer the Washington Embassy to Edward

Heath in 1979, an offer that was similarly declined, as Heath had
made it perfectly clear in his own constituency after his re-election
there that he wished to remain in the House of Commons.

Selwyn's refusal to go to Washington put the Conservative managers in a quandary. In November 1970 Horace King formally
announced that he was going and on 1 December Boyd-Carpenter
sought a further meeting with William Whitelaw to see how the land
lay. He was now told that the choice was between Selwyn and himself,
not what he had been led to believe at the Carlton Club lunch in the
summer. Two factors had tipped the balance towards Selwyn. The
first was the support he had in Cabinet from Alec Home (on 10
December Whitelaw told Boyd-Carpenter that the Cabinet's choice
was Selwyn) and the second was the attitude of the Shadow Cabinet,
who had voted 12–8 in favour of Selwyn.[5] At this stage the unknown
factor was how the backbenchers would react. Selwyn was soon left in
no doubt about the virulence of the opposition to him in certain
quarters by a letter he received from Sir Brandon Rhys Williams,
Conservative MP for Kensington South. Selwyn wrote to Whitelaw
on 2 December:

> My dear Willie,
> I am getting a little disturbed as to the way the Speakership issue
> is going. Too many people seem to be going round saying 'Selwyn
> does not really want it', 'He would be too lonely' etc.
> I want to make it quite clear that if offered the job, I will gladly
> accept it. I have been into the financial and living arrangements. I
> am completely satisfied with what I have been told about them.
> Therefore the position is this. I definitely would like the job. I
> think there is a job to be done which I would like to try to do.
> As to age, my Dr. tells me that I have the blood pressure, heart
> condition and arteries of someone 20 years younger than my age
> (famous last words!!)
>
> Yours ever,
> Selwyn.[6]

Selwyn was now very pessimistic about his prospects and told
Geoffrey Hardy-Roberts early in December that he was out of the
running. Privately he put the contested Speakership on a par with his
divorce and his sacking as a time of personal unhappiness. But he was
unaware that the tide was flowing in his favour. On 17 December he
met Nigel Fisher to give him his recollections of Iain Macleod for
Fisher's forthcoming biography. Later that day Fisher wrote to
Selwyn, thanking him for his help over the biography and saying that

he would do all he could to ensure that there were no hiccups on the Conservative side about the Speakership:

> The matter was discussed in the 1922 Executive and in the main Committee. The *large majority* view was that a public contest between two members of our own Party on the floor of the House *must* be avoided. And that therefore your nomination should receive the unanimous support of the Tory Party. This is being conveyed to the Whips, & I think & hope the crisis is now over.[7]

Yet one of the things that weighed with backbenchers (particularly on the Labour side) when the question of the Speakership came up was how Selwyn had not been found wanting in the test of character he had faced after 13 July 1962. There was a general feeling that he had been badly done by. This is not to say that Selwyn acquired the Speakership as a compensation for bad luck (as was the case with Rab Butler and the Foreign Office in October 1963), but there was a combination of sympathy and a feeling that he could cope. The old Tories, like the middle class, were great ones for guilt and they always felt rather guilty about Selwyn, 'poor Selwyn' as they referred to him. Selwyn had drawn the short straw twice – in 1956 and 1962 – and had smothered the hurts, but never turned against the hand that 'bit' him. As a potential Speaker he therefore had a character that commended itself. The Speakership is a curiously mysterious role. Stoicism was what clinched it for him.

It was not only Nigel Fisher who felt the crisis was over, for Selwyn now received letters of congratulation from all sides of the House. The issue had, in effect, been decided by Boyd-Carpenter's press statement on 30 December that he was stepping down. Lord Shawcross offered Selwyn his full-bottomed wig. When Selwyn became Speaker he thus did so wearing a wig which had seen legal service on the Northern Circuit. Because of his uncertainty about the outcome of the election (and his reluctance to be seen taking anything for granted) he made no pre-order for Speaker's clothes. He went to the House on 12 January 1971 for the election with considerable apprehension. The Press were waiting for him at St Stephen's Entrance. At 2.30 p.m. the House proceeded to the choice of a new Speaker. Dame Irene Ward moved: 'That the Right. Hon. Selwyn Lloyd do take this chair as Speaker',[8] a motion seconded by the Labour Privy Councillor Charles Pannell. At 2.55 p.m. the objections began, the Liberal MP John Pardoe, expressing a 'backbencher's dissatisfaction with the way in which this election procedure has been handled'. He argued that a former senior minister ('any senior minister not just this one') would be imbued with the thinking of the executive rather than of the legislature and could not fail to be a figure of controversy. At 3.10 p.m. the Conservative Member for Tiverton, Robin Maxwell-Hyslop, said that he agreed with the points made by Pardoe and nominated Sir Geoffrey de Freitas as an alternative candidate. (Without a contest it appeared there could be no Division, a procedural point later amended by a Standing Order.) Willie Hamilton, Labour Member for West Fife, seconded Maxwell-Hyslop's proposal. 'This afternoon we are going through the farce of pretending that this House is electing its Speaker. We all know that whatever the theory might be, the fact is that this has been fixed and decided upon by the two front benches.' There was nothing personal in his attack, he said. Selwyn Lloyd was 'one of the best Leaders of the House under whom I have had the privilege to serve', but he returned to Suez and the freezing of nurses' pay. Sir Geoffrey de Freitas then promptly rose to renounce his involuntary candidature and said that he would be voting for Selwyn Lloyd. When the House proceeded to a Division there were 294 Ayes and 55 Noes. Among the Noes were Richard Crossman, David Owen and Michael Stewart. Selwyn then submitted to the will of the House, though out of deference to the age of his two proposers he did not put on a show of reluctance and force them to drag him to the Chair. Standing on the upper step, he said: 'Before I take the Chair as Speaker-Elect, I wish to thank the House for the very great honour it has paid me by electing me to the chair. As has been pointed out, my political past has not been entirely free from controversy. Therefore I was not surprised that there was some controversy today.' Selwyn did not realise that many Speakership elections are difficult and that there was potential for a far bigger row than there was. But that hurdle was now cleared. Many politicians are lucky if they have one reincarnation; for Selwyn, the Speakership was not a second, but a third and the culmination of a unique career. After the anxieties of the contested election there were now feelings of elation. Congratulations came from many sides, but Selwyn was soon brought down to earth by Kenneth Rose, a friend of some years' standing, who reminded him (while promising not to quote it in his 'Albany' column in the *Sunday Telegraph*) of Lord Rosebery's view of the Speakership:

There is much exaggeration about the attainments requisite for a Speaker. All Speakers are highly successful, all Speakers are deeply regretted and are generally announced to be irreplaceable. But a Speaker is soon found, almost invariably, among the medio-crities of the House.[9]

Selwyn now had to sever all links with the Conservative Party. Privately, one of the first things he said on becoming Speaker was that it was a great relief that he no longer had to pretend to be a Tory.[10] Although this was said with his customary tongue-in-cheek attitude, it contained more than a grain of truth. Like many professional figures who came to political consciousness in the 1920s, Selwyn was an old-style Gladstonian Free Trade Liberal. The controversy over Tariffs in 1931 had taken him to the Conservatives. Megan Lloyd George never really forgave him for leaving the Liberals (unless it had been for Labour, like herself). Selwyn was, in later parlance, a Tory 'wet' and his attitudes on many social issues (notably capital punishment) were decidedly liberal and he did not always have the easiest ride in certain sections of his Wirral constituency. He was never a party hack. Nevertheless many loyal Conservative workers in the Wirral were keenly disappointed that nominally they no longer had a Conservative MP.

Business associations were also severed. He wrote to Howard Hicks on 15 January, resigning from IDC Ltd and adding: 'It was a little unpleasant for me but I think it turned out all right in the end and at least there does not seem to be much personal feeling against me.'[11] Although Selwyn had to forgo his directorships, he was paid £8,500 as Speaker (of which the first £4,000 was tax free). Of greater significance to him was the fact that it was the first pensionable job he had ever held. He also delighted in the historical associations of the office – sixth in order of precedence after the Royal Family, tenant of Speaker's House ('the best tied cottage in London' as he described it, usually with the accompanying direction 'first on the left over Westminster Bridge'), even the right to order a peal of bells at St Margaret's, Westminster, for 6 guineas.

There was of course another side to the coin, as Selwyn soon found. To be imprisoned in the House – 'embedded in that pompous tomb' in Lord Rosebery's words – from Monday to Friday week after week was a heavy price. As he could never dine out when the House was sitting, he had people to lunch and dine with him. In seconding Irene Ward's motion Charles Pannell had expressed the hope that the new Speaker would not be so remote as previous Speakers had been. On 28 January Selwyn's first innovation was what he called his 'experimental' lunches, when he invited a cross section of members (usually three Conservative, three Labour, one Liberal plus an Independent or an official of the House) on a weekly basis. He broadened the range of invitations (on 25 March that first year he entertained the Cambridge Boat Race crew to tea) and opened up Speaker's House, so that it became more like a home than a Gothic mausoleum. As Selwyn's hospitality was one of cases, not bottles (he always had great disdain for what he called 'a two sardine barbecue'), this was widely appreciated, especially on family occasions like his great-niece's wedding reception. Selwyn had never been extravagant with money and now when he got into the full swing of things he spent some £200 a week on entertaining when Parliament was in session. He spent that amount, not in a self-indulgent flamboyant manner, but believing that it was part of the responsibility of his position; and he kept careful lists of the MPs he entertained to ensure the hospitality was spread correctly. The loneliness of the job was not, as many had warned him, one of being bereft of companions but in the political isolation and the solitariness of the decisions that had to be taken in the Chair. An early indication of his new hybrid status between public figure and individual citizen came twelve days after his election when he appeared as a witness for the defence in the case that had been brought against Jonathan Aitken under the Official Secrets Act.[12] When the charge had originally been brought Selwyn had promised to give a character reference, and once he had given his word he kept it, even though fourteen months elapsed between this and the case coming to court. By that time he was Speaker and his appearance was a source of some constitutional and legal niceties. Could or should the Speaker appear in court, and if so should it be 'in full fig'? (Selwyn thought it would be rather appropriate to do so.) But after consulting with Lord Goodman he turned up in a tail coat. After the acquittal Selwyn was invited to a celebration party, but that he declined as he did not think it constitutionally proper. As Speaker he was excessively punctilious. When the Lord Chancellor, Lord Hailsham, in his flat at one end of the Palace of Westminster invited Selwyn for a drink in the evening he would never go as he thought it constitutionally incorrect for the two Speakers to be meeting unofficially lest members should hear of it and consider they were arranging things privately.

Like many Speakers, Selwyn's term of office (he was to be re-elected in February 1974 and October 1974) went through clearly defined phases. He started off with an anxiety to please and to be fair. Gradually this gave way to a nervousness and a worry as to whether he actually was being fair. Finally he became irritated at his own irritability. Members noticed that he often had a rolled up piece of paper in his hand which he then used to bang impetuously against his wrist when he was not happy. In assessing the performance of a Speaker, the House of Commons is particularly responsive to the legacy of the previous incumbent. In this Selwyn was fortunate. He took over after the declining months of Horace King, who had not been well, and handed the office to George Thomas after many important reforms and improvements. This was despite the fact that he was one of the few Speakers in recent times not to have been Deputy Speaker or Deputy Chairman of the Ways and Means Committee. He therefore leant very heavily for the first six months of his tenure on Robert Grant-Ferris (later Lord Harvington), help he never adequately acknowledged in his book on the Speakership. He began by being interested, not in the post itself, but by what it represented. Though he was a procedural man who worked well within the procedural conventions, much of the daily grind of the work bored him. It was thus a job into which he grew. As Speaker Selwyn was not without his vulnerability, but this was part of his strength in that people were reluctant (even at the time of the disputed election) to 'chip' at him. In a skilful way he traded on the fact that ambitious and influential people did not like offending the Speaker. Contrary to the expectation of many backbenchers, who have an instinctive preference for one of their own as Speaker, the best Speakers are often those who have had some experience of ministerial responsibility. The career backbencher is a thing of the past and if the Speakership were restricted to non-ministers it would tend to exclude the most able. Selwyn was a man of the political world, he carried around with him the folk memory of Cabinet. When people came to the Chair and pressurised him, as happens to all Speakers, he was able to deal with it. As the Labour MP J. P. Mackintosh noted: 'It was said, that, having held most of the senior offices of state, other than the premiership, he might be a little too partial to former ministerial colleagues. In practice, his seniority meant that most of the Conservative ministers of the 1970–1974 government had been mere underlings in his time and he treated them as such.'[13]

The most important of Selwyn's reforms was the introduction of the third Deputy. Selwyn had seen what the long hours had done to Horace King, and to his predecessor, Sir Harry Hylton-Foster, who had died in harness in 1965, and though there was an element of self-interest in the reform, it was also one that worked to the benefit of the House. Selwyn was determined that he would not take the Chair after 10 p.m. (though he had to be present in the Palace of Westminster when the House was sitting). This meant the amendment of certain rules, for instance to allow one of the Deputies to 'name' an MP. Selwyn knew his physical limitations (he was nearly 67 when he became Speaker) and he wanted to conserve himself for the important periods of the day in mid-afternoon and parliamentary questions. By having three Deputies – Lance Mallalieu, Labour MP for Brigg, was appointed Second Deputy Chairman of Ways and Means in 1971 – some argued that Selwyn over-egged the pudding, but he believed it to be an error in the right direction. Another innovation was his 'Blue Book'. As a former Cabinet minister Selwyn was aware of the accommodations that would have led a Cabinet to have decided on such and such a course (something not always apparent to a backbencher), yet despite that knowledge he never considered it part of his function to be accommodating to the government on that account. He remained a backbenchers' Speaker. 'All parts of the orchestra must be heard', he used to say, 'not just the violins, but also the so-and-so who plays the triangle.' To enable backbenchers to have a fair crack of the whip he kept in his 'Blue Book' details of those who had spoken, the subjects, dates and length of the speeches (even putting 'F' against those who had drawn a Friday morning, so that it should only count as a proportion of a reckoning.) Any MP who made an unjustified complaint soon received chapter and verse. He also believed in the importance of Parliamentary Private Notice questions. George Thomas was to reduce the permitted number, but Selwyn allowed over forty in each session, always aware that a Speaker's power resides in the Member's knowledge that he can be cold-shouldered. That was why he believed it right that a Speaker should go in mid-Parliament (as he did in 1976) as not only does that give MPs an opportunity to elect a successor on a basis of personal knowledge, but also because it does not diminish the residual power of the Speaker. He made sure that he never sheathed his Damoclean sword. He believed it was the job of the Speaker to let Parliament reflect what was going on in the country, even if that was division. He was criticised at times for 'waffling' from the Chair, but this was a studied and deliberate way of defusing tension. Of the two kinds of Speaker – those in the foreground, and those who keep themselves as far as possible in the background, blowing the whistle when necessary – Selwyn was as clearly in the second category as his successor was in the first.

He was the hub of a Westminster team as surely as Speaker's House is the hub of a parliamentary village. Apart from Sir Robert Grant-Ferris, he was greatly helped by Brigadier Noel Short, Speaker's Secretary, Sir Robert Speed, Speaker's Counsel, and in the House by Sir Myer Galpern, Miss Betty Harvie Anderson (later Baroness Skrimshire), Sir Lance Mallalieu and Oscar Murton. He loved the ceremonial and appreciated the help of his three trainbearers, Mr Green, Mr Canter and Mr Lord. He delighted in the eccentricities of the official furniture, the ancient double bed in the main bedroom with its inscription 'Thy master will look after thee', the view from his private dining room on the corner of the Tower with its sweeping panorama over Speaker's Green and the Thames. Eric Cockeram, MP for neighbouring Bebington in the Wirral until February 1974, took much of the load of party political constituency work. In May 1972 Selwyn appointed Christopher Spence as his personal assistant and this made a vast difference to the smooth running of Selwyn's public life, both in London and in the Wirral. Christopher Spence handled day-to-day matters, Selwyn's dealings with the officials of the House, MPs and Deputies. In the constituency he liaised with public authorities and local bodies such as the Liverpool School of Tropical Medicine (of which Selwyn was to become President in 1976), Merseyside Young Volunteers, WASP and Abbeyfield. He travelled on official visits to Rumania and Yugoslavia and in the two General Elections of 1974 helped Gilbert Stephenson, Selwyn's agent, Selwyn always insisting that his agent should be described as Agent for the Wirral Conservative Association and never agent for Mr Selwyn Lloyd as Speaker.

Selwyn was not, however, Speaker at an easy time. The years of the Heath administration proved to be highly controversial with two miners' strikes, contentious industrial relations legislation and the 'three day week'. The troubles in Ireland were an ever present worry. From February 1974 there was a minority Labour government with all the difficulties that parliamentary situation involved. It was a time of bitter rowdiness in the Chamber, far more serious and intense than the knockabout stuff Selwyn had witnessed in the late 1940s. Nevertheless he took comfort from the fact that there was nothing new in such rowdiness. Some of the incidents were, however, very ugly, as he found in his first weeks in the Chair.

On 18 January 1971 the Committee Stage of the Industrial Relations Bill was being considered. In announcing the business for the next week, the Leader of the House, William Whitelaw, said that the parliamentary guillotine would be applied on the following Monday (25 January). Towards 10 p.m. that day sixty Labour members crowded on to the floor of the House in front of the table to prevent Robert Carr, the Minister of Labour, from completing his speech. 'This is getting almost as boring as a standing ovation', said Selwyn, before being forced to suspend the sitting for fifteen minutes. When the House re-assembled Selwyn cleared the lobby and called for a division, which the government won by 308 votes to 276. 'You're nothing but a government stooge', said one Opposition front-bencher as he passed the Chair later. Not for the first time as Speaker Selwyn applied selective deafness.

An even more serious episode came on 31 January 1972. The Home Secretary, Reginald Maudling, was making a statement to the House about events in Londonderry the previous day in which there had been a tragic number of fatalities. Bernadette Devlin, the MP for Mid Ulster, called Maudling a liar and a murdering hypocrite. Then, without warning, she rushed across the floor of the House, pushing past the Foreign Secretary, Alec Douglas-Home, and physically attacked Maudling. Robert Mellish, the Opposition Chief Whip, and Oscar Murton restrained the attack and hurried Bernadette Devlin from the Chamber. A deathly silence fell momentarily (some present have thought it might have been like the silence in Whitehall at the moment of Charles I's execution), broken by the clop of the feet as she was bustled away. Selwyn's handling (or as some saw it, non-handling) of this episode came in for much criticism. All Speakers have their bad moments. 31 January 1972 was Selwyn's. (The space he devoted to it in his book on the Speakership was an indication of his retrospective unease.) Both William Whitelaw and Francis Pym came (in their official capacities as Leader of the House and Government Chief Whip) to express their concern. Selwyn made a statement that did not satisfy all Members and some went so far as to put down a motion of censure on the Speaker, though it never came to debate. There are two views on Selwyn's handling of this episode. There are those who thought that it was a storm in a tea-cup and that by not reacting Selwyn had made the best of a bad job and denied Bernadette Devlin any status as a parliamentary martyr. Selwyn later said, 'The greatest mistake a Speaker can make is to be firm against his better judgment for fear of being thought weak.'[14] The other view is harsher. Although this was a time of unruliness (and even the throwing of CS gas canisters and manure from the public gallery) a physical assault on one of Her Majesty's Ministers is of the utmost constitutional gravity. On three occasions before the attack unparliamentary language had streamed forth. Many MPs felt that at the very least Bernadette Devlin should have been 'named'. Selwyn had a sense at the time of having failed the House, but in his diary at the end of the 1971–2 session he wrote: 'Bernadette Devlin had her outburst. I was much criticised for ignoring it, but judging by her behaviour since, I was right (touch wood).'[15] He talked it over with his friends as though seeking reassurance. After one such talk on 29 March 1972 Jonathan Aitken wrote in his diary:

There had been some sort of a tussle, then Bob Mellish, the Opposition Chief Whip, had just simply put his arm round her and bundled her out of the chamber in a matter of seconds, very quickly and very efficiently. Selwyn at that moment had to decide what to do, but the day before there had been the killings in Londonderry and he thought that supposing he was to ban Bernadette Devlin from the House of Commons there would probably be more shootings and more deaths, so his mind worked very fast and he decided that he wouldn't make her a martyr, and he wouldn't take any more risks, but he would let tempers cool down for 24 hours, and as things turned out it was a very wise decision.[16]

On balance it was an episode that did no lasting damage to Parliament, but it had been a close thing.

After a year in the post Selwyn wrote down his impressions of the office of Speaker. The physical strain he had found much greater than he had expected. 'Possibly the rather agonising preliminaries to the Election, and the tension of the Chair, coupled with a move, new domestic arrangements etc.' Sleep too he found a real problem before the advent of the third Deputy. 'With only two deputies, it was not possible for me to be off completely any night – 1 of them would share duty with me – this often meant I was in the Chair until after 2 a.m., i.e. asleep not before 3.' He also found that he had been under fire for not getting through enough parliamentary questions.

The problems are:
  a) supplementaries are too verbose
  b) Ministerial answers are too verbose
  c) if the Speaker allows only one Supplementary, he is accused of protecting Ministers – and what about the Opposition Front Bench?
  d) for any real probing, several supplementary questions are necessary.

He felt uneasy also about Points of Order. 'Bogus ones are the most difficult. How does one know it is bogus until it has been put. If one waits until the end, the Member has got his stuff out.'[17]

As Speaker Selwyn had a unique vantage point. He recorded his impressions of the issues and the personalities. The 1971–2 session had been dominated by the EEC. After the unexpectedly large majority for entry in principle on the terms negotiated, the Bill proved a very different affair.

I had the impression that the Labour pro-Marketeers were better organised than they admitted, and were determined to have enough abstentions to let the Bill through. Roy Jenkins, George Thomson & Harold Lever were in an extremely difficult position, and I think were much happier after resigning from the Front Bench.

His comments were shrewdly reflective:

Wilson looks a very unhappy man. One feels all the time that he is under great strain in his own party. His relations with Heath are very bad. Their personalities at Question Time are embarrassing to both sides . . .

Heath is as difficult to comprehend as ever. He is very civil to me publicly . . . yet in the Chamber, he is difficult, and makes audible comments as he passes the Chair – 'Must this go on for ever' etc . . .

Callaghan strikes me as playing a deep game . . . I think he would be the best leader Labour could have & very dangerous to the Tories . . .

The Government made a great mistake in taking on the miners. Willie Whitelaw said to me the week before 'I don't much like taking on the miners'. Harold Macmillan said to me that these were the sort of people who died in droves in World War 1, whether well led or badly, whether right or wrong, they weren't going to be beaten. So it turned out. The Govt. must have been very badly advised about stocks and picketing. Picketing has now become Problem No 1 after N Ireland . . .

Peter Walker's Empire has done quite well, although he has some terrible problems tied round his neck . . .

Margaret Thatcher has improved considerably.[18]

In his neutral position, Selwyn was the recipient of many confidences. 'After the diplomatic Party at the Palace, I went in to have supper with the Queen', wrote Selwyn in his diary for 11 November 1972. At this function the Queen spoke to him in private about her concern over a recent political development. He was now a trusted elder statesman. He began to see Macmillan again more often and learned some interesting things about his position in the early 1960s. 'Macmillan told me that he had nominated me in place of Derry Amory as person to decide on pressing button for nuclear war if he was not available.'[19] He found it easy to talk over old times with Harold Wilson too. He wrote in his diary on 11 April 1972: 'Harold Wilson . . . made a curious reference to the past. He said that I had been the first to "interest him" in the Common Market. He remembered a talk which we had had in the Smoking Room, which he had reported to Gaitskell . . . He ended with the usual reference to how well we had got on when I was Chancellor and he was Shadow

Chancellor. Politics had been fun in those days because we both knew how to conduct ourselves!'[20] Not that Selwyn was dismissive of the more recent intake. Dennis Skinner, for instance, the Labour MP for Bolsover he found a knowing and effective member and had regard for his intentions.

In his first term as Speaker he announced a Conference on Electoral Reform, which led to the Representation of the People Act 1974 and clarified the law on election expenditure. Various honours came his way. In 1971 he was made a Deputy High Steward of Cambridge University, which he hoped (unavailingly) would be a stepping stone to the Chancellorship of his old university on the retirement of Lord Tedder. In 1972 he received the freedom of Ellesmere Port, the Labour stronghold in his Wirral constituency. This pleased him as much as any honour he ever received. This idea had been mooted by Councillor F. W. Venables, his Labour opponent at the 1959 General Election, and had been unanimously accepted by the Labour group on the Council, and although two of the younger Labour members absented themselves on 22 September when the freedom was conferred, Selwyn thought they were quite right not to forgo the football at Anfield. However busy he was with national affairs he always found time for the Wirral. 'We knew we had a friend there, who would support us in government circles', recalled F. W. Venables.[21] One of the things that gratified his constituents at this time was that problems seemed to be tackled quicker because Selwyn always seemed to know the right man to approach.

Selwyn was more relaxed than he had been for years, though there could still be flashes of impetuosity. The reflationary Budget that Anthony Barber introduced on 21 April 1972 (in which taxation was reduced by £1,380m and an annual growth rate of 5 per cent targeted, with the consequent rise in the Public Sector Borrowing Requirement) led him to one of his few displays of anger. One of his relatives can remember him stumping the corridors of Speaker's House that evening, bitterly complaining, 'This is against all I ever taught him.' He knew that inflation was just round the corner and the 1973 rise in oil prices merely exacerbated the situation. By 1975 weekly wage rate increases in the public sector had risen 232 per cent since he had left the Treasury. The stock market crash of 1973 was a heavy personal blow to Selwyn. He had had shares since he was a young man, usually in what he felt were ultra safe concerns, like insurance companies, though he was not averse to taking a risk with his investments. When the recession came even his best investments were vulnerable. But he was more concerned for local people in Liverpool than for himself.

The plight of Liverpool at this time affected him deeply and it worried him to contrast the Liverpool he had known in its heyday with the Liverpool he saw as Speaker. He watched with dismay as the very fabric of society seemed to be threatened in the winter of 1973–4. The government declared a State of Emergency on 13 November 1973 and minimum lending rate (which had replaced the Bank Rate) was raised to 13 per cent. It was all a far cry from the guiding light and the July measures of 1961, severe though they had seemed. A three-day working week followed with continued industrial deadlock between the government and the TUC. One of the few olive branches that was offered at this time came at the meeting of the NEDC on 9 January 1974 when the General Council of the TUC undertook that any settlement between the government and the miners would not be used by other unions as the basis for the settlement of their own outstanding claims. On 7 February, before the decision was publicly announced, Edward Heath wrote to Selwyn in his capacity as Speaker to tell him that there would be a General Election on 28 February.

The convention, though not an absolute one, had grown up that the Speaker should be returned unopposed at parliamentary elections. The decision of the Liberal Party to contest the Wirral seat therefore disappointed Selwyn, not because he could not campaign, but because of the wider implication. He felt that if it became accepted that the Speaker was fair game at an election then only those members with the safest seats would be considered for the office and he did not think this the best criterion for choosing a Speaker. Once the Liberals had entered the contest, then the Labour Party also put up a candidate. Selwyn's cautious and constitutionally correct behaviour during the two general election campaigns of 1974 later served as a model for Speaker Weatherill's in 1987, some of Speaker Weatherill's green leaflets (Selwyn's choice of colour because of the upholstery of the parliamentary benches) containing direct quotations from material produced in the Wirral in 1974, largely by Selwyn's new agent-designate, Peter Robinson. Selwyn emphasised that, 'a Member while holding the office of Speaker remains the Member of Parliament for his constituency. He can take up matters of public interest, for example to do with planning permissions, the green belt, housing, welfare services or transport.'[22] In his first three years as Speaker Selwyn, who was against the idea that the Speaker should sit for a nominal seat such as St Stephen's, had dealt with over 7,000 letters on individual problems. Despite being opposed and not taking part directly in the campaign, Selwyn was returned comfortably. The figures were:

Lloyd, J. S. B. (The Speaker)	38,452
Whipp, A. J. (Labour)	22,605
Gayford, M. (Liberal)	14,123
Speaker's majority	15,847

The national result was far more indecisive. As in 1951 when the Labour Party gained most votes, but fewer seats than the Conservatives, now the Conservatives found themselves marginally winning the race for votes, but losing the one on which the result hinged, with only 297 of the 635 available seats. The Labour Party (with 301 seats) were also well short of an overall majority. After unsuccessful attempts to form an alliance with the Liberals, and after consulting the constitutional historian Lord Blake, Edward Heath tendered his resignation and Harold Wilson formed a minority government. It was clear that a second election would soon follow.

Selwyn's first three years as Speaker had been set against a difficult political background. The eight months from February 1974 were constitutionally even more sensitive. The General Election had failed to produce a stable government with a working majority. There was talk of the need for a government of national unity. The catalyst for such a government during the financial crisis of 1931 had been King George V, but it was now tacitly accepted that the Queen could not be expected in 1974 to take such an active part as her grandfather, though ultimately the Monarchy might well be the stabilising force. Questions of devolution and proportional representation were also to the fore (the six million Liberal votes had produced only 14 seats) and some felt that the Speaker might have some significant role to play in any constitutional crisis that might arise in the course of the year. Selwyn was not convinced that this was part of the Speaker's function (how could a Speaker subsequently be seen as impartial if he had been seen to take part in horse-trading?) and knew that if a go-between was necessary it would have been Sir Martin Charteris, the Queen's Private Secretary, as Sir Clive Wigram had been in many crises before and including that of 1931. In the event the situation was resolved (as ultimately it had to be) by the second General Election in October 1974. The telling fact as far as Selwyn was concerned was that some people felt that the combination of his office and his character made him an appropriate figure to serve in such a capacity had it been required.

On 18 September Harold Wilson wrote to Selwyn giving him advance notice that polling day would be on 10 October. It was the first time since 1910 that two General Elections had been held in one year. Selwyn now stood for Parliament for the last time. The national

result was as unexpected as that in Feburary. The Conservative aim
was to avoid any repetition of the 1966 result, a large Labour victory.
It was the campaign for damage limitation. Against expectations,
Labour only scraped the barest of overall majorities, winning 319 of
the 635 seats. For the tenth time the Wirral returned Selwyn with a
comfortable majority, the figures being:

Lloyd, J. S. B. (The Speaker)	35,705
Thomas, P. R. (Labour)	22,217
Gayford, M. R. D. (Liberal)	12,345
Speaker's Majority	13,488

The thing that Selwyn remembered most about his third spell as
Speaker was how he could see demonstrations coming over Westminster Bridge before other people knew about them. Selwyn made it
clear to the Leader of the House, Edward Short (later Lord Glena-
mara), that he did not intend to stay for a full Parliament. On 16
October he had a talk with the Government Chief Whip, Robert
Mellish, when he reiterated his belief that it was right for a Speaker to
retire in mid-term. They pencilled in January 1977 as a possible time
for retirement.[23] Selwyn was always convinced that George Thomas,
Deputy Speaker since 1974, should be his successor, though he was
not above teasing George by saying that he had never felt better for
years and intended to go on until he was eighty. But before Selwyn
retired there was to be a more dramatic parliamentary election.
Although Heath's leadership of the Conservative Party had not been
in danger after the heavy defeat of March 1966, the two defeats of
1974 (like the two defeats Balfour suffered in 1910) proved to be the
writing on the wall. On 16 December William Whitelaw came to
Speaker's House for a talk about the political situation. He told
Selwyn that he was 'profoundly unhappy about the state of the
Conservative Party', saying that Selwyn was the only person, except
for Home, whom he could consult. Selwyn wrote in his diary:

> Heath was being v. difficult over the leadership issue. He was
> furious with the new rules, which would mean that a candidate had
> to get 50% of those entitled to vote, & 15% more than his nearest
> rival. In fact Willie thought that the introduction of annual elec-
> tions might save Heath this time. Willie would not stand against
> Heath in the first round. He did not seem so certain about a second
> ballot.[24]

With that bowing to the inevitable that seemed to have come over
Rab Butler in the summer of 1963 (when in a chance meeting in the
street with Reginald Maudling he had said that he would serve under

the younger man)[25] Whitelaw was now facing the prospect that he would never be Conservative leader. 'Willie said that reluctantly he would serve under Margaret Thatcher, but never under Edward du Cann.'[26]

In February 1975, to the surprise of many outsiders, but not to those like Selwyn with their ear close to the ground, Margaret Thatcher was elected Leader of the Conservative Party. Although Selwyn was not to live to see the first woman Prime Minister of the United Kingdom take office, he had many dealings with Mrs Thatcher in his last year as Speaker, though his relationship with the Conservative Party inevitably altered as a new and younger generation came to the fore. However, as with Bonar Law in 1911, he felt that the Conservatives had chosen their best candidate, though this time not by accident. Selwyn continued to groom George Thomas as his successor. He knew that Thomas had been far more pro-Labour than he himself had ever been pro-Tory, so he took to allaying doubts in the appropriate quarters about Thomas's suitability for Speaker (there were actually far more worries on this score than there had been with Selwyn in 1971, difficult though this may be to appreciate some years later with the folk memories of that mellifluous Welsh voice sounding 'Order, Order' over the air waves or reading the lesson at the Prince of Wales's wedding.) Selwyn and George Thomas (despite their Methodism* and the fact that they were single) were very different Speakers. One only has to compare Selwyn's book on the Speakership with George Thomas's memoirs to appreciate the difference. As an ex-Speaker, Selwyn would never have written a book like George Thomas's *Mr. Speaker*, which revealed in detail the pressures put on the Speaker by the Labour Party.

On 3 November 1975 Selwyn issued a statement saying that he did not intend to seek re-election at the next General Election. 'I intend, when I retire, to continue to live in the constituency and to maintain my local ties.'[27] On 21 November he wrote to Harold Wilson, 'As I think you know, it is my intention to go in the fairly near future.'[28] A portrait was commissioned from Michael Noakes, which broke precedent in two ways. First, Selwyn was not wearing his wig, that was on a stand in the background, and second, he was painted sitting down. Prints (borrowed from the Department of the Environment) of the Treasury and the Foreign Office were incorporated. With memories of a pastel portrait that had been drawn in his childhood, he felt that he ought to wear what he called his Little Lord Fauntleroy suit. The

---

* George Thomas completed a hat-trick of Methodist Speakers after Horace King and Selwyn Lloyd.

finished portrait, which has austere dignity, was the first to be placed in the ante-room next to the state dining room of Speaker's House. He was very pleased with it. Later when Michael Noakes wished to show the portrait in the annual Exhibition of the Royal Society of Portrait Painters, despite Selwyn's request for it to be lent official permission was not forthcoming. This brought home to Selwyn how, once out of that great office, all the deferential bows had faded into oblivion. A second portrait (for Gray's Inn) was painted by Kenneth Green, which caught a kind of lonely melancholy.

Selwyn's decision to retire when he did coincided with the vacancy for the Chancellorship of Cambridge University for which he had ambitions. There was thus an element of haste about the arrangements as his Party Chairman, Mr Pocock, and his agent, Peter Robinson, were summoned to Hilbre House to be told that he wanted his successor nominated by Christmas 1975. (As Deputy High Steward of Cambridge University Selwyn was notified on 29 January 1976 that the Duke of Edinburgh had been offered the Chancellorship.)[29] By interviewing against the clock, a decision was made by 19 December 1975. Selwyn had wanted his personal assistant Christopher Spence to succeed him as MP, but though Spence got on to the 'long' short list (out of deference to Selwyn) to Selwyn's disappointment he did not proceed to the final four. (Of the final 24 shortlisted out of 300 applications 16 did eventually become MPs, which showed the strength of the field.) Many Liberals in the Wirral had hopes of capturing the seat, which was one of the reasons why David Hunt, a young Liverpudlian with family connections in the Wirral was chosen. Selwyn did all that he could to make the changeover smooth and gave David Hunt much valuable advice – as well eventually as the chairmanship of nearly thirty charitable organisations ranging from the British Heart Foundation to the Deeside Gilbert and Sullivan Society, Selwyn writing to each local organisation individually asking them to invite David Hunt to take over. In confidence he also gave David Hunt a black list of correspondents whose letters should be acknowledged but with whom he should not get unduly involved. Shortly after his election David Hunt received a letter from one of the people on this black list, complaining about unfair dismissal. It sounded such a deserving case that he disregarded Selwyn's advice and took up the cudgels. He then received a suitcase of correspondence going back to 1933 when the dismissal had occurred. David Hunt met Selwyn on 6 January 1976 for the first of many talks about the Wirral constituency which had seen Selwyn through good times and bad for over three decades. It was Twelfth Night and the decorations were in the hall. As David Hunt made to leave Selwyn said, 'Tonight's the night we take down the decorations. I'm one of the decorations that will shortly be taken down.' Thus ended thirty-one years as Member of Parliament for the Wirral.

Selwyn retired as Speaker on 3 February 1976. Tributes were paid by the Prime Minister and by the Leader of the Opposition. 'In the Shakespearean sense you have played many parts', said Mrs Thatcher.[30] As Bottom the Weaver at Fettes in July 1923 he had expressed the wish to undertake many parts. Now he had accomplished that wish. He returned his wig to Hartley Shawcross and on 11 February vacated his seat in the Commons on being appointed Steward and Bailiff of the Manor of Northstead. When he was offered a peerage Selwyn thought first of taking the title Lord Hilbre, 'to fox the foreigners', as he joked, but decided in the end that he did not wish to change his name. The problem was that there were other Lord Lloyds. He took advice from his old friend Lord Geoffrey-Lloyd on how to avoid these difficulties. The vogue for double-barrelled titles (Gordon-Walker, George-Brown) had been tolerated rather than approved and so to forestall objections he had his name changed by deed poll to Selwyn-Lloyd, before being gazetted Baron Selwyn-Lloyd of the Wirral. He was introduced into the House of Lords on 10 March by Baroness Hylton-Foster and Lord Maybray-King, the day the Wirral by-election gave David Hunt the largest Conservative majority in the country. Among other things, his coat of arms incorporated the Welsh dragon, an oyster catcher perched on a golf ball (Hilbre Island and Hoylake) and the Fettes bee (*Industria*). Characteristically he chose as his motto *Vendere et vincere obstinatus* (Determined Sell – Win). One of the first congratulatory letters on his peerage came from Harold Macmillan. Harold Wilson told Selwyn that his performance as Speaker had made him revise his opinion about not having ex-Ministers in the Chair. The letter that pleased him most came from Nigel Fisher. 'After sitting under every Speaker from Clifton Brown onwards, you were – in my view – immeasurably the best; because you had all the qualities of fairness, firmness, humour and tolerance – & of course total impartiality – which are required.'[31] Though not without its moments of controversy, his Speakership was widely acknowledged as a fulfilled ending to a long and unique parliamentary career. He had earned his *Nunc Dimittis*.

Selwyn made his maiden speech in the House of Lords on 16 June, but in the last eighteen months of his life played no prominent part in the deliberations of the Upper Chamber. As a former Speaker he was, in any case, precluded from taking part in controversy. He sat on the Cross Benches, coming in from time to time for Questions, then the most interesting part of the Lords proceedings. He appeared to many peers as a shy, retiring figure, taking his lunch often alone and always promptly at 12.30 p.m., and disappearing after questions to the flat he had now taken at 7 Gray's Inn. His main retirement occupation was writing and gardening, one visitor to Hilbre House recalling him with an extraordinary woollen cap on his head and a huge sack of twigs over his shoulder, looking for all the world like an Anatolian peasant. There was time for the laughter of friends and the door was always open. Publishers began to knock again too and after taking advice he contracted with Jonathan Cape to write about the Speakership (modelled on Patrick Gordon Walker's *The Cabinet*, which he hoped would be a useful guide for students and of interest to the general reader.) But Selwyn was not a naturally gifted writer with a flair for the telling phrase and Cape regarded *Mr Speaker, Sir* as the sprat to catch the Suez whale, the disappointment for Cape being that when the Suez book came along it turned out to be a bit of a mackerel. The book Selwyn really wanted to write was *A Middle Class Lawyer from Liverpool* and the first two were intended as trial runs. He found the process of writing irksome and after an hour of somewhat desultory work he would be out in the garden, weaving his way round hidden tree trunks on his tractor mower. Nevertheless the Speakership book was well received. 'The book mirrors the man', wrote David Wood in *The Times* 'modest, open-minded, friendly and honest.'[32] Selwyn was very generous in the distribution of copies to family and friends. He sent a signed copy to the Queen. This generosity later led Magdalene College to claim posthumously a free copy of the Suez book on the grounds that as an Honorary Fellow he would undoubtedly have given them a copy had he lived.[33] He worked hard in promoting the Speakership book, travelling to literary lunches in Yorkshire and in Oxford, the latter in company with Lord Home. It was on this train journey that he waxed lyrical to the former Prime Minister about the advantages of an old age pensioner's rail card, yet Home did not really understand what Selwyn was getting at and in some mysterious way thought that British Rail were being done out of their fare. However, when the Wirral constituency proposed a presentation to him, he directed the generosity of his constituents away from himself towards a Selwyn Lloyd Charitable Trust (which still flourishes) to help local charities.

As an elder statesman who had been involved in great events, Selwyn was much in demand from historians and biographers. This was not confined to Suez. In June 1977 he talked to Nigel Fisher, who was researching his biography of Harold Macmillan. Two other historians who were indebted to him him were Professor Keith Sainsbury (for *British Foreign Secretaries since 1945*) and Anthony Seldon for his pioneering history of the first post-war Conservative government (*Churchill's Indian Summer*). Such help he regarded as a historical duty, akin to the keeping of full records for the use of his biographer. Yet he never allowed people to take advantage. One American researcher who arrived unannounced and uninvited at Lower Farm House, while Selwyn was boat-hooking the stream at the end of the garden, was soon sent packing. One book he very much took against was Robert Lacey's *Majesty*, a study of Queen Elizabeth II, which he regarded as premature and inaccurate. He wrote to Lacey on 31 August 1976:

> I regret the fact that you should have written a book about political events with which the Queen was concerned, without allowing an appropriate lapse of time. She cannot comment on your allegations and therefore I would have thought 25 years a decent interval before you should start writing about her part in such events.
>
> On each of the situations in which I myself was concerned, you are inaccurate in detail according to my recollection.
>
> I do not agree with your deductions or inferences, so far as they relate to matters of which I have knowledge.
>
> Perhaps, therefore, it is just as well that there is not time for us to meet before your text must go to the printers![34]

Selwyn was inundated with requests for television and radio interviews and on 23–24 June 1976 allowed Kenneth Harris of the *Observer* to film an extended retrospect on his career, extracts from which were subsequently broadcast by the BBC.

He paid his last visit to Magdalene for a College feast in July 1977. Over Christmas 1977 he wrote to many of those involved in the Suez operation. It was now the military aspect that interested him most, as he told Marshal of the Royal Air Force Sir William Dickson in February 1978. He even toyed with the idea of writing Dempsey's biography, and in March 1978, only two months before his death, he helped in the sorting of Dempsey's papers before they were deposited at the Public Record Office at Kew. It was his last public act.

With the death of Anthony Eden in January 1977 Selwyn had felt himself to be the senior survivor of Suez. He found the task of sifting through the Foreign Office files (which he began to do in 1976) increasingly wearing and the small flat at Gray's Inn totally unsuitable for cataloguing the vast paperwork. As he wandered through the Foreign and Commonwealth library or the courts of Gray's Inn, he seemed in these last months like a figure from a C. P. Snow novel,

whereas in earlier days he had been something of Anthony Powell's
Widmerpool in a succession of unexpected promotions. Over Christmas 1977 his eldest sister Dorice had been concerned at Selwyn's
uncharacteristic forgetfulness. Pulling into the petrol station on the
motorway on a journey south he had at first been unable to find the
pumps. Then he drove away without filling up and later wondered
why the gauge was so low. He began to complain of headaches.
Things came to a head on Friday 10 March 1978. Without telling Jill
Pinsent that he would be coming to Lower Farm House for the
weekend (he was usually most punctilious about giving advance
warning) he set off quite late from London and crashed his car into a
stationary vehicle on the hard shoulder of the M40. As nobody was in
the parked vehicle Selwyn wandered across the fields to a nearby
farmhouse for help. When he finally arrived at Preston Crowmarsh it
was clear that more than the accident was involved. Dr King-Lewis
arranged for an examination in the National Hospital for Nervous
Diseases in London. Selwyn was an intuitive man and when the
Ensesas visited Lower Farm House shortly afterwards with plans for
the summer holidays Selwyn would not commit himself. 'I'm not
sure', he said, 'I don't know whether I'll have the time.' The Ensesas
were staying when news came of the date of his admission to hospital.
Carmona Ensesa offered to help with the packing. Taking his father's
copy of the Bible down from a shelf, Selwyn said, 'This is the only
luggage I'll need.'

He underwent surgery in London, but the brain tumour that was
discovered was incurable. The family in the Wirral was unprepared
for the suddenness of his decline as Selwyn returned for the last time
to Preston Crowmarsh to the countryside he had come to love.
Selwyn began to speak of his memorial service at the Abbey when the
daffodils would be blooming. Alerted by Dr King-Lewis, the family
issued a statement on 14 May saying that his condition was giving
grave cause for concern. It had been a last week of chocolate truffles
and champagne, as Selwyn wished. Jill Pinsent and Christopher
Spence were already at Lower Farm House. Joanna and her mother
came soon afterwards, together with Dorice Shone and Barbara
Stileman. By one of those coincidental quirks of history, Sir Robert
Menzies, another major participant in the Suez story, had died on 15
May and on the day of Selwyn's death the papers were again full of
Suez. At 6.15 p.m. on Wednesday 17 May Selwyn Lloyd died
peacefully in his sleep. He was two months short of his seventy-fourth
birthday.

16

Who Goes Home?

'When our long days of work are over here there is nothing in our oldest customs which so stirs the imagination of the young member as the cry which goes down the Lobbies, "Who Goes Home?"', said Stanley Baldwin in the House of Commons on the death of Sir Austen Chamberlain in 1937. With that combination of fine sentiment and high rhetoric that was on such occasions uniquely his, he continued: 'Sometimes when I hear it I think of the language of my own country-side and my feeling that for those who have borne the almost insupportable burden of public life there may well be a day when they will be glad to go home.'[1]

For many of those who gathered in the orchard at Lower Farm House, Preston Crowmarsh, on 20 May to bid farewell to Selwyn before the last journey to the Wirral, it seemed that he too was going home from the green heart of England. It was a day of sun and apple blossom and above all, as Selwyn wanted, champagne for his friends in the summer garden. Many of his close relatives had been attending the family funeral for Bishop Treacy of Wakefield (Howard Shone's brother-in-law) in the north. This was a farewell from those in the south. Joanna and Bae were there and Christopher Spence and Jill Pinsent. Many elements of Selwyn's life came together. The Glanvill Benns were there, the Ensesas, the Hardy-Roberts, the Hayters, the King-Lewises, the Profumos, Jonathan Aitken and Donald Logan. It was a roll call of Cambridge and the Second Army, of Parliament and the Foreign Office, but above all of the companionship of the foster-filial world of godchildren and friends. The Rev. Andrew Henderson, a neighbour, conducted a short service together with the Vicar of Benson, Canon Alfred Barton. Sir Geoffrey Hardy-Roberts read the lesson 'To everything there is a season' from Ecclesiastes before Selwyn's coffin was taken from under the shade of the mulberry tree through Lower Farm House for the last time.

The news of Selwyn Lloyd's death was accorded the prominence appropriate to a figure of his political rank. It was the main item in the television and radio bulletins and assessments filled both the daily and the weekly journals. *The Times* headed its lengthy obituary: 'A career of paradox as well as distinction marked by public loyalty to the team', the virtue most prized by the Tories, particularly when it was displayed, as in Selwyn's case, 'in the face of personal discomfiture'. He was, the obituarist wrote, 'the chief of staff, meticulous and effective behind the scenes.'[2] The *Daily Telegraph* stressed his political durability: 'He survived both Suez and Macmillan's knife',[3] while for the *Guardian* it was his role in the Suez affair which made it 'certain that he will be remembered by future historians'.[4]

The funeral took place at the Westbourne Road Methodist Church, West Kirby on 25 May. It was the church where he had been baptised in 1904 and where as a child he had fidgeted in the family pew. In all essentials, except for the stained glass window in memory of Dr and Mrs Lloyd, it remained as it had been in the early years of the century. The church was half a mile from where he had been born at Red Bank and in the same road as the hall in which he had made his speech to his constituents on 19 July 1962. Then, as now, Westbourne Road was crowded with people and the sprawlings of television equipment. At the funeral the address was given by Lord Home. The lesson, again from Ecclesiastes, was read by Brigadier Sir Douglas Crawford, Lord Lieutenant of Merseyside, and a contemporary of Selwyn both at the Leas and at Magdalene. In his address Lord Home said that 'a time to keep silence, and a time to speak' was Selwyn's special hallmark. 'He never courted the crowd – he shunned it. He never tried the showmanship of oratory – he disdained it. He was content to be himself – a nice, good, companionable and compassionate man.'[5] After the service the cortege wound its way the short distance uphill to the Grange cemetery, the road lined with people, many of them Lowry-like figures who took off their caps as the hearse passed by. Selwyn was laid to rest with his parents and Eileen in the family grave. The site commands a fine view over the Wirral looking to the Irish Sea and to the distant smudge of Liverpool on the far horizon. The inscription records that he was a Member of Parliament for the area for thirty-one years.

After the two local tributes came the national one. On 5 July a memorial service was held at Westminster Abbey, which was attended by the great and the good, but even more in the body of the nave by the rank and file of the Wirral constituency, and by no means all Conservatives. At Selwyn's own request the lessons were read by John Profumo and Lord Home. The Queen was represented and the

Prime Minister, James Callaghan, attended, together with his two predecessors, Harold Wilson and Edward Heath. The only notable absentee was Harold Macmillan. The names of others attending filled four columns of *The Times*. The address was given, most fittingly, by Selwyn's successor as Speaker, George Thomas, who spoke of Selwyn's rare ability to accept both success and disappointment with philosophical calm.

'It is an open secret', he continued, 'that Selwyn Lloyd regarded his election as Speaker of the House of Commons as the crowning glory of his career. To be given the affection and the complete trust of Members of all Parties, as he was, gave him cause for humble pride. The sense of history that surrounds the Office of Speaker was never far from his mind. Thus the dignity and grace which distinguished his Speakership was matched only by the sense of fairness and kindness with which he fulfilled his task.'[6]

After the immediate batch of newspaper obituaries, other tributes followed. Two are of special interest. 'He was a political animal from the first, and a Liberal who followed Lloyd George, and was often in argument with myself who was of the Asquith breed', wrote Lord Ramsey of Canterbury in the *Magdalene College Magazine and Record*. 'I think that in his Cambridge days Selwyn had already the kind of popularity, coming less from bonhomie than from integrity, which in the end led the House of Commons to want to have him as its Speaker.'[7] Sir Edward Gardner, like Selwyn a Bencher of Gray's Inn, a QC, a Recorder and a Member of Parliament for a North West constituency, wrote in *Graya*, the magazine of Gray's Inn:

> I shall always remember his great affection for Gray's Inn. It is, of course, the small things that fix themselves firmly in the memory. I shall remember his reply to someone who did not recognise him at a private party when he was Speaker of the House of Commons and asked what he did, 'Oh', he said, 'I'm just a Civil Servant.' I shall remember his happy reply when the Opposition taunted him on his return to the front bench under a new Prime Minister about his summary dismissal by the old. 'Well, I'm back now', he declared as warm laughter broke on both sides of the House. And I shall remember the sadness and the silence in the members' dining room when we heard that he had died.[8]

A man's life is not to be measured by the list of his achievements, however various, nor his worth assessed against a benchmark of failings, whether innate or venial. 'I've no time for ologies and degrees', Selwyn said to the young in his later years, 'people are what matter.' As a result there was a generosity of spirit in his attitudes, particularly towards those for whom he did not care. As a friend who knew him for over forty years wrote: 'I do not recall Selwyn ever saying a nasty, cutting or unkind word to or of anyone.'[9] Although he could be tactless to the point of mischief, this was the product of the sense of insecurity that never left him. He cultivated a protective outer skin as a guard against closeness and this was difficult at times for even family to penetrate, for casual acquaintances almost impossible. Thus those who worked for him for short spells (as at the Ministry of Supply or the Ministry of Defence) never met with the inner man and it took time for him to establish himself at the Foreign Office and the Treasury. 'Why didn't everyone love him as we did?', asked one of his close circle after his death, the answer being his combination of touchiness and insensitivity. He was inhibited emotionally and inhibited about things such as social position and money, though he loved talking about his investments, which were shrewdly made, although some (which he called his 'bets') had a higher degree of risk. There was always this tension in Selwyn between his 'humble' beginnings (which were far from humble) and the grand world he inhabited, rubbing shoulders with grandees, yet never accepting that he was really one of them. He was sensitive and minded a lot about reverses, but he cultivated a thick skin to make it seem otherwise when he was bruised in the battle of larger creatures. He loved the beautiful, but with economy.

His consequent loneliness was not a lame duck kind of loneliness. Some surprising and varied friendships cropped up in his life. Sidney Silverman, Bessie Braddock, Hartley Shawcross and David Ormsby-Gore might seem to have little in common, but they were all bound by ties of friendship to Selwyn. Similarly in the military world a man whose friendships embraced Montgomery, Dempsey and Bomber Harris (a frequent visitor in the latter years to Preston Crowmarsh) had a richness of experience not given to many. He loved his family to meet the famous that he met, whether it was a hurried word with Bulganin and Khrushchev at the door of the Carlton Gardens lift or a meal at Chequers with a visiting dignitary, and he liked to surround himself with what he called the three-tiers of the generations. To the nephews he was 'Uncle Sel', but the great-nephews called him 'Sel' and he had an instinctive sense of communion with the young, as when young himself he had had with the old. He would sometimes use his family to rehearse arguments before the real battles elsewhere. He did not give his friendship easily. The desire for privacy, based on an innate shyness, extended into his life in other ways. He loved his golf (the Royal Liverpool Golf Club was a comfortable haven in the constituency), but the open expanses of the first tee at Aldeburgh Golf Club, for instance, were not to his liking, for here he could be recognised and introduced to other golfers as a public figure. So staying in the clubhouse until the last minute, he invariably rushed his opening drive and only settled to the round when out of sight of other players. His charitable contributions – whether to Fettes or Wesley's City Road Chapel – were anonymous and unheralded.

He was never at home with the High Tories. His world was that of his Methodist upbringing, industry and diligence. He got up in the morning and he worked. Not knowing the High Tories' habits he did not understand how they would behave when the going got rough and tough. He came from a background where people were honest and straight, therefore, when he was embroiled in a world where people told lies and put the knife in he was completely out of his depth. No more unsuitable person could have been sent to Sèvres than Selwyn. As he did not like hurting people's feelings he would say 'Maybe' rather than 'No' and at times suffered because of it.

At a private gathering of the Cambridge University Conservative Association the conversation turned to the subject of Moral Rearmament, which Selwyn did not condemn out of hand. The next weekend at the D-Day reunion at Christ Church, Portsdown a Press reporter asked Selwyn whether it was true he was a member of the movement.[10] This upset Selwyn dreadfully. As the meeting had been off the record he felt that he had been badly let down, but a more worldly, less kind man would not have given any such hostage to fortune. There remained an element of the unsuspicious and naïve about him, which combined strangely with his feeling that fate could always be waiting round the next corner with a piece of lead piping. When the Profumo affair broke Selwyn's first reaction was, 'But he couldn't have had the time'.[11]

His hesitations demanded the reassurance of structure. His family had provided this abundantly in his childhood, then when he set up on his own and the alternative structure failed he fell back on a series of substitute structures – the Cambridge college, the Inn of Court, the Northern Circuit, the Army, the Conservative Party, the country house world, the club, Parliament, the Foreign Office, all with their different rituals and hierarchies. Thus Macmillan's sacking was all the more painful as it removed the supportive structure for which the temporary financial reassurances of the business community never adequately compensated. In his last years the Speakership gave him the grandest structure of all. It was the perfect ending to his career (like the Mastership of Trinity College was for Rab Butler) and Selwyn knew it.

Yet within even the grandest of these structures his personal life was low-key, even simple. His tastes were old fashioned. At a weekend at Preston Crowmarsh he liked his piece of Battenberg cake at 4 p.m. and then a little rest before his house guests arrived. Salmon featured on his menus at some stage as he liked salmon fish-cakes for breakfast the next morning. The timetable of social drinking had a ritualistic air to it. If champagne was uncorked at noon he liked his house guests to be ready. For him the cultural and aesthetic aspects of life were not a high priority. He liked films about the Spanish Main, Westerns, the novels of Georgette Heyer, vingt-et-un, companionable games of Scrabble and competitive games of Racing Demon. (During interminable debates while Speaker he would while away the time seeing how many words he could make out of the names of those taking part in the proceedings.) He played tapes of *South Pacific* in his car. Staying at Rab Butler's one weekend he was anxious to ascertain the whereabouts of a television set so that Joanna could watch the next episode of *Robin Hood*. As the clock moved to the appointed hour Rab Butler said, 'You don't have to go, Joanna. We know who really wants to see it.'[12] Selwyn could be a tease too. At the time of his first Budget he read out extracts from a Budget speech to a friend, who was much embarrassed at being used as a sounding board, particularly as the measures seemed ruthlessly inappropriate to the prevailing conditions. Only then did Selwyn reveal it was Philip Snowden's 1931 statement. When the Soviet Ambassador invited Selwyn as Foreign Secretary to attend the prestigious closing performance of the visiting Moscow Arts Theatre production of Chekhov's *The Cherry Orchard*, Selwyn said that as earlier in the week he had sat through *Uncle Vanya* then he had done all that heroism could require. He told Harold Wilson that in twenty years' time he would be remembered as the husband of a famous poet. As befitted a pupil of Walter Sellar, author of *1066 And All That*, he loved a play on words (as the motto on his crest of arms showed). Of his Cambridge days, he recalled, 'One never knew whether a combination room was a pantry or a vestry.' When told that a schoolboy had written that a nun was 'a virgin in confinement', he replied, 'What a peculiar conception, obviously a clerical error.' Travelling as the Shadow Commonwealth Secretary down a primitive road on one of his fact-finding missions he delighted in the wayside sign that warned: BEWARE WIDE CURVES AND SOFT SHOULDERS. *Private Eye*, on whose first cover he appeared, he called the Working Man's Erskine May. When giving one godson a cheque for £21 on his 21st birthday, he wrote, 'Don't expect £100 on your hundredth birthday'.[13]

For a man who was never wealthy (his will was proved for £154,169 but much of that consisted of Hilbre House, the bequest of Mrs Macdona) he was exceptionally generous, particularly over large things. Help to members of the family was kept secret, one of his 'deadlies' as he termed it. His Christmas presents were always thoughtful and of the best. But like many generous people he often niggled over small amounts. He had a keen eye for what would later be termed 'a freebie'. The long list of aristocratic scions among his Parliamentary Private Secretaries and assistants led to some social misapprehensions among those who saw him as a political William Walton, riding in the wake of the Westminster Sitwells. This was misreading his motives. In a way he was flattered to be included in the London social scene, but he never deceived himself that he was part of it. He was there as Selwyn Lloyd, the Foreign Secretary, not as Selwyn Lloyd of the Wirral. At Bruern Abbey or Cliveden he could blend into the background, be himself, he did not have to shine, whereas in the Wirral he was expected to be the local patriarch – not a role he sought. In the country house he was allowed anonymity, and in return he brought insights from the world of politics, 'a dry wine, but an exceptionally fine one', as Viola, Dowager Duchess of Westminster recalled.[14] He was a man free of envy.

When he went to the Bar his friend Sidney Cope-Morgan gave him advice he remembered all his life. 'Don't let the green-eyed monster get hold of you. Don't be jealous. Don't be envious. If someone in your chambers gets a bigger brief than you, don't be jealous. If you get beaten in a case, don't resent it, don't make it a personal matter. If you want a happy life you'll educate yourself out of any kind of jealousy or resentment at the other fellow's success.'[15] As a godparent Selwyn tried to hand this on to the next generation. At confirmation times he sent out his *Letter to a Young Relative*:

> If you can force yourself to acquire as a habit, as something coming naturally to you, the feeling of pleasure at the successes of others, even though you are yourself in direct competition with them, you will gain much in happiness. Friendship is giving, not getting. You must disburse if you are to receive, love if you are to be loved, push out if you are to draw in. Life is not a single engagement, it is a campaign. One can lose a number of engagements and yet win the campaign.[16]

Selwyn lost many engagements in his political life. The great disappointments were the defeat of the Yellow Book strategy of Lloyd George in 1926–7, *We Can Conquer Unemployment* and the failure of the New Party in 1930–1. Commercial radio and television never fulfilled what he had hoped for in the Minority Report. He was disappointed by the gradual withdrawal from the Middle East and the Gulf and the failure to establish a bipartisan approach to an incomes policy. He was apprehensive about the local government reforms of the early 1970s and the gradual government detachment from the National Economic Development Council. The disbanding of the Territorial Army grieved him, as did the failure in his lifetime to build on the Test Ban Treaty of 1963. But he felt that he had done good during the armistice talks of the Korean war, the integration of the service Ministries which began while he was at Defence, the improvement of the conditions of service of MPs and in helping the Young Volunteer Force Foundation. It was a characteristic undervaluing by a man who never came to terms with the position he achieved. When Alan Lennox-Boyd went to a Shadow Play in 1963 in a remote village in Pahang, one of the puppets was of Selwyn. He was astonished when Lennox-Boyd told him about it. 'Who would have believed that Dulles's death could cause all this brouhaha?', wrote Rupert Hart-Davis to George Lyttelton in May 1959. 'Will the court go into mourning when Selwyn Lloyd shuffles off this mortal coil?'[17] Selwyn would not have considered this an unkind question.

Yet, even by his own criteria, Selwyn did not fall short. The essential political attributes he listed as:

Integrity – judgment – Energy i.e. capacity for hard work – ability – good health – personality (gift of gab, TV performances) – a liking for people (interest in them and their problems) – Faith i.e. belief in high ethical standards – patriotism – some other interests (professional, artistic, industrial) – self confidence and a thick skin.[18]

Most of these he possessed in abundance. He lacked self-confidence and knew that he would never gain the highest rung by oratory or charisma. His was the route of the staff officer and his career an object lesson in making the most of one's talents. He had no time for those who had good opportunities and then later were bitter for having missed the tide. He was a judgmental rather than an inspirational figure, 'Celluloid' or Mr Hoylake UDC to those who did not know him. But his integrity and his stamina were a powerful combination. The British political system (unlike the French) is uniquely hard on those who seek, in addition to their constituency work, a ministerial office. From Second Army days Selwyn knew how to pace himself. Like Macmillan he worked every hour that was necessary, though he was never really at ease when attempting to relax. There was always a job to do, whether dead-heading the roses stained with the blood of his dragooned guests, or writing articles for

the *Sunday Telegraph* or tidying up the accounts of a family investment trust. Although he rose, without the advantage of birth or
inherited wealth to some of the highest positions in the land it was
only in the latter days that he found calm. Fame exacted its price. He
left his mark on his times, but time left its mark too. Harold
Macmillan felt that Selwyn would have been at home in an Asquith
Cabinet, with people like Sir Edward Grey or Haldane, a man of the
solid professional class, with a lawyer's mind, a kind of latter-day
Augustine Birrell. His roots were in the Liberalism of the Nonconformist tradition, respectful, discreet, the best of the solid middle
ground, and he was, in the words of Churchill on Neville
Chamberlain, 'an English worthy and laboured doughtily'.

What will be his political epitaph? He was a man to be taken
seriously in everything he did, who was concerned to play a constructive part in his country's welfare. His contribution was practical,
rather than intellectual. He hated to lose, whether it was a game of
croquet against General Norstad on the North lawn of Chequers or
standing out against the ranged company of the Beveridge Committee. But he accepted that there were times when he must lose, as over
Schedule A on the eve of the 1962 Budget. He was instinctively a
good-housekeeping sort of politician, not as an end in itself, but
because through that could come a setting free. His ability to master a
brief was outstanding and he was a notable constituency MP.

Yet Selwyn Lloyd was never a politician of the very front rank. He
saw himself not as the opening batsman who would play a lot of
dashing strokes, but the solid, dependable man who would bolster up
the innings if there were difficulties. He was never a serious contender
for the Leadership of the Conservative Party, though at times he felt
the Premiership could possibly have come his way. 'He said that he
reckoned he'd badly misjudged not making a row with Macmillan
about being sacked in July 1962', wrote a colleague. 'If he had, he
thinks he would have stayed and been made Prime Minister. Also
thinks he would have been Prime Minister if he'd resigned over Suez.
He said he wanted to resign but, in fact, felt he couldn't, basically for
financial reasons . . . A good argument for becoming financially
independent of politics before doing anything else.'[19] In retrospect
this may have been wishful thinking, but there are many good
Cardinals who never become Pope. Joseph Chamberlain was clearly
a figure of the topmost rank, more than his contemporaries such as
Lord Rosebery and Sir Henry Campbell-Bannerman who achieved
the Premiership. Rab Butler made more of a political mark than Lord
Home. Selwyn was not in that league, but in Cambridge terms he was
a 2:1 figure (or as one of his Oxford friends put it 'more Exeter than

Balliol'), but at the very top of that division. He always knew that his memorial service would be in Westminster Abbey, rather than St Margaret's.

Selwyn Lloyd lived a life of paradox and about his achievement there will be disagreement and division. On the one hand it could be said with justice that he had a negligible political following. Selwyn Lloyd was not a name to fill the benches of the Chamber. He had no power base, either in the House of Commons, or in the country. His geographical roots were ones to which he was bound by ties of emotion and family loyalty. The Wirral never provided a party caucus in the manner of Joseph Chamberlain's Birmingham. Unlike Derby or Bentinck he never led a particular brand of Conservatism, nor did he allow himself to become the focus of parliamentary dissent. The cave of Adullam was not his spiritual home. Although his reputation was that of a rather old-fashioned family lawyer ('a dry old stick', as George Forsyte was wont to call his cousin Soames) and the values for which he stood may have seemed dated in the 'swinging Sixties', he was never backward-looking. Even when driving through London in retirement pointing out all the buildings and ministries in which he had served – Supply, Defence, the Foreign Office, the Treasury, Speaker's House – he added the comment that he was not (and ironically it was usually in Latin) *'laudator temporis acti se puero'*.*[20] He had no wish to be the critic and censor of the new generation. At his death there was no sense of national trauma. The tributes were restrained, concentrating largely on what had haunted him for twenty-two years, the events of a long ago summer.

However, Selwyn Lloyd carved out for himself a career that was unique in twentieth-century politics. 'I would ask leave to say that for every man who has taken part in the noble conflicts of parliamentary life', said Sir William Harcourt, when he retired as Leader of the House of Commons in 1895, 'the chiefest ambition, whether in the majority or the minority, must be to stand well with the House of Commons.'[21] Selwyn stood well with the House of Commons. After his death a political library was set up in his memory at Fettes at the instigation of Ian Harvey, for the benefit of a new generation. Politicians of all persuasions sent their books and gifts of others, many suitably inscribed.[22] It was one kind of epitaph. Selwyn's own preferred epitaph was the one inscribed at the foot of Tell's Tower in the garden of Hilbre House in memory of the champion St Bernard: *He was majestic in appearance, noble in character, affectionate in*

---

* 'inclined to praise the way the world went when he was a boy.'

disposition and of undaunted courage. 'That will do for me, if I deserve it', he said to Kenneth Rose, who added (after an unsatisfactory parliamentary picnic) 'and his wit was as dry as a House of Commons sandwich'.[23]

Born into the Edwardian age with its illusory certainties, Selwyn Lloyd lived through some of the most transitional years in history. His school days were passed in the shadow of one great war; in his manhood he achieved distinguished service in a second. He was a collector of Imperial stamps as a boy and the death of his sister Eileen in the service of Empire was the most important early stimulus to his own career. Yet the Empire he read about in ochre-coloured volumes of Henty had faded to a memory by the time of his death and he was a closer witness than most of its disintegration. He came into politics when the aristocratic element in the Conservative Party was to the fore. Over a quarter of a century later he was prominent in a very different kind of political world. He survived many transitions. But one thing was constant. From the age of sixteen he was determined to enter the House of Commons, which was for him the centre of events, the focus of public life. Despite blandishment he did not willingly relinquish his place there. Few moments matched the State Opening of Parliament on 15 August 1945 when he wrote that he 'could see the King & Queen intermittently by standing on my toes, & could just hear the King.'[24] To be elected to that company was to participate in the comity of the nation, to take one's place on the benches of history. At first this was adventure enough, but as the years passed Selwyn became more than a bystander. In short, he belonged decisively to that select group of figures who have influenced the times in which they have lived. He aimed to do the State some service and leave the country the better for his living. The burden of public life may at times have seemed insupportable, but once he had set his mind to it he would never have passed up the opportunity to 'undertake' his part in what was for him the greatest of all vocations and what Stanley Baldwin lovingly called the endless adventure of ruling men.

Appendix A

Report of the Broadcasting Committee (1949) Cmd 8116

Minority Report
SUBMITTED BY MR SELWYN LLOYD
Disagreement with Majority Report

1. Although I am substantially in agreement with my colleagues on a considerable number of matters contained in their Report, I regret that I am unable to agree with them upon the most important matter submitted to us. I do not believe that broadcasting in this country should be compelled to continue its development within the structure of a single Corporation.

2. I do not wish to imply by that statement condemnation of the work of the BBC in the past. I readily join my colleagues' tributes. The view that the time has come for a change is not a vote of censure on the BBC, but rather a recognition of the expansion accomplished and of the great possibilities ahead.

3. Technical progress is continuously improving the coverage of the BBC's sound programmes. It is now technically possible for most listeners to hear the three national programmes. If V.H.F. transmissions were to be undertaken, it would probably be possible to give the majority of listeners a further choice of at least four local programmes. It should also be technically possible for most viewers to have a choice of two or three television programmes. It should be remembered that in New York City the listener has now a choice among about 45 sound programmes and the viewer has a choice among seven television programmes. The availability of wavelengths in Britain is not likely ever to be as favourable as that in the U.S.A. so long as the V.H.F. broadcasting band is required to be used for other purposes such as the Fire, Police and Mobile services. But the number of channels available should provide ample scope for variety in local broadcasting. Similarly, sufficient extra television channels should be available to provide for a

choice of programmes. Receivers of each type could have adapters fitted at a small cost.

4. Against that forecast of the technical possibilities, the actual and potential power and influence of broadcasting can be measured. In paragraph 544 of the Majority Report, it is described as

> 'the most pervasive, and therefore one of the most powerful of agents for influencing men's thoughts and actions, for giving them a picture, true or false, of their fellows and of the world in which they live, for appealing to their intellect, their emotions and their appetites, for filling their minds with beauty or ugliness, ideas or idleness, laughter or terror, love or hate.'

To use less striking words, broadcasting is a very fine medium for the oral and visual transmission of information, education and entertainment.

5. It therefore seems that the most important question submitted to us is whether it is right that the control and development of this means of informing, educating and entertaining should remain with a single body of men and women. While acknowledging gladly the great gifts and high principles of those in authority at Broadcasting House, I cannot agree that it is in the public interest that all this actual and potential influence should be vested in a public or private monopoly.

EVILS OF MONOPOLY

6. Disquiet on this issue of leaving broadcasting in the hands of a public monopoly was shown by many of the witnesses who gave evidence. It was not confined to one interest or school of political thought. It came from many of those concerned with broadcasting, from commercial and advertising interests, and from both the Fabian and Liberal Research Groups. An outstanding warning is contained in paragraph 25 of the Memorandum of Evidence of Sir Robert Watson-Watt and Mr Geoffrey Crowther (page 341 of Appendix H). I will refer to four of the principal evils inherent in monopoly:

(a) *Size and Unwieldiness.* In 1935 the BBC had about 2,500 employees. At present it employs about 12,000 people. As the activities of an organisation grow, there is an inevitable tendency towards over-staffing, centralisation and bureaucracy. Those in authority cannot help being far removed from the rank and file. As Television and V.H.F. broadcasting develop, the tendency will increase. This is not criticism of the way in which the BBC have managed their affairs. It is the unavoidable result of the centralised control of a large and varied organisation.

(b) *Hindrance of development.* It is also unavoidable that monopoly should lead to complacency and rigidity. Throughout the whole organisation there must be a fear of taking risks and of making mistakes. Nor is it possible for an organisation built up upon the use of one technique readily to accept the introduction of a new one. Either the new technique will be held back for fear of mistakes, as possibly has been the case with the development of V.H.F., or the new technique will be dominated by the old, as in the view of some people has happened with television.

(c) *Only one employer.* Thirdly, with a monopoly there can be only one employer. This affects efficiency and freshness of outlook in two ways. If a man has spent many years of his working life in broadcasting and he knows that if he loses his job there is no alternative source of employment, he is bound to think twice about differing from his superior, let alone quarrelling with him. Conversely, if a man has been employed for many years and then shows signs of falling off, his superior will be chary of reporting adversely upon him if such a report may mean the end of any chance of employment for that individual, or perhaps some public controversy.

(d) *Excessive power.* Fourthly and most important, there is the danger of abuse of power. It is true as suggested above that a public monopoly may be so timid of making mistakes that it divests itself of initiative and purpose. On the other hand, there is no knowing when it may swing to the other extreme and exercise its power excessively and so as to abuse it. The BBC state in effect in their evidence that it is the BBC's duty to decide what it is good for people to hear or to see, and that the BBC must elevate the public taste and constantly be ahead of public opinion and public wishes in their programmes. It is just as though a British Press Corporation were to be set up with a monopoly of publishing newspapers and were to decide what choice of newspapers people were to have and what it was good for them to read in them. Again, we might have a British Publishing Corporation with a monopoly of publishing books deciding what books should be published; or a British Theatre Corporation with a monopoly of producing stage plays deciding what plays it was good for people to see. These national Corporations might all be staffed by good and worthy people, animated by the loftiest principles, but it would be the negation of freedom and democracy to vest in them such powers. The argument that ordinary people cannot be trusted to make wise decisions for themselves is the stock argument of dictators.

7. These arguments against monopoly are formidable. To me the most serious of them is the last. Lord Reith on the other hand gloried in the power of the BBC:

'It was the brute force of monopoly that enabled the BBC to become what it did; and to do what it did; that made it possible for a policy of moral responsibility to be followed.' (Page 364 of Appendix H.)

I do not like this 'brute force of monopoly' and I am afraid that its dangers in regard to this medium of expression are both insidious and insufficiently appreciated by the public.

SAFEGUARDS PROPOSED IN MAJORITY REPORT

8. My colleagues in their Report have shown that they are very much aware of these dangers and have suggested certain measures which may be

regarded as safeguards. Before I review them, it is only fair also to add that I believe that these dangers are also a matter of constant concern to the present Director General of the BBC. My colleagues' relevant proposals are as follows:

(a) *The National Commissions.* I welcome warmly this proposal, and have entered fully into the preparation of the portion of the Majority Report dealing with them. Whether or not my suggestions for the future organisation of broadcasting are accepted, I support this proposal.

(b) *The development of local broadcasting.* Here again I welcome wholeheartedly this proposal; my fear is that in so far as this development is left to the BBC it will either not happen at all or be painfully slow and restricted.

(c) *Devolution for Television.* I support this proposal. I should prefer that the devolution should be carried even further; meanwhile I believe it to be a step in the right direction.

(d) *Internal criticism.* Great importance is attached in the Majority Report to the institution of a new Public Representation Service. I do not object to this if the BBC are to continue to have their monopoly, although its success will depend upon the use made of it by the BBC. It could be so developed as merely to involve adding to the committees, paper work, and bureaucracy. In this event its effect would be to divorce still further those in authority from the rank and file.

(e) *Quinquennial Review.* Finally, my colleagues attach importance to the Quinquennial Review. I agree that it is important to have a periodic review. Its usefulness will depend upon the terms of reference of the Committee set up, but I favour such a review whatever the future pattern of broadcasting.

9. If broadcasting is to continue under a single organisation, I welcome most of these proposals. Even if the new framework suggested by me later in this Report were to be adopted, I still consider that the proposals under sub-paragraphs (a) and (e) of paragraph 8 should be implemented. My difficulty however is that I believe that the only effective safeguard is competition from independent sources. Without that competition the basic evils and dangers of monopoly will remain.

ALTERNATIVES TO THE PRESENT SINGLE
PUBLIC SERVICE CORPORATION

10. Although it may be admitted that certain dangers will remain if a single corporation continues to control broadcasting, it may be argued that the practical alternatives are such that it is preferable to retain the monopoly and run the risks. It is therefore necessary to consider what are the alternatives and whether the remedy would be worse than the disease.

(a) *Direct Parliamentary Control.* It would be possible to put the BBC in the same relation to Parliament as the Post Office. Either the Postmaster General or some new Minister would be answerable for the work of the Corporation and each Member of Parliament would be able to raise in the House every detail of the daily running of broadcasting, just as every act of every Post Office servant can be queried in Parliament at present. Like my colleagues, I reject this course without hesitation. The running of a broadcasting service, in particular the part of it dealing with culture, entertainment, and discussion of public issues, is in my view quite unsuitable for the same treatment as the organisation of a postal service. This alternative would bring the service under the direct control of the Government of the day, which would be wholly undesirable.

(b) *The substitution for the public monopoly of a number of separate agencies, independent of one another, each responsible for the transmission of programmes.* This could be done in a variety of ways:

(i) *The United States pattern.* This would entail no public service system at all. No licence fee would be paid, programmes would be provided by reason of the financial backing of those wishing to sell goods or services, or of those wishing to propagate certain ideas. This interplay of commercial competition would be regulated by a licensing authority, which would be responsible for the maintenance of certain standards.

(ii) *The Canadian or Australian patterns.* This would mean a composite system. In each of these countries, a public service system, wholly financed by licence fees in the case of Australia and partly so in Canada, exists alongside of commercial radio stations.

(iii) *The proposals of Sir Robert Watson-Watt and Mr. Crowther.* It would be possible to set up three public service corporations to compete with one another both in sound and television programmes for the same types of listener. All three would be financed from licence fees, with some sort of bonus for the most popular.

(iv) *Separate functional Corporations.* Finally, as suggested by several witnesses, it would be possible to have a number of public corporations (say three or four) set up on a functional basis, one to do the Home Service, one Television, one the Light Programme, and possibly a fourth for the Overseas Services or some other distinctive type of programme.

Commercial radio would be essential if (i) or (ii) were adopted. It would not be essential if (iii) or (iv) were adopted although it might be permitted. Accordingly I will consider firstly whether independent competition is to be desired and secondly whether it is tolerable that any or all of that independent competition should come from sponsored programmes. This consideration is certainly not a task to be undertaken lightheartedly. Great issues are at stake. What is good in the BBC's work must be preserved. Can that be done if any of the above changes are made? Before an answer can be given, it is necessary to consider the arguments put forward by the BBC for the continuance of the monopoly.

BBC'S DEFENCE OF THEIR MONOPOLY

11. The BBC defend their monopoly with vigour. I will not set out their case in any detail; it appears in Appendix H. They say that public monopoly is indispensable if high standards are to be maintained, if broadcasting is to have a social purpose and if taste is to be elevated. If competition is allowed, it will become competition for numbers of listeners. That will lower standards. The BBC argue this point against any form of competition, whether from other public service corporations or not, and whether the other public service corporations are organised as suggested by Mr. Crowther or on a functional basis as the Fabian and Liberal Research Groups wish. Against competition depending in any way on commercial sponsoring the BBC put forward additional arguments. They say that the social purpose of the BBC will be lost, and that programme content will pass to the hands of people caring only for the making of money, and no doubt they think that the air will be sullied by advertising matter.

12. I will deal first with the argument that any competition must debase standards. The most extravagant statements are current about the effect of competition in the U.S.A. It is alleged that unrestricted competition there has forced everything worthwhile off the air at good listening times. This is quite untrue so far as large cities like New York are concerned (see page 307 Appendix G). In New York the normal choice given by the 45 programmes is far wider and in many respects better than the normal choice given by the 3 programmes in Great Britain. Nevertheless there is the real danger that in this country with its fewer wavelengths, unrestricted competition might affect adversely the interests of listeners who are in a minority. Perusal of the Audience Research figures shows how low down in the list of popular choices come symphony concerts, poetry readings, chamber music, grand opera and the like. Therefore in the absence of the profusion of wavelengths which exists in the large centres of population in the U.S.A., I fully accept the necessity for one public service system, one of the functions of which would be to cater for minorities. Subject to that proviso I see no harm in the bulk of other programmes being intended to cater for as large a number of listeners as possible. In fact that is the case with much of the Home and Light programmes of the BBC at present. In paragraph 359 of the Majority Report an extract is quoted from the evidence given on behalf of the Labour Party to the effect that the vast majority of listeners who naturally prefer to be entertained rather than educated would listen to the best entertainment, if there was competition, and would miss the improving items interspersed in the BBC's programmes. The Labour Party considered that that was a good reason for maintaining the public monopoly. It appears to me a most undemocratic reason. I am not attracted by the idea of compulsory uplift achieved by 'the brute force of monopoly' to use Lord Reith's phrase. If people are to be trusted with the franchise, surely they should be able to decide for themselves whether they want to be educated or entertained in the evening. As long as provision is made for those who wish to listen to classical music or plays or poetry readings, etc., I see no reason why there

should not be competition for listeners in the rest of the field. Actually listeners are not showing themselves very willing to be improved even by the BBC. In paragraph 227 of the Majority Report it is stated that in the third quarter of 1949, 63 per cent. of evening listeners were listening to the Light Programme (the least 'improving' programme) as compared with 44 per cent. in the third quarter of 1945. Therefore provided that there is a public service system with its finances secured, able to set a high standard, to give a lead, and to cater for minorities, I much prefer to leave the rest to freedom of choice rather than to 'the brute force of monopoly.' I am strongly in favour of a constant endeavour to improve standards, but in a free society it should be by choice and not compulsion. In the field of entertainment and discussion, competition might well give a vitality which on occasion is now lacking. I read with interest a sentence in the evidence of the Electrical Association for Women (page 308 of Appendix H).

> 'A member who has experienced nothing but commercial broadcasting until the last two years, points out that, while at first she was delighted with the BBC system and the lack of sales talk, she finds on experience that the programmes lack something of the keenness to find new features apparent where there is competition.'

13. The next matter to be considered is whether if there is to be independent competition, it is tolerable that any of it should be from sponsored programmes. The BBC argue that, under the existing system, broadcasting has a social purpose. I do not accept the view that it is impossible for a company broadcasting programmes with the primary object of making a profit, to fulfil a social purpose. I believe that the milk retailer who retails milk at a profit and the ice cream merchant who sells ices to children on the seashore also at a profit are fulfilling social purposes. Newspapers run at a profit for their shareholders, in my view a social purpose rather more than the Government Department which distributes literature at the taxpayers' expense. Profits can be made only by providing a service appreciated by a number of people. If the service is anti-social, then that is matter for legal prohibition or control. Defence of public monopoly on the presumption that it alone can fulfil a social purpose can so easily degenerate into a cover for administrative incompetence or for the most vicious bureaucratic control or for tyranny itself. I admit that there are certain jobs which may not be done by profit-making bodies, for example, the Overseas Services and School Broadcasting; therefore, in rejecting t'ie BBC's argument about the profit makers and the social purpose, I again add the proviso that a public network should be retained.

14. Another BBC argument is that quite apart from the iniquity of profit making, programmes would be put on the air for the wrong reasons, not in furtherance of the art of broadcasting but to enable their sponsors either to sell goods or to propagate certain ideas. Is not this splitting hairs? Goods would not be sold nor ideas propagated unless an audience were to be attracted. The main purpose in putting on a programme would be to get

people to listen to it or to view it. May there not be hope of thus getting the best entertainment, the best type of drama, the outstanding sporting events and the most popular forms of discussions and talks? Programme producers would constantly be on the lookout for new types of discussions, etc. The true comment is less that the wrong people would be preparing the programmes than that the listeners would be the choosers. If they did not choose to listen, the item would not be sponsored. In the realm of entertainment and amusement at least, the desire to obtain a large audience is certainly not a bad motive and it seems to me idle to pretend that that is not what the BBC try to do. In this field, however, there are also minorities. Therefore this view is put forward again subject to the proviso that there should be in parallel a non-commercial public service programme.

ADVERTISEMENT CONTENT

15. The fourth argument is that the air will be sullied by advertisements. Many listeners have had experience of advertisements in continental programmes directed to this country, and I myself have listened to them in programmes in Canada and the U.S.A. and have viewed them in the U.S.A. Many advertisements directed to North American ears and eyes seemed to me to be boring, repetitive and lacking in subtlety. Many Americans agreed with me. On the other hand there were some in television programmes which were amusing and entertaining. I agree that strict control of advertisement matter would be needed. There would have to be a controlling body to deal with matters such as limitation or prohibition of advertisement of certain goods, rules against interrupting an item otherwise than at a recognised interval, rules governing the time to be allowed for the advertisement and the periods for a number of 'spot' advertisements, and rules for the protection of the small advertiser. I believe that it should be possible for British advertisers to co-operate in the formulation of rules and standards which would mitigate the force of most of the objections to advertisements on the air.* But on this aspect of the matter also, I would repeat the proviso about a non-advertisement alternative sound programme being available. No one would have to listen to advertisements in order to hear a radio programme. In the case of television, similar control would be required, although I am sure that there would be less objection to advertisement on the screen than in sound programmes. We are much more used to seeing advertisements than to hearing them. Owing to development difficulties, a non-advertisement alternative programme might not be feasible for some considerable time.

16. Having considered these arguments put forward by the BBC on behalf of monopoly, I am of the opinion that independent competition will be healthy for broadcasting. A BBC should remain to set the standards, and with the duty of providing the News, Education and Overseas Services, and that Corporation should be given adequate financial resources. In addition

* I should ban 'give away' programmes from the outset.

to this BBC there should be independent agencies to provide and transmit programmes and I do not object to those agencies being financed by means other than an Exchequer Grant or the revenue from licence fees, in other words by revenue from sponsors. On this basis it should be possible to halve the licence fee for sound, and later to reduce that for television. My proposals for the framework for a new system are set out in the following paragraphs. If this view should prove unacceptable, my second preference is for competition between a number of non-commercial corporations along the lines set out in paragraph 25 below.

ALTERNATIVE PROPOSALS

17. The following proposals may seem to entail sweeping changes. I admit that the process of transition might be delayed by difficulties about physical resources and manpower, although I believe that these difficulties can be greatly exaggerated. A process of slow transition, however, would have its own advantage in that it would offer scope for experiment.

18. *Commission for British Broadcasting*. To regulate* British broadcasting there should be established a new Commission with the following tasks:

    (a) the allotment of frequencies for broadcasting;

    (b) the licensing of broadcasting stations;

    (c) the regulation of a variety of matters such as political controversy at Election time, religious broadcasts, protection of small advertisers, affiliation of local stations to national programmes and anti-monopoly action;

    (d) the enforcement of certain standards and rules for advertising.

On general matters, the Lord President of the Council would be the appropriate Minister to answer to Parliament with regard to the activities of this body. On technical matters the Postmaster General would reply.

19. *The British Broadcasting Corporation*. The BBC should be licensed by the Commission to continue the Home and Regional Services. It would be under a duty to provide the News, School Broadcasting and the Overseas Services. Its revenue would come from a fixed licence fee for receivers, possibly 10s., and the Grant-in-Aid for the Overseas Services. It should not be allowed to include advertising matter. The fee to be fixed should be sufficient to give it financial independence and adequate resources to carry out the duties laid upon it.

20. *Other National Programmes*. Either one or two Companies (or Corporations) should be formed to run national programmes on commercial lines, that is to say programmes the items in which would be produced or sponsored by those willing to buy time. Although I believe that sufficient wavelengths would be available for two such bodies, it might be wiser to hasten slowly and at first to have only one. Its constitution, the degree of public control, its Memorandum and Articles of Association if a public

    * In his original draft, Selwyn Lloyd had written 'At the head of'.

company, the method of financing it, the terms of the licence and the arrangement for transfer of assets no longer required by the BBC are all matters for detailed examination.

21. *Local Stations.* These should be licensed to transmit local programmes. The capital cost of each station would not necessarily be large. One witness stated that the cost of a 100 Watt transmitter would be £1,500. It is to be hoped that universities, local authorities, newspapers, and companies formed for the purpose would make application for licences to set up such local stations. No concern should be permitted to run more than one station. The existence of advertising facilities on local programmes should enable the smaller business concerns to take advantage of this facility. As these local stations grow in numbers, the Commission might need to set up a subsidiary body to deal with them. I wholeheartedly agree with my colleagues that there is wide scope for local broadcasting and that it could make a great contribution to local patriotism, local interest, the development of local talent and culture, and to the diversification of broadcasting as a whole. An interesting memorandum submitted to us on this point is summarised at page 367 of Appendix H.

22. *British Television Corporation.* This Corporation should be licensed by the Commission to put on television programmes with the power as an interim measure to accept advertisements for sponsored items. I should expect that the support from sponsors would be sufficient to enable the licence fee also to be reduced.

23. *Other Television Corporations.* In due course one or more other Companies or Corporations could be licensed to provide the alternative television programmes which sooner or later the public will certainly demand and which are now technically possible. When that has taken place, it might be desirable to follow the same pattern as with sound broadcasting, a public non-commercial programme financed by a licence fee and alongside it one or more other agencies financed commercially.

24. *Advantages of above proposals.* The benefits accruing from the scheme outlined in the above paragraphs would be as follows:

(a) The monopoly would be broken up and there would be some competition. This would be a painful process, but its difficulty is no reason for failing to undertake it. It is one of the great drawbacks to monopoly that it is always difficult to break it.

(b) The BBC News, School Broadcasting, Overseas Services, and other distinctive programmes (paragraph 39 of the Majority Report) would be retained. The BBC would continue to give the authentic public service national programme, seeking to set the standard for the other agencies, with adequate revenue for that task.

(c) No one would have to listen to programmes containing advertisements unless of his or her free choice.

(d) Local broadcasting would develop. Local talent would have its chance in local programmes.

(e) Television could develop unimpeded by the influence of sound broadcasting. Contributions would come towards its very costly development from sources other than licence fees.

(f) Entertainment programmes would gain in vitality. The best would almost certainly be better.

(g) Those in the broadcasting profession or industry would no longer be tied to a single employer.

(h) A new facility would be provided for trade and industry, and advertising techniques would be acquired which would be of great advantage in export markets.

(i) A new impetus would be given to the development of the entertainment industry, and so to increased earnings of foreign currencies. The same would apply to certain types of equipment.

(j) Licence fees would be reduced, and at the same time the very large sums required for proper development of broadcasting would be made available.

(k) If broadcasting continues under the present system, commercially sponsored programmes will certainly be directed at this country to an increasing extent from overseas (Radio Luxembourg for example). This scheme would ensure that commercial programmes would be under our own control.

COMPETITION BETWEEN NON-COMMERCIAL CORPORATIONS

25. If the above proposals do not find favour with a majority of those responsible for deciding the pattern of broadcasting for the future, I favour an alternative method of breaking up the monopoly. I doubt whether the proposal of Sir Robert Watson-Watt and Mr. Crowther for three independent public service corporations all competing nationally for the same listeners with the same variety of programmes is practicable. The cost in materials and manpower and the difficulty in determining the method of financial reward appear to me to be grave disadvantages. I therefore support, as an alternative, the views of some of those who advocated competition between public service Corporations with different functions. The Fabian Research Group (Appendix H, pages 320 seq.) suggested one corporation to be responsible for two national programmes, a second corporation to develop local and regional broadcasting, a third corporation for overseas broadcasting and a television corporation. The Liberal Research Group (Appendix H, pages 382 seq.) made very much the same suggestions, except that it proposed that instead of the second corporation for local broadcasting there should be separate chartered organisations in each region. Other suggestions were put forward by other witnesses. My own view is that if this method of breaking up the monopoly were to be adopted, a beginning should be made by setting up a separate television corporation and a separate corporation to encourage and develop local broadcasting. If sponsoring were not to be permitted, the Television Corporation would have to be financed out of licence fees with power to borrow

for capital expenditure, and the Corporation for developing local broadcasting would have to receive a proportion of the sound licence fee with similar power to borrow. This split might have certain practical disadvantages but I believe that they would be outweighed by the correctives to the dangers of monopoly which would be provided.

CONCLUSION

26. If my proposals set out in paragraphs 18 to 23 or if the alternatives set out in paragraph 25 are adopted, they will involve substantial changes. Many men and women have given devoted service to make the BBC, and some of them will feel surprised and hurt that any change should be suggested. In particular in the present Director General, the BBC have a public servant of outstanding distinction. Nothing that I have written in this Minority Report is meant to reflect adversely upon any individual. The evil lies in the system, the control by a monopoly of this great medium of expression. It involves the concentration of great power in the hands of a few men and women, and the tendency to create a uniform pattern of thought and culture. At a time when every other tendency is towards the concentration of power at the centre and a uniform society, this issue in broadcasting is of outstanding importance for the country. About one matter there can be reasonable certainty. The present time when television is young and V.H.F. broadcasting has not begun is the most suitable for a change. If the opportunity is not taken now, and if it should recur, the task of breaking the monopoly will be many times more difficult.

27. One advantage of writing a minority report is that it gives the writer an opportunity for paying tribute to his colleagues. No body of men and women could have disagreed with me more courteously. Lord Beveridge by the magnitude of his exertions and the thoroughness of his inquiries has rendered a great public service. It is a matter of personal regret that I cannot accept his conclusions.

28. I would end by expressing – and not as a mere formality – my gratitude for the help given to me by Mr Parsons, Mr Baker and the excellent staff.

SELWYN LLOYD

15th December, 1950.

Appendix B

THE CHANCELLOR OF THE EXCHEQUER'S LETTER
ABOUT THE NEDC

Selwyn Lloyd's letter of 23 September 1961 to the Trades Union Congress, the Federation of British Industries, the British Employers' Confederation, the Association of British Chambers of Commerce and the National Union of Manufacturers:

Following upon my meetings with both sides of industry about a new approach to economic planning on a national scale, I have given careful thought to the various suggestions which have been made. In order to forward our joint consideration of these matters I set out in this letter, as promised, some specific proposals.

I believe that the time has come to establish new and more effective machinery for the co-ordination of plans and forecasts for the main sectors of our economy. There is a need to study centrally the plans and prospects of our main industries, to correlate them with each other and with the Government's plans for the public sector, and to see how in aggregate they contribute to, and fit in with, the prospects for the economy as a whole, including the vital external balance of payments. The task of keeping claims on our resources within our capacity is the responsibility of Government. But experience has shown the need for a closer link between Government and Industry in order to create a climate favourable to expansion and to make possible effective action to correct weaknesses in our economic structure. This new machinery should therefore assist in the promotion of more rapid and sustained economic growth.

I am anxious to secure that both sides of industry, on whose co-operation the fulfilment of our objectives must significantly depend, should participate fully with the Government in all stages of the process. I hope they would, under the arrangements proposed below, obtain a picture, more continuous and comprehensive than has hitherto been available, of the long-term problems in the development of our economy; and this should enhance the value of their advice on, and efforts in, the search for solutions. They would also have better opportunities to help in the moulding of the economic policies of the Government at the formative stage.

Clearly, we shall need some new machinery for this work. I envisage that this might take the following form. First, I propose the creation of a National Economic Development Council. The Chancellor of the Exchequer would be the Chairman and one or two other Ministers, such as the President of the Board of Trade and the Minister of Labour, would be members. The other members of the Council, who would be appointed by the Chancellor after appropriate consultations, would be drawn from the trade unions and from the management side of private and nationalised industry, with perhaps some additional members. I would aim at a total membership of, say, about twenty.

The functions of the Council would be to examine, and if necessary, commission studies relevant to the economic objectives which I have indicated earlier in this letter, and to consider how these objectives could best be secured. Responsibility for final decisions on matters of Government policy must remain with the Government, but the view expressed by the Council would carry great weight both with the Government and with industry. It would be for the Council to consider how far, and in what form, the results of its work should be made public.

The effectiveness of the Council's work would depend on the establishment of a full-time staff of the right calibre. This staff which would work under a Director to be appointed from outside the Civil Service, although under the aegis of Government, would not be part of the ordinary Government machine. It would act under the general direction of, and be responsible to, the Council. The Government for their part would be prepared to make available from the Civil Service an appropriate portion of the staff. I would hope that the rest would be drawn from both sides of industry, the commercial world and elsewhere. Normally individual members of the staff would be regarded as on temporary secondment for, say, two to three years.

The function of this staff would be to examine the plans for development of the main industries in the private sector and, in the light of such examinations and of discussions with Government Departments about other sectors of the economy, e.g. the nationalised industries, to prepare, for the consideration of the Council, studies of the kind envisaged in the second paragraph of this letter. The staff would make the fullest use of existing channels of information and consultation in Government and industry, and in the studies of particular industries would work in association with the Government Departments and other public bodies, e.g. the Iron and Steel Board and the Cotton Board, normally concerned with them.

With the setting up of the new organisation, I would propose that the present Economic Planning Board should come to an end. My present thought is that the National Production Advisory Council on Industry might be continued but, in that event, it should in future meet less frequently. The Minister of Labour's National Joint Advisory Council would continue as at present.

I am writing similarly to the (employers' organisations/the other employers' organisations and to the Trades Union Congress). If you agree, I suggest that we have a meeting with similar representation to that which attended the meeting I held on (22nd/23rd) August. Alternatively, if you and the others concerned preferred it, the meeting could be a joint one with representatives of both management and labour. In either case I should like, if it is convenient to you, to hold the meeting during the first ten days of October, and my private secretary will be getting in touch with you shortly to make a firm appointment.

In view of the public interest in the topic, I propose, if you have no objection, to make this letter available to the Press. I should be grateful if you would inform me whether this would be acceptable to you.

Notes

SELO refers to the Selwyn Lloyd Collection at Churchill College, Cambridge. The first number refers to the box in that collection and the second (in parenthesis) to the file within that box. e.g. SELO 123 (4). PRO refers to papers deposited at the Public Record Office, Kew.

PREFACE

1 Two expectations about the release of the Suez papers in 1987 (the paucity of material and the crowds of researchers at the Public Record Office) were confounded. The material released was extensive and the numbers at Kew on 2 January 1987 no more than on many a 'normal' day – but one saw some old friends.
2 The late Mrs A. Howard Shone to the author, 17 December 1984.
3 SELO 180 (4).
4 Ibid.
5 SELO 38 (4).

I A MIDDLE CLASS LAWYER FROM LIVERPOOL

1 The origin of this remark has been traced to several sources. One of the first occasions on which it was used was on the resignation of Lord Lambton on 16 May 1957. 'What a pity', Harold Macmillan told Victor Raikes, 'that we should have had to sacrifice an aristocrat for a middle class lawyer from Liverpool.' Victor Raikes told this to Randolph Churchill and so shortly afterwards the remark became part of the general political currency.
2 SELO 308 (2).
3 The others, according to many of his colleagues, were industry, integrity and loyalty.
4 SELO 308 (2).
5 SELO 179 (2).
6 Sir Evelyn Shuckburgh, *Descent to Suez*, 1986, p. 312.
7 George Borrow, *Wild Wales*, 1862, Ch. LXXIX.
8 Rev. Henry Rees, *Lest We Forget*, 1936, p. 55.
9 Kingswood School Records (Kingswood School, Bath).

10 SELO 118 (2).
11 SELO 308 (2).
12 SELO 307 (2).
13 SELO 308 (2).
14 Leys School Records (Cambridge University Library).
15 SELO 375 (1).
16 SELO 129 (2).
17 SELO 308 (2).
18 Ibid.
19 SELO 398 (4).
20 Ibid.
21 Interview with Kenneth Harris, 23–4 June 1976 (BBC).
22 Westbourne Road Methodist Church Records (Westbourne Road Methodist Church, West Kirby).
23 SELO 451 (1).
24 SELO 308 (5).
25 Ibid.
26 SELO 180 (4).
27 SELO 171 (5).
28 The late Mrs A. Howard Shone to the author, 17 December 1984.
29 Ibid.
30 Letter of 18 May 1971, SELO 265 (1).
31 Michael Noakes, letter to the author, 15 November 1985.
32 SELO 419 (2).
33 SELO 308 (2).
34 Michael McAfee, letter to the author, 12 September 1987.
35 SELO 396 (4).
36 SELO 180 (4).
37 The late Henry Silcock to the author, 16 December 1984.
38 Nicholas Monsarrat, *Life is a Four Letter Word*, 1966, p. 90.
39 SELO 130 (4).
40 SELO 171 (5).
41 SELO 180 (4).
42 Ibid.
43 SELO 171 (5)
44 Dr Ian Blake to the author, November 1984. He was the master.
45 SELO 374 (9).
46 SELO 180 (4).
47 SELO 35 (1).
48 SELO 398 (5).
49 Ibid.
50 Letter in the possession of Mrs David Stileman.
51 Ian Kemp, *Tippett: The Composer and his Music*, 1984, p. 9.
52 Private information.
53 SELO 443 (3).
54 SELO 396 (4).
55 SELO 180 (4).

56 SELO 443 (3).
57 SELO 123 (4).
58 SELO 258 (5).
59 SELO 300 (5).
60 SELO 171 (5).
61 SELO 443 (3).
62 *Fettesian*, vol. XLI.
63 Letter in the possession of the family.
64 George Hodson, letter to the author, 23 July 1985.
65 M. C. Leslie, letter to the author, 30 November 1984.
66 SELO 119 (1).
67 SELO 352 (1).
68 Fettes College *Vive-La*, 23 July 1923, printed privately.
69 SELO 468 (4).
70 Alasdair Macdonald to the author, 15 July 1985.
71 SELO 303 (4).
72 SELO 122 (1).
73 Private information.
74 T. S. Eliot, *Notes towards the Definition of Culture*, Faber & Faber, 1948, p. 43.
75 Samuel Smiles, *Self Help*, 1859, ch. V.
76 Quoted by Roy Lewis and Angus Maude, *The English Middle Classes*, Penguin edition, 1953, p. 26.

2 CAMBRIDGE AND LIBERALISM

 1 Percy Cradock (ed.), *Recollections of the Cambridge Union*, 1953, p. 1.
 2 SELO 304 (6).
 3 Ibid.
 4 SELO 308 (2).
 5 David Newsome, *On the Edge of Paradise*, 1980, p. 154.
 6 SELO 438 (2).
 7 SELO 80 (1).
 8 SELO 308 (2).
 9 Lord Ramsey of Canterbury to the author, 21 August 1985.
10 SELO 443 (1).
11 Speech at Sidney Sussex, Cambridge, 5 June 1975.
12 SELO 80 (1).
13 Ibid.
14 SELO 104 (8).
15 Ibid.
16 Ibid.
17 Dame Olwen Carey Evans to the author, 25 July 1985.
18 Ibid.
19 Mrs Ronald Clayton to the author, 14 April 1986.
20 Letter in the possession of the family.
21 SELO 26 (4).
22 SELO 438 (2).

23 SELO 443 (1).
24 SELO 289 (6).
25 SELO 104 (8).
26 Ibid.
27 Ibid.
28 Ibid.
29 SELO 122 (3).
30 SELO 396 (4).
31 SELO 443 (1).
32 Ibid.
33 Philip M. Williams, *Hugh Gaitskell: A Political Biography*, 1979, p. 18.
34 For a full account of Cambridge attitudes to the General Strike see T. E. B. Howarth, *Cambridge Between Two Wars*, 1978, pp. 141–50.
35 SELO 443 (1).
36 Ibid.
37 SELO 104 (8).
38 SELO 443 (1).
39 *Cambridge Daily News*, 19 October 1926.
40 SELO 306 (1).
41 SELO 443 (1).
42 Cambridge Union Society Records (University Library, Cambridge).
43 SELO 104 (8).
44 SELO 396 (3).
45 Sir Hugh Foot, *A Start in Freedom*, 1964, p. 25.
46 SELO 396 (3).
47 Ibid.
48 Ibid.
49 Ibid.
50 Ibid.
51 SELO 38 (4).
52 SELO 374 (4).
53 SELO 439 (2).
54 SELO 443 (1).
55 SELO 396 (3).
56 Maurice Cowling, *The Impact of Labour 1920–1924*, 1971, p. 419.
57 SELO 38 (2).
58 Ibid.
59 SELO 304 (6).
60 SELO 179 (3).
61 SELO 38 (2).
62 SELO 443 (2).
63 SELO 38 (2).
64 SELO 443 (2).

3 MR HOYLAKE UDC

1 David Lloyd George, Speech at the Free Trade Hall, Manchester, 12 April 1929.

2 SELO 289 (6).
3 SELO 292 (1).
4 SELO 104 (8).
5 *People*, 1 January 1928.
6 SELO 179 (3).
7 SELO 404 (3).
8 SELO 289 (6).
9 Ibid.
10 Ibid.
11 SELO 180 (4).
12 Personal information from several members of the family.
13 Attlee papers, ATLE 2/4.
14 SELO 443 (2).
15 SELO 289 (6).
16 SELO 50 (1).
17 SELO 9 (3).
18 SELO 204 (1).
19 Speech of 4 October 1948 on appointment as Recorder of Wigan, SELO 201.
20 Private information.
21 SELO 289 (6).
22 SELO 10 (1).
23 SELO 267 (1).
24 SELO 325 (1).
25 SELO 188 (4).
26 SELO 38 (2).
27 Private information.
28 Information from those who worked in the Chambers at Cook Street and Castle Street before the war.
29 SELO 289 (6).
30 SELO 204 (2).
31 Patric Dickinson, *A Round of Golf Courses*, 1951, p. 57.
32 SELO 86.
33 SELO 10 (1).
34 SELO 204 (4).
35 Unpublished memorandum, 'The Suspension of the Death Penalty', SELO 219 (4).
36 See in particular David Marquand, *Ramsay Macdonald*, 1977, ch. 26.
37 Stephen Roskill, *Hankey: Man of Secrets*, Volume 2, 1919–31, 1972, p. 569.
38 C. L. Mowat, *Britain between the Wars: 1918–1940*, 1955, p. 412.
39 SELO 293 (1).
40 Interview with Kenneth Harris, 23–24 June 1976.
41 SELO 396 (1).
42 Ibid.
43 Ibid.
44 SELO 281 (1).

45 SELO 300 (5).
46 SELO 289 (6).
47 SELO 179 (3).
48 SELO 267 (5).
49 SELO 491 (6).
50 SELO 491 (1).
51 Speech at Institute of Public Administration, 8 February 1949, SELO 487 (4).
52 SELO 86.
53 SELO 491 (6).
54 Minutes of Hoylake UDC, 16 March 1937, SELO 374 (8).
55 SELO 86.
56 SELO 491 (6).
57 SELO 109 (1).
58 SELO 182 (2).
59 Evidence of a colleague of the time.
60 See Bernard Levin, writing as Taper, *Spectator*, *passim*.
61 Mr Anthony Shone showed me from a hillock on the Royal Liverpool Golf Course the routes of these childhood journeyings.
62 The late Lord Mancroft to the author, 30 November 1985.
63 Minutes of the 25 Club (25 Club, Liverpool).
64 SELO 86.

4 WILLINGLY TO WAR

1 Wilfred Owen, 'Dulce et Decorum Est'.
2 Army Reminiscences, SELO 435 (1).
3 'One's rum account of the war years', SELO 308 (2).
4 SELO 224 (1).
5 Hore-Belisha papers, 5/46.
6 SELO 436 (1).
7 Ibid.
8 SELO 435 (1).
9 Hore-Belisha papers, 5/66.
10 SELO 308 (2).
11 Ibid.
12 Ibid.
13 Interview with Kenneth Harris, 23–4 June 1976.
14 Lt-Gen. Sir Brian Horrocks, *A Full Life*, 1960, p. 75.
15 SELO 435 (1).
16 SELO 190 (1).
17 SELO 108 (6).
18 Ibid.
19 Ibid.
20 Ibid.
21 Ibid.
22 Ibid.
23 SELO 443 (5).

24 SELO 435 (1).
25 This had been in September 1936. See Richard Griffiths, *Fellow Travellers of the Right: British Enthusiasts for Nazi Germany*, 1980, pp. 222–3. Selwyn Lloyd's diary entry is in SELO 71 (1).
26 SELO 435 (1).
27 Ibid.
28 Ibid.
29 SELO 108 (7).
30 SELO 435 (1).
31 SELO 108 (7).
32 Ibid.
33 Ibid.
34 Ibid.
35 SELO 289 (6).
36 SELO 443 (6).
37 Ibid.
38 Interview with Kenneth Harris, 23–4 June 1976.
39 Correspondence 1961, SELO 70 (1).
40 SELO 180 (4).
41 SELO 443 (6).
42 SELO 190.
43 The late T. E. B. Howarth to the author, 14 March 1987.
44 SELO 443 (4).
45 Nigel Hamilton, *Monty: The Making of a General, 1887–1942*, 1981, p. 561.
46 SELO 443 (4).
47 SELO 180 (4).
48 SELO 443 (4).
49 Ibid.
50 *The Times*, 18 May 1978.
51 SELO 108 (7).
52 *Troilus and Cressida*, I. iii. 200.
53 SELO 443 (4).
54 Private information.
55 WO 171/192 (PRO).
56 SELO 488 (8).
57 Private information from Ashley Gardens personnel.
58 *An Account of the Operations of Second Army in Europe 1944–1945*, 1945, vol. 1 Ch. 2, Appendix H, pp. 150–1.
59 The late T. E. B. Howarth to the author, 14 March 1987.
60 SELO 71 (1).
61 SELO 443 (7).
62 SELO 438 (1).
63 SELO 443 (7).
64 Interview with Kenneth Harris, 23–24 June 1976.
65 SELO 443 (7).
66 Ibid.

67 Ibid.
68 SELO 108 (3).
69 Ibid.
70 Ibid.
71 Letters in the possession of Mr Anthony Shone.
72 Interview with Kenneth Harris, 23–4 June 1976.
73 Pyman papers, File 15.
74 Colonel Michael Osborn in a letter to the author, 8 August 1986.
75 One of the most moving moments for the author in the preparation of
    this biography was when he was the catalyst for a reunion of Selwyn
    Lloyd's Second Army colleagues at a luncheon in July 1986. Many of
    those present had not met since the last reunion at the D-Day Service at
    Christ Church, Portsdown in 1969, the year of General Dempsey's
    death. The convivial atmosphere as they relived those days was an
    eloquent testimony to the teamwork that was displayed in 1944–5. As
    we parted, one of those present said to the author, 'Now you can see
    how we worked at Second Army.'
76 SELO 108 (2).
77 WO 285/22 (PRO).
78 SELO 108 (2).
79 Ibid.
80 Interview with Kenneth Harris, 23–24 June 1976.
81 SELO 108 (2).
82 SELO 443 (8).
83 Ibid.
84 *An Account of the Operations of Second Army in Europe 1944–1945*,
    1945, vol. 2.
85 Pyman papers, File 15/23.
86 Pyman papers, File 4/19.
87 SELO 443 (8).
88 Ibid.
89 Ibid.
90 SELO 272 (1).
91 Ibid.
92 SELO 181 (4).
93 Sir John Smyth, *Milestones: A Memoir*, 1979, p. 219.
94 SELO 86 (5).
95 CAB 106/1049 (PRO).
96 SELO 443 (9).
97 Ibid.
98 Ibid.
99 *Hansard*, 11 February 1960 (col. 792).
100 SELO 443 (9).
101 WO 285/22 (PRO).
102 H. E. Pyman, *Call to Arms*, 1971, pp. 82–3.
103 SELO 54 (2) and private information from those present.
104 SELO 443 (8).

105 SELO 488 (8).

5 MEMBER FOR THE WIRRAL

1 Anthony Howard, 'The British General Election of 1945', in Michael Sissons and Philip French (eds), *The Age of Austerity*, 1963.
2 D. R. Thorpe, *The Uncrowned Prime Ministers*, 1980, p. 182.
3 SELO 443 (9).
4 *Birkenhead News*, 2 June 1945.
5 SELO 232 (2).
6 *Birkenhead News*, 16 and 30 June 1945.
7 *Birkenhead News*, 30 June 1945.
8 SELO 272 (1).
9 SELO 315 (1).
10 *Birkenhead News*, 16 June 1945.
11 Information from several members of the family.
12 Dr J. W. Lloyd diary, SELO 86 (5).
13 *Birkenhead News*, 7 July 1945.
14 Ibid.
15 SELO 86 (5).
16 Mr John Shone to the author, 16 April 1986.
17 SELO 86 (5).
18 Ben Pimlott (ed.), *The Political Diary of Hugh Dalton 1918–40, 1945–60*, 1986, p. 512.
19 SELO 122 (4).
20 SELO 300 (5).
21 Ibid.
22 Private information.
23 *Hansard*, 12 February 1946 (cols 268–74).
24 Private information.
25 SELO 314 (2).
26 SELO 201.
27 Ibid.
28 SELO 300 (5).
29 SELO 374 (5).
30 SELO 104 (1).
31 SELO 424 (1).
32 D. R. Thorpe, op. cit., pp. 186–7.
33 SELO 300 (5).
34 Sir Robert Shone to the author, 21 March 1985.
35 J. D. Hoffman, *The Conservative Party in Opposition*, 1964, p. 207.
36 SELO 219 (4).
37 Ibid.
38 The late Sir Austin Strutt to the author, 1975.
39 SELO 122 (2).
40 SELO 392 (2).
41 SELO 329 (1).
42 *Wigan Observer*, 2 October 1948.

43 SELO 48.
44 SELO 287 (1).
45 SELO 122 (2).
46 Sir Robert Speed and David Natzler, *The Parliamentary Golfing Society: A Short History*, 1985.
47 SELO 122 (2).
48 Ibid.
49 T. E. B. Howarth, *Prospect and Reality: Great Britain 1945–1955*, 1985, p. 222.
50 Grace Wyndham Goldie, *Facing the Nation*, 1977, p. 72.

6 'THE FATHER OF COMMERCIAL TELEVISION'

 1 HO 254/2 (PRO).
 2 Correlli Barnett, *The Audit of War: the Illusion and Reality of Britain as a Great Nation*, 1986, p. 26.
 3 *Hansard*, 24 May 1949 (col. 1050).
 4 CAB 129/51 (PRO).
 5 The late Sir Hugh Greene to the author, 4 February 1987.
 6 Letter of 25 September 1948, SELO 122 (2).
 7 David Dilks, *Neville Chamberlain; Volume I, 1869–1929*, 1984, p. 303.
 8 *The Broadcasting Committee Report (August 1923)*, Cmd 1951.
 9 Asa Briggs, *The BBC: The First Fifty Years*, 1979, p. 49.
10 *Report of the Broadcasting Committee 1935* (1936), Cmd 5091.
11 CAB 65/41 (PRO).
12 CAB 128/2 (PRO).
13 CAB 129/10 (PRO).
14 Reith evidence to the Crawford Committee, 1925.
15 *The Times*, 26 June 1946.
16 *Broadcasting Policy*, Cmnd 6852.
17 HO 245/3 (PRO).
18 Interview with Phillip Whitehead, SELO 254 (3).
19 HO 254/3 (PRO).
20 Broadcasting Committee, Paper No. 91.
21 HO 254/4 (PRO).
22 HO 254/5 (PRO).
23 Broadcasting Committee, Paper No. 165, HO 254/6 (PRO).
24 HO 254/6 (PRO).
25 Broadcasting Committee, Paper No. 226.
26 HO 254/8 (PRO).
27 Ibid.
28 Interview with Phillip Whitehead, SELO 254 (3).
29 SELO 387 (1).
30 Andrew Boyle, *Only the Wind will Listen: Reith of the BBC*, 1972, footnote p. 343.
31 Harman Grisewood, *One Thing at a Time*, 1968, pp. 175–6.
32 Ibid., p. 176.
33 BBC Records, Caversham, R4/1/10/11.

34 Ibid.
35 Diary 15 June 1950, SELO 104 (1).
36 Diary 20 July 1950, SELO 104 (1).
37 SELO 74 (1).
38 BBC Records, Caversham, R 4/1/25.
39 HO 254/10 (PRO).
40 Ibid.
41 BBC Records, Caversham, R 4/1/25.
42 Mary Stocks, *My Commonplace Book*, 1970, p. 173.
43 SELO 122 (2).
44 Ibid.
45 Ibid.
46 Ibid.
47 BBC Records, Caversham, R 4/1/25.
48 SELO 267 (2).
49 *Broadcasting in the USA*, HO 254/9 (PRO).
50 Broadcasting Committee, Paper No. 317, HO 254/9 (PRO).
51 Ibid.
52 Private information.
53 Christopher Mayhew, *Dear Viewer*, 1953.
54 SELO 267 (2).
55 HO 254 (1) (PRO).
56 Grace Wyndham Goldie, *Facing the Nation*, 1977, p. 104.
57 HO 254/1 (PRO).
58 H. H. Wilson, *Pressure Group: The Campaign for Commercial Television*, 1961, p. 54.
59 Asa Briggs, op. cit., p. 264.
60 *Spectator*, 19 January 1951.
61 *New Statesman* and *Nation*, 20 January 1951.
62 *Hansard*, 19 July 1951 (cols 1423–61).
63 Ibid., (cols 1495–8).
64 SELO 122 (2).
65 SELO 447 (1).
66 Minority Report (See Appendix A).
67 Asa Briggs, *The History of Broadcasting in the United Kingdom: Volume 4, Sound and Vision*, 1979, p. 392.
68 *Listener*, 3 October 1985.
69 *Attlee paper on Broadcasting Policy*, Cmnd 8291.
70 *Broadcasting: Memorandum on the Report of the Broadcasting Committee, 1949* (1952), Cmd 8550.
71 CAB 129/52 (PRO).
72 *White Paper: Television Policy* (November 1953), Cmd 9005.
73 CAB 129/50 C (52) 99 (PRO).
74 SELO 384 (2).
75 Ibid.
76 *Hansard*, 27 June 1963 (col. 1782).
77 SELO 166 (4).

78 SELO 22 (1).
79 *Hansard*, 27 June 1963 (col. 1782).
80 The late Sir Hugh Greene to the author, 4 February 1987.
81 Ibid.
82 SELO 180 (4).

7 ON THE LADDER

1 Megan Lloyd George wrote to Attlee on 25 April 1955, saying that she was joining the Labour Party as only there could she be 'true to the Radical spirit'. Attlee papers, ATLE 2/4.
2 SELO 392 (1).
3 Nigel Fisher, *Iain Macleod*, 1973, p. 77.
4 Lord Carr of Hadley to the author, 13 October 1987.
5 BBC Records, Caversham, R 34/562/1.
6 SELO 122 (2).
7 *Evening Standard*, 6 December 1950.
8 *Daily Despatch*, 7 December 1950.
9 SELO 122 (2).
10 Private information.
11 SELO 122 (2).
12 Ibid.
13 Harold Nicolson, *Diaries and Letters, Volume 3 1945–1962*, 1968, p. 164.
14 Lord Butler of Saffron Walden papers, RAB H 46.
15 Ibid, RAB G 23$^{2-5}$.
16 Ibid, RAB H 94.
17 Conservative Party Records, Bodleian Library, CRD 2/49/22.
18 Ibid., CRD 2/49/24.
19 Lord Butler of Saffron Walden papers, RAB H 34 (Letter of 11 September 1951).
20 J. D. Hoffman, *The Conservative Party in Opposition, 1945–1951*, 1964, p. 204.
21 SELO 86.
22 Private information.
23 Anthony Seldon, *Churchill's Indian Summer*, 1981, p. 78.
24 SELO 299 (4).
25 The *Daily Record*, reporting these comings and goings, referred to the five as 'prominent' Conservatives, *Daily Record* 30 October 1951.
26 Private information.
27 SELO 16 (2).
28 Selwyn Lloyd, *Suez 1956: A Personal Account*, 1978, p. 4.
29 Private information.
30 Robert Rhodes James, *Anthony Eden*, 1986, p. 344.
31 SELO 222 (4).
32 SELO 329 (1).
33 SELO 299 (4).
34 SELO 86.

35 SELO 201 (3).
36 Private information.
37 SELO 16 (2).
38 PREM 11/305 (PRO).
39 SELO 16 (2).
40 Ibid.
41 SELO 299 (4).
42 *Winnipeg Tribune*, 27 December 1955.
43 Evelyn Shuckburgh, *Descent to Suez*, 1986, p. 26.
44 Anthony Eden, *Full Circle*, 1960, pp. 7–9.
45 FO 371/95656 (PRO).
46 SELO 16 (2).
47 See also Anthony Seldon, *Churchill's Indian Summer*, 1981, p. 385.
48 FO 371/95678 (PRO).
49 FO 371/95656 (PRO).
50 SELO 441 (1).
51 Ibid.
52 Ibid.
53 SELO 16 (2).
54 Ibid.
55 Ibid.
56 Ibid.
57 *Hansard*, 5 February 1952 (col. 925).
58 SELO 16 (2).
59 SELO 29 (5).
60 CAB 129/60 C (53) 108 (PRO).
61 FO 371/99622 (PRO).
62 SELO 300 (5).
63 SELO 166 (3).
64 Ibid.
65 Ibid.
66 SELO 300 (5).
67 SELO 166 (3).
68 SELO 16 (2).
69 SELO 25 (5).
70 SELO 166 (4).
71 SELO 16 (2).
72 Ibid.
73 Private information.
74 SELO 16 (2).
75 Private information.
76 SELO 25 (5).
77 SELO 16 (2).
78 Private information.
79 FO 800/692 (PRO).
80 CAB 129/50 (PRO).
81 CAB 131/12 (PRO).

82 CAB 128/25 (PRO).
83 CAB 129/54 (PRO).
84 Anthony Eden, op. cit., 1960, p. 229.
85 PREM 11/544 (PRO).
86 SELO 15 (4).
87 Ibid.
88 FO 800/695 (PRO).
89 Selwyn Lloyd, op. cit., p. 14.
90 CAB 129/60 (PRO).
91 Evidence from the Private Office.
92 SELO 16 (1).
93 SELO 129 (1).
94 Private information.
95 SELO 16 (1).
96 FO 800/699 (PRO).
97 SELO 88 (3).
98 SELO 65 (2).
99 SELO 313 (1).
100 FO 800/700.
101 SELO 16 (1).
102 SELO 193 (2).
103 Private information.
104 Sir John Leahy to the author, 29 June 1987.
105 Ibid.
106 Private information.
107 PREM 11/544 Sudan Papers (PRO).
108 MAF 255/87 (PRO).
109 Sir John Colville to the author, 20 June 1985.
110 SELO 278 (3).
111 See Sir John Colville, *The Churchillians*, 1981, ch. 10 *passim*.
112 Private information.
113 D. R. Thorpe, *The Uncrowned Prime Ministers*, 1980, p. 198.
114 Private information.
115 CAB 128/27 C (54) 29 (PRO).
116 See Evelyn Shuckburgh, op. cit., p. 129.
117 SELO 16 (1).
118 Evelyn Shuckburgh, op. cit., p. 133.
119 1954 Diary, SELO 363.
120 FO 371/108352 (PRO).
121 Ibid.
122 Private information.
123 SELO 16 (1).
124 Ibid.
125 SELO 363.
126 Private information. Churchill had asked Selwyn to represent the government at a minor negotiation at the United Nations. Selwyn had misunderstood his brief, which was to be non-committal. He proceeded

to a signed settlement which occasioned Churchill's remark in 10 Downing Street.

127 SELO 329 (1).

8 HIS MASTER'S VOICE?

1 SELO 88 (3).
2 Ibid.
3 Private information.
4 SELO 95 (1).
5 Private information.
6 SELO 35 (1).
7 SELO 363.
8 CAB 128/27 (PRO).
9 Mary Soames, *Clementine Churchill*, 1979, p. 501.
10 *The Supply of Military Aircraft* (February 1955), Cmnd 9388.
11 CAB 128/28 (PRO).
12 Richard Crossman, *The Backbench Diaries of Richard Crossman*, edited by Janet Morgan, 1981, p. 394.
13 CAB 128/28 (PRO).
14 SELO 249 (4).
15 DEFE 7/556 (PRO).
16 SELO 56 (1).
17 SELO 180 (5).
18 Hailes Papers, HAIS 2/12.
19 SELO 56 (1).
20 Lord Carr of Hadley to the author, 13 October 1987.
21 SELO 180 (4).
22 Harold Macmillan, *Tides of Fortune*, 1969, p. 579.
23 Ismay Papers, ISMAY III/4/40–1.
24 SELO 56 (1).
25 Private information.
26 CAB 129/77 (PRO).
27 Ibid.
28 SELO 56 (1).
29 Harold Macmillan, op. cit., p. 688.
30 SELO 180 (4).
31 SELO 168 (3).
32 Most recently by Richard Lamb in *The Failure of the Eden Government*, 1987, p. 52.
33 Interview with Kenneth Harris, 23–24 June 1976.
34 Anthony Eden, *Facing the Dictators*, 1962, p. 594.
35 SELO 180 (4).
36 SELO 106 (1).
37 Ibid.
38 Ben Pimlott (ed.), *The Political Diary of Hugh Dalton, 1918–40, 1945–60*, 1986, p. 506.
39 Speech at the Military Academy, West Point, 5 December 1962.

40 Lord Strang Papers, STRN 4/1.
41 Private information.
42 The late Sir Denis Laskey to the author, 6 August 1985.
43 CAB 129/78 (PRO).
44 CAB 128/30 (PRO).
45 Letter in the possession of the family.
46 Makins Papers, FO 800/437 (PRO).
47 CAB 128/30 (PRO).
48 Ibid.
49 Selwyn Lloyd, *Suez 1956: A Personal View*, 1978, p. 44.
50 Private information.
51 SELO 129 (1).
52 Selwyn Lloyd, op. cit., p. 47.
53 Private information.
54 PREM 11/1476 (PRO).
55 Mohammed Heikal, *Nasser: The Cairo Documents*, 1972, p. 88.
56 CAB 128/30 (PRO).
57 Philip M. Williams (ed.), *The Diary of Hugh Gaitskell*, 1983, p. 493.
58 PREM 11/1516 (PRO).
59 Philip M. Williams (ed), op. cit., p. 595.
60 Ibid., p. 595.
61 Anthony Eden, *Full Circle*, 1960, p. 357.
62 Ibid., p. 362.
63 Private information.
64 SELO 477 (1).
65 Ibid.
66 Private information.
67 Private information.
68 Tony Benn, *Out of the Wilderness: Diaries 1963–1967*, 1987, pp. 39–40.
69 Richard Crossman, op. cit., p. 501.
70 SELO 308 (2).
71 Anthony Eden, *Full Circle*, 1960, p. 318.
72 Richard Crossman, op. cit., p. 501.
73 Sir John Leahy in a letter to the author, 17 July 1987.
74 SELO 308 (2).

9 SUEZ

1 David Carlton, *Anthony Eden: A Biography*, 1981, p. 472.
2 SELO 237 (1).
3 Ibid.
4 Nigel Fisher, *The Tory Leaders: Their Struggle for Power*, 1977, p. 75.
5 Robert Rhodes James, *Anthony Eden*, 1986, p. 628.
6 It is in Box 237 of the Selwyn Lloyd Papers, File 3.
7 Sir Donald Logan, 'Collusion at Suez', *Financial Times*, 8 November 1956. The Secrets of Suez (BBC Television), 12 November 1986.
8 Private information.
9 Selwyn Lloyd, *Suez 1956: A Personal View*, 1978, p. 21.

10 SELO 278 (4).
11 SELO 180 (3).
12 Selwyn Lloyd, op. cit., p. 204.
13 Anthony Eden, *Full Circle*, 1960, p. 419.
14 CAB 128/30 (PRO).
15 Selwyn Lloyd. op. cit., p. 71. The British Ambassador was Sir Roger Makins (later Lord Sherfield).
16 Lord Sherfield, private letter of 2 August 1978.
17 SELO 278.
18 Charles Dickens, *Oliver Twist*, ch. 17.
19 SELO 169.
20 Selwyn Lloyd, op. cit., p. 89.
21 CAB 128/30 (PRO).
22 SELO 278 (4).
23 Philip M. Williams (ed.), *The Diary of Hugh Gaitskell 1945–1956*, 1983, p. 552.
24 Ibid., p. 553.
25 Roy Fullick and Geoffrey Powell, *Suez: The Double War*, 1979, p. 13.
26 Philip Ziegler, *Mountbatten: The Official Biography*, 1985, p. 538.
27 Quoted by Anthony Eden in *Full Circle*, p. 425.
28 Speech in the House of Commons, 16 May 1957, *Hansard*, vol. 570, cols 679–89.
29 CAB 128/30 (PRO).
30 Ibid.
31 CAB 134/1216 (PRO).
32 J. P. Mackintosh, *The British Cabinet*, 3rd edition, 1977, p. 24.
33 Ibid., p. 25.
34 CAB 134/1216 (PRO).
35 Ibid.
36 SELO 278 (4).
37 SELO 112 (1).
38 Michael A. Guhin, *John Foster Dulles: a Statesman and His Times*, 1972, p. 292.
39 FO 800/728 (PRO).
40 CAB 134/1216 (PRO).
41 *Listener*, 16 August 1956. BBC Records, Caversham (Microfilm T 299).
42 FO 800/728 (PRO).
43 CAB 128/30 (PRO).
44 Selwyn Lloyd, op. cit., p. 114.
45 Stephen Roskill, *Hankey: Man of Secrets, Vol. 3*, 1974, p. 636.
46 FO 800/714 (PRO).
47 CAB 128/30 (PRO).
48 Private information from several Foreign Office officials of the time.
49 CAB 134/1216 (PRO).
50 SELO 278 (4).
51 SELO 129 (1).
52 SELO 278 (4).

53 CAB 128/30 (PRO).
54 In particular Foreign Office Telegram 1942, SELO 278 (4).
55 Selwyn Lloyd, op. cit., p. 144.
56 SELO 278 (4).
57 Ibid.
58 SELO 129 (2).
59 Ibid.
60 Ibid.
61 CAB 128/30 (PRO).
62 SELO 278 (4).
63 Selwyn Lloyd, op. cit., p. 150.
64 CAB 134/1216 (PRO).
65 FO 800/728 (PRO).
66 See Selwyn Lloyd, op. cit., Appendix IV.
67 Mohammed H. Heikal, *Cutting the Lion's Tail: Suez through Egyptian Eyes*, 1986, p. 174.
68 SELO 236 (3).
69 SELO 129 (1).
70 PREM 11/1102 (PRO).
71 Selwyn Lloyd, op. cit., p. 165.
72 Terence Robertson, *Crisis: The Inside Story of the Suez Conspiracy*, 1965, p. 144.
73 Ibid., p. 145.
74 SELO 237 (3).
75 Ibid.
76 Ibid.
77 Selwyn Lloyd, op. cit., p. 166.
78 Sir Anthony Nutting, *No End of a Lesson*, 1967, p. 98.
79 Hugh Thomas, *The Suez Affair*, revised edition, 1986, p. 113.
80 FO 800/725 (PRO).
81 CAB 134/1216 (PRO).
82 Selwyn Lloyd, op. cit., p. 175.
83 The fact that Sir Gladwyn Jebb might resign as British Ambassador in Paris also had to be considered by the government at this time.
84 Lord Butler, *The Art of the Possible*, revised edition, 1973, p. 192.
85 SELO 129 (1).
86 CAB 128/30 (PRO).
87 Selwyn Lloyd, op. cit., p. 178.
88 PREM 11/1152 (PRO).
89 SELO 298 (3).
90 Patrick Shone diary 20 October 1956 (courtesy of Mr Patrick Shone).
91 SELO 169 (1).
92 FO 800/745.
93 SELO 129 (1).
94 Selwyn Lloyd, op. cit., p. 180.
95 David Carlton, op. cit., p. 435.
96 Private information.

97 FO 800/716 (PRO).
98 SELO 278 (4).
99 Selwyn Lloyd, op. cit., p. 181.
100 Sir John Colville, *The Fringes of Power: Downing Street Diaries 1939–1955*, 1985, p. 759.
101 The Secrets of Suez, BBC Television 12 November 1986.
102 Clarissa Eden diary, 23 October 1956.
103 CAB 128/30 (PRO).
104 SELO 253 (2).
105 FO 800/725 (PRO).
106 Christian Pineau, *1956 Suez*, 1976, p. 137.
107 CAB 128/30 (PRO).
108 Ibid.
109 SELO 236 (3).
110 SELO 237 (3).
111 SELO 329 (1).
112 SELO 237 (1).
113 SELO 278 (3).
114 *Hansard*, 20 December 1956 (cols 1491–518).
115 Lord Gladwyn papers.
116 SELO 116 (1).
117 CAB 128/30 (PRO).
118 Private information from those concerned.
119 *Hansard*, 31 October 1956 (col. 1568).
120 Shimon Peres, *David's Sling*, 1970, p. 200.
121 SELO 308 (2).
122 FO 800/727 (PRO).
123 SELO 129 (2).
124 Selwyn Lloyd, op. cit., p. 205.
125 CAB 134/1216 (PRO).
126 CAB 128/30 (PRO).
127 Lord Gladwyn papers.
128 SELO 129 (2).
129 CAB 134/1216 (PRO).
130 FO 800/742 (PRO).
131 Ibid.
132 Lord Caccia's Visitors' Book, Washington Embassy (courtesy Lord Caccia).
133 SELO 129 (1).
134 SELO 129 (2).
135 FO 800/741 (PRO).
136 Selwyn Lloyd, op. cit., pp. 224–227.
137 Krishna Menon was a constant thorn in the flesh. When Selwyn did not take to a person he was reticent in his comments. In October 1962 Krishna Menon's biographer (Professor Crown of Princeton University) interviewed Selwyn. 'Fairly careful what I said', Selwyn noted in his diary. SELO 351 (1).

138 Selwyn Lloyd, op. cit., p. 228.
139 CAB 128/30 (PRO).
140 SELO 313 (1).
141 CAB 128/30 (PRO).
142 Private information.
143 The printed words in *Hansard* are only an indication of the difficulties faced by Selwyn Lloyd in this debate. See *Hansard*, 3 December 1956 (col. 877 onwards).
144 *Hansard*, 5 December 1956 (col. 1276).
145 SELO 237 (3).
146 Patrick Gordon Walker diary, 23 December 1956. Gordon Walker papers, Churchill College, File GNWR 1/13 (which also contains much interesting material on the Labour Party response to the Suez crisis).
147 SELO 123.
148 CAB 128/30 (PRO).
149 *Guardian*, 18 May 1978.
150 SELO 88 (3).
151 SELO 129 (1).
152 Harold Wilson, *Memoirs: The Making of a Prime Minister 1916–1964*, 1986, p. 165.
153 SELO 129 (1).
154 Robert Rhodes James, op. cit., p. 512.
155 SELO 128 (1).
156 SELO 237 (3).
157 Ibid.
158 Ibid.
159 Ibid.
160 Ibid.
161 Ibid.
162 *The Times*, 6 July 1978.
163 Nigel Nicolson in a letter to the author, 7 September 1985.
164 SELO 129 (2).
165 SELO 254 (5).
166 SELO 129 (2).
167 SELO 88 (3).
168 Sir Donald Logan in a letter to the author, 23 January 1988.
169 SELO 129 (1).
170 Ibid.
171 Douglas Jay, *Change and Fortune: A Political Record*, 1980, p. 261.
172 Robert Blake, Eden chapter, in *British Prime Ministers in the Twentieth Century, Volume 2: Churchill to Callaghan*, ed. J. P. Mackintosh, 1978, pp. 112–13.
173 Lord Moran, *Winston Churchill: The Struggle for Survival 1940–1965*, 1966, p. 711.

10 MACMILLAN'S FOREIGN SECRETARY

1 *Daily Worker*, 10 January 1957. Selwyn kept a copy with his news-

paper cuttings. Not surprisingly, it was one of his favourites, SELO 253 (1).

2 SELO 88 (3).
3 D. R. Thorpe, *The Uncrowned Prime Ministers*, 1980, p. 209.
4 The late Lord Butler to the author, 20 November 1975.
5 Harold Macmillan, *Riding the Storm*, 1971, p. 186.
6 SELO 88 (3).
7 *Evening Standard*, 11 January 1957.
8 *Daily Mirror*, 16 January 1957.
9 SELO 329 (1).
10 SELO 180 (4).
11 Ibid.
12 I am indebted to the late Wing Commander Vera Thomas, Curator at Chequers until her death in 1986, for showing me the correspondence regarding this transaction and for explaining the legal niceties.
13 The late Earl of Stockton to the author, 27 March 1985.
14 *Hamlet*, Act 3, Scene 2.
15 Private information.
16 Sir Douglas Dodds-Parker, *Political Eunuch*, 1986, pp. 88–9.
17 Harold Macmillan, op. cit., p. 287.
18 SELO 123 (1).
19 Private information.
20 Speech of 27 February 1968 to the British American Parliamentary Group in Bermuda, SELO 34 (1).
21 SELO 314 (2).
22 *Hansard*, 16 May 1957 (col. 586). Notes for the speech are in SELO 49.
23 SELO 88 (3).
24 SELO 5 (2).
25 SELO 174 (2).
26 SELO 308 (2).
27 SELO 174 (2).
28 SELO 313 (1).
29 SELO 21.
30 John Campbell, *Nye Bevan and the Mirage of British Socialism*, 1987, p. 337.
31 Harold Macmillan, op. cit., p. 472.
32 SELO 180 (4).
33 SELO 329 (1).
34 Selwyn Lloyd to Sir Thomas Harley, 25 February 1958 (letter in the possession of Sir Thomas Harley).
35 Private information.
36 FO 800/728 (PRO).
37 Note of conversation of 25 June 1958, SELO 258 (3).
38 *The Times*, 11 October 1958.
39 Hugh Foot, *A Start in Freedom*, 1964, pp. 151–2.
40 SELO 364 (3).
41 Private information.

42 SELO 308 (1).
43 SELO 88 (3).
44 Ibid.
45 SELO 313 (1).
46 Sir Patrick Reilly, letter of 8 March 1959 (Reilly papers).
47 Private information.
48 Memorandum, 'Visit of the Prime Minister and Foreign Secretary to the Soviet Union' (Reilly papers).
49 SELO 32 (5).
50 Memorandum, 'The Foreign Ministers' Conference at Geneva July–August 1959' (Reilly papers).
51 Harold Macmillan, *Pointing the Way*, 1972, p. 63.
52 *The Times*, 1 June 1959.
53 Harold Macmillan to Michael Fraser, 12 July 1959.
54 SELO 18 outfiles.
55 SELO 32 (1).
56 SELO 18.
57 Ibid.
58 *Annual Register*, 1959, p. 35.
59 Letter of 22 October 1959, SELO 378 (1).
60 Councillor F. W. Venables to the author, 12 July 1987.
61 SELO 378 (1).
62 Ibid.
63 Harold Macmillan, *Pointing the Way, 1959–1961*, 1972, p. 17.
64 SELO 308 (1).
65 Harold Macmillan, op. cit., p. 57.
66 SELO 308 (1).
67 SELO 308 (2).
68 SELO 18.
69 SELO 308 (1).
70 Ibid.
71 Ibid.
72 Ibid.
73 Ibid.
74 Private information from several sources.
75 SELO 308 (1), Diary of 9 February 1960.
76 SELO 308 (1), Diary of 11 February 1960.
77 SELO 308 (1).
78 Ibid.
79 SELO 308 (1), Diary of 14 May 1960.
80 Ibid.
81 Michael R. Beschloss, *Mayday: Eisenhower, Khrushchev and the U2 Affair*, 1986, p. 277.
82 Private information.
83 SELO 308 (1).
84 Ibid.
85 Private information.

86 SELO 308 (1).
87 Private information.
88 Reminiscence of a British delegate.
89 *Hansard*, 25 July 1960 (col. 625).
90 SELO 308 (1).
91 Ibid.
92 The opinion of virtually every member of the Foreign Service with whom I spoke.
93 Hugh Thomas, *The Suez Affair*, revised edition, 1986, p. 42.
94 Nigel Nicolson in a letter to the author, 7 September 1985.
95 Sir William Hayter, *A Double Life*, 1974, p. 156.

11 CHANCELLOR OF THE EXCHEQUER
  1 SELO 308 (1).
  2 Ibid.
  3 SELO 180 (4).
  4 SELO 308 (1).
  5 SELO 180 (4).
  6 SELO 308 (1).
  7 Ibid.
  8 Ibid.
  9 SELO 180 (4).
 10 SELO 308 (1).
 11 SELO 88 (3).
 12 SELO 308 (1).
 13 Harold Macmillan, *Riding the Storm*, 1971, p. 19.
 14 Samuel Brittan, *The Treasury under the Tories*, 1964, p. 208.
 15 Private information.
 16 Ibid.
 17 Ibid.
 18 Samuel Brittan, op. cit., p. 211.
 19 *Monthly Digest of Statistics*, July 1963, Table 6.
 20 Ibid., Table 133.
 21 SELO 300 (3).
 22 Speech to Glasgow Chamber of Commerce, 10 February 1961, SELO 300 (3).
 23 Samuel Brittan, op. cit., p. 242.
 24 SELO 277 and SELO 88 (3).
 25 SELO 88 (3).
 26 Ibid.
 27 Ibid.
 28 John Elsom and Nicholas Tomalin, *History of the National Theatre*, 1978, p. 119.
 29 Ibid., p. 123.
 30 SELO 387 (1).
 31 SELO 88 (3).
 32 SELO 61 (6).

33 SELO 88 (3).
34 Ibid.
35 SELO 240 (4).
36 SELO 88 (3).
37 Private information.
38 SELO 88 (3).
39 Selwyn Lloyd's Budget speech, *Hansard*, 17 April 1961 (col. 791 onwards).
40 SELO 179 (2).
41 *The Times*, 18 April 1961.
42 *Financial Times*, 18 April 1961.
43 *Guardian*, 18 April 1961.
44 Harold Macmillan, *Pointing the Way*, 1972, p. 376.
45 SELO 88 (3).
46 SELO 241 (3).
47 Geoffrey Goodman, *The Awkward Warrior: Frank Cousins: His Life and Times*, 1979, p. 293.
48 SELO 300 (3).
49 SELO 88 (3).
50 NEDC Minutes, 7 March 1962 (National Economic Development Council).
51 SELO 88 (3).
52 Ibid.
53 BBC Records, Caversham, Microfilm 33–4.
54 SELO 299 (1) and SELO 88 (3).
55 Selwyn Lloyd's Budget Speech, *Hansard*, 9 April 1962 (cols 960 onwards).
56 BBC News Bulletin, 17 April 1962. BBC Records, Caversham, Microfilm 32.
57 Letter of 10 April 1962, SELO 170 (3).
58 SELO 88 (3).
59 *Sunday Times*, 15 April 1962.
60 SELO 88 (3).
61 SELO 300 (4).

12 THE NIGHT OF THE LONG KNIVES

1 *Hansard*, 12 April 1962 (col. 1623).
 2 *Incomes Policy: the next step* (1962), Cmnd 1626.
 3 SELO 88 (3).
 4 SELO 300 (3).
 5 Private information.
 6 SELO 300 (3).
 7 SELO 88 (3).
 8 NEDC Minutes, 9 May 1962.
 9 Harold Macmillan, *At the End of the Day*, 1973, p. 89.
10 Selwyn Lloyd diary, 1 August 1962, recording conversation with Reginald Maudling, SELO 88 (3).

11 Nigel Fisher, *Iain Macleod*, 1973, p. 220.
12 SELO 300 (3).
13 Harold Macmillan, op. cit., p. 91.
14 Ibid., p. 92.
15 *Daily Mail*, 12 July 1962.
16 SELO 180 (4).
17 Unless otherwise indicated, all subsequent quotations in this chapter are from Selwyn Lloyd's Memorandum on the events of July and August 1962, contained in SELO 88 (3).
18 SELO 180 (4).
19 Harold Macmillan, op. cit., p. 96.
20 *The Times*, 14 July 1962.
21 Private information from several people, including one Conservative MP, who over the years heard all three versions at different times in the dining room at Pratt's. They were that it was imperative to reduce the overall age of the Cabinet, that Selwyn was a bad Chancellor, and that he was the focus of rebellion against Macmillan personally.
22 Anthony Howard, 'Monarch of Glencoe', *New Statesman*, 20 July 1962, Copy in SELO 53 (1).
23 SELO 53 (1).
24 Private information.
25 Harold Macmillan, op. cit., p. 100.
26 SELO 53 (1).
27 SELO 30 (1).
28 Cecil Taylor in a letter to the author, 7 December 1985.
29 SELO 180 (4).
30 *Sunday Telegraph* 15 July 1962, *Financial Times* 17 July 1962, *The Times* 14 July 1962.
31 SELO 78 (1).
32 SELO 120 (7).
33 SELO 202 (2).
34 SELO 162 (1).
35 SELO 202 (2).
36 In SELO 202 (7).
37 NEDC Minutes, 18 July 1962.
38 Roger Wilmut (ed.), *The Complete Beyond the Fringe*, Methuen, 1987, p. 54.
39 *Queen* magazine, 31 July 1962.
40 SELO 180 (4).
41 SELO 184 (3).
42 Private information.
43 Sir Alec Cairncross diary, 29 August 1962.
44 SELO 383 (1).
45 Samuel Brittan, *The Treasury under the Tories*, 1964, p. 211.
46 Private information.
47 Michael Stewart, *Life and Labour*, 1980, p. 124 and communicated to the author from Lord Stewart of Fulham via the family.

13 REHABILITATION

1 Richard Crossman, *The Diaries of a Cabinet Minister*, Vol. 2, 1976, p. 167.
2 Bodleian Library, Conservative Party Records, CCO 120/4/1.
3 SELO 180 (4).
4 Letter to Jonathan Aitken, 16 February 1963.
5 Ibid.
6 Bodleian Library, CCO 120/4/26.
7 SELO 299 (2).
8 Bodleian Library, CCO 120/4/1.
9 SELO 8 (2).
10 SELO 69 (1).
11 Ibid.
12 SELO 147.
13 Russell Davies and Liz Ottaway, *Vicky*, 1987, p. 154.
14 SELO 391 (3).
15 SELO 426 (2).
16 Woolton Papers, Mss Woolton File 82 (Bodleian Library, Oxford).
17 SELO 63 (6).
18 Harold Macmillan, *At the End of the Day*, 1973, p. 500.
19 Anthony Howard, *Rab: the Life of R. A. Butler*, 1987, p. 314.
20 *Dictionary of National Biography*, 1971–80, (ed. Lord Blake), 1986, p. 546.
21 Private information.
22 Ibid.
23 Letter to Jonathan Aitken, 13 October 1963.
24 The late Lord Butler to the author, 20 November 1975.
25 SELO 61 (6).
26 Ibid.
27 Ibid.
28 'One Man Dog', unpublished memoirs of Sir Knox Cunningham (lent to author by the late Sir Knox Cunningham in 1975).
29 SELO 61 (6).
30 John Boyd-Carpenter, *Way of Life*, 1980, p. 180.
31 Ibid.
32 SELO 16 (6).
33 John Boyd-Carpenter, op. cit., p. 181.
34 SELO 61 (6).
35 John Boyd-Carpenter, op. cit., p. 181.
36 SELO 61 (6).
37 Ibid.
38 Private information.
39 SELO 61 (6).
40 SELO 449 (1).
41 *Hansard*, 19 November 1963 (col. 929).
42 *The Times*, 20 November 1963.
43 SELO 61 (6).

44 Memorandum of 4 September 1964, SELO 61 (5).
45 SELO 252 (3).
46 Letter of 22 June 1964, SELO 232 (3).
47 SELO 61 (3).
48 Letter of 29 October 1964, SELO 232 (3).

14 IN OPPOSITION
  1 SELO 232 (2).
  2 *Financial Times*, 18 May 1978.
  3 SELO 309 (1).
  4 Anthony Trollope, *The Prime Minister*, 1876.
  5 Kenneth Rose to the author, 30 April 1985.
  6 SELO 60 (1).
  7 SELO 60 (2).
  8 Ibid.
  9 Ibid.
 10 Ibid.
 11 Ibid.
 12 Ibid.
 13 Ibid.
 14 Several colleagues believe that Selwyn had his eyes fixed on the Speakership as early as July 1962.
 15 Jonathan Aitken diary, 10 December 1965.
 16 SELO 238 (1).
 17 Ibid.
 18 SELO 430 (1).
 19 Jonathan Aitken diary, 3 February 1966.
 20 Ibid., 7 February 1966.
 21 SELO 430 (2).
 22 SELO 430 (1) and SELO 312. Jonathan Aitken diary, 9 February 1966.
 23 Jonathan Aitken diary, 10 February 1966.
 24 SELO 312.
 25 SELO 430 (2).
 26 Ibid.
 27 Tim Dartington, *Task Force*, 1971, p. 7.
 28 Selwyn Lloyd to Dame Olwen Carey Evans, 19 November 1969 (letter in possession of Dame Olwen Carey Evans).
 29 Dingle Foot Papers, Churchill College, File DGFT 7/12.
 30 *Hansard*, 22 June 1967 (cols 2009–11).
 31 SELO 308 (2).
 32 *Liverpool Echo*, 13 August 1968.
 33 SELO 311 (3).
 34 SELO 91 (1).
 35 Diary 3 January 1968, SELO 124 (2).
 36 SELO 124 (2).

37 See David Butler and Michael Pinto-Duschinsky, *The British General Election of 1970*, 1971, *passim*.
38 Edward Heath in a letter to Selwyn Lloyd, 24 June 1970, SELO 209 (1), quoted by permission of the Rt Hon. Edward Heath, MP.
39 Peter Hennessy and Anthony Seldon (eds), *Ruling Performance: British Governments from Attlee to Thatcher*, 1987, p. 219.
40 Viscount Tonypandy to the author, 5 December 1984.

15 MR SPEAKER

1 SELO 171 (4).
2 Letter of 27 July 1970, SELO 171 (4).
3 As was pointed out by Sir Edward Gardner in his obituary of Selwyn in *Graya*, the magazine of Gray's Inn.
4 See John Boyd-Carpenter, *Way of Life*, chapter 20, 'The Affair of the Speakership', 1980, *passim*.
5 Private information.
6 SELO 181.
7 SELO 392 (3).
8 See *Hansard*, 12 January 1971 (col. 1 onwards for the proceedings in full).
9 SELO 392 (3).
10 Private information.
11 SELO 171 (2).
12 Jonathan Aitken, *Officially Secret*, 1971, p. 184.
13 J. P. Mackintosh, in a review of Selwyn Lloyd's *Mr Speaker, Sir*, in the *Listener* 18 November 1976.
14 Speech at *Yorkshire Post* lunch, 6 January 1977, SELO 129 (2).
15 SELO 127 (2).
16 Jonathan Aitken diary, 29 March 1972.
17 SELO 104 (9).
18 SELO 127 (2).
19 Ibid.
20 SELO 166 (2).
21 Councillor F. W. Venables to the author, 12 July 1987.
22 SELO 51 (2).
23 SELO 313 (2).
24 Ibid.
25 Reginald Maudling to the author, 4 September 1975.
26 SELO 313 (2).
27 Press Statement, 3 November 1975.
28 SELO 59 (1).
29 SELO 54 (1).
30 *Hansard*, 3 February 1976 (col. 1144).
31 SELO 25 (3).
32 *The Times*, 4 November 1976.
33 Jonathan Cape Records, Publishers' Archives, Reading University.
34 SELO 125 (3).

16 WHO GOES HOME?

1 Stanley Baldwin, *Service of our Lives*, Hodder & Stoughton, 1937, pp. 91–2.
2 *The Times*, 18 May 1978.
3 *Daily Telegraph*, 18 May 1978.
4 *Guardian*, 18 May 1978.
5 Funeral address by Lord Home, 25 May 1978 (copy in possession of the family).
6 Address by George Thomas at the Memorial Service, Westminster Abbey, 5 July 1978 (copy in possession of the family).
7 *Magdalene College Magazine and Record*, No. 22, 1977–8.
8 *Graya*, No. 82.
9 J. S. Watson in a letter to the author, 2 August 1986.
10 Private information.
11 Ibid.
12 Ibid.
13 Peter King-Lewis to the author, 4 June 1985.
14 Letter to the author from Viola, the late Dowager Duchess of Westminster (quoted by permission of Her Grace Viola, Dowager Duchess of Westminster).
15 Interview with Kenneth Harris, 23–24 June 1976.
16 SELO 88 (2).
17 *The Lyttelton Hart-Davis Letters, Volumes Three and Four 1958–1959*, John Murray, paperback edition, 1986, p. 249.
18 SELO 308 (2).
19 Jonathan Aitken diary, 19 December 1965.
20 Horace, *Ars Poetica*, line 173.
21 Cited by Lord Boyle in a letter to Selwyn Lloyd on his retirement from the Speakership, 1 Feburary 1976, SELO 364 (2).
22 The first donations were from Lord Eccles, Lord Hailsham, Edward Heath, Lord Longford, Harold Macmillan, Maurice Macmillan, Lord Mayhew, Enoch Powell, David Steel and George Thomas. Two Fettesians, Lord Fraser of Kilmorack and Ian Harvey, did much to establish the Library and were generous benefactors.
23 Kenneth Rose to the author, 30 April 1985.
24 SELO 122 (4).

Select Bibliography

PRIVATE PAPERS

1 *Selwyn Lloyd Papers*

The private papers of Baron Selwyn-Lloyd of the Wirral were deposited by his literary executors at Churchill College, Cambridge.

The SELWYN LLOYD collection (Catalogue Classification SELO) consists of 495 boxes and 3 parcels of framed photographs. The catalogue is only a general guide to the multiplicity of material contained in upwards of 3,000 files. No area of Selwyn Lloyd's life is left unrecorded, though some periods are more comprehensively covered than others. The papers are not organised in chronological order but by subject, a compartmentalised system which well matches the structured manner of his own life.

2 *Other Private Papers*

Jonathan Aitken papers (courtesy of Jonathan Aitken MP).

Earl Alexander of Tunis papers (Public Record Office).

Ernest Bevin papers (Churchill College, Cambridge and Public Record Office).

Brendan Bracken papers (Churchill College, Cambridge).

Lord Butler of Saffron Walden papers (Trinity College, Cambridge).

Sir Alec Cairncross diary (courtesy of Sir Alec Cairncross).

Lord Chandos papers (Churchill College, Cambridge).

Sir Miles Dempsey papers (Liddell Hart Centre for Military Papers, King's College, London and Public Record Office).

Dr James Dyce papers (courtesy of Dr James Dyce).

Sir Dingle Foot papers (Churchill College, Cambridge).

Lord Gladwyn papers (courtesy of Lord Gladwyn).

Lord Gordon-Walker papers (Churchill College, Cambridge).

Sir James Grigg papers: P. J. Grigg – Field Marshal Montgomery correspondence (Churchill College, Cambridge).

Lord Hailes papers (Churchill College, Cambridge).

Lord Hankey papers (Churchill College, Cambridge).

Sir Thomas Harley papers: correspondence with Selwyn Lloyd (courtesy of Sir Thomas Harley).

Lord Hore-Belisha papers (Churchill College, Cambridge).

Lord Ismay Papers (Liddell Hart Centre for Military Papers, King's College, London).

Lord Kilmuir papers (Churchill College, Cambridge).

Sir Basil Liddell Hart papers (Liddell Hart Centre for Military Papers, King's College, London).

Lady Megan Lloyd George: Attlee correspondence, Attlee papers (Churchill College, Cambridge).

Prime Ministerial correspondence of Harold Macmillan (PREM 11, Public Record Office).

Sir Roger Makins papers (Public Record Office).

Gilbert Murray papers (Bodleian Library, Oxford).

Lord Noel-Baker papers (Churchill College, Cambridge).

Lord Peyton of Yeovil: correspondence with Selwyn Lloyd (courtesy of Lord Peyton of Yeovil).

Sir Harold Pyman papers (Liddell Hart Centre for Military Papers, King's College, London).

Sir Patrick Reilly papers (courtesy of Sir Patrick Reilly).

Kenneth Rose papers (courtesy of Kenneth Rose).

Lord Sherfield (Sir Roger Makins): private correspondence (courtesy of Lord Sherfield).

Sir Hugh Stockwell papers (Liddell Hart Centre for Military Papers, King's College, London).

Lord Strang papers (Churchill College, Cambridge).

Lord Swinton papers (Churchill College, Cambridge).

Lord Woolton papers (Bodleian Library, Oxford).

PUBLIC AND INSTITUTIONAL RECORDS

I   *State Papers* (Public Record Office, Kew):

i The Foreign Office Papers of the Rt Hon. J. Selwyn Lloyd: FO 800/691–749.

ii Departmental Papers: Ministry of Aviation (AVIA 11); Cabinet Committees (CAB 21, CAB 44, CAB 65, CAB 66, CAB 69, CAB 78, CAB 80, CAB 87, CAB 106, CAB 118, CAB 124, CAB 127, CAB 128, CAB 130, CAB 131, CAB 133, CAB 134); Cabinet Minutes and Conclusions (CAB 128, CAB 129); Ministry of Defence (DEFE 4, DEFE 7, DEFE 11); Foreign Office Records (FO 370, FO 371, FO 800); Home Office Records (HO 254, HO 256); Miscellaneous Ministerial Correspondence (MAF 255); Prime Minister's Office (PREM 1, PREM 4, PREM 8, PREM 11); Ministry of Supply (AB 16); War Office (WO 171, WO 185, WO 205).

2   *Broadcasting Records*

BBC Written Archives (Caversham Park, Reading).

The Broadcasting Committee Report (August 1923), Cmd 1951.

Report of the Broadcasting Committee 1925 (1926), Cmd 2599.

Report of the Broadcasting Committee 1935 (1936), Cmd 5091.

Broadcasting: Memorandum by the Postmaster-General on the Report of the Broadcasting Committee, 1935 (June 1936), Cmd 5207.

Report of the Television Committee 1943 (1945), HMSO.

Broadcasting Policy (July 1946), Cmd 6852.

Broadcasting: Draft of Royal Charter for the Continuance of the British Broadcasting Corporation for which the Postmaster-General proposes to apply (December 1946), Cmd 6974.

Broadcasting: Copy of the Licence and Agreement, dated the 29th day of November, 1946, between His Majesty's Postmaster-General and the British Broadcasting Corporation (1946), Cmd 6975.

Report of the Broadcasting Committee, 1949, Cmd 8116.

Report of the Broadcasting Committee, 1949: Memoranda Submitted to the Committee, Cmd 8117.

Broadcasting: General Survey of the Broadcasting Service (May 1949), BBC Memorandum.

Broadcasting: Memorandum on the Report of the Broadcasting Committee, 1949 (1951), Cmd 8291.

Broadcasting: Draft of Royal Charter (1951), Cmd 8416.

Broadcasting: Memorandum on the Report of the Broadcasting Committee, 1949, (1952), Cmd 8550.

Broadcasting: Copy of the Licence and Agreement (1952), Cmd 8579.

Broadcasting: Copy of a New Charter (1952), Cmd 8675.

White Paper: Television Policy (November 1953), Cmd 9005.

Pilkington Committee on Broadcasting: Report (1962), Cmd 1753.

3   *Other Records*

County Assize Records (Public Record Office, Chancery Lane).

Fettes College, Edinburgh.

Hoylake Urban District Council Minutes.

Jonathan Cape Ltd: Selwyn Lloyd files (Publishers' Archives, Reading University).

Keesing's Contemporary Archives, 1945–78.

Leas School, Hoylake.

National Economic Development Council.

Royal Liverpool Golf Club, Hoylake.

Second Army Planning and Intelligence Papers (Liddell Hart Centre for Military Papers, King's College, London).

25 Club Minutes, 1932–47.

Union Society, Cambridge (Cambridge University Library).

Who's Who, 1945–78 (A & C Black).

Who Was Who 1971–1980, 1981 (A & C Black).

4   *Published Official and Party Documents*

An Account of the Operations of Second Army in Europe 1944–1945 (2 vols), compiled by HQ Second Army, 1945.

Conditions Favourable to Faster Growth (NEDC), HMSO, 1963.

Conservative Party Archives (Bodleian Library, Oxford).

Conservative Political Centre Pamphlets, 1946–59.

Control of Public Expenditure (The Plowden Report), 1961, Cmd 1432.
D Notice Matters: Report of the Committee of Inquiry (June 1967), Cmd 3309.
The D Notice System: Presented to Parliament by the Prime Minister (June 1967), Cmd 3312.
'Despatches by General Sir Charles Keightley', *London Gazette* No. 41172, 10 September 1957.
The Financial and Economic Obligations of the Nationalised Industries (April 1961), Cmd 1337.
Hansard: House of Commons Debates (HC Debs) – Vol. 413 (1 August 1945) to Vol. 907 (19 March 1976). (Selwyn Lloyd's annotated personal volumes, loaned to the library at Fettes College, Edinburgh).
Incomes Policy: The Next Step, Presented to Parliament by the Chancellor of the Exchequer (February 1962), Cmd 1626.
Law Reports: King's Bench Division, 1930–9 (Butterworth & Co.).
Liberal Party, *We Can Conquer Unemployment*, Cassell, 1929.
Paris Summit Documents relating to the meetings between the President of the French Republic, the President of the United States of America, the Chairman of the Council of Ministers of Soviet Socialist Republics and the Prime Minister of the United Kingdom: Paris, 15–17 May 1960, Cmd 1052.
Resolutions adopted by the General Assembly during its first Emergency Special Session from 1–10 November 1956 (Official Records Supplement, No. 1) (A/3354).
Royal Commission on the Constitution, 1969–73, Volume 1: *The Report* (October 1973), Cmd 5460.
The Supply of Military Aircraft, Cmd 9388.
Sir Peter Thorne, *Serjeant for the Commons*, HMSO (December 1985).

THE PRESS AND PERIODICAL LITERATURE

1 National and Foreign
Daily Despatch, Daily Express, Daily Herald, Daily Mail, Daily Mirror, Daily Record, Daily Telegraph, Daily Worker, Evening Standard, Financial Times, Guardian, Manchester Guardian, News Chronicle, Observer, People, Sun, Sunday Express, Sunday Telegraph, Sunday Times, The Times, Winnipeg Tribune.

2 Local and Regional
Birkenhead Advertiser & Wallasey Guardian, Birkenhead News, Birmingham Post, Cambridge Daily News, Coventry Evening Telegraph, Glasgow Herald, Hoylake & West Kirby News, Huddersfield Examiner, Leicester Mercury, Liverpool Daily Post, Liverpool Echo, Liverpool Post & Mercury, Macclesfield Courier & Herald, Macclesfield Reporter, Scotsman, Sheffield Morning Telegraph, Stockport Advertiser, Western Mail, Wigan Observer, Wirral News, Yorkshire Post.

3 Journals and Periodicals
Aeroplane, Benson Parish News, Cambridge Review, Crossbow, The

Economist, The Fettesian, Graya, Leas School Magazine, Listener, Magdalene College Magazine & Record, Methodist Recorder, Monthly Digest of Statistics, New Statesman & Nation, Spectator, TV Times, Varsity.

PUBLISHED WORKS BY SELWYN LLOYD

1   *Books*
Mr Speaker, Sir, Jonathan Cape, London, 1976.
Suez 1956: A Personal View, Jonathan Cape, London, 1978.

2   *Other Published Works*
i *Report of the Broadcasting Committee* (1949): *The Selwyn Lloyd Minority Report*, Cmd 8116.
The Selwyn Lloyd Report, 1963 (Conservative Central Office).
ii 'A Foreign Secretary Remembers', *Listener*, 4 November 1976.
'The Future of Broadcasting', *National & English Review*, June 1951.
'How to live at peace with the Russians', *Reader's Digest*, April 1959.
'It's time the Commons put their House in Order', *Reader's Digest*, May 1970.
'Libel and slander', *Spectator*, 29 October 1948.
'The London Conference on the Suez Canal', *Listener*, 16 August 1956.
'Neddy and Parliament', *Crossbow*, October–December 1963.
'Recollections of the Union', *Varsity* newspaper (Cambridge), February 1965.

3   *Unpublished Memorandum*
'The Suspension of the Death Penalty', 1948, SELO 219 (4).

SECONDARY SOURCES

1   *Published Works*
(All books are published in London, unless otherwise indicated)

Dean Acheson, *Present at the Creation*, Hamish Hamilton, 1970.
Jonathan Aitken, *Officially Secret*, Weidenfeld & Nicolson, 1971.
Stephen E. Ambrose, *Eisenhower The President: Volume 2, 1952–1969*, Allen & Unwin, 1984.
Sidney Aster, *Anthony Eden*, Weidenfeld & Nicolson, 1976.
Michael Astor, *Tribal Feeling*, John Murray, 1963.
Correlli Barnett, *The Audit of War; The Illusion and Reality of Britain as a Great Nation*, Macmillan, 1986.
Michael Bar-Zohar, *The Armed Prophet: A Biography of Ben Gurion*, Arthur Barker, 1967.
André Beaufre, *The Suez Expedition*, Faber, 1969.
David Ben Gurion, *Israel: Years of Challenge*, Blond, 1964.
Tony Benn, *Out of the Wilderness: Diaries 1963–1967*, Hutchinson, 1987.
Michael R. Beschloss, *Mayday: Eisenhower, Khrushchev and the U2 Affair*, Faber, 1986.
Lord Beveridge, *Power and Influence*, Hodder, 1953.

Reginald Bevins, *The Greasy Pole*, Hodder, 1965.

Earl of Birkenhead, *The Prof in Two Worlds: The official life of Professor F. A. Lindeman, Viscount Cherwell*, Collins, 1961.

——*The Life of Lord Halifax*, Hamish Hamilton, 1965.

——*Walter Monckton: The Life of Viscount Monckton of Brenchley*, Weidenfeld & Nicolson, 1969.

Robert Blake, *The Conservative Party from Peel to Thatcher*, Methuen, 1985.

——*The Decline of Power 1915–1964*, Granada, 1985.

Robert Blake and C. S. Nicholls (eds), *The Dictionary of National Biography 1971–1980*, Oxford University Press, Oxford, 1986.

Lord Boothby, *My Yesterday, Your Tomorrow*, Hutchinson, 1962.

——*Recollections of a Rebel*, Hutchinson, 1978.

Robert R. Bowie, *Suez*, New York, 1956.

Francis Boyd, *Richard Austen Butler*, Rockcliff, 1956.

John Boyd-Carpenter, *Way of Life: The Memoirs of John Boyd-Carpenter*, Sidgwick & Jackson, 1980.

Andrew Boyle, *Only the Wind will Listen: Reith of the BBC*, Hutchinson, 1972.

Alan Brack, *The Wirral*, Batsford, 1980.

Russell Braddon, *Suez: Splitting of a Nation*, Collins, 1973.

General Omar N. Bradley, *A Soldier's Story of the Allied Campaign from Tunis to the Elbe*, Eyre & Spottiswode, 1952.

Asa Briggs, *The BBC: The First Fifty Years*, Oxford, 1979.

——*Governing the BBC*, British Broadcasting Corporation, 1979.

——*The History of Broadcasting in the United Kingdom: Volume 4, Sound and Vision*, Oxford, 1979.

Samuel Brittan, *The Treasury under the Tories*, Secker & Warburg, 1964.

——*Steering the Economy*, Penguin Books, Harmondsworth, 1971.

George Brown, *In My Way*, Gollancz, 1971.

R. H. Bruce Lockhart, *My Scottish Youth*, Putnam, 1937.

Alan Bullock, *Ernest Bevin, Foreign Secretary 1945–1951*, Heinemann, 1983.

Ivor Bulmer-Thomas, *The Growth of the British Party System: Volume 2, 1924–1966*, John Baker, 1967.

Trevor Burridge, *Clement Attlee: A Political Biography*, Jonathan Cape, 1985.

David Butler, *The British General Election of 1951*, Macmillan, 1952.

——*The British General Election of 1955*, Macmillan, 1955.

David Butler and Richard Rose, *The British General Election of 1959*, Macmillan, 1960.

David Butler and Anthony King, *The British General Election of 1964*, Macmillan, 1965.

——*The British General Election of 1966*, Macmillan, 1966.

David Butler and Michael Pinto-Duschinsky, *The British General Election of 1970*, Macmillan, 1971.

David Butler and Dennis Kavanagh, *The British General Election of February 1974*, Macmillan, 1974.

——*The British General Election of October 1974*, Macmillan, 1975.

David Butler and Anne Sloman, *British Political Facts 1900–1975*, Macmillan, 1975.

Lord Butler, *The Art of the Possible*, revised edition, Penguin Books, Harmondsworth, 1973.

——*The Art of Memory: Friends in perspective*, Hodder, 1982.

Mollie Butler, *August and Rab: A Memoir*, Weidenfeld & Nicolson, 1987.

John Campbell, *Lloyd George: The Goat in the Wilderness*, Jonathan Cape, 1977.

——*F. E. Smith: First Earl of Birkenhead*, Jonathan Cape, 1983.

——*Nye Bevan and the Mirage of British Socialism*, Weidenfeld & Nicolson, 1987.

E. W. Capleton, *Shabash – 149: The War Story of the 149th Regiment RA, 1939–1945*, printed privately, 1963.

Olwen Carey Evans, *Lloyd George was my Father*, Gomer Press, 1985.

David Carlton, *Anthony Eden: A Biography*, Allen Lane, 1981.

Barbara Castle, *The Castle Diaries 1974–1976*, Weidenfeld & Nicolson, 1976.

Alun Chalfont, *Montgomery of Alamein*, Weidenfeld & Nicolson, 1976.

Erskine B. Childers, *The Road to Suez*, MacGibbon & Kee, 1962.

Randolph S. Churchill, *The Rise and Fall of Sir Anthony Eden*, MacGibbon & Kee, 1959.

——*The Fight for the Tory Leadership*, Heinemann, 1964.

William Clark, *From Three Worlds – Memoirs*, Sidgwick & Jackson, 1986.

John Cloake, *Templer: Tiger of Malaya*, Harrap, 1985.

John Colville, *The Churchillians*, Weidenfeld & Nicolson, 1981.

——*The Fringes of Power: Downing Street Diaries 1939–1955*, Hodder, 1985.

John Connell, *The Most Important Country*, Cassell, 1957.

Chris Cook, *Sources in British Political History 1900–1951, 5 volumes*, Macmillan, 1975.

Chris Cook and John Ramsden, *By-Elections in British Politics*, Macmillan, 1973.

Chester Cooper, *The Lion's Last Roar: Suez 1956*, Harper & Row, 1978.

Patrick Cosgrave, *R. A. Butler: An English Life*, Quartet, 1981.

Maurice Cowling, *The Impact of Labour 1920–1924*, Cambridge University Press, Cambridge, 1971.

Francis A. Cowper, *A Prospect of Gray's Inn*, Second revised edition, Graya, 1985.

Percy Cradock (ed.), *Recollections of the Cambridge Union 1815–1939*, Bowes & Bowes, Cambridge, 1953.

J. A. Cross, *Lord Swinton*, Clarendon Press, Oxford, 1982.

Richard Crossman, *The Diaries of a Cabinet Minister*, Volume 2, (edited by Janet Morgan), Hamish Hamilton and Jonathan Cape, 1976.

——*Selections from the Diaries of a Cabinet Minister 1964–1970* (edited by

Anthony Howard), Hamish Hamilton and Jonathan Cape, 1979.
——*The Backbench Diaries of Richard Crossman* (edited by Janet Morgan), Hamish Hamilton and Jonathan Cape, 1981.
Ian Curteis, *Suez 1956: A Television Play*, BBC Publications, 1972.
Hugh Dalton, *High Tide and After, Memoirs 1945–1960*, Muller, 1962.
Tim Dartington, *Task Force*, Mitchell Beazley, 1971.
Russell Davies and Liz Ottaway, *Vicky*, Secker & Warburg, 1987.
Moshe Dayan, *Diary of the Sinai Campaign*, Weidenfeld & Nicolson, 1966.
——*Story of My Life*, Weidenfeld & Nicolson, 1976.
Patric Dickinson, *A Round of Golf Courses*, Evans Brothers, 1951.
David Dilks, *Neville Chamberlain: Volume 1 1869–1929*, Cambridge University Press, Cambridge, 1984.
Piers Dixon, *Double Diploma: The Life of Sir Pierson Dixon*, Hutchinson, 1968.
Sir Douglas Dodds-Parker, *Political Eunuch*, Springwood Books, 1986.
Bernard Donoughue and G. W. Jones, *Herbert Morrison: Portrait of a Politician*, Weidenfeld & Nicolson, 1973.
Robert Dougall, *In and Out of the Box*, Collins Harvill, 1973.
J. C. R. Dow, *The Management of the British Economy 1945–1960*, Cambridge University Press, Cambridge, 1970.
Lord Drogheda, *Double Harness*, Weidenfeld & Nicolson, 1978.
Abba Eban, *My Country*, Weidenfeld & Nicolson, 1972.
Anthony Eden, *Full Circle*, Cassell, 1960.
——*Facing the Dictators*, Cassell, 1962.
Dwight D. Eisenhower, *Crusade in Europe*, Heinemann, 1949.
——*The White House Years: Mandate for Change 1953–1956*, New York, 1963.
——*The White House Years: Waging Peace 1956–1961*, New York, 1965.
Major L. F. Ellis, *Victory in the West*, 2 volumes, 1962 and 1968, HMSO.
John Elsom and Nicholas Tomalin, *History of the National Theatre*, Jonathan Cape, 1978.
Leon D. Epstein, *British Politics in the Suez Crisis*, Pall Mall Press, 1964.
Harold Evans, *Downing Street Diary: The Macmillan Years 1957–1963*, Hodder, 1981.
Fettes College Register: 1870–1953, T. and A. Constable, Edinburgh, 1954.
Fettes College Register: 1870–1970, T. and A. Constable, Edinburgh, 1970.
Herman Finer, *Dulles Over Suez: The Theory and Practice of his Diplomacy*, Heinemann, 1964.
Nigel Fisher, *Iain Macleod*, Deutsch, 1973.
——*The Tory Leaders: Their Struggle for Power*, Weidenfeld & Nicolson, 1977.
——*Harold Macmillan*, Weidenfeld & Nicolson, 1982.
Hugh Foot, *A Start in Freedom*, Hodder & Stoughton, 1964.
Michael Foot, *Aneurin Bevan: Volume 2 1945–1960*, Davis Poynter, 1973.
Joseph Frankel, *The Making of Foreign Policy*, Oxford, 1963.
——*British Foreign Policy 1945–1973*, Oxford, 1975.

Roy Fullick and Geoffrey Powell, *Suez: The Double War*, Hamish Hamilton, 1979.

Martin Gilbert, *Road to Victory: Winston S. Churchill 1941–1945*, Heinemann, 1986.

——*Never Despair: Winston S. Churchill 1945–1965*, Heinemann, 1988.

Cynthia Gladwyn, *The Paris Embassy*, Collins, 1976.

Lord Gladwyn, *The Memoirs of Lord Gladwyn*, Weidenfeld & Nicolson, 1972.

Sir John Glubb, *The Changing Scenes of Life: An Autobiography*, Quartet Books, 1983.

Geoffrey Goodman, *The Awkward Warrior: Frank Cousins: His Life and Times*, Davis Poynter, 1979.

Richard Goold-Adams, *John Foster Dulles: A Reappraisal*, Greenwood Press, Connecticut, 1962.

Patrick Gordon Walker, *The Cabinet*, Jonathan Cape, 1972.

James Griffiths, *Pages from Memory*, Dent, 1969.

Richard Griffiths, *Fellow Travellers of the Right: British Enthusiasts for Nazi Germany 1937–1939*, Constable, 1980.

Jo Grimond, *Memoirs*, Heinemann, 1979.

Harman Grisewood, *One Thing at a Time: An Autobiography*, Hutchinson, 1968.

Michael A. Guhin, *John Foster Dulles: A Statesman and His Times*, Columbia University Press, Columbia, 1972.

Lord Hailsham, *The Door Wherein I Went*, Collins, 1975.

Nigel Hamilton, *Monty: The Making of a General, 1887–1942*, Hamish Hamilton, 1981.

——*Monty: Master of the Battlefield 1942–1944*, Hamish Hamilton, 1983.

——*Monty: The Field Marshal, 1944–1976*, Hamish Hamilton, 1986.

Jose Harris, *William Beveridge: A Biography*, Clarendon Press, Oxford, 1977.

Kenneth Harris, *Attlee*, Weidenfeld & Nicolson, 1982.

Ralph Harris, *Politics without Prejudice: A Political Appreciation of the Rt Hon. Richard Austen Butler*, Staples Press, 1956.

Ian Harvey, *To Fall Like Lucifer*, Sidgwick & Jackson, 1971.

Max Hastings, *Overlord: D-Day and the Battle for Normandy 1944*, Michael Joseph, 1984.

Sir William Hayter, *The Kremlin and the Embassy*, Hodder, 1966.

—— *A Double Life*, Hamish Hamilton, 1974.

Cameron Hazlehurst and C. Woodland, *A Guide to the Papers of British Cabinet Ministers, 1900–1951*, Royal Historical Society, London, 1974.

Mohammed H. Heikal, *Nasser: The Cairo Documents*, New English Library, 1972.

——*Cutting the Lion's Tail: Suez through Egyptian Eyes*, Deutsch, 1986.

Sir Nicholas Henderson, *The Private Office*, Weidenfeld & Nicolson, 1984.

Peter Hennessy and Anthony Seldon (eds), *Ruling Performance: British Governments from Attlee to Thatcher*, Blackwell, Oxford, 1987.

Lord Hill, *Both Sides of the Hill*, Heinemann, 1964.

J. D. Hoffman, *The Conservative Party in Opposition, 1945–1951*, Mac-Gibbon & Kee, 1964.

Lord Home, *The Way the Wind Blows*, Collins, 1976.

Lt-Gen. Sir Brian Horrocks, *A Full Life*, Collins, 1960.

Anthony Howard, *RAB: The Life of R. A. Butler*, Jonathan Cape, 1987.

T. E. B. Howarth, *Cambridge between Two Wars*, Collins, 1978.

——*Prospect and Reality: Great Britain 1945–1955*, Collins, 1985.

Emrys Hughes, *Sidney Silverman: Rebel in Parliament*, Charles Skilton, 1969.

Douglas Hurd, *An End to Promises: A Sketch of Government 1970–1974*, Collins, 1979.

George Hutchinson, *The Last Edwardian at No. 10*, Quartet Books, 1980.

Robert Jackson, *Suez 1956: Operation Musketeer*, Ian Allan, 1980.

Douglas Jay, *Change and Fortune: A Political Record*, Hutchinson, 1980.

Clive Jenkins, *Power behind the Screen: Ownership, Control and Motivation in British Commercial Television*, MacGibbon & Kee, 1961.

Roy Jenkins, *Nine Men of Power*, Hamish Hamilton, 1974.

——*Truman*, Collins, 1986.

Paul Johnson, *The Suez War*, MacGibbon & Kee, 1957.

Lucy Kavaler, *The Astors*, Harrap, 1966.

John Keegan, *Six Armies in Normandy*, Jonathan Cape, 1982.

Ian Kemp, *Tippett: The Composer and his Music*, Eulenberg Books, 1984.

Major-General Sir John Kennedy, *The Business of War: The War Narrative of Major-General Sir John Kennedy* (ed. B. Fergusson), Hutchinson, 1957.

Earl of Kilmuir, *Political Adventure, The Memoirs of the Earl of Kilmuir*, Weidenfeld & Nicolson, 1964.

Cecil King, *Diary 1970–1974*, Jonathan Cape, 1975.

Alan King-Hamilton, *Nothing but the Truth*, Weidenfeld & Nicolson, 1982.

Sir Ivone Kirkpatrick, *The Inner Circle: Memoirs of Ivone Kirkpatrick*, Macmillan, 1959.

Richard Lamb, *Montgomery in Europe*, Buchan and Enright, 1983.

——*The Failure of the Eden Government*, Sidgwick & Jackson, 1987.

Joseph Lash, *Dag Hammarskjöld: a Biography*, Cassell, 1962.

Roy Lewis and Angus Maude, *The English Middle Classes*, Penguin Books, Harmondsworth, 1953.

Kennett Love, *Suez: The Twice Fought War*, Longman, 1969.

P. B. Lucas, *Five Up: A Chronicle of Five Lives*, Sidgwick and Jackson, 1978.

James Lunt, *Glubb Pasha: A Biography*, Harvill Press, 1984.

Oliver Lyttelton, Viscount Chandos, *The Memoirs of Lord Chandos*, Bodley Head, 1962.

R. B. McCallum and Alison Readman, *The British General Election of 1945*, Oxford University Press, Oxford, 1947.

H. F. Macdonald (ed.), *A Hundred Years of Fettes*, T. and A. Constable, Edinburgh, 1970.

Donald MacDougall, *Don and Mandarin: Memoirs of an Economist*, John Murray, 1987.

Robert McKenzie, *British Political Parties*, Heinemann, 1967.

J. P. Mackintosh, *The British Cabinet*, 3rd edition, Stevens & Sons, 1977.

——(ed.), *British Prime Ministers in the Twentieth Century, Volume 2: Churchill to Callaghan*, Weidenfeld & Nicolson, 1978.

Harold Macmillan, *Blast of War 1939–1945*, Macmillan, 1967.

——*Tides of Fortune 1945–1955*, Macmillan, 1969.

——*Riding the Storm, 1956–1959*, Macmillan 1971.

——*Pointing the Way, 1959–1961*, Macmillan, 1972.

——*At the End of the Day, 1961–1963*, Macmillan, 1973.

Norman Macrae, *Sunshades in October*, George Allen & Unwin, 1963.

David Marquand, *Ramsay Macdonald*, Jonathan Cape, 1977.

Reginald Maudling, *Memoirs*, Sidgwick & Jackson, 1978.

Christopher Mayhew, *Time to Explain: An Autobiography*, Hutchinson, 1987.

Golda Meir, *My Life*, Weidenfeld & Nicolson, 1975.

Robert Menzies, *Afternoon Light: Some Memories of Men and Events*, Cassell, 1967.

Keith Middlemass, *Industry, Unions and Government: 21 years of NEDC*, Macmillan, 1983.

Anthony Moncrieff (ed.), *Suez: Ten Years Later*, BBC Publications, 1967.

Viscount Montgomery, *Normandy to the Baltic*, 21st Army Group, privately printed edition, 1946.

——*The Memoirs of Field Marshal the Viscount Montgomery of Alamein, KG*, Collins, 1958.

Nicholas Monsarrat, *Life is a Four Letter Word*, Cassell, 1966.

Lord Moran, *Winston Churchill: The Struggle for Survival, 1940–1965*, Constable, 1966.

Kenneth O. Morgan, *Labour in Power 1945–1951*, Clarendon Press, Oxford, 1984.

James Morris, *Farewell the Trumpets: An Imperial Retreat*, Faber, 1978.

Leonard Mosley, *Dulles*, Hodder, 1978.

Charles Mott-Radclyffe, *Foreign Body in the Eye*, Leo Cooper, 1955.

C. L. Mowat, *Britain Between the Wars, 1918–1940*, Methuen, 1955.

Robert Murphy, *Diplomat among Warriors*, Collins, 1964.

Sir Gerald Nabarro, *NAB 1: Portrait of a Politician*, Robert Maxwell, 1969.

David Newsome, *On the Edge of Paradise: A. C. Benson Diarist*, John Murray, 1980.

H. G. Nicholas, *The British General Election of 1950*, Macmillan, 1951.

Harold Nicolson, *Diaries and Letters: Volume 3 1945–1962* (edited by Nigel Nicolson) Collins, 1968.

Nigel Nicolson, *People and Parliament*, Weidenfeld & Nicolson, 1958.

——*Alex: The Life of Field Marshal Earl Alexander of Tunis*, Weidenfeld & Nicolson, 1973.

F. S. Northedge, *Descent from Power: British Foreign Policy 1945–1973*, Allen and Unwin, 1975.

Sir Anthony Nutting, *No End of a Lesson: the Story of Suez*, Constable, 1967.

——*Nasser*, Constable, 1972.

John Osborne, *The Entertainer*, Faber, 1957.

Frank Owen, *Tempestuous Journey: Lloyd George His Life and Times*, Hutchinson, 1954.

Vance Packard, *The Hidden Persuaders*, Longmans Green, 1957.

Henry Pelling, *Winston Churchill*, Macmillan, 1974.

Shimon Peres, *David's Sling*, Weidenfeld & Nicolson, 1970.

——*From These Men: 7 Portraits*, Weidenfeld & Nicolson, 1979.

Ben Pimlott, *Hugh Dalton*, Jonathan Cape, 1985.

Ben Pimlott (ed.), *The Political Diary of Hugh Dalton, 1918–1940, 1945–1960*, Jonathan Cape, 1986.

Christian Pineau, *1956 Suez*, Robert Laffont, Paris, 1976.

G. Polanyi, *Planning in Britain: The Experience of the 1960s*, Institute of Economic Affairs, 1967.

H. R. Pyatt (ed.), *Fifty Years of Fettes: Memories of Old Fettesians 1870 –1920*, T. and A. Constable, Edinburgh, 1931.

H. E. Pyman, *Call to Arms*, Leo Cooper, 1971.

Rev. Henry Rees, *Lest We Forget: Being the Life Story of Rev. John Lloyd 1802–1869*, J. D. Davies, Blaenau Festiniog, 1936.

Robert Rhodes James, *Anthony Eden*, Weidenfeld & Nicolson, 1986.

Brian Roberts, *Randolph: A Study of Churchill's Son*, Hamish Hamilton, 1984.

Terence Robertson, *Crisis: The Inside Story of the Suez Conspiracy*, Hutchinson, 1965.

Eric Roll, *Crowded Hours*, Faber, 1985.

Stephen Roskill, *Hankey: Man of Secrets*, Volume 2, 1919–31, Volume 3, 1931–63, Collins, 1972, 1974.

Peter Rowland, *Lloyd George*, Barrie & Jackson, 1975.

Arthur Salter, *Slave of the Lamp*, Weidenfeld & Nicolson, 1967.

Anthony Sampson, *The Anatomy of Britain*, Hodder, 1962.

——*Macmillan: A Study in Ambiguity*, Allen Lane, 1967.

——*The New Anatomy of Britain*, Hodder, 1971.

Avi Schlaim, Peter Jones and Keith Sainsbury, *British Foreign Secretaries since 1945*, David & Charles, Newton Abbot, 1977.

Anthony Seldon, *Churchill's Indian Summer: The Conservative Government 1951–1955*, Hodder, 1981.

Bernard Sendall, *Independent Television in Britain*, 2 volumes, Macmillan, 1983.

Andrew Shonfield, *British Economic Policy since the War*, revised edition, Penguin Books, Harmondsworth, 1959.

——*Modern Capitalism: The Changing Balance of Private and Public Power*, Oxford University Press, Oxford, 1965.

Evelyn Shuckburgh, *Descent to Suez: Diaries 1951–1956*, Weidenfeld & Nicolson, 1986.

Viscount Simon, *Retrospect*, Hutchinson, 1952.

Michael Sissons and Philip French (eds), *The Age of Austerity*, Hodder, 1963.

Robert Skidelsky, *Politicians and the Slump: the Labour Government of 1929–1931*, Macmillan, 1967.

——*John Maynard Keynes: Hopes Betrayed 1883–1920*, Macmillan, 1983.

Samuel Smiles, *Self Help*, centenary edition, John Murray, 1958.

Anthony Smith, *British Broadcasting*, David & Charles, Newton Abbot, 1974.

Sir John Smyth, *Milestones: A Memoir*, Sidgwick & Jackson, 1979.

C. P. Snow, *Corridors of Power*, Macmillan, 1964.

Mary Soames, *Clementine Churchill by her daughter Mary*, Cassell, 1979.

Gerald Sparrow, *RAB: Study of a Statesman*, Odhams, 1965.

Michael Stewart, *Life and Labour*, Sidgwick & Jackson, 1980.

Mary Stocks, *My Commonplace Book*, Peter Davies, 1970.

——*Still more Commonplace*, Peter Davies, 1973.

Lord Strang, *Home and Abroad*, André Deutsch, 1956.

Charles Stuart (ed.), *The Reith Diaries*, Collins, 1975.

James Stuart, *Within the Fringe*, Bodley Head, 1967.

Earl of Swinton, *Sixty Years of Power*, Hutchinson, 1966.

A. J. P. Taylor, *English History 1914–1945*, Clarendon Press, Oxford, 1965.

——*Beaverbrook*, Hamish Hamilton, 1972.

——*A Personal History*, Hamish Hamilton, 1983.

Lord Tedder, *With Prejudice: The War Memoirs of Marshal of the Royal Air Force Lord Tedder, GCB*, Cassell, 1966.

George Thomas, *Mr Speaker: The Memoirs of George Thomas, the Viscount Tonypandy*, Century, 1985.

Hugh Thomas, *The Suez Affair*, revised edition, Weidenfeld & Nicolson, 1986.

Alan Thompson and John Barnes, *The Day Before Yesterday*, Sidgwick & Jackson, 1971.

D. R. Thorpe, *The Uncrowned Prime Ministers*, Darkhorse Publishing, 1980.

Humphrey Trevelyan, *The Middle East in Revolution*, Macmillan, 1970.

Harold Watkinson, *Turning Points: A Record of our Times*, Michael Russell, Salisbury, 1986.

E. T. Williams and Helen H. Palmer (eds), *The Dictionary of National Biography 1951–1960*, Clarendon Press, Oxford, 1971.

E. T. Williams and C. S. Nicholls (eds), *The Dictionary of National Biography 1961–1970*, Clarendon Press, Oxford, 1981.

Philip M. Williams, *Hugh Gaitskell: A Political Biography*, Jonathan Cape, 1979.

——(ed.), *The Diary of Hugh Gaitskell 1945–1956*, Jonathan Cape, 1983.

Harold Wilson, *Final Term: The Labour Government 1974–1976*, Weidenfeld & Nicolson/Michael Joseph, 1979.

——*Memoirs: The Making of a Prime Minister 1916–1964*, Weidenfeld & Nicolson/Michael Joseph, 1986.

H. H. Wilson, *Pressure Group: The Campaign for Commercial Television*, Secker & Warburg, 1961.

Trevor Wilson, *The Downfall of the Liberal Party 1914–1935*, Collins, 1966.

C. M. Woodhouse, *British Foreign Policy since the Second World War*, Hutchinson, 1961.

Lord Woolton, *The Memoirs of the Rt Hon. the Earl of Woolton*, Cassell, 1959.

Grace Wyndham Goldie, *Facing the Nation: Television and Politics 1936–1976*, Bodley Head, 1977.

Kenneth Young, *Sir Alec Douglas-Home*, Dent, 1970.

Philip Ziegler, *Mountbatten: the official biography*, Collins, 1985.

2   Articles, Essays, Lectures and Pamphlets

Abbeyfield Hoylake & West Kirby Society: *Lord Selwyn-Lloyd and Abbeyfield*, printed privately, July 1980.

'BBC for Ever', *Spectator*, 19 January 1951.

Francis Boyd, 'Selwyn Lloyd's Report', *Guardian*, 26 March 1963.

Broadcasting: A study of the case for and against commercial broadcasting under State Control in the United Kingdom, Institute of Incorporated Practitioners in Advertising, 1946.

John Corner, ' "Culture" versus Popular Taste', *Listener*, 3 October 1985.

Leslie Edwards, *The Royal Liverpool Golf Club 1869–1969: A Short History of the Club and of the Championships played over the Hoylake Links*, printed privately, 1969.

Sir Michael Fraser, 'The Conservative Research Department & Conservative Recovery after 1945', circulated privately, August 1961.

Sir William Haley, *The Responsibilities of Broadcasting*, The Lewis Fry Memorial Lectures, University of Bristol, 11–12 May 1948.

——*Moral Values in Broadcasting*, Address to the British Council of Churches, 2 November 1948.

——*Affairs: The Journal of the Hansard Society*, Vol. II, No. 2, Spring 1949.

——*Sound and Television Broadcasting*, Address, 18 May 1949. (PRO, HO 254/2.)

Peter Hennessy, 'The Scars of Suez', *Listener*, 5 February 1986.

—— 'Suez and the Ponting Factors', *New Statesman*, 6 February 1987.

Anthony Howard, 'Monarch of Glencoe', *New Statesman*, 20 July 1962.

Sir Donald Logan, 'Collusion at Suez', *Financial Times*, 8 November 1986.

Gilbert Longden, *Let's Look into This – Some Thoughts on Television*, printed privately, 1953.

Iain Macleod, 'The Tory Leadership', *Spectator*, 17 January 1964.

Christopher Mayhew, *Dear Viewer*, LP Publishers, 1953.

——*Commercial Television – What is to be Done?* Fabian Society Tract 318, September 1959.

President Nasser, 'My Side of Suez', *Sunday Times* 24 June 1962.

'Observer Profile: Selwyn Lloyd', *Observer* 10 May 1959.

Bill Patrick, 'The Night of the Long Knives: The True Story', *Oxford Tory*, Michaelmas Term, 1967.

William Rees-Mogg, 'The Right Moment to Change', *Sunday Times*, 18 July 1965.

Robert Rhodes James, 'Eden at Suez: The Diplomat who went uncertainly to War', *The Times*, 27 October 1986.

—— 'Anthony Eden and the Suez Crisis', *History Today*, November 1986.

Sir Robert Speed and David Natzler, *The Parliamentary Golfing Society: A Short History*, printed privately for the Parliamentary Golfing Society, 1985.

Laurence Thompson, 'Man in the Red', 5 articles on R. A. Butler, *News Chronicle*, September 1955.

Professor Geoffrey Warner, '"Collusion" and the Suez Crisis of 1956', *International Affairs*, lv, 1979.

J. R. Warren Evans, *A Short History of the Cambridge Union*, printed privately, 1963.

Philip Whitehead, 'Politics in Camera', *Listener*, 21 November 1985.

Squadron Leader R. Wickham Partridge, 'The Education of the Children of Regular Personnel of Her Majesty's Forces', *The Conservative Teacher*, Vol. 1, No. 4, Autumn 1954.

3   *Unpublished Theses, Etc*

Rosemary Brown, 'The General Election of 1945: Wirral Division', Ethel Wormald College of Education.

Sir Knox Cunningham, 'One Man Dog: the Memoirs of Harold Macmillan's Private Secretary', in the possession of the Drapers' Company.

T. A. Hart, 'Research Notes prepared for Mr Selwyn Lloyd on his Period at the Treasury, July 1960–July 1962', Churchill College, Cambridge.

Sir Donald Logan, 'Meetings at Sèvres', unpublished memorandum on the events of 22–24 October 1956 (by courtesy of Sir Donald Logan).

H. E. Pyman, 'The Story of Second Army in North West Europe', manuscript, February 1969, Liddell Hart Centre for Military Papers, King's College, London, Pyman Papers File 15.

A. L. Teasdale, 'Interpreting the Crisis of October 1963', Ph.D. thesis, Nuffield College, Oxford.

BROADCAST PROGRAMMES

1   *Radio*

Transcripts in BBC Archives, Caversham:

'Crisis 1956', 5 July 1966.

'Egyptian Outlook', 7 July 1966.

'Israel & the Middle East', 14 July 1966.

'Some Evidence of Collusion', 18 July 1966.

'A Canal Too Far', Radio 3, 31 January 1987.

2   *Television*

'At the End of the Day', Harold Macmillan/Robert McKenzie interview, BBC TV 1973.

'The Day before Yesterday', Thames Television, 1971.

'End of Empire', Granada Television, 1985.

'Nasser', Tyne Tees Television, 1986.
'The Secrets of Suez', BBC Television, 12 November 1986.

GRAMOPHONE RECORDINGS

The Sixties, BBC Records, RESR 8. Contains extracts of Selwyn
Lloyd's speech to his constituents in West Kirby on 19 July 1962 after
his sacking as Chancellor of the Exchequer.

Index

Notes: SL = Selwyn Lloyd; n. = footnote

JANUARY 3. 1956

DEAR SIR ANTHONY,

I HAVE BEEN WANTING TO WRITE TO YOU EVER SINCE YOU RESHUFFLED YOUR GOVERNMENT TO TELL YOU OF THE PLIGHT OF THE CARTOONISTS. WE HAVE HAD A DISASTROUS YEAR HAVING LOS, MOST OF OUR FAVOURITE CHARACTERS !

THE FAMOUS CIGAR HAS DISAPPEARED FROM THE SCENE, — AS HAS THE FAMILIAR, BENIGN SMILE OF "UNCLE WOOLTON. THE MASSIVE FRAME OF ARTHUR DEAKIN HAS GONE ... THE BALD HEAD OF CLEM - ER, SORRY - EAR ATTLEE HAS BEEN OBSCURED BY A CORONET— AND THE COCKY QUIFF HAS BEEN ECLIPSED.

MOST OF YOUR MINISTERS RUN TO A PATTERI BOTH IN FEATURES AND DRESS. JUST LOOK AT —

SIR D. ECCLES, MR. BUCHAN-HEPBURN, MR. SANDYS, MR. NUTTING, etc. etc.